The Dissent of the Governed

The Dissent of the Governed

Readings on the Democratic Process

JOHN C. LIVINGSTON

Sacramento State College

ROBERT G. THOMPSON

Sacramento State College

The Macmillan Company, New York

Preface

When we agreed with our publisher to put together a book of readings on American politics, we contemplated the casual and enjoyable job of culling some of our favorite pieces on politics and looking at new materials we wanted to read anyway. The task has turned out differently. For the last six months we have been thrashing about in a sea of material that washes over an almost endless number of topics, which, in turn, could be organized in a seemingly infinite number of ways. Ultimately, procrastination and argument and reorganization had to end and here are our decisions.

Selections of topics were made on a general criterion that our readers should gain an understanding of the total framework of American politics ranging from philosophical and ideological concepts of democracy to the smell of cigar smoke in a back room. Individual articles were selected on the basis of how sharply they penetrated to the matter under examination as well as on their accuracy and their interest. We have tried to avoid articles that are unduly "heavy" or that are laden with prolix circumlocutions or esoteric jargon. We have also thought it pointless and mistaken to try to present all sides of every issue (particularly since we know neither all the issues nor all the sides), or to try to insure that our articles were selected from a "balanced" list of publications.

We have organized our selections into a loose confederation of themes, which we know overlap one another and may even duplicate a point now and then. We also decided to let the articles speak for themselves, and so disciplined ourselves to keep the headnotes brief. How well we have succeeded in these several objectives will, of course, depend on the judgment of our readers. We hope you will share our views of what is interesting and important.

Our thanks go to our editor, James J. Carroll, Jr., for his patience and help, and to Ethel Livingston, for maintaining her equanimity while keeping order in a jungle of materials. Our biggest debt, of course, is to the very able authors of the readings we have merely selected. It is their knowledge and creativity that give this book its reason for being.

J. C. L.
R. G. T.

Contents

vii

Section III. Pluralism at Work: Stability and Change or Stalemate at Dead Center?   91

Section IV. The Manipulative Arts   151

Section V. Law and Order: Liberty, Law, and Violence   213

American Politics in the Seventies: Where Did Man's "Last, Best Hope" Go Wrong?

To read today about politics is to read about crisis, legitimacy, credibility, alienation, revolt, confrontation, violence. One reads about the meaninglessness of elections these days; if elections have become meaningless, can the people still be said to control the government? What, then, distinguishes us from peoples who are not democratic? The justice and the urgency of the cause of the black, the brown, the poor, are generally recognized, but the system seems unable to respond. How long will they wait? When the system does respond, it is often to their marching feet or threatening rage rather than to the justice of their cause. What does this mean for the future? Will the backlash of an aroused "silent majority" be reactionary and oppressive? The political air echoes with serious talk of revolution. Should it be taken seriously? The war in Southeast Asia has made it a commonplace for Presidents to lie to and deceive the American people. It has raised the question of American war crimes (My Lai *and* "free fire zones," *and* aerial "interdiction") on a scale that dulls the capacity for moral reaction. Has the American political conscience, as David Halberstam tells us, been "vietnamized"?

We begin with a view from abroad: A British novelist tells us why he feels sorry for America. How can this be, that an outsider can talk this way about the land that men once thought to have been created especially by God himself as the setting for the grand experiment in the creation of a "new man" who could live in peace and freedom?

The several short essays that follow give us some sample answers to the question of what it feels like to be a politically informed citizen of America in the 1970's. They are intended to convey the flavor of the criticism, the upheaval, the urgency, the despair and the hope, the anguish and the sense of betrayal, the rage and the outrage, the alienation and rejection, the commitment and rededication that surround and influence American public life. It is a time of crisis. Here are some of its dimensions and characteristics.

In the reaction of Americans to these pressures and conflicts, a new political force has emerged: middle America, the new "forgotten man." In the revolt of the "silent majority" the nature of the crisis is more clearly revealed and an important portent for the future is outlined. In the final selections in this section the characteristics and implications of this new political phenomenon are discussed.

J. B. PRIESTLEY

I Feel Sorry for America

I have been feeling genuinely and deeply sorry for the American people—the ordinary decent Americans as distinct from the bloodthirsty half-barmy riff-raff. I am sorry for them because, bewildered, saddened or maddened, they are trying to grope their way out of a long dangerous dream.

In this dream, which closed over them from childhood onwards, not only was their country the richest and most powerful in the world, which of course it is, but also the wisest, the kindest, the purest, offering a supreme example to all mankind. It was a new sort of country, not simply a place where a lot of people had lived a long time, like Britain or France. It had come out of a revolution, made too in an enlightenment when men were assumed to be entirely rational. It represented a truly magnificent idea. An idea all had to accept and uphold. Any lack of warm patriotic feeling amounted to a rejection of the grand idea, a cynical betrayal of a new way of life.

While Americans have been far bolder at muck-racking than we have—and any dictionary of American slang shows how far-reaching and inventive their cynicism can be—nevertheless they have been brought up and have lived under this vast blue canopy of glory and wonder and communal self-praise.

Now, when reality has come crashing through over and over again and the canopy is all gaps and patches, it looks as if most of the American people are reacting in sharply different ways. Somewhere in the middle are the people who tend to be deeply immersed in political apathy and routine TV. Such people feel fairly secure behind a mild cynicism, a sort of family inheritance, but even so I feel that a demagogue of genius, somebody several cuts above the George Wallaces, could start them stumbling after him.

However, it is the reaction of the other two groups that I find far more significant. They are both comparative minorities, but both have strong if very different assets. Let us look first at the one on the Left, showing us so many young rebels. Suddenly they discovered they had been told a lot of thumping great lies. All that stuff about America they had been handed out was just a load of bullshit.

Americans weren't better than other people; they were mostly much worse;

Source: Mr. Priestley is a British novelist, essayist, dramatist. This selection originally appeared in the *New Statesman* (London), Dec. 12, 1969; the portion reproduced here is reprinted from *Atlas*, March 1970, pp. 18–19, by permission of the *New Statesman*.

they were in no position to teach other people anything except advanced and dangerously suspect technology. It is now time the U.S. started all over again and did much better. This is more or less what they think, and, really much more important, what they feel.

Now many of us over here are not at all out of sympathy with these disillusioned young Americans. We also dislike the society they dislike. We are wearily contemptuous of its self-glorification. Nevertheless, I for one think a lot of these youngsters go too far in utterly rejecting the American idea, the big dream. Because some of its claims are fraudulent, there is a danger that the rebels may destroy what remains good and true in it. One example will show what I mean. There still exists in America, very much to its credit, a tradition of free speech. Too many young protesters clearly no longer believe in free speech, being ready to howl down any speaker who happens to disagree with them. Once in power, they could create the very conditions that drove so many spirited men and women from Europe to America. Again, it seems to me that democracy depends on a common standard of decency and good manners. If you are against a university president, you don't prove it by defecating all over his study. This takes us back to the Nazis.

Now for the third group, away to the far right, still a minority but a very powerful minority indeed, occupying many seats of power. These people— and now I have dismissed the mere idiots—have had shocking doubts about the great idea, the big dream; so that simple honest, God-fearing American folk were soon ringed round with menacing faces—Reds, of course, socialist agitators, long-haired intellectuals, the only sexually promiscuous eunuchs the world has ever known, the treacherous eggheads, most journalists and TV newscasters, in fact anybody not jumping up and cheering Old Glory all the time.

This psychological situation, making any mature integration quite impossible, not only encourages instant anger, always a bad sign, but also, like an evil spell, can freeze men not utterly brainless into a rigid stupidity. Men who were bright at school and college are turned into blockheads. Alternatively, more sensitive and neurotic types, refusing to recognize what is there in the dark of their minds, quietly go mad, when they may still be making decisions that affect the whole country, perhaps the whole world. Others again are so determined to be completely extravert, that they now appear to be existing short of a dimension or two and suggest a curious and sinister emptiness, with no thickness, no warmth, no juice. And, because reality has been rejected, because honest doubt has been savagely suppressed, because these people are so perilously one-sided, mixed with their stupidity, bigotry and instant anger is a certain cruelty their grandfathers never knew.

So a great country, based on a noble revolutionary idea, is now tearing itself apart, and may experience more anger, violence, shame and sorrow before it can heal itself. I for one am desperately sorry.

ART HOPPE

To Root Against Your Country

The radio this morning said the Allied invasion of Laos had bogged down. Without thinking, I nodded and said, "Good."

And having said it, I realized the bitter truth: Now I root against my own country.

This is how far we have come in this hated and endless war. This is the nadir I have reached in this winter of my discontent. This is how close I border on treason:

Now I root against my own country. How frighteningly sad this is. My generation was raised to love our country and we loved it unthinkingly. We licked Hitler and Tojo and Mussolini. Those were our shining hours. Those were our days of faith.

They were evil; we were good. They told lies; we spoke the truth. Our cause was just, our purposes noble, and in victory we were magnanimous. What a wonderful country we were! I loved it so.

But now, having descended down the torturous, lying, brutalizing years of this bloody war, I have come to the dank and lightless bottom of the well: I have come to root against the country that once I blindly loved.

I can rationalize it. I can say that if the invasion of Laos succeeds, the chimera of victory will dance once again before our eyes—leading us once again into more years of mindless slaughter. Thus, I can say, I hope the invasion fails.

But it is more than that. It is that I have come to hate my country's role in Vietnam.

I hate the massacres, the body counts, the free fire zones, the napalming of civilians, the poisoning of rice crops. I hate being part of My Lai. I hate the fact that we have now dropped more explosives on these scrawny Asian peasants than we did on all our enemies in World War II.

And I hate my leaders who, over the years, have conscripted our young men and sent them there to kill or be killed in a senseless cause simply because they can find no honorable way out—no honorable way out for them.

I don't root for the enemy. I doubt they are any better than we. I don't give

Source: Mr. Hoppe is a political satirist and newspaper columnist. This is from "Our Man Hoppe," *San Francisco Chronicle*, March 1, 1971. Copyright © 1971 by the Chronicle Publishing Company. Reprinted by permission of the publisher.

a damn any more who wins the war. But because I hate what my country is doing in Vietnam, I emotionally and often irrationally hope that it fails.

It is a terrible thing to root against your own country. If I were alone, it wouldn't matter. But I don't think I am alone. I think many Americans must feel these same sickening emotions I feel. I think they share my guilt. I think they share my rage.

If this is true, we must end this war now—in defeat, if necessary. We must end it because all of Southeast Asia is not worth the hatred, shame, guilt and rage that is tearing Americans apart. We must end it not for those among our young who have come to hate America, but for those who somehow manage to love it still.

I doubt that I can ever again love my country in that unthinking way I did when I was young. Perhaps this is a good thing.

But I would hope the day will come when I can once again believe what my country says and once again approve of what it does. I want to have faith once again in the justness of my country's causes and the nobleness of its ideals.

What I want so very much is to be able once again to root for my own, my native land.

ART HOPPE

The Light Will Shine Again

The other day, in a sad and bitter mood, I wrote a column about how I had come to root against my own country in Vietnam because of this ugly, inane, interminable war.

I tried to say how it had been when I was young—how shining and noble and right my country had seemed to me. I tried to tell how this brutal, senseless war had tainted and degraded the love I had once felt for my own land. I tried to express the shame, the rage and the hopelessness that was in me.

Source: From "Our Man Hoppe," *San Francisco Chronicle*, March 5, 1971. Copyright 1971 Chronicle Publishing Company. Reprinted by permission of the publisher.

These were depressing things to say. I said them because I thought they should be said. Then I waited for the mail to come in. I waited with dread.

In this business, you can usually predict the tone of the mail that any particular column will draw. I expected a few approving letters from the Left and a flood of hate mail from the Right. Those without strong views seldom bother to write a columnist.

The mail is coming in. And now I have something more to say because I think it should be said.

The first thing that surprised me about the mail was its volume. Never have I written a column that has attracted so many letters.

I opened the first few nervously. They were approving. The first dozen, the first score—all were approving. Of the first 300, there were only four angry letters and three of those were unsigned.

Gradually, as I read through these letters agreeing with my stand and approving my expressing it, my spirits lifted. Where I had been depressed, I was now elated. Where I had been sick and bitter, I was now proud.

Part of it, of course, was the approval. Every man cherishes approval. But it was more than that.

These letters were from people like me. A few, a very few, were from professional America haters. But the rest were from doctors, lawyers, accountants, housewives and one grand lady who typed under her signature, "A small, female and old voice from Santa Rosa."

Surprisingly many were from military men including four ex-army Colonels. Surprisingly few were from college students. Most were of my generation, a probation officer, a policeman, a construction worker.

What they said, most of them, was that they, too, had seen their love for their country eroded by this endless war. And they, too, mourned it.

It was this, more than anything, that heartened me. In only a few societies could I have written what I wrote. In most, I would be clapped into jail. Yet these people, with nothing to gain, expressed their agreement and approval.

And they signed their names.

In this land, in these times, you can still stand up and say your country's wrong. More importantly, if you do, those who agree will stand up with you.

This, by God, is the greatness of this country.

This country is still sunk in the decaying mess that is Vietnam. We will be there, I think, for months or years to come. But my hopelessness has passed.

For even in that decaying mess, that which shone in my youth still glimmers. And now, for the first time in years, I believe with all my heart that it will shine again.

JOHN GARDNER

Everybody's Organized but the People

I know that many of you share my concern over what is happening to our country.

That is why I am coming to you; to ask you to join me in forming a new, independent, non-partisan organization that could be an effective force in rebuilding America.

It is called *Common Cause*.

It will not be a third party, but a third force in American life which will uphold the public interest against all comers, particularly the special interests that dominate our national life today. Common Cause will not support candidates; it will confine itself to issues.

Wherever you touch the public process in this country today, almost without exception, you will find a failure of performance.

The air we breathe is foul. The water we drink is impure. Our public schools are in crisis. Our courts cry out for reform. Race conflict is deepening. Unemployment is rising. The housing shortage has driven rents through the roof. Inflation runs rampant, sapping the initiative of our people and wiping out the life's savings of our senior citizens.

The things that government is supposed to do, it is not doing. The things it is not supposed to do—encroaching upon the lives and liberties of its citizens —it *is* doing.

One of our aims will be to revitalize politics and government. The need is great. State governments are mostly feeble. City government is archaic. The Congress of the United States is in grave need of overhaul. The parties are becoming useless as instruments of the popular will. We can no longer accept such obsolescence.

Let's Get Together and Do Something About It

The first thing Common Cause will do is to assist you to speak and act in behalf of legislation designed to solve the nation's problems. We will keep

Source: Mr. Gardner is former Secretary of Health, Education, and Welfare and currently Chairman of Common Cause. This article is reprinted from a full-page advertisement in *The National Observer*, Jan. 11, 1971, p. 15, by permission of the author.

you up to date on crucial issues before Congress. We will suggest when and where to bring pressure to bear.

I shall not attempt to list here all the issues with which Common Cause will be concerned.

We believe there is urgency in ending the war in Indochina *now*. We believe there must be a major reordering of national priorities, and that the Government cannot go on spending $200,000,000 a day for "national defense." We believe the problems of poverty and race must be among our first concerns. We will call for new solutions in housing, employment, education, health, consumer protection, environment, family planning, law enforcement and the administration of justice.

We intend to take the phrase "Common Cause" seriously. The things that unite us as a people are more important than the things that divide us. No particular interest group can prosper for long if the nation is disintegrating. Every group must have an overriding interest in the well-being of the whole society.

A Good Place to Begin: Abolish the Seniority System

All efforts to bring about constructive social change come down to specific battles to accomplish specific goals.

We have already plunged into the fight to end the tyrannical seniority system in Congress. Committee chairmen in the Senate and House have absolute, unchecked power. They hold their chairmanships for life (sometimes to the point of senility), as long as they continue to be re-elected to Congress and their party holds a majority. They are immovable and responsible to no one.

Their decisions affect the lives of every American, and sometimes the deaths. And by what criterion are they chosen? Intelligence? Wisdom? Character? Leadership?

None of these qualities makes the slightest difference. *Committee chairmen get the job strictly and automatically on length of continuous service in the Senate or House.* If that means that a man of limited intelligence or character moves into a position crucial to the nation's future, so much the worse for the nation.

Also, the system unfairly favors one-party states and districts, since those are the areas that send the same man back to Congress for twenty, thirty, *even forty years*.

The seniority principle is not written into the Constitution. It is not even a law. It is simply a custom of the Congress and could be changed with ease.

This is just one of the practical steps that could be taken immediately to make Congress more responsive. But there has been no active, powerful, hard-hitting constituency to fight for such steps. We can provide that kind of constituency.

We Have Not Behaved like a Great People

Many of you share my anger at institutions and individuals that have behaved irresponsibly. But, if we're going to focus our anger, a good place to begin is with ourselves.

We are not being the people we set out to be. We have not lived by the values we profess to honor. And we will never get back on course until we take some tough, realistic steps to revitalize our institutions. We had better get on with it.

In recent years we have seen too much complacency, narrow self-interest, meanness of mind and spirit, irrational hatred and fear. But as I travel around the country, I see something else. I see great remaining strength in this nation. I see deeper reserves of devotion and community concern than are being tapped by present leadership. I see many, many Americans who would like to help rebuild this nation but don't know where to begin. . . .

With a large and active membership, we can begin to remake America.

TOM WICKER

The Politics Before Us

I was asked to talk today about the results of the 1970 elections and where they may have left us. I'm going to pass over the numbers game that we've played in Washington since those elections. I'm going to pass over the question of whether or not there is an ideological majority of one kind or another in the Senate. I'm going to get right down to the literal fact and say that it

Source: Mr. Wicker is a prominent journalist and columnist. This article is based on the transcript of an extemporaneous speech to a meeting sponsored by the New Democratic Coalition on Jan. 12, 1970; reprinted from the *New York Review of Books*, Feb. 11, 1971, pp. 14–16, by permission of Paul R. Reynolds, Inc. Copyright © 1971 by NYREV, Inc.

seems to me that the only thing you can say about the 1970 elections is that the Democrats picked up nine seats in the House and the Republicans one and a half senators. If you wonder how there can be a half-senator, you haven't met some of those fellows.

Getting beyond the numbers game to some results of the 1970 elections that may mean something, I would say first that there was no further swing to the Republicans in the South. After at least a decade and a half of a steady Republican trend in the South, the Republicans did not make any further gains.

In fact, they lost two governorships they had held, and two more they had hoped very much to win. They won only one seat in Congress and that was from the valley of Virginia. So I would suggest that Nixon may be in a good deal more trouble in 1972 in achieving even as many electoral votes in the South as he did in '68, particularly since Governor Wallace now appears to be ready to run entirely as a Southern candidate, trying to consolidate the Southern vote as best he can. And after his four years in office, it will not be as easy for Southern voters to delude themselves that somehow the election of Richard Nixon will turn back the tide of the civil rights movement.

There are some other consequences. There is no real evidence, it seems to me, of the kind of conservative trend that had been predicted. I'm not talking necessarily about conservatism as against the old New Deal or conservatism in economics or anything of that sort. I have in mind a sort of law-and-order conservatism, a crackdown on the dissidents. I saw no evidence of any such trend in the 1970 elections, despite the assiduous efforts of the Administration and most of the press to convince us that there was such a trend.

Another thing I didn't see in the 1970 elections was a vast, overwhelming demand for the Democratic party. People like to cite all the governorships the party won. They should look at the governorship in Nebraska, for instance, in which the man who was elected there was about as far to the right, particularly in economic matters, as you could get, even though he ran in the Democratic party. In fact, he displaced a relatively moderate, progressive Republican governor who committed the sin of raising taxes in order to try to provide services for the people. So I saw no overwhelming trend to the Democrats, particularly since so many of their victories were won out of a rather sterile dependence on the economic dislocations that the Democratic party itself had managed to produce in the 1960s.

Another result of those elections is that there seemed to me to be no vast demand for the Republican party either. As I've said, they lost nine seats in the House, despite the fact that they hadn't carried the House in '68, which meant that there was no reservoir of weak Republican seats there, ready to be taken back by the Democrats. They failed to gain much in the Senate despite the fact that in the two previous elections for this class of senators—1958 and 1964—there had been a Democratic landslide.

And finally, it seemed to me that there was no evidence that the leadership of the Republican party, the President and the Vice President—in their strategy, their personal performances, or their actual appearances in the various states—had any overwhelming effect on the electorate, except negative.

I saw no vast demand for either party in those elections and therefore the only real conclusion that I'd venture about 1970 is that President Nixon did not improve himself. He did not, as the quarterbacks say, get good field position for 1972 or for his party, except in one sense. Politics being what they are, I would suggest that his willingness to expose himself to every lost cause from Ralph Smith to George Murphy and to work as hard as he could for the party probably cemented his intraparty leadership. At the same time, the failure of Reagan to reach the majority predicted for him by such experts as Evans and Novak seems to me to have lessened the possibility of a right-wing challenge to Nixon. Now a recent column by Kevin Phillips has raised the possibility of a left-wing challenge to Nixon, if indeed there are those who can regard a challenge from Governor Rockefeller as a left-wing challenge. But I would think that President Nixon's party leadership and hold on the party probably are now a little bit stronger than one might have expected.

Another more obvious conclusion is that Senator Muskie is now the front runner for the Democratic party, and the polls seem to confirm this. But I think that that's a mixed benefit. I can recall when Governor Romney was the front runner at just about this same time in 1967. I wouldn't want to compare the two but, generally speaking, I would say that a front runner at this stage does have a number of problems to contend with.

He's everyone's target in both parties. Every time that some issue arises he's expected to comment on it. And in this case, there's another doubly difficult problem for Senator Muskie: he is in danger of becoming identified suddenly and right away as the candidate of the LBJ–Mayor Daley–John Connally wing of the Democratic party. And I don't think there's any doubt at the moment that this wing of the party, with certain reservations, is indeed in favor of Muskie because he appears to be a man who might reconcile it with other wings of the party. Finally, I think Muskie's position as front runner is endangered by the fact that he still must face what I expect to be vigorous opposition in the Democratic primaries in 1972.

A final conclusion that I would draw from the election, after these two, is that American politics are still unsettled and not moving in any clear direction. I see no evidence, for example, that there's some huge right-wing swing in the Atlantic community, heralded by the election of Edward Heath, and that Nixon and the Republicans are simply following suit along that line.

Nor is there evidence of a great left-wing swing. I think it is useful here to compare the Presidential elections of 1960 and 1968. The election of 1964 was exceptional because it followed so closely after the death of President Kennedy. In retrospect there was never any doubt that the Democratic nominee was going to be elected to complete that period as best people thought it could be. People didn't want three Presidents in the space of a little over a year. But if you look at the elections of 1960 and 1968, they were both, as we say in the South, as tight as Dick's hatband: very close elections in which very few votes either way could have changed the outcome. In fact, if you look at all the Presidential elections, excluding 1964, since 1948, and if you add up all the votes cast for Republicans and all the votes cast for Democrats they come to just about the same numerical total.

During this entire period, there hasn't been a clear trend in American politics, except toward the ultimate bankruptcy of the New Deal. Certainly there has not been a clear ideological trend and I don't think there is one now, nor that the 1970 elections suggested anything of the kind.

I would think then that this means, as we look ahead to 1972 and beyond, that we are in for a continuation of the rather turbulent and embittered politics that we have become accustomed to in recent years, a politics with a very strident base of moral enthusiasm, of ideological sentiment, of zeal on the part of partisans of both sides—a politics in sharp contrast to that of only ten or fifteen years ago, which was much more nearly compromise, coalition politics.

A more turbulent and embittered politics will mean that people like the New Democratic Coalition in New York and the ethnic groups and the blacks and the young are going to demand, or try to find, forms to make ends mean something. They will demand participation in politics, that their views be taken into account. So I think turbulance and a demand for participation can be expected to continue for many years and are not something peculiar to a particular generation in America.

I also suggest that we've probably entered an era of one-term Presidencies. This has nothing particularly to do with Mr. Nixon. President Johnson, I suggest, is the first victim of that circumstance.

Until now in the twentieth century we have, by and large, expected that our Presidents would win two terms. The only Presidents who have sought re-election in the twentieth century and failed to win it were Taft, who went down in the Bull Moose split, and Hoover, who went down in the Depression. Just this week in a column advocating a six-year Presidency, William S. White stated the assumption that, generally speaking, American Presidents win two terms. I think that that assumption now ought to be changed. The assumption now ought to be, in my judgment, that a President seeking re-election probably is going to be in deep trouble. That doesn't mean that he can't get elected— the opposition party might help elect him, as could happen in '72. But he's going to be in deep trouble, rather than having an easy time.

The most obvious reason for this is that communications are beginning to work for the outs too, as we saw on election eve last year, when the President's speech was seen by Democratic politicians as helpful. While the White House is a "bully pulpit," as Theodore Roosevelt said, when the man in the White House goes on television, he's not necessarily a bully preacher.

Communications can work for the outs and after our twenty-odd years of experience with television, I am beginning to believe that television burns out politicians about the same way it does comedians. (This seems a possible explanation for the decline and fall of Spiro T. Agnew.)

The man in office appears very often on television in turbulent surroundings. He seems to be the man who is struggling with difficulties, with controversies. Whereas the fellow who is seeking his office, like Senator Muskie coming out of his den on the banks of the Allagash River in Maine, speaks very pleasantly about how things could be.

Perhaps this danger of politicians being burned out has something to do with the nature of the Presidency itself. Many profound things happened in the American soul in 1960. But in particular, I think that the monarchical sense that we once had of the Presidency—the willingness to rally 'round the Presidency, no matter who the occupant was—has been diminished by the revelations that this institution too has feet of clay, that we cannot necessarily trust what it tells us, that its wisdom is not necessarily far-reaching.

Incidentally, I think the very office itself has lost something of the magical aura that it once had. In Dean Acheson's *Present at the Creation,* for instance, that particular aura infuses every page. In Acheson's book, which is preeminently a book of a man of the Forties and Fifties, there is a sense that the President, no matter who he is or what he's been, somehow is all of a sudden set apart from the rest of us.

I think there are not many of us who believe that any more. And I think this has diminished the power of the politician President to use the institutional office to protect himself.

But the major reason why we may be coming into an era of one-term Presidencies is that the problems are becoming too difficult. We expect the President today to be everything from the mayor of Hoboken to the leader of the free world. We expect him to wear a Green Beret and a hard hat and to throw out the first ball for the Washington Senators.

At the same time we have had a shift in American politics from the old, relatively simplistic issue of improving the standard of living to a great many more complicated, difficult issues that don't necessarily yield to legislation. Many of us have been disillusioned since the late Fifties, when we expected the civil rights legislation to have a tremendous impact on racial amity in this country. It hasn't. If anything, this legislation had the opposite effect.

So we begin to see that passing bills and proclaiming policies don't really have the impact that we once thought they did. Presidents, therefore, it seems to me, are victims of the pace of change. I think it's a fair assessment of Mr. Nixon's first two years that he came to office having spent the preceding four years not noticing what was happening in the country while he ran for office: you can't notice what's happening in the country if you're running. So in his first two years in office he attempted to be an Eisenhower President, and also, in a way, a Kennedy President, someone who could deal with the chessboard problems of the world—a checkmate here, a gambit to be pulled on

Nasser there—without realizing that the house was coming down around his ears.

And if anything is encouraging in Washington today it is that the pundits say that Mr. Nixon, in preparing to get himself re-elected in 1972, is turning to domestic affairs. It's encouraging because I think the word may have gotten through to him that his view, expressed to Theodore White before the election, that you don't really need a President for domestic affairs, you just need a Cabinet, isn't good enough any more. It isn't the era of Eisenhower.

The problems in the country are intractable. They don't necessarily respond to politics or to policy but they all have the effect of reacting against the man who's in the White House. That's why I think Presidents are going to come up every four years from now on and find themselves in deep trouble because they will not have been able to deal with the matters that people see as their real problems.

The real problem in America today, and the gut issue of our politics, does not, as I've said, have very much to do with the standard of living. We're glutted in this country with the standard of living. Nor do I think we are undergoing some kind of psychological breakdown because all of a sudden, as some have argued, we've been projected into history. We were projected into history a half-century ago. And a half-century, the way time moves nowadays, is five centuries. Nor do I think we're entering Professor Reich's Consciousness III either. I might myself welcome it if we were, but I don't think it's happening.

What has really got us in its grip today in my judgment is the general concern, a lament from the farthest right to the farthest left, and from the poorest to the richest, with the breakdown of American life, because American life doesn't work any more. You can't get your garbage picked up and you can't get a quick and easy ride to work on the subway. Or if you get on the freeway with your car, the traffic doesn't move. Or if you walk you get hit over the head and somebody takes your wallet. As George Wallace says, the crook will be out of court before you're out of the hospital and that is a fact, even if George Wallace did say it.

Because every time that the publisher of *The New York Times* gives you a handsome raise, well deserved for the work that you've done so beautifully the past year, prices go up faster, and taxes go up, and in the long run your check shows you have less net money at the end of the month.

Because you can't stand to breathe the air, and if you live in Washington the Potomac River will make you sick when you drink it. And because of the lack of quality from top to bottom in American life. Because when you turn on the television you don't see anything but junk. And when you go down to the store and buy something you don't get anything but junk.

Last year at Christmas we bought my daughter a radio record player. And by God we had to take it back because it didn't work. And then the second one they gave us, we had to take that back because it didn't work. And finally we had to take the third one we got to a shop and get them to adjust the speed of the turntable.

At the same time we bought for our son one of those little mini-bikes and we had to take that back because it didn't work, and that tells you something about materialism in American life as well as the lack of quality. It sometimes seems there's not any damn thing you can buy that's worth a damn. And we all know that.

What's bothering the people today is that life has broken down in this country. In the midst of wealth, in the midst of plenty, above all, in the midst of pretensions, life has broken down. We can't hear ourselves think for the noise in the streets and most of the noise in the streets comes from where we are tearing down our heritage and everything that's worthwhile in this country, and putting up plastic and pressed concrete that twenty years from now we'll have to tear down and put up all over again.

It's not just the war in Vietnam and it's not just that we're shipping all those arms abroad. It's that we're concealing from ourselves the fact that we're doing those things, as the recent Senate hearings have just revealed.

It's the persistence of racial strife in this country, despite all the legislation that we've passed, and all that we've tried to do. What does that mean?

The persistence of racial strife in this country means that there's something wrong with us, not something wrong with the laws, and we know that. Welfare—it doesn't matter how liberal you are or how conservative you are, you know that the way we give out welfare is wrong. It's a bad system. There's something wrong with it and yet we can't change it.

So I think the general concern from the poorest black to the richest white and everybody in between is that American life has broken down; it doesn't work; in the midst of pretensions and wealth it doesn't work.

Why doesn't it work?

I don't know all the reasons why, but perhaps I can try to suggest some of them. One reason is that the pace of change has moved like a bullet. In the twenty-five years since World War II, technology has made this country move, as none of Detroit's automobiles will move. And while this has happened, all of our institutions have grown old, their arteries have hardened and they've dug in their heels and they're entrenched.

And I would say that there are really four of these institutions that matter, in the broadest sense:

There is the bureauracy, federal, state, and local.

There are the labor unions.

There are the corporations.

And there are the political parties.

All of them are overaged and entrenched and dug in and refuse to change, and all of them are holding us back. That's what we've got to go for.

Here I get to the weakest part of my thesis, because now you say, all right, how are we going to do it? I don't know. But I know this: If we're going to do it in any way, we're not going to do it by moderation.

I want to say that, in the interests of saving America, moderation is no virtue and extremism is no vice. And I stand behind that.

We've got to have a political movement in America, a political movement that will be at least of the courage and foresightedness of the consumer movement under Ralph Nader. We've got to have something that goes beyond the embryonic lobby movement headed by John Gardner. We've got to incorporate the various environmental movements that have shown what can be done here. The SST has been beaten in the Senate. Or if it hasn't been beaten it may at least be whipped into some kind of shape that the human race can live with.

Something else we've got to do, if we're going to have a political movement that comes anywhere close to matching these other movements, and I say this with some regional pride. We've got to go back and study the George Wallace example. George Wallace is a man who stands on a side of the spectrum which I don't share, but I come from people who do share it; and those people who do share it are good people. The mere fact that they vote for George Wallace doesn't mean that they're bad people; it means that they're upset like the rest of us about things that affect their lives. George Wallace showed that you don't have to take it.

The importance of George Wallace in 1968 was not so much what we thought it was and what I thought it was, that he might throw the election into the House of Representatives or hold the balance of power in the Electoral College or something of that sort. The importance of George Wallace was the influence he had on Richard Nixon, on Richard Nixon's campaign and on his administration. It behooves not so much the Democratic party as all those who would seek faith in the Democratic party to learn that lesson. The Democratic party is not going to be moved by anything less than the same amount of power that George Wallace wields on the Republican party.

I'm not opposed to Senator Muskie. But whether it's Senator Muskie or anyone else, I don't think that a moderate, centrist candidate, nominated by the Democratic party in 1972, even though he may defeat the present incumbent in the White House, is going to make one damn bit of difference.

The question is how *do* we make a difference? And I confess I don't know how. But the best that I can say is that George Wallace made a difference in the Republican party, and a difference that we all deplore.

When the Democratic party goes into convention—no doubt in Chicago again in 1972, because of course that blot must be wiped from the escutcheon of our leading Democrat—unless it is confronted with a monumental threat that has behind it more than words, a threat that has behind it people who have said and have made their intention plain, that if necessary they're going to be on the ballot, and they're going to be on the ballot in fifty states, and they're going to advocate certain things. I make the prediction here today that the Democratic party will nominate someone who will, as they say, "pull us together." And who will then be elected—and who will not make any difference.

GEORGE WALD

A Generation in Search of a Future

All of you know that in the last couple of years there has been student unrest breaking at times into violence in many parts of the world: in England, Germany, Italy, Spain, Mexico and needless to say, in many parts of this country. There has been a great deal of discussion as to what it all means. Perfectly clearly it means something different in Mexico from what it does in France, and something different in France from what it does in Tokyo, and something different in Tokyo from what it does in this country. Yet unless we are to assume that students have gone crazy all over the world, or that they have just decided that it's the thing to do, there must be some common meaning.

I don't need to go so far afield to look for that meaning. I am a teacher, and at Harvard, I have a class of about 350 students—men and women—most of them freshmen and sophomores. Over these past few years I have felt increasingly that something is terribly wrong—and this year ever so much more than last. Something has gone sour, in teaching and in learning. It's almost as though there were a widespread feeling that education has become irrelevant.

A lecture is much more of a dialogue than many of you probably appreciate. As you lecture, you keep watching the faces; and information keeps coming back to you all the time. I began to feel, particularly this year, that I was

Source: Dr. Wald is a professor of biology at Harvard and winner of the Nobel Prize in 1967 for his contribution to medicine. This article is from an extemporaneous speech to a group of faculty and students at Massachusetts Institute of Technology. Reprinted from *The Boston Globe*, March 8, 1969, by permission of the author.

missing much of what was coming back. I tried asking the students, but they didn't or couldn't help me very much.

But I think I know what's the matter, even a little better than they do. I think that this whole generation of students is beset with a profound uneasiness. I don't think that they have yet quite defined its source. I think I understand the reasons for their uneasiness even better than they do. What is more, I share their uneasiness.

What's bothering those students? Some of them tell you it's the Vietnam War. I think the Vietnam War is the most shameful episode in the whole of American history. The concept of War Crimes is an American invention. We've committed many War Crimes in Vietnam; but I'll tell you something interesting about that. We were committing War Crimes in World War II, even before the Nuremburg trials were held and the principle of war crimes stated. The saturation bombing of German cities was a War Crime. Dropping atom bombs on Hiroshima and Nagasaki was a War Crime. If we had lost the war, some of our leaders might have had to answer for those actions.

I've gone through all of that history lately, and I find that there's a gimmick in it. It isn't written out, but I think we established it by precedent. That gimmick is that if one can allege that one is repelling or retaliating for an *aggression*—after that everything goes. And you see we are living in a world in which all wars are wars of defense. All War Departments are now Defense Departments. This is all part of the double talk of our time. The aggressor is always on the other side. And I suppose this is why our ex-Secretary of State, Dean Rusk—a man in whom repetition takes the place of reason, and stubbornness takes the place of character—went to such pains to insist, as he still insists, that in Vietnam we are repelling an aggression. And if that's what we are doing—so runs the doctrine—anything goes. If the concept of war crimes is ever to mean anything, they will have to be defined as categories of acts, regardless of alleged provocation. But that isn't so now.

I think we've lost that war, as a lot of other people think, too. The Vietnamese have a secret weapon. It's their willingness to die, beyond our willingness to kill. In effect they've been saying, you can kill us, but you'll have to kill a lot of us, you may have to kill all of us. And thank heavens, we are not yet ready to do that.

Yet we have come a long way—far enough to sicken many Americans, far enough even to sicken our fighting men. Far enough so that our national symbols have gone sour. How many of you can sing about "the rockets' red glare, bombs bursting in air" without thinking, those are *our* bombs and *our* rockets bursting over South Vietnamese villages? When those words were written, we were a people struggling for freedom against oppression. Now we are supporting real or thinly disguised military dictatorships all over the world, helping them to control and repress peoples struggling for their freedom.

But that Vietnam War, shameful and terrible as it is, seems to me only an immediate incident in a much larger and more stubborn situation.

Part of my trouble with students is that almost all the students I teach were born since World War II. Just after World War II, a series of new and abnormal procedures came into American life. We regarded them at the time as temporary aberrations. We thought we would get back to normal American life some day. But those procedures have stayed with us now for more than 20 years, and those students of mine have never known anything else. They think those things are normal. Students think we've always had a Pentagon, that we have always had a big army, and that we always had a draft. But those are all new things in American life; and I think that they are incompatible with what America meant before.

How many of you realize that just before World War II the entire American army including the Air Force numbered 139,000 men? Then World War II started, but we weren't yet in it; and seeing that there was great trouble in the world, we doubled this army to 268,000 men. Then in World War II it got to be 8 million. And then World War II came to an end, and we prepared to go back to a peacetime army somewhat as the American army had always been before. And indeed in 1950—you think about 1950, our international commitments, the Cold War, the Truman Doctrine, and all the rest of it— in 1950 we got down to 600,000 men.

Now we have 3.5 million men under arms: about 600,000 in Vietnam, about 300,000 more in "support areas" elsewhere in the Pacific, about 250,000 in Germany. And there are a lot at home. Some months ago we were told that 300,000 National Guardsmen and 200,000 reservists—so half a million men—had been specially trained for riot duty in the cities.

I say the Vietnam War is just an immediate incident, because so long as we keep that big an army, it will always find things to do. If the Vietnam War stopped tomorrow, with that big a military establishment, the chances are that we would be in another such adventure abroad or at home before you knew it.

As for the draft: Don't reform the draft—get rid of it.

A peacetime draft is the most un-American thing I know. All the time I was growing up I was told about oppressive Central European countries and Russia, where young men were forced into the army; and I was told what they did about it. They chopped off a finger, or shot off a couple of toes; or better still, if they could manage it, they came to this country. And we understood that, and sympathized, and were glad to welcome them.

Now by present estimates four to six thousand Americans of draft age have left this country for Canada, another two or three thousand have gone to Europe, and it looks as though many more are preparing to emigrate.

A few months ago I received a letter from the Harvard Alumni Bulletin posing a series of questions that students might ask a professor involving what to do about the draft. I was asked to write what I would tell those students. All I had to say to those students was this: If any of them had decided to evade the draft and asked my help, I would help him in any way I could. I would feel as I suppose members of the underground railway felt in pre-Civil War days, helping runaway slaves to get to Canada. It wasn't altogether a popular position then; but what do you think of it now?

A bill to stop the draft was recently introduced in the Senate (S. 503), sponsored by a group of senators that ran the gamut from McGovern and Hatfield to Barry Goldwater. I hope it goes through; but any time I find that Barry Goldwater and I are in agreement, that makes me take another look.

And indeed there are choices in getting rid of the draft. I think that when we get rid of the draft, we must also cut back the size of the armed forces. It seems to me that in peacetime a total of one million men is surely enough. If there is an argument for American military forces of more than one million men in peacetime, I should like to hear that argument debated.

There is another thing being said closely connected with this: that to keep an adequate volunteer army, one would have to raise the pay considerably. That's said so positively and often that people believe it. I don't think it is true.

The great bulk of our present armed forces are genuine volunteers. Among first-term enlistments, 49 percent are true volunteers. Another 30 percent are so-called "reluctant volunteers," persons who volunteer under pressure of the draft. Only 21 percent are draftees. All re-enlistments, of course are true volunteers.

So the great majority of our present armed forces are true volunteers. Whole services are composed entirely of volunteers: the Air Force for example, the Navy, almost all the Marines. That seems like proof to me that present pay rates are adequate. One must add that an Act of Congress in 1967 raised the base pay throughout the services in three installments, the third installment still to come, on April 1, 1969. So it is hard to understand why we are being told that to maintain adequate armed services on a volunteer basis will require large increases in pay; that they will cost an extra $17 billion per year. It seems plain to me that we can get all the armed forces we need as volunteers, and at present rates of pay.

But there is something ever so much bigger and more important than the draft. That bigger thing, of course, is the militarization of our country. Ex-President Eisenhower warned us of what he called the military-industrial complex. I am sad to say that we must begin to think of it now as the military-industrial-labor union complex. What happened under the plea of the Cold War was not alone that we built up the first big peace time army in our history, but we institutionalized it. We built, I suppose, the biggest government building in our history to run it, and we institutionalized it.

I don't think we can live with the present military establishment and its $80–100 billion a year budget, and keep America anything like we have known it in the past. It is corrupting the life of the whole country. It is buying up everything in sight: industries, banks, investors, universities; and lately it seems also to have bought up the labor unions.

The Defense Department is always broke; but some of the things they do with that $80 billion a year would make Buck Rogers envious. For example: the Rocky Mountain Arsenal on the outskirts of Denver was manufacturing a deadly nerve poison on such a scale that there was a problem of waste disposal. Nothing daunted, they dug a tunnel two miles deep under Denver, into which they have injected so much poisoned water that beginning a couple of years ago Denver began to experience a series of earth tremors of increasing severity. Now there is a grave fear of a major earthquake. An interesting debate is in progress as to whether Denver will be safer if that lake of poisoned water is removed or left in place. (N.Y. Times, July 4, 1968; Science, Sept. 27, 1968.)

Perhaps you have read also of those 6000 sheep that suddenly died in Skull Valley, Utah, killed by another nerve poison—a strange and, I believe, still unexplained accident, since the nearest testing seems to have been 30 miles away.

As for Vietnam, the expenditure of fire power has been frightening. Some of you may still remember Khe Sanh, a hamlet just south of the Demilitarized Zone, where a force of U.S. Marines was beleaguered for a time. During that period we dropped on the perimeter of Khe Sanh more explosives than fell on Japan throughout World War II, and more than fell on the whole of Europe during the years 1942 and 1943.

One of the officers there was quoted as having said afterward, "It looks like the world caught smallpox and died." (N.Y. Times, Mar. 28, 1968.)

The only point of government is to safeguard and foster life. Our government has become preoccupied with death, with the business of killing and being killed. So-called Defense now absorbs 60 percent of the national budget, and about 12 percent of the Gross National Product.

A lively debate is beginning again on whether or not we should deploy antiballistic missiles, the ABM. I don't have to talk about them, everyone else here is doing that. But I should like to mention a curious circumstance. In September, 1967, or about 1½ years ago, we had a meeting of M.I.T. and Harvard people, including experts on these matters, to talk about whether anything could be done to block the Sentinel system, the deployment of ABM's. Everyone present thought them undesirable; but a few of the most knowledgeable persons took what seemed to be the practical view, "Why fight about a dead issue? It has been decided, the funds have been appropriated. Let's go on from there."

Well, fortunately, it's not a dead issue.

An ABM is a nuclear weapon. It takes a nuclear weapon to stop a nuclear weapon. And our concern must be with the whole issue of nuclear weapons.

There is an entire semantics ready to deal with the sort of thing I am about to say. It involves such phrases as "those are the facts of life." No—they are the facts of death. I don't accept them, and I advise you not to accept them. We are under repeated pressure to accept things that are presented to us as settled—decisions that have been made. Always there is the thought: let's go on from there! But this time we don't see how to go on. We will have to stick with those issues.

We are told that the United States and Russia between them have by now stockpiled in nuclear weapons approximately the explosive power of 15 tons of TNT for every man, woman and child on earth. And now it is suggested that we must make more. All very regrettable, of course; but those are "the facts of life." We really would like to disarm; but our new Secretary of Defense has made the ingenious proposal that now is the time to greatly increase our nuclear armaments so that we can disarm from a position of strength.

I think all of you know there is no adequate defense against massive nuclear attack. It is both easier and cheaper to circumvent any known nuclear defense system than to provide it. It's all pretty crazy. At the very moment we talk of deploying ABM's, we are also building the MIRV, the weapon to circumvent ABM's.

So far as I know, the most conservative estimates of Americans killed in a major nuclear attack, with everything working as well as can be hoped and all foreseeable precautions taken, run to about 50 millions. We have become callous to gruesome statistics, and this seems at first to be only another gruesome statistic. You think, Bang!—and next morning, if you're still there, you read in the newspapers that 50 million people were killed.

But that isn't the way it happens. When we killed close to 200,000 people with those first little, old-fashioned uranium bombs that we dropped on Hiroshima and Nagasaki, about the same number of persons was maimed, blinded, burned, poisoned and otherwise doomed. A lot of them took a long time to die.

That's the way it would be. Not a bang, and a certain number of corpses to bury; but a nation filled with millions of helpless, maimed, tortured and doomed persons, and the survivors of a nuclear holocaust will be huddled with their families in shelters, with guns ready to fight off their neighbors, trying to get some uncontaminated food and water.

A few months ago Sen. Richard Russell of Georgia ended a speech in the Senate with the words: "If we have to start over again with another Adam and Eve, I want them to be Americans; and I want them on this continent and not in Europe." That was a United States senator holding a patriotic speech. Well, here is a Nobel Laureate who thinks that those words are criminally insane. (Prolonged applause.)

How real is the threat of full scale nuclear war? I have my own very inexpert idea, but realizing how little I know and fearful that I may be a little paranoid on this subject, I take every opportunity to ask reputed experts. I asked that question of a very distinguished professor of government at Harvard about a month ago. I asked him what sort of odds he would lay on the possibility of full-scale nuclear war within the foreseeable future. "Oh," he said comfortably,

"I think I can give you a pretty good answer to that question. I estimate the probability of full-scale nuclear war, provided that the situation remains about as it is now, at 2 percent per year." Anybody can do the simple calculation that shows that 2 percent per year means that the chance of having that full-scale nuclear war by 1990 is about one in three, and by 2000 it is about 50-50.

I think I know what is bothering the students. I think that what we are up against is a generation that is by no means sure that it has a future.

I am growing old, and my future so to speak is already behind me. But there are those students of mine who are in my mind always; and there are my children, two of them now 7 and 9, whose future is infinitely more precious to me than my own. So it isn't just their generation; it's mine too. We're all in it together.

Are we to have a chance to live? We don't ask for prosperity, or security; only for a reasonable chance to live, to work out our destiny in peace and decency. Not to go down in history as the apocalyptic generation.

And it isn't only nuclear war. Another overwhelming threat is the population explosion. That has not yet even begun to come under control. There is every indication that the world population will double before the year 2000; and there is a widespread expectation of famine on an unprecedented scale in many parts of the world. The experts tend to differ only in the estimates of when those famines will begin. Some think by 1980, others think they can be staved off until 1990, very few expect that they will not occur by the year 2000.

That is the problem. Unless we can be surer than we now are that this generation has a future, nothing else matters. It's not good enough to give it tender loving care, to supply it with breakfast foods, to buy it expensive educations. Those things don't mean anything unless this generation has a future. And we're not sure that it does.

I don't think that there are problems of youth, or student problems. All the real problems I know are grown-up problems.

Perhaps you will think me altogether absurd, or "academic," or hopelessly innocent—that is, until you think of the alternatives—if I say as I do to you now: we have to get rid of those nuclear weapons. There is nothing worth having that can be obtained by nuclear war: nothing material or ideological, no tradition that it can defend. It is utterly self-defeating. Those atom bombs represent an unusable weapon. The only use for an atom bomb is to keep somebody else from using one. It can give us no protection, but only the doubtful satisfaction of retaliation. Nuclear weapons offer us nothing but a balance of terror; and a balance of terror is still terror.

We have to get rid of those atomic weapons, here and everywhere. We cannot live with them.

I think we've reached a point of great decision, not just for our nation, not only for all humanity, but for life upon the Earth. I tell my students, with a feeling of pride that I hope they will share, that the carbon, nitrogen and oxygen that make up 99 percent of our living substance, were cooked in the deep interiors of earlier generations of dying stars. Gathered up from the ends of the universe, over billions of years, eventually they came to form in part the substance of our sun, its planets and ourselves. Three billion years ago life arose upon the Earth. It seems to be the only life in the solar system. Many a star has since been born and died.

About two million years ago, man appeared. He has become the dominant species on the Earth. All other living things, animal and plant, live by his sufferance. He is the custodian of life on Earth. It's a big responsibility.

The thought that we're in competition with Russians or with Chinese is all a mistake, and trivial. Only mutual destruction lies that way. We are one species, with a world to win. There's life all over this universe, but in all the universe we are the only men.

Our business is with life, not death. Our challenge is to give what account we can of what becomes of life in the solar system, this corner of the universe that is our home and, most of all, what becomes of men—all men of all nations, colors and creeds. It has become one world, a world for all men. It is only such a world that now can offer us life and the chance to go on.

JACK NEWFIELD

What Kind of Democracy?

It is now two years since that instant of insanity in a chaotic hotel kitchen pantry in Los Angeles robbed us of Robert Kennedy. It is now June 1970 and America has become another country.

Almost 15,000 more Americans have died in Vietnam in the interim. Cambodia, a neutral nation, has been invaded without the Congress even being consulted. The President has called student activists "bums," and a week later four students were killed by National Guardsmen at Kent State.

Source: Mr. Newfield is assistant editor of the *Village Voice* in New York City and author of *A Prophetic Minority.* This article is from *The New York Times Magazine,* June 7, 1970, pp. E 1, 4. © 1970 by The New York Times Company. Reprinted by permission.

Desegregation has been slowed in the South, and a bus carrying black school children has been burned in Lamar, S.C. The Chicago Eight were indicted even though the previous attorney general refused to indict them and tried to testify for the defense at their trial.

Fred Hampton was shot to death in his bed in Chicago and James Rector died on a rooftop in Berkeley during the movement for the People's Park. The ABM is being built, and Daniel Moynihan has counseled the President that we need a period of "benign neglect" of the racial issue that involves 20 million black citizens. G. Harrold Carswell and Clement Haynsworth were nominated for the Supreme Court seats once occupied by Brandeis and Frankfurter.

All of this has happened since the hopeful day Robert Kennedy won both the California and South Dakota primaries and seemed, for the first time, within reach of his party's nomination for president.

In recent days, two things have happened to remind me again of what we lost and how much the nation has unraveled since June 6, 1968, and why it is that Robert Kennedy's assassination, unlike any of the others in that awful litany, is the one that hurts more, not less, as time passes.

One of the most vivid memories I have of Robert Kennedy is the first day of his truncated run for the presidency. It was two in the afternoon of March 19 at the University of Kansas, in rural Lawrence. KU was a quiet college. There had been no bitter protests, no violent demonstrations. The students were provincial and hardworking. Their parents were farmers and many of them wanted only to be farmers. They looked as straight as a junior chamber of commerce committee. Short hair, ties and jackets, long skirts, no beards, no sandals, no sweet smell of pot hanging in the air. It was a sea of 18,000 wholesome, corn-fed, prairie faces, turned upwards in Phog Allen Fieldhouse, as Kennedy nervously began to talk in a flat monotone.

After about 10 minutes he started to speak of Vietnam and the students began to cheer and applaud and Kennedy began to feel their emotion, and be nourished by it, and he built on its playback.

"I am concerned (he said) that at the end of it all, there will only be more Americans killed, more of our treasure spilled out . . . so that they may say, as Tacitus said of Rome: 'They made a desert and called it peace.' I don't think that is satisfactory for the United States of America. . . ."

The cheering, bouncing off the walls and scoreboard and rafters, grew still louder, and Kennedy candidly confessed his own errors in shaping the early Vietnam policy.

I am willing to bear my share of the responsibility, before history and my fellow citizens. But past error is no excuse for its own perpetuation. . . . If the South Vietnamese troops will not carry the fight for their own cities, we cannot ourselves destroy them. That kind of salvation is not an act we can presume to perform for them. For we must ask ourselves and we must ask our government: Where does such logic end? If it becomes necessary to destroy all of South Vietnam to save it, will we do that too? And if we care so little about South Vietnam that we are willing to see its land destroyed, and its people dead, then why are we there in the first place?

It was now near the end of the speech. Kennedy's hair was flopping over his perspiring temple. He was jabbing the air with his small clenched fist, thumb extended, pouring all his pent-up passion into the final peroration.

So I come here today to this great university to ask your help, not for me, but for your country, and for the people of Vietnam . . . I urge you to learn the harsh facts that lurk behind the mask of official illusion with which we have concealed our true circumstances from even ourselves. Our country is in danger: Not just from foreign enemies, but above all, from our own misguided policies, and what they can do to the nation that Thomas Jefferson once said was the last, best hope of man. . . .

It was over and the basketball fieldhouse sounded like it was inside Niagara Falls; it was like a soundtrack gone haywire. The sound of screaming filled the arena and thousands of those Kansas students began moving toward Kennedy on the platform, knocking over wooden folding chairs. They engulfed him, pulled off his cufflinks, shouted his name, and a few girls even sobbed in hysteria.

That was in March of 1968. Last month I read that the Student Union at the University of Kansas was burned down.

The last time I had had seen Joe Kennedy, Bobby's eldest son, was when he unexpectedly walked through the cars of his father's funeral train, big and strong in a blue pinstripe suit, stuck out his 16-year-old hand and saying, "Hiya. I'm Joe Kennedy and I'm glad to see you. Thank you for coming."

And then I saw Bobby's son again four weeks ago. It was in the midst of the hot, gentle throng massed at the Ellipse behind the White House to protest the invasion of Cambodia and the renewed bombing of North Vietnam. Joe Kennedy, now a senior at Milton Academy, anonymous in the assembly of 100,000, was naked to the waist, his hair very long, and he was saying to me, "How could Nixon do it? Why doesn't he go and fight himself if he believes in war so much? Why can't the politicians stop him from invading a new country?"

This is what we lost with Robert Kennedy—a leading politician willing to try to stop a president from doing such a thing. Bobby Kennedy was not a saint and not a genius. He was a politician with his fair share of human frailties and failings. He waited too long before he began to criticize the Vietnam war and he waited too long before he decided to seek the presidency in 1968. He could not redefine the role of a politician and so like a fly he was trapped in the flypaper of local politics in New York. He was a transitional figure between the old politics and the new.

But he was also the most humane, the most curious and the least phony politician I have ever seen. He was the first to go to the Mississippi Delta and Appalachia and Delano, Calif., and say, yes, hunger is an urgent political issue in this richest nation in the history of mankind.

He was the first liberal politician to say, yes, the conservatives are right, ordinary people do feel powerless and need more local control and more "participatory democracy," and yes, the traditional liberals have become too dependent on federal centralization and top-to-bottom bureaucracy.

He was the only antiracist politician in the land to have the trust of the ironworkers and steelworkers and cops and secretaries and taxi drivers, who after his death would switch their earthy allegiance to George Wallace.

He was the only politician I ever met who could be obsessed with the suffering of minorities that don't vote—migrant workers, Eskimos and Indians —obsessed to the point where he sometimes couldn't talk after visiting an Indian reservation or a migrant worker camp.

He was perhaps the only person in the country over whose coffin in St. Patrick's Cathedral Mayor Richard Daley and Tom Hayden—the opposing generals in "the battle of Chicago"—could both weep for what each had lost. Kennedy was the only politician in the system who might have put together, among the young, the poor, the blacks, a new majority for change.

We can say of Kennedy now what Guy Dumar said of Albert Camus after his death: "He would have been a force in reserve, a bridge between the past and the future; he would have been one from whom we awaited a response that, when it came, would have been heard by all."

Since my memoir of Robert Kennedy was published in paperback last March, I have received almost 100 letters, nearly all from students, sweet, moderate students, asking for an answer to their frustration and anger.

The other day, I received such a letter from Debby Davis, an undergraduate at the University of Missouri in Columbia. It was dated May 4, the day of the shootings at Kent State. It said, in part:

"I just can't keep from thinking that maybe Bobby could have found a solution—but thinking about him does nothing but make things seem even more futile.

"Where does one go from here? The campaigns don't work—Nixon is as bad as Johnson—worse now. Demonstrations have gotten us nowhere, not nationally or locally. Nixon is definitely tone deaf. We protested near here at Sedalia, Mo., the Saturday after Earth Day, against the deployment of the ABM. Nobody heard us. Nobody came or cared, except those who already agreed. We are up against a brick wall with the Agnews and Nixons knocking our heads together.

"Bobby said we would have to answer to somebody and explain what we did for our fellow human beings. I believe that, and I'm ready to run and work and fight to help but my sense of direction is hopelessly screwed up . . . it really scares me. I feel totally helpless and empty. . . ."

I don't have many answers for Debby or the others who write and ask whether Teddy Kennedy or John Lindsay is a new Bobby, or why they shouldn't burn ROTC buildings since there is no Kennedy left to save the system.

There are millions of Debbys on college campuses and in high schools who have no objective correlative for their desperation in the world of adult politics. They are just as likely to vote as sit in or go on strike or throw a rock at a National Guardsman because all strategies seem equally hopeless.

This is what I wrote back to Debby:

At the end of my book about Bobby I said that the best, the most compassionate national leaders were all part of memory now, not hope, that things would get worse from now on, and not better; that Kennedy was "irreplaceable" and that the stone was at the bottom of the hill and we were alone.

I still believe most of that. . . . There is still no one to replace Bobby within Establishment politics. Lindsay can move the young and the black, but he lacks Bobby's identification with the white workingman. George McGovern is a good and decent man but the blacks and Chicanos don't know who he is. Muskie is like Ed Sullivan, relaxed, rehearsed, vacant.

So all I can do is share with you a few rock-bottom notions I have come to since Los Angeles.

Don't depend on leaders any more because there are too many Sirhans in America. Only look to strong, authentic movements—antiwar, blacks, Women's Lib, those who preach respect for the earth. And trust the power of ideas and small, young institutions. Work to elect a new Congress but understand that is only one small part of a long and complex struggle.

Become a radical within your own chosen profession, whether it is teaching, law, medicine. Rudi Dutschke is probably right—we will have to make the long, hard march through the existing institutions to transform them.

In an era of repressive politics and harsh conflict, don't forget the importance of private virtue and good character. Perhaps all I've ever tried to say about Robert Kennedy is that he had better character than anyone else.

Keep stretching your consciousness. Go back and really read Wright Mills and Camus and Paul Goodman. Try to get Tom Hayden and Allen Ginsberg and Staughton Lynd to speak at your university. And listen to Bob Dylan and The Band—they're good for the soul.

Right now there is no country, no political party, no politician inside the system we can look to as a model. The brittle, visible surface of national politics is now too authoritarian, too sick for anything healthy to grow in it. Our energies and plans are by necessity inchoate now, below surface, literally underground and formless until a more fertile time. All we can do for now is try and push the stone back up the hill once again. You and me, Debby, because there is no Robert Kennedy to make it easier.

Peace,
Jack Newfield

DAVID McREYNOLDS

Are We in the Middle of the "Second American Revolution"?

Are we in the beginning of a Second American Revolution? Yes and no. Paradox: revolutions can occur only after they have occurred. Marx's call for revolution in 1848 was based on the revolutionary changes that had already occurred—the emergence of the proletariat. Revolution as we usually use the word means the violent effort to create new institutions to help share power among new social forces. In England and in the Scandinavian countries, the creation of democratic political parties (a debt we owe the Marxists), trade unions and cooperatives all served to distribute political power to the proletariat without a violent convulsion. In Russia, the revolution occurred less because of the proletariat—a small group in 1917—than because of the inflexibility of Russian institutions combined with the disaster of the war. When the Czar stumbled from power in April, 1917, it was a surprise to everyone, including Lenin. (Which suggests that while we may talk about revolutions, we cannot predict them.)

Revolutions do not occur because of revolutionaries but because of massive social tensions that demand change, combined with a political establishment unwilling or unable to make those changes. That situation exists today in America. Nixon has made the fatal mistake of declaring war on our youth (through his noisome little mouthpiece, Spiro Agnew) and of seeking the allegiance of Southern whites rather than the confidence of American blacks and American youth. In the short run, it is a successful strategy. In the long run, it will prove a disaster.

Blacks, Chicanos, Puerto Ricans, and youth do not constitute a majority, but they are a massive force of social energy and they are unable to feel respect for—or any sense of shared power in—the present white Establishment, made up of the military, the corporations, the conservative A.F.L.–C.I.O. The Chicago trial, the search and destroy missions the police carry out against the Black Panthers, the nomination of Carswell, the absolutely unconstitutional

Source: Mr. McReynolds is field secretary of the War Resisters' League and author of a forthcoming collection of essays, *We Have Been Invaded by the 21st Century.* This article is from the *New York Times Magazine,* May 17, 1970, p. 26. © 1970 by The New York Times Company. Reprinted by permission.

expansion of the war into Cambodia, the failure of the Government to check inflation or to wage a meaningful war on poverty—all of these provoke a loss of confidence in the legitimacy of the Establishment. (The hypocrisy of the "respectable Establishment" is demonstrated by New York Times editorials demanding immediate criminal prosecution of the handful of terror bombers in our nation, while failing to demand similar criminal prosecution of Nixon and all officers of the Government who have conspired in the massive bombing of Vietnam and the waging of a war in which more than a million have died and an entire nation has been ravaged.)

The Pentagon is a greater threat to American institutions than the Weathermen. Spiro Agnew is the real organizer for the violent fringe—every speech he makes drives a few more deeply concerned youths into the tragic tactic of armed resistance. The most "revolutionary agent" of the moment is simply the war itself, which daily persuades more Americans of the criminal nature of the central Government.

When is a revolution justified? Is America in such a bad state that a revolution is justified now? Revolutions are like earthquakes. They are tragic, they cannot be predicted, they do not require justification, they cannot really be organized. Revolutions occur when they occur. They are not caused by conspiracies but, as the Russian theologian Nicholas Berdyaev pointed out, by the indifference and inhumanity and inflexibility of existing institutions. America is in a bad state now and it would be in a bad state after a violent revolution.

What is the aim, beyond destroying the system, of present-day revolutionaries? Revolutions, from our own of 1776 through the Russian, Chinese and Cuban, share a common set of values: freedom, justice, wider distribution of power to previously powerless and oppressed elements of the society. Few revolutions have a blueprint of what they will actually do, and those blueprints are usually scrapped as unusable once the revolution has occurred. For myself, I favor wider distribution of power away from the central Government directly to communities. And I favor the unilateral dismantling of our military machine, so that it cannot oppress us or anyone else. (I would fear a revolutionary military machine as much as I fear the present one.) Such an act would more likely revolutionize the world as a whole, including the Soviet Union, than lead to our facing an invasion. The large corporations need to be broken into smaller units with ownership and control vested in communities and regions. Centralization of economic or political power is dangerous to a free society.

What chances of success do the revolutionaries have? On our own, very little. The central Government still commands the support of the vast majority of citizens, though discussion of revolution helps to remind people that revolution is a very American process. Terror bombings do more to build support for a police state than for revolution, and I suspect that Government agents are involved in some of the bombings. It is possible there will be no revolution but that America, the most advanced power in the world, will prove unable to govern itself in any way and sink into chaos. Youths need to read less Lenin and Mao and more about America. Chants of "Ho, Ho, Ho Chi Minh" are not revolutionary. Ho didn't win power in Vietnam by chanting about Russia or China, but by dealing with Vietnamese problems. The breakfast program of the Panthers is far shrewder than their earlier display of guns. The nonviolence of César Chavez and the nonviolence of the draft-resistance movement suggest that the compassionate tradition of American radicalism, the tradition of Eugene Debs and Martin Luther King, is not yet played out.

Is the revolution here? Something is happening, Mr. Jones, but I'm not sure what it is. The bombings. The campus unrest. Hundreds jailed for resisting the draft, thousands jailed on drug charges, tens of thousands fleeing into Canada, black leaders shot to death in their beds by Chicago cops. Listen to rock music. Observe the culture heroes of the youth.

Popular as Nixon and Agnew may be with a frightened middle America, they lack the charisma needed to sustain the kind of police state the Attorney General is trying so hard to fashion. I won't try to predict the future—just urge those of us who believe in democracy and nonviolence to keep struggling. The editor of Crawdaddy, a leading "rock culture" paper, put the thing perfectly when he said: "Agnew, Nixon and Mitchell have set to sea in a sieve." Sink they will—nothing in today's politics is more certain. The question is whether America will sink with them. . . .

RICHARD H. ROVERE

We Must Assume That There Is Hope

So many things are out of joint in this country that if they were all, or nearly all, set right, or nearly right, the changes, by whatever means accomplished, would constitute a revolution of great magnitude.

None of us can know, at this point in our history, how much in the way of change is within the realm of the possible—a realm in which time is now a crucial dimension. If we go by the form sheets—election returns, opinion polls—we have to see ourselves as a conservative people, and getting more so from month to month. Yet the conservative powers-that-be are capable of at least some innovation—e.g., family-assistance programs. And some kinds of change seem to commend themselves on an almost wholly non-ideological basis—e.g., protection of the environment, abortion reform. But this seems to me about to exhaust the categories. Most of the rest involve struggle. Power has to change hands. Wealth has to be redistributed. Institutions have to be junked or reshaped. Most social and political change is brought about through social and political conflict.

Conflict can and usually does take many forms, one of which is violence. For my own part, I see little point in discussing violence as a means toward revolutionary ends in this country in this part of this century. I think I would oppose it under almost any circumstances because I find it abhorrent and corrupting. But even if I felt otherwise and felt also that conditions in this country were so intolerable as to justify an attempt at revolution by violence, I would still oppose it on the ground that the likeliest—indeed, the certain—outcome would be to make conditions even more intolerable There have been exceptions (fewer than are claimed, though), but this has been the general history of violence, and I should suppose that anyone in possession of his wits and able to give the matter a few moments of thought would find this conclusion inescapable. This country might benefit from revolutionary change, but the overwhelming majority of its people think otherwise. Our society may be deteriorating, but the news hasn't reached deeply into the masses. Of those

Source: Mr. Rovere is a well-known author; in addition to several books and essays, he writes the "Letter from Washington" column in the *New Yorker*. This article is from *The New York Times Magazine*, May 17, 1970, p. 27. © 1970 by The New York Times Company. Reprinted by permission.

it has reached, probably a majority blame the deterioration on those who would make the revolution.

In other words a revolution would be quite promptly crushed. Before that happened, a few, perhaps many, edifices would topple, and guerrillas might make life hazardous for a time. But the more bombings there were and the more guerrillas in the streets, the bloodier the retribution and the more repressive the repression. This is not Vietnam. The masses may be deceived and exploited, but political education has not brought them to the point of much awareness on this score. Nor are they apathetic. They are overwhelmingly on the side of authority, legitimate or otherwise, and wish it were used less sparingly than it is. And although certain outbreaks of violence—particularly in the ghettoes—may have had some value as "demonstration effect," the kind of concerted violence that is revolution would bring into the streets not only the police and the military but millions of self-appointed and well-armed vigilantes and counter-revolutionaries.

I said—or tried to say—some of this to some young revolutionaries on a television show recently and was quickly put down as a "cynic" and a "defeatist." My analogies were all from the past—where else can one find any?—and one of them enjoined me to forget history and "study the future." I plead not guilty to cynicism, but guilty of first-degree defeatism when it comes to the proposition of turning this country leftward with guns and bombs. That, at least, is what my study of "the future" leads me to conclude.

Beyond this, I conclude very little. I have my visions of what I would like this country to be and do in the world, and I think they accord with at least some of those who are in the process of persuading themselves that violence is the only answer. I am not sure they are wrong in believing there is no hope in any of the other approaches. In other words, it could be that our American situation is hopeless. But I see no choice but to proceed on the assumption that there is hope. The argument, in any case, is not closed as of now. The record of democracy, where it has been practiced in some limited fashion, is often far from exhilarating, particularly when it comes to wars and other instruments of foreign policy. It has produced injustices as gross as those produced in many totalitarian societies. But it has had its triumphs, and it is the only system that I know of to be worth trying to bring to something approaching perfection. It cannot be improved or perfected by revolutionary violence. But it can surely be wrecked by counterrevolutionary violence.

PAUL COWAN

Dissolution Before Decay!

I'm writing this a few hours after the Ohio National Guard murdered four students at Kent State; a few days after President Nixon incited such violence by calling students "bums," announced the invasion of Cambodia, resumed the bombings of North Vietnam. New declarations of war on two fronts, a redeclaration of war on one. Who knows what will have happened by the time this is printed?

We got rich too quickly in this country, defined our freedom as the right to exploit others, replaced our cultural and moral roots with a crazed desire to chase the big buck. We prided ourselves on an undefeated, untied, un-scored-upon war record, lost all personal feeling for what it's like to be devastated. We decided that our affluence was willed by God and immunized ourselves to the complexity and tragedy of life, the suffering of others.

I have serious doubts about presenting a fuller, reasoned argument here. Are there words that will persuade you that The New York Times, Time and Newsweek should print articles exploring the psyches of the clean-cut generals who order the wanton destruction of thousands of Asians, not of radicals who respond to such provocations by fighting? That the white-collar fascists in power now hope to gain total control of this country by insulting, imprisoning and even murdering young people, black people and poor people? Can you be convinced that Richard Nixon and his advisers are war criminals who should be tried accordingly? That there are no conventional means at all by which the problems of this country can be solved?

Here are seven proposals. Some readers may have mind sets that make it hard for them to take such suggestions seriously. To me, and many people I've talked to, such ideas—not necessarily these specific ones—represent the minimum necessary for survival.

(1) Force the United States to admit and accept defeat in Southeast Asia.

(2) That means that the end of the war in Indochina—and of the war against dissenters at home—must become the absolute first priority of every American institution.

Strikes can be organized like those on the campuses. Social workers can

Source: Mr. Cowan is a former Peace Corps member and author of *The Making of an Un-American*. This article is from *The New York Times Magazine*, May 17, 1970, p. 116.
© 1970 by The New York Times Company. Reprinted by permission.

force their agencies to join clients in combating the war and its disastrous effect on poor people. Teachers and students; poverty lawyers and their clients; doctors, nurses and their patients can enter into similar sorts of alliances. People in agencies like the Peace Corps and AID can organize to shut down those operations. Liberal Justice Department lawyers, if there still are any, can disrupt the functioning of that thoroughly corrupt agency. Federal employes in agencies like Health, Education and Welfare and the O.E.O. can stage massive demonstrations at the Pentagon for a reversal of national priorities. Workers throughout the country can organize antiwar strikes in their unions. Such actions could inspire a nationwide general strike.

(3) Also, petition the United Nations General Assembly (where the U.S. has no veto) to brand this country the aggressor in Southeast Asia and recruit an international army to fight it in a sort of reverse Korea.

(4) Impeach Nixon—then the rest of the ghostly parade of successors who have complied with the United States' criminal policies: Agnew, John McCormack, Richard Russell, etc.

(5) Force the Government, private institutions and large corporations to recognize that America's affluence is largely based on the exploitation of domestic colonies. Negotiate reparations treaties with blacks, Indians, Puerto Ricans, Mexican-Americans. Free political prisoners like Huey Newton, Bobby Seale and Martin Sostre, some of the bravest, most far-sighted members of their communities.

(6) Establish new communities, "liberated zones," in cities or sections of states.

There we can build the kind of humane institutions we believe in—schools, hospitals, child-care centers, old peoples' homes, mental institutions that are dedicated to serving people. Our loyalties will not be to the piggish United States, but to people throughout the world. In such communities, we will have to learn to transcend the racism, egotism and product addition that we have developed during our lives in this culture of greed—to undergo personal revolutions that parallel the political revolution we are trying to bring about.

If we can create such communities and defend them, people throughout the country will relate to them enthusiastically, see them and the politics and life style they represent as vibrant alternatives to the horrors of Nixonia.

(7) Work toward the eventual dissolution of the United States into a number of smaller autonomous regions. Only indispensible technological systems like communications and transportation should be continental—and those should include Canada and Mexico as equal partners with the rest of the separate North American states.

In some regions, of course, people will form alliances with Europeans, Asians, Africans or Latins that are closer than their alliances with other parts of the present United States.

This nation is too big for any group to govern it humanely. Few people really identify with it except in a commercial sense: they get tears in their eyes when they go overseas and hear some patriotic or popular song that reminds them of the hamburgers or huge hunks of steak they miss. Living in smaller, self-governing regions, Americans might recover some of the roots they lost when they came to this country, recover some of the modesty. We might become decent citizens of the world.

But maybe that is impossible. Maybe our history has injected a poison into our blood stream that forces us to be violent. Then, I would rather see Kansans fight Oklahomans than be part of a country where Kansans and Oklahomans are drafted into an army which forces them to drop bombs on Cambodians, Laotians, Vietnamese, their houses, schools and hospitals.

My slogan is: Dissolution before decay!

Of course, much of America's ruling class will suffer if any such ideas are adopted. The Nixon Administration knows that. It is terrified by all threats to its greedy plans to turn the United States into a giant factory town and use its mechanized people to control this planet and space.

It will try to stifle even small threats with repression at first, as it is doing now. Perhaps, when that doesn't work, there will be a military dictatorship. If that happens, the bloodshed will be ghastly. Could anything humane survive the wreckage that would be in store for this country?

I often think that the name of the thing we are headed for is not fascism, not revolution, but national suicide.

SCOTT BUCHANAN

Revolution—Permanent Possibility

A common principle underlies both revolutions and politics. If we have lost the rationale of revolutions, we have also lost the reasons that support genuine political life. Stated simply, perhaps too simply for quick comprehension, the principle is that every human being has a responsibility for injustice anywhere in the community. Governments—that is, the laws and the institutions that the laws establish—are the proper political means for discharging that responsibility. But, no matter how well conceived and founded, governments may gradually or suddenly, depending on the rates of change in the community, become functionless, overloaded, or positive hindrances to the processes of justice. The ordinary processes of government, lawmaking and repealing, administration and adjudicating, are elastic and capable of adjusting themselves to the course of history; but they may also become rigid and cumbersome when the issues are heavy and when the rate of change is high, as in the British, French, and American Revolutions of the seventeenth and eighteenth centuries.

In such times the will to maintain the legalistic details of custom and tradition and the consequent failure to adjust and invent may lead to the rapid accumulation of injustices. The will to create laws and institutions is replaced by the habit of domination on the part of the beleaguered authorities. Reason gives way to force and legality takes on the sinister meaning of the phrase "law and order." It is in such circumstances that the individual, or some fraction of the public, rediscovering not only the right but the duty of revolution, is moved to grasp the means at hand and to invent new methods for discharging the basic responsibility for restoring justice. This amounts to the recognition that the permanent possibility of revolution is a necessary condition of responsible government.

If we are to extend our public intelligence to comprehend, tolerate, and use both the domestic and foreign incipient revolutions of our time, we would do well to conceive of our task in terms of membership in a permanent con-

Source: The late philosopher, Scott Buchanan, was a Senior Fellow at the Center for the Study of Democratic Institutions. This article was originally written in 1967. Reprinted with permission from pp. 21ff. of the September 1969 issue of *The Center Magazine*, a publication of the Center for the Study of Democratic Institutions in Santa Barbara, California.

stitutional convention, first on a national scale and then later on a world scale. If we are to deal with revolutions and wars responsibly, we would do well not to suppress their causes by police or military force. This is no longer a matter of nineteenth-century liberal sentiments of decency and idealism; it is, strictly speaking, a matter of life and death for any government.

As parliamentary government, with its systems of representation, deliberation, and voting, comprehended incipient revolutions of the eighteenth century and turned into what we now call democratic self-government, so we must provide constitutional conventions that will turn current causes of war and revolution into institutions and laws. We should extend the due processes of law to the deeper processes of justice which revolutions present to communities that exist because they respect justice, peace, freedom, and order.

PETER SCHRAG

The Forgotten American

There is hardly a language to describe him, or even a set of social statistics. Just names: racist-bigot-redneck-ethnic-Irish-Italian-Pole-Hunkie-Yahoo. The lower middle class. A blank. The man under whose hat lies the great American desert. Who watches the tube, plays the horses, and keeps the niggers out of his union and his neighborhood. Who might vote for Wallace (but didn't). Who cheers when the cops beat up on demonstrators. Who is free, white, and twenty-one, has a job, a home, a family, and is up to his eyeballs in credit. In the guise of the working class—or the American yeoman or John Smith— he was once the hero of the civics book, the man that Andrew Jackson called "the bone and sinew of the country." Now he is "the forgotten man," perhaps the most alienated person in America.

Nothing quite fits, except perhaps omission and semi-invisibility, America

Source: Mr. Schrag is editor of *Change*, editor-at-large of *Saturday Review*, and an author of penetrating social commentary. "The Forgotten American" appeared in *Harper's Magazine*, August 1969, pp. 27–34. Copyright © 1969 by Peter Schrag. Reprinted from *Out of Place in America*, by Peter Schrag, by permission of Random House, Inc.

is supposed to be divided between affluence and poverty, between slums and suburbs. John Kenneth Galbraith begins the foreword to *The Affluent Society* with the phrase, "Since I sailed for Switzerland in the early summer of 1955 to begin work on this book. . . ." But *between* slums and suburbs, between Scarsdale and Harlem, between Wellesley and Roxbury, between Shaker Heights and Hough, there are some eighty million people (depending on how you count them) who didn't sail for Switzerland in the summer of 1955, or at any other time, and who never expect to. Between slums and suburbs: South Boston and South San Francisco, Bell and Parma, Astoria and Bay Ridge, Newark, Cicero, Downey, Daly City, Charlestown, Flatbush. Union Halls, American Legion posts, neighborhood bars and bowling leagues, the Ukrainian Club and the Holy Name. Main Street. To try to describe all this is like trying to describe America itself. If you look for it, you find it everywhere: the rows of frame houses overlooking the belching steel mills in Bethlehem, Pennsylvania, two-family brick houses in Canarsie (where the most common slogan, even in the middle of a political campaign, is "curb your dog"); the Fords and Chevies with a decal American flag on the rear window (usually a cut-out from the *Reader's Digest*, and displayed in counter-protest against peaceniks and "those bastards who carry Vietcong flags in demonstrations"); the bunting on the porch rail with the inscription, "Welcome Home, Pete." The gold star in the window.

When he was Under Secretary of Housing and Urban Development, Robert C. Wood tried a definition. It is not good, but it's the best we have:

He is a white and employed male . . . earning between $5,000 and $10,000. He works regularly, steadily, dependably, wearing a blue collar or white collar. Yet the frontiers of his career expectations have been fixed since he reached the age of thirty-five, when he found that he had too many obligations, too much family, and too few skills to match opportunities with aspirations.

This definition of the "working American" involves almost 23-million American families.

The working American lives in the gray area fringes of a central city or in a close-in or very far-out cheaper suburban subdivision of a large metropolitan area. He is likely to own a home and a car, especially as his income begins to rise. Of those earning between $6,000 and $7,500, 70 per cent own their own homes and 94 per cent drive their own cars.

94 per cent have no education beyond high school and 43 per cent have only completed the eighth grade.

He does all the right things, obeys the law, goes to church and insists—usually—that his kids get a better education than he had. But the right things don't seem to be paying off. While he is making more than he ever made—perhaps more than he'd ever dreamed—he's still struggling while a lot of others—"them" (on welfare, in demonstrations, in the ghettos) are getting most of the attention. "I'm working my ass off," a guy tells you on a stoop in South Boston. "My kids don't have a place to swim, my parks are full of glass, and I'm supposed to bleed for a bunch of people on relief." In New York a man who drives a Post Office trailer truck at night (4:00 P.M. to midnight) and a cab during the day (7:00 A.M. to 2:00 P.M.), and who hustles radios for his Post Office buddies on the side, is ready, as he says, to "knock somebody's ass." "The colored guys work when they feel like it. Sometimes they show up and sometimes they don't. One guy tore up all the time cards. I'd like to see a white guy do that and get away with it."

Nobody knows how many people in America moonlight (half of the eighteen million families in the $5,000 to $10,000 bracket have two or more wage earners) or how many have to hustle on the side. "I don't think anybody has a single job anymore," said Nicholas Kisburg, the research director for a Teamsters Union Council in New York. "All the cops are moonlighting, and the teachers; and there's a million guys who are hustling, guys with phony social-security numbers who are hiding part of what they make so they don't get kicked out of a housing project, or guys who work as guards at sports events and get free meals that they don't want to pay taxes on. Every one of them is cheating. They are underground people—*Untermenschen*. . . . We really have no systematic data on any of this. We have no ideas of the attitudes of the white worker. (We've been too busy studying the black worker.) And yet he's the source of most of the reaction in this country."

The reaction is directed at almost every visible target: at integration and welfare, taxes and sex education, at the rich and the poor, the foundations and students, at the "smart people in the suburbs." In New York State the legislature cuts the welfare budget; in Los Angeles, the voters reelect Yorty after a whispered racial campaign against the Negro favorite. In Minneapolis a police detective named Charles Stenvig, promising "to take the handcuffs off the police," wins by a margin stunning even to his supporters: in Massachusetts the voters mail tea bags to their representatives in protest against new taxes, and in state after state legislatures are passing bills to punish student demonstrators. ("We keep talking about permissiveness in training kids," said a Los Angeles labor official, "but we forget that these are our kids.")

And yet all these things are side manifestations of a malaise that lacks a language. Whatever law and order means, for example, to a man who feels his wife is unsafe on the street after dark or in the park at any time, or whose kids get shaken down in the school yard, it also means something like normality—the demand that everybody play it by the book, that cultural and social standards be somehow restored to their civics-book simplicity, that things shouldn't be as they are but as they were supposed to be. If there is a revolution in this country—a revolt in manners, standards of dress and obscenity, and, more importantly, in our official sense of what America is—there is also a counter-revolt. Sometimes it is inarticulate, and sometimes (perhaps most of the time) people are either too confused or apathetic—or simply too polite and too decent—to declare themselves. In Astoria, Queens, a white working-class district of New York, people who make $7,000 or $8,000 a year (sometimes in two jobs) call themselves affluent, even though the Bureau of Labor Statistics regards an income of less than $9,500 in New York inadequate to a moderate standard of living. And in a similar neighborhood in Brooklyn a truck driver who earns $151 a week tells you he's doing well, living in a two-story frame house separated by a narrow driveway from similar houses, thousands of them in block after block. This year, for the first time, he will go on a cruise—he and his wife and two other couples—two weeks in the Caribbean. He went to work after World War II ($57 a week) and he has lived in the same house for twenty years, accumulating two television sets, wall-to-wall carpeting in a small living room, and a basement that he recently remodeled into a recreation room with the help of the two moonlighting firemen. "We get fairly good salaries, and this is a good neighborhood, one of the few good ones left. We have no smoked Irishmen around."

Stability is what counts, stability in job and home and neighborhood, stability in the church and in friends. At night you watch television and sometimes on a weekend you go to a nice place—maybe a downtown hotel—for dinner with another couple. (Or maybe your sister, or maybe bowling, or maybe, if you're defeated, a night at the track.) The wife has the necessary appliances, often still being paid off, and the money you save goes for your daughter's orthodontist, and later for her wedding. The smoked Irishmen —the colored (no one says black; few even say Negro)—represent change and instability, kids who cause trouble in school, who get treatment that your kids never got, that you never got. ("Those fucking kids," they tell you in South Boston, "raising hell, and not one of 'em paying his own way. Their fucking mothers are all on welfare.") The black kids mean a change in the rules, a double standard in grades and discipline, and—vaguely—a challenge to all you believed right. Law and order is the stability and predictability of established ways. Law and order is equal treatment—in school, in jobs, in the courts—even if you're cheating a little yourself. The Forgotten Man is Jackson's man. He is the vestigial American democrat of 1840: "They all know that their success depends upon their own industry and economy and that they must not expect to become suddenly rich by the fruits of their toil." He is also Franklin Roosevelt's man—the man whose vote (or whose father's vote) sustained the New Deal.

There are other considerations, other styles, other problems. A postman in a Charlestown (Boston) housing project: eight children and a ninth on the way. Last year, by working overtime, his income went over $7,000. This year, because he reported it, the Housing Authority is raising his rent from $78 to $106 a month, a catastrophe for a family that pays $2.20 a day for milk, has never had a vacation, and for which an excursion is "going out for ice cream." "You try and save for something better; we hope to get out of here to some-place where the kids can play, where there's no broken glass, and then something always comes along that knocks you right back. It's like being at the bottom of the well waiting for a guy to throw you a rope." The description becomes almost Chaplinesque. Life is humble but not simple; the terrors of insolent bureaucracies and contempuous officials produce a demonology that loses little of its horror for being partly misunderstood. You want to get a sink fixed but don't want to offend the manager; want to get an eye operation that may (or may not) have been necessitated by a military injury five years earlier, "but the Veterans Administration says I signed away my benefits"; want to complain to someone about the teen-agers who run around breaking windows and harassing women but get no response either from the management or the police. "You're afraid to complain because if they don't get you during the day they'll get you at night." Automobiles, windows, children, all become hostages to the vague terrors of everyday life; everything is vulnerable. Liabilities that began long ago cannot possibly be liquidated: "I never learned anything in that school except how to fight. I got tired of being caned by the teachers and so at sixteen I quit and joined the Marines. I still don't know anything."

American culture? Wealth is visible, and so, now, is poverty. Both have become intimidating clichés. But the rest? A vast, complex, and disregarded world that was once—in belief, and in fact—the American middle: Greyhound and Trailways bus terminals in little cities at midnight, each of them with its neon lights and its cardboard hamburgers; acres of tar-paper beach bungalows in places like Revere and Rockaway; the hair curlers in the supermarket on Saturday, and the little girls in the communion dresses the next morning; pinball machines and the *Daily News*, the *Reader's Digest* and Ed Sullivan; houses with tiny front lawns (or even large ones) adorned with statues of the Virgin or of Sambo welcomin' de folks home; Clint Eastwood or Julie Andrews at the Palace; the trotting tracks and the dog tracks—Aurora Downs, Connaught Park, Roosevelt, Yonkers, Rockingham, and forty others —where gray men come not for sport and beauty, but to read numbers, to study and dope. (If you win you have figured something, have in a small way controlled your world, have surmounted your impotence. If you lose, bad luck, shit. "I'll break his goddamned head.") Baseball is not the national pastime; racing is. For every man who goes to a major-league baseball game there are four who go to the track and probably four more who go to the candy store or the barbershop to make their bets. (Total track attendance in 1965: 62 million plus another 10 million who went to the dogs.)

There are places, and styles, and attitudes. If there are neighborhoods of aspiration, suburban enclaves for the mobile young executive and the aspiring worker, there are also places of limited expectation and dead-end districts where mobility is finished. But even there you can often find, however vestigial, a sense of place, the roots of old ethnic loyalties, and a passionate, if often futile, battle against intrusion and change. "Everybody around here," you are told, "pays his own way." In this world the problems are not the ABM or air pollution (have they heard of Biafra?) or the international population crisis; the problem is to get your street cleaned, your garbage collected, to get your husband home from Vietnam alive; to negotiate installment payments and to keep the schools orderly. Ask anyone in Scarsdale or Winnetka about the schools and they'll tell you about new programs, or about how many are getting into Harvard, or about the teachers; ask in Oakland or the North Side of Chicago, and they'll tell you that they have (or haven't) had trouble. Somewhere in his gut the man in those communities knows that mobility and choice in this society are limited. He cannot imagine any major change for the better; but he can imagine change for the worse. And yet for a decade he is the one who has been asked to carry the burden of social reform, to integrate his schools and his neighborhod, has been asked by comfortable people to pay the social debts due to the poor and the black. In Boston, in San Francisco, in Chicago (not to mention Newark or Oakland) he has been telling the reformers to go to hell. The Jewish schoolteachers of New York and the Irish parents of Dorchester have asked the same question: "What the hell did Lindsay (or the Beacon Hill Establishment) ever do for us?"

The ambiguities and changes in American life that occupy discussions in university seminars and policy debates in Washington, and that form the backbone of contemporary popular sociology, become increasingly the conditions of trauma and frustration in the middle. Although the New Frontier and Great Society contained some programs for those not already on the rolls of social pathology—federal aid for higher education, for example—the public priorities and the rhetoric contained little. The emphasis, properly, was on the poor, on the inner cities (*e.g.*, Negroes) and the unemployed. But in Chicago a widow with three children who earns $7,000 a year can't get them college loans because she makes too much; the money is reserved for people on relief. New schools are built in the ghetto but not in the white working-class neighborhoods where they are just as dilapidated. In Newark the head of a white vigilante group (now a city councilman) runs, among other things, on a platform opposing pro-Negro discrimination. "When pools are being built in the Central Ward—don't they think white kids have got frustration? The white can't get a job; we have to hire Negroes first." The middle class, said Congressman Roman Pucinski of Illinois, who represents a lot of it, "is in revolt. Everyone has been generous in supporting anti-poverty. Now the middle-class American is disqualified from most of the programs."

The frustrated middle. The liberal wisdom about welfare, ghettos, student revolt, and Vietnam has only a marginal place, if any, for the values and life of the working man. It flies in the face of most of what he was taught to cherish and respect: hard work, order, authority, self-reliance. He fought, either alone or through labor organizations, to establish the precincts he now considers his own. Union seniority, the civil-service bureaucracy, and the petty professionalism established by the merit system in the public schools become sinecures of particular ethnic groups or of those who have learned to negotiate and master the system. A man who worked all his life to accumulate the points and grades and paraphernalia to become an assistant school principal (no matter how silly the requirements) is not likely to relinquish his position with equanimity. Nor is a dock worker whose only estate is his longshoreman's card. The job, the points, the credits become property:

Some men leave their sons money [wrote a union member to the *New York Times*], some large investments, some business connections, and some a profession. I have only one worthwhile thing to give: my trade. I hope to follow a centuries-old tradition and sponsor my sons for an apprenticeship. For this simple father's wish it is said that I discriminate against Negroes. Don't all of us discriminate? Which of us . . . will not choose a son over all others?

Suddenly the rules are changing—all the rules. If you protect your job for your own you may be called a bigot. At the same time it's perfectly acceptable to shout black power and to endorse it. What does it take to be a good American? *Give the black man a position because he is black, not because he necessarily works harder or does the job better.* What does it take to be a good American? Dress nicely, hold a job, be clean-cut, don't judge a man by the color of his skin or the country of his origin. What about the demands of Negroes, the long hair of the students, the dirty movies, the people who burn draft cards and American flags? Do you have to go out in the street with picket signs, do you have to burn the place down to get what you want? What does it take to be a good American? *This is a sick society, a racist society, we are fighting an immoral war.* ("I'm against the Vietnam war, too," says the truck driver in Brooklyn. "I see a good kid come home with half an arm and a leg in a brace up to here, and what's it all for? I was glad to see *my kid* flunk the Army physical. Still, somebody has to say no to these demonstrators and enforce the law.") What does it take to be a good American?

The conditions of trauma and frustration in the middle. What does it take to be a good American? Suddenly there are demands for Italian power and Polish power and Ukrainian power. In Cleveland the Poles demand a seat on the school board, and get it, and in Pittsburgh John Pankuch, the seventy-three-year-old president of the National Slovak Society demands "action, plenty of it to make up for lost time." Black power is supposed to be nothing but emulation of the ways in which other ethnic groups made it. But have they made it? In Reardon's Bar on East Eighth Street in South Boston, where the workmen come for their fish-chowder lunch and for their rye and ginger, they still identify themselves as Galway men and Kilkenny men; in the newsstand in Astoria you can buy *Il Progresso, El Tiempo*, the *Staats-Zeitung*, the *Irish World*, plus papers in Greek, Hungarian, and Polish. At the parish of Our Lady of Mount Carmel the priests hear confession in English, Italian, and Spanish and, nearby, the biggest attraction is not the stickball game, but the *bocce* court. Some of the poorest people in America are white, native, and have lived all of their lives in the same place as their fathers and grandfathers. The problems that were presumably solved in some distant past, in that prehistoric era before the textbooks were written—problems of assimilation, of upward mobility—now turn out to be very much unsolved. The melting pot and all: millions made it, millions moved to the affluent suburbs; several million—no one knows how many—did not. The median income in Irish South Boston is $5,100 a year but the community-action workers have a hard time convincing the local citizens that any white man who is not stupid or irresponsible can be poor. Pride still keeps them from applying for income supplements or Medicaid, but it does not keep them from resenting those who do. In Pittsburgh, where the members of Polish-American organizations earn an estimated $5,000 to $6,000 (and some fall below the poverty line), the Poverty Programs are nonetheless directed primarily to Negroes, and almost everywhere the thing called urban backlash associates itself in some fashion with ethnic groups whose members have themselves only a precarious hold on the security of affluence. Almost everywhere in the old cities, tribal neighborhoods and their styles are under assault by masscult. The Italian grocery gives way to the supermarket, the ma-and-pa store and the walk-up are attacked by urban renewal. And almost everywhere, that assault tends to depersonalize and to alienate. It has always been this way, but with time the brave new world that replaces old patterns becomes increasingly bureaucratized, distant, and hard to control.

Yet beyond the problem of ethnic identity, beyond the problems of Poles and Irishmen left behind, there are others more pervasive and more dangerous. For every Greek or Hungarian there are a dozen American-Americans who are past ethnic consciousness and who are as alienated, as confused, and as angry as the rest. The obvious manifestations are the same everywhere—race, taxes, welfare, students—but the threat seems invariably more cultural and psychological than economic or social. What upset the police at the Chicago convention most was not so much the politics of the demonstrators as their manners and their hair. (The barbershops in their neighborhoods don't advertise Beatle Cuts but the Flat Top and the Chicago Box.) The affront comes from middle-class people—and their children—who had been cast in the role of social exemplars (and from those cast as unfortunates worthy of public charity) who offend all the things on which working class identity is built: "hippies [said a San Francisco longshoreman] who fart around the streets and don't work"; welfare recipients who strike and march for better treatment; "all those [said a California labor official] who challenge the precepts that these people live on." If ethnic groups are beginning to organize to get theirs, so are others: police and firemen ("The cop is the new nigger"); schoolteachers; lower-middle-class housewives fighting sex education and bussing; small property owners who have no ethnic communion but a passionate interest in lower taxes, more policemen, and stiffer penalties for criminals. In San Francisco the Teamsters, who had never been known for such interests before, recently demonstrated in support of the police and law enforcement and, on another occasion, joined a group called Mothers Support

Neighborhood Schools at a school-board meeting to oppose—with their presence and later, apparently, with their fists—a proposal to integrate the schools through bussing. ("These people," someone said at the meeting, "do not look like mothers.")

Which is not to say that all is frustration and anger, that anybody is ready "to burn the country down." They are not even ready to elect standard model demagogues. "A lot of labor people who thought of voting for Wallace were ashamed of themselves when they realized what they were about to do," said Morris Iushewitz, an officer of New York's Central Labor Council. Because of a massive last-minute union campaign, and perhaps for other reasons, the blue-collar vote for Wallace fell far below the figures predicted by the early polls last fall. Any number of people, moreover, who are not doing well by any set of official statistics, who are earning well below the national mean ($8,000 a year), or who hold two jobs to stay above it, think of themselves as affluent, and often use that word. It is almost as if not to be affluent is to be un-American. People who can't use the word tend to be angry; people who come too close to those who can't become frightened. The definition of affluence is generally pinned to what comes in, not to the quality of life as it's lived. The $8,000 son of a man who never earned more than $4,500 may, for that reason alone, believe that he's "doing all right." If life is not all right, if he can't get his curbs fixed, or his streets patrolled, if the highways are crowded and the beaches polluted, if the schools are ineffectual he is still able to call himself affluent, feels, perhaps, a social compulsion to do so. His anger, if he is angry, is not that of the wage earner resenting management—and certainly not that of the socialist ideologue asking for redistribution of wealth—but that of the consumer, the taxpayer, and the family man. (Inflation and taxes are wiping out most of the wage gains made in labor contracts signed during the past three years.) Thus he will vote for a Louise Day Hicks in Boston who promises to hold the color line in the schools or for a Charles Stenvig calling for law enforcement in Minneapolis but reject a George Wallace who seems to threaten his pocketbook. The danger is that he will identify with the politics of the Birchers and other middle-class reactionaries (who often pretend to speak for him) even though his income and style of life are far removed from theirs; that taxes, for example, will be identified with welfare rather than war, and that he will blame his limited means on the small slice of the poor rather than the fat slice of the rich.

If you sit and talk to people like Marjorie Lemlow, who heads Mothers Support Neighborhood Schools in San Francisco, or Joe Owens, a house painter who is president of a community-action organization in Boston, you quickly discover that the roots of reaction and the roots of reform are often identical, and that the response to particular situations is more often contingent on the politics of the politicians and leaders who appear to care than on the conditions of life or the ideology of the victims. Mrs. Lemlow wants to return the schools to some virtuous past; she worries about disintegration of the family and she speaks vaguely about something that she can't bring herself to call a conspiracy against Americanism. She has been accused of leading a bunch of Birchers, and she sometimes talks Birch language. But whatever the form, her sense of things comes from a small-town vision of national virtues, and her unhappiness from the assaults of urban sophistication. It just so happens that a lot of reactionaries now sing that tune, and that the liberals are indifferent.

Joe Owens—probably because of his experience as a Head Start parent, and because of his association with an effective community-action program—talks a different language. He knows, somehow, that no simple past can be restored. In his world the villians are not conspirators but bureaucrats and politicians, and he is beginning to discover that in a struggle with officials the black man in the ghetto and the working man (black or white) have the same problems. "Every time you ask for something from the politicians they treat you like a beggar, like you ought to be grateful for what you have. They try to make you feel ashamed."

The imponderables are youth and tradition and change. The civics book and the institution it celebrates—however passé—still hold the world together. The revolt is in their name, not against them. And there is simple decency, the language and practice of the folksy cliché, the small town, the Boy Scout virtues, the neighborhood charity, the obligation to support the church, the rhetoric of open opportunity: "They can keep Wallace and they can keep Alabama. We didn't fight a dictator for four years so we could elect one over here." What happens when all that becomes Mickey Mouse? Is there an urban ethic to replace the values of the small town? Is there a coherent public philosophy, a consistent set of beliefs to replace family, home, and hard work? What happens when the hang-ups of upper-middle-class kids are in fashion and those of blue-collar kids are not? What happens when Doing Your Own Thing becomes not the slogan of the solitary deviant but the norm? Is it possible that as the institutions and beliefs of tradition are fashionably denigrated a blue-collar generation gap will open to the Right as well as to the Left? (There is statistical evidence, for example, that Wallace's greatest support within the unions came from people who are between twenty-one and twenty-nine, those, that is, who have the most tenuous association with the liberalism of labor.) Most are politically silent; although SDS has been trying to organize blue-collar high-school students, there are no Mario Savios or Mark Rudds—either of the Right or the Left—among them. At the same time the union leaders, some of them old hands from the Thirties, aren't sure that the kids are following them either. Who speaks for the son of the longshoreman or the Detroit auto worker? What happens if he doesn't get to college? What, indeed, happens when he does?

Vaguely but unmistakably the hopes that a youth-worshiping nation historically invested in its young are becoming threats. We have never been unequivocal about the symbolic patricide of Americanization and upward mobility, but if at one time mobility meant rejection of older (or European) styles it was, at least, done in the name of America. Now the labels are blurred and the objectives indistinct. Just at the moment when a tradition-bound Italian father is persuaded that he should send his sons to college—that education is the only future—the college blows up. At the moment when a parsimonious taxpayer begins to shell out for what he considers an extravagant state university system the students go on strike. Marijuana, sexual liberation, dress styles, draft resistance, even the rhetoric of change becomes monsters and demons in a world that appears to turn old virtues upside down. The paranoia that fastened on Communism twenty years ago (and sometimes still does) is increasingly directed to vague conspiracies undermining the schools, the family, order and discipline. "They're feeding the kids this generation-gap business," says a Chicago housewife who grinds out a campaign against sex education on a duplicating machine in her living room. "The kids are told to make their own decisions. They're all mixed up by situation ethics and open-ended questions. They're alienating children from their own parents." They? The churches, the schools, even the YMCA and the Girl Scouts, are implicated. But a major share of the villainy is now also attributed to "the social science centers," to the apostles of sensitivity training, and to what one California lady, with some embarrassment, called "nude therapy." "People with sane minds are being altered by psychological methods." The current major campaign of the John Birch Society is not directed against Communists in government or the Supreme Court, but against sex education.

(There is, of course, also sympathy with the young, especially in poorer areas where kids have no place to play. "Everybody's got to have a hobby," a South Boston adolescent told a youth worker. "Ours is throwing rocks." If people will join reactionary organizations to protect their children, they will also support others: community-action agencies which help kids get jobs; Head Start parent groups, Boys Clubs. "Getting this place cleaned up" sometimes refers to a fear of young hoods; sometimes it points to the day when there is a park or a playground or when the existing park can be used. "I want to see them grow up to have a little fun.")

Beneath it all there is a more fundamental ambivalence, not only about the young, but about institutions—the schools, the churches, the Establishment—and about the future itself. In the major cities of the East (though perhaps not in the West) there is a sense that time is against you, that one is living "in one of the few decent neighborhoods left," that "if I can get 125 a week upstate (or downstate) I'll move." The institutions that were supposed to mediate social changes and which, more than ever, are becoming priesthoods of information and conglomerates of social engineers, are increasingly suspect. To attack the Ford Foundation (as Wright Patman has done) is not only to fan the embers of historic populism against concentrations of wealth and power, but also to arouse those who feel that they are trapped by an alliance of upper-class Wasps and lower-class Negroes. If the foundations have done anything for the blue-collar worker he doesn't seem to be aware of it. At the same time the distrust of professional educators that characterizes the black militants is becoming increasingly prevalent among a minority of lower-middle-class whites who are beginning to discover that the schools aren't working for them either. ("Are all those new programs just a cover-up for failure?") And if the Catholic Church is under attack from its liberal members (on birth control, for example) it is also alienating the traditionalists who liked their minor saints (even if they didn't actually exist) and were perfectly content with the Latin Mass. For the alienated Catholic liberal there are other places to go; for the lower-middle-class parishioner in Chicago or Boston there are none.

Perhaps, in some measure, it has always been this way. Perhaps none of this is new. And perhaps it is also true that the American lower middle has never had it so good. And yet surely there is a difference, and that is that the common man has lost his visibility and, somehow, his claim on public attention. There are old liberals and socialists—men like Michael Harrington —who believe that a new alliance can be forged for progressive social action:

From Marx to Mills, the Left has regarded the middle class as a stratum of hypocritical, vacillating rear-guarders. There was often sound reason for this contempt. But is it not possible that a new class is coming into being? It is not the old middle class of small property owners and entrepreneurs, nor the new middle class of managers. It is composed of scientists, technicians, teachers, and professionals in the public sector of the society. By education and work experience it is predisposed toward planning. It could be an ally of the poor and the organized workers—or their sophisticated enemy. In other words, an unprecedented social and political variable seems to be taking shape in America.

The American worker, even when he waits on a table or holds open a door, is not servile; he does not carry himself like an inferior. The openness, frankness, and democratic manner which Tocqueville described in the last century persists to this very day. They have been a source of rudeness, contemptuous ignorance, violence—and of a creative self-confidence among great masses of people. It was in this latter spirit that the CIO was organized and the black freedom movement marched.

There are recent indications that the white lower middle class is coming back on the roster of public priorities. Pucinski tells you that liberals in Congress are privately discussing the pressure from the middle class. There are proposals now to increase personal income-tax exemptions from $600 to $1,000 (or $1,200) for each dependent, to protect all Americans with a national insurance system covering catastrophic medical expenses, and to put a floor under all incomes. Yet these things by themselves are insufficient. Nothing is sufficient without a national sense of restoration. What Pucinski means by the middle class has, in some measure, always been represented. A physician earning $75,000 a year is also a working man but he is hardly a victim of the welfare system. Nor, by and large, are the stockholders of the

Standard Oil Company or U.S. Steel. The fact that American ideals have often been corrupted in the cause of self-aggrandizement does not make them any less important for the cause of social reform and justice. "As a movement with the conviction that there is more to people than greed and fear," Harrington said, "the Left must . . . also speak in the name of the historic idealism of the United States."

The issue, finally, is not *the program* but the vision, the angle of view. A huge constituency may be coming up for grabs, and there is considerable evidence that its political mobility is more sensitive than anyone can imagine, that all the sociological determinants are not as significant as the simple facts of concern and leadership. When Robert Kennedy was killed last year, thousands of working-class people who had expected to vote for him—if not hundreds of thousands—shifted their loyalties to Wallace. A man who can change from a progressive democrat into a bigot overnight deserves attention.

Pluralist Democracy and Its Critics

When John Gardner makes a plea for support for "Common Cause" on the ground that "everybody's organized but the people" he is pointing to a central characteristic of American politics: It is primarily a process in which organized groups contend for power. In American politics, despite our rhetoric, a majority does not typically rule. Elections are, of course, decided by majority vote, but policies are not determined by elections. If a majority does not typically rule, must we conclude that a minority does? Most political scientists would say no, that what we actually observe in American politics is the rule of *minorities* through an endless process of negotiation, bargaining, accommodation, and compromise among organized groups. In the process, of course, some interest groups get more than others. But everyone, at least all organized groups, gets something, and usually it is enough to create sufficient satisfaction to keep the game going.

Politicians tend to play the role of neutral brokers, responding to shifting coalitions of interests, helping the elites who represent the interests to work out mutually satisfactory accommodations of their rivalries. These political processes—variously described as pluralism, broker rule, minorities rule, polyarchy, or interest-group liberalism—are fundamentally different from what our traditional democratic ideals led us to expect. In a pluralist system, for example, the electoral process does not present citizens with meaningful policy choices; politicians do not act on principle, but respond to pressures and seek to please; candidates and political parties put winning above everything else; voters are expected to approach politics in the spirit of "what's-in-it-for-me," and are not expected to be informed or active. As these differences suggest, there are fundamental conflicts between our inherited ideology of democracy and our current pluralist practices.

Pluralism is a normative as well as a descriptive theory of politics. That is, there are those who argue not only that it provides us with a model of how our politics actually does operate, but that it gives us answers to the question of how a democratic political system *ought* to be organized and to function. The essays in this section describe the major characteristics of pluralist politics; they part company over the questions of how well the process works and whether Americans should be satisfied with the results. They should be read carefully and critically: carefully, because they provide the conceptual tools necessary for understanding much of the materials in the following sections; critically, because in the issues that divide the several authors in this section are the major problems of modern democracy.

PETER F. DRUCKER

A Key to American Politics: Calhoun's Pluralism

The American party system has been under attack almost continuously since it took definite form in the time of Andrew Jackson. The criticism has always been directed at the same point: America's political pluralism, the distinctively American organization of government by compromise of interests, pressure groups and sections. And the aim of the critics from Thaddeus Stevens to Henry Wallace has always been to substitute for this "unprincipled" pluralism a government based as in Europe on "ideologies" and "principles." But never before—at least not since the Civil War years—has the crisis been as acute as in this last decade; for the political problems which dominate our national life today: foreign policy and industrial policy, are precisely the problems which interest and pressure-group compromise is least equipped to handle. And while the crisis symptoms: a left-wing Third Party and the threatened split-off of the Southern Wing, are more alarming in the Democratic Party, the Republicans are hardly much better off. The 1940 boom for the "idealist" Willkie and the continued inability to attract a substantial portion of the labor vote, are definite signs that the Republican Party too is under severe *ideological* pressure.

Yet, there is almost no understanding of the problem—precisely because there is so little understanding of the basic principles of American pluralism. Of course, every politician in this country must be able instinctively to work in terms of sectional and interest compromise; and the voter takes it for granted. But there is practically no awareness of the fact that organization on the basis of sectional and interest compromise is both the distinctly American form of political organization and the cornerstone of practically all major political institutions of the modern U.S.A. As acute an observer as Winston Churchill apparently does not understand that Congress works on a basis entirely different from that of Britain's Parliament; neither do nine out of ten Americans and 999 out of a 1000 teachers of those courses in "Civics." There is even less understanding that sectional and interest-group pluralism is not

Source: Economist, management expert, philosopher, and historian, Mr. Drucker is the author of several books and many articles. "A Key to American Politics: Calhoun's Pluralism" appeared in *The Review of Politics*, October 1968, pp. 412–426, and in *Men, Ideas & Politics* by Peter F. Drucker. Copyright © 1971 by Peter F. Drucker. Reprinted by permission of Harper & Row, Publishers, Inc.

just the venal expediency of that stock-villain of American folklore, the "politician," but that it in itself is a basic ideology, a basic principle—and the one which is the very foundation of our free society and government.[1]

I

To find an adequate analysis of the principle of government by sectional and interest compromise we have to go back almost a hundred years to John C. Calhoun and to his two political treatises [2] published after his death in 1852. Absurd, you will say, for it is practically an axiom of American history that Calhoun's political theories, subtle, even profound though they may have been, were reduced to absurdity and irrelevance by the Civil War. Yet, this "axiom" is nothing but a partisan vote of the Reconstruction Period. Of course, the specific occasion for which Calhoun formulated his theories, the Slavery issue, has been decided; and for the constitutional veto power of the states over national legislation, by means of which Calhoun proposed to formalize the principle of sectional and interest compromise, was substituted in actual practice the much more powerful and much more elastic but extra-constitutional and extra-legal veto power of sections, interests and pressure groups in Congress and within the parties.[3] But *his basic principle itself: that every major interest in the country, whether regional, economic or religious, is to possess a veto power on political decisions directly affecting it*, the principle which Calhoun called—rather obscurely—"the rule of concurrent majority," has become the organizing principle of American politics. And it is precisely this principle that is under fire today.

What makes Calhoun so important as the major key to the understanding of American politics, is not just that he saw the importance in American political life of sectional and interest pluralism; other major analysts of our government, Tocqueville, for instance, or Bryce or Wilson, saw that too. But Calhoun, perhaps alone, saw in it more than a rule of expediency, imposed by the country's size and justifiable by results, if at all. He saw in it a basic principle of free government.

Without this (*the rule of concurrent majority based on interests rather than on principles*) there can be . . . no constitution. The assertion is true in reference

[1] A perfect illustration was the outraged amazement with which most book reviewers greeted Edward J. Flynn's *You're the Boss*—a simple and straight recital of facts every American should really have known and understood all along.

[2] A *Disquisition on Government*; and A *Discourse on the Constitution and Government of the United States*.

[3] Calhoun's extreme legalism, his belief that everything had to be spelled out in the written Constitution—a belief he shared with his generation—is one of the major reasons why the importance of his thesis has not been generally recognized. Indeed it is of the very essence of the concept of "concurrent majority" that it cannot be made official and legal in an effective government—the express veto such as the UN Charter gives to the Great Powers makes government impossible.

to all constitutional governments, be their forms what they may: It is, indeed, the negative power which makes the constitution,—and the positive which makes the government. The one is the power of acting;—and the other the power of preventing or arresting action. The two, combined, make constitutional government.

. . . it follows, necessarily, that where the numerical majority has the sole control of the government, there can be no constitution . . . and hence, the numerical, unmixed with the concurrent majority, necessarily forms, in all cases, absolute government.

. . . The principle by which they (governments) are upheld and preserved . . . in constitutional governments is *compromise;*—and in absolute governments is *force.* . . .[4]

And however much the American people may complain in words about the "unprincipled" nature of their political system, by their actions they have always shown that they too believe that without sectional and interest compromises there can be no constitutional government. If this is not grasped, American government and politics must appear not only as cheap to the point of venality, but must appear as utterly irrational and unpredictable.

II

Sectional and interest pluralism has molded all American political institutions. It is the method—entirely unofficial and extra-constitutional—through which the organs of government are made to function, through which leaders are selected, policies developed, men and groups organized for the conquest and management of political power. In particular it is the explanation for the most distinctive features of the American political system: the way in which the Congress operates, the way in which major government departments are set up and run, the qualifications for "eligibility" as a candidate for elective office, and the American party structure.

To all foreign observers of Congress two things have always remained mysterious: the distinction between the official party label and the "blocs" which cut across party lines; and the power and function of the Congressional Committees. And most Americans though less amazed by the phenomena are equally baffled.

The "blocs"—the "Farm Bloc" the "Friends of Labor in the Senate," the "Business Groups," etc.—are simply the expression of the basic tenet of sectional and interest pluralism that major interests have a veto power on legislation directly affecting them. For this reason they must cut across party lines—that is, lines expressing the numerical rather than the "concurrent" majority. And because these blocs have (a) only a negative veto, and (b) only on measures directly affecting them, they cannot in themselves be permanent groupings replacing the parties. They must be loosely organized; and one and the same member of Congress must at different times vote with different

---

[4] Quotations from A *Disquisition on Government* (Columbia, S.C., 1852), pp. 35 to 37.

blocs. The strength of the "blocs" does not rest on their numbers but on the basic mores of American politics which grant every major interest group a limited self-determination—as expressed graphically in the near-sanctity of a senatorial "filibuster." The power of the "Farm Bloc" for instance, does not rest on the numerical strength of the rural vote—a minority vote even in the Senate with its disproportionate representation of the thinly populated agricultural states—but on its "strategic" strength, that is on its being the spokesman for a recognized major interest.

Subordination of a major interest is possible; but only in a "temporary emergency." Most of the New Deal measures were, palpably, neither temporary nor emergency measures; yet their sponsors had to present them, and convincingly, as "temporary emergency measures" because they could be enacted only by over-riding the extra-constitutional veto of the business interests.

Once the excuse of the "temporary emergency" had fully lost its plausibility, that major interest could no longer be voted down; and the policy collapsed. By 1946, for instance, labor troubles could be resolved only on a basis acceptable to both labor and employer: higher wages *and* higher prices. (Even if a numerical majority had been available to legislate against either party—and the business group could probably still have been voted down two and half years ago—the solution had to be acceptable to both parties.)

The principle of sectional and interest compromise leads directly to the congressional committee system—a system to which there is no parallel anywhere in the world. Congress, especially the House, has largely abdicated to its committees because only in the quiet and secrecy of a committee room can sectional compromise be worked out. The discussion on the floor as well as the recorded vote is far too public and therefore largely for the folks back home. But a committee's business is to arrive at an agreement between all major sectional interests affected; which explains the importance of getting a bill before the "right" committee. In any but an American legislature the position of each member, once a bill is introduced, is fixed by the stand of his party which, in turn, is decided on grounds that have little to do with the measure itself but are rather dictated by the balance of power within the government and by party programs. Hence it makes usually little difference which committee discusses a bill or whether it goes before a committee at all. In the United States, however, a bill's assignment to a specific committee decides which interest groups are to be recognized as affected by the measure and therefore entitled to a part in writing it ("who is to have standing before the committee"), for each committee represents a specific constellation of interests. In many cases this first decision therefore decides the fate of a proposed measure, especially as the compromise worked out by the committee is generally accepted once it reaches the floor, especially in the House.

It is not only Congress but every individual member of Congress himself who is expected to operate according to the "rule of concurrent majority."

He is considered both a representative of the American people and responsible to the national interest and a delegate of his constituents and responsible to their particular interests. Wherever the immediate interests of his constituents are not in question, he is to be a statesman; wherever their conscience or their pocketbooks are affected, he is to be a business agent. This is in sharp contrast to the theory on which any parliamentary government is based—a theory developed almost two hundred years ago in Edmund Burke's famous speech to the voters at Bristol—according to which a member of Parliament represents the commonwealth rather than his constituents. Hence in all parliamentary countries, the representative can be a stranger to his constituency— in the extreme, as it was practiced in Weimar Germany, there is one long national list of candidates who run in all constituencies—whereas the Congressman in this country must be a resident of his constituency. And while an American Senator considers it a compliment and an asset to be called "Cotton Ed Smith," the Speaker of the House of Commons not so long ago severely reprimanded a member for calling another member—an official of the miners' union—a "representative of the coal miners."

The principle of sectional and interest pluralism also explains why this is the only nation where Cabinet members are charged by law with the representation of special interests—labor, agriculture, commerce. In every other country an agency of the government—any agency of the government—is solemnly sworn to guard the public interests against "the interests." In this country the concept of a government department as the representative of a special interest group is carried down to smaller agencies and even to divisions and branches of a department. This was particularly noticeable during the war in such fights as that between OPA—representing the consumer—and the War Production Board representing the producer, or, within WPB between the Procurement branches speaking for the war industries and the Civilian Requirements Branch speaking for the industries producing for the "home front."

The mystery of "eligibility"—the criteria which decide who will make a promising candidate for public office—which has baffled so many foreign and American observers, Bryce for instance—also traces back to the "rule of the concurrent majority." Eligibility simply means that a candidate must not be unacceptable to any majority interest, religious or regional group within the electorate; it is primarily a negative qualification. Eligibility operates on all levels and applies to all elective offices. It has been brilliantly analyzed in "Boss" Flynn's *You're the Boss*. His classical example is the selection of Harry Truman as Democratic vice-presidential candidate in 1944. Truman was "eligible" rather than Wallace, Byrnes or Douglas precisely because he was unknown; because he was neither Easterner nor Westerner nor Southerner, because he was neither New Deal nor Conservative, etc., in short because he had no one trait strong enough to offend anybody anywhere.

But the central institution based on sectional pluralism is the American party. Completely extra-constitutional, the wonder and the despair of every foreign observer who cannot fit it into any of his concepts of political life, the American party (rather than the states) has become the instrument to realize Calhoun's "rule of the concurrent majority."

In stark contrast to the parties of Europe, the American party has no program and no purpose except to organize divergent groups for the common pursuit and conquest of power. Its unity is one of action, not of beliefs. Its only rule is to attract—or at least not to repel—the largest possible number of groups. It must, by definition, be acceptable equally to the right and the left, the rich and the poor, the farmer and the worker, the Protestant and the Catholic, the native and the foreign-born. It must be able to rally Mr. Rankin of Mississippi and Mr. Marcantonio of New York—or Senator Flanders and Colonel McCormick—behind the same presidential candidate and the same "platform."

As soon as it cannot appeal at least to a minority in every major group (as soon, in other words, as it provokes the veto of one section, interest or class) a party is in danger of disintegration. Whenever a party loses its ability to fuse sectional pressures and class interests into one national policy—both parties just before the Civil War, the Republican Party before its reorganization by Mark Hanna, both parties again today—the party system (and with it the American political system altogether) is in crisis.

It is, consequently, not that Calhoun was repudiated by the Civil War which is the key to the understanding of American politics but that he has become triumphant since.

The apparent victors, the "Radical Republicans," Thaddeus Stevens, Seward, Chief Justice Chase, were out to destroy not only slavery and states rights but the "rule of the concurrent majority" itself. And the early Republican Party—before the Civil War and in the Reconstruction Period—was indeed determined to substitute principle for interest as the lodestar of American political life. But in the end it was the political thought of convinced pluralists such as Abraham Lincoln and Andrew Johnson rather than the ideologies of the Free Soilers and Abolitionists which molded the Republican Party. And ever since, the major development of American politics have been based on Calhoun's principle. To this the United States owes the strength as well as the weaknesses of its political system.

III

The weaknesses of sectional and interests compromise are far more obvious than its virtues; they have been hammered home for a hundred years. Francis Lieber, who brought the dominant German political theories of the early nineteenth century to this country, attacked pluralism in Calhoun's own state of South Carolina a century ago. Twenty years later Walter Bagehot contrasted, impressively, General Grant's impotent administration with those of Gladstone and Disraeli to show the superiority of ideological party organization. The most thorough and most uncompromising criticism came from Woodrow Wilson; and every single one of the Professor's points was amply borne out by his later experience as President. Time has not made these weaknesses any less dangerous.

There is, first of all, the inability of a political system based on the "rule of the concurrent majority" to resolve conflicts of principles. All a pluralist system can do is to deny that "ideological" conflicts (as they are called nowadays) do exist. Those conflicts, a pluralist must assert are fundamentally either struggles for naked power or friction between interest groups which could be solved if only the quarreling parties sat down around a conference table. Perhaps, the most perfect, because most naive, expression of this belief remains the late General Patton's remark that the Nazis were, after all, not so very different from Republicans or Democrats. (Calhoun, while less naive, was just unable to understand the reality of "ideological" conflict in and around the slavery problem.)

In nine cases out of ten the refusal to acknowledge the existence of ideological conflict is beneficial. It prevents fights for power, or clashes of interests, from flaring into religious wars where irreconcilable principles collide (a catastrophe against which Europe's ideological politics have almost no defense). It promotes compromise where compromise is possible. But in a genuine clash of principles—and, whatever the pluralists say, there *are* such clashes—the "rule of concurrent majority" breaks down; it did, in Calhoun's generation, before the profound reality of the slavery issue. A legitimate ideological conflict is actually aggravated by the pluralists' refusal to accept its reality: the compromisers who thought the slavery issue could be settled by the meeting of good intentions, or by the payment of money, may have done more than the Abolitionists to make the Civil War inevitable.

A weakness of sectional and interest pluralism just as serious is that it amounts to a principle of inaction. The popular assertion "it's better to make the wrong decision than to do nothing at all," is, of course, fallacious; but no nation, however unlimited its resources, can have a very effective policy if its government is based on a principle that orders it to do nothing important except unanimously. Moreover, pluralism increases exorbitantly the weight of well organized small interest groups, especially when they lobby *against* a decision. Congress can far too easily be high-pressured into emasculating a bill by the expedient of omitting its pertinent provisions; only with much greater difficulty can Congress be moved to positive action. This explains, to a large extent, the eclipse of Congress during the last hundred years, both in popular respect and in its actual momentum as policy-making organ of government. Congress, which the Founding Fathers had intended to be the central organ of government—a role which it fulfilled up to Andrew Jackson—became the compound representative of sections and interests and, consequently, progressively incapable of national leadership.

Pluralism gives full weight—more than full weight—to sections and interests; but who is to represent the national welfare? Ever since the days of
Calhoun, the advocates of pluralism have tried to dodge this question by
contending that the national interest is equal to the sum of all particular
interests, and that it therefore does not need a special organ of representation.
But this most specious argument is contradicted by the most elementary
observation. In practice, pluralism tends to resolve sectional and class conflicts at the expense of the national interest which is represented by nobody
in particular, by no section and no organization.

These weaknesses had already become painfully obvious while Calhoun
was alive and active—during the decade after Andrew Jackson, the first
President of pluralism. Within a few years after Calhoun's death, the inability
of the new system to comprehend and to resolve an ideological conflict—
ultimately its inability to represent and to guard the national interest—had
brought catastrophe. For a hundred years and more, American political
thought has therefore resolved around attempts to counteract if not to overcome these weaknesses. Three major developments of American constitutional life were the result: the growth of the functions and powers of the
President and his emergence as a "leader" rather than as the executive agent
of the Congress; the rise of the Supreme Court, with its "rule of law," to the
position of arbiter of policy; the development of a unifying ideology—the
"American Creed."

Of these the most important—and the least noticed—is the "American
Creed." In fact I know of no writer of major importance since Tocqueville
who has given much attention to it. Yet even the term "un-American" cannot
be translated successfully into any other language, least of all into "English"
English. In no other country could the identity of the nation with a certain
set of ideas be assumed—at least not under a free government. This unique
cohesion on principles shows, for instance, in the refusal of the American
voter to accept Socialists and Communists as "normal" parties, simply because
both groups refuse to accept the assumption of a common American ideology.
It shows, for another example, in the indigenous structure of the American
labor movement with its emphasis on interest pressure rather than on a
political philosophy. And this is also the only country in which "Civics" could
be taught in schools—the only democratic country which believes that a
correct social philosophy could or should be part of public education.

In Europe, a universal creed would be considered incompatible with a
free society. Before the advent of totalitarianism, no European country had
ever known anything comparable to the flag salute of the American school
child.[5] For in Europe all political activity is based on ideological factions;
consequently, to introduce a uniform ideology in a European country is to

[5] The perhaps most profound discussion of the American ideological cohesion can be
found in the two decisions of the Supreme Court on the compulsory flag salute, and in the
two dissents therefrom, which deserve high rating among American state papers.

stamp out *all* opposition. In the United States ideological homogeneity is the very basis of political diversity. It makes possible the almost unlimited freedom of interest groups, religious groups, pressure groups, etc.; and in this way it is the very fundament of free government. (It also explains why the preservation of civil liberties has been so much more important a problem in this country—as compared to England or France, for instance.) The assumption of ideological unity gives the United States the minimum of cohesion without which its political system simply could not have worked.

IV

But is even the "American dream" enough to make a system based on the "rule of the concurrent majority" work today? Can pluralism handle the two major problems of American politics—the formulation of a foreign policy, and the political organization of an industrial society—any more successfully than it could handle the slavery issue? Or is the American political system as much in crisis as it was in the last years of Calhoun's life—and for pretty much the same reasons?

A foreign policy can never be evolved by adding particular interests— regional, economic or racial—or by compromising among them; it must supersede them. If Calhoun's contention that the national interest will automatically be served by serving the interests of the parts is wrong anywhere, it is probably wrong in the field of foreign affairs.

A foreign policy and a party system seem to be compatible only if the parties are organized on programmatic grounds, that is on principles. For if not based on general principles, a foreign policy will become a series of improvisations without rhyme or reason. In a free society, in which parties compete for votes and power, the formulation of a foreign policy may thus force the parties into ideological attitudes which will sooner or later be reflected in their domestic policies too.

This was clearly realized in the early years of the Republic when foreign policy was vital to a new nation, clinging precariously to a long seaboard without hinterland, engaged in a radical experiment with new political institutions, surrounded by the Great Powers of that time, England, France and Spain, all of them actually or potentially hostile. This awareness of foreign policy largely explains why the party system of the Founding Fathers— especially of Hamilton—was an ideological one; it also explains why the one positive foreign-policy concept this country developed during the entire nineteenth century—the Monroe Doctrine—was formulated by the last two politically active survivors of the founding generation, Monroe and John Quincy Adams. No matter how little Calhoun himself realized it, his doctrine would have been impossible without the French Revolution and the Napoleonic Wars which, during the most critical period of American integration, kept its potential European enemies busy. By 1820, the country had become too strong, had taken in too much territory, to be easily attacked; and it was still not strong enough, and far too much absorbed in the development of its own interior, to play a part in international affairs. Hence Calhoun, and all America with him, could push foreign policy out of their minds —so much so that this is the only country in which it is possible to write a comprehensive work on an important historical period without as much as a mention of foreign affairs, as Arthur M. Schlesinger, Jr. managed to do in his *The Age of Jackson.*

But today foreign policy is again as vital for the survival of the nation as it ever was during the administrations of Washington and Jefferson. And it has to be a foreign *policy,* that is, a making of decisions; hence neither "isolationism" nor "internationalism" will do. (For "internationalism"—the search for formulae which will provide automatic decisions, even in advance— is also a refusal to have a foreign policy; it may well have done this country, and the world, as much harm as "isolationism"—perhaps more.) To survive as the strongest of the Great Powers, the United States might even have to accept permanently the supremacy of foreign policies over domestic affairs, however much this may go against basic American convictions, and indeed against the American grain. But no foreign policy can be evolved by the compromise of sectional interests or economic pressures; yet neither party, as today constituted, could develop a foreign policy based on definite principles.

The other great national need is to resolve the political problems of an industrial society. An industrial society is by nature ultrapluralistic, because it develops class and interest groups that are far stronger, and far more tightly organized, than any interest group in a pre-industrial age. A few big corporations, a few big unions, may be the actually decisive forces in an industrial society. And these groups can put decisive pressure on society: they can throttle social and economic life.

The problem does not lie in "asocial behavior" of this or that group but in the nature of industrial society which bears much closer resemblance to feudalism than to the trading nineteenth century. Its political problems are very similar to those which feudalism had to solve—and failed to solve. It is in perpetual danger of disintegration into virtually autonomous fiefs, principalities, "free cities," "robber baronies" and "exempt bishoprics"—the authority and the interest of the nation trampled underfoot, autonomous groups uniting to control the central power in their own interest or disregarding government in fighting each other in the civil conflict of class warfare. And the alternative to such a collapse into anarchy or civil war—the suppression of classes and interest groups by an all-powerful government—is hardly more attractive.

An industrial society cannot function without an organ able to superimpose the national interest on economic or class interests. More than a mere arbiter is needed. The establishment of the "rules of civilized industrial warfare," as was done by both the Wagner Act and the Taft-Hartley Acts, tries to avoid the need for policies by equalizing the strength of the conflicting sections; but that can lead only to deadlock, to collusion against the national interest or, worse still, to the attempt to make the national authority serve the interest of one side against the other. In other words, an industrial society cannot fully accept Calhoun's assumption that the national good will evolve from the satisfaction of particular interests. An industrial society without national policy will become both anarchic and despotic.

Small wonder that there has been increasing demand for a radical change which would substitute ideological parties and programmatic policies for the pluralist parties and the "rule of the concurrent majority" of the American tradition. Henry Wallace's Third-Party Movement, while the most publicized, may well be the least significant development; for third parties are, after all, nothing new in our political history. But for the first time in a hundred years there is a flood of books—and by serious students of American government—advocating radical constitutional reform. However much Senator Fulbright, Henry Hazlitt and Thomas Fineletter disagree on details, they are one in demanding the elimination—or at least the limitation—of the "rule of the concurrent majority," and its replacement by an ideological system functioning along parliamentary lines. More significant even may be Walter Reuther's new unionism with its blend of traditional pressure tactics and working-class, that is ideological, programs and aims.

V

Yet all these critics and reformers not only fail to ask themselves whether an ideological system of politics would really be any better equipped to cope with the great problems of today—and neither the foreign nor the industrial policy of England, that most successful of all ideologically organized countries, look any too successful right now; the critics also never stop to consider the unique strength of our traditional system.

Our traditional system makes sure that there is always a legitimate government in the country; and to provide such a government is the first job of any political system—a duty which a great many of the political systems known to man have never discharged.

It minimizes conflicts by utilizing, rather than suppressing conflicting forces. It makes it almost impossible for the major parties to become entirely irresponsible: neither party can afford to draw strength from the kind of demagogic opposition, without governmental responsibility, which perpetually nurtures fascist and communist parties abroad. Hence, while the two national parties are willing to embrace any movement or any group within the country that commands sufficient following, they in turn force every group to bring its demands and programs into agreement with the beliefs, traditions and prejudices of the people.

Above all, our system of sectional and interest compromise is one of the only two ways known to man in which a free government and a free society can survive—and the only one at all adapted to the conditions of American life and acceptable to the American people.

The central problem in a free government is that of factions, as we have known since Plato and Aristotle. Logically, a free government and factions are incompatible. But whatever the cause—vanity and pride, lust for power, virtue or wickedness, greed or the desire to help others—factionalism is inherent in human nature and in human society. For 2000 years the best minds in politics have tried to devise a factionless society—through education (Plato), through elimination of property (Thomas More), through concentration on the life of the spirit outside of worldly ambition (the political tradition of Lutheranism). The last great attempt to save freedom by abolishing faction was Rousseau's. But to create the factionless free society is as hopeless as to set up perpetual motion. From Plato to Rousseau, political thought has ended up by demanding that factions be suppressed, that is, that freedom, to be preserved, be abolished.

The Anglo-American political tradition alone has succeeded in breaking out of this vicious circle. Going back to Hooker and Locke, building on the rich tradition of free government in the cities of the late middle ages, Anglo-American political realism discovered: that if factions cannot be suppressed, they must be utilized to make a free government both freer and stronger. This one basic concept distinguishes Anglo-American political theory and practice from continental European politics, and accounts for the singular success of free and popular governments in both countries. Elsewhere in the western world the choice has always been between extreme factionalism which makes government impotent if not impossible and inevitably leads to civil war, and autocracy which justifies the suppression of liberty with the need for effective and orderly government. Nineteenth-century France with its six revolutions, or near revolutions, stands for one, the totalitarian governments of our time for the other alternative of continental politics.

But—and this is the real discovery on which the Anglo-American achievements rests—factions can be used constructively only if they are encompassed within a frame of unity. A free government on the basis of sectional interest groups is possible only when there is no ideological split within the country. This is the American solution. Another conceivable solution is to channel the driving forces, the vectors of society, into ideological factions which obtain their cohesion from a program for the whole of society, and from a creed. But that presupposes an unquestioned ruling class with a common outlook on life, with uniform mores and a traditional, if not inherent, economic security. Given that sort of ruling class, the antagonist in an ideological system can be expected to be a "loyal opposition," that is, to accept the rules of the game and to see himself as a partner rather than as a potential challenger to civil war. But a ruling class accepted by the people as a whole, and feeling itself responsible to the people as a whole, cannot be created by fiat or overnight. In antiquity only Rome, in modern times only England, achieved it. On the Continent, all attempts to create a genuine ruling class have failed dismally.

In this country, the ruling-class solution was envisaged by Alexander Hamilton and seemed close to realization under the presidents of the "Virginia Dynasty." Hamilton arrived at his concept with inescapable consistency; for he was absorbed by the search for a foreign policy and for the proper organization of an industrial society—precisely the two problems which, as we have seen, pluralism is least equipped to resolve. But even if Hamilton had not made the fatal mistake of identifying wealth with rulership, the American people could not have accepted his thesis. A ruling class was incompatible with mass immigration and with the explosive territorial expansion of nineteenth-century America. It was even more incompatible with the American concept of equality. And there is no reason to believe that contemporary America is any more willing to accept Hamilton's concept, Mr. James Burnham's idea of the managerial elite notwithstanding. This country as a free country has no alternative, it seems, to the "rule of the concurrent majority," no alternative to sectional pluralism as the device through which factions can be made politically effective.

It will be very difficult, indeed, to resolve the problems of foreign and of industrial policy on the pluralist basis and within the interest-group system, though not provably more difficult than these problems would be on another, ideological, basis. It will be all the harder as the two problems are closely inter-related; for the effectiveness of any American foreign policy depends, in the last analysis, on our ability to show the world a successful and working model of an industrial society. But if we succeed at all, it will be with the traditional system, horse-trading, log-rolling and politicking all included. An old saying has it that this country lives simultaneously in a world of Jeffersonian beliefs and in one of Hamiltonian realities. Out of these two, Calhoun's concept of "the rule of the concurrent majority" alone can make one viable whole. The need for a formulated foreign policy and for a national policy of industrial order is real—but not more so than the need for a real understanding of this fundamental American fact: the pluralism of sectional and interest compromise is the warp of America's political fabric—it cannot be plucked out without unravelling the whole.

BERNARD R. BERELSON

Democratic Practice and Democratic Theory

. . . .

Requirements for the Individual

Perhaps the main impact of realistic research on contemporary politics has been to temper some of the requirements set by our traditional normative theory for the typical citizen. "Out of all this literature of political observation and analysis, which is relatively new," says Max Beloff, "there has come to exist a picture in our minds of the political scene which differs very considerably from that familiar to us from the classical texts of democratic politics."

Experienced observers have long known, of course, that the individual voter was not all that the theory of democracy requires of him. As Bryce put it:

> How little solidity and substance there is in the political or social beliefs of nineteen persons out of every twenty. These beliefs, when examined, mostly resolve themselves into two or three prejudices and aversions, two or three prepossessions for a particular party or section of a party, two or three phrases or catch-words suggesting or embodying arguments which the man who repeats them has not analyzed.

While our data do not support such an extreme statement, they do reveal that certain requirements commonly assumed for the successful operation of democracy are not met by the behavior of the "average" citizen. The requirements, and our conclusions concerning them, are quickly reviewed.

Interest, Discussion, Motivation. The democratic citizen is expected to be interested and to participate in political affairs. His interest and participation can take such various forms as reading and listening to campaign materials, working for the candidate or the party, arguing politics, donating money, and voting. In Elmira the majority of the people vote, but in general they do not give evidence of sustained interest. Many vote without real involvement in the election, and even the party workers are not typically motivated by ideological concerns or plain civic duty.

Source: Mr. Berelson is a professional political scientist who specializes in public opinion and voting behavior. This essay is abridged from the final chapter in *Voting*, by Berelson, Paul F. Lazarsfeld, and William N. McPhee. Copyright 1954 by The University of Chicago Press. Reprinted by permission of the publisher.

If there is one characteristic for a democratic system (besides the ballot itself) that is theoretically required, it is the capacity for and the practice of discussion. "It is as true of the large as of the small society," says Lindsay, "that its health depends on the mutual understanding which discussion makes possible; and that discussion is the only possible instrument of its democratic government." . . . In this instance there was little true discussion between the candidates, little in the newspaper commentary, little between the voters and the official party representatives, some within the electorate. On the grass-roots level there was more talk than debate, and, at least inferentially, the talk had important effects upon voting, in reinforcing or activating the partisans if not in converting the opposition.

An assumption underlying the theory of democracy is that the citizenry has a strong motivation for participation in political life. But it is a curious quality of voting behavior that for large numbers of people motivation is weak if not almost absent. It is assumed that this motivation would gain its strength from the citizen's perception of the difference that alternative decisions made to him. Now when a person buys something or makes other decisions of daily life, there are direct and immediate consequences for him. But for the bulk of the American people the voting decision is not followed by any direct, immediate, visible personal consequences. Most voters, organized or unorganized, are not in a position to foresee the distant and indirect consequences for themselves, let alone the society. The ballot is cast, and for most people that is the end of it. If their side is defeated, "it doesn't really matter."

Knowledge. The democratic citizen is expected to be well informed about political affairs. He is supposed to know what the issues are, what their history is, what the relevant facts are, what alternatives are proposed, what the party stands for, what the likely consequences are. By such standards the voter falls short. Even when he has the motivation, he finds it difficult to make decisions on the basis of full information when the subject is relatively simple and proximate; how can he do so when it is complex and remote? The citizen is not highly informed on details of the campaign, nor does he avoid a certain misperception of the political situation when it is to his psychological advantage to do so. The electorate's perception of what goes on in the campaign is colored by emotional feeling toward one or the other issue, candidate, party, or social group.

Principle. The democratic citizen is supposed to cast his vote on the basis of principle—not fortuitously or frivolously or impulsively or habitually, but with reference to standards not only of his own interest but of the common good as well. Here, again, if this requirement is pushed at all strongly, it becomes an impossible demand on the democratic electorate.

Many voters vote not for principle in the usual sense but "for" a group to which they are attached—their group. The Catholic vote or the hereditary vote is explainable less as principle than as a traditional social allegiance. The ordinary voter, bewildered by the complexity of modern political problems, unable to determine clearly what the consequences are of alternative lines of action, remote from the arena, and incapable of bringing information to bear on principle, votes the way trusted people around him are voting. A British scholar, Max Beloff, takes as the "chief lesson to be derived" from such studies:

Election campaigns and the programmes of the different parties have little to do with the ultimate result which is predetermined by influences acting upon groups of voters over a longer period. . . . This view has now become a working hypothesis with which all future thinking on this matter will have to concern itself. But if this is admitted, then obviously the picture of the voter as a person exercising conscious choice between alternative persons and alternative programmes tends to disappear.

On the issues of the campaign there is a considerable amount of "don't know"—sometimes reflecting genuine indecision, more often meaning "don't care." Among those with opinions the partisans *agree* on most issues, criteria, expectations, and rules of the game. The supporters of the different sides disagree on only a few issues. Nor, for that matter, do the candidates themselves always join the issue sharply and clearly. The partisans do not agree overwhelmingly with their own party's position, or, rather, only the small minority of highly partisan do; the rest take a rather moderate position on the political considerations involved in an election.

Rationality. The democratic citizen is expected to exercise rational judgment in coming to his voting decision. He is expected to have arrived at his principles by reason and to have considered rationally the implications and alleged consequences of the alternative proposals of the contending parties. Political theorists and commentators have always exclaimed over the seeming contrast here between requirement and fulfillment. . . . In any rigorous or narrow sense the voters are not highly rational; that is, most of them do not ratiocinate on the matter, e.g., to the extent that they do on the purchase of a car or a home. Nor do voters act rationally whose "principles" are held so tenaciously as to blind them to information and persuasion. Nor do they attach efficient means to explicit ends.

The fact that some people change their minds during a political campaign shows the existence of that open-mindedness usually considered a component of rationality. But among whom? Primarily among those who can "afford" a change of mind, in the sense that they have ties or attractions on both sides —the cross-pressured voters in the middle where rationality is supposed to take over from the extremes of partisan feeling. But it would hardly be proper to designate the unstable, uninterested, uncaring middle as the sole or the major possessor of rationality among the electorate. As Beloff points out: "It is likely that the marginal voter is someone who is so inadequately identified with one major set of interests or another and so remote, therefore, from the group-thinking out of which political attitudes arise, that his voting record is an illustration, not of superior wisdom, but of greater frivolity."

The upshot of this is that the usual analogy between the voting "decision" and the more or less carefully calculated decisions of consumers or businessmen or courts, incidentally, may be quite incorrect. For many voters political preferences may better be considered analogous to cultural tastes—in music, literature, recreational activities, dress, ethics, speech, social behavior. Consider the parallels between political preferences and general cultural tastes. Both have their origin in ethnic, sectional, class, and family traditions. Both exhibit stability and resistance to change for individuals but flexibility and adjustment over generations for the society as a whole. Both seem to be matters of sentiment and disposition rather than "reasoned preferences." While both are responsive to changed conditions and unusual stimuli, they are relatively invulnerable to direct argumentation and vulnerable to indirect social influences. Both are characterized more by faith than by conviction and by wishful expectation rather than careful prediction of consequences. . . .

II

If the democratic system depended solely on the qualifications of the individual voter, then it seems remarkable that democracies have survived through the centuries. After examining the detailed data on how individuals misperceive political reality or respond to irrelevant social influences, one wonders how a democracy ever solves its political problems. But when one considers the data in a broader perspective—how huge segments of the society adapt to political conditions affecting them or how the political system adjusts itself to changing conditions over long periods of time—he cannot fail to be impressed with the total result. Where the rational citizen seems to abdicate, nevertheless angels seem to tread.

The eminent judge, Learned Hand, in a delightful essay on "Democracy: Its Presumptions and Reality," comes to essentially this conclusion.

I do not know how it is with you, but for myself I generally give up at the outset. The simplest problems which come up from day to day seem to me quite unanswerable as soon as I try to get below the surface. . . . My vote is one of the most unimportant acts of my life; if I were to acquaint myself with the matters on which it ought really to depend, if I were to try to get a judgment on which I was willing to risk affairs of even the smallest moment, I should be doing nothing else, and that seems a fatuous conclusion to a fatuous undertaking.

Yet he recognizes the paradox—somehow the system not only works on the most difficult and complex questions but often works with distinction. "For, abuse it as you will, it gives a bloodless measure of social forces—bloodless, have you thought of that?—a means of continuity, a principle of stability, a relief from the paralyzing terror of revolution."

Justice Hand concludes that we have "outgrown" the conditions assumed in traditional democratic theory and that "the theory has ceased to work." And yet, the system that has grown out of classic democratic theory, and, in this country, out of quite different and even elementary social conditions, does continue to work—perhaps even more vigorously and effectively than ever.

That is the paradox. *Individual voters* today seem unable to satisfy the requirements for a democratic system of government outlined by political theorists. But the *system of democracy* does meet certain requirements for a going political organization. The individual members may not meet all the standards, but the whole nevertheless survives and grows. This suggests that where the classic theory is defective is in its concentration on the *individual citizen*. What are undervalued are certain collective properties that reside in the electorate as a whole and in the political and social system in which it functions.

The political philosophy we have inherited, then, has given more consideration to the virtues of the typical citizen of the democracy than to the working of the *system* as a whole. Moreover, when it dealt with the system, it mainly considered the single constitutive institutions of the system, not those general features necessary if the institutions are to work as required. For example, the rule of law, representative government, periodic elections, the party system, and the several freedoms of discussion, press, association, and assembly have all been examined by political philosophers seeking to clarify and to justify the idea of political democracy. But liberal democracy is more than a political system in which individual voters and political institutions operate. For political democracy to survive, other features are required: the intensity of conflict must be limited, the rate of change must be restrained, stability in the social and economic structure must be maintained, a pluralistic social organization must exist, and a basic consensus must bind together the contending parties.

Such features of the system of political democracy belong neither to the constitutive institutions nor to the individual voter. It might be said that they form the atmosphere or the environment in which both operate. In any case, such features have not been carefully considered by political philosophers, and it is on these broader properties of the democratic political system that more reflection and study by political theory is called for. In the most tentative fashion let us explore the values of the political system, as they involve the electorate, in the light of the foregoing considerations.

Requirements for the System

Underlying the paradox is an assumption that the population is homogeneous socially and should be homogeneous politically: that everybody is about the same in relevant social characteristics; that, if something is a political virtue (like interest in the election), then everyone should have it; that there is such a thing as "the" typical citizen on whom uniform requirements can be imposed. The tendency of classic democratic literature to work with an image of "the" voter was never justified. For, as we will attempt to illustrate here, some of the most important requirements that democratic values impose on a system require a voting population that is not homogeneous but heterogeneous in its political qualities. . . .

In short, our electoral system calls for apparently incompatible properties—which, although they cannot all reside in each individual voter, can (and do) reside in a heterogeneous electorate. What seems to be required of the electorate as a whole is a *distribution* of qualities along important dimensions. We need some people who are active in a certain respect, others in the middle, and still others passive. The contradictory things we want from the total require that the parts be different. This can be illustrated by taking up a number of important dimensions by which an electorate might be characterized.

Involvement and Indifference. How could a mass democracy work if all the people were deeply involved in politics? Lack of interest by some people is not without its benefits, too. True, the highly interested voters vote more, and know more about the campaign, and read and listen more, and participate more; however, they are also less open to persuasion and less likely to change. Extreme interest goes with extreme partisanship and might culminate in rigid fanaticism that could destroy democratic processes if generalized throughout the community. Low affect toward the election—not caring much —underlies the resolution of many political problems; votes can be resolved into a two-party split instead of fragmented into many parties (the splinter parties of the left, for example, splinter because their advocates are *too* interested in politics). Low interest provides maneuvering room for political shifts necessary for a complex society in a period of rapid change. Compromise might be based upon sophisticated awareness of costs and returns—perhaps impossible to demand of a mass society—but it is more often induced by indifference. Some people are and should be highly interested in politics, but not everyone is or needs to be. Only the doctrinaire would deprecate the moderate indifference that facilitates compromise.

Hence, an important balance between action motivated by strong sentiments and action with little passion behind it is obtained by heterogeneity within the electorate. Balance of this sort is, in practice, met by a distribution of voters rather than by a homogeneous collection of "ideal" citizens.

Stability and Flexibility. A similar dimension along which an electorate might be characterized is stability-flexibility. The need for change and adaptation is clear, and the need for stability ought equally to be. . . .

How is political stability achieved? There are a number of social sources of political stability: the training of the younger generation before it is old enough to care much about the matter, the natural selection that surrounds the individual voter with families and friends who reinforce his own inclinations, the tendency to adjust in favor of the majority of the group, the self-perpetuating tendency of political traditions among ethnic and class and regional strata where like-minded people find themselves socially together. Political stability is based upon social stability. Family traditions, personal associations, status-related organizational memberships, ethnic affiliations, socioeconomic strata—such ties for the individual do not change rapidly or sharply, and since his vote is so importantly a product of them, neither does it.

What of flexibility? Curiously, the voters least admirable when measured against individual requirements contribute most when measured against the aggregate requirement for flexibility. For those who change political preferences most readily are those who are least interested, who are subject to conflicting social pressures, who have inconsistent beliefs and erratic voting histories. Without them—if the decision were left only to the deeply concerned, well-integrated, consistently-principled ideal citizens—the political system might easily prove too rigid to adapt to changing domestic and international conditions. . . .

Progress and Conservation. Closely related to the question of stability is the question of past versus future orientation of the system. In America a progressive outlook is highly valued, but, at the same time, so is a conservative one. Here a balance between the two is easily found in the party system and in the distribution of voters themselves from extreme conservatives to extreme liberals. But a balance between the two is also achieved by a distribution of political dispositions through time. There are periods of great political agitation (i.e., campaigns) alternating with periods of political dormancy. Paradoxically, the former—the campaign period—is likely to be an instrument of conservatism, often even of historical regression. . . .

Political campaigns tend to make people more consistent both socially and psychologically; they vote more with their social groups and agree more with their own prior ideas on the issues. But new ideas and new alignments are in their infancy manifested by inconsistency psychologically and heterogeneity socially; they are almost by definition deviant and minority points of view. To the extent that they are inhibited by pressure or simply by knowledge of what is the proper (i.e., majority) point of view in a particular group, then the campaign period is not a time to look for the growth of important new trends.

This "regressive tendency" may appear as a reaction to intense propaganda during decisive times. The term "regressive" need not imply a reversion to less-developed, less-adaptive behavior; in fact, one might argue that the revival of a Democratic vote among workers was functional for their interests. What it refers to is simply the reactivation of prior dispositions—dispositions in politics that date back years and decades, often to a prior political era.

Its counterpart, of course, is what we believe to be an important potential for progress during the periods of relaxed tension and low-pressure political and social stimuli that are especially characteristic of America between political campaigns. The very tendency for Americans to neglect their political system most of the time—to be "campaign citizens" in the sense that many are "Sunday church-goers"—is not without its values. Change may come best from relaxation.

Again, then, a balance (between preservation of the past and receptivity to the future) seems to be required of a democratic electorate. The heterogeneous electorate in itself provides a balance between liberalism and conservatism; and so does the sequence of political events from periods of drifting change to abrupt rallies back to the loyalties of earlier years.

Consensus and Cleavage. . . . American opinion on public issues is much too complex to be designated by such simple, single-minded labels as *the* housewife opinion or *the* young people's opinion or even *the* workers' opinion. If one uses as a base the central Republican-Democratic cleavage, then one finds numerous "contradictions" within individuals, within strata and groups, and within party supporters themselves. There are many issues presented, cafeteria-style, for the voter to choose from, and there are overlaps in opinion in every direction.

Similarly there are required *social* consensus and cleavage—in effect, pluralism—in politics. Such pluralism makes for enough consensus to hold the system together and enough cleavage to make it move. Too much consensus would be deadening and restrictive of liberty; too much cleavage would be destructive of the society as a whole. . . .

Thus again a requirement we might place on an electoral system—balance between total political war between segments of the society and total political indifference to group interests of that society—translates into varied requirements for different individuals. With respect to group or bloc voting, as with other aspects of political behavior, it is perhaps not unfortunate that "some do and some do not."

Individualism and Collectivism. Lord Bryce pointed out the difficulties in a theory of democracy that assumes that each citizen must himself be capable of voting intelligently:

Orthodox democratic theory assumes that every citizen has, or ought to have, thought out for himself certain opinions, i.e., ought to have a definite view, defensible by argument, of what the country needs, of what principles ought to be applied in governing it, of the man to whose hands the government ought to be entrusted. There are persons who talk, though certainly very few who act, as if they believed this theory, which may be compared to the theory of some ultra-Protestants that every good Christian has or ought to have . . . worked out for himself from the Bible a system of theology.

In the first place, however, the information available to the individual voter is not limited to that directly possessed by him. True, the individual casts his own personal ballot. But . . . that is perhaps the most individualized action he takes in an election. His vote is formed in the midst of his fellows in a sort of group decision—if, indeed, it may be called a decision at all—and the total information and knowledge possessed in the group's present and past generations can be made available for the group's choice. Here is where opinion-leading relationships, for example, play an active role.

Second, and probably more important, the individual voter may not have a great deal of detailed information, but he usually has picked up the crucial *general* information as part of his social learning itself. He may not know the parties' positions on the tariff, or who is for reciprocal trade treaties, or what are the differences on Asiatic policy, or how the parties split on civil rights, or how many security risks were exposed by whom. But he cannot live in an American community without knowing broadly where the parties stand. He has learned that the Republicans are more conservative and the Democrats were liberal—and he can locate his own sentiments and cast his vote accordingly. After all, he must vote for one or the other party, and, if he knows the big thing about the parties, he does not need to know all the little things. The basic role a party plays as an institution in American life is more important to his voting than a particular stand on a particular issue.

It would be unthinkable to try to maintain our present economic style of life without a complex system of delegating to others what we are not competent to do ourselves, without accepting and giving training to each other about what each is expected to do, without accepting our dependence on others in many spheres and taking responsibility for their dependence on us in some spheres. And, like it or not, to maintain our present political style of life, we may have to accept much the same interdependence with others in collective behavior. We have learned slowly in economic life that it is useful not to have everyone a butcher or a baker, any more than it is useful to have no one skilled in such activities. The same kind of division of labor— as repugnant as it may be in some respects to our individualistic tradition—is serving us well today in mass politics. There is an implicit division of political labor within the electorate.

III

CONCLUSION

In short, when we turn from requirements for "average" citizens to requirements for the survival of the total democratic system, we find it unnecessary for the individual voter to be an "average citizen" cast in the classic or any other single mold. With our increasingly complex and differentiated citizenry has grown up an equally complex political system, and it is perhaps not simply a fortunate accident that they have grown and prospered together.

But it is a dangerous act of mental complacency to assume that conditions found surviving together are, therefore, positively "functional" for each other. The apathetic segment of America probably has helped to hold the system together and cushioned the shock of disagreement, adjustment, and change.

But that is not to say that we can stand apathy without limit. Similarly, there must be some limit to the degree of stability or nonadaptation that a political society can maintain and still survive in a changing world. And surely the quality and amount of conformity that is necessary and desirable can be exceeded, as it has been in times of war and in the present Communist scare, to the damage of the society itself and of the other societies with which it must survive in the world.

How can our analysis be reconciled with the classical theory of liberal political democracy? Is the theory "wrong"? Must it be discarded in favor of empirical political sociology? Must its ethical or normative content be dismissed as incompatible with the nature of modern man or of mass society? That is not our view. Rather, it seems to us that modern political theory of democracy stands in need of revision and not replacement by empirical sociology. The classical political philosophers were right in the direction of their assessment of the virtues of the citizen. But they demanded those virtues in too extreme or doctrinal a form. The voter does have some principles, he does have information and rationality, he does have interest—but he does not have them in the extreme, elaborate, comprehensive, or detailed form in which they were uniformly recommended by political philosophers. Like Justice Hand, the typical citizen has other interests in life, and it is good, even for the political system, that he pursues them. The classical requirements are more appropriate for the opinion leaders in the society, but even they do not meet them directly. Happily for the system, voters distribute themselves along a continuum:

Sociable Man	Political Man	Ideological Man
(Indifferent to public affairs, nonpartisan, flexible . . .)		(Absorbed in public affairs, highly partisan, rigid . . .)

And it turns out that this distribution itself, with its internal checks and balances, can perform the functions and incorporate the same values ascribed by some theorists to each individual in the system as well as to the constitutive political institutions!

Twentieth-century political theory—both analytic and normative—will arise only from hard and long observation of the actual world of politics, closely identified with the deeper problems of practical politics. Values and the behavior they are meant to guide are not distinctly separate or separable parts of life as it is lived; and how Elmirans choose their governors is not completely unrelated to the considerations of how they are *supposed* to choose them. We disagree equally with those who believe that normative theory about the proper health of a democracy has nothing to gain from analytic studies like ours; with those who believe that the whole political tradition from Mill to Locke is irrelevant to our realistic understanding and assessment of modern democracy; or with those like Harold Laski who believe that "the decisions of men, when they come to choose their governors, are influenced by considerations which escape all scientific analysis."

We agree with Cobban: "For a century and a half the Western democracies have been living on the stock of basic political ideas that were last restated toward the end of the eighteenth century. That is a long time. . . . The gap thus formed between political facts and political ideas has steadily widened. It has taken a long time for the results to become evident; but now that we have seen what politics devoid of a contemporary moral and political theory means, it is possible that something may be done about it."

To that end we hope this book will contribute.

ROBERT PAUL WOLFF

A Critique of Pluralism: "Beyond Tolerance"

Like most political theories, democratic pluralism has both descriptive and prescriptive variants. As a description, it purports to tell how modern industrial democracy—and particularly American democracy—really works. As a prescription, it sketches an ideal picture of industrial democracy as it could and should be. Both forms of the theory grew out of nineteenth century attacks on the methodological individualism of the classical liberal tradition.

According to that tradition, political society is (or ought to be—liberalism is similarly ambiguous) an association of self-determining individuals who concert their wills and collect their power in the state for mutually self-

Source: Dr. Wolff is a professor of philosophy and author of several books, including *The Poverty of Liberalism.* This selection is from his essay "Beyond Tolerance," in Wolff, Barrington Moore, Jr., and Herbert Marcuse, *A Critique of Pure Tolerance* (Boston: Beacon Press, 1965), pp. 5–17; 40–50. Copyright © 1965 by Robert Paul Wolff. Reprinted by permission of Beacon Press.

interested ends. The state is the locus of supreme power and authority in the community. Its commands are legitimated by a democratic process of decision and control, which ensures—when it functions properly—that the subject has a hand in making the laws to which he submits. The theory focuses exclusively on the relationship between the individual citizen and the sovereign state. Associations other than the state are viewed as secondary in importance and dependent for their existence on the pleasure of the ṣtate. Some liberal philosophers counsel a minimum of state interference with private associations; others argue for active state intervention. In either case, non-governmental bodies are relegated to a subsidiary place in the theory of the state. The line of dependence is traced from the people, taken as an aggregate of unaffiliated individuals, to the state, conceived as the embodiment and representative of their collective will, to the private associations, composed of smaller groupings of those same individuals but authorized by the will of the state.

Whatever the virtues of classical liberalism as a theory of the ideal political community, it was very quickly recognized to be inadequate as a portrait of the industrial democracy which emerged in the nineteenth century. The progressively greater divergence of fact from theory could be traced to two features of the new order. The first was the effective political enfranchisement of the entire adult populations of the great nation-states; the second was the growth of an elaborate industrial system in the private sphere of society, which gave rise to a new "pluralistic" structure within the political framework of representative government.

Traditional democratic theory presupposed an immediate and evident relation between the individual citizen and the government. Whether in the form of "direct democracy," as Rousseau desired, or by means of the representative mechanism described by Locke, the state was to confront the citizen directly as both servant and master. The issues debated in the legislature would be comprehensible to every educated subject, and their relevance to his interests easily understood. With the emergence of mass politics, however, all hope of this immediacy and comprehensibility was irrevocably lost. The ideal of a small, self-governing, autonomous political society retained its appeal, finding expression in the utopian communities which sprang up in Europe and America throughout the nineteenth century. As a standard by which to judge the great industrial democracies of the new era, however, it suffered from the greatest possible failing—irrelevance. Permanent, complex institutional arrangements became necessary in order to transmit the "will of the people" to the elected governors.

At the same time, great industrial corporations appeared in the economic world and began to take the place of the old family firms. As labor unions and trade associations were organized, the classical picture of a market economy composed of many small, independent firms and a large, atomized labor supply, became less and less useful as a guide to economic reality. Individuals entered the marketplace and came in contact with one another through their associations in groups of some sort. The state in its turn brought its authority to bear on the individual only indirectly, through the medium of laws governing the behavior of those groups. It became necessary to recognize that, both politically and economically, the individual's relation to the state was mediated by a system of "middle-size" institutional associations.

The size and industrial organization alone of the modern state destroy any possibility of classical liberal democracy, for the intermediating bureaucratic organizations are necessary whether the economy is private and capitalist or public and socialist in structure. In addition, however, three factors historically more specific to the American experience have combined to produce the characteristic form which we call pluralism.

The first factor, in importance as well as in time, is the federal structure of the American system. From the birth of the nation, a hierarchy of local governments, formerly sovereign and autonomous, interposed itself between the individual and the supreme power of the state. The United States, as its name implied, was an association of political communities rather than of individuals. The natural ties of tradition and emotion binding each citizen to his native colony were reinforced by a division of powers which left many of the functions of sovereign authority to the several states. Hence the relation of the individual to the federal government was from the beginning, and even in theory, indirect and mediated by intervening bodies. Furthermore, as the eighteenth century debates over unification reveal, the constitution took form as a series of compromises among competing interests—large states versus small, agriculture versus commerce, slave-holding versus free labor. The structure of the union was designed to balance these interests, giving each a voice but none command. The conception of politics as a conflict of more or less permanent groups was thus introduced into the foundation of our government. By implication, an individual entered the political arena principally as a member of one of those groups, rather than as an isolated agent. Conversely, the government made demands upon the individual and responded to his needs, through the intercession of local authorities. As the volume of government activity grew throughout the nineteenth and twentieth centuries, this federal structure embedded itself in countless judicial and executive bodies. In America today, it is impossible to understand the organization of education, the regulation of commerce, or the precise allocation of responsibility for law enforcement without acknowledging the historically special relationship of the states to the federal government.

A second factor which has shaped the character of American democracy is our oft-chronicled penchant for dealing with social problems by means of voluntary associations. This phenomenon was made much of by Tocqueville and has since been portrayed by students of American politics as our peculiar contribution to the repertory of democratic techniques. It seems that whereas some peoples turn to God when a problem looms on the social horizon, and others turn to the state, Americans instinctively form a committee, elect a president and secretary-treasurer, and set about finding a solution on their own. The picture is idealized and more than a trifle self-congratulatory; it evokes images of the prairie or a New England town meeting, rather than a dirty industrial slum. Nevertheless, it is a fact that a remarkable variety of social needs are met in America by private and voluntary institutions, needs which in other countries would be attended to by the state. Religion, for example, is entirely a non-governmental matter because of the prohibition of an established church. The burdens of primary and secondary education are borne jointly by local governments and private institutions; higher education is dominated by the great private universities and colleges with state institutions of any sort only recently playing a significant role. The subsidy and encouragement of the arts and letters has been managed by the great charitable foundations, and until the advent of military research and development, the natural sciences found their home solely in the laboratories of universities and private industry. In addition to industry, agriculture, religion, education, art, and science, countless other dimensions of social activity have been organized on the basis of voluntary, non-governmental associations.

In order to clarify the relationship between the government and this network of private associations, we must first observe that while some groups perform their function and achieve their goal directly, others are organized as pressure groups to influence the national (or local) government and thus achieve their end indirectly. Needless to say, most associations of the first sort engage in political lobbying as well. Nevertheless, the distinction is useful, for it enables us to identify the two principal "pluralist" theories of the relationship between group and government.

The first, or "referee" theory, asserts that the role of the central government is to lay down ground rules for conflict and competition among private associations and to employ its power to make sure that no major interest in the nation abuses its influence or gains an unchecked mastery over some sector of social life. The most obvious instance is in the economic sphere, where firms compete for markets and labor competes with capital. But according to the theory a similar competition takes place among the various religions, between private and public forms of education, among different geographic regions, and even among the arts, sports, and the entertainment world for the attention and interest of the people.

The second theory might be called the "vector-sum" or "give-and-take" theory of government. Congress is seen as the focal point for the pressures which are exerted by interest groups throughout the nation, either by way of the two great parties or directly through lobbies. The laws issuing from the government are shaped by the manifold forces brought to bear upon the legislators. Ideally, congress merely reflects these forces, combining them—or "resolving" them, as the physicists say—into a single social decision. As the strength and direction of private interests alters, there is a corresponding alteration in the composition and activity of the great interest groups—labor, big business, agriculture. Slowly, the great weathervane of government swings about to meet the shifting winds of opinion.

More important than federalism or interest-group politics in fostering the ideology of pluralism has been the impact on the American consciousness of religious, ethnic, and racial heterogeneity. Many of the original colonies were religiously orthodox communities, deliberately created in order to achieve an internal purity which was unattainable in the hostile political climate of England. The Reformation split Europe first into two, then into many, warring camps, and it was quite natural to view the nation as an association of religious communities rather than of individuals. Where some compromise could be achieved among the several sects, as eventually occurred in England, political society became in a sense a community of communities. In the United States, the deliberate prohibition of an established church made it necessary to acknowledge a diversity of religious communities within the nation. Eventually, this acceptance of heterogeneity was extended to the Roman Catholic community, and then even to the Jews.

The ethnic diversity brought about by the great immigrations of the nineteenth century produced a comparable effect in American life. The big cities especially came to be seen as agglomerations of national enclaves. Little Italies, Chinatowns, Polish ghettos, German communities, grew and flourished. America became a nation of minorities, until even the descendants of the original settlers acquired an identifying acronym, WASP.

The ethnic and religious communities in American society encountered one another through the pluralistic mechanisms of politics and private associations which already existed. The typical "hyphenated" community (Italian-American, Polish-American, etc.) had its own churches, in which the religious practices of the old country—special saints, holy days, rituals—were kept up. There were newspapers in the mother tongue, men's clubs, folk societies, businessmen's associations, trade union branches, all based on the ethnic or religious unity of the local community.

The religious and ethnic groups entered the political system at the precinct, city, or county level, using the unified mass of their voting populations as a weight to be thrown on the political scales. The decentralized, hierarchical federal structure of American government was perfectly suited to ethnic politics. The first matters of social importance which impinged on the consciousness of the group were, typically, of a sort that could be decided at the level of city government, where only a rudimentary organization and political knowledge was necessary. As Italian, Irish, Polish, or Jewish politicians ascended the ladder of elective office, they encountered the larger, multi-ethnic and multi-religious community. There they acted first as spokesmen for their own kind, and later as statesmen capable of acknowledging the greater public good.

If we draw together all these descriptive fragments, we have a portrait of pluralist democracy. America, according to this account, is a complex interlocking of ethnic, religious, racial, regional, and economic groups, whose members pursue their diverse interests through the medium of private associations, which in turn are coordinated, regulated, contained, encouraged, and guided by a federal system of representative democracy. Individual citizens confront the central government and one another as well through the intermediation of the voluntary and involuntary groups to which they belong. In this way, pluralist democracy stands in contrast to classical democracy of the liberal model; indeed, it is curiously like feudal society, in which the individual played a political role solely as a member of a guild, incorporated town, church, or estate rather than as a subject *simpliciter*. As in medieval political society, so in pluralist democracy, the guiding principle is not "one man—one vote" but rather, "every legitimate group its share." In modern America, it is taken for granted that a rough equality should be maintained between labor and business or among Catholics, Protestants, and Jews. The fact that "labor" constitutes the overwhelming majority of the population or that there are ten times as many Catholics as Jews is rarely seen as a reason for allotting influence in those proportions.

Pluralism is a theory of the way modern industrial democracies work, with particular applicability to the United States; it is also an ideal model of the way political society ought to be organized, whether in fact it is or not. As a descriptive theory, pluralism requires empirical verification, of the sort which hosts of political scientists have sought to provide in recent decades. As a normative theory, however, pluralism must be defended by appeal to some principle of virtue or ideal of the good society. In the history of the discussion of pluralism three distinct sorts of justification have been offered.

The earliest argument, dating from the preindustrial period of religious conflict between Catholics and Protestants, Nonconformists and Anglicans, asserts that the toleration of divergent religious practices is a necessary evil, forced upon a society which either cannot suppress dissidence or else finds the social cost of suppression too high. Orthodoxy on this view is the ideal condition, intolerance of heresy even a duty in principle. It is now an historical commonplace that the great Anglo-American tradition of religious liberty can be traced to just such a grudging acceptance of *de facto* heterodoxy and not to early Protestant devotion to the freedom of individual conscience.

The second argument for pluralism presents it as a morally neutral means for pursuing political ends which cannot be achieved through traditional representative democracy. In this view, the ideal of democracy is a citizen-state, in which each man both makes the laws and submits to them. The political order is just and the people are free to the extent that each individual plays a significant and not simply symbolic role in the political process of decision. But for all the reasons catalogued above, genuine self-government is impossible in a large industrial society organized along classic democratic lines. The gulf is so broad between the rulers and the ruled that active citizen participation in the affairs of government evaporates. Even the periodic election becomes a ritual in which voters select a president whom they have not nominated to decide issues which have not even been discussed on the basis of facts which cannot be published. The result is a politics of style, of image, of faith, which is repugnant to free men and incompatible with the ideal of democracy.

But decisions will be taken, whether by democratic means or not, and so some other way than elections must be found to submit the rulers to the will of the ruled. Pluralism is offered as the answer. Within the interest groups which make up the social order, something approximating democracy takes place. These groups, in turn, through pressure upon the elected representatives, can make felt the will of their members and work out the compromises with opposed interests which would have been accomplished by debate and deliberation in a classical democracy. The government confronts not a mass of indistinguishable and ineffectual private citizens, but an articulated system of organized groups. Immediacy, effectiveness, involvement, and thus democratic participation are assured to the individual in his economic, religious or ethnic associations—in the union local, the church, the chapter of the American Legion. Control over legislation and national policy is in turn assured to the associations through their ability to deliver votes to the legislator in an election. The politician, according to this defense of pluralism, is a middleman in the power transactions of the society. He absorbs the pressures brought to bear upon him by his organized constituents, strikes a balance among them on the basis of their relative voting strength, and then goes onto the floor of the Congress to work out legislative compromises with his colleagues, who have suffered different compositions of pressures and hence are seeking different adjustments of the competing social interests. If all goes well, every significant interest abroad in the nation will find expression, and to each will go a measure of satisfaction roughly proportional to its size and intensity. The democratic ideal of citizen-politics is preserved, for each interested party can know that through participation in voluntary, private associations, he has made his wishes felt to some small degree in the decisions of his government. To paraphrase Rousseau, the citizen is a free man since he is at least partially the author of the laws to which he submits.

The first defense of pluralism views it as a distasteful but unavoidable evil; the second portrays it as a useful means for preserving some measure of democracy under the unpromising conditions of mass industrial society. The last defense goes far beyond these in its enthusiasm for pluralism; it holds that a pluralistic society is natural and good and an end to be sought in itself. . . .

One might think that whatever faults the theory of pluralism possessed, at least it would be free of the dangers of ideological distortion. Does it not accord a legitimate place to all groups in society? How then can it be used to justify or preserve the dominance of one group over another? In fact, I shall try to show that the application of pluralist theory to American society involves ideological distortion in at least three different ways. The first stems from the "vector-sum" or "balance-of-power" interpretation of pluralism; the second arises from the application of the "referee" version of the theory; and the third is inherent in the abstract theory itself.

According to the vector-sum theory of pluralism, the major groups in society compete through the electoral process for control over the actions of the government. Politicians are forced to accommodate themselves to a number of opposed interests and in so doing achieve a rough distributive justice. What are the major groups which, according to pluralism, comprise American society today? First, there are the hereditary groups which are summarized by that catch-phrase of tolerance, "without regard to race, creed, color, or national origin." In addition there are the major economic interest groups among which—so the theory goes, a healthy balance is maintained: labor, business, agriculture, and—a residual category, this—the consumer. Finally, there are a number of voluntary associations whose size, permanence, and influence entitle them to a place in any group-analysis of America, groups such as the veterans' organizations and the American Medical Association.

At one time, this may have been an accurate account of American society. But once constructed, the picture becomes frozen, and when changes take place in the patterns of social or economic grouping, they tend not to be acknowledged because they deviate from that picture. So the application of the theory of pluralism always favors the groups in existence against those in process of formation. For example, at any given time the major religious, racial, and ethnic groups are viewed as permanent and exhaustive categories into which every American can conveniently be pigeonholed. Individuals who fall outside any major social group—the non-religious, say—are treated as exceptions and relegated in practice to a second-class status. Thus agnostic conscientious objectors are required to serve in the armed forces, while those who claim even the most bizarre religious basis for their refusal are treated with ritual tolerance and excused by the courts. Similarly, orphanages in America are so completely dominated by the three major faiths that a non-religious or religiously-mixed couple simply cannot adopt a child in many states. The net effect is to preserve the official three-great-religious image of American society long after it has ceased to correspond to social reality and to discourage individuals from officially breaking their religious ties. A revealing example of the mechanism of tolerance is the ubiquitous joke about "the priest, the minister, and the rabbi." A world of insight into the psychology of tolerance can be had simply from observing the mixture of emotions with which an audience greets such a joke, as told by George Jessel or some other apostle of "interfaith understanding." One senses embarrassment, nervousness, and finally an explosion of self-congratulatory laughter as though everyone were relieved at a difficult moment got through without incident. The gentle ribbing nicely distributed in the story among the three men of the cloth gives each member of the audience a chance to express his hostility safely and acceptably, and in the end to reaffirm the principle of tolerance by joining in the applause. Only a bigot, one feels, could refuse to crack a smile!

Rather more serious in its conservative falsifying of social reality is the established image of the major economic groups of American society. The emergence of a rough parity between big industry and organized labor has been paralleled by the rise of a philosophy of moderation and cooperation between them, based on mutual understanding and respect, which is precisely similar to the achievement of interfaith and ethnic tolerance. What has been overlooked or suppressed is the fact that there are tens of millions of Americans—businessmen and workers alike—whose interests are completely ignored by this genial give-and-take. Non-unionized workers are worse off after each price-wage increase, as are the thousands of small businessmen who cannot survive in the competition against great nationwide firms. The theory of pluralism does not espouse the interests of the unionized against the non-unionized, or of large against small business; but by presenting a picture of the American economy in which those disadvantaged elements do not appear, it tends to perpetuate the inequality by ignoring rather than justifying it.

The case here is the same as with much ideological thinking. Once pluralists acknowledge the existence of groups whose interests are not weighed in the labor-business balance, then their own theory requires them to call for an alteration of the system. If migrant workers, or white-collar workers, or small businessmen are genuine *groups*, then they have a legitimate place in the system of group-adjustments. Thus, pluralism is not explicitly a philosophy of privilege or injustice—it is a philosophy of equality and justice whose *concrete application* supports inequality by ignoring the existence of certain legitimate social groups.

This ideological function of pluralism helps to explain one of the peculiarities of American politics. There is a very sharp distinction in the public domain between legitimate interests and those which are absolutely beyond the pale. If a group or interest is within the framework of acceptability, then it can be sure of winning some measure of what it seeks, for the process of national politics is distributive and compromising. On the other hand, if an interest falls *outside* the circle of the acceptable, it receives no attention whatsoever and its proponents are treated as crackpots, extremists, or foreign agents. With bewildering speed, an interest can move from "outside" to "inside" and its partisans, who have been scorned by the solid and established in the community, become presidential advisers and newspaper columnists.

A vivid example from recent political history is the sudden legitimation of the problem of poverty in America. In the post-war years, tens of millions of poor Americans were left behind by the sustained growth of the economy. The facts were known and discussed for years by fringe critics whose attempts to call attention to these forgotten Americans were greeted with either silence or contempt. Suddenly, poverty was "discovered" by Presidents Kennedy and

Johnson, and articles were published in *Look* and *Time* which a year earlier would have been more at home in the radical journals which inhabit political limbo in America. A social group whose very existence had long been denied was now the object of a national crusade.

A similar elevation from obscurity to relative prominence was experienced by the peace movement, a "group" of a rather different nature. For years, the partisans of disarmament labored to gain a hearing for their view that nuclear war could not be a reasonable instrument of national policy. Sober politicians and serious columnists treated such ideas as the naive fantasies of bearded peacenicks, communist sympathizers, and well-meaning but hopelessly muddled clerics. Then suddenly the Soviet Union achieved the nuclear parity which had been long forecast, the prospect of which had convinced disarmers of the insanity of nuclear war. Sober reevaluations appeared in the columns of Walter Lippmann, and some even found their way into the speeches of President Kennedy—what had been unthinkable, absurd, naive, dangerous, even subversive, six months before, was now plausible, sound, thoughtful, and—within another six months—official American policy.

The explanation for these rapid shifts in the political winds lies, I suggest, in the logic of pluralism. According to pluralist theory, every genuine social group has a right to a voice in the making of policy and a share in the benefits. Any policy urged by a group in the system must be given respectful attention, no matter how bizarre. By the same token, a policy or principle which lacks legitimate representation has no place in the society, no matter how reasonable or right it may be. Consequently, the line between acceptable and unacceptable alternatives is very sharp, so that the territory of American politics is like a plateau with steep cliffs on all sides rather than like a pyramid. On the plateau are all the interest groups which are recognized as legitimate; in the deep valley all around lie the outsiders, the fringe groups which are scorned as "extremist." The most important battle waged by any group in American politics is the struggle to climb onto the plateau. Once there, it can count on some measure of what it seeks. No group ever gets all of what it wants, and no *legitimate* group is completely frustrated in its efforts.

Thus, the "vector-sum" version of pluralist theory functions ideologically by tending to deny new groups or interests access to the political plateau. It does this by ignoring their existence in practice, not by denying their claim in theory. The result is that pluralism has a braking effect on social change; it slows down transformation in the system of group adjustments but does not set up an absolute barrier to change. For this reason, as well as because of its origins as a fusion of two conflicting social philosophies, it deserves the title "conservative liberalism."

According to the second, or "referee," version of pluralism, the role of the government is to oversee and regulate the competition among interest groups in the society. Out of the applications of this theory have grown not only countless laws, such as the antitrust bills, pure food and drug acts, and

Taft-Hartley Law, but also the complex system of quasi-judicial regulatory agencies in the executive branch of government. Henry Kariel, in a powerful and convincing book entitled *The Decline of American Pluralism*, has shown that this referee function of government, as it actually works out in practice, systematically favors the interests of the stronger against the weaker party in interest-group conflicts and tends to solidify the power of those who already hold it. The government, therefore, plays a conservative, rather than a neutral, role in the society.

Kariel details the ways in which this discriminatory influence is exercised. In the field of regulation of labor unions, for example, the federal agencies deal with the established leadership of the unions. In such matters as the overseeing of union elections, the settlement of jurisdictional disputes, or the setting up of mediation boards, it is the interests of those leaders rather than the competing interests of rank-and-file dissidents which are favored. In the regulation of agriculture, again, the locally most influential farmers or leaders of farmers' organizations draw up the guidelines for control which are then adopted by the federal inspectors. In each case, ironically, the unwillingness of the government to impose its own standards or rules results not in a free play of competing groups, but in the enforcement of the preferences of the existing predominant interests.

In a sense, these unhappy consequences of government regulation stem from a confusion between a theory of interest-conflict and a theory of power-conflict. The government quite successfully referees the conflicts among competing *powers*—any group which has already managed to accumulate a significant quantum of power will find its claims attended to by the federal agencies. But legitimate *interests* which have been ignored, suppressed, defeated, or which have not yet succeeded in organizing themselves for effective action, will find their disadvantageous position perpetuated through the decisions of the government. It is as though an umpire were to come upon a baseball game in progress between big boys and little boys, in which the big boys cheated, broke the rules, claimed hits that were outs, and made the little boys accept the injustice by brute force. If the umpire undertakes to "regulate" the game by simply enforcing the "rules" actually being practiced, he does not thereby make the game a fair one. Indeed, he may actually make matters worse, because if the little boys get up their courage, band together, and decide to fight it out, the umpire will accuse them of breaking the rules and throw his weight against them! Precisely the same sort of thing happens in pluralist politics. For example, the American Medical Association exercises a stranglehold over American medicine through its influence over the government's licensing regulations. Doctors who are opposed to the A.M.A.'s political positions, or even to its medical policies, do not merely have to buck the entrenched authority of the organization's leaders. They must also risk the loss of hospital affiliations, speciality accreditation, and so forth, all of which powers have been placed in the hands of the medical establishment by state and federal laws. Those laws are written by the government in cooperation with the very same A.M.A. leaders; not surprisingly, the interests of dissenting doctors do not receive favorable attention.

The net effect of government action is thus to weaken, rather than strengthen, the play of conflicting interests in the society. The theory of pluralism here has a crippling effect upon the government, for it warns against positive federal intervention in the name of independent principles of justice, equality, or fairness. The theory says justice will emerge from the free interplay of opposed groups; the practice tends to destroy that interplay.

Finally, the theory of pluralism in all its forms has the effect in American thought and politics of discriminating not only against certain social groups or interests, but also against certain sorts of proposals for the solution of social problems. According to pluralist theory, politics is a contest among social groups for control of the power and decision of the government. Each group is motivated by some interest or cluster of interests and seeks to sway the government toward action in its favor. The typical social problem according to pluralism is therefore some instance of distributive injustice. One group is getting too much, another too little, of the available resources. In accord with its modification of traditional liberalism, pluralism's goal is a rough parity among competing groups rather than among competing individuals. Characteristically, new proposals originate with a group which feels that its legitimate interests have been slighted, and the legislative outcome is a measure which corrects the social imbalance to a degree commensurate with the size and political power of the initiating group.

But there are some social ills in America whose causes do not lie in a maldistribution of wealth, and which cannot be cured therefore by the techniques of pluralist politics. For example, America is growing uglier, more dangerous, and less pleasant to live in, as its citizens grow richer. The reason is that natural beauty, public order, the cultivation of the arts, are not the special interest of any identifiable social group. Consequently, evils and inadequacies in those areas cannot be remedied by shifting the distribution of wealth and power among existing social groups. To be sure, crime and urban slums hurt the poor more than the rich, the Negro more than the white—but fundamentally they are problems of the society as a whole, not of any particular group. That is to say, they concern the general good, not merely the aggregate of private goods. To deal with such problems, there must be some way of constituting the whole society a genuine group with a group purpose and a conception of the common good. Pluralism rules this out in theory by portraying society as an aggregate of human communities rather than as itself a human community; and it equally rules out a concern for the general good in practice by encouraging a politics of interest-group pressures in which there is no mechanism for the discovery and expression of the common good.

Pluralism at Work:
Stability and Change
or Stalemate at Dead Center?

Is pluralism the doctrine of the rich and the powerful? Does it hold sway by offering the weak and the poor the opportunity to organize, but with the smug knowledge that those who lack power usually lack the means of acquiring it? Or does it simply expose the levers of power to an open and free competition? Can reformers and radicals use those levers as readily as conservatives and vested interests?

Does the pluralist system provide effective checks on the exercise of presidential power in foreign policy? Can it provide adequately for the protection of the rights of ethnic and other oppressed minorities? Can it protect the rights of eccentric individuals and the fundamental values of democracy? Can it respond to a long-range public interest that transcends the interests or goals of private groups? Can it respond rapidly enough to such major problems as urban decay and ecology?

In the selections that follow we look first at a series of examples and case studies of pluralism in operation which may shed some light on these questions. They examine the operation of pluralism in "consensus politics" and its implications for political parties, campaigns, elections, legislative practices, and interest groups. They ask about the operation and the adequacy of pluralist politics in dealing with such problems as racial justice and civil rights, the "urban crisis," and ecology. It is of some interest that John Fischer, who describes how the inability of the system to avoid ecological disaster has radicalized him, had written in 1948 one of the earliest and best defenses of pluralism.

IRVING KRISTOL

The Old Politics, the New Politics, the New New Politics

Many people, these past months, have been talking about a New Politics; but so far as I can see, no one seemed to have a clear idea as to what this New Politics meant. In the light of the election returns, there will now be a tendency to surmise that it never meant anything at all. This, I think, would be a mistake. I have a feeling that, in the course of the nineteen-sixties, American politics has indeed been in the process of moving, not simply and familiarly from left to right or from right to left, but on to a new political spectrum altogether. Which is to say: There may well be a new politics emerging— but this new politics is only too likely to be poles apart from what the advocates of the New Politics have in mind.

As enunciated by such spokesmen as the late Robert Kennedy, Eugene McCarthy, and—at least during the latter part of his campaign—by Nelson Rockefeller, the New Politics seemed to signify an especially keen sensitiveness to the political mood of young people on the campuses and black militants in the ghettos. The mood of both these groups is certainly turbulent, often to the point of rebelliousness, and it would be exceedingly difficult not to pay attention to it, even if one wanted not to. (A great many Americans obviously want not to.) On the other hand, there is this to be said about the mood: (1) it is not easy to tell what the purpose and intent of this turbulence is; and (2) it is the mood of two minority groups—and not especially influential minorities at that.

It is the second point about which many people still have a great number of illusions. Any man who thinks that he can stake out a political career by appealing to young students or black militants has failed to do his political arithmetic. There aren't enough of either. Though, as a result of the postwar baby boom, the median age of the American population has been lowered, it has not been lowered by all *that* much. It is now about 26 years, and as a

Source: Mr. Kristol is co-editor of *The Public Interest*; his work appears frequently in serious but popular journals of social criticism. This article is from *The New York Times Magazine*, Nov. 24, 1968, pp. 49–51 and 162–180 passim. © 1968 by The New York Times Company. Reprinted by permission.

consequence of the decline in the birth rate that set in a decade ago, it is not likely to get much beneath this figure in your lifetime or mine.

The United States is certainly a somewhat younger country than it was in 1950, when the median age was 30. But the change has not been of such an order as to permit one to say that some kind of deep and far-reaching demographic transformation has occurred. After all, the median age of the American *electorate* in 1968 was 45 years. Even if the vote were given to the 18-year-olds by 1972, that would only reduce the median age of the electorate to 42 years. So, if the young are to inherit the earth, someone else will have to vote them the legacy.

Moreover, not all young people are on campuses—a majority of those between the ages of 18 and 22 still work for a living. And of those who are on campuses, the polls show that only a minority—perhaps 20 per cent—are sufficiently dissatisfied with the political and social arrangements now existing to be attracted to a left-of-center New Politics. In addition, there is the fact that among young workers, resistance to this kind of New Politics is especially strong. At one point in this recent campaign, close to a third of the young workers in the 21–29 age group said they would vote for George Wallace. It is nice to know that not all that many actually did. But it would nevertheless appear beyond doubt that there are all sorts of ways of making a particular appeal to young people.

A not too dissimilar kind of conclusion emerges when one examines the question of black militancy. A majority of American blacks—65 per cent— are not poor (though they are certainly poorer than their white counterparts). The majority of American blacks do not live in central-city slums—unless one automatically defines a slum as a place where Negroes live. (As Nathan Glazer has pointed out, the proportion of nonwhites now living in substandard housing is about 30 per cent.) And, as opinion polls indicate, the majority of American blacks, while intensely dissatisfied with their present condition and desirous of a faster movement toward equality, do not think that revolutionary changes are necessary for them to achieve this accelerated rate of progress. The black militants certainly have their constituency, but despite the best efforts of the mass media—which have a fondness for militancy because it comes across so well on film and makes for more dramatic headlines—this constituency is of minor significance in our political system.

Indeed, one often is tempted to conclude that the cry for a New Politics really has amounted to little more than a demand from certain groups that the political process concede to them greater power and influence than they are entitled to under our traditional democratic formulas. The young students have all sorts of thoughts about how to make this a better country to live in, and they see no reason why they should have to persuade the majority of the validity of ideas which seem to them self-evident. Similarly, the black militants feel that a redress of the all-too-real injustices the Negroes have suffered in the past, or still suffer, should entitle them to something more than one man, one vote.

Was there more than this in the cry for a New Politics? As a matter of fact, I think there was, and is. I do believe that there may well be a new politics emerging in the United States—emerging slowly, incoherently, amid vast confusion. Of only one thing I am absolutely certain: The new politics that is in fact emerging will, in the event, have little connection with what people who now talk so much about "the New Politics" have in mind. For the *real* new politics will emerge from the condition of the *majority* of Americans, and will reflect their strong but contradictory sentiments about this condition. More important, it will have to do something about resolving this contradiction which afflicts the American mood.

This contradiction has many aspects, but let us begin with the simplest and plainest: The American people today have a far greater degree of material prosperity than ever before, but somehow seem to be enjoying it less. How is this to be explained?

Most of our liberal social critics, wedded to a quite vulgar, materialistic notion of politics, can only reply that the dissatisfaction arises from needs that are still unfulfilled. This won't wash, however, as is evidenced by the fact that these same critics have a terribly difficult time in defining these needs—or, when they think they have, arousing any great popular interest in them. I cannot, in my lifetime, remember a moment when liberal reformers were so barren of legislative proposals. Medicare was their last great popular cause. They won that handsomely, and have been searching for new issues ever since, without much success. American liberalism, during these past four decades, was able to mobilize a political majority in order to have the Federal Government pass laws that would obviously, instantly and tangibly benefit this majority. It no longer seems able to mobilize a majority in this way and for this purpose. And this is a fact of the greatest importance, marking as it does the end of a political era in American history.

To be sure, there are a great many *minorities* within the American population that clearly need help. But what liberal reformers have discovered in these past eight years is that their habitual response—passing a law which funds a program—is inadequate. It is inadequate for two reasons:

First, it is not so easy to get majority support for such a program. It is not merely that a majority is inevitably somewhat callous and inattentive toward minority problems—though, human nature being what it is, this is sadly true. But what is also true is that this majority, though affluent by historical standards, isn't all *that* affluent. (Probably no more mischievous phrase has been invented in our time than "the affluent society.") The median family income in this country is about $8,000—and it just isn't easy to persuade a family with such an income that its tax burden should be increased substantially for the benefit of those who earn $4,000 a year or so—or who even, as in New York City, receive that sum annually in welfare benefits.

And this increase in taxes would have to happen for any significant income redistribution in favor of the poor to take place. You can't finance what we now call an anti-poverty program merely by taxing the rich. There just aren't enough of them. As a matter of fact, there never were enough of them. The social expenditures of the New Deal, Fair Deal, New Frontier and Great Society did not to any important extent represent a redistribution of wealth from rich to poor. Mainly, the money came from putting the idle resources of the economy to work—it was *new* money, created by the new economics.

Once that has been done, however, and the economy is fairly efficiently using its available resources, as is now the case, such social expenditures have to come from general taxation—i.e., from the average taxpayer. And the average taxpayer resists, because he is probably in debt and is persuaded he needs the money as much as anyone else. In country after country—in England, France, Germany, Sweden, and now in the United States—the proliferation of welfare programs is running head-on into a stonewall of taxpayers' resistance. In any kind of political system short of a police state, that stonewall will prevail.

Secondly, we have discovered in these past years that it just doesn't suffice to pass a law in order to solve minorities' problems. Precisely because they are minorities, the laws run into immense administrative problems. It is far easier, in a democracy, to help everyone over 65 than it is, say, to help poor blacks over 65 who live in central-city ghettos. These "special purpose" programs have a way of not quite hitting the mark. Somehow, the money never seems to reach the people for whom it is intended—or, if it does, it never has the effect it was supposed to have.

The widespread disillusionment with our welfare system is a case in point. And the disillusionment is well-earned. After all, we in New York City have abolished poverty—we really have—in the sense that the dole for a family of four now puts this family above the Administration's poverty line. Somehow, this statistical abolition of poverty in New York City has changed hardly anything at all, and the poor seem not even aware that it has happened. No wonder that, within the ranks of liberal reformers themselves, there has been an increasing skepticism about all such government programs.

So this, then, is the dilemma of American liberalism today. It cannot come up with legislative programs that appeal to the majority, and it has not been able to create viable programs for the various minorities that need help. And it would seem fair to conclude that the future of American politics in the decades immediately ahead will be shaped along lines quite different from those familiar liberal ones we have all grown accustomed to.

This does not mean, however, that it will be shaped along familiar conservative ones. Indeed, it is quite certain that it will not be.

The conservatives in the United States today do have some real opportunities, and it is not altogether inconceivable that the Republican Administration will be able to take advantage of some of them during the next four years. Above all, they might undertake an overhaul of the welfare state. Such an overhaul would aim at having the Government provide money (or its equivalent—i.e., vouchers) with which the individual citizens could purchase social welfare in the open market, instead of having the Government try to provide, directly and institutionally, such services as education, housing, medical care, etc. There is now considerable dissatisfaction among all levels of the population at the bumbling and ineffectual way Government bureaucrats go ahead providing such things. There has also arisen, during the past 10 years, an eminently respectable and increasingly influential body of economic analysis—emanating largely from the University of Chicago—which persuasively argues the desirability of so redefining the idea of "the welfare state" as to have the Government act as a kind of financial guarantor against "ill-fare" without the Government attempting to estimate, provide, and distribute differential benefits to each individual. (Prof. Milton Friedman's "negative income tax," as a substitute for our divers welfare programs—aimed, as the case may be, at the old, the sick, the blind, the abandoned, the unemployed, the underemployed, etc.—is the most notable example of this approach.) It is possible, therefore, that action along these lines will be taken by a Republican Administration, and I, for one, would be interested to see if it could work.

Aside from such a possible overhaul of the welfare state, however, conservatives in this country today do not have much of a program. They have no particular views on what to do about the universities, for instance—an area which is obviously becoming more of a mess every day. They do not even have any kind of consensus on what to do about trade unions, though the present state of trade unions continually affronts conservative opinion. In both cases, American conservatives have simply failed *intellectually*. They have not been able to come up with—have not really tried very hard to come up with—any kind of thoughtful analysis that could lead to workable reforms.

Conservatives in America have always been more than a little weak-minded, and sometimes positively anti-intellectual in their bias. This attitude has been extremely costly. It means that when a conservative administration does take office, it pursues no coherent program but merely takes satisfaction in not doing the things that the liberals may be clamoring for. This, in effect, is what happened during the two terms of President Eisenhower—eight relatively placid years, in retrospect, but also years that permitted various problems to build up in an explosive way, and ensured that this period would in the end, amount to little more than an interregnum.

Not only are conservatives lacking a program that an administration in Washington can refer to. They also share with liberals—indeed, with all modern political creeds—a basic orientation that is inherently self-defeating for conservatives. This orientation affirms that we are living through a "revolution of rising expectations," that this revolution is a good thing, and that the prime function of government is to satisfy the demands generated by this revolution.

That we are in fact living through a revolution of rising expectations is indisputable. This revolution arises partly out of economic growth itself—the knowledge that one's condition will be better in the future makes all present limitations and restraints particularly irksome. (People have far more patience with the inevitable than they do with the temporary.) It also arises out of the very nature of contemporary society, which can only achieve growth through the constant creation and expansion of demand. So it is not a revolution anyone has much control over. And yet left to run its own course, it is ultimately frustrating to its presumed beneficiaries.

It is frustrating for two reasons:

(1) Even when economic growth is rapid, people are still disappointed with the results. This is not simply explained by the fact that the human appetite is an unruly and insatiable force. It also derives from the fact that economic growth never provides people with the goods and benefits that they anticipate. As Bertrand de Jouvenel has pointed out, the future always disappoints us because it is so unimaginably different. A woman living in the year 1900, and being told of the economic growth that was in store for her society in the decades ahead, would have expected perhaps to be able to hire a maid or two. Instead, she was given the vacuum cleaner and washing machine. Similarly, we today automatically assume that economic growth will give us, for example, more commodious living space. But it will almost certainly not give us any such thing. Instead, we may have the opportunity to visit the moon. This whole process is very unsettling; the psychological costs of economic growth are real even if they aren't measurable.

(2) It is fantastic to believe that we can just project current rates of economic growth indefinitely. The current rate in the United States is at about double the historic rate that prevailed for the century and a half before World War II. Were this current rate to continue, and to compound itself uninterruptedly, all Americans would be enormously rich 50 years from now. The median income of the American family would be something like $35,000 (in constant dollars).

That just isn't going to happen; history is not a fairy tale and the more extravagant a long mathematical projection appears, the more ridiculous it is to take it seriously. Something will go wrong—inflation will get out of hand, we'll stumble into an expensive little war or even a big one, etc.; this projection will be interrupted; and the social and political order will stand indicted for breach of promise. I still recall vividly the assurance of one of President Kennedy's staff, five years ago, that the big problem looming up was how to spend the "surplus" $6-billion a year that the economy was "automatically" generating.

Now, this revolution of rising expectations is a problem for all political creeds, as I have said. But it is an especially acute problem for conservatism. The political ethos of conservatism is more naturally inclined to revere the past and appreciate the present than it is to exult in the future. It has no natural claim, therefore, to be the manager of a revolution of rising expectations. One can even put it more strongly: There is a kind of self-betrayal and self-contradiction in conservatism pretending to be capable of "superior performance" in this task of management.

If conservatism means anything, it means that existing institutions and social arrangements derive their legitimacy, not from superior performance as measured by some abstract standard, but from the presumption that they embody a kind of accumulated wisdom—accumulated over generations, incrementally and organically—that is beyond the contrivance of any set of living politicians, no matter how clever. Though many people usually think of liberalism as "idealistic" and conservatism as "materialistic," the reverse is more nearly true. Conservatism cannot take honest root in a situation where the criteria of success or failure are ruthlessly materialistic.

What this comes down to, in political terms, is that conservatism can take advantage of the inevitable failures of liberal administrations to achieve a temporary power. But it cannot, in our terms, offer a viable alternative. It is always *faute de mieux*.

In view of the difficulties besetting liberalism and conservatism, radicalism would seem to have an awful lot going for it. And so it does—except that this awful lot just doesn't go very far. Ours is an age that breeds radicals with an almost awesome ease. But it is also an age that breeds disillusioned radicals with an equal degree of fertility.

The basic trouble with modern radicalism is that it can never become radical enough without at the same time becoming irrelevant. Thus, sooner or later every radical movement confronts the fact that, if it wishes to capitalize on the revolution of rising expectations, if it aims to increase the material welfare of the people, it must come to terms with the structure and functioning of modern society—and this society, whatever its ostensible political creed, does not permit too many liberties to be taken with it before it balks and malfunctions.

I am not suggesting that it is impossible for the modern industrial system to support different kinds of political regimes: It clearly is possible, and the differences are by no means negligible. What I am suggesting is that any regime which tries to impose a priori radical goals or revolutionary ideals on a modern industrial system will find that this imposition can only be maintained by political violence and political repression—not a single, modern radical movement has been able to create a society in which, over the longer term, people are freer, or feel freer, than they were before. And this would seem to imply (what I believe to be the case) that the relationship between modern radicalism and modern industrial society is inherently perverse.

An instance of this perversity is represented by the demand of the New Left that our representative democracy be transformed into a "participatory democracy." Now, as it happens, we know quite a great deal about what we now call "participatory democracy." It is precisely what most political theorists, prior to the American and French Revolutions, meant by "democracy" when they used that term. It is the kind of democracy that prevailed in classical Athens, in some of the theocratic city-states of the Reformation period, in some of our own early colonial settlements, on the Israeli kibbutzim. It is the kind of democracy that works only in small communities, ethnically homogeneous communities, ideologically homogeneous communities, and economically homogeneous communities.

Our Founding Fathers discussed this whole matter very acutely in "The Federalist Papers." They decided that this kind of democracy, in so large and varied a nation as the United States, could only lead to incessant civil conflict, chaos and eventually tyranny. So they opted for a *democratic republic*, constructed around the principle of representation. Such a republic allows for ideological and economic diversity, and also for a high degree of civil concord. Representatives are able to bargain, to compromise, to coexist with one another in a way that active participating masses of citizens cannot.

It is no accident that those who begin by demanding "participatory democracy" almost invariably end up by celebrating the virtues of a one-party dictatorship which mystically incarnates the "participatory" people. It is also no accident that such a one-party dictatorship, when it tries to manage a modern, modernized economy, ends up in a blind alley—for such an economy naturally moves toward innovation and differentiation, which in turn threatens the stability of the regime.

I would say that the only really radical group in American society today are the hippies and their associated sects. They are truly radical because they are dropouts from the revolution of rising expectations and reject the materialistic ethos that is the basis of the modern social order. Unfortunately, their kind of radicalism is also tainted at the source: Though they are not materialists, they are certainly hedonists, and hedonism cannot of itself generate the kind of self-discipline and self-denial that would make a radical alternative viable. If you want to reject the bourgeois, acquisitive, affluent society, you need people who are oriented toward the production of transcendental values, not the consumption of temporal goods. And the hippies, alas, are as consumption-oriented as the rest of us, even if they prefer to consume sex and drugs rather than, say, detergents and automobiles.

I seem to have landed this analysis in a dead end, in that I have outlined a very troubled situation to which the liberal, conservative and radical responses are all desperately inadequate. But, in political analysis as in mathematics, an impasse can tell us something about the way we have been looking at a problem. And in this case, what I think it tells us is the following: Our problem is not really political at all. It is cultural, in the largest sense of that term. It is not the case that our institutions are functioning badly; by all the familiar "objective" indices—increasing wealth, increasing education, increasing leisure—they are working quite well. What is happening to our institutions is that they are being inexorably drained of their legitimacy.

One can put it this way: We have, over these past decades, created pretty much the kind of economic, social and political order that was intended. Any social critic of the year 1900 who could observe America today would have to concede that truly remarkable progress has been made. As a matter of fact, if you go back only to the nineteen-thirties and forties, and read the radical social criticism of that time, you will discover that most of the economic promises which were made in the name of radically reconstructed social order have in fact been more than fulfilled by our unreconstructed but evolving one. (You don't have to be very old to recall the derision that greeted Henry Wallace's promise of 60 million jobs. Yet we surpassed that figure long ago.) *But*, at the same time, we have created a moral and cultural order which is dismissive of—more than that: contemptuous of—these very intentions. The Old Politics didn't fail, it succeeded, and that is precisely what is held against it.

This reality is obscured by the fact that so many critics of the Old Politics have failed to come up with a new, adequate vocabulary and habitually speak in the older, familiar jargon of socio-economic criticism. They talk stridently of the problem of poverty and the problem of the Negroes, both of which are indeed problems, but neither of which in itself is a crisis beyond our management. Even if we don't do much better than we have these past 10 years—and I believe we can—it is still demonstrable by simple arithmetic that in 15 years' time the proportion of poor people in this country will have sharply decreased and that the blacks will be much, much closer to economic equality. (The poverty population is shrinking at a rate of about 3 to 4 per cent a year, even as the total population grows. As for the Negroes, some 30 per cent of Negro families now earn more than $7,000 a year, as against less than half that percentage only eight years ago.)

In any kind of reasonable historical perspective, these are not critical or intractable challenges to the present system. But a reasonable historical perspective is of the least possible appeal to the advocates of the New Politics. They don't really mean to criticize the established order because it has not successfully coped with this or that particular problem. Rather, they seize upon the problem because they have lost all belief in the legitimacy of the established order.

The real clue to what is going on is the revolt on the campus. Here, too, the students bewilder us by talking of new things in an old way—they insist that their "rights" are unrecognized, that they are "underprivileged" when it comes to the distribution of power. But these students aren't 19th-century farmers or 20th-century factory workers in avant-garde costume. They are largely from the upper-middle classes and the heart of their complaint is spiritual, not material. They feel that American life and American society are devoid of both moral authority and moral significance. And what they really mean by a New Politics is one that would give moral direction and moral purpose to American life.

Now, this sounds innocuous enough, even rather uplifting. But it is a truly radical, a profoundly radical demand—more radical, even, than the overwhelming majority of students realize. For if there is any single cardinal principle around which the American polity is constructed, it is that it is *not* the function of government to define the moral purpose of American life—or to provide the social discipline necessary to achieve this moral purpose.

I am not saying that the American republic is a morally neutral institution, or a morally indifferent one. Rather, I am pointing to the fact that the American political tradition explicitly leaves the governance of moral life to our nonpolitical institutions—to the family, the churches, the schools. Our is a *limited* government of a *free* society, and it is rooted in the assumption that it is the task of government to reconcile conflicting interests in a reasonable way. But this assumption, in turn, is only valid if our nongovernmental institutions see to it that the American people, no matter how diverse, all do behave in a reasonable way—i.e., a self-disciplined way. And this kind of discipline is learned in the home, in church, in school. If you want a polity with an overriding moral purpose, then you want a government that *rules*, that *forms* the young citizen according to some preconceived political end, and that (subtly or crudely) *represses* all deviations from its orthodoxy.

It is a truism of political philosophy that no social order can have an enduring stability which is not based on some kind of consensus among its citizens as to (1) what is good or bad, and (2) what are the proper actions to take to settle the inevitable differences of opinion over what is good or bad. In the American political tradition, the purpose of government is confined to the second part of that proposition; it is left to free, nonpolitical institutions to cope with the first part.

Yet it is obvious that, in the course of recent decades, our nonpolitical institutions have been coping ever more ineffectually with the obligations that the American political tradition imposes upon them. Young people are emerging in our society who find themselves deprived of any sense of personal moral purpose—who see the institutions of their society as mere incarnations of power and prejudice, who have been thoroughly instructed in their rights as Americans but hardly at all in their obligations as Americans, and who in the end can find moral purpose only in a wild explosion of moral outrage. Nor is it any surprise that they then begin to cast longing eyes on other political regimes—Castro's Cuba, or Mao's China—where the Government mobilizes the people for purported moral ends. People, especially young people, fear a meaningless life more than they do an unfree one.

I do not need to recount how we came to reach our present condition. The broad outlines are familiar enough, since this is something that anyone over 40 has seen with his own eyes in his own lifetime. Suffice it to say that we reached our present condition as the result of making progress. We have progressively diminished the moral authority of all existing institutions and have successfully instructed our children to take a skeptical, critical, "creative" attitude toward them. So far as concerns religion and the family, this has been going on for a long time, but its consequences were muted by the fact that, more and more, the traditional functions of family and church in transmitting values were taken over by our schools.

Now, that last bastion is beginning to crumble. Our schools no longer transmit values for the most part; they regard it as their job to question values. One can hardly blame the schools, though many are tempted to do so. Why should they, and they alone, be the sustainers of traditional authority? If parents can't and won't do it, and if clergymen can't and won't do it, how can one reasonably ask educators and teachers to do it? They, too, want a part of the cultural action. They, too, want to be "progressive," just like everyone else. And so they are.

Thus we have a void, created by the progressive diminution of traditional authorities. And into this void spills a debased version of avant-garde culture —an antibourgeois culture, an "adversary culture," in Lionel Trilling's phrase —which was originally limited to a handful of bold artists and thinkers, but which is now being diffused through the popular arts and the educational system. This avant-garde culture used to be a "highbrow" culture, and set itself up in opposition to "lowbrow" or "middlebrow" culture. One hears very little of such opposition these days, since it has in truth ceased to exist. Twenty years ago, avant-garde intellectuals would have scorned Playboy magazine as an opiate for the masses. Now they write regularly for it, are well paid for their contributions—and, at the same time are more often than not respected professors in our universities.

It is not easy to say who has taken over whom. There has been a merger, based on money (which the organs of mass culture always had) and an arty pornography and a vague antibourgeois radicalism, both of which used to be the property of the avant-garde. And out of this merger there has been born a new cultural mode, a mass culture that is compared with the mass cultures of the past, of fairly high artistic quality, but which is also filled to overflowing with an instructive animus to, and rejection of, all traditional authorities, all traditional moral values, and most especially of the bourgeois order, in its moral, political and socio-economic aspects. It is this culture, moreover, which is more and more becoming the substance of the educational curriculum in our colleges and even our high schools.

Where all this will end, I haven't the faintest idea. But I do know it does have a crucial connection with the New Politics. Up to now, the New Politics signified a process of accommodation to this trend—it speaks for all those alienated youngsters and self-denigrating, upper-middle-class parents who think "The Graduate" is an absolutely wonderful and utterly truthful movie. But I believe the election of 1968 revealed that this is only a passing and temporary phenomenon. Most Americans do not despise themselves, do not think they are unfit to be parents, do not think their way of life is irremediably nasty or corrupt. And we have seen evidence, especially in the unexpected national appeal of George Wallace, that they, too, will be moving toward their own version of a New Politics—one that will be considerably less liberal, considerably less tolerant, and perhaps even downright repressive.

I see the future of American politics as being considerably less liberal than it has been in past decades, while being in no true sense of the term conservative. We are headed for a time of trouble, in which our political authorities are going to have to cope with an unreasonable revolution of rising material expectations on the part of the majority, an equally unreasonable revolution of utopian spiritual expectations on the part of a significant minority, and with a general breakdown of individual and social discipline. Not since the Civil War has this republic faced so fundamental a challenge. Whether the American Republic can cope with it remains to be seen. But I fear that, in attempting to cope with it, this republic will find itself involved with a *new* New Politics that will not be very congenial to those of us who rather liked the Old Politics, for all its deficiencies—or to those who set great store on yesterday's New Politics.

JAMES MacGREGOR BURNS

The Corruption of Consensus

"I am the President of the United States, the only President you will have, God willing, until January of next year," Lyndon Johnson said a few months after his election, before a group of newspaper editors assembled in the flower garden. "One of the hardest tasks that a President faces is to keep the time

Source: Mr. Burns is a well-known political scientist and author, among whose best-known books are *Roosevelt: The Lion and the Fox* and *The Deadlock of Democracy.* This essay is from *Presidential Government: The Crucible of Leadership* by James MacGregor Burns, pp. 323–335. Copyright © 1965 by James MacGregor Burns. Reprinted by permission of the publisher, Houghton Mifflin Company.

scale of his decisions always in mind and to try to be the President of all the people. He is not simply responsible to an immediate electorate, either. He knows over the long stretch of time how great can be the repercussions of all that he does or that he fails to do, and over that span of time the President always has to think of America as a continuing community.

"He has to try to see how his decisions will affect not only today's citizens, but their children and their children's children unto the third and fourth generation. He has to try to peer into the future, and he has to prepare for that future.

". . . Irresistible forces of change have been unleashed by modern science and technology, and the very facts dissolve and regroup as we look into them. To make no predictions is to be sure to be wrong. . . .

"The President of this country, more than any other single man in the world, must grapple with the course of events and the directions of history. What he must try to do, try to do always, is to build for tomorrow in the immediacy of today, for if we can, the President, and the Congress, and you leaders of the communities throughout the Nation, will have made their mark in history. Somehow we must ignite a fire in the breast of this land, a flaming spirit of adventure that soars beyond the ordinary and the contented, and really demands greatness from our society, and demands achievement in our Government. . . ." [1]

No presidential speech could have caught more aptly the paradox of the modern Presidency. To serve the needs of the present and the future, to satisfy current electorates and future ones, to conceive of America as a present community and a continuing one, to anticipate the future by preparing for it now, to make long-run predictions in the face of opaque facts, to "build for tomorrow in the immediacy of today," to foster greatness in the midst of so much that is mediocre and complacent—all these alternatives pose dilemmas for the President who aspires to his own greatness in history but must work in a tangle of day-to-day problems.

The crowning paradox is an old one for the American President—the need to be both the "President of all the people" and yet to respond to the interests and expectations of the majority that elected him. Since the beginning the President has had to serve both as the ceremonial and symbolic head of the whole nation and also as the head politician. He has had to be Chief of State at the same time that he has served as legislative and party chief. He has had to combine roles that are neatly divided in parliamentary countries between a king and a prime minister, or between a largely ceremonial president and a *premier*. He has had to be both a unifier and a divider of the people.

Filling these two roles has been awkward but not impossible. The President has had almost literally to don and doff his partisan or ceremonial costume for differing occasions. The shift from a "President of all the people" stance

[1] Remarks of President Johnson to American Society of Newspaper Editors, Office of the White House Press Secretary, April 17, 1964.

to a "politician looking for votes" stance is marked rather cleanly during election years by the day that the President formally begins his campaign for re-election and no longer can command television and radio channels free. The shifting back and forth between the roles has led to humorous byplays, as when reporters used to question Franklin Roosevelt as to whether his campaign-year inspection trips were part of his presidential or his electioneering responsibilities. The inconsistency and tension between the two roles, indeed, served a useful purpose in reminding people—including the President himself—that as leader of the whole nation he was always subject to the claims of the people who voted for him, and that as party chief he had obligations to the whole nation. The President could never be seen simply as a hero, for he had crass political obligations, but neither could he be perceived as a mere politician. The two roles both complemented each other and held each other in check. Their very inconsistency was a sign of health.

Note the striking contrast with today. As the modern Presidency has become increasingly the expression of a consensus over political goals—the goals of freedom through equality—the holder of the office has come increasingly to represent the same kind of national unity and harmony in his political role as in his symbolic and ceremonial. The old tension—and hence the balance and safeguards—between the two roles is disappearing. Columnists have poked fun at Lyndon Johnson because he clothed the most obviously political ideas and goals in the most bland and magisterial phrases. But this is not simply Lyndon Johnson's doing. The fact is that any President articulating the modern values of freedom and equality *seems* to be speaking for the great bulk of the nation for the simple reason that he *is* so speaking.

The implications of this development for the future can be grasped if we consider what has also been happening to the President's role as ceremonial and symbolic and even heroic leader. That role is of course an old one—even older than the Presidency itself, having begun when George Washington, in resplendent array, stepped out on the balcony overlooking Wall Street and took his solemn oath. By the end of the nineteenth century Henry Jones Ford was noting that in the Presidency America had revived the oldest political institution of the race, the elective kingship—precisely what Patrick Henry had feared. The sheer magnitude of the President's ceremonial duties today is staggering. "He lights the national Christmas tree on the White House lawn in the season of good will to men," Herman Finer has summed it up; "he issues the Thanksgiving Day message in the season of thankfulness and bicarbonated repletion; his office sends greetings to societies and persons on their birthdays, offering national recognition and a reason for gratitude; he throws out the first baseball of the season and attends the Army-Navy football game in a spirit of good-fellowship and as a votary of the sport; he is host at brilliant banquets for kings and queens and potentates, representing America in its dignity in the comity of nations; he sponsors movements for health and wealth and happiness; gigantic dams and electric works pound into operation

as his finger touches the proper button, enhancing America's pride; and he is
in mourning on Memorial Day, his hat over his heart, one with the heroes of
the past, one with those who mourn the men who died so that the nation
might live; at military parades on the Fourth of July he embodies the vigor
of American independence; and he is at home, for hand-shaking, to scores of
thousands of worthy and ordinary citizens throughout the year. And with him
is the First Lady of the land, presiding, the smartly dressed descendant of
Dolly Madison and the rest, over the social life of the capital, the epitome of
grace for the women of the nation." [2] The facilities of the White House have
been augmented to permit the President's home to be almost continuously on
show, both to the hordes of tourists and the stream of dignitaries. The
ceremonial and symbolic life of the Presidency has become almost as formal
and stylized as that of the court of Versailles. The White House has even had
court jesters about, and the Gridiron Club, now in its seventh decade of
existence, serves as the occasion when men can try to make fools of Presidents
and get away with it.

All this is familiar; what we must gauge is the long-time effect of this kind
of symbolism on attitudes toward the Presidency. Consider the attitudes that
children develop toward the office during their most formative years. Since the
beginning of the Republic, no doubt, little boys have wanted to be President,
but recent investigations of children's perceptions of the President make one
pause. In a study of the grade-school student's image of political authority,
Hess and Easton discovered that two figures appear first on the horizon of the
child's political awareness—the local policeman and the President of the
United States. The children's attitudes toward the President were highly
idealized. They saw him as much more hardworking than most men, more
honest, having more liking for people, knowing much more. As a person he
was "best in the world" to 61 percent of the second-graders, and either best
in the world or "good" to all but a very small minority of the children. They
saw him also as a potent figure, having the main part in making the laws,
with congressmen as helpers and governors and mayors as subordinates. The
children have ideas about the office, not just the man; there was, report the
authors, "a base line of expectations about the conduct and qualifications of
the man who occupies or seeks to occupy it." [3] While the perception of the
President in positive terms decreases a bit with age, it stays high, and it did
not seem to be dependent on social status or partisanship (or the child's
parents). In commenting on this and other studies, Roberta Sigel has suggested
that the school is probably one of the important sources of the child's image
of political authority and that most children's books "are designed to increase
pride in our Presidents and our history." And she notes that the "President

[2] Herman Finer, *The Presidency: Crisis and Regeneration* (Chicago: University of
Chicago Press, 1960), pp. 111–12.

[3] Robert D. Hess and David Easton, "The Child's Changing Image of the President,"
Public Opinion Quarterly, vol. 24, no. 4 (Winter 1960), pp. 632–44.

being far away enjoys an added advantage over local authority figures: the child has no opportunity to check against reality the idealized image taught him by the adult world." [4] From her own set of findings about children's reactions to President Kennedy's assassination she concluded that the image of the Presidency remained highly positive despite a slight decrease in the power image and that the children could in a rudimentary way distinguish between the person of the President and the institution of the government. "Their sense of political security seems to be a function of their faith in the institution of government as well as of their faith in individual Presidents." [5] These early attitudes inevitably shape people's views of the Presidency in their adult years.

The increasing dominance of the Presidency over the rest of the government, its embodiment of the national purpose, its symbolic expression of the nation's glory and solidarity, its tremendous impact on Americans during their most formative years—what does all this imply for the future of the nation and of the Presidency?

The old and accepted fears of presidential power, I have contended in the last chapter, do not seem justified on the basis of actual experience. Increased authority and scope have not made the Presidency a tyrannical institution; on the contrary, the office has become the main governmental bastion for the protection of individual liberty and the expansion of civil rights. The office "represents" the electorate at least as effectively and democratically as does Congress, though in a different way. The office has attracted neither power-mad politicians nor bland incompetents but the ablest political leaders in the land, and these leaders in turn have brought the highest talent to the White House. We must, under modern conditions, reassess the old idea that the *main* governmental protection of civil liberty, social and economic rights, and due process of law lies in the legislature or the courts or state and local government. The main protection lies today in the national executive branch. As a general proposition the Presidency has become the chief protector of our procedural and substantive liberties; as a general proposition, the stronger we make the Presidency, the more we strengthen democratic procedures and can hope to realize modern liberal democratic goals.

The danger of presidential dominance lies in a different and more subtle tendency. It lies not in presidential failure but in presidential success. It lies not in the failure to achieve our essential contemporary goals of freedom and equality but in their substantial realization and in the incapacity of presidential government to turn to new human purposes.

The prospects seem good that presidential government will continue to help broaden equality of opportunity at the same time that it protects our basic freedoms. All the Presidencies since that of Hoover have made some

[4] Roberta S. Sigel, "Death of a President and School Children's Reaction To It—An Exploration into Political Socialization," Wayne State University, 1964.
[5] Ibid.

kind of commitment to this goal; they have aroused strong expectations; they have perfected the governmental machinery necessary to realize the goals; and we can expect that the contest between the presidential parties on domestic issues will turn mainly on the incumbent Administration's successes and failures in combating poverty, expanding opportunity, and enlarging civil rights, especially for Negroes. In foreign policy the election tests will be the efficient management of crisis plus the long-run effectiveness of military and economic programs abroad designed to strengthen the foundations of freedom and equality in other nations. Given the harmony between ends and means—between the ends of freedom and equality and the means of presidential government—we can expect that well before the end of this century, and perhaps much sooner, we will have achieved substantial equality of opportunity in this nation. We need not expect equality of *condition*, nor full equality of opportunity, for gray areas of deprivation and discrimination will remain. Some of the old tension between equality and freedom will always be found in a diverse and changing society. But to the extent that public and private measures can realize freedom and equality, the goals will be substantially achieved.

And precisely here lies the problem. As freedom and equality are achieved presidential government will exhaust the purpose for which it has been such an eminently suited means. The great machinery of government that has been shaped to distribute welfare and overcome poverty and broaden opportunity and protect liberty will become devoted to increasingly automatic tasks. The passion will long since have disappeared, and increasingly the compulsion of purpose will be dissipated. Purpose will no longer be toughened in conflict; creativity will no longer rise from challenge and crisis. As the ends of government become increasingly agreed upon among the people, between the parties, between President and Congress, between national and state and local governments, issues will resolve mainly around questions of technique. And the more humdrum these matters become, the more the President will turn to his ceremonial and symbolic role to provide circuses to the people—the bread already being in abundance.

According to Morgenthau, we are already facing this problem, even with the goals of freedom and equality not yet achieved. In this nation there have been purposes, he reminds us, to which we could pledge our lives, our fortunes, and our sacred honor. "There is no such issue today. None of the contemporary issues of domestic politics of which the public at large is aware commands for its alternative solutions those loyalties out of which great political conflicts are made. There are divergent opinions and interests, to be sure; but there is no great issue that men deem worthy of sacrifice and risk. In consequence, the integrating principle of American society has lost both its dynamic and its substantive qualities. . . . The American consensus, which in the past was monistic in form and pluralistic in substance, has become monistic in both respects. In consequence, conformism now extends to the substance of policies and constitutional arrangements. Since no issue is any longer worth fighting over, a position must be 'moderate,' and what was once a compromise between seemingly irreconcilable positions now transforms itself into the adjustment of positions differing only in degree. Since the purpose of America seems to have been achieved—the need for improvement notwithstanding—the *status quo* tends to become as sacred as the purpose itself, and an attack upon the *status quo* almost as unpalatable as dissent from the purpose. Since there is nothing left to fight for, there is nothing to fight against. . . ." [6] Morgenthau was writing during the Eisenhower Administration, and he did not anticipate the force of Kennedy's challenge to Republicanism and of the Negroes' revolt against the status quo in the early 1960's. But he was right in a broader sense, for it was precisely Eisenhower's acceptance of the purposes of the New Deal and the Fair Deal, and his blandness in his methods of realizing them, that made his administration an ominous indication of the likely nature of late twentieth century politics in America.

Many would reject any call today for high purposes and fighting issues. They prefer a polity that is not rent by great issues, scarred by savage conflict, absorbed in passionate controversy, or even distracted by political problems. Considering the nature of the early and middle epochs of the twentieth century, they would cherish a period of calm in which people could indeed, in John Adams' words, turn to painting, poetry, music, architecture, statuary, tapestry and porcelain. The very realization of the grand aims of freedom and equality, they believe, would create a basis on which people could turn to the enduring problems of the richness and quality of life, and could forsake some of the old ideological quarrels.

Those who spurn ideology will contend, moreover, that progress emerges not from the pursuit of central, synoptic visions or plans or purposes, but from the pursuit of a wide range of alternative policies, from flexible methods, from refusal to make an ultimate commitment to any means or any end, from incremental and adjustive tactics that permit day-to-day reconciliation of differences. Such an approach, they hold, produces innovation, creativity, and excitement. It rejects the grand formulations of interrelated ends and means in favor of special angles of vision, sharpened individual or group motivation, the social dynamics of a loosely articulated, highly accessible, and open-ended polity. The incrementalists would proceed step by step, renouncing passion and commitment in favor of prudence and calculation.

Yet many who have lived through the decades of traumatic and even bloody political conflict, at home or abroad, will wonder about a nation in which the great issues have dwindled to matters of technique. They will worry first about a people so bored by the relatively trivial political issues of the day that they have become largely absorbed in the minutiae of their private lives.

[6] Hans J. Morgenthau, *The Purpose of American Politics* (New York: Vintage Books, 1964), pp. 213–14.

They will doubt whether in the long run even architecture and poetry can be kept out of politics. They will worry that people might fall into adjustment, conformity, undiscriminating tolerance, and aimless, time-filling activities, and that this will lead to the acceptance of mediocrity and a compulsive together-ness rather than the pursuit of excellence and individuality.

They will be concerned about the governors as well as the governed. For a government agreed on the larger issues and proceeding by calculation and adjustment is likely to attract to its service the little foxes who know many little things—the operators, the careerists, the opportunists, the technicians, the fixers, the managers. Some of these men may be resourceful, zealous, dedi-cated, flexible, and adjustable. But they will be so absorbed in technique that it will be difficult for them to separate issues of policy from questions of their own immediate self-enhancement. Certainly there would be little room for the Churchills who give up office in the pursuit of broader principles, or even for the administrative innovators who wish to create something more exalted than a better administrative mousetrap. Thus the governors too would lose their way, become lost in technique, would become absorbed in private mo-tives, would substitute means for ends.

For this is the corruption of concensus—the attempt to find universal agree-ment on so many issues that great public purposes are eroded by a torrent of tiny problems solved by adjustment and adaptation. Ways and means are more and more rationally elaborated by increasing numbers of technicians for a society having less and less human purpose. In government this would mean Hamiltonianism gone wild; in the Presidency it would mean the sub-mergence of the nation's supreme political decision-maker in an ever widening tide of incremental adjustments. The President might still be a hero to most of his people, but his policy and program would not be heroic, only his image. He would still seem a potent figure to children—and grownups—but his actual influence over events would be dwindling. He would still be visible as he mediated among the technicans and occasionally coped with crisis; but it would be the visibility of the tightrope walker whom the great public watches with emotional involvement but without actual participation. The defeat of presidential government would be inherent in its very success. Having taken over the Cabinet and the rest of the government, presidential government would finally have taken over the President.

HARRY S. ASHMORE AND LINUS PAULING

Party Politics or Protest Politics: "What Can a Man Do?"

Harry S. Ashmore:

My assignment is to answer the question of what a man can do within the traditional party system of this country. I might start with an anecdote. It was a standard story in South Carolina when I first became active as an observer of, and participant in, partisan politics. The state, of course, was a one-party area, and the actual electing was done in the Democratic primary. The winner had to have a majority vote; if there was no majority in the first primary, the two top men had a run-off.

The long-time political leader in my county was a man named Tom Henderson, whom I had known from childhood. In this campaign for governor, Mr. Henderson and his henchmen had been backing a candidate who was eliminated in the first primary. The morning after, Mr. Henderson called in the faithful to inform them that they were about to come out for Cole Blease. This caused some consternation among the constituency. One innocent fellow said, "Well, Mr. Tom, I don't understand that because just last week I heard you say that Cole Blease was the worst son of a bitch who ever stood for public office in this state." Mr. Henderson replied, "Yes, I said it and he is, but he's our son of a bitch now." The questioner was really very innocent and so he went: "But, Mr. Tom, couldn't we come out for the other fellow?" And Henderson said, "No, goddam it, our folks won't switch that way."

I draw two morals from this story. One is that party politics has always been an exercise in compromise. Party politics—obviously in view of the kind of story I have just related—has always been offensive to intellectuals; it has been offensive to moralists; it has been offensive to people who feel strongly that principle must prevail and compromise is bad. But the second moral is contrary. It is that the political bosses, as in the case of Mr. Tom, are, in fact,

Source: Mr. Ashmore is a newspaper editor, journalist, and author. Dr. Pauling is a Nobel prize-winning physicist and prominent peace activist. This article is reprinted with permission from pp. 66–68 of the September 1968 issue of *The Center Magazine*, a publication of the Center for the Study of Democratic Institutions in Santa Barbara, California.

never entirely able to deliver in exactly the way that the public thinks they can and that they would have the public believe they can. Old man Henderson couldn't switch his voters in a direction they didn't want to go. In any case, this kind of conventional party politics is disappearing rapidly in this country. I believe it has been eroded to the point that it has virtually disappeared, and I predict that in a short time it will disappear entirely.

But, while it lasts, the party system still provides at least a partial answer to the question: What can a man do? I couldn't have made that statement with any degree of assurance if I had had to deliver those remarks before March 31st. But now we have seen a powerful President brought down on a moral issue—an event comparable to a vote of no confidence under a parliamentary system. And this happened because disaffected Americans, many of them of tender age, marched into the party primaries and made their indignation known.

The primary function of the parties in our political process has been to nominate candidates, and they are still doing that. Another function was to provide the organization that made it possible for rising politicians to reach the electorate. This is no longer needed because rising politicians can now do it through television as long as they can afford it. The third thing party organizations traditionally did was to raise money for political campaigns. Clearly they no longer do that. The individual candidates do it as best they can, or if they are fortunate they come in with their own bankrolls. The fourth thing the parties did was to define the issues in a crude sort of way. They did this by gathering intelligence, as Mr. Tom Henderson gathered intelligence about what the folks in Greenville County were really worried about, how they might respond to a candidate, and what a candidate ought to tell them if he wanted their votes. This function has been taken over by the polling systems, public and private, that have grown up out of social science. The decay of these last three functions of party politics has left a great void, and this seems to me a disturbing phenomenon indeed.

I was with a convention of pollsters recently. One of them was defending his colleagues by saying that they provided a democratic device that was very important to the political process. They made the primary an endless event; between official elections the country had a continual election. Candidates were always being advised of what the people thought about the big issues of the day. I suppose this is true, but I would not say it is the best thing I have heard lately. I believe the leadership of the country needs intervals between public reaction and decision-making. I believe it needs to do what it has not been doing effectively for some time, and that is leading. It has been depending on what it thought was public reaction rather than attempting to influence public reaction. I do not absolve the pollsters from having a role in this process. The burdens of leadership are great, and one of them is to be unpopular when necessary. A politician can't become permanently unpopular or he becomes a retired politician. Nevertheless, the role of advocacy, of arguing the case and presenting alternatives to the public, is not being adequately performed by the leadership.

One of the reasons for this is the erosion of the old party structure and the failure to replace it with something more responsive and more effective, some better channel from the public to the leadership and, equally, from the leadership to the people.

At the meeting of the pollsters, I listened to a learned paper, one of those objective "value-free" social-science papers. The burden of it was that the polls are having a great influence on our elections but the pollsters do not intend them to and do not really care how it all comes out. The conclusion was that, as a result of the polls, and of television, and of the way we now practice politics in general, we are moving our politics irrevocably into the middle ground. I must agree that this is what is happening. However, if we fail to restore or replace the kind of political process that this country grew up with, it might well turn out that the middle ground is the burying ground.

Linus Pauling:

Party politics as we have known it is not going to solve the great problems that need to be solved now. There is a struggle going on in the world, and its outcome will determine the fate of the hundreds of millions, even billions, of people who are suffering from increasing starvation and disease owing to extreme malnutrition, and who occupy a position of virtual serfdom. I do not believe that the wealth of the world, which is now largely controlled by a rather few powerful people, should be used in the way that it is being used. On the other hand, I do not believe that this control will be voluntarily shared by them with the rest of the world in a just and moral way.

When I remember what has happened since the Civil War among the Negroes in the United States, I am skeptical about the success of anything except protest politics. I believe that it is only through continued and vigorous protest by large groups of people, through demonstrations by the mass of the people, through revolution, that the evil future for the world that I foresee as a possibility can be averted. The Negroes are revolting now, and their equal-rights revolution will be successful. I am encouraged that the students are revolting too, and not only in the United States. Some of them in the United States are revolting against the C.I.A., and what better protest could our students make than against the C.I.A., which I believe is the most immoral institution in the world?

How many people have died because of the C.I.A.? In the Indonesian massacre estimates of the deaths range from three hundred thousand to a million left-wingers. This was carried out because the C.I.A. was afraid of the operation of democracy in Indonesia. In Guatemala the agrarian revolution under President Jacobo Arbenz was stopped by an invasion of right-wing exiles organized by the C.I.A. And the poor and miserable people in twenty other countries have been made poorer and more miserable by the C.I.A.-supported military dictatorships. Why is the United States opposed to land reform in underdeveloped countries? Whenever a constitutional government begins to move in the direction of land reform in a Latin-American country the C.I.A. arranges for it to be overthrown by a military dictatorship, which we then support.

Why do we waste ten per cent of our wealth on militarism year after year? The rest of the world follows our lead and as a result ten per cent of the world's wealth is wasted. These are efforts to continue the trend in the world that Pope Paul described as one that makes the rich richer and the poor poorer.

I always feel more certain about my understanding of a problem if I have some figures, and so I have factored something out: five per cent of the people in the United States, or ten million people, receive twenty per cent of our national income. This amounts to about two hundred billion dollars. In the world as a whole three billion poor people have a total income of the same amount, two hundred billion dollars. This ratio of dollars to people is 300–1, which means that two-thirds of the people in the world have an individual income one three-hundredths of that of the most affluent ten million in the United States. This two hundred billion dollars is less than the amount the world has been spending on militarism. If we were to use this two hundred billion dollars for the benefit of the poor people of the world instead of for militarism, it would double their income and obviously alleviate their misery greatly.

The United States, with six per cent of the world's people, owns sixty-five per cent of the world's wealth, and the world's wealth increases every year. There is no evidence to suggest that this trend will be reversed except through protest politics. As an American I believe in revolution. I believe that all men are created equal and are endowed with certain unalienable rights, and that among these are life, liberty, and the pursuit of happiness. I believe that whenever any form of government becomes destructive of these ends, the people have the right to alter it or to abolish it, and to institute a new government, "laying its foundation on such principles and organizing its powers in such form, as to them shall seem most likely to effect their safety and happiness." Our government and the governments of the world are now destructive of the ends of life, liberty, and the pursuit of happiness for the great majority of the people. These governments, I believe, must be altered, and perhaps Harry Ashmore said the same thing in indicating that he thought party politics as it has been in the past will not continue much longer.

I believe that we the people must protest the evil and injustice of the present world system. I don't think that party politics, even if it changes somewhat, can abolish the evil system of which it is a part. Only mass protest can achieve this goal. I believe in non-violence. The problem is that the Establishment believes in violence, in force, in napalm, in police power, aerial bombing, B-52's, B-58's, nuclear weapons, war. As long as the selfishness of the Establishment remains the determining factor, our hope that the coming revolution will be non-violent has little basis in reality.

ANDREW M. GREELEY

Mayor Daley As Honest Broker: Take Heart from the Heartland

Both Kevin Phillips and the team of Richard Scammon and Ben Wattenberg are agreed that the Middle West is crucial in American politics. Whether it be called the "Heartland" or the "Quadracali," it is the "swing region" in Presidential elections; and as the elections of 1970 quickly become an unpleasant memory, one is forced to say that the heartland has moved to the left. In the massive block of America between the Ohio River and the Rocky Mountains, Democrats managed to hold almost all of their supposedly tenuous Senate seats, score most of their House gains, send a bright new liberal face to the United States Senate, and grab just about every governorship in sight.

How can this be? What happened to the silent majority? Where is the backlash? What became of the crime issue? Apparently, they've all migrated east of the Hudson River.

And, if the heartland has become liberal once again, its capital is the despised Second City on the shores of Lake Michigan. For the hated Daley Organization won what may be its greatest victory. Adlai Stevenson III now holds the Senate seat his father always wanted, having obtained 2,065,154 against his opponent's 1,519,718 votes. Two other attractive Democratic candidates—Alan Dixon, the new state treasurer, and Professor Michael Bakalis, the superintendent of public instruction—joined with Stevenson in leading the first major success for the Organization in previously solid Republican

Source: Mr. Greeley is program director of the National Opinion Research Center at the University of Chicago. This article is from *The New Republic*, Dec. 12, 1970, pp. 16–19. Reprinted by permission of *The New Republic*, © 1970, Harrison-Blaine of New Jersey, Inc.

suburbs of Chicago; the Republicans find themselves with almost nothing left in Cook County, and the Democrats dominate the state legislature in Springfield for the first time in the twentieth century. Not bad at all for the last hurrah.

While Democrats and liberals in New York and Connecticut were busily engaged in committing suicide, Richard J. Daley was picking up every marble on the playground. While progressive New York was helping Mr. Agnew put James Buckley in the United States Senate, benighted, hard-hat Illinois was giving an overwhelming victory to a man whose family name symbolizes all that was supposedly dear in American liberalism. Is it possible that those who do most of the thinking and writing about American politics, who shape the issues and campaigns, who author the columns and the articles in the liberal journals have missed something critical about American politics?

One of my colleagues remarked the day after election that "of course you can elect a liberal in Illinois if his name happens to be Adlai Stevenson." Leaving aside the fact that there was a liberal called Paul Douglas and another called Charles Percy, the question remains why a name which symbolizes the "liberal permissiveness" that Mr. Agnew so cheerfully denounced is political magic in a state supposedly dominated by the silent majority and, to use a term bandied about at a meeting of the American Sociological Association in 1968, "shanty Irish bigots"?

I am contending that the Chicago system deserves a fair investigation in the wake of November 3 to see what it may tell us about the operation of the political process. Martin Meyerson, Edward Banfield and James Q. Wilson have made such investigations on the scholarly level but their investigations are systematically ignored, even by their sometime colleagues at the University of Chicago. And the journalists from the East—to say nothing of their alienated imitators from Chicago—are interested only in telling it like they knew it was before they bothered to investigate it in any depth. Let me illustrate.

1. An Eastern paper the day after the election wrote of a "deal" by which Stevenson agreed to support Daley candidates in return for Daley's support of his senatorial candidacy. The article added that while Stevenson had won easily, the Daley machine had not done well. The facts are that such "deals" do not exist in Chicago politics (they are not necessary), that Stevensen *was* a Daley candidate, and that the Daley organization *had* won the greatest victory in its history.

2. The normally fair Howard K. Smith lumped Stevenson (though not by name) with Agnew on the night before the election as an example of campaign demagoguery because Adlai wore an American flag on his lapel, emphasized the crime issue, and put a famous prosecutor on his campaign staff. The facts are that Stevenson had authored crime legislation before it was fashionable to do so and that the prosecutor in question, Thomas Aquinas Foran, receives more hate mail for prosecuting a school integration case in a Chicago suburb,

indicting police for the convention disturbances, and pushing faculty integration in the public schools.

3. Roy Newquist, writing obviously for non-Chicagoans in Fielding's *Guide to Chicago*, observes, "the political complexion of Chicago seems to be undergoing a change. The 1968 Democratic Convention riots upset the natives more than anything else that has happened in decades and citizens of all colors are taking harsh second and third looks at the regular Democratic (or Daley) machinery." Newquist is right, of course, that the natives were upset by the convention demonstrations, but the slightest glance at the public opinion polls ought to have indicated that it was not the organization at which they were angry.

4. A prize-winning Chicago journalist has quoted several times a sentence from a speech of Foran's after the conspiracy trial in which the prosecutor said, "Our children are shocked when they hear us saying "wop" and "nigger." He never bothers to add that the next sentence was, "And they are right to be shocked." Nor does he point out that on racial and economic matters Foran has always been a liberal. Indeed, one of the most fascinating interludes of the campaign was Foran—an impressive TV personality—upstaging Jesse Jackson on a TV talk show with ploys like, "I agree with you completely, Reverend Jackson, but I'd want to go further and take an even more radical stand."

5. A New Yorker once observed to me, "Everyone knows that Julius Hoffman is the most corrupt judge who ever bought a seat on the bench from Dick Daley." Hoffman is a Republican appointed by Dwight Eisenhower before Daley was mayor of Chicago, and judgeships are not "bought" in Chicago. They *are* frequently a reward for loyalty, but Chicago has no monopoly on this method of judicial selection.

6. The ordinary explanation for the "Machine's" triumphs implies that in part the votes are bought or stolen, and that in part they are cast by a patronage army. One gets the picture of vast, unthinking Slavic hordes marching in tight discipline to the polls. The facts are that you cannot steal or buy a half-million votes, and that the patronage army is tiny compared to the size of the city. Furthermore, the black and Slavic voters of Chicago are no less intelligent than voters elsewhere. The blacks have had alternative candidates to the Daley candidates and have, with one or two exceptions, soundly rejected them. Nor are the Polish voters who overwhelmingly endorsed Adlai Stevenson unaware of his racial stand. To explain the Organization's ability to get more than three-fourths of the Polish vote and three-fourths of the black vote in terms of fraud, fear, and theft is to turn the voters of Chicago into dull, stereotypical automatons. Such a strategy is useful for those who don't want to face the possibility that there may be some extremely important political truth that the Organization has discovered. But it is also prejudice in the strict sense of that word.

One moderately militant black summarized the position of many of his colleagues when he told me, "We're loyal to the organization because it works, because we know of no better way of improving our position in Chicago, and because, while it can't give everyone everything he wants, it can give most Chicago groups enough to keep them happy." Such a comment may sound cynical and, from a black, even treasonable. But, from the point of view of Chicago Democrats, it represents the essence of the political process.

The masters of ethnic politics are not intellectuals; they are not given to articulating abstract ideas; only Foran and one or two others look good on TV; their insight into the city and what makes it tick is not phrased in slick social science terminology, but is concrete and instinctual. Any attempt to state their model of the political process in formal terms—such as I will shortly engage in—is bound to lose something of the vigor and flavor of the original. On the other hand, while intellectual types may find the poor diction and malapropisms of some of the ethnic politicians vastly amusing, their amusement should not blind them to the fact that the best of politicians have an intuitive grasp of the city that would make the most skillful social scientist look naive.

The first assumption of ethnic politics is that the city is composed of various groups, national, racial, economic, religious. It is the politician's role to act as a broker among these groups, arranging and rearranging power and resources in such a way as to prevent one group from becoming so unhappy with the balance that they will leave the system. He arranges, usually indirectly and informally, and almost always gradually, compromises among the various power elements, within the city, that these elements could not achieve by direct negotiation among themselves. Thus, Irish aldermen or congressmen are slowly phased out to be replaced by Poles and then blacks (there are three Polish Democratic congressmen, two blacks, two Jews, one Irishman, and one Italian from Chicago, and in the next aldermanic elections about 30 percent of the city council seats will be held by blacks); but there is no great fanfare accompanying such changes. Does the organization slate a black congressman to represent Cicero and Berwyn? It surely does; but it doesn't issue press releases claiming that it is engaged in a revolution.

The "balanced ticket" is a symbol of this power brokerage game. To exclude a group its "place" on the ticket is to insult and offend them. If you should tell an ethnic politician that in one state (New York) the Democratic slate was made up of three Jews and a black and that the party still expected to get the Irish and Italian vote, he will simply not believe you. And if you tell him that in another state (Connecticut) a Unitarian minister with an Irish name and a liberal background led a slate on which, for the first time in many years, there were no Irish Catholics he would assume that the Irish vote would go Republican and wonder who was responsible for such an inept decision.

Nor would he be able to understand why some would consider piece-of-the-pie demands to be immoral. The model of the new politics—enthusiastic college students from "out of the neighborhood," vigorous ideological liberalism, passionate moral self-righteousness—would baffle him. The ethnic politician knows that in most of the districts of his city this model will not win elections.

In his frame of reference you can't afford to lose one economic or racial or ethnic group. If you win an election at the price of turning off one such segment of the city and setting the others against this scapegoat group you're simply asking for trouble. No political leader can afford to lose a major group from his consensus, for he will find it difficult to govern without this group and even more difficult to be reelected.

The ethnic politician also realizes that most people are not ideologues. He knew long before Amitai Etzione's brilliant article in *Transaction* that most people are quite "inconsistent" in their political attitudes; they are "liberal" on some issues, "conservative" on others. Furthermore, the ethnic politician realizes that for all the attention they get on the media, self-appointed "spokesmen" usually represent only themselves and a tiny band of friends. Most citizens are not interested in ideology but are moved by more concrete and pressing matters—jobs, sidewalks, garbage removal, streets, transportation, housing, access to the government to get assistance when needed. The vast network of precinct captains is not merely, or even principally a downward channel of communication designed to convey voting instructions. It is also a technique—frequently more effective than public opinion polling—for determining what is on people's minds and providing them with a feeling of access to the system.

Why do you slate an obvious liberal like Adlai Stevenson at a time when the pundits are all persuaded that there is a "shift to the right"? Partly you may do it because you don't read the pundits, but partly because your instincts and your organization say that Adlai is a winner. Why are you undismayed when a smooth advertising firm, relying on poll data and White House advice, turns out clever ads suggesting your candidate is "soft" on student radicals? Mostly because your instincts and your organization tell you that the student issue is not all that important and that Adlai is still a winner. And why do you rejoice when the Vice President arrives on the scene as part of the "realignment" strategy and accuses Adlai of disgracing his father's name? Because you know your voters well enough to know that they are not going to be "realigned" by such foolishness and will certainly resent such an attack on someone about whom they have already made up their minds.

The ethnic politician is also free from the pundit's uncertainty about the nature of the electorate. Before the election, there was much fear that the voter was a narrow, frightened, easily swayed member of the silent majority, and maybe a hard-hat to boot. After the election, he looked more like a responsible, discriminating, and sophisticated person. But from the ethnic politician's viewpoint, both images are incomplete. He is well aware of the unpredictability, the strain towards bigotry, the extreme sensitivity to slights, the fear, the impatience with all politicians. But he also realizes that there is a strain towards rationality, openness and trust, and a sympathy for social reform, and that, in his better moments, John Q. Voter is capable of civility, intelligence and generosity. Thus, the ethnic politician is not too surprised when he rises to heights. In other words, you appeal to both the voter's fears and his idealism, his selfishness and his integrity; and, after awhile, you hope that you have become skillful in the art of blending the two kinds of appeals.

The ethnic politician's slogan that social progress is good politics is neither phony nor cynical but simply a statement of political reality as he sees it. He knows that if he is too "conservative" the balance he has established will not shift rapidly enough to keep up with the changing state of his city; and if he is too "liberal" he may attempt to force change on the city before there is a broad enough consensus to support it. In the thirties he supports the trade unions and in the sixties the black demand for power, but he supports both such demands in ways that will not drive other groups out of his coalition. There may be a tendency in such an approach to move too slowly, especially if the organization has poor communication links with a minority group. But the political leader is much less sanguine than his academic critic about the ability of any leadership to correct most social problems in a brief period of time.

The two Stevensons, Paul Douglas, Otto Kerner (who presided over the extremely liberal report on Civil Disturbances), and the present Lt. Governor, Paul Simon, represent a liberal tradition of which any state might be proud. Michael Bakalis, a thirty-two year old university professor (of Greek origin, conveniently enough), and U.S. Congressman Abner Mikva are liberal enough to please Professor Galbraith. The ethnic politician knows that there is a strong liberal strain in his electorate and that an articulate and intelligent liberal can have strong voter appeal. The liberal must of course be able to win, he must want to win (frequently a difficulty for many American liberals) and he must not forget who helped him to win—or run the risk of not winning again. Furthermore, he must realize that he and his fellows cannot claim a monopoly on all offices. From the point of view of the ethnic politician, liberalism is good politics, especially when he can find a liberal who is willing to admit that politics can be good liberalism.

While his critics contend that it is patronage which holds the organization together, he knows himself that "loyalty" is more important than jobs. As one young Irish lawyer put it, "a man who is not loyal to his friends will never be loyal to an idea." The mockery to which Arthur Goldberg was subjected by those who thrust him into the political limelight would be unthinkable to an ethnic politician. You stand by your own, even if they have made mistakes, or if they have perhaps grown a bit too old. You wait patiently in line until it's "your turn" to be slated. You accept the decisions of the organization with good grace and work for the success of the ticket even though you are personally disappointed. You do so because you're convinced that there is no other way to engage in politics and that the alternative is what New York Democrats are currently calling Balkanization.

In his book, *The Irish and Irish Politicians*, Edward Levine tells the story of Nineteenth Ward Committeeman John Duffy who supported Martin Kennelly against Daley in 1955 because of the loyalty that Duffy's mentor, Thomas Nash, felt for Kennelly. According to Levine, Daley is reputed to have said, "If I were Duffy I would bolt." Later Duffy became the organization's president of the county board and worked closely with the mayor. There is a nice etiquette required of those who must balance loyalties, but the phrase "do what you have to do" is fully understood by the ethnic politicians. When he hears that this is "clanishness" the ethnic politician is puzzled. What are the alternatives? To quote one of Levine's informants, "The only thing you have in politics is your word. Break your word and you're dead. The most successful politician is the politician who kept his word." But if he is puzzled by the failure of the "liberal" to understand this truism, the ethnic politician would probably be astonished that such new left political theorists as John Schaar are demanding the same kind of personal fealty from their political leaders. The ethnic leader and the hippy guru may have more in common than they know.

There are obvious faults in such a political model in addition to those which are inevitable in any political model. Its very flexibility and amorphousness may make dishonesty and corruption somewhat easier than the so-called Reform models of politics, but ethnic systems are much less corrupt in most American cities than they have been in the past and ethnic politicians have no monopoly on corruption. Nor is the charge that the ethnic system is not open to the major forces of social change a valid one; quite the contrary, if the system is working properly social change is precisely what it is open to, though it distinguishes between actual social change and that announced by academic theorists.

There are three critical weaknesses however. First, the responsiveness of the system to groups depends to some extent on how well organized and articulate a given group is. The ethnic politician does not readily spot a situation where a given group may need his help in organizing itself and articulating its demands.

Second, small but potentially explosive groups can be missed. The basic problem at root of the 1968 turmoil was that the organization had little experience with the Youth Culture and was unprepared to deal with it. It learned quickly and there has been no repetition of the scene in front of the Conrad Hilton, but the mistake of playing into the hands of the radicals was a function of the fact that until the convention Youth Culture was not seen as a serious problem to cope with.

Finally, while the ethnic politician is not likely to be swayed by the moralism, the dogmatism and the perfectionism of the academic, his own proclivity to a concrete and instinctual style makes it hard for him to communicate with the intellectual and make use of the intellectual's important contribution to the political process—and, in particular, the intellectual's ability to spot long-range trends and problems.

It is difficult to write such an article for non-Chicago readership. The mere mention of "Chicago politics" or "Richard Daley" or "Irish politicians" erects a barrier in certain segments of American society which is hard to pierce. The system is immoral and corrupt or, to use Mr. Goldberg's word, cheap.

But the "liberal" may want to ponder the thought that the alternative is Nelson Rockefeller and James Buckley till the year 2000. And the "radical" may feel that ethnic politics are part of the "establishment" which must be overthrown in "the revolution"—whether it be the peaceful revolution of Consciousness III or something more bloody. But the "radical" may want to ponder the fact that even after the revolution he will have to contend with the same social groups in the large city with which the ethnic politician must cope, and that if he does not come up with a better method, he will either have to fall back on the ethnic strategy or maintain a very efficient secret police and a very large system of concentration camps.

TOM KELLY

Mayor Daley's Smart, but What Else?

In his defense of Mayor Richard Daley and Chicago machine politics Andrew Greeley ("Take Heart from the Heartland" NR, December 12, 1970) correctly argues that Daley is a master practitioner of ethnic politics. Daley's shrewd slating of Adlai Stevenson III for the Senate is only one of countless examples of his skill. There is little doubt that in the Senate Stevenson will vote to substantially reorient priorities, a *sine qua non* for social change. As Greeley pointed out, the Chicago machine has helped elect reformers such as Paul Douglas and the present senator's father. But to imply that the slating of such men in 1948 or 1970 signifies the machine's commitment to reform is

Source: Mr. Kelly teaches urban studies at Malcolm X College. This article is from *The New Republic*, Dec. 26, 1970, pp. 9–11. Reprinted by permission of *The New Republic*, © 1970 by Harrison-Blaine of New Jersey, Inc.

nonsense. Such men as Douglas or Stevenson are nominated by the machine only when it needs straight-ticket voting because it is in trouble locally, and to the machine a Senator is unimportant in comparison to local—city and county—offices with their abundant patronage and powers of tax-assessment and fraud investigation. To Daley and the machine, the political goal is preservation of jobs and power. By rolling up a 500,000-vote plurality in Cook County, Stevenson carried Daley's hacks to victory in the patronage-rich sheriff and assessor races. In the sheriff's race, for example, Democrat Richard Elrod, whose credentials consist primarily of a flying tackle on Brian Flanegan during the Weathermen "Days of Rage," won by only 10,000 votes.

Greeley's ethnic breakdown of Chicago's new congressional delegation is correct but misleading in that it implies the machine grants fair representation to ethnic groups and minorities. Chicago's machine has been and still is dominated by the Irish. Poles, Jews, Italians, but especially blacks and Spanish-speaking groups, have been and are discriminated against. (Sexual discrimination is almost total.) Chicago *will* send its second black machine man to the next Congress, but while the city's black population is conservatively estimated at 35 percent of the total, black Chicagoans have: 22 percent of the congress-man, 20 percent of the alderman, six percent of the mayor's cabinet, innumer-able white precinct captains and ward committeemen, 16 percent of the police force (virtually unrepresented among the brass), 27 percent of the public school board and four percent of the school principals (57 percent of the students are black). Though the figures are more disproportionate for other categories from judgeships to firemen, the percentage game itself is misleading. ADA voting profiles and other studies (e.g. Greenstone, *Labor in American Politics*) establish that nationally and locally Chicago machine Democrats, white and black, are significantly less liberal than their non-machine urban Democratic peers. According to *The New Republic* ratings (October 24, 1970) Chicago Democrats (excluding Rep. Abner Mikva whose initial bid for office was opposed by the machine) voted the recommended way less than 66 percent of the time. In comparison, the percentage of the New York City Democrats whom Greeley lectures is 84 percent. Again, such figures are mis-leading, for Chicago Democrats are much more liberal in Congress than in Chicago!

Throughout the agitation by blacks during the 1960s, Mayor Daley labelled demonstrators "Communists" and sought injunctions and ordinances to curb demonstrations. In 1959 the U.S. Commission on Civil Rights found Chicago the most residentially segregated city in the country. Daley has yet to enforce existing laws and revoke a single realtor's license for racial discrimination. In 1965 when federal Commissioner of Education Keppel suspended federal funds to Chicago's segregated schools, the mayor immediately obtained release of the funds. Daley's promises to Martin Luther King after the 1966 open occupancy marches have yet to be kept. Rampant discrimination persists at the public school that trains apprentices for the building trades, despite repeated pledges and plans by Daley. Greeley argued that Daley stumbled at the 1968 convention because of his lack of familiarity with the "youth culture." There is another explanation. Chicago police react according to how they are expected to react. When civil rights activists peacefully picketing Daley's home were assulted by a white mob, Daley denounced the demonstrators; the police ignored the mob and arrested the marchers. When 11 blacks were killed by police and guardsmen during a riot five months before the convention, Daley criticized the restraint of the police and issued a "shoot to kill" order.

It is said that demonstrations by blacks arouse the fears of white ethnics and thus force Daley to act tough, but that elsewhere the mayor "supports . . . such demands in ways that will not drive other groups out of his coalition." Does he? Throughout the 1960s there were no demonstrations over hospital discrimination. And studies show there was no change in the rigid discrimination practiced by white, private hospitals either. The public hospital is swamped by blacks (40 percent of whom are *not* charity patients; they are able to pay but unable to get admitted elsewhere) to a degree that hospital accreditation has been a problem for a decade. In 15 years the only time Daley revoked the license of a private hospital was when negligence resulted in the death of an infant of a middle-class white couple.

Daley is powerful for three reasons. First, the Republicans in Illinois—despite Senator Percy and Representative John Anderson—are so reactionary, so opposed to civil rights and social welfare legislation, that blacks and to a lesser degree white ethnics have no real alternative. Second, Daley uses the resources of the machine not to solve social problems but to combat the possibility of an independent alternative arising on the left. The Stevensons are slated to help elect the hacks. The local NAACP is neutralized by packing its meetings and officer board with black patronage workers. A black, independent aldermanic candidate is mysteriously shot. Black ministers whose congregations suffer from inadequate building code enforcement but who offer their churches to Dr. King and his marchers are suddenly visited by the building inspectors and presented with the alternatives of expensive remodeling, closing their facilities or being less hospitable to Dr. King. Black street gangs and their violence are largely ignored until the gangs turn political and then Daley gets into bed with Senator McClellan to stop such dangerous goings-on. Finally, while ignoring the needs of the black and the poor, Daley consistently supported the interests and prejudices of the business and upper-income white community.

Greeley's attempt to have academics and students extend their concern to the lower-middle-class ethnic and his problems is commendable. But Greeley is seriously mistaken in saying that the mayor is an asset to the little man, white or black. Though they are hidden under Chicago's relative prosperity, Daley's manner and record are quite similar, *mutatis mutandis*, to those of the machine boys in the South. Both value power and office above all else. Both deny justice to blacks. Both manipulate racism and deliver largely symbolic benefits to poor whites. Both devote their power and energy to satisfying the businessman and the rich.

During his 15 years as mayor, Daley has accomplished much in physically renewing Chicago. But this has been at the expense of the man at or near the bottom, both white (unless he's a member of the building trades) and black. Expressways and urban renewal projects which Daley pushes serve suburban commuters and downtown businessmen but increase the severe shortage of low-cost housing. The mayor's projects have destroyed Polish and Italian homes and communities as well as those of blacks. The average white ethnic does not want blacks in his neighborhood. Daley publicly responds to this fear by denouncing demonstrations and failing to enforce anti-discrimination ordinances. Yet his construction projects have forced the black community and the white ethnics to fight it out over the available housing.

Greeley did not mention: that Daley's anti-pollution board is packed with steel and utility polluters/executives; that one of the hacks carried to reelection as tax assessor on Stevenson's coattails was exposed for failure to adequately assess the property of the rich; that Daley's head of housing is not only a slumlord but is receiving over $100,000 from businessmen to arrange an urban renewal project that will displace white and black poor. Nor did Greeley explain why Chicago businessmen, strongly Republican and conservative in state and national politics, have repeatedly contributed to and campaigned for the reelection of Richard Daley.

HERBERT J. GANS

We Won't End the Urban Crisis
Until We End "Majority Rule"

In 1962, a group of us, planners and social scientists, assembled a book of essays about the city, and we called it "The Urban Condition." Had the book been published only a couple of years later, it would probably have been entitled "The Urban Problem," and today it would surely come out as "The Urban Crisis." But these catch phrases are misleading, for they divert attention from the real issues. Although American cities are in deep trouble, the real crisis is not urban but national, and stems in large part from shortcomings in American democracy, particularly the dependence on majority rule.

The troubles of the city have been catalogued in long and by now familiar lists, but I would argue that, in reality, they boil down to three: *poverty and segregation*, with all their consequences for both their victims and other urban residents; and *municipal decay*, the low quality of public services and the declining tax revenues which are rapidly leading to municipal bankruptcy. Moreover, the first two problems are actually the major cause of the third, for the inability of the poor to pay their share of keeping up the city, as well as the crime and other pathology stimulated by poverty and segregation have brought about much of the municipal decay. In addition, the fear of the ghetto poor has recently accelerated the middle-class exodus, thus depriving cities of an important source of taxes at the very moment their expenditures have been increased by the needs of the poor. Consequently, the elimination of urban poverty and segregation would go far toward relieving the other problems of the city.

Neither poverty and segregation nor municipal decay are unique to the city, however; indeed, they are often more prevalent in rural areas. More important, all three problems are caused by nationwide conditions. Poverty is to a considerable extent a by-product of the American economy, which is today growing only in the industries and services that employ the skilled, semi-professional and professional worker, and, in fact, many of the unskilled now living in urban slums were driven out of rural areas where the demand for

Source: Mr. Gans, a sociologist and planner, is the author of *The Levittowners* and *People and Plans*. This article is from *The New York Times Magazine*, Aug. 3, 1969, pp. 12–15, 20, 24, 26–28. © 1969 by The New York Times Company. Reprinted by permission.

126

their labor had dried up even earlier than in the cities. Municipal decay is similarly national in cause, for small communities can also no longer collect enough in taxes to provide the needed public services, and their populations, too, are becoming increasingly poor and black as the nationwide suburbanization of the middle class proceeds.

In short, the so-called urban crisis is actually an American crisis, brought on largely by our failure to deal with the twin evils of poverty and segregation. This failure has often been ascribed to a lack of national will, as if the country were an individual who could pull himself together if he only wanted to, but even the miraculous emergence of a national consensus would not be sufficient, for the sources of our failure are built into our most important economic and political institutions.

One major source of failure is the corporate economy, which has not realized, or been made to realize, that the rural and urban unskilled workers it has cast aside are part of the same economic process which has created affluence or near-affluence for most Americans. As a result, private enterprise has been able to improve productivity and profit without having to charge against its profit the third of the population which must live in poverty or near-poverty. Instead, government has been left the responsibility for this by-product of the economic process, just as it has often been given the task of removing the waste materials that are a by-product of the production process.

But government has not been able or willing to require private enterprise—and its own public agencies—to incorporate the employable poor into the economy. Not only is there as yet little recognition among the general public or most of our leaders of the extent to which urban and rural poverty result from the structure of the economy, but private enterprise is powerful enough to persuade most people that government should take care of the poor or subsidize industry to create jobs for them.

However, government—whether Federal, state or local—has not been able or willing to absorb responsibility for the poor either, and for several important political reasons.

First, most voters—and the politicians that represent them—are not inclined to give the cities the funds and powers to deal with poverty, or segregation. This disinclination is by no means as arbitrary as it may seem, for the plight of the urban poor, the anger of the rebellious, and the bankruptcy of the municipal treasury have not yet hurt or even seriously inconvenienced the vast majority of Americans.

Rural and small-town America make little use of the city anyway, except for occasional tourist forays, and the city financial institutions which play an influential part in their economies are not impaired in their functioning by the urban condition. Suburbanites may complain about the dirt, crime and traffic congestion when they commute to city jobs, but they can still get downtown without difficulty, and, besides, many of their employers are also moving out to the suburbs.

But even the city-dwellers who are neither poor nor black can pursue their daily routines unchanged, for most of them never need to enter the slum areas and ghettos. Only the urbanites who work in these areas or live near them are directly touched by the urban condition—and they are a small minority of America's voters.

Second, many Americans, regardless of where they live, are opposed to significant governmental activity on behalf of the poor and black—or, for that matter, to further governmental participation in the economy. Not only do they consider taxes an imposition on their ability to spend their earnings, but they view governmental expenditure as economic waste, whereas private enterprise expenditures are proudly counted in the Gross National Product. The average American taxpayer is generous in paying for the defense of the country and for projects that increase American power and prestige in the world, be it a war in Vietnam or a moon shot, but he is often opposed to governmental activities that help anyone other than himself. The very corporations and workers whose incomes depend on government contracts often fight against Federal support of other activities and groups—and without ever becoming aware of the contradiction.

Consequently, many taxpayers and voters refuse to see the extent to which governmental activities create jobs and provide incomes, and how much government subsidizes some sectors of American life but not others. By and large, these subsidies go to people who need them less: there are tax exemptions for homeowners, Federal highway programs and mortgage insurance for suburbanites; direct subsidies to airlines, merchant shipping, large farms, colleges and college students; and, of course, the depletion allowance for oil producers. Grants to the poor are fewer and smaller; the most significant one is public welfare, and it is called a handout, not a subsidy.

Subsidies are generally provided not on the basis of merit but power, and this is a *third* reason for the lack of action in the cities. Even though many Americans live in the city, urban areas and their political representatives have relatively little power, and the poor, of course, yet less. The poor are powerless because they are a minority of the population, are often difficult to organize, and are not even a homogeneous group with similar interests that could be organized into an effective pressure group.

The cities are relatively powerless because of the long-time gerrymandering of American state and Federal governments in favor of rural and small-town areas. As a result, rural-dominated state legislatures can use the tax receipts of the cities to subsidize their own areas, and Congressmen from these areas have been able to outvote the representatives of urban constituencies. The Supreme Court's requirement of one man-one vote is now bringing about reapportionment, but it may be too late for the cities. As more and more Americans leave for the suburbs, it appears that the cities will not be able to increase their power, for voters and politicians from rural and suburban areas who share a common interest in not helping the cities can unite against them.

In effect, then, the cities and the poor and the black are politically out-numbered. This state of affairs suggests the *fourth* and perhaps most important reason for the national failure to act: the structure of American democracy and majority rule.

America, more so than other democratic nations in the world, runs its political structure on the basis of majority rule. A majority vote in our various political institutions determines who will be nominated and elected to office, what legislation will be passed and funded, and who will be appointed to run the administering and administrative agencies. Of course, the candidates, laws and budgets which are subject to the vote of the majority are almost always determined by minorities; the only men who can run for office these days are either affluent or financed by the affluent groups who donate the campaign funds, and the legislation these men vote on is often suggested or even drafted by campaign-fund donors or other small groups with specific interests in government action. Properly speaking then, American democracy allows afflu-ent minorities to propose, and the majority to dispose.

There is nothing intrinsically conspiratorial about this phenomenon, for it follows from the nature of American political participation. Although every citizen is urged to be active in the affairs of his community and nation, in actual practice participation is almost entirely limited to organized interest groups or lobbies who want something from government.

As a result, legislation tends to favor the interests of the organized: of businessmen, not consumers, even though the latter are a vast majority; of landlords, not tenants; doctors, not patients. Unorganized citizens may gripe about the lack of consumer legislation or even the defense budget, but only when their interests are similar and immediately threatened so that they can organize or be organized are they able to affect governmental affairs.

This is not to say that governmental decisions often violate the wishes of a majority of Americans, for, by and large, that majority is usually happy—or at least not too unhappy—with the decisions of its governments. The almost $100-billion spent annually for defense and space exploration are appropriated because, until recently, the majority of the voters wanted a victory in Vietnam and a man on the moon before the Russians. There is no Federal mass-transit program because the majority of Americans, even in the cities, prefer to use their cars; and Congress can pay more attention to a small number of tobacco farmers and producers than to the danger of cigarette smoking because the majority is not sufficiently concerned about this danger, and, as a recent study showed, many heavy smokers do not even believe that smoking leads to cancer or heart disease.

But while the American political structure often satisfies the majority, it also creates *outvoted minorities* who can be tyrannized and repressed by majority rule, such as the poor and the black, students, migrant workers and many others. In the past, such minorities have had to rely on the goodwill of the majority, hoping that it would act morally, but it generally offered them only charity, if that much. For example, the majority has granted the poor miserly welfare payments, and then added dehumanizing regulations for obtaining and spending the funds.

Today, many outvoted minorities have tired of waiting for an upturn in public altruism and are exerting political pressure on the majority. Thus, the poor and the black have been organizing their own pressure groups, forming coalitions with more powerful minorities (like the progressive wing of the labor movement) and getting support from liberals, other advocates of social justice and guilty whites. Indeed, such methods enabled the poor and the black to achieve the civil rights and antipoverty programs of the nineteen-sixties.

Even so, these gains, however much of an improvement they represent over the past, remain fairly small, and have not significantly improved the living conditions of large numbers in the slums and ghettos. Moreover, the activities of ghetto demonstrators and rioters have cooled some of the ardor of white liberals and trade unionists, and it is questionable whether many other groups would derive much benefit from coalition with poor or black organizations. Like all outvoted minorities, they can offer little to a coalition except the moral urgency of their cause.

Consequently, the poor and the black are caught in an almost hopeless political bind, for any programs that would produce significant gains, such as a massive antipoverty effort, an effective assault on segregation or even a workable community control scheme, are likely to be voted down by the majority, or the coalitions of minorities that make up majorities in American political life. *Moreover, since the poor and the black will probably always be outvoted by the majority, they are thus doomed to be permanently outvoted minorities.*

But if I am correct in arguing that the urban condition cannot be improved until poverty and segregation are eliminated or sharply reduced, it is likely that *under the present structure of American government there cannot be and will not be a real solution to the problem of the cities.*

The only other source of power left to outvoted minorities is *disruption,* upsetting the orderly processes of government and of daily life so as to inconvenience or threaten more powerful groups. This explains why the ghettos have rebelled, why young people sometimes resort to what adults consider to be meaningless delinquency, or students to occupations of school buildings, or working-class people to occasionally violent forms of white backlash.

Although disruption is bitterly attacked as antisocial by defenders of the existing social order, strikes were also once considered antisocial, but are now so legitimate that they are no longer even thought of as a form of disruption. The disrupters of today do not strike, but their methods have not been so unproductive as their opponents would have us believe. The ghetto rebellions have been responsible for stimulating private enterprise to find jobs for the so-called hard-core unemployed; the sit-ins—as well as the organizational activity—of the Welfare Rights movement have won higher grants for welfare recipients in some cities and have helped to arouse the interest of the Nixon Administration in re-examining the Federal welfare program; and the uprisings by college and high school students have been effective in winning them a voice in their schools.

Needless to say, disruption also has disadvantages: the possibility that it will be accompanied by violence and that it will be followed by counter-disruption—for example, police or vigilante violence—and by political efforts of more powerful groups to wipe out the gains achieved through disruption. Thus, the backlash generated by the ghetto rebellions has been partly responsible for the cutback in antipoverty and civil-rights efforts, and the disruptions by welfare recipients and college students are now producing repressive legislation against both groups. But disruption also creates serious costs for the rest of society, particularly in terms of the polarization of opposing groups, the hardening of attitudes among other citizens, and the hysterical atmosphere which then results in more repressive legislation. Clearly, disruption is not the ideal way for outvoted minorities to achieve their demands.

Nevertheless, disruption has become an accepted political technique, and may be used more widely in the nineteen-seventies, as other groups who feel they are being short-changed by American democracy begin to voice their demands. Consequently, perhaps the most important domestic issue before the country today is whether outvoted minorities—in the cities and elsewhere —must resort to further disruption, or whether more peaceful and productive ways of meeting their needs can be found.

If the outvoted minorities are to be properly represented in the political structure, two kinds of changes are necessary. First, they must be counted fairly, so that they are actually consulted in the decision-making process, and are not overpowered by other minorities who would be outvoted were they not affluent enough to shape the political agenda. But since even a fairer counting of the voters would still leave the outvoted minorities with little influence, ways of restricting majority rule must be found when that rule is always deaf to their demands.

Majority rule is, of course, one of the unquestioned traditions of American political life, for the first axiom of democracy has always been that the majority should decide. But democracy is not inviolably equivalent to majority rule, for government of the people, by the people and for the people need not mean that a majority is "the people." Indeed, despite its traditional usage in democracies, majority rule is little more than an easily applied quantitative formula for solving the knotty problems of how the wishes of the people are to be determined. Moreover, traditions deserve to be re-examined from time to time, particularly if society has changed since they came into being.

And American society has changed since its government was created. What might be called *majoritarian democracy* was adopted when America was a small and primarily agrarian nation, with a great degree of economic and cultural homogeneity, few conflicting interest groups, and a since-rejected tradition that the propertyless should have fewer rights than the propertied. As a result, there were few serious disputes between majorities and minorities, at least until the Civil War, and majoritarian democracy could be said to have worked. Today, however, America is a highly heterogeneous and pluralistic nation, a society of minority groups, so to speak, and every important political decision requires an intense amount of negotiation and compromise so that enough minorities can be found to create a majority coalition. And even then, America is so pluralistic that not all minorities can be accommodated and must suffer all the consequences of being outvoted.

America has been a pluralistic society for almost a century, but the shortcomings of majority rule have not become a public issue before, mainly because previous generations of outvoted groups had other forms of redress. The outvoted of the past were concentrated among poor ethnic and racial minorities, as they are today, but in earlier years the economy needed their unskilled labor, so that they had less incentive to confront the majority, except to fight for the establishment of labor unions. Moreover, they had little reason even to think about majority rule, for government played a smaller role in the economy and in their lives.

Now all this has changed. When governmental policies and appropriations very nearly decide the fate of the poor, the black, draft-age college students, disadvantaged high school students, and not so affluent blue-collar workers, such groups must deal with government; and more often than not, their demands are frustrated by the workings of majority rule.

Thus, it becomes quite pertinent to ask whether majoritarian democracy is still viable, and whether the tradition of majority rule should not be re-examined. If three-fourths of the voters or of a legislative body are agreed on a course of action, it is perhaps hard to argue against majority rule, but what if that rule seriously deprives the other fourth and drives it to disruption? And what if the majority is no more than 55 per cent, and consists only of an uneasy and temporary coalition of minorities? Or if the remaining 45 per cent are unable to obtain compromises from the slender majority?

I believe that the time has come to modernize American democracy and adapt it to the needs of a pluralistic society; in short, to create a *pluralistic democracy*. A pluralistic form of democracy would not do away with majority rule, but would require systems of proposing and disposing which take the needs of minorities into consideration, so that when majority rule has serious negative consequences, outvoted minorities would be able to achieve their most important demands, and not be forced to accept tokenism, or resort to despair or disruption.

Pluralistic democracy would allow the innumerable minorities of which America is made up to live together and share the country's resources more equitably, with full recognition of their various diversities. Legislation and appropriations would be based on the principle of "live and let live," with different programs of actions for different groups whenever consensus is impossible. Groups of minorities could still coalesce into a majority, but other minorities would be able to choose their own ways of using public power and funds without being punished for it by a majority.

It would take a book to describe how the American political system might be restructured to create a pluralistic democracy, but I can suggest some specific proposals toward this goal. They fall into two categories: those that incorporate outvoted minorities into the political structure by increasing the responsiveness of governments to the diversity of citizen interests—and to all citizens; and those which restrict majority rule so as to prevent the tyrannization of minorities. Many of my proposals have drawbacks, and some are outright utopian, but I suggest them more to illustrate what has to be done than to provide immediate feasible solutions.

The responsiveness of governments can be increased in several ways.

First, the one man-one vote principle must be extended to all levels of government and the political parties. County and municipal bodies need to be reapportioned to eliminate gerrymandering of the poor and the black; party leaders, high and low, should be elected by party members, and party candidates should be nominated by primaries, rather than by conventions or closed meetings of party leaders.

Second, the seniority system must be abolished in all legislatures, so that politicians can no longer obtain undue power simply because their own districts re-elect them time after time. The power of committee chairmen who may represent only a small number of voters to block legislation wanted by a larger number must also be eliminated.

Third, the administrative agencies and their bureaucracies must become more accountable, perhaps by replacing appointive officers with elective ones, or by requiring such bodies to be run by elected boards of directors.

Fourth, all election campaigns should be funded by government, to discourage the near-monopoly that wealthy individuals now have in becoming candidates, and to prevent affluent interest groups from making demands on candidates as a price for financing their campaigns. If equal amounts—and plenty of free television time—were given to all candidates, even from third, fourth and fifth parties, the diversity of the population would be better represented in the electoral process. This might lead to election by plurality rather than majority, although in a highly diverse community or state such an outcome might not be undesirable, and run-offs can always be required to produce a final majority vote.

Fifth, methods by which the citizenry communicates with its elected representatives ought to be improved. Today, legislators tend to hear only from lobbyists, people in their own social circles, and the writers of letters and newspaper editorialists—a highly biased sample of their constituencies. Indeed, the only way an ordinary citizen can communicate is by organizing or writing letters. Of course, such methods make sure that a legislator hears only from deeply interested citizens, protecting him from being overwhelmed by too much feedback, but they also discriminate against equally interested people who cannot organize or write.

One possible solution is for governments to make postage-free forms available for people who want to write letters to their representatives, to be picked up in banks, post offices, stores and taverns. Another solution is for governments to finance the establishment of regular but independently run public-opinion polls on every major issue, so that government officials can obtain adequate feedback from a random sample of their constituents, and not only on the few issues a handful of private pollsters today decide are worth polling about.

Yet another solution is for governments to encourage people to organize politically, by allowing them to claim as tax deductions the dues and contributions to lobbying organizations (other than political parties). Limits on the size of such deductions would have to be set to prevent affluent minorities from using their funds to gain extra power; and organizations of the poor, whose members cannot afford to pay dues and do not benefit from tax deductions, could be given government grants if they could prove that two-thirds of their members were poor.

Feasible methods for increasing the power of minorities at the expense of majority rule are more difficult to formulate. One approach is to enhance the power of existing institutions that represent minority interests—for example, the courts and Cabinet departments. If constitutional amendments to establish an economic and racial bill of rights could be passed, for instance, a provision giving every American citizen the right to a job or an income above the poverty-line, the power of the poor would be increased somewhat.

Cabinet departments also represent minority interests, particularly at the Federal and state levels, although more often than not they speak for affluent minorities. Nevertheless, if the Office of Economic Opportunity were raised to full Cabinet status and a Department of Minorities established in Washington, at least some new legislation and higher appropriations for the poor and the black would result. In other Cabinet departments, new bureaus should be set up to represent the interests of outvoted minorities; in Housing and Urban Development (now dominated by builders and mayors), to look after the needs of slum dwellers; in Health, Education and Welfare, to deal with the concerns of patients, students and welfare recipients, respectively. Moreover, the policy-making boards that I suggested earlier to oversee Cabinet departments and other administrative agencies should include their clients. Thus, all school boards should include some students; welfare departments, some welfare recipients; and housing agencies, some residents of public housing and F.H.A.-supported projects.

The financial power of poor minorities could be increased by extending the principles of the progressive income tax and of school-equalization payments to all governmental expenditures. Funding of government programs could be based in part on the incomes of eventual recipients, so that the lower their income, the higher the government grant. Poorer communities would thus obtain more Federal money per capita for all public services, and subsidies for mass transit programs would automatically be higher than for expressways to suburbia.

In addition, changes in the electoral system would be needed. One solution would be election by proportional representation. P.R. has not been popular in America, partly because it wreaks havoc with the two-party system, but it is not at all clear whether a pluralistic society is best served by a two-party system to begin with. Proportional representation by race or income would go against the American grain, but as long as racial and economic integration seems to be unachievable in the near future, this solution might be more desirable than forcing the poor or the black to resort to disruption.

Actually, proportional representation is already practiced informally in many places; in New York City, election slates have always been "balanced" to include candidates from the major ethnic and religious groups. Perhaps we should even think about proportional representation by occupational groups, for job concerns are often uppermost in the voters' choices. After all, many pro-Wallace factory workers voted for Humphrey at the last minute, realizing that their job interests were more important than their fear of black militancy.

Another approach would restrict majority rule directly, by making all elections and voting procedures in legislative branches of government go through a two-step process, with majority rule applying only to the final step. This system, somewhat like the runoff used in some state and municipal elections, would require that if any legislative proposal or appropriation obtains at least 25 per cent of the total vote, it must be revised and voted on again until it is either approved by a majority or rejected by 76 per cent of the voting body. In the meantime, compromises would have to be made, either watering down the initial proposal so that a majority could accept it, or satisfying other demands of the minority through the time-honored practice of log-rolling so that they would allow 76 per cent of the voting body to reject the original proposal.

For example, if at least a quarter of a Congressional committee supported a strong negative income tax, it is likely that the second vote would produce at least a weaker version of the tax that the majority could live with. Of course, such a system would work only if outvoted minority groups were able to elect representatives in the first place. (Also, it is always possible that legislators who favored a highly regressive income tax or segregationist policies would be able to obtain legislation for *their* minorities, but if an economic and racial bill of rights were added to the Constitution, such legislation would be thrown out by the courts.)

Outvoted minorities can also achieve greater political power by the alteration of existing political boundaries and powers so that they could even

become majorities in their own balliwicks. Current proposals for decentraliza-
tion and community control are boundary-altering schemes with just this
political consequence, and some of the disadvantages of these schemes today
could be alleviated by my previous proposal for progressive methods of government funding to provide more money to poorer communities.

But the concept of redrawing boundaries ought to be applied more broadly,
for many existing political subdivisions are anachronistic. For example, it is
difficult to justify the existence of many of the states as political units today,
and it might be useful to think about creating smaller and more homogeneous
units in highly urbanized parts of the country, perhaps of county size, particularly in order to reduce the number of outvoted minorities. (Norman
Mailer has suggested just that in proposing statehood for New York City.)

Along the same line, the old idea of replacing geographical political units
by groupings along economic and other interests deserves re-examination. For
instance, the welfare recipient's lot would probably be improved if he or she
became part of a regional governmental body of welfare recipients which
could determine how the welfare system ought to be run.

Sometimes, outvoted minorities are tyrannized because their demands are
diametrically opposed to the majority's. When this happens within a school
or other institution, the minority should have the right to secede, establishing
its own institution without being financially punished by the majority. If
some parents want a Summerhill education for their children, they should be
given tax money to start their own school, just as determined black nationalists
should be free to build their own community if and when public aid for new
towns becomes available. In a pluralistic nation, all impulses for diversity that
do not clearly harm the rest of society should be encouraged.

Finally, changes in the rules of the political system must be supplemented
by changes in the economic system, for ultimately it is the major obstacle to
improving the lot of many outvoted minorities—and even of the unorganized
majority. Some of my earlier proposals are equally applicable here.

The one-man, one-vote principle might be extended to stockholders who
elect corporate boards of directors; a Cabinet department to represent consumers and other corporate customers should be set up; feedback from stockholders and customers to the corporate "legislature" should be improved,
and they, as well as workers, should sit on corporate boards. In an era when
many firms are subsidized by government contracts and tax credits, it is
certainly possible to argue that at least such firms should become more
democratic.

Most of the proposals for a pluralistic democracy are purposely intended
to enhance the power of poor and black minorities; for, as I noted earlier, this
seems to me the only way of solving the problems of the cities. But such a
democracy is needed by all minorities who stand in danger of being outvoted
by a majority, whatever their income or color. As the current demands of
more people for greater equality and more control over their lives accelerate,

and the role of government in society continues to mount at the same time, the need for more political pluralism will become increasingly urgent. What we so inaccurately describe as the urban crisis is in reality the beginning of a national political crisis. But it is also an opportunity for Americans to develop new ways of living together.

JOHN FISCHER

How I Got Radicalized:
The Making of an Agitator for Zero

To my astonishment, the political convictions that I had cherished for most of my life have suddenly deserted me. Like my children, these were convictions I loved dearly and had nurtured at considerable expense. When last seen they were—like all of us—somewhat battered by the events of the last decade, but they looked durable enough to last out my time. So I was disconcerted when I found that somehow, during the past winter, they sort of melted away, without my consent and while I was looking somewhere else.

Their place has been usurped by a new set of convictions so radical that they alarm me. If the opposite kind of thing had happened, I would have felt a little melancholy but not surprised, since people traditionally grow more conservative as they get older. But to discover that one has suddenly turned into a militant subversive is downright embarrassing; at times I wonder whether it signals the onset of second childhood.

Except that I seem to be a lot more radical than the children. Those SDS youngsters who go around breaking windows and clubbing policemen now merely depress me with their frivolous irrelevance. So do most other varieties of New Leftists, such as the Women's Liberation movement; if some dire

Source: Mr. Fischer is the author of several books and writes "The Easy Chair" column in *Harper's Magazine*. This article is from *Harper's Magazine*, April 1970, pp. 18, 20, 26, 28–29. Copyright © 1970, by Minneapolis Star and Tribune Co., Inc. Reprinted from the April 1970 issue of *Harper's Magazine* by permission of the author.

accident should, God forbid, throw one of those ladies into my clutches, she can be sure of instant liberation. I am equally out of tune with those old fogies, the Communists. The differences between capitalism and Communism no longer seem to me worth fighting about, or even arguing, since they are both wrong and beside the point. Or so it seems to me, since the New Vision hit me on my own small road to Damascus.

Let me make it plain that none of this was my doing. I feel as Charles Darwin must have felt during the last leg of his voyage on the *Beagle.* When he embarked he had been a conventional (if slightly lackadaisical) Christian, who took the literal truth of Genesis for granted. He had been raised in that faith, as I was raised a Brass Collar Democrat, and had no thought of forsaking it. Only gradually, while he examined fossil shellfish high in the Andes and measured the growth of coral deposits and the bills of Galapagos finches, did he begin to doubt that the earth and all its inhabitants had been created in six days of October, 4004 B.C., according to the pious calculations of Archbishop James Ussher. By the time he got back to England, he found himself a reluctant evolutionist, soon to be damned as a heretic and underminer of the Established Church. This was not his fault. It was the fault of those damned finches.

Recently I too have been looking at finches, so to speak, although mine are mostly statistical and not nearly as pretty as Darwin's. His gave him a hint about the way the earth's creatures came into being; mine, to my terror, seem to hint at the way they may go out. While I am by no means an uncritical admirer of the human race, I have become rather fond of it, and would hate to see it disappear. Finding ways to save it—if we are not too late already—now strikes me as the political issue which takes precedence over all others.

One of the events which led to my conversion was my unexpected appointment to a committee set up by Governor John Dempsey of Connecticut to work out an environmental policy for our state. Now I had been fretting for quite a while about what is happening to our environment—who hasn't?— but until the work of the committee forced me into systematic study, I had not realized that my political convictions were in danger. Then after looking at certain hairy facts for a few months, I found myself convinced that the Democratic party, and most of our institutions of government, and even the American Way of Life are no damned good. In their present forms, at least, they will have to go. Either that, or everybody goes—and sooner than we think.

To begin with, look at the American Way of Life. Its essence is a belief in growth. Every Chamber of Commerce is bent on making its Podunk grow into the Biggest Little City in the country. Wall Street is dedicated to its search for growth stocks, so that Xerox has become the American ideal— superseding George Washington, who expressed *his* faith in growth by speculating in land. Each year Detroit prays for a bigger car market. Businessmen spend their lives in pursuit of an annual increase in sales, assets, and net profits. All housewives—except for a few slatterns without ambition—yearn for bigger houses, bigger cars, and bigger salary checks. The one national goal that everybody agrees on is an ever-growing Gross National Product. Our modern priesthood—the economists who reassure us that our mystic impulses are moral and holy—recently announced that the GNP would reach a trillion dollars early in this decade. I don't really understand what a trillion is, but when I read the news I rejoiced, along with everybody else. Surely that means that we were in sight of ending poverty, for the first time in human history, so that nobody would ever again need to go hungry or live in a slum.

Now I know better. In these past months I have come to understand that a zooming Gross National Product leads not to salvation, but to suicide. So does a continuing growth in population, highway mileage, kilowatts, plane travel, steel tonnage, or anything else you care to name.

The most important lesson of my life—learned shamefully late—was that nonstop growth just isn't possible, for Americans or anybody else. For we live in what I've learned to recognize as a tight ecological system: a smallish planet with a strictly limited supply of everything, including air, water, and places to dump sewage. There is no conceivable way in which it can be made bigger. If Homo sapiens insists on constant growth, within this system's inelastic walls, something has to pop, or smother. Already the United States is an overpopulated country: not so hopelessly overcrowded as Japan or India, of course, but well beyond the limits which would make a good life attainable for everybody. Stewart Udall, former Secretary of Interior and now a practicing ecologist, has estimated that the optimum population for America would be about 100 million, or half of our present numbers. And unless we do something, drastic and fast, we can expect another 100 million within the next thirty years.

So our prime national goal, I am now convinced, should be to reach Zero Growth Rate as soon as possible. Zero growth in people, in GNP, and in our consumption of everything. That is the only hope of attaining a stable ecology: that is, of halting the deterioration of the environment on which our lives depend.

This of course is a profoundly subversive notion. It runs squarely against the grain of both capitalism and the American dream. It is equally subversive of Communism, since the Communists are just as hooked on the idea of perpetual growth as any American businessman. Indeed, when Khrushchev was top man in the Kremlin, he proclaimed that 1970 would be the year in which the Russians would surpass the United States in output of goods. They didn't make it: a fact for which their future generations may be grateful, because their environment is just as fragile as ours, and as easily damaged by headlong expansion. If you think the Hudson River and Lake Erie are unique examples of pollution, take a look at the Volga and Lake Baikal.

No political party, here or abroad, has yet even considered adopting Zero Growth Rate as the chief plank in its platform. Neither has any politician dared to speak out loud about what "protection of the environment" really means—although practically all of them seem to have realized, all of a sudden, that it is becoming an issue they can't ignore. So far, most of them have tried to handle it with gingerly platitudes, while keeping their eyes tightly closed to the implications of what they say. In his January State of the Union message, for instance, President Nixon made the customary noises about pollution; but he never even mentioned the population explosion, and he specifically denied that there is any "fundamental contradiction between economic growth and the quality of life." He sounded about as convincing as a doctor telling a cancer patient not to worry about the growth of his tumor.

The Democrats are no better. I have not heard any of them demanding a halt to all immigration, or a steeply progressive income tax on each child beyond two, or an annual bounty to every woman between the ages of fifteen and forty-five who gets through the year without becoming pregnant. Neither Ted Sorensen nor any of the other Kennedy henchmen has yet suggested that a politician with a big family is a spacehog and a hypocrite, unworthy of public trust. No Democrat, to my knowledge, has ever endorsed the views of Dr. René Dubos of Rockefeller University, one of the truly wise men of our time. In an editorial in the November 14, 1969, issue of *Science* he predicted that in order to survive, "mankind will have to develop what might be called a steady state . . . a nearly closed system" in which most materials from tin cans to sewage would be "recycled instead of discarded." His conclusion—that a viable future depends on the creation of "social and economic systems different from the ones in which we live today"—apparently is too radical for any politician I know.

Consequently I feel a little lonesome in my newfound political convictions. The only organization which seems to share them is a tiny one, founded only a few months ago: Zero Population Growth, Inc., with headquarters at 367 State Street, Los Altos, California 94022. Yet I have a hunch that I may not be lonesome for long. Among college students a concern with ecology has become, almost overnight, nearly as popular as sideburns. On many campuses it seems to be succeeding civil rights and Vietnam as The Movement. For example, when the University of Oregon announced last January a new course, "Can Man Survive?", it drew six thousand students, the biggest class in the university's history. They had to meet in the basketball court because no classroom would hold them.

Who knows? Maybe we agitators for Zero may yet turn out to be the wave of the future.

At the same time I was losing my faith in the virtues of growth, I began to doubt two other articles of the American credo.

One of them is the belief that technology can fix anything. Like most of us, I had always taken it for granted that any problem could be solved if we just applied enough science, money, and good old American know-how. Is the world's population outrunning its food supply? Well, then, let's put the laboratories to work inventing high-yield strains of rice and wheat, better fertilizers, ways to harvest seaweed, hydroponic methods for growing food without soil. If the air is becoming unbreathable, surely the technologists can find ways to clean it up. If our transportation system is a national disgrace, all we have to do is call in the miracle men who built a shuttle service to the moon; certainly they should be able to figure out some way to get a train from New York to New Haven on time.

I was in East Haddam, Connecticut, looking at an atomic power plant, when I began to suspect that technology might not be the answer after all. While I can't go along with the young Luddites who have decided that science is evil and that all inventions since the wheel ought to be destroyed, I am persuaded that technology is a servant of only limited usefulness, and highly unreliable. When it does solve a problem, it often creates two new ones—and their side effects are usually hard to foresee.

One of the things that brought me to East Haddam was curiosity about the automobile. Since the gasoline engine is the main polluter of the air, maybe it should be replaced with some kind of electric motor? That of course would require an immense increase in our production of electric power, in order to recharge ten million batteries every night. Where would it come from? Virtually all waterpower sites already are in use. More coal- and oil-fired power stations don't sound like a good idea, since they too pour smoke into the atmosphere—and coal mining already has ruined countless streams and hundreds of thousands of acres of irreplaceable land. Atomic power, then?

At first glance, the East Haddam plant, which is fairly typical of the new technology, looked encouraging. It is not as painful an eyesore as coal-burning stations, and not a wisp of smoke was in sight. When I began to ask questions, however, the company's public-relations man admitted that there are a few little problems. For one thing, the plant's innards are cooled with water pumped out of the Connecticut River. When it flows back in, this water raises the river's temperature by about twenty degrees, for a considerable distance. Apparently this has not yet done any serious damage to the shad, the only fish kept under careful surveillance; but its effect on other fish and algae, fish eggs, microorganisms, and the general ecology of the river is substantial though still unmeasured.

It would be possible, though expensive, for the company to build cooling towers, where the water would trickle over a series of baffles before returning to the river. In the process it would lose its heat to the atmosphere. But this, in turn, threatens climatic changes, such as banks of artificial fog rolling eastward over Long Island Sound, and serious wastage of water through evaporation from a river system where water already is in precarious supply. Moreover, neither this process nor any other now known would eliminate the slight, but not negligible, radiation which every atomic plant throws off, nor the remote but still omnipresent chance of a nuclear accident which could take thousands of lives. The building of an additional twenty plants along the banks of the

Connecticut—which some estimates call for, in order to meet future demand for electricity—would be a clear invitation to an ecological disaster.

In the end I began to suspect that there is no harmless way to meet the demands for power of a rising population, with rising living standards—much less for a new herd of millions of electric cars. Every additional kilowatt levies some tax upon the environment, in one form or another. The Fourth Law of Thermodynamics seems to be: "There is no free lunch."

Every time you look at one of the marvels of modern technology, you find a by-product—unintended, unpredictable, and often lethal. Since World War II American agriculture has performed miracles in increasing production. One result was that we were able for years to send a shipload of free wheat every day to India, saving millions from starvation. The by-products were: (1) a steady rise in India's population; (2) the poisoning of our streams and lakes with insecticides and chemical fertilizers; (3) the forced migration of some ten million people from the countryside to city slums, as agriculture became so efficient it no longer needed their labor.

Again, the jet plane is an unquestionable convenience, capable of whisking a New Yorker, say, to either the French Riviera or Southern California in a tenth of the time he could travel by ship or car, and at lower cost. But when he reaches his destination, the passenger finds the beaches coated with oil (intended to fuel planes, if it hadn't spilled) and the air thick with smog (thanks in good part to the jets, each of which spews out as much hydrocarbon as ten thousand automobiles).

Moreover, technology works best on things nobody really needs, such as collecting moon rocks or building supersonic transport planes. Whenever we try to apply it to something serious, it usually falls on its face.

An obvious case in point is the railroads. We already have the technology to build fast, comfortable passenger trains. Such trains are, in fact, already in operation in Japan, Italy, and a few other countries. Experimental samples —the Metroliners and Turbotrains—also are running with spectacular success between Washington and Boston. If we had enough of them to handle commuter and middle-distance traffic throughout the country, we could stop building the highways and airports which disfigure our countryside, reduce the number of automobiles contaminating the air, and solve many problems of urban congestion. But so far we have not been able to apply the relatively simple technology needed to accomplish these aims, because some tough political decisions have to be made before we can unleash the scientists and engineers. We would have to divert to the railroads many of the billions in subsidy which we now lavish on highways and air routes. We would have to get rid of our present railroad management—in general, the most incompetent in American industry—and retire the doddering old codgers of the Railway Brotherhoods who make such a mess out of running our trains. This might mean public ownership of a good many rail lines. It certainly would mean all-out war with the unions, the auto and aviation industries, and the highway lobby. It would mean ruthless application of the No Growth principle to roads, cars, and planes, while we make sensible use instead of something we already have: some 20,000 miles of railways.

All this requires political action, of the most radical kind. Until our Great Slob Society is willing to take it, technology is helpless.

My final apostasy from the American Creed was loss of faith in private property. I am now persuaded that there no longer is such a thing as truly private property, at least in land. That was a luxury we could afford only when the continent was sparsely settled. Today the use a man makes of his land cannot be left to his private decision alone, since eventually it is bound to affect everybody else. This conclusion I reached in anguish, since I own a tiny patch of land and value its privacy above anything money can buy.

What radicalized me on this score was the Department of Agriculture and Dr. Ian McHarg. From those dull volumes of statistics which the Department publishes from time to time, I discovered that usable land is fast becoming a scarce resource—and that we are wasting it with an almost criminal lack of foresight. Every year, more than a million acres of farm and forest land is being eaten up by highways, airports, reservoirs, and real-estate developments. The best, too, in most cases, since the rich, flat bottom lands are the most tempting to developers.

Since America is, for the moment, producing a surplus of many crops, this destruction of farmland has not yet caused much public alarm. But some day, not too far off, the rising curve of population and the falling curve of food-growing land inevitably are going to intersect. That is the day when we may begin to understand what hunger means.

Long before that, however, we may be gasping for breath. For green plants are our only source of oxygen. They also are the great purifiers of the atmosphere, since in the process of photosynthesis they absorb carbon dioxide—an assignment which gets harder every day, as our chimneys and exhaust pipes spew out ever-bigger tonnage of carbon gases. This is a function not only of trees and grass, but also of the tiny microorganisms in the sea. Indeed, its phytoplankton produces some 70 percent of all the oxygen on which life depends. These are delicate little creatures, easily killed by the sewage, chemicals, and oil wastes which already are contaminating every ocean in the world. Nobody knows when the scale will tip: when there are no longer enough green growing things to preserve the finely balanced mixture of gases in the atmosphere, by absorbing carbon dioxide and generating oxygen. All we know is that man is pressing down hard on the lethal end of the scale.

The Survivable Society, if we are able to construct it, will no longer permit a farmer to convert his meadow into a parking lot any time he likes. He will have to understand that his quick profit may, quite literally, take the bread out of his grandchildren's mouths, and the oxygen from their lungs. For the same reasons, housing developments will not be located where they suit the whim of a real-estate speculator or even the convenience of the residents.

They will have to go on those few carefully chosen sites where they will do the least damage to the landscape, and to the life-giving greenery which it supports.

This is one of the lessons taught by Ian McHarg in his extraordinary book, *Design with Nature*, recently published by Natural History Press. Alas, its price, $19.95, will keep it from reaching the people who need it most. It ought to be excerpted into a pocket-size volume—entitled, perhaps, "The Thoughts of McHarg"—and distributed free in every school and supermarket.

The current excitement about the environment will not come to much, I am afraid, unless it radicalizes millions of Americans. The conservative ideas put forth by President Nixon—spending a few billion for sewage-treatment plants and abatement of air pollution—will not even begin to create the Survivable Society. That can be brought about only by radical political action— radical enough to change the whole structure of government, the economy, and our national goals.

How the Survivable State will work is something I cannot guess; its design is a job for the coming generation of political scientists. The radical vision can, however, give us a glimpse of what it might look like. It will measure every new law, every dollar of investment by a cardinal yardstick: Will this help us accomplish a zero rate of growth and a stabilized environment? It will be skeptical of technology, including those inventions which purport to help clean up our earthly mess. Accordingly it will have an Anti-Patent Office, which will forbid the use of any technological discovery until the Office figures out fairly precisely what its side effects might be. (If they can't be foreseen, then the invention goes into deep freeze.) The use of land, water, and air will not be left to private decision, since their preservation will be recognized as a public trust. The landlord whose incinerator smokes will be pilloried; the tanker skipper who flushes his oil tanks at sea will be hanged at the nearest yardarm for the capital crime of oxygen destruction. On the other hand, the gardener will stand at the top of the social hierarchy, and the citizen who razes a supermarket and plants its acreage in trees will be proclaimed a Hero of the Republic. I won't live to see the day, of course; but I hope somebody will.

DANIEL M. BERMAN

Congress Enacts Civil Rights Legislation

"The Civil Rights Act of 1960 isn't worth the paper it's written on." This bitter comment was made, shortly after enactment of the law, by Thurgood Marshall, who argued the School Segregation Cases in the Supreme Court and is now Solicitor General of the United States. Subsequent events did not indicate that Marshall had been guilty of exaggeration. In the 1960 election, no use was made of the referee plan, though it had been heralded as the most important part of the bill. Southern judges were also reluctant to apply the law in 1962. On the few occasions when they did act, Negroes were deterred from using the procedure by the requirement that they would first have to approach local election officials and try to register with them. Considering the amount of time and energy that went into the making of the law and the pressing need that existed for legislative protection of the Negro, the revelation of how weak a statute Congress produced in 1960 was sharply disillusioning.

On the subject of voting, there was also disillusionment after the passage of the Civil Rights Act of 1964. Within months, the failure of the new law to deal effectively with racial disfranchisement had become so glaringly obvious that Congress was once again compelled to grapple with the problem and pass the Voting Rights Act of 1965.

But unlike the 1960 law, the statute passed in 1964 had important provisions on subjects other than voting. There were also sections on discrimination in public accommodations, schools, employment, and programs assisted by the federal government. On these subjects, at least some concrete results could be observed immediately. With respect to public accommodations, for example, there was swift compliance in a large number of southern cities, and at least a dim awareness in the rural areas that defiance could do no more than postpone the inevitable. Of the 1964 law, then, it cannot be said that it "isn't worth the paper it's written on."

What accounted for the palpable difference between 1960 and 1964? What

Source: The late Mr. Berman was a political scientist and a leading authority on Civil Rights legislation and on congressional procedure. This article is from the "Conclusion" in *A Bill Becomes a Law*, Second Edition (New York: The Macmillan Company), pp. 135–142. Reprinted with permission of The Macmillan Company from *A Bill Becomes a Law* by Daniel M. Berman. Copyright © by Daniel M. Berman, 1966.

factors operated in 1960 to frustrate the proponents of civil rights at every turn? And why was the importance of these factors diminished in 1964?

There is little doubt that President Eisenhower must shoulder some responsibility for the fact that the Civil Rights Act of 1960 was so weak. Only with the firm support of a President, particularly in his role as party leader, can there ever be a favorable prognosis for liberal legislation in Congress. Mr. Eisenhower, however, chose equivocation and inaction rather than resolute leadership on civil rights. Yet the President's attitude by no means provides the entire explanation for what happened. Even if Mr. Eisenhower had thrown himself wholeheartedly into the struggle, the final outcome might have been much the same, for a powerful conservative coalition was in firm control of Congress.

That coalition had been functioning for more than two decades. Because of its effectiveness, almost any session of Congress furnished examples of legislative measures whose final versions were far different from the bold and original bills they had once been. Moreover, the strength of the coalition was affected only slightly by popular elections, although most Americans believe that these elections determine the political complexion of Congress. For regardless of which party would achieve a formal majority, the reality of power —something very different from the appearance of power—remained in the same hands. Both groups comprising the coalition—the southern Democrats and the right-wing Republicans—generally sought identical goals: an end to positive federal legislation on social and economic issues. The southerners, who desired to defeat or dilute civil rights legislation, and the Republicans, whose principal desire was the scrapping of social welfare proposals, cooperated closely to assure the death of both types of measures.

If it were not for the strangely ambivalent character of the Democratic party, such a peculiar situation could not exist. As Peter Finley Dunne once heard Mr. Dooley say, "Th' dimmycratic party ain't on speakin' terms with itself." It would be hard to imagine, for instance, two individuals separated more widely by philosophical differences than Paul Douglas and James Eastland. Yet the liberal and the segregationist belong to the same party, and each benefits from the election of the other since both share in the rewards that Democratic control of the Senate brings.

The nature of the Democratic party as an uneasy collaboration of polar opposites has generally led it to exclude from positions of national leadership those individuals with reputations as extremists. Southern segregationists are not nominated for the presidency, yet neither are those men with uncompromisingly liberal records; a racist will never become the Democratic leader in the Senate, but neither will a Wayne Morse. The Democrat who is the ideal leader is one who has learned to subordinate all other values to party unity. On Lyndon Johnson, the mantle of leadership rested comfortably during the fight over civil rights in 1959 and 1960.

Johnson's position as an honest broker did not mean that he could always adopt positions precisely midway between the extremes, or that he could side with the liberals just as frequently as with the conservatives. There is no task more difficult than to convince conservatives that they ought to support positive actions offensive to them; it is far easier to make liberals believe that progress against entrenched social and economic evils must of necessity be slow. Not surprisingly, therefore, Johnson's conception of the middle of the road was considerably to the right of dead center. During the debate in 1960, for example, he concentrated far more on trimming the demands of the liberals than on prodding the southerners. As on many occasions in the past, he worked more closely with Everett Dirksen, the Republican leader in the Senate, than with the civil rights Democrats.

If conservatives benefited from the alliance between Johnson and Dirksen, they were aided even more by another phenomenon: the conservative nature of several important congressional procedures.

Perhaps the most conspicuous example of the conservative bias in Congress was the Rules Committee of the House. When the Republicans held a majority, the conservative domination of this committee was assured, and liberal measures on both economic issues and civil rights scarcely had a chance. The result was not very different, however, when a resurgence of liberalism in the country gave a majority in the House to the Democrats. In the Eighty-sixth Congress, for example, the four conservative Republicans on the committee found to their delight that they had precisely the number of southern Democratic allies they needed to bottle up liberal legislation.

The filibuster was another congressional procedure that was anything but neutral in its political effects. Like the Rules Committee in the House, it had become primarily an instrument of conservative power. It had, in fact, seldom been used successfully for anything except to force the abandonment or emasculation of civil rights proposals.

Although the power of the Rules Committee and the threat of the filibuster were the best known elements of the conservative bias in Congress, they were by no means the only ones. The disproportionate number of southerners at the head of standing committees—almost entirely a product of the seniority system—was at least as important. And even the bare fact that the rules were so cumbersome was significant. The procedures that follow the introduction of a bill and its reference to committee are so formidable that they might well have been devised by men who hated the thought that legislation would ever be enacted. In an age when liberals are insisting that the federal government take positive steps to fashion a more equitable and democratic society, a barrier to all congressional action hurts their cause directly. Conservatives, who demand far less of government, lose little.

The newspaper columnist, Joseph Alsop, has argued that something else was to blame for the civil rights debacle in 1960. The liberals, he says, were both stubborn and inept, and thus did grave damage to their cause. They were "less interested in the dusty legislative process than in striking noble, popular postures." Undoubtedly the liberals did not understand parliamentary procedures as well as the southern conservatives (partly because not too many of them had been in Congress as long). Certainly they had no leaders whose generalship could equal that of Lyndon Johnson, Sam Rayburn, Richard Russell, or Howard Smith. Yet these factors had only slight bearing on the defeat they suffered. Even if they had been past masters of legislative procedure and experts in the art of compromise, they would still have had no chance at all to overcome the awesome power marshalled against them by the conservative coalition.

Although the coalition was far from defunct in 1964, a new condition had arisen that reduced it to impotence. That condition was the increased militance of the Negro protest movement and the threat of ruinous violence created in parts of the Deep South by the intransigence and brutality with which the protest was met. First President Kennedy and then President Johnson, as well as the bipartisan leadership in Congress, came to the conclusion that only a strong civil rights bill could possibly prevent widespread racial bloodshed and utter catastrophe for the nation. Given such bipartisan determination, which was particularly pronounced after the events in Birmingham in the spring of 1963, obstacles in Congress tended to melt away.

It is a sad commentary on the American system of government that the Negro had to go into the streets before anything even approximating serious attention was paid to his legitimate grievances. Those who glorify the system in terms of its responsiveness to the long-range public interest will not find it easy to explain why it required street demonstrations and the imminence of chaos to awaken presidents and congressmen to their responsibilities.

Tragically, the awakening may have come too late. The civil rights movement had built up so much momentum by 1964 that even the new law was seen as not going far enough. The demand, unanswerable in its own terms, was for "freedom now!" Particularly among northern Negroes—for whom the 1964 law did relatively little—pent-up frustrations had combined with rising expectations to create a highly inflammable situation. Understandably, the Negro community in both the North and South was not ready to concede the good faith of the white political elite merely on the basis of a law whose enactment had been compelled by marching feet. Only the most militant tactics had finally persuaded Congress to act. These tactics, it was certain, would be used again and again.

Things might have been very different had Congress moved a little earlier. Even 1960 might not have been too late. The Legislative Branch, however, was immobilized by a combination of factors: a President who was the epitome of complacency; a Senate Majority Leader who sensed no insistent national demand for a strong bill; and congressional procedures, such as the filibuster, that made it difficult to pass anything more than an innocuous civil rights law.

When the Eighty-ninth Congress convened in January 1965, it turned its attention to a few of these procedures and actually stripped the House Rules Committee of some of its powers.[1] But a movement for liberalization of the cloture rule made no headway, and a new joint committee on congressional reform was specifically prohibited from recommending any changes in the rules of either House. Battles for civil rights would continue to be fought in the streets.

How long will Congress continue to make such a negligible contribution to the solution of national problems? How long will it tolerate institutional arrangements making it so excruciatingly difficult—except in time of crisis— to pass the simplest ameliorative legislation?

The Promised Land is still far away. There is at this time no agreement even on the direction that reform of the congressional system should take. The most thoroughgoing remedy that has been suggested would involve a realignment of the two major parties, with a new liberal party opposing a grouping of former Democrats from the South and conservative Republicans. Such a solution has much to recommend it. The voter would enjoy a clear-cut choice between alternative policies promoted by disciplined parties, and the party in power could be held responsible for its actions by the electorate. Yet the idea is seldom discussed seriously, for we are told that its adoption would encourage the development of irreconcilable antagonisms which might crack the underlying unity of the American people. The tendency to celebrate rather than examine the institutions of American government is deep-seated. It is not easy to win a hearing for moderate plans to democratize some congressional procedures, let alone for grandiose schemes to recast the two-party system.

There is, however, a strong possibility that in the foreseeable future the conservative bias in Congress will be eliminated and the conservative coalition will entirely disappear. When the subjection of the Negro ends and racial equality ceases to be a scare word, whites in the South will begin increasingly to expect other actions from their congressmen than mere opposition to civil rights. They will want their representatives to be leaders in the fight for social welfare measures—because what region of the nation, after all, needs these measures more desperately than the South? When the bulk of southern legislators start voting for such things as strong labor unions, a high minimum wage, and federal health insurance, it is inevitable that the props under the conservative coalition will collapse, for the Democrat from the South will no longer have any basis for partnership with the Republican from the North.

[1] The House adopted a 21-day rule that was far more meaningful than the rule that had been in effect in 1949 and 1950. Now it would be possible for the Speaker to wrest any bill from the Rules Committee as long as he had the support of a majority in the House. This was a major step in the direction of a system of party responsibility, under which the elected leadership of the majority party would not be able to claim that it was helpless to enact the legislative program to which it was pledged.

The precondition of all this is the total emancipation of the Negro. To this cause, the Civil Rights Act of 1960 contributed little. But the contribution of the Civil Rights Act of 1964 was more significant. And the battle is continuing on other fronts—the voter registration line, the school, the factory, and the street—where filibusters and committee obstruction are out of order. The outcome of these contests may be different. If it is, the legislative process will surely not be immune from the changes that will be wrought.

The Manipulative Arts

A phenomenon of modern politics that attracts a great deal of attention is the use of manipulative techniques to convince the citizenry that they should behave toward politicians and governmental policies much as they would toward the selection of a new automobile or a deodorant. The techniques of hawking a presidential candidate, Republican or Democrat, do not differ much from those used to try to get us to join the "Dodge rebellion," nor do the government's efforts to persuade us that we need a supersonic transport differ markedly from those used to convince us that we need a deodorant or a mouthwash. In fact, governmental propaganda efforts are a huge business. For example the Pentagon spends, by their own admission, $30 million a year on "public relations," but according to Roger Mudd's C.B.S. documentary "The Selling of the Pentagon," [1] more like $190 million is used to "sell" the public on the Pentagon's programs and policies.

Most importantly, however, the government is moving increasingly away from a candid revelation of information and news to the use of techniques designed to "manage" the information it releases. There is a growing tension between reporters and governmental press officers. Presidential press secretaries, for example, tilt mightily with reporters trying to penetrate their defense mechanisms. Bill Moyers, during the Johnson administration, told the reporters, "All right, gentlemen, I'll take the planted questions first." The reporters retorted that these kinds of encounters were "goat-feeding" sessions that left them not only angry and frustrated but empty-handed.

The basic problem, however, is the severe damage official propagandizing or even lying does to the faith of the people in their government. Sadly, there has been so much of this in recent history that the term *credibility*

[1] *Newsweek*, March 8, 1971, p. 74.

gap has been invented to describe the reaction of press and public to official prevarications and distortions. Government officials have tried to extricate themselves from the doubts cast upon their credibility by blaming the press for poor, if not dishonest, reporting. Attacking the press was a recent assignment Vice President Agnew so energetically fulfilled for President Nixon that many people became concerned that the still vigorous fraternity of journalists and television reporters would be severely intimidated. The articles and essays in this section deal with techniques of persuasion and the media, their use in politics, and the implications of these developments for democratic theory and practice.

VICTOR S. NAVASKY

Advertising Is $\left\{\begin{array}{l} \textbf{\textit{a Science?}} \\ \textbf{\textit{an Art?}} \\ \textbf{\textit{a Business?}} \end{array}\right.$

In the thirties, economists knocked advertising. In the forties, novelists knocked advertising. In the fifties, sociologists knocked advertising and Hollywood began making movies out of the novels of the forties. In the sixties, the politicians who saw the movies began to attack advertising as its volume zoomed to what Printer's Ink estimates will be $16.3-billion by the end of 1966.

Toynbee has said it is "evil." Galbraith says it is wasteful. And Arthur Schlesinger Jr. says it is awful. It has been muckraked, ridiculed, chastised, satirized and Vance Packardized. It has been attacked for "arousing anxieties and manipulating the fears of consumers to coerce them into buying" and at the same time it has been dismissed as impotent, misdirected and irrelevant —vide the millions of dollars wasted on promoting the Edsel. As Martin Solow, president of Solow/Wexton, notes: "Madison Avenue has replaced Wall Street as the whipping boy. There has been a transference of villainies from the principals to the agents." Madison Avenue has an image problem.

One of the reasons why Madison Avenue is misunderstood has to do with the fact that Madison Avenue and its critics don't speak the same language. This is partly the fault of "the professors" (as one of advertising's trade magazines has referred to its critics) but mostly the fault of Madison Avenue which, while it is supposed to consist of communications experts, actually speaks a language all its own. Some words change every year. For instance, last year's word was Beautiful and this year's word is Fantastic. Benton & Bowles vice president Whit Hobbs observes that "everybody calls everybody else pussycat or baby, not out of endearment but because it's a heckuva lot easier than bothering to remember names."

But the significant semantic fact about Madison Avenue is that the adver-

Source: Mr. Navasky is the editor of *Monocle,* an occasional journal of political satire. This article is from *The New York Times Magazine,* Nov. 20, 1966, pp. 52–153, 162–177 passim. © 1966 by The New York Times Company. Reprinted by permission.

tising community has captured the language and sees everything from its own perspective. Radio, television, magazines, newspapers and even the U.S. mails are "advertising media." People are "consumers." Words are "copy." Stealing a client is "account switching" and stealing an idea is "keeping up with the latest trend." Twelve executives sitting in a room trying to adjust a "copy strategy" so that it meshes with a "marketing strategy" are known as a "creative group." Even the standard jokes are told from an agency perspective ("Let's get down on all fours and look at this from the client's point of view").

As a result, the professors often aim their criticism at Madison Avenue en masse and ignore (a) the changes which have taken place, especially over the last decade, and (b) the internal philosophic and esthetic divisions which characterize contemporary Madison Avenue. (According to a Mediascope survey, only 25 per cent of New York's advertising agencies can actually be found on Madison Avenue.)

Some of these divisions are well illustrated in a story currently making the rounds of what happened when three agency presidents were invited to make presentations to a potential client. Calling them in one by one, he asked each the same question: "What time is it?" The first replied: "Just a minute. I'll send down to research." The second responded: "What time would you like it to be?" And the third said: "The hell with the time, read the copy." (In another version, the third is rumored to have said: "Wait while I steal you a watch.")

My theory is that if the professors appreciated the profound implications of each of these three approaches, the annual professorial assaults might give way to a genuine dialogue between the Academy and the Avenue. It is in this ecumenical spirit that I propose for Madison Avenue's consideration the adoption of a new vocabulary, one that speaks to the professors in their own language. Since each of the three approaches represents a philosophy (that advertising is a science, that it is a business, that it is an art), and since the works of the great philosophers have already been market-tested on the academic community, I propose that when Madison Avenue speaks for the record it employ the language of philosophy.

Take David Ogilvy of Ogilvy & Mather. Mr. Ogilvy, who has given us the eye-patched man in the Hathaway shirt, Commander Whitehead of Schweppes and the information that "At 60 miles an hour, the loudest noise in this new Rolls-Royce comes from the electric clock," is an articulate student of advertising theory. A former chef, he is generally recognized as a man of creative stature. But when you talk with him you realize that basically he believes advertising has a great deal to learn from science.

Roaming around his spacious office he will tell you, as he snaps his red suspenders, that "it pays to pre-test advertising with consumers." Without such pre-testing, he says, "I cannot predict what advertising will work and what won't. Any advertiser who thinks he can is an irresponsible gambler."

Mr. Ogilvy observes that "a lot of advertisers are more interested in the *originality* of their advertising than in its power to sell their product. I won't play that silly game. I spend every waking moment trying to create advertising which will increase our clients' sales—and profits. If it also happens to be exciting and original, that's nice, too."

Ogilvy's basic idea is that every product needs a personality, a "brand-image." In addition, he is an informaniac, believing in long lists of product benefits and general information. His book, "Confessions of an Advertising Man," is chock-full of quasi-scientific principles and observations such as, "Five times as many people read headlines as body copy." "Research shows that it is dangerous to use negatives in headlines." "What you say is more important than how you say it." "Readership falls off rapidly up to 50 words of copy but drops very little between 50 and 500 words." "Always use testimonials." "Over and over, research has shown that photographs sell more than drawings."

Ogilvy's print ads are recognizable by the photo near the top of the page, the newsy bold headline and what is usually a heavy dose of body copy ("The more you tell, the more you sell").

Now it should be obvious that professors who have written volumes which run into hundreds of thousands of words are not going to take Mr. Ogilvy very seriously when he talks about readership falling off rapidly up to 50 words. But suppose Ogilvy were to point out that all he is doing is putting some of Plato's theories into practice. After all, Plato argued that knowledge leads to virtuous action, and if you give consumers the facts—for instance, a long essay (under a photo and headline) on "Why Mercedes-Benz has the nerve to charge $4,305 for a car with a funny-sounding Diesel engine"—you can assume that the by now virtuous man, will at least send in for the 24-page brochure offered at the bottom of the page, giving even more facts.

In providing product testimonials by men like Comdr. Whitehead, Ogilvy has also recognized the wisdom of Plato's technique in the Dialogues, using personalities like Socrates to stand for ideas. And while many scholars might wriggle uncomfortably at the notion that every product must have a "brand image," Ogilvy could do worse than recall Plato's belief that for every object there is an ideal object.

Of course an agency like Ted Bates, which under the leadership of Rosser Reeves (now retired) won a reputation for "hard sell" and as "the rat-tat-tat" agency, representing such package goods as Carter's Liver Pills and Anacin, is a more extreme example of the scientific approach to advertising. Reeves even had a formula for the creation of an ad, which he called U.S.P. (Unique Selling Proposition) and he was proud of ugly, irritating repetitive commercials as long as they worked.

In his own book, "Reality in Advertising," he was delighted to recall that when 25 top creative people in advertising were asked to pick the three worst TV commercials of the past several years, they picked two of the most "electric successes." To the extent that the Reeves approach is still dominant, my recommendation is that Bates invoke the unlikely philosophy of Epicurus.

According to Bertrand Russell: "It was Epicurus who first maintained that a man could be happy on a rack." He believed that "absence of pain is in itself pleasure, indeed in his ultimate analysis the truest pleasure." With the Stoics, he felt that the absence of pain is the wise man's goal. Are you suffering from headaches, neuritis or neuralgia? Try a little Epicureanism, of the 270 B.C. variety.

While the recent hiring of some "creative" types has led to speculation that Bates is moving away from the old hard sell, they certainly have not relinquished their emphasis on scientific research. President Archie Foster recently estimated that "KOOL cigarettes will have spent about $5-million per word on its current advertising message by the end of this year, and Colgate Dental Cream, somewhat more per word."

At the Southern Conference of the Advertising Federation of America in October, Foster made a speech which would entitle him to claim that if Doyle Dane Bernbach, known for its imagination and creativity, is the Athens of Madison Avenue, Bates is the Sparta:

> We are a regiment of Marines. We are on ridge 101 and our mission is to advance to ridge 102 and secure it in 8 hours. Ladies and gentlemen, the regimental commander had better have a plan before he begins shooting his way forward. He had better know everything he can find out about the enemy's dispositions, and the nature of the terrain between him and ridge 102. . . .
> The battle for market share points is not dissimilar. The advertiser is on a ridge called Market Share 6 per cent. His mission is to advance to the next one ahead, called Market Share 7 per cent. Between him and that next ridge are the enemy—the 94 per cent of the market he hasn't got. . . . He'd better have a plan, drawing on whatever he can learn about them, before he begins shooting his dollars, no matter how sharp the words and pictures.

Agencies like Bates operate on the same principle as the logical positivists, who hold that if a proposition is not verifiable it is meaningless. But perhaps the most ambitious empiricists on Madison Avenue are The Interpublic Group of Companies, Inc., which bills itself as "the world's largest marketing communications enterprise" and consists of 26 companies (including McCann-Erickson and the creative Jack Tinker and Partners). Recently, it announced that nine of these companies would henceforth operate under the name of Market Planning Corporation, including a company called The Applied Science Group which "develops advanced 'software' programs for computers as well as simulation and model-making techniques for media selection."

Paul Foley, chairman of the board of McCann and director of its new creative offspring, The Center for Advanced Practice, says that while the complex layers of testing, quality control, creative review, etc. "can't guarantee creativity, the system does operate as a safety net. It prevents us from falling on our faces." Dan Stern, creative director at McCann, who writes novels and reviews books in his spare time, adds: "One of the main roles of advertising is to be a pipeline from the university to industry. This is the trend. Who knows? By 1975, we may have to open an office in Cambridge."

One complaint of these empirically rigorous agencies is that many advertising awards, like the Gold Key Awards and the Andy Awards and others, often seem to be based on esthetic considerations rather than proven sales value. Norman B. Norman, president of Norman, Craig & Kummel, claims to have compiled a list of ads and commercials which received awards from various juries over a five-year period and discovered that the majority of award-winning campaigns were no longer in existence and in most cases had been abandoned as unsuccessful.

It would be an intelligent strategy for the logical positivist agencies to band together and denounce the whole system of awards as "metaphysical."

William Bernbach, the mild-mannered president of Doyle Dane Bernbach, is generally recognized as the Dean of the Advertising-Is-an-Art school, although he is the first to tell you that if it doesn't sell it's worthless. Students, fellow travelers and sympathizers include agencies like Carl Ally, Tinker, Wells Rich Greene, Solow/Wexton, de Garmo, Leber Katz Paccione and Freeman & Gossage on the West Coast.

Bernbach's attitude toward research was best expressed when $3,864 worth of research on the Avis campaign suggested that it should be dropped because "people aren't interested in doing business with No. 2." Doyle Dane threw out the research but kept the campaign because, according to Bernbach, "We knew we weren't saying Avis is Number 2. We were saying Avis tries harder."

This willingness to rely on intuition over the protests of doubtful clients is an important element of the Bernbach approach. "We use research when we have to," says Bernbach, "but nine times out of 10 you know where to go. You don't need research to tell you. What counts is how you get there. That has to do with artistry, with believability, with freshness."

Where Ogilvy believes content to be more important than form, Bernbach believes, as Martin Mayer reported in his book, "Madison Avenue, U.S.A.," "form can become content."

Because of this emphasis on artistry, on the importance of *how* you say something, one is tempted to classify Bernbach as an Aristotelian (Aristotle, it will be recalled, argued that form was the essence of matter and that without form, matter is only potential). But Bernbach's real contribution was the discovery that on Madison Avenue the shock of honesty pays. With such credentials he can rightfully stake out his claim as advertising's first existentialist.

Existentialism holds that man's existence precedes his essence. And Bernbach starts with the assumption that before you can get to the *essence* of advertising, you need the *existence* of a product which is superior, unique or different. If it's none of these you don't take the account. With Camus, he believes that man must create his own meaning out of the absurd commercial world in which he finds himself. With Sartre, he believes that preconceived rules and value judgments impede rather than advance the creative process. For instance: "You don't have to be Jewish to like Levy's Real Jewish Rye" ignores the rule about negatives in headlines.

And if they ever wish to make out an existentialist case for themselves, Doyle Dane should emphasize the deep strain of Kierkegaardian despair which permeates their work. Why else would they single out Avis as "No. 2," Volkswagen as a "lemon," and ask, "What idiot changed the [Chivas Regal] bottle?" (The client liked the last ad except for one word. It wanted to change "idiot" to "genius." Doyle Dane said no.)

Carl Ally, a spectacular successful young practitioner of the Doyle Dane approach, confirms its existential quality when he says: "The singular feature of the ad business is that most of it stinks. Thirty per cent of it is downright offensive and insulting, another 55 per cent is irrelevant, which leaves 15 per cent which actually does something. Three per cent of that is outstanding. There is a hierarchy of values in most agencies which closely resembles the values of the society in which it finds itself. The fundamental flaw in most advertising has nothing to do with talent or ability—that's around and for sale. The real flaw is lack of commitment. The well-they-won't-buy-that mentality. We don't ask what the client wants. We test everything on ourselves. If we like it, it's good. If we don't, it stinks. What the client wants is merely essential. It's not decisive."

Ally, who has been running his own agency only since 1962, recently assumed the driver's seat at Hertz. The first thing he did was to abandon Norman, Craig & Kummel's "Let Hertz Put You in the Driver's Seat" campaign in favor of a direct confrontation with his hero. The new Hertz campaign has a banner headline which violates every rule in Ogilvy's book, Reeves's book and probably even some of the rules in the Consumers' Union book, which frowns on mentioning a competitor's name in one's own ads. It reads: "For Years Avis Has Been Telling You Hertz Is No. 1. Now We're Going To Tell You Why." The last sentence in the ad says, "No. 2 says he tries harder. Than who?"

When Leon Meadow, a Doyle Dane copy executive, ran into Ed McCabe, Carl Ally's copy group chief, at a meeting of the Advertising Writers' Association, he was overhead to say: "I want to thank you for the free plug."

"There'll be many more," promised McCabe.

Wells Rich Greene, who gave the Alka-Seltzer people a headache when they resigned from Jack Tinker, where they had helped create the famous Alka-Seltzer television commercials, to form their own agency, are generally reported to be the "hottest" exponent of the irreverent Doyle Dane approach. While still with Tinker, they made their reputations by painting Braniff planes the colors of the rainbow, putting Pucci gowns on the stewardesses and then taking them off in the famous "air strip."

What W.R.G. has done is to challenge Bernbach's idea that a good ad emphasizes a product's point of difference. The comely but aggressive Mary Wells has stated, "We prefer to handle a product which is the *same* as its competitors. That's what we're best at." In thus abandoning any commitment to the idea of product superiority or distinctiveness, it appears that W.R.G. has left behind conventional existentialism in favor of the Theater of the Absurd. Wells Rich is a Madison Avenue Happening.

"I think our philosophy is as necessary for this era as Bernbach's was for his," says Mrs. Wells, implying that Bernbach's era is past, a judgment in which not many concur. But then, as Richard Rich told Newsweek, "Our motto is, 'If we were modest, we'd be perfect.'"

Howard Gossage of Freeman & Gossage in San Francisco is another man usually identified with the advertising-as-an-art approach because of his zany ads for Eagle Shirts and Land-Rover. His theory is that "an ad ought to be like one end of an interesting conversation." Putting that theory into practice, he once pulled a record 11,342 responses from an Eagle shirt ad in The New Yorker. What Gossage instinctively recognized is that with all its departments and far-flung correspondents, The New Yorker is in large part a series of letters to its readers. What he did was invite them to R.S.V.P.

Peter Spelman, public relations director of The New Yorker, says that "Gossage is the James Thurber of advertising. He's one of the few geniuses in the business." But what Gossage *really* is is the Socrates of San Francisco. A recent series of Socratic questions caused much dismay to governmental authorities; they had to cancel plans to build two dams that would have flooded parts of the Grand Canyon when Gossage and a colleague named Jerry Mander mounted a protest advertising campaign on behalf of the Sierra Club, asking, "Shall we flood the Sistine Chapel so the tourists can get closer to the ceiling?"

On one side, then, are the Platonists and positivists who look upon advertising primarily as a science based on accumulated knowledge; and on the other are the existentialists and individualists who regard it primarily as an art, based in varying degrees on commitment, intuition and creativity. Each school, of course, represents merely a degree of emphasis. And somewhere between those polarities lies the great mass of larger and smaller agencies searching for Aristotle's Golden Mean, who look upon advertising as a business.

As Charles Brower, chairman of the board of Batten Barton Durstine & Osborn says:

I think the pretense that advertising is either a profession or an art form is a lot of bunk. It's a trade, like bricklaying. You can make a cathedral by laying bricks but it's tradesmen who make it. Our particular theory is that since every product is different, each campaign should be tailor-made.

For instance, our Dodge campaign was designed to blast the stodginess image. Our research showed that Dodge sales were to an older group because the major part of the ad expenditure was on the Lawrence Welk Show, which was attracting older folks. We wanted to cure this so we came up with Pam Austin and the Dodge Rebellion.

I don't believe in this "hot" agency business. Thompson's Mustang campaign is as creative as anything you'll see this year. But they are too big and old to be called "hot" and so everybody forgets about it.

What does Mr. Brower think of the Wells Rich rebellion and the Braniff campaign? "I heard a rumor that the paint job slows down the airplane."

Dan Seymour, president of J. Walter Thompson, the largest advertising agency in the U.S. with worldwide billings of $530-million, shares Mr. Brower's skepticism about schools of advertising.

We are dedicated to constant discontent with the status quo. We don't believe in styles or schools. We don't believe in the idea of presenting a client with one ad and saying, take it or leave it. It depends on the client. For some clients we may do that. For others we may make up to 50 ads and let him make his choice. The only thing we know for sure is that there is no such thing as a J. Walter Thompson ad.

We have no organization chart. Everybody's door is always open. Our role is simple—to increase our clients' sales. Look at our Ford ad. Our research showed that people identify quietness with quality. So we came up with the slogan, "Ford rides quieter than Rolls-Royce." People said nobody would believe it but we had scientific proof! Our testing service installed audiometers. We don't care about being different. We care about sales. Leo Burnett said it all when he said, "If you want to be different, come to breakfast some morning with your socks in your mouth."

Perhaps the chief chronicler of the advertising-as-a-business approach is Bernard Gallagher, whose Gallagher Report, an inside dope sheet on Madison Avenue comings and goings, hirings and firings, seems to be read, if not respected, by all. Gallagher maintains that "the fastest-growing agency today is Grey Advertising. That's because they are merchandise-minded. They're not interested in squandering a client's money to make their commissions. They've come up from Seventh Avenue and they haven't forgotten it. The same goes for Doyle Dane and Papert Koenig Lois."

P.K.L., incidentally, seems to be an agency in transition. Originally exponents of the Doyle Dane school, of which the principals in the agency are alumni, they are said to have had their brains laundered when they got Procter and Gamble as a client.

But if Madison Avenue goes around saying that advertising is a business like any other business, John Kenneth Galbraith, who has a questionable attitude toward business anyway, is simply going to take it as an affirmation of his thesis that millions of dollars which might more profitably go to schools, hospitals and highways—the public sector—are being frittered away on the creation of artificial private wants.

To help forestall such criticism, the great mass of agencies should make it clear that they are operating in the great instrumentalist tradition of John Dewey and William James, America's home-grown exponents of pragmatism.

Like James and Dewey, these agencies don't adhere to any theoretical or metaphysical constructs. They look upon life as *process*—in this case, the marketing process. Every product presents a new problem and the job of the agency is simply to solve that problem.

Thus when Young & Rubicam, perhaps the most creative of the larger agencies, breaks precedent by placing the first hi-fi ad in a general circulation newspaper or attempts to buy a column on the letters-to-the-editor page, it should not boast that "we are known for our innovative media buys." Rather, they should mention that, as Dewey made clear in his pioneering work, "Human Nature and Conduct," choices are always relative to particular situations in which certain ends-in-view (sales) are tentatively fixed, and in which value-deliberations (conferences) consist in weighing these ends and the means (media) in relation to each other to find a solution (the ad) to the problem (market share).

Among the less pressing problems confronting today's Madison Avenue pragmatists are such questions as: Should clients be on a fee or a commission basis? "The commission system has all the earmarks of a kickback," says Howard Gossage, of Freeman & Gossage, San Francisco. "It is as sensible as paying a lawyer for the number of lawsuits he gets you into rather than the number he keeps you out of." Should agencies judge the morality of products? "As far as I am concerned, the Bible, whisky and cigarettes are all the same. We aren't the moral arbiters of the country," says Brower. But Ogilvy and others refuse to handle cigarette advertising. If a client doesn't like an ad, do you tell him to try another agency, as Bernbach does, or do you go back to the drawing board, like the vast majority of agencies? Should an agency handle political accounts? "Yes," says an agency like P.K.L., which followed up Senator Jacob Javits's senatorial campaign with Robert F. Kennedy's senatorial campaign. "No," says Ogilvy, who feels it's not fair to the members of the opposition party who may be working in the office. It also disrupts work on other accounts. And, of course, the big question of the year is, should chalk-white armored knights on armored horses gallop around chasing dirt? "Yes," says Norman B. Norman, who calls this "empathy" advertising a form of therapy for the consumer as well as an effective sales device. "No," says Fairfax Cone, chairman of the executive committee of Foote Cone & Belding, who believes that "there is a group of people in advertising who are not truly advertising people, who have attached themselves to it in the mistaken belief that advertising is part and parcel of show business."

However these various disputes are resolved, McCann's Paul Foley is convinced that "in the next aspect of advertising, it must be the legitimate voice of the consumer that we've been hearing so much about. We live in a persuasion society. Man is *homo communicans*—man in communication with other men. What's exciting about this business is that we are the experts in persuasion. The public is ultimately interested only in what serves them so that's what we'll have to do."

If Mr. Foley is right, Madison Avenue's image problem should dissolve. But in the interim, I am happy to report that my idea of relating the role of advertising to a more inspirational tradition is no radical departure from Madison Avenue's heritage. As long ago as 1925, Bruce Barton, one of the founders of B.B.D.&O., remarked in a book called "The Man Nobody Knows" that Jesus was really something of an executive. "He picked up 12 men from the bottom ranks of business and forged them into an organization that conquered the world." If He were alive today, said Barton, He'd be a "national advertiser."

RICHARD C. SCAMMON AND BEN J. WATTENBERG

Strategy for Democrats

It is neither likely nor proper, nor potentially profitable for Democrats in 1972 to nominate a candidate who would be, or would be perceived as, antiblack. Morality aside for the moment, any such candidacy would destroy itself on the rocks of credibility; the national party of Stevenson, Kennedy, Johnson and Humphrey will not be believed as a party advocating a go-slow-on-civil-rights policy; a party that attracted so much of the black vote in 1968 will not be perceived as the line on the ballot to voice antiblack sentiments, certainly not with a Republican and an American Independent also on the ballot.

What to do?

Stating the problem points toward its solution. Liberal Democrats must attempt to split off the Race Issue from the rest of the Social Issue.

Source: The ideas in this essay were further developed in a best-selling and highly respected book, *The Real Majority* (New York: Coward-McCann, Inc., 1970). From *The New Republic*, Aug. 15, 1970, pp. 17–21, 30–31. Copyright 1970 by Richard C. Scammon and Ben J. Wattenberg. Reprinted by permission of the Harold Matson Company, Inc. The letter to the editors and the authors' response, which follow the essay, appeared shortly after its initial publication, in the issue of September 26, 1970.

This split-off of race from crime may not be as difficult as it seems. To begin, it is inherently a phony linkup. The Social Issue would be present in America if every black American vanished tomorrow morning. Campus disruptions, drugs, pornography, Vietnam dissent, the generation gap certainly are not caused by blacks. There would still be a crime problem without blacks —white crime rates are increasing, too. There are poverty and urban decay in inner-city neighborhoods that are neither black nor threatened by blacks, and there are middle-class whites who are distinctly unhappy when poor whites begin to move into a neighborhood, "destroying property values." To some extent, then, blacks in America have become only a lightning rod that attracts white resentment over already existing problems.

If the Social Issue and the Race Issue are *not* the same, then Democrats, if prudent, should be able to remain a pro-civil-rights party without being an antilaw-and-order party or a pro-mugger party. The law-and-order issue can be finessed as it was in Detroit, Pittsburgh, and Seattle. Or it can be turned partially into a ping-pong issue working against the party in power: Republicans.

The rhetoric for such a position is not hard to imagine:

—Do *not* say, "Well, I don't agree with the Students for a Democratic Society when they invade a college president's office, but I can understand their deep sense of frustration."
—Do say, "When students break laws they will be treated as lawbreakers."
—Do *not* say, "Crime is a complicated sociological phenomenon and we'll never be able to solve the problem until we get at the root causes of poverty and racism."
—Do say, "I am going to make our neighborhoods safe again for decent citizens of every color. I am also in favor of job training, eradication of poverty, etc., etc."

. . . and so on. After each utterance, it is further suggested to add this rhetorical suffix: "and what have Richard Nixon and the Republicans done about it? Nothing!"

This is more than opportunistic political rhetoric. It is viable rhetoric because it is valid, and it should be a *Democratic* issue. If there is to be a political party in America deeply concerned about law and order, then by logic and history, it most certainly ought to be the Democratic Party.

—The law-and-order issue today is essentially a civil libertarian's issue and the question that must be asked is: What about the civil liberties of hardworking, crime-scared Americans today, black and white, many of whom happen to be *Democrats?*
—It is black *Democrats* who face the worst crime rates in America, and who have the most legitimate fears of mugging, rape, robbery, and drugs. It is white *Democrats* in inner-city neighborhoods—the so-called ethnics—who are also more than casually threatened by violent crime.
—It is *Democratic* intellectuals in all those colleges and universities whose way of life is disrupted, bulldozed, and brutalized by student anarchists.

That being "liberal" should equate with being soft on mugging or soft on disruption is absurd. In point of fact, being liberal *demands* a firm stand on freedom from fear in society. Democrats have made a major national issue of the "environment." Fine. Let them include in that position the key element of a decent urban environment: safety of the citizenry from the pollution of violence.

If Nixon's the One. If we assume that Mr. Nixon will be a candidate to succeed himself in 1972, as Harry Dent has announced, then it is fair to speculate about Nixon's merits as a candidate. Dent, a Nixon political lieutenant, told District of Columbia Young Republicans that things were going so well under Mr. Nixon's leadership that "I don't have much question now that his Administration will be in for two terms."

Mr. Nixon will be the incumbent; he will fly around in Air Force One; he will draw large crowds because he is President; he will likely have a united party behind him; he will create, or time, certain events for his own benefit; he will have a certain amount of political arm-twisting power because of his position—all to the good for Mr. Nixon.

But we know more about him, as well. He has, after all, run for President twice, and in neither instance did he get a majority of the vote. In neither instance did he demonstrate that he was a particularly devastating television personality. In the first year of his Presidency he has shown some improvement as a television performer, but not enough to make an observer think that he will build up the huge and intense personal sort of following that President Eisenhower or President Kennedy had. His popularity seems somewhat hollow, a popularity that is extremely vulnerable to a bad turn of events.

So, if we assume that Mr. Nixon will be the candidate of the Republicans in 1972, we can assume *only* that the Republicans will have a competent, well-known, centrist candidate—but that's all. Not an Eisenhower.

Mr. Nixon was perhaps described best by his English adviser on Vietnam, Sir Robert Thompson. After meeting with Mr. Nixon, Sir Robert remarked upon how good it was that America now had a "professional President." Strange phrase, that. Probably accurate. But is a "professional President," a super-civil servant, a GS 100, is that an appealing political image? Not very, we'd venture. If the Democratic candidate in 1972 is a man of the center, he may do very well on a personality versus personality contest.

Wallace. That Wallace will run in 1972 seems likely. That Wallace will move toward the center, toward the realities of political power in the seventies, seems obvious. But he can't really move far enough unless the character of the events of the seventies helps by moving the center toward him. If social turbulence and disorder, school problems, and riots deepen and intensify the Social Issue, Wallace might benefit from such circumstances, but even then only if *both* major parties were seen by the voters as mired deep in non-responsive dogmas about these problems.

But the whole nature of American politics is responsive. Should the public attitudes go so far as to come closer to Wallace policies or to what these policies may become, then in all probability one (or both) of the major parties will co-opt Wallace rhetoric or Wallace strategy. Mr. Agnew has already been called, pejoratively, a "white-collar Wallace," read as a "semi-demagogue." Should the times and conditions demand it, some patriot in some party will step forward as a "white-collar Agnew," substantively in tune with an intensified Social Issue, but "nondemagogic," no doubt denouncing Wallace and Agnew while picking up their rhetoric.

In a very real sense it is because American two-party Presidential politics *is* so close to the people that Wallace's chances in the seventies seem dim. Wallace will likely be co-opted by the major parties. He personally will not likely be President. But because he may still carry many votes (10,000,000 in 1968), his electoral presence may well determine who the next Presidents are. The Wallace voter and the decrease or increase of Wallace voters may well be the kingmaking factors in the 1970s.

These votes are obviously an alluring target, particularly so for President Nixon, for we may recall that about seven of every ten Wallace voters would have gone for Nixon in 1968 had Wallace not run.

An alluring target, but a mixed blessing.

President Nixon might conceivably think of making a deal to keep Wallace from running, but then he'd think twice about it and realize that deals don't stay secret for long and that the spectacle of an American President dealing with a politician still perceived by many as a red-neck racist would undoubtedly cost more votes than it would gain. (In effect, Goldwater made such a deal with Wallace in 1964; Wallace was implored not to split the conservative vote. He didn't. Goldwater got 39 percent of the total vote.) Wallace, after all, drew only 46 electoral votes—about the number California will have after the 1970 reapportionment of electoral seats that follows each decennial census. Nixon carried California by only 223,346 votes, a margin over Humphrey of 3.1 percent. In any attempt to win some of the five Southern Wallace states, Mr. Nixon must be very careful not to lose 112,000 votes in California, or perhaps his margin for error is a bit more if he can get some of California's Wallace vote. In New Jersey, a switch of 32,000 gives 17 electoral votes to the Democrats; in Illinois 68,000 switches provide 26 votes to the Democrats. Just let the voters feel that their President is trying to outbid George Wallace in the South, and watch those slim non-Southern pluralities melt all over the nation. Let Richard Nixon say he's going to run over a demonstrator with his car, and watch the seepage from voters who might well like to run over demonstrators with *their* car but would find such rhetoric unseemly from a President.

Furthermore, there is another, but very potent, reason to believe that Nixon will not deal with Wallace, nor will he try any number of cute political tricks that the strategists will conjure up. Presidents, strange as it may seem, are honorable men, honestly trying to do their best for the nation. This notion is apparently indigestible to large segments of the political press that find cabals and conspiracies beneath every press release. But in fact, being President places very real constraints on political operations. A *candidate*—some candidates and some tacticians anyway—can plot a nifty antiblack ploy that will allow Nixon to pick up Wallace votes. But Richard Nixon is not only a *candidate*, but a *President* running for reelection. And no President who is responsible is going to play the race-hatred game in the already tense racial climate in America. That may seem to some to be a naive view of the Presidency, but we submit it as a valid one, duly demonstrated by each of the recent Presidents in America: They do what they feel is in the best interests of the nation, even when it hurts them politically. Richard Nixon does not believe that turning back the clock on civil rights or that drumming upon antiblack sentiments is in the best interests of the nation. Accordingly, he will not so act.

The Young. Candidate Nixon vowed, in the argot of a man who forgot the argot, that he would "sock it to them." Yet, Nixon ended up as the man who allegedly appealed least to the young, turned-on college generation. He won the election.

There are two critical questions to ask about young voters when we think about their electoral impact. First: Can they by their votes actually elect anyone? Second: Can young people by their influence or activity get others to help elect a candidate?

To the first question we may answer: Few groups are as electorally weak as are young people.

There are many, many more people over thirty than there are between twenty-one and thirty:

Percent of Total Vote, by Age, 1968

Age	Percent of Total Vote
Under 30	17%
30–64	68%
65 and over	15%

(*U.S. Census Bureau*)

Furthermore, although the rhetoric of the "kids" in 1968 dealt heavily with "participatory democracy," the cold fact is that young people eligible to vote are far less likely to participate than their elders:

Estimated Percent of Eligible Population
Who Voted, by Age, 1968

Age	Percent Voted
18–20	
21–24	51%
25–29	60%
30–64	72%
65 and over	66%

(U.S. Census Bureau)

[Editor's note: When this article was written only four states permitted persons under twenty-one to vote. Since then, of course, the Twenty-Sixth Amendment to the Constitution has been ratified, giving eighteen-year-olds the right to vote in federal elections.]

In part, this lack of participation is accounted for by the difficulties encountered by first-time registration and absentee ballot voting for students and military personnel. But regardless of reason, they simply take less part in elections than do their elders.

Still, one of every six voters is under thirty. This, of course, could be vitally important in a Presidential contest *if* young people voted monolithically. Some groups in American political life do. Young people don't.

On the eve of the Presidential election, at a time when young people were pictured in the press as liberal, college-educated, dovish on Vietnam, pro-Kennedy, pro-McCarthy intellectuals:

Vietnam—Hawks and Doves (Self-identified)

	Under 30	30–49	50 and over
Hawk	45%	48%	40%
Dove	43%	40%	42%
No Opinion	12%	12%	18%

(Gallup, October, 1968)

Young people were *more* hawkish than the over-fifty generation.

Surveys of 1968 voting tell us that young people were also slightly more likely to vote for *Wallace* than older voters although they were also more pro-Humphrey. Obscured during the dramatic primary campaigns that pitted Senator McCarthy against Senator Kennedy was the fact that many young Americans were not for either one of them. It is too easy to forget that the hands which held the tire chains threatening Martin Luther King, Jr., when he marched to Cicero, Illinois, were young white hands. Being a young American apparently connotes nothing more than a chronological fact: Some are liberal, some conservative; some are of the right, some of the left; many are in the center. As a Daniel Yankelovich survey for Columbia Broadcasting showed in 1969, there is a much greater class gap between the attitudes of those young people in college and those not in college than there is a generation gap between young people generally and their parents.

The second question is harder to answer: Can young people, particularly the activist college youth, influence other voters? Are they a key electoral target for this reason?

That is certainly so, but it is a two-way street. When the McCarthy kids assembled thousands strong in New Hampshire and Wisconsin and rang every doorbell in sight, they showed that an ancient tactic of the Old Politics could be refitted and made to work on a grander scale. Door-to-door campaigning had been usually effective in the United States only when the candidate himself did it, typically in a local election. The idea of mounting a troop of 5000 clear-eyed, articulate, appealing campaign workers in a state the size of New Hampshire would normally have been unthinkable. Had such a political troop been raised in more normal times it would likely have consisted of middle-aged women beginning to sag and middle-aged men smoking cigars—and there would always have been the question of whether they would gain votes for their candidates or repel them. There was little question of the effectiveness of the "Be Clean for Gene" kids. They were effective campaigners.

Yet consider the two-edged sword of strong identification with activist youth. In the spring of 1968, the students of Columbia took over the campus; in April 1968, on the night of Martin Luther King's death, there was looting and burning in 100 cities, and Americans watched as (mostly young) black militants proclaimed their televised incantations about burning down a corrupt white society; in August 1968, young peace demonstrators shouting obscenities clashed with Mayor Daley's police. Rather suddenly, there was a legitimate question about "kidlash": Might not youth support be the kiss of death for any candidate who sought to appeal to the broad middle class of America?

The fact that youths today are more likely to be college-educated would not normally correlate to a more Democratic or more liberal electorate in the future. In the past, the more educated a voter, the more likely he has been to be affluent, and the more educated and affluent the voter, the more likely he has been to vote Republican and think conservatively. This happened even though the 1930s equivalents of the "kids" were radicals, agitators, Communists, or what have you. There would not seem to be any good reason for this pattern to change. Only a small percentage of the current college youth are categorized as "revolutionaries," 3.5 percent in the Yankelovich/CBS survey. Another 9.5 percent are categorized as "radical reformers." The balance, about 87 percent, are "moderate reformers," "middle of the road," or "conservatives," and there are, incidentally, slightly more "conservatives" than "radical reformers." In short, the college experience may be regarded as liberalizing, but not revolting. And doctors who will be making $60,000 a year in the 1970s or 1980s would not seem to be good bets to be throwing rocks through hospital windows.

By the decade's end a projection based on Census data reveals that only 10 percent of the electorate will be "young college graduates" (i.e., under age forty in 1980). Later on in the century, in the elections of 1984, 1988, 1992, 1996, the percentage of college-educated in the electorate will be rising substantially. But an interesting question arises: In the land of the one-eyed is the one-eyed king? When most people are college-educated, will the fact of college education mean much politically? Isn't it likely then that the elitist will not be the "college graduate," but perhaps the PhD, while the mere college graduates are relegated to the ranks of the unwashed?

The Radical Left. The ideal of confrontation politics, of confusing cops with pigs, of justifying riots, of sympathy for muggers and rapists, of support of the drug culture or the gay culture—seem to have an extremely limited constituency. Not only are these ideas thoroughly and totally rejected by an overwhelming majority of Middle Americans, but they are rejected by a large portion of their supposed natural constituency as well: blacks, Mexican-Americans, poor people, Jews, young people. The more radical aspects of the New Left are a psephological [electoral] fraud. It has no constituency worth counting. Furthermore, even sympathy for, let alone espousal of, those radical aspects can poison the well of any sincere candidate for public office.

This seems to leave the Radical Left with four basic choices:

Choice One: Back to the drawing boards. Rethink. Examine again the propositions; question the validity and justifications of radicalism versus the backlash it breeds. Take a deep breath of fresh air, and come up brainwashed—reconstituted as Old Liberals. An admittedly difficult choice.

Choice Two: Retain the radical beliefs, but sear into one's political soul the idea that they are psephological poison. Accordingly, clam up on the radical aspects of the Social Issue, and concentrate on making the best compromise possible with the Democratic center. The center of the Democratic Party supports most, if not all, of the nonradical substantive demands of the left. The issues of better housing, aid to education, low unemployment are not the exclusive province of radicals. Nor is integration a taboo issue. The center of the Democratic Party is receptive to demands for bettering the conditions of blacks in the United States. It is sometimes a difficult political issue these days, but not an impossible one.

Choice Three: Withdraw from major-party politics. Form a fourth party that is ideologically as pure as the driven snow, a party unwilling to compromise intellectually with the center of the national Democratic Party. Be prepared that such a fourth party will have a very limited appeal and won't elect anyone to anything and that it will probably split into several factions within three years. This choice is not offered facetiously. It is the choice that a peaceful man like Norman Thomas took, and Mr. Thomas eventually wielded great influence on political thought in America and lived to see many of his "radical" ideas enacted into law and become a beneficial part of American life. Remember, the center is a moving center and can be moved in many ways. The process of changing society does not always come about through the machinery of a political party power. It can come simply from the articulation of an idea whose time has come—or almost come—from a minor party or from no party at all. The Anti-Saloon League brought about Prohibition— but it was not a political party.

As a subvariant of Choice Three, a further choice is offered: Depoliticize completely. Perhaps politics is not the answer to the real problems that so much of the New Left is concerned with: alienation, identity, rootlessness, and the harsh fact that life is at least somewhat absurd. There is no denying that these are major human problems, but there is room to question whether there is any beneficial reason to clutter up major-party national politics with the distracting notion that living is not as easy as it seemed in high school.

It is unlikely that an extreme left party would meet with the same relative success that greeted the Wallace right. Because of the electoral college system, Wallace's strength in the South brought him electoral votes. An extreme left party would not be regional; would not, therefore, get any electoral votes; and would therefore be in a minimal bargaining position. (This would change in the event of the passage of a popular vote for President system.) Furthermore, unlike the Wallace situation, an extreme left party would take almost all of its votes from one party—the Democratic Party. If it ever got strong, then, it could only be a "spoiler" ensuring Republican victories. As a weak party, however, an extreme left party might be helpful to Democrats, by getting the crazies out of the tent, decreasing the identification of "Democrats" as "radicals."

A final possibility: If Senator McCarthy should be a fourth-party candidate he might try to go for the center rather than the extreme, attempting to bridge the Republican-Democratic gap. He had some Republican/suburban-type strength in 1968 and might try to take some of Nixon's vote and go for a 26 percent-type victory in a four-man race. It won't work. In a showdown, those Republican votes will stay with Nixon.

Choice Four: Become real revolutionaries; attempt violently to take control of the national government, or the campus, or the city hall. Prepare against the possibility of languishing in jail for long periods of time under extremely inhospitable surroundings, sure only that a movement toward "real" revolution will trigger "real" repression.

Correspondence: Real Majorities *

Sirs:

In their "Strategy for Democrats" (August 15) Richard C. Scammon and Ben J. Wattenberg once again illustrate the faulty conclusions that can be reached by relying exclusively on projections from historical statistical data as a means for analyzing the future of electoral politics. The interesting quality of the future is the promise that the future will differ from the present and from the past. Unlike Scammon and Wattenberg, we believe that the reasons why voters in the 21 to 29 age bracket in 1968 failed to vote at the higher levels of those 30 and over are crucial in formulating both a winning and progressive strategy for the Democrats to recapture the White House in 1972.

A principal reason for this failure to vote at the percentage levels reached by older Americans was that many younger voters felt they had no one with whom they might identify and for whom they might vote in November, 1968. It is quite likely that a Democratic Presidential candidate who appeals to younger voters and who sponsors a vigorous registration campaign directed to them will be able to substantially increase their percentage participation at the polls. This development would be significant in view of the fact that U.S. Census figures show that although voters under 30 cast 17 percent of the total vote in 1968 they comprised 21 percent of the voting-age population in 1968. If the Supreme Court sustains the recent congressional statute lowering the voting age to 18, this will provide immediately a large number of new voters in the 18–21 range (10 to 12 million).

The authors tell us that there are only two "critical" questions to ask about young voters and their electoral impact: "Can they by their votes actually elect anyone? Can young people by their influence or activity get others to help elect a candidate? As to the first question, we are told that the answer is no because young voters do not comprise an absolute majority of the electorate and because they don't vote "monolithically." We would restate the first of these questions to read: "Can the Democratic candidate for President in 1972 excite enough interest among voters under 30 to increase the turnout enough and shift the party-vote distribution enough to win the election?" The answer to this question is a resounding, yes! Only a modest increase in turnout or a modest shift in party preference would be necessary. Young voters do not need to vote monolithically to produce this result. To illustrate, Richard Nixon won 43.4 percent of the vote in 1968 to Hubert Humphrey's 42.7 percent. Voters under 30 cast 17 percent of the vote in 1968. It is self-evident that if younger voters had selected Humphrey in only very slightly greater numbers than they in fact did, he would have won the election.

It is in the authors' comments on the second "critical" question that they exhibit a particular myopia. As the authors admit, "the idea of mounting a troop of 5000 clear-eyed, articulate, appealing campaign workers in a state the size of New Hampshire" was "unthinkable" to professionals in 1968— but highly successful. Yet the authors now posit a "kidlash" brought about by the events since 1968. There is little basis for believing that a troop of campaign workers similar to that used in New Hampshire would arouse a "kidlash" against a candidate today. Such workers won the 1970 Democratic primary for Bella Abzug in New York and almost won it for Peter Eikenberry. (Naturally a door-to-door campaign mounted by a group of Abbie Hoffmans in full hippie regalia would bring about a negative reaction.) There is no reason to believe that Americans in 1970 or 1972 will react distastefully to young, clear-eyed, and articulate campaigners, whereas in 1968 they reacted favorably.

The authors' comments about the radical left and the juxtaposition of their remarks with their comments about the young raise a host of questions. Who comprise the "radical left?" Who are those who adhere to "extreme left" positions? What are "radical beliefs?" The authors have lumped together "confrontation politics," with "confusing cops and pigs," "justifying riots," "sympathy for muggers and rapists," and "support of the drug culture or the gay culture" in defining the "radical left." Why should confrontation politics be lumped together with these other concepts? Is not confrontation traditional to American politics, and, indeed, one crucial element that has brought the workingman, the blacks, and other groups into fuller participation in our system? Why should one who believes in confrontation be labeled "radical left," a "crazy," and written off as a sympathizer with muggers and rapists who have no legitimate constituency. . . .

There are many different ways to mold a majority coalition to win a Presidential election and govern the country. None of these majorities is any more "real" than the others. We prefer a majority that can both win and deal with the problems of our society. We have had such majorities before; we can have them again.

Peter F. Rousselot
Raymond E. Vickery, Jr.

In reply:
If, indeed, younger voters were to turn out in greatly increased numbers, and if they were to vote heavily (not even massively) one way *or* the other, it would certainly have an effect.

My own guess, however, is that both premises, while certainly not impossible, are less likely, as indeed was the case with Goldwater in 1964. The language then was almost exactly the duplicate of Rousselot's and Vickery's, only then it was the American conservative who ". . . felt they had no one with whom they might identify and for whom they might vote in November, 1968 . . .," substituting 1964 for 1968.

There is, of course, another point here which has real possibilities. The premise of many observers (including possibly your correspondents), is that American youth are left-oriented on Vietnam and will turn out heavily for a candidate who rejects this "immoral" conflict and promises to get out yesterday. But is this correct?

Let us examine a specific Gallup Poll in May of this year. To the query, "Do you think the U.S. made a mistake sending troops to fight in Vietnam?," the response, nationally and by age, was:

	Yes	No	No Opinion
National	56%	36%	8%
Under 30	49	48	3
30 to 49	53	41	6
50 and over	61	26	13

Note that the *most hawkish group are those under 30.* Though the whole country shows a solid "Yes, it was a mistake" opinion, young people are almost evenly divided. Though those over 50 think our action was a mistake by better than two-to-one, young voters think so by one percentage point.

Richard Scammon
Washington, D.C.

STUART H. LOORY

How We Could Succeed in
Making Our Elections Meaningless

Let me start by saying that if I do violence to the ideas of Richard C. Scammon and Ben J. Wattenberg, it's all intentional. They have written a clever book, *The Real Majority*, and the problem is that politicians have been taking it too seriously. Hubert Humphrey used to tell the voters back in 1968: "If you want to live like a Republican, vote Democratic." Scammon and Wattenberg—and here's where my friends say I do them violence—say that if a Democrat wants to get elected these days, he has to act like a Republican.

I find that idea deeply disturbing; not necessarily because I am anti-Republican but because I am pro-freedom-of-choice when it comes to elections.

The Scammon-Wattenberg (S&W) idea is not to face issues but to finesse them. Their strategy is not to lead the great, vast center of the American body politic in the directions necessary for national survival but to pander to the center. They say that candidates are not judged by what they actually are but rather by what the voters perceive them to be.

No sooner had their book found its way into the stores than Establishmentarian politicians of all persuasions adopted it as a text. And so there was Adlai E. Stevenson III proudly displaying an American flag in his lapel in Illinois, Richard M. Nixon hiring a union hall in East Baltimore, and Hubert H. Humphrey proclaiming his love for guns and hunting in Minnesota.

The 1970 election was a test for the Scammon-Wattenberg thesis. It was to 1972 as the Spanish Civil War was to World War II, an experimental conflict for the bigger one to come. It was the proving ground for the idea that candidates could be packaged en masse as Richard Nixon was packaged in 1968.

It was not the Model T that revolutionized the automobile industry. It was the assembly-line technique that Henry Ford gave us. And similarly, it

Source: Mr. Loory is White House correspondent for the Los Angeles *Times*. He covered all of President Nixon's journeys during the 1970 election campaign. With David Kraslow he wrote *The Secret Search for Peace in Vietnam*, which won the Raymond Clapper Memorial Award. Reprinted from *The Progressive*, January 1971, pp. 18–20, by permission of the publisher.

174

was not the results of the 1970 election that were of most importance. Rather it was the nature of the campaigns that were the proving grounds for the finesse-the-issue strategy and the mass-produced image.

Political image-making *circa* 1968 was still pretty much a custom-built job. By 1970, the consulting firms, the media experts, and the Scammon-Wattenberg type of strategists had turned it into an assembly-line product. From Murphy to Muskie, from Bumpers to Buckley, the political packagers had themselves such an orgy that when it was all over they could afford to hire, as they did, a hall in New York's Lincoln Center for a two-day idea-exchanging session.

Among other things they learned at the conference, if they needed to be told at all, was that it was good politics to be taunted by "hippies." Mickey Smith, a Texas packager who handled Democratic Governor Preston Smith's winning campaign for re-election, related how the governor was threatened with a bomb scare while speaking at the University of Houston.

"The story that the governor was chased off the stage by a hippie with a broom was not exactly true," Smith told his colleagues. "The governor was heckled by some students, all right, and he decided to walk out. And there was this guy with a broom. But I don't know whether he was a hippie or not; he might have been a janitor. But the press ran it the other way and that was all right with us. The governor had a lot of sympathy as a result."

What was good for a Texas Democrat was considered terrific for a Vermont Republican. One Saturday morning in October, President Nixon flew to Burlington, Vermont, to speak at a rally for incumbent Republican Senator Winston L. Prouty, who was facing a challenge from former Democratic Governor Philip Hoff. There was a handful of anti-war demonstrators on hand—maybe several handfuls—outside the National Guard hangar building when Mr. Nixon arrived, and enough police and National Guardsmen to stave off an attack on the Japanese Diet by hordes of snake-dancing leftists.

The Burlington demonstrators were only a small proportion of a crowd of several thousand good, solid Green Mountaineers who had braved bitter, damp cold to come out to greet their President. Few could even see Mr. Nixon. Their view was blocked by two rows of helmeted, visored state police and National Guardsmen, each wielding a big riot stick, many carrying cans of mace on their belts, in an ominous looking cordon around the crowd.

As the President advanced from Air Force One to the hangar building, a single, large-size stone (call it a small rock, if you will) lofted softly out of the crowd and landed harmlessly on the periphery of the official party, nowhere near the President. The Secret Service showed an utter lack of concern over the missile at the time. Later, Pat Lahey, the local state's attorney, said that at a post-mortem of the rally by the Secret Service, state police, and local officials, "The incident was dismissed as inconsequential. No one seemed concerned."

But you never would have gotten that impression from the President or his staff. Flying away from Burlington aboard Air Force One, Charles Colson, a political aide to Mr. Nixon, was ecstatic over the incident, telling newsmen:

"One rock is worth 10,000 votes to Senator Prouty."

How that rock was to grow. In the following week, Mr. Nixon referred to the Burlington incident no less than thirteen times in eight speeches. Typical was the passage on the State House steps in Columbus, Ohio:

I know people are concerned where there are those that throw rocks at the President of the United States, as they did in Vermont. I know there are those who are concerned when people shout four letter obscenities, as this crowd over here is doing. And so they say, what do we do? . . .

My friends, here is what you do on November 3rd. The answer to those who shout obscenities, who throw rocks, who engage in violence, is not to answer in kind, but with the most powerful voice in the history of mankind, one vote. . . .

Meanwhile, on a lower road, Vice President Spiro T. Agnew, two days after the rock was lobbed, expressed indignation that the press had not made more of it. Imagine, criticizing the press for not blowing up an incident only two years after another Administration had criticized it for making far too much out of the Chicago convention street scene.

Agnew, who happened to be speaking in Chicago, of all places, said that Mr. Nixon, in Burlington, had been the target for a "shower of rocks thrown by radical young thugs" and complained that "that physical attack on the President . . . was buried in some news columns and went unmentioned in others."

Burlington proved to be little more than a road-show tryout for San Jose, California. No one can prove that he did it deliberately but, nonetheless, Mr. Nixon provoked an already anxious crowd of demonstrators (standing atop a car, giving the peace sign with both hands, and saying, "That's what they hate to see") and then his motorcade, instead of taking an already open route, took a route which the police had to open through the crowd.

The limousine, a veritable fortress on wheels, was hit with eggs, placards, and other missiles of unknown description as it led the long motorcade through the crowd. Senator George Murphy, who was riding with the President, described the objects, from the sound, as something the size of half-bricks. If a stone is worth 10,000 votes, what is the value of a half-brick?

The San Jose incident occurred on a Thursday. The following Monday, the day before the election, Murphy's campaigners inundated California with radio and newspaper advertisements headlined ANARCHY (the type was 120 point black face—1200 per cent bigger than this type—in the *Los Angeles Times*). The message read:

The riot last Thursday night at the Murphy rally in San Jose, which threatened the lives of President Richard Nixon, Governor Reagan and Senator Murphy, had ought to make it clear that the decision you will make tomorrow will be between:

ANARCHY
or
LAW AND ORDER

Senator George Murphy
Has Supported Every Law and Order Bill.
Rep. John Tunney
Has Not. It's That Simple.

But it wasn't quite that simple. When the moment of decision came, Tunney defeated Murphy, and one post-election survey revealed that Californians threw out the song-and-dance man mainly because they thought an early end to the Vietnam war was a more important issue than law and order. If the survey is correct, the voters' perceptions were at sharp variance with those of most politicians.

Texas, Vermont, and California, to take only three examples, were Scammon-Wattenberg concepts carried to their logical extreme on the so-called "social issue." Be firm on law and order and you can say whatever else you want. Their strategic axiom: The votes are cast by the unyoung, the unpoor, the nonblack.

In 1970, this dictated the political tactic of campaigning *against* the young. It was that simple, to borrow Murphy's campaign line, and that shoddy. And who is to say that in 1971 we might not see politicians campaigning against the poor and the black as well? That is a downright frightening prospect.

The problem of taking S&W too seriously was only one of the dangers of the 1970 elections. Another involved the manner in which the nation's law enforcement officers were drawn into the political process not as protectors of the peace but as imposers of a point of view.

One can argue that in an age of assassination extraordinary measures are necessary to protect the President of the United States against bodily danger. But when the National Guard is called out, as it was at Burlington, and forms an olive-drab gamut at the entrance to the meeting hall down which all who wanted to hear the President had to pass, that is another matter.

And so it is when local police in Teterboro, New Jersey, actually frisked many—but not all—of those who wanted to hear the President, selecting as their victims those who were not dressed properly (in the estimation of the police) or whose hairdos and beards were too long. Similarly, in Anaheim, California, local police were used to screen out youngsters with long hair or sloppy dress trying to get into a Murphy rally at which the President spoke.

It is a mistake to chalk all this up to security, particularly since hecklers were deliberately allowed into many of the rallies. After all the indignity of the friskings, the police, on White House orders, threw the doors wide open in Teterboro to let hecklers in. And one White House official has told me he saw a memo from an Administration advance man which related just where in the audience a group of hecklers would be located at a rally two days hence.

Further, on at least three occasions in 1970, I saw police and the Secret Service—acting almost certainly on orders from the White House staff—beckon crowds *closer* to the President without any regard for the possible danger. It happened in San Diego, New Orleans, and Limerick, Ireland. In each case the purpose appeared to be to allow photographers to get pictures of crowds adulating The Leader.

I can only draw the conclusion that the police—and even the National Guard—are being used to manipulate crowds for political purposes. As one who has lived for two years in the Soviet Union and has scoffed at the manner in which the Communist Party there could rely on the mythical agency, "Rent-A-Crowd," to turn out hundreds of thousands of spectators to line a parade route, or a cheering audience at a party rally, or rock-throwing demonstrators in front of the American Embassy, I find it most unsettling to see the introduction of the same techniques in the United States.

For all its faults, the electoral process is still an important part of the foundation of American democracy. When such blatant police state techniques are introduced, one begins to wonder whether democracy can survive its own self-protection.

Finally, something must be said about the use of radio and television in the 1970 campaign. The crowds along the motorcade routes, the flesh to be pressed at airport barricades, the multitudes in the hangar buildings, convention halls, city squares, and university campuses were important not because they could be talked to—and perhaps convinced—but because they were actors on the larger stage, the stage projected across the land into the living rooms of the nation.

The tube carried the important message, which might have been all right if it had not been packaged to conceal truth from the voters rather than reveal it.

Take Utah for example. Early on, the consulting firm of Joseph Napolitan Associates, Inc., of Washington, tested the electorate there and found that the firm's client, Senator Frank E. Moss, the Democratic incumbent, would have a close race against Representative Laurence J. Burton, the Republican challenger. Another poll showed that if only the race were between Moss' running mate, Democratic Governor Calvin S. Rampton, and Mr. Nixon, Rampton would win easily.

"So we ran a Rampton-Nixon race," one of Napolitan's associates said, "and Moss won easily." He got fifty-five per cent of the vote after a campaign in which Rampton appeared in a saturation television and radio campaign.

Once again, it was S&W raised to the nth degree. If you can finesse issues, why not finesse candidates as well?

It is easy to document the case that the Scammon-Wattenberg strategy and its embellishment by the image-producing tacticians did not work, that the voters showed more common sense than the politicians. But the uneasy feeling persists that the results were ambiguous enough for those who practice manipulatory politics to learn the wrong lessons. They *could* decide to make their candidates more responsive to the voters in 1972. They will probably decide instead to improve on the strategy and technology designed to make the public vote in the best interests of their candidates rather than in those of the country.

During 1970, citizens all over the country were concerned about the apocryphal Rand Corporation study of whether the country could withstand the cancellation of the elections in 1972. Of course no such study was ever made. Yet, if the perversion of the electoral process continues to spread, who is to say that the 1972 elections, by becoming a meaningless formality, will not in effect be cancelled? We scoff at the way the Communist Party of the Soviet Union engineers an election. We have not looked carefully enough at what is happening in this country by comparison.

ROBERT WERNICK

The Perfect Candidate

At intervals through the winter and early spring, variations on the following small ad appeared in a Los Angeles newspaper: "Leading public relations firm with top-flight experience in state-wide campaigns wants state senator candidate."

A number of interested parties made their way to the headquarters of the Public Relations Center on Wilshire Boulevard and subsequently into the office of the Center's boss, a swarthy, jowly, bubbly 50-year-old gentleman named Hal Evry. With the brisk dynamism of his trade, Evry then explained the modern scientific techniques for getting elected to public office. To be sure, an unknown like Pennsylvania's Milton Shapp may still manage to win a gubernatorial primary (*Life*, May 27) with the help of hard work, speeches and taped TV spots, but Evry considers such methods to be both obsolete

Source: Reprinted from *Life*, June 10, 1966, by permission of Cyrilly Abels, agent for the author. Copyright © 1966 by Robert Wernick.

and—worse—risky. For next week's California primaries he has masterminded the campaigns of a half dozen candidates—both local and statewide, including one for state senator. Evry is confident that all six of his men will win.

Other P.R. men start with a candidate and an Issue, then try to sell them to the people. Hal Evry starts with the people, and 90 or more per cent of the time he ends up with a winner. (He says he has elected 35 out of the 39 clients whom he has represented in the past 10 years.) He has persuaded dozens of southern California towns to incorporate as cities, and he has persuaded dozens of others not to incorporate. He has pushed through dozens of school bond issues, and he could have beaten an equal number except that what he calls "a certain emotional immaturity" keeps him from ever taking the anti-school side. Evry and his Center have been so successful that already they are branching out to run campaigns this year in Newark, in Baltimore and in Alaska. They also hold $100-a-day seminars for would-be candidates and their managers to expound their techniques for winning elections.

If it's so easy, why can't you or I be elected to some high office?

Well, we can. Hal Evry will do it with pleasure. All he asks from us in return are these three things:

First, enough cash to pay for a campaign: $60,000 for state senator; $100,000 for a seat in the U.S. Congress; and so on. The Center's fee is a flat 20%. The operative word is *cash*.

Prospective clients are always coming in to the Center and saying, "I've just seen my important old friend Joe Bonanza and he's 100% for me. Isn't that great?" Hal Evry doesn't believe in dream worlds. "Gee, that's great, it really is," he answers. "Now, would you mind telling me to just what extent Old Joe is 100% behind you? Fifty thousand dollars worth? Two thousand? Two hundred? Oh, I see."

Second, we must present a character, or least the appearance of a character, which fits into what Evry calls the "code of the great middle cluster of normality."

Presumably there has to be some sort of reality behind the appearance, but it's the appearance that counts. After all, Evry says, people voted for Eisenhower because he looked like a typical benign American father, and for Kennedy because he looked like a typical virile American young man; but no one outside of their immediate families and circle of close acquaintances could have known for sure whether these public images corresponded in any way to reality.

The other day a man came into the Center waving large sums of money and insisting that he had to beat Pat Brown and become governor of California this year because having all the money in the world didn't mean anything any more in modern society; you needed political power, and he had to start getting power right away because he didn't want to run against Bobby—he wanted to run against Humphrey. Evry could not help being impressed by the scope of these ambitions, not to speak of the millions of dollars the man claimed to have made. But Evry turned him down: "When it comes to the public taste, you have to avoid anything that's too different. Goldwater tried to be different, and look what happened to *him*."

And third, we must take an intelligence test and score at least 120 on the Stanford-Binet scale.

The reason for this last is not any residual puritanism in Evry's nature. He is not a nut on the subject of improving the quality of our public servants. In fact, he is fond of repeating the maxim, "You can't upgrade society." The reason is simply that people with only an average I.Q. or less find it difficult to understand Evry's approach, and it takes so much effort to argue with them that it isn't worth the time and money. And yet his approach, as it applies to the conduct of the individual candidate, is simple indeed. It can be summed up in the single adjuratory phrase: Shut up.

According to Evry, all candidates talk too much. From the magic moment when first they feel that shaft of light from heaven, that ghostly finger touching their shoulder and summoning them to a life of public service, they also feel a compulsion to get out and bend the ears of their fellow-citizens—with messages, with arguments, with Issues; and their fellow-citizens couldn't care less.

"Have you ever noticed the audience at a political speech?" asks Evry. "Reporters are always looking at the candidate, but the interesting part of the scene is the audience. Have you seen them when the man gets to Point Five of his eleven-point program for reforming the world? How they're all fidgeting and sneaking looks at their watches?

"Hell, we had a lunch the other day for one of our candidates. I wouldn't let him show up. Some of his friends insisted on making speeches, so I let five of them do it—for one and a half minutes each. That's the absolute maximum anyone will pay attention to a speech."

Evry may stretch a point in a particular case. At present he is running Ivy Baker Priest, ex-treasurer of the U.S. for treasurer of California, and since she is, as he says, "a glib, eloquent person," he lets her prowl a bit on the lecture circuit. But fundamentally he considers all such speeches a waste of time.

The object of Mrs. Priest's campaign, according to Evry, is not to put across theories of high finance but simply to get people to know that there is such a person as Ivy Baker Priest and such an office as treasurer of California.

The goal of recognition can be reached more easily with less expense and worry by taking a big ad in the local paper saying *I Like Ivy* than by sending her off to make a speech, even a good speech before a couple of hundred people who would probably vote for her anyway. Furthermore, Evry points out, after even the best speech in the world—a one-and-a-half minute knockout —what is to prevent some kook in the audience from getting up and asking a question like, "Should we impeach Earl Warren?" The candidate has to answer the question, and *then* where is he—or she?

As Evry says, there are three ways of answering a question: Yes, No, or something in between. Whatever answer you give is going to irritate the people holding the other two positions, so in the long run if you keep on answering all sorts of questions you may end up alienating two-thirds of the voters. That is why Evry candidates are urged to spend a maximum amount of time at the bowling alley, or in Disneyland.

"The ideal campaign," says Evry, "is like Teddy Kennedy's. Where was he? Flat on his back in a hospital. No speeches, and he gets the biggest majority in the history of Massachusetts. Or Lodge winning those primaries. Where was he? In Saigon.

"Whereas you look at the people who have thrown it away because they couldn't keep their big mouths shut. Why did Nixon have to let himself get murdered in those debates with Kennedy? You say the people would have disapproved if he ducked out? What people? How many people? How many people cared when Johnson wouldn't debate Goldwater? Just look at Goldwater! Oh, he learned his lesson finally—he wouldn't talk to anybody. But by that time it was too late."

But aren't there some candidates associated in the voters' minds with intellectual brilliance? Who would have heard of Stevenson if he hadn't made all those stirring speeches?

"Stirring speeches?" says Evry. "What did he stir with them—soup? Sure, millions of people loved his speeches. They loved William Jennings Bryan's speeches. But how many elections did those boys win? If Stevenson had consulted me, I'd have told him: Get rid of Schlesinger and all those guys. I would have run him as 'Old Joe' Stevenson, with that hole in his shoe. He would have had a chance that way."

It isn't just speeches that Evry wants to get rid of, it's the whole standards of the past, it should be a safe seat for Mr. Beilenson.

But here comes Alex Campbell. "He is one of the finest men I ever met," says Evry. "A pioneer oil developer. Quiet, mild-mannered, utterly objective— he makes me look biased, he's so objective—48 years old. What I'd call an average American, a typical Presbyterian Scotsman. He was hanging around the Joe Shell headquarters—remember, Shell was running against Nixon for the Republican nomination for governor a few years back—and he saw all these party workers scurrying around, and got to wondering what they really did. He came to me and said, 'Do they really do anything?' I said, 'No.' So a little later he said, 'Why don't I run for state senator—just for the heck of it? I've done everything else, just about. It would be sort of nice.'

"So now we're running him. He can't lose. *In the Lincoln Tradition*, we call it.

"First we win the primary next week. Alex is registered as a Republican. At first he didn't know which party he wanted to run in, but we told him he was registered and he couldn't switch. There's a publisher of some sort running against him, and it will look good when we beat him.

"Then, by November, we'll have had time to really work on the voters.

They'll be going for Lincoln or for Campbell's soup, or both. You can't beat the combination."

To observers who charge that this type of campaign degrades the level of politics by making possible the election of unqualified candidates, Evry replies that unqualified candidates are being elected all the time under the old methods, and the new methods may actually improve the level of politics by bringing in candidates who would not have run in the old unsophisticated days. And, he adds, the way things are now, only noisy boisterous types are apt to run for public office—people who love to press the flesh of thousands of their sweaty countrymen and who love to talk at the top of their voices. But under Evry's methods of candidacy—or noncandidacy, if you prefer— refined introverted types as well can run and win: they certainly won't wear themselves out by trying. All they have to do is have the courage of Evry's convictions and pay no attention to critics.

"In the long run," reads a document prepared by the Center, "only he will achieve basic results in influencing public opinion who is able to reduce problems and issues to the simplest terms and who has the courage to keep forever repeating them in this simplified form despite the objection of the intellectuals."

Let doubters chew over the story of the 1964 elections. An unknown named Jerry Pettis came to Evry and Dresser, and asked for help in running for Congress in the 33rd District. They were willing, and they ran a campaign based entirely on cartoons of a little boy and a little girl lying on their backs with warm folksy words ballooning out of their mouths on the order of: "I like Jerry Pettis. He likes us kids."

Jerry Pettis outdrew every single candidate of both parties in the primaries. Then he got cold feet, called in a bigger, fancier public-relations outfit, which outfitted him with a good deal of ponderous material about Issues. Pettis compounded *that* sin by making speeches—and he was defeated in November.

Though the lesson should be plain for all to see, prospective candidates still come forward and run on tired old slogans like, *It's Time for a Change.* But the computers at the Center have conclusively proved that this is one of the worst of all possible slogans: the average person doesn't like change. (On the other hand, if you simply want to *improve* things, he'll buy that.) The computers also indicate that politicians are out of their minds when they insist on making their positions clear on offshore oil, balance of payments, water pollution and all that esoteric jazz. What the voters really worry about is bound to be closer to home. As a matter of fact, the thing that most voters of California worry about most is Parking Meters. Evry is looking for a man brave enough to run the Evry way for Attorney General of the State. The campaign would cost a quarter of a million dollars and would consist of one giant slogan: *End the Parking-Meter Racket!* It would be a shoo-in.

Hal Evry does not want power or even glory for himself. He is just an unassuming, politically unambitious, horse-playing, average American. But his brown eyes light up when he talks of that day—coming soon, he says, perhaps not precisely in 1984 but thereabouts—when the techniques of motivational analysis and sampling and polling will be so refined that, instead of going through the sweat and strain of a national election, a flick of an IBM machine will poll a cross-section of American voters. They will be intensively questioned on just what they want their President to be: dark or fair, tall or short, paternally benign or youthfully virile, grandiloquent or soft-spoken, hawk or dove. Their answers will be tabulated and constructed into a profile of the ideal President the people want.

Then, all the people who want to be President will have their characteristics coded and fed into a machine. *Whir! Clack!*—and the one candidate whose card most closely corresponds to the ideal will be chosen. Finally, a guaranteed-typical, central cluster of 1,000 All-American voters will vote. The peoples' choice—the Evry Man—wins again.

WILLIAM SAFIRE

The All-Purpose Political Speech, 1968

Political argot, in its refined form, permits some candidates to take firm stands on all sides of every issue. If he applies his skill, the man who deeply understands the language of politics can earn the supreme accolade: "Nobody can quarrel with that." Here is the unassailable, meaningful, knowledgeable speech of 1968, lavishly footnoted to show derivations.

My friends:
In this campaign, the burning questions and paramount issues cannot be straddled by me-tooers and yes-butters who would be all things to all men.[1]

Source: Mr. Safire is author of *The New Language of Politics: An Anecdotal Dictionary of Catchwords, Slogans and Political Usage* (Random House, 1968). This article is from *The New York Times Magazine*, June 9, 1968, pp. 39, 42, 47, 49, 52. © 1968 by The New York Times Company. Reprinted by permission of the publisher.

[1] *All things to all men:* now two-facedness, but originally the strategy of the Apostle Paul, quoted in the Bible as, "I am made all things to all men, that I might by all means save some."

We will talk sense to the American people in this grassroots crusade to throw the rascals out—the hacks, hangers-on, henchmen and hatchetmen, the wardheelers and wheelhorses, the gophers [2] and snollygosters [3] who feed at the public trough.

At the outset, let me make clear that I will not join a cabal of any stop movements, dump movements, powergrabs or whispering campaigns; at the same time, I will not be steamrollered, smoke-screened or subjected to gag rule by any bloc of sachems, satraps, high mucky mucks,[4] solons or kingmakers power-brokering their hand-picked dark horses [5] in smoke-filled rooms, nor stampeded at a rigged convention by gallery-packing or a voice from the sewer.[6]

I am neither running like a dry creek nor running for the exercise; in this crunch, I am running scared, like a singed cat, despite my above-politics role as noncandidate.

Mine shall be a whirlwind,[7] whistle-stopping,[8] flat-out campaign; on the hustings I shall eschew the front porch; I am hell-bent for election and throw my hat in the ring to joyfully stump the rubber-chicken circuit.

Though I am a regular and against insurgents, I am for reform; while I would like to see a new face at the top of the ticket, I will not turn my back on an old pro willing to press the flesh and lay on the hands.

To the angry young men, I say: I was once a Young Turk [9] myself and reject the prophets of gloom and doom who make up the standpatters and mossbacks of the Old Guard. However, mavericks and mugwumps only

[2] *Gopher:* a political volunteer willing to "go for" coffee and assume other menial tasks.

[3] *Snollygoster:* according to Harry Truman, who reactivated this Civil War epithet, "a man born out of wedlock."

[4] *High mucky mucks:* big shots; from Chinook Indian jargon, *hiu* (plenty) *muck-a-muck* (food); hence, one who has plenty to eat, a powerful chieftain. Powwows of political party elders also include "sachems" and "mugwumps," both American Indian words, though the latter has gained a pejorative connotation, as an insurgent who straddles a fence with "his mug on one side and his wump on the other."

[5] *Dark horse:* a long-shot or compromise candidate; coined in a novel by Benjamin Disraeli in 1831. Probably first used politically sometime between the elections of James Polk in 1844 and Franklin Pierce in 1852. "We Polked You in 1844, We'll Pierce You in 1852" was Pierce's slogan, despite which he won. Other horseracing metaphors in politics include "bolt," "running mate" and "shoo-in."

[6] *Voice from the sewer:* the voice that began the chant, "We Want Roosevelt," when it appeared that F.D.R. was unwilling to run for a third term; later identified as a member of Chicago Mayor Kelly's staff at the 1940 Democrat convention, working at a microphone in a subterranean chamber. Now, any offstage voice that seeks to stampede.

[7] *Whirlwind campaign:* any mildly aggressive effort. Disaster metaphors abound in politics: support grows like a "prairie fire," leading to "avalanches" and "landslides"; politicians pray for "lightning to strike." Almost any natural catastrophe is synonymous with good news in politics.

[8] *Whistle-stopping:* a political term unintentionally coined in 1948 by Senator Robert A. Taft.

[9] *Young Turk:* insurgent or restive element; from the reformers who seized power in the Ottoman Empire in 1908 from the aging sultans. First used in U.S. to describe a group of Republican Senators who broke with the leadership in 1929 over tariff legislation.

splinter our power bases, and though I may decide to go fishing, I frown on going off the reservation and condemn those who take a walk.[10]

My front-running opponent is a lightweight, no heft at all, devoid of a *weltanschauung* and unfamiliar with *realpolitik*,[11] a straw man and stalking horse for the fat cats and special interests.

He cannot see the wave of the future or feel the winds of change, which, like a cloud no bigger than a man's hand, will one day thunder on the left and pour a storm of criticism and hail of dead cats [12] on those who, like the floo-floo bird,[13] cannot begin a meaningful dialogue with the charismatic movers and shakers [14] who have a rendezvous with destiny.

Though I never engage in personalities, my opponent is a captive candidate of a palace guard, surrounded by a kitchen cabinet or brain trust—including a rustling behind the jalousies [15] who make up a government by crony,[16] caucusing all too often to strike a blow for freedom.[17]

But my own political coloration is not that of a chameleon on plaid: I am against black power, white racism, red menaces, yellow perils and gray eminences. I turn away from the bleeding hearts,[18] the Comsymps, the welfare staters, the fellow travelers; with equal vehemence, I reject the radical right, the lunatic fringe,[19] the little old ladies in tennis shoes, the old fogies (who

10 *Go fishing*: to refuse to support a candidate of one's party, but without supporting his opponent. *Off the reservation*: to temporarily stray—to support an opposing party's nominee with the intent of returning to the party after the election. *Take a walk*: an outright bolt, coined by Al Smith in 1936.

11 *Weltanschauung*: German for "world view," something people like Joseph Alsop have. *Realpolitik*, pronounced re-AL-pol-i-TIK: often used in the U.S. to mean the realities of politics, or practical politics. In Europe, the German word means power politics, international diplomacy based on strength rather than appeals to world opinion. The use of foreign words in political discourse adds cachet and confusion to a speech.

12 *Hail of dead cats*: criticism accompanying the resignation of an unpopular public figure, coined in 1934 by the department head of the National Recovery Administration, Gen. Hugh Johnson.

13 *Floo-floo bird*: one which flies backward because it is more interested in where it has been than where it is going; a jocular symbol of reaction.

14 *Movers and shakers*: influentials; coined by a 19th-century English poet, Arthur O'Shaughnessy, to mean artists and poets: "We are the music-makers,/ And we are the dreamers of dreams,/ . . . Yet we are the movers and shakers/ Of the world for ever, it seems." Now applied mainly to mucky mucks (see footnote 4), rarely to poets.

15 *Rustling behind the jalousies*: unsolicited advice on political matters from the candidate's wife.

16 *Government by crony*: the buddy system in national affairs; often attributed to F.D.R.'s Interior Secretary, Harold Ickes, but coined in 1946 by an anonymous "press gallery wit" quoted by columnist Arthur Krock; Mr. Krock now admits that the wit was himself.

17 *Strike a blow for freedom*: to enjoy an alcoholic beverage in the privacy of a politician's office.

18 *Bleeding hearts*: conservative's epithet for ultraliberals, possibly derived from the semi-religious "Order of the Bleeding Heart," founded in the Middle Ages to honor the Virgin Mary, whose "heart was pierced with many sorrows."

19 *Lunatic fringe*: originally applied to leftists by Theodore Roosevelt in 1913, as "every reform movement has its lunatic fringe"; currently used to refer to extremists of the right.

are not to be confused with our constructively conservative senior citizens). The middle-of-the-roaders are not dynamic enough for me; my own politics of hope can be found in the mainstream of the vital center, implacably opposed to consensus.

What is the thrust of my own position papers?

In foreign policy, where partisanship should end at the water's edge, I believe in containment and the domino theory, though I feel it is time to make an agonizing reappraisal of brinkmanship and entangling alliances.[20] The Foggy Bottom cookie-pushers, with their no-win policy, should unleash the shirt-sleeve diplomats unafraid of go-it-alone,[21] eyeball-to-eyeball confrontations. Only by honoring our genuine commitments and developing situations of strength in our proper spheres of influence can we avoid becoming the policemen of the world.[22]

I don't want to see another Munich, but we must guard against another Sarajevo. We cannot implement a craven let-the-dust-settle policy when the exacerbating exigencies of overkill call for a bold strategy of watchful waiting.

My defense policy is equally in-depth:

Within given parameters, we must maximize our options to escalate the state of the art—especially the software—which will quantify a credible deterrent, restructure the infrastructure, crank in a fallback position, and make a quantum leap to a pre-emptive strike contingency. Any less viable scenario would be counterproductive.

As for fiscal integrity, I stand for a hold-the-line policy on inflation's cruel spiral, hard money but not tight money, trade-offs to redirect the gold flow, judicious pump-priming to overcome profitless prosperity, and an application of the new economics to get our affluent society out of any rolling readjustments, avoiding boom-and-bust cycles that could curl your hair.

For those of you who have never had it so good, I say don't let them take it away; for those of you who have had enough, I say let's get this country moving again.

On civil rights, I am against Jim Crow and against crime in the streets; I am for all deliberate speed,[23] and I am for law and order and against police brutality during the long hot summer ahead.

I stand foursquare against the logrolling tactics of those who would dip into

[20] *Entangling alliance:* usually misattributed to George Washington; written by Thomas Jefferson.

[21] *Go-it-alone:* forthrightly independent or foolishly isolationist; a metaphor from the card game of four-handed euchre (not "cut-throat" euchre), in which the player doubles his point total if he takes in his tricks without the help of his partner.

[22] *Policemen of the world:* coined in 1888 by Benjamin Harrison as, "We Americans have no commission from God to police the world."

[23] *With all deliberate speed:* a jarring juxtaposition of words going in different directions —verging on the oxymoronic; an old phrase from the English Chancery, first used in U.S. law by Supreme Court Justice Oliver Wendell Holmes in 1912 and applied in 1954 to school desegregation.

the pork barrel and pass the Christmas-tree bills,[24] but hasten to assure the swing voters whose turnout in squeakers is crucial that my advice and consent [25] will never be given to shortchange this banner district.

In my dealings with the pundits of the fourth estate, I have not stooped to backgrounders, leaks, dope stories or trial balloons. Instead, I insist that what I say is not for attribution, preferring the plant to come from reliable sources or official circles, thereby avoiding the foot-in-mouth disease associated with the news-management bloopers of the opposition standard-bearer.

A few simple moral precepts have been my guidelines:

"You Scratch My Back, and I'll Scratch Yours"; "If You Can't Stand the Heat, Get Out of the Kitchen"; "When the Water Reaches the Upper Deck, Follow the Rats." [26]

On that platform, which I call the Great New Just Fair Square Deal Frontier Society, I plump for vox populi's [27] mandate, consistent with my previous Sherman statements and my conviction that the office seeks the man.

---

[24] *Christmas-tree bill:* legislation that contains a variety of pet projects attached as riders; not to be confused with *"put in a Christmas tree,"* a directive to include a note of idealism in a factual speech.

[25] *Advice and consent:* perhaps the oldest English political phrase still in active current use; best known for its use in Article II, section 2, of the U.S. Constitution, the phrase is traceable to Anglo-Saxon King Sigiraed's gift of land to Bishop Eardwolf in 759 A.D. "with the advice and consent of my principal men."

[26] In order, these political proverbs are attributed to (1) Simon Cameron, Lincoln's first Secretary of War; (2) Harry Truman; (3) Claude Swanson, F.D.R.'s first Navy Secretary.

[27] *Vox populi:* the voice of the people, most effectively used as doggerel in the Harding-Cox race in 1920; "Cox or Harding, Harding or Cox/ You tell 'em, populi, you got the vox."

JAMES M. PERRY

Psst, Image Maker, You're Naive

The ink-stained wretches of the print media have been having a ball lately, chortling in knee-slapping glee over the failure of the TV boys on Nov. 3. It is pretty funny, at that.

Whooee. Just look at the losers.

Harry Treleaven, right out of the pages of Joe McGinniss' *The Selling of the President 1968*. He had another go at image making this year, in five campaigns—and he lost four of them. Like, wow!

Charles Guggenheim, the famous award-winning documentary maker. He was image making in eight campaigns—and lost three of them. Way to go, Charlie!

Roger Ailes, Treleaven's skeptical sidekick in Joe McGinniss' book. He was making images in four campaigns; he lost two of them. Roger, Roger, and out!

So now we can all sit back—smugly—and say the American voters aren't so stupid after all. You can't con them with a lot of slick, Madison Avenue commercials. And, from there, a lot of us proceed to this further assumption: Slick professionalism in politics gets the candidate nowhere.

And that simply isn't true.

We need to stop laughing for a while and put this situation in perspective.

Slick professionalism in politics does not mean, by definition, Harry Treleaven, Roger Ailes, and Charles Guggenheim. They are specialists in the art of making TV commercials; they are dabblers in the trade of organizing campaigns.

A lot of people have come to believe that a political campaign is simply an immense TV campaign. For that, we can lay a good bit of the blame on Joe McGinniss. It is the thesis of his immensely successful book that slick image makers took Richard Nixon in hand in 1968, laid him out on a slide under a microscope, decided the creature they beheld needed reshaping, and thereafter employed television to create the "new" Richard Nixon. And that, we are to believe, is why Nixon is President today.

Not so. Nixon's television was, in fact, bland and unconvincing. Although

Source: Mr. Perry is an astute observer of the political scene whose column, "Politics by Perry," appears in *The National Observer*. Reprinted from *The National Observer*, Nov. 16, 1970, by permission of the publisher.

millions were spent on the tube, Nixon's standing in the polls never improved. On the other hand, when Hubert Humphrey's television finally went on the air, his standing began to soar. Television was a factor—one of *several* factors —in bringing Humphrey back to life.

. . . *One of several factors.* That's the key. Television is one of several tools available to campaign managers. Sometimes, it is more important than all the other tools put together.

For examples:

1. A candidate with lots of money can use television to create self-identity. With TV, a politician can become a household word almost overnight (which isn't, of course, a guarantee that he will be elected).

2. A candidate with lots of money can blitz an opponent in a *primary* election—as long as the opponent doesn't have the money to blitz back. The evidence is steadily mounting, in fact, that it is in primaries that TV counts most. Note, this year, Howard Metzenbaum's defeat of John Glenn in Ohio; Lloyd Bentsen's defeat of incumbent Sen. Ralph Yarborough in Texas.

3. Once in a very long while, a candidate with lots and lots of money can blitz a destitute opponent in a general election. It is possible, for example, that Nelson Rockefeller's saturation TV campaign was the deciding factor in his victory in New York's general election in 1966.

For most campaign managers, the problem is that no tool is going to work on huge numbers of voters. John Deardourff, a professional campaign manager, puts it this way:

Before the campaign even begins, 50 per cent or more of the voters already have their minds made up. These are the regular, straight-ticket Republican and Democratic voters. They are going to vote their party come hell or high water. Nothing can change them.

So cross them off. Then, in addition, there are lots of voters who are "leaners"— that is, they tend to vote Democratic regularly or vote Republican regularly. They are very hard to convince.

That leaves maybe 10 or 15 per cent of the electorate that is independent and susceptible. These are the people that a professional campaign is aimed at.

This is where slick professionalism begins to play a part. The question in most campaigns is this: How can the candidate best hang on to his basic party support and how can he best appeal to the "leaners" and the "independents"?

Polls are taken, not to see who's ahead but to see what the issues are, what the people are thinking, how the voters perceive the candidates. A "campaign plan" is written. Issues are given priority. Position papers are written. The candidate's schedule is prepared; he is dispatched to those communities where the "leaners" and the "independents" live.

Television is used two ways. First, the candidate tries to get as much free television as he can, using all kinds of gimmicks to attract the attention of the TV news directors. Second, the candidate purchases TV time and delivers his message in the most dramatic, the most convincing way he can. He uses radio too, and direct mail and rallies and canvassers and press releases.

"If we do our job," says Deardourff, "we can make a difference. But it is not a big difference. I would guess that the spread between a well-managed campaign and a run-of-the-mill campaign would be on the order of eight to ten points. Sometimes, that's enough to win; sometimes, it isn't."

Candidates and issues still count.

Deardourff's firm managed the U.S. Senate campaign this year of Republican Nelson Gross in New Jersey. Gross' campaign, presumably, was well-managed. Everything that should have been done was done. Gross won 42.9 per cent of the vote; his opponent, Democrat Sen. Harrison A. Williams, Jr., won 54.5 per cent of the vote.

How come?

Problems that no image makers could overcome. Gross is Jewish, but doesn't practice his religion. Some gentiles voted against Gross because he is Jewish; some Jews voted against him because he isn't Jewish enough.

Gross had been Republican state chairman. At the GOP convention in 1968, he bolted from support of favorite-son Sen. Clifford Case to vote for Richard Nixon. That made Case angry. Furthermore, voters perceived Gross as a partisan Republican—and, in fact, a partisan Nixon Republican.

New Jersey is heavily Democratic. The more Gross tried to appeal to the "leaners" and the "independents" (in the early stages of the campaign) the more Agnew talked about Democrats as "radiclibs."

The Agnew line, later taken up by the President himself, forced candidates like Gross to make a decision: Follow the party line or be labeled a maverick. He followed the line, attacking the liberal record of his opponent. Ultimately, largely because of events beyond his and his managers' control, his support was shrunk to include only regular Republicans and Republican "leaners."

Deardourff's firm also managed the campaign of Kit Bond in Missouri, for the office of state auditor. Bond is exceedingly bright, highly personable, and very ambitious. In that campaign, everything went on schedule.

The incumbent auditor, a Democrat, was aging and politically inept. He had not been doing much auditing, and a series of scandals had turned up in various state departments. Bond's theme was simple: Elect an "independent" auditor; elect a watchdog.

Bond is very young, so a TV commercial was prepared that showed older people saying nice things about him. In another commercial, Bond held the annual report of Missouri's auditor in one hand, the annual report of Michigan's auditor in the other. The Michigan report is a tome, the Missouri report is a pamphlet. The point was clear—and visually effective. Republican Bond won by 200,000 votes while Republican John C. Danforth, running for the Senate, lost to Stuart Symington by 37,000 votes.

"I think Bond would have won without our help," says Deardourff. "But I think we made a difference."

Two points:

Bond was a good candidate, Gross was a mediocre candidate.

Bond had a compelling issue, Gross' major issue was counterproductive.

Bond won; Gross lost.

So, finally, some aphorisms:

Television is a useful political tool—but it is not all that some people crack it up to be.

Professionalism does count, within rather narrow limits, but no one can work miracles when the candidate is second-rate and when the issues are non-existent.

Joe McGinniss is naive—and so, perhaps, is Harry Treleaven.

NICHOLAS JOHNSON

The Media Barons and the Public Interest

Before I came to the Federal Communications Commission my concerns about the ownership of broadcasting and publishing in America were about like those of any other generally educated person.

Most television programming from the three networks struck me as bland at best. I had taken courses dealing with propaganda and "thought control," bemoaned (while being entertained by) *Time* magazine's "slanted" reporting, understood that Hearst had something to do with the Spanish-American War, and was impressed with President Eisenhower's concern about "the military-industrial complex." The changing ownership of the old-line book publishers and the disappearance of some of our major newspapers made me vaguely uneasy. I was philosophically wedded to the fundamental importance of "the marketplace of ideas" in a free society, and a year as law clerk to my idol,

Source: Federal Communications Commissioner Nicholas Johnson has a well-earned reputation as a crusader against special privilege and is the author of *How to Talk Back to Your Television Set* (Atlantic–Little, Brown; Bantam, 1970). Reprinted from *The Atlantic Monthly*, June 1968, pp. 43–51, by permission of the author. Copyright © 1968 by Nicholas Johnson.

Supreme Court Justice Hugo L. Black, had done nothing to weaken that commitment.

But I didn't take much time to be reflective about the current significance of such matters. It all seemed beyond my ability to influence in any meaningful way. Then, in July, 1966, I became a member of the FCC. Here my interest in the marketplace of ideas could no longer remain a casual article of personal faith. The commitment was an implicit part of the oath I took on assuming the office of commissioner, and, I quickly learned, an everyday responsibility.

Threats to the free exchange of information and opinion in this country can come from various sources, many of them outside the power of the FCC to affect. Publishers and reporters are not alike in their ability, education, tolerance of diversity, and sense of responsibility. The hidden or overt pressures of advertisers have long been with us.

But one aspect of the problem is clearly within the purview of the FCC— the impact of *ownership* upon the content of the mass media. It is also a part of the responsibility of the Antitrust Division of the Justice Department. It has been the subject of recent congressional hearings. There are a number of significant trends in the ownership of the media worth examining—local and regional monopolies, growing concentration of control of the most profitable and powerful television stations in the major markets, broadcasting-publishing combines, and so forth. But let's begin with a look at the significance of media ownership by "conglomerate corporations"—holding companies that own, in addition to publishing and broadcasting enterprises, other major industrial corporations.

During my first month at the FCC I studied the cases and attended the meetings, but purposefully did not participate in voting on any items. One of the agenda items at the July 20 commissioners' meeting proposed two draft letters addressed to the presidents of International Telephone and Telegraph and the American Broadcasting Company, ITT and ABC, Messrs. Harold Geneen and Leonard Goldenson. We were asking them to supply "a statement specifying in further detail the manner in which the financial resources of ITT will enable ABC to improve its program services and thereby better to serve the public interest." This friendly inquiry was my first introduction to the proposed ITT-ABC merger, and the Commission majority's attitudes about it. It was to be a case that would occupy much of my attention over the next few months.

There wasn't much discussion of the letters that morning, but I read carefully the separate statements filed with the letter by my two responsible and experienced colleagues, Commissioners Robert T. Bartley and Kenneth A. Cox, men for whom I was already feeling a respect that was to grow over the following months.

Commissioner Bartley, a former broadcaster with the deep and earthy wisdom one would expect in a Texas-born relative of the late Speaker Sam Rayburn, wrote a long and thoughtful statement. He warned of "the probable far-reaching political, social and economic consequences for the public interest of the increasing control of broadcast facilities and broadcast service by large conglomerate corporations such as the applicants." Commissioner Cox, former lawyer, law professor, counsel to the Senate Commerce Committee, and chief of the FCC's Broadcast Bureau, characterized the proposed merger as "perhaps the most important in the agency's history." He said the issues were "so significant and far-reaching that we should proceed immediately to designate the matter for hearing."

Their concerns were well grounded in broadcasting's history and in the national debate preceding the 1934 Communications Act we were appointed to enforce. Precisely what Congress intended the FCC to do was not specified at the time or since. But no one has ever doubted Congress' great concern lest the ownership of broadcasting properties be permitted to fall into a few hands or to assume monopoly proportions.

The 1934 Act was preceded by the 1927 Radio Act and a series of industry Radio Conferences in the early 1920s. The conferences were called by then Secretary of Commerce Herbert C. Hoover. Hoover expressed concern lest control over broadcasting "come under the arbitrary power of any person or group of persons." During the congressional debates of the 1927 Act a leading congressman, noting that "publicity is the most powerful weapon that can be wielded in a republic," warned of the domination of broadcasting by a "single selfish group." Should that happen, he said, "then woe to those who dare to differ with them." The requirement that licenses not be transferred without Commission approval was intended, according to a sponsoring senator, "to prevent the concentration of broadcast facilities by a few." Thirty years later, in 1956, Senate Commerce Committee Chairman Warren G. Magnuson was still warning the Commission that it "should be on guard against the intrusion of big business and absentee ownership."

These concerns of Congress and my colleagues were to take on fuller meaning as the ITT-ABC case unfolded, a case which eventually turned into an FCC *cause célèbre*. It also demonstrated the enormity of the responsibility vested in this relatively small and little-known Commission, by virtue of its power to grant or withhold membership in the broadcast industry. On a personal level, the case shook into me the realization, for the first time in my life, of the dreadful significance of the ownership structure of the mass media in America.

The ITT-ABC Merger Case

ITT is a sprawling international conglomerate of 433 separate boards of directors that derives about 60 percent of its income from its significant holdings in at least forty foreign countries. It is the ninth largest industrial corporation in the world in size of work force. In addition to its sale of electronic equipment to foreign governments, and operation of foreign countries' telephone systems, roughly half of its domestic income comes from U.S. Government defense and space contracts. But it is also in the business of consumer finance, life insurance, investment funds, small loan companies, car rentals (ITT Avis, Inc.), and book publishing.

This description of ITT's anatomy is taken (as is much of this ITT-ABC discussion) from opinions written by myself and Commissioners Bartley and Cox. We objected, vigorously, to the four-man majority's decision to approve the merger. So did some senators and congressmen, the Department of Justice, the Commission's own staff, the American Civil Liberties Union, a number of independent individuals and witnesses, and a belated but eventually insistent chorus of newspaper and magazine editorialists.

What did we find so ominous about the take-over of this radio and television network by a highly successful conglomerate organization?

In 1966, ABC owned 399 theaters in 34 states, 5 VHF television stations, 6 AM and 6 FM stations (all in the top 10 broadcasting markets), and, of course, one of the 3 major television networks and one of the 4 major radio networks in the world. Its 137 primary television network affiliates could reach 93 percent of the then 50 million television homes in the United States, and its radio network affilates could reach 97 percent of the then 55 million homes with radio receivers. ABC had interests in, and affiliations with, stations in 25 other nations, known as the "Worldvision Group." These, together with ABC Films, made the parent corporation perhaps the world's largest distributor of filmed shows for theaters and television stations throughout this country and abroad. ABC was heavily involved in the record production and distribution business, and other subsidiaries published three farm papers.

The merger would have placed this accumulation of mass media, and one of the largest purveyors of news and opinion in America, under the control of one of the largest conglomerate corporations in the world. What's wrong with that? Potentially a number of things. For now, consider simply that the integrity of the news judgment of ABC might be affected by the economic interests of ITT—that ITT might simply view ABC's programming as a part of ITT's public relations, advertising, or political activities. This seemed to us a real threat in 1966, notwithstanding the character of the management of both companies, and their protestations that no possibility of abuse existed. By 1967 the potential threat had become reality.

ITT's Empire

ITT's continuing concern with political and economic developments in foreign countries as a result of its far-flung economic interests was fully documented in the hearing. It showed, as one might expect, ITT's recurrent concern with internal affairs in most major countries of the world, including rate problems, tax problems, and problems with nationalization and reimbursement, to say nothing of ordinary commercial dealing. Its involvement with the United States government, in addition to defense contracts, included the Agency for International Development's insurance of 5.8 percent of all ITT assets.

Testimony was offered on the fascinating story of intrigue surrounding "Operation Deep Freeze" (an underwater cable). It turned out that ITT officials, using high-level government contracts in England and Canada, had brought off a bit of profitable international diplomacy unknown to the United States State Department or the FCC, possibly in violation of law. Further inquiry revealed that officers and directors of ITT's subsidiaries included two members of the British House of Lords, one in the French National Assembly, a former premier of Belgium, and several ministers of foreign governments and officials of government-owned companies.

As it seemed to Commissioners Bartley and Cox and to me when we dissented from the Commission's approval of the merger in June, 1967, a company whose daily activities require it to manipulate governments at the highest levels would face unending temptation to manipulate ABC news. Any public official, or officer of a large corporation, is necessarily clearly concerned with the appearance of some news stories, the absence of others, and the tone and character of all affecting his personal interests. That's what public relations firms and press secretaries are all about. We concluded, "We simply cannot find that the public interest of the American citizenry is served by turning over a major network to an international enterprise whose fortunes are tied to its political relations with the foreign officials whose actions it will be called upon to interpret to the world."

Even the highest degree of subjective integrity on the part of chief ITT officials could not ensure integrity in ABC's operations. To do an honest and impartial job of reporting the news is difficult enough for the most independent and conscientious of newsmen. Eric Sevareid has said of putting on a news program at a network relatively free of conglomerate control: "The ultimate sensation is the feeling of being bitten to death by ducks." And ABC newsmen could not help knowing that ITT had sensitive business relations in various foreign countries and at the highest levels of our government, and that reporting on any number of industries and economic developments would touch the interests of ITT. The mere awareness of these interests would make it impossible for those news officials, no matter how conscientious, to report news and develop documentaries objectively, in the way that they would do if ABC remained unaffiliated with ITT. They would advance within the news organization, or be fired, or become officers of ABC—perhaps even of ITT—or not, and no newsman would be able to erase from his mind the idea that his chances of doing so might be affected by his treatment of issues on which ITT is sensitive.

Only last year CBS was reportedly involved, almost Hearst-like, in a nightmarish planned armed invasion of Haiti. It was an exclusive, and would have made a very dramatic start-to-finish documentary but for the inglorious end:

U.S. Customs wouldn't let them leave the United States. Imagine ITT, with its extensive interests in the Caribbean, engaged in such undertakings.

The likelihood of at least some compromising of ABC's integrity seemed inherent in the structure of the proposed new organization. What were the *probabilities* that these potentials for abuse would be exercised? We were soon to see the answer in the bizarre proceedings right before our eyes.

During the April, 1967, hearings, while this very issue was being debated, the *Wall Street Journal* broke the story that ITT was going to extraordinary lengths to obtain favorable press coverage of this hearing. Eventually three reporters were summoned before the examiner to relate for the official record the incidents that were described in the *Journal's* exposé.

An AP and a UPI reporter testified to several phone calls to their homes by ITT public relations men, variously asking them to change their stories and make inquiries for ITT with regard to stories by other reporters, and to use their influence as members of the press to obtain for ITT confidential information from the Department of Justice regarding its intentions. Even more serious were several encounters between ITT officials and a New York *Times* reporter.

On one of these occasions ITT's senior vice president in charge of public relations went to the reporter's office. After criticizing her dispatches to the *Times* about the case in a tone which she described as "accusatory and certainly nasty," he asked whether she had been following the price of ABC and ITT stock. When she indicated that she had not, he asked if she didn't feel she had a "responsibility to the shareholders who might lose money as a result of what" she wrote. She replied, "My responsibility is to find out the truth and print it."

He then asked if she was aware that I (as an FCC Commissioner) was working with a prominent senator on legislation that would forbid any newspaper from owning any broadcast property. (The New York *Times* owns station WQXR in New York.) In point of fact, the senator and I had never met, let alone collaborated, as was subsequently made clear in public statements. But the ITT senior vice president, according to the *Times* reporter, felt that this false information was something she "ought to pass on to [her] . . . publisher before [she wrote] . . . anything further" about the case. The obvious implication of this remark, she felt, was that since the *Times* owns a radio station, it would want to consider its economic interests in deciding what to publish about broadcasting in its newspaper.

To me, this conduct, in which at least three ITT officials, including a senior vice president, were involved, was a deeply unsettling experience. It demonstrated an abrasive self-righteousness in dealing with the press, insensitivity to its independence and integrity, a willingness to spread false stories in furtherance of self-interest, contempt for government officials as well as the press, and an assumption that even as prestigious a news medium as the New York *Times* would, as a matter of course, want to present the news so as to serve best its own economic interests (as well as the economic interests of other large business corporations).

But for the brazen activities of ITT in this very proceeding, it would never have occurred to the three of us who dissented to suggest that the most probable threat to the integrity of ABC news could come from *overt* actions or written policy statements. After the hearing it was obvious that that was clearly possible. But even then we believed that the most substantial threat came from a far more subtle, almost unconscious, process: that the questionable story idea, or news coverage, would never even be proposed—whether for reasons of fear, insecurity, cynicism, realism, or unconscious avoidance.

Concentration of Control over the Media

Since the ITT-ABC case left the Commission I have not ceased to be troubled by the issues it raised—in many ways more serious (and certainly more prevalent) for wholly domestic corporations. Eventually the merger was aborted by ITT on New Year's Day of this year, while the Justice Department's appeal of the Commission's action was pending before the U.S. Court of Appeals. However, I ponder what the consequences might have been if ITT's apparent cynicism toward journalistic integrity had actually been able to harness the enormous social and propaganda power of a national television network to the service of a politically sensitive corporate conglomerate. More important, I have become concerned about the extent to which such forces *already* play upon important media of mass communication. Pehaps such attitudes are masked by more finesse than that displayed in the ITT-ABC case. Perhaps they are even embedded in the kind of sincere good intentions which caused former Defense Secretary (and former General Motors president) Charles Wilson to equate the interests of his company with those of the country.

I do not believe that most owners and managers of the mass media in the United States lack a sense of responsibility or lack tolerance for a diversity of views. I do not believe there is a small group of men who gather for breakfast every morning and decide what they will make the American people believe that day. Emotion often outruns the evidence of those who argue a conspiracy theory of propagandists' manipulation of the masses.

On the other hand, one reason evidence is so hard to come by is that the media tend to give less publicity to their own abuses than, say, to those of politicians. The media operate as a check upon other institutional power centers in our country. There is, however, no check upon the media. Just as it is a mistake to overstate the existence and potential for abuse, so, in my judgment, is it a mistake to ignore the evidence that does exist.

In 1959, for example, it was reported that officials of the Trujillo regime in the Dominican Republic had paid $750,000 to officers of the Mutual Radio Network to gain favorable propaganda disguised as news. (Ownership of the Mutual Radio Network changed hands once again last year without any review whatsoever by the FCC of old or new owners. The FCC does not regulate networks, only stations, and Mutual owns none.) RCA was once charged with using an NBC station to serve unfairly its broader corporate interests, including the coverage of RCA activities as "news," when others did not. There was speculation that after RCA acquired Random House, considerable pressure was put on the book publishing house's president, Bennett Cerf, to cease his Sunday evening service as a panelist on CBS's *What's My Line?* The Commission has occasionally found that individual stations have violated the "fairness doctrine" in advocating causes serving the station's economic self-interest, such as pay television.

Virtually every issue of the *Columbia Journalism Review* reports instances of such abuses by the print media. It has described a railroad-owned newspaper that refused to report railroad wrecks, a newspaper in debt to the Teamsters Union which gave exceedingly favorable coverage to Jimmy Hoffa, the repeated influence of the DuPont interests in the editorial functions of the Wilmington papers which it owned, and Anaconda Copper's use of its company-owned newspapers to support political candidates favorable to the company.

Edward P. Morgan left ABC last year to become the commentator on the Ford Foundation-funded Public Broadcasting Laboratory. He has always been straightforward, and he used his final news broadcast to be reflective about broadcasting itself. "Let's face it," he said. "We in this trade use this power more frequently to fix a traffic ticket or get a ticket to a ballgame than to keep the doors of an open society open and swinging. . . . The freest and most profitable press in the world, every major facet of it, not only ducks but pulls its punches to save a supermarket of commercialism or shield an ugly prejudice and is putting the life of the republic in jeopardy thereby."

Economic self-interest *does* influence the content of the media, and as the media tend to fall into the control of corporate conglomerates, the areas of information and opinion affecting those economic interests become dangerously wide-ranging. What *is* happening to the ownership of American media today? What dangers does it pose? Taking a look at the structure of the media in the United States, I am not put at ease by what I see.

Most American communities have far less "dissemination of information from diverse and antagonistic sources" (to quote a famous description by the Supreme Court of the basic aim of the First Amendment) than is available nationally. Of the 1500 cities with daily newspapers, 96 percent are served by single-owner monopolies. Outside the top 50 to 200 markets there is a substantial dropping off in the number of competing radio and television signals. The FCC prohibits a single owner from controlling two AM radio, or two television, stations with overlapping signals. But it has only recently expressed any concern over common ownership of an AM radio station and an FM radio station and a television station in the same market. Indeed, such ownership is the rule rather than the exception and probably exists in your community. Most stations are today acquired by purchase. And the FCC has, in part because of congressional pressure, rarely disapproved a purchase of a station by a newspaper.

There are few statewide or regional "monopolies"—although some situations come close. But in a majority of our states—the least populous—there are few enough newspapers and television stations to begin with, and they are usually under the control of a small group. And most politicians find today, as Congress warned in 1926, "woe be to those who dare to differ with them." Most of our politics is still state and local in scope. And increasingly, in many states and local communities, congressmen and state and local officials are compelled to regard that handful of media owners (many of whom are out-of-state), rather than the electorate itself, as their effective constituency. Moreover, many mass media owners have a significant impact in more than one state. One case that came before the FCC, for example, involved an owner with AM-FM-TV combinations in Las Vegas and Reno, Nevada, along with four newspapers in that state, seven newspapers in Oklahoma, and two stations and two newspapers in Arkansas. Another involved ownership of ten stations in North Carolina and adjoining southern Virginia. You may never have heard of these owners, but I imagine the elected officials of their states return their phone calls promptly.

National Power

The principal national sources of news are the wire services, AP and UPI, and the broadcast networks. Each of the wire services serves on the order of 1200 newspapers and 3000 radio and television stations. Most local newspapers and radio stations offer little more than wire service copy as far as national and international news is concerned. To that extent one can take little heart for "diversity" from the oft-proffered statistics on proliferating radio stations (now over 6000) and the remaining daily newspapers (1700). The networks, though themselves heavily reliant upon the wire services to find out what's worth filming, are another potent force.

The weekly newsmagazine field is dominated by *Time, Newsweek,* and *U.S. News.* (The first two also control substantial broadcast, newspaper, and book or publishing outlets. *Time* is also in movies (MGM) and is hungry for three or four newspapers.) Thus, even though there are thousands of general and specialized periodicals and program sources with significant national or regional impact, and certainly no "monopoly" exists, it is still possible for a single individual or corporation to have vast national influence.

What we sometimes fail to realize, moreover, is the political significance of the fact that we have become a nation of cities. Nearly half of the American people live in the six largest states: California, New York, Illinois, Pennsylvania, Texas, and Ohio. Those states, in turn, are substantially influenced (if not politically dominated) by their major population-industrial-financial-media centers, such as Los Angeles, New York City, Chicago, and Philadelphia—the nation's four largest metropolitan areas. Thus, to have a major newspaper or television station influence in *one* of these cities is to have significant national power. And the number of interests with influence in *more* than one of these markets is startling.

Most of the top fifty television markets (which serve approximately 75 percent of the nation's television homes) have three competing commercial VHF television stations. There are about 150 such VHF commercial stations in these markets. Less than 10 percent are today owned by entities that do not own other media interests. In 30 of the 50 markets at least one of the stations is owned by a major newspaper published in that market—a total of one third of these 150 stations. (In Dallas-Fort Worth *each* of the network affiliates is owned by a local newspaper, and the fourth, an unaffiliated station, is owned by Oklahoma newspapers.) Moreover, half of the newspaper-owned stations are controlled by seven groups—groups that also publish magazines as popular and diverse as *Time, Newsweek, Look, Parade, Harper's, TV Guide, Family Circle, Vogue, Good Housekeeping,* and *Popular Mechanics*. Twelve parties own more than one third of all the major-market stations.

In addition to the vast national impact of their affiliates the three television networks each *own* VHF stations in all of the top three markets—New York, Los Angeles, and Chicago—and each has two more in other cities in the top ten. RKO and Metromedia each own stations in both New York City and Los Angeles. Metromedia also owns stations in Washington, D.C., and California's other major city, San Francisco—as well as Philadelphia, Baltimore, Cleveland, Kansas City, and Oakland. RKO also owns stations in Boston, San Francisco, Washington, Memphis, Hartford, and Windsor, Ontario— as well as the regional Yankee Network. Westinghouse owns stations in New York, Chicago, Philadelphia *and* Pittsburgh, Pennsylvania, Boston, San Francisco, Baltimore, and Fort Wayne. These are but a few examples of today's media barons.

There are many implications of their power. Groups of stations are able to bargain with networks, advertisers, and talent in ways that put lesser stations at substantial economic disadvantage. Group ownership means, by definition, that few stations in major markets will be locally owned. (The FCC recently approved the transfer of the last available station in San Francisco to the absentee ownership of Metromedia. The only commercial station locally owned today is controlled by the San Francisco *Chronicle*.) But the basic point is simply that the national political power involved in ownership of a group of major VHF television stations in, say, New York, Los Angeles, Philadelphia, and Washington, D.C., is greater than a democracy should unthinkingly repose in one man or corporation.

Conglomerate Corporations

For a variety of reasons, an increasing number of communications media are turning up on the organization charts of conglomerate companies. And the incredible profits generated by broadcast stations in the major markets (television broadcasters *average* a 90 to 100 percent return on tangible investment annually) have given FCC licensees, particularly owners of multiple television stations like the networks, Metromedia, Storer Broadcasting, and others, the extra capital with which to buy the New York Yankees (CBS), Random House (RCA), or Northeast Airlines (Storer). Established or up-and-coming conglomerates regard communications acquisitions as prestigious, profitable, and often a useful or even a necessary complement to present operations and projected exploitation of technological change.

The national problem of conglomerate ownership of communications media was well illustrated by the ITT-ABC case. But the conglomerate problem need not involve something as large as ITT-ABC or RCA-NBC. Among the national group owners of television stations are General Tire (RKO), Avco, Westinghouse, Rust Craft, Chris Craft, Kaiser, and Kerr-McGee. The problem of *local* conglomerates was forcefully posed for the FCC in another case earlier this year. Howard Hughes, through Hughes Tool Company, wanted to acquire one of Las Vegas' three major television stations. He had recently acquired $125 million worth of Las Vegas real estate, including hotels, gambling casinos, and an airport. These investments supplemented 27,000 acres previously acquired. The Commission majority blithely approved the television acquisition without a hearing, overlooking FCC precedents which suggested that a closer examination was in order. In each of these instances the potential threat is similar to that in the ITT-ABC case—that personal economic interests may dominate or bias otherwise independent media.

Concentration and Technological Change

The problem posed by conglomerate acquisitions of communications outlets is given a special but very important twist by the pendency of sweeping technological changes which have already begun to unsettle the structure of the industry.

President Johnson has appointed a distinguished task force to evaluate our national communications policy and chart a course for realization of these technological promises in a manner consistent with the public interest. But private interests have already begun to implement their own plans on how to deal with the revolution in communications technology.

General Sarnoff of RCA has hailed the appearance of "the knowledge industry"—corporate casserole dishes blending radio and television stations, networks, and programming; films, movie houses, and record companies; newspaper, magazine, and book publishing; advertising agencies; sports or other entertainment companies; and teaching machines and other profitable appurtenances of the $50 billion "education biz."

And everybody's in "cable television"—networks, book publishers, newspapers. Cable television is a system for building the best TV antenna in town and then wiring it into everybody's television set—for a fee. It improves signal quality and number of channels, and has proved popular. But the new technology is such that it has broadcasters and newspaper publishers worried. For the same cable that can bring off-the-air television into the home can also bring programming from the cable operator's studio, or an "electronic newspaper" printed in the home by a facsimile process. Books can be delivered (between libraries, or to the home) over "television" by using the station's signal during an invisible pause. So everybody's hedging their bets—including the telephone company. Indeed, about all the vested interests can agree upon is that none of them want us to have direct, satellite-to-home radio and television. But at this point it is not at all clear who will have his hand on the switch that controls what comes to the American people over their "telephone wire" a few years hence.

What Is to Be Done?

It would be foolish to expect any extensive restructuring of the media in the United States, even if it were considered desirable. Technological change can bring change in structure, but it is as likely to be change to even greater concentration as to wider diversity. In the short run at least, economics seems to render essentially intractable such problems as local monopolies in daily newspapers, or the small number of outlets for national news through wire services, newsmagazines, and the television networks. Indeed, to a certain extent the very high technical quality of the performance rendered by these news-gathering organizations is aided by their concentration of resources into large units and the financial cushions of oligopoly profits.

Nevertheless, it seems clear to me that the risks of concentration are grave.

Chairman Philip Hart of the Senate Antitrust and Monopoly Subcommittee remarked by way of introduction to his antitrust subcommittee's recent hearings about the newspaper industry, "The products of newspapers, opinion and information, are essential to the kind of society that we undertake to make successful here." If we are serious about the kind of society we have undertaken, it is clear to me that we simply must not tolerate concentration of media ownership—except where concentration creates actual countervailing social benefits. These benefits cannot be merely speculative. They must be identifiable, demonstrable, and genuinely weighty enough to offset the dangers inherent in concentration.

This guideline is a simple prescription. The problem is to design and build machinery to fill it. And to keep the machinery from rusting and rotting. And to replace it when it becomes obsolete.

America does have available governmental machinery which is capable of scotching undue accumulations of power over the mass media, at least in theory and to some extent. The Department of Justice has authority under the antitrust laws to break up combinations which "restrain trade" or which "tend to lessen competition." These laws apply to the media as they do to any other industry.

But the antitrust laws simply do not get to where the problems are. They grant authority to block concentration only when it threatens *economic* competition in a particular economic *market*. Generally, in the case of the media, the relevant market is the market for advertising. Unfortunately, relatively vigorous advertising competition can be maintained in situations where competition in the marketplace of ideas is severely threatened. In such cases, the Justice Department has little inclination to act.

Look at the Chicago *Tribune's* recent purchase of that city's most popular and most successful FM radio station. The *Tribune* already controlled two Chicago newspapers, one (clear channel) AM radio station, and the city's only independent VHF television station. It controls numerous broadcast, CATV, and newspaper interests outside Chicago (in terms of circulation, the nation's largest newspaper chain). But, after an investigation, the Antitrust Division let this combination go through. The new FM may be a needless addition to the *Tribune's* already impressive battery of influential media; it could well produce an unsound level of concentration in the production and supply of what Chicagoans see, read, and hear about affairs in their community, in the nation, and in the world. But it did not threaten the level of competition for advertising money in any identifiable advertising market. So, it was felt, the acquisition was not the business of the Justice Department.

Only the FCC is directly empowered to keep media ownership patterns compatible with a democracy's need for diversified sources of opinion and information.

In earlier times, the Commission took this responsibility very seriously. In 1941, the FCC ordered NBC to divest itself of one of its two radio networks (which then became ABC), barring any single network from affiliating with more than one outlet in a given city. (The Commission has recently waived this prohibition for, ironically, ABC's four new national radio networks.) In 1941 the Commission also established its power to set absolute limits on the total number of broadcast licenses any individual may hold, and to limit the number of stations any individuals can operate in a particular service area.

The American people are indebted to the much maligned FCC for establishing these rules. Imagine, for example, what the structure of political power in this country might look like if two or three companies owned substantially all of the broadcast media in our major cities.

But since the New Deal generation left the command posts of the FCC, this agency has lost much of its zeal for combating concentration. Atrophy has reached so advanced a state that the public has of late witnessed the bizarre spectacle of the Justice Department, with its relatively narrow mandate, intervening in FCC proceedings, such as ITT-ABC, to create court cases with names like *The United States vs. The FCC.*

This history is an unhappy one on the whole. It forces one to question whether government can ever realistically be expected to sustain a vigilant posture over an industry which controls the very access of government officials themselves to the electorate.

I fear that we have already reached the point in this country where the media, our greatest check on other accumulations of power, may themselves be beyond the reach of any other institution: the Congress, the President, or the Federal Communications Commission, not to mention governors, mayors, state legislators, and city councilmen. Congressional hearings are begun and then quietly dropped. Whenever the FCC stirs fitfully as if in wakefulness, the broadcasting industry scurries up the Hill for a congressional bludgeon. And the fact that roughly 60 percent of all campaign expenses go to radio and television time gives but a glimmer of the power of broadcasting in the lives of senators and congressmen.

However, the picture at this moment has its more hopeful aspect. There does seem to be an exceptional flurry of official concern. Even the FCC has its proposed rulemaking outstanding. The Department of Justice, having broken into the communications field via its dramatic intervention before the FCC in the ITT-ABC merger case, has also been pressing a campaign to force the dissolution of joint operating agreements between separately owned newspapers in individual cities, and opposed a recent application for broadcasting properties by newspaper interests in Beaumont, Texas. It has been scrutinizing cross-media combinations linking broadcasting, newspaper, and cable television outlets. On Capitol Hill, Senator Phil Hart's Antitrust and Monopoly Subcommittee and Chairman Harley Staggers' House Interstate and Foreign Commerce Committee have both summoned the Federal Communications Commission to appear before them in recent months, to acquaint the Commission with the committees' concern about FCC-approved increases in broadcast holdings by single individuals and companies, and about cross-ownership of newspapers, CATV systems, and broadcast stations. Representatives John Dingell, John Moss, and Richard Ottinger have introduced legislation which would proscribe network ownership of any nonbroadcast interests. And as I previously mentioned, President Johnson has appointed a task force to undertake a comprehensive review of national communications policy.

Twenty years ago Robert M. Hutchins, then chancellor of the University of Chicago, was named chairman of the "Commission on Freedom of the Press." It produced a thoughtful report, full of recommendations largely applicable today—including "the establishment of a new and independent [nongovernmental] agency to appraise and report annually upon the performance of the press," and urged "that the members of the press engage in vigorous mutual criticism." Its proposals are once again being dusted off and reread.

What is needed now, more than anything else, is to keep this flurry of interest alive, and to channel it toward constructive reforms. What this means, in practical fact, is that concern for media concentration must find an institutional home.

The Department of Justice has already illustrated the value of participation by an external institution in FCC decision-making. The developing concept of a special consumers' representative offers a potentially broader base for similar action.

But the proper place to lodge continuing responsibility for promoting diversity in the mass media is neither the FCC nor the Justice Department nor a congressional committee. The initiative must come from private sources. Plucky Nader-like crusaders such as John Banzhaf (who single-handedly induced the FCC to apply the "fairness" doctrine to cigarette commercials) have shown how responsive government can be to the skillful and vigorous efforts of even a lone individual. But there are more adequately staffed and funded private organizations which could play a more effective role in policy formation than a single individual. Even the FCC, where the public interest gets entirely too little representation from private sources, has felt the impact of the United Church of Christ, with its interest in the influence of broadcasting on race relations and in the programming responsibility of licensees, and of the American Civil Liberties Union, which submitted a brief in the ITT-ABC case.

Ideally, however, the resources for a sustained attack on concentration might be centered in a single institution, equipped to look after this cause with the kind of determination and intelligence that the Ford Foundation and the Carnegie Corporation, for example, have brought to bear in behalf of the cause of public broadcasting and domestic satellites. The law schools and their law reviews, as an institution, have performed well in this way for the courts, but have virtually abdicated responsibility for the agencies.

Such an organization could devote itself to research as well as representation. For at present any public body like the FCC, which has to make determinations about acceptable levels of media concentration, has to do so largely on the basis of hunch. In addition, private interest in problems of concentration would encourage the Justice Department to sustain its present vigilance in this area. It could stimulate renewed vigilance on the part of the FCC, through participation in Commission proceedings. And it could consider whether new legislation might be appropriate to reach the problem of newspaper-magazine-book publishing combinations.

If changes are to be made (or now dormant standards are to be enforced) the most pressing political question is whether to apply the standards prospectively only, or to require divestiture. It is highly unlikely, to say the least, that legislation requiring massive divestiture of multiple station ownership, or newspaper ownership of stations, would ever pass through Congress. Given the number of station sales every year, however, even prospective standards could have some impact over ten years or so.

In general, I would urge the minimal standard that no accumulation of media should be permitted without a specific and convincing showing of a continuing countervailing social benefit. For no one has a higher calling in an increasingly complex free society bent on self-government than he who informs and moves the people. Personal prejudice, ignorance, social pressure, and advertiser pressure are in large measure inevitable. But a nation that has, in Learned Hand's phrase, "staked its all" upon the rational dialogue of an informed electorate simply cannot take any unnecessary risk of polluting the stream of information and opinion that sustains it. At the very least, the burden of proving the social utility of doing otherwise should be upon him who seeks the power and profit which will result.

Whatever may be the outcome, the wave of renewed interest in the impact of ownership on the role of the media in our society is healthy. All will gain from intelligent inquiry by Congress, the Executive, the regulatory commissions—and especially the academic community, the American people generally, and the media themselves. For, as the Supreme Court has noted, nothing is more important in a free society than "the widest possible dissemination of information from diverse and antagonistic sources." And if we are unwilling to discuss *this* issue fully today we may find ourselves discussing none that matter very much tomorrow.

EDITORS OF *PROGRESSIVE*

The Word from Washington

The ritual is called the goat-feeding. Twice a day, the White House correspondents—the goats—assemble to be fed such tidbits of information as the President's press secretary—the feeder—may chose to pass along. The fare is usually thin: a glimpse at the President's schedule for the day, a proclamation of National Chilblaims Week, the naming of some deserving Republican greengrocer as Ambassador Plenipotentiary to Transylvania. From time to time the hungry goats become restive and even mutinous. Since the President is inordinately inaccessible, the twice-a-day feeding provides about the only opportunity to obtain a square meal.

Since April 30, the White House goats have displayed an enormous appetite for news about the Administration's intentions in Cambodia—a craving that has hardly been sated by the few rancid scraps thrown the correspondents' way. On June 1, when both the President and the correspondents happened to be at the Western White House in San Clemente, California, the goat feeding conducted by Press Secretary Ron Ziegler took a particularly lively turn. We present the following extracts from the official transcript as a contribution to public appreciation of one of our quainter art forms:

MR. ZIEGLER: The U.S. operation in the Cambodian sanctuaries is proceeding well. The President has said that U.S. forces would begin to come out of the Cambodian sanctuary area throughout June, mid-June, but that the operation will be complete by June 30, the U.S. operation.

We also said that in response to a question in a press conference that logistical and air support also would be completed by June 30. That stands as the President has stated it. He went on to say that he anticipated or that he expected that the South Vietnamese would be completing the mop-up operations and perhaps for a longer period of time beyond June 30.

In relation to what ARVN actions are in Cambodia after the sanctuary operations are complete, we have said before that this would be dependent on the actions of the other side and that I am not in a position, nor are we

Source: Reprinted from the editor's column "The Word from Washington," *The Progressive,* July 1970, p. 11, by permission of the publisher.

in a position, to discuss the deployment of ARVN forces. We have said that any actions that the U.S. takes in relation to Cambodia would relate to the security of the U.S. forces in South Vietnam. . . .

Q: Ron, I am sorry. But I don't yet find that you have answered the basic question here, despite the fact that you have repeated what you have said in the past. The basic question is still whether you are leaving open the possibility that U.S. air and logistical support will be given to the South Vietnamese.

MR. ZIEGLER: On June 30—the President has said this—logistical personnel will be withdrawn from Cambodia and air support will not be used.

Q: Ron, let's get this clear now, because many of us have interpreted, from what the Secretary of Defense has said and from what you have said and from what others have said in the recent past, that American air and logistic support will be continued for the South Vietnamese operation. Now, if I understand you correctly, you are saying that is not true; that if they stay in there they will not get U.S. air and logistic support. Could you clarify that?

MR. ZIEGLER: Bob, the way I would clarify it would be to refer you to what the President has said. . . . The President said in his May 8 press conference—and I am quite precise on this because I have looked at it frequently— the fact that on June 30 the Cambodian sanctuary operation will be completed, and he said that he expected that the ARVN forces will be coming out shortly thereafter as the logistical and air support would be coming out at that time.

Q: Ron, the ARVN forces right now are not confined to the twenty-one-mile limit that U.S. forces are confined to. They are operating deeper into Cambodia and they are operating now, as I understand it, with American support and American logistics.

MR. ZIEGLER: Not beyond twenty-one miles.

Q: Who gives them the rifles they are using, Ron?

MR. ZIEGLER: Of course they have U.S. supplies.

Q: Is this not logistical support?

MR. ZIEGLER: Then we are getting into a definition of logistical support. Obviously the ARVN forces have operated with U.S. equipment, U.S. rifles.

Q: They get logistical support from the United States.

MR. ZIEGLER: Quite obviously they have U.S. equipment. When we refer to logistical support, it is logistical support involving U.S. personnel in the territory of Cambodia providing the supply flow to ARVN forces. That is a moot question. It is quite obvious that ARVN forces have U.S. materiel.

Q: When you say that there will be no logistical support and all their ammunition and food and everything else is furnished by Americans—

MR. ZIEGLER: I am referring to logistical support. It is quite obvious that what we mean by logistical support, which is U.S. personnel being in the territory of Cambodia. That is how we have always addressed the question.

Q: You are talking about U.S. personnel and not U.S. supplies?

MR. ZIEGLER: We are talking about U.S. personnel forming the process of logistical support.

Q: You are not talking about U.S. supplies; is that correct, Ron?

MR. ZIEGLER: The ARVN forces receive, without question, U.S. ammunition to go in there, M-16s which they use and have been using for years.

Q: In two backgrounders that we have had with an eminent personality in the White House, he has left open the question of air support after June 30.

MR. ZIEGLER: We are reserving on U.S. air support following June 30.

Q: What do you mean, "reserving"?

MR. ZIEGLER: Reserving from the standpoint of discussing what action the U.S. will take in relation to air support following June 30.

We have said that any action that we take in relation to air support will be in direct relation to the security of U.S. forces in South Vietnam. However—and I will repeat this finally, because this is almost a direct pickup of a briefing we had in Washington a couple of days ago or a few days ago—the President in his May 8 press conference said the operation in Cambodia will be complete by June 30 and that logistical and air support would be completed by that time. Moving beyond that into a future date is what I am not discussing.

Q: You mean they can come back in later? That is what you are saying?

MR. ZIEGLER: Who can come back later?

Q: The Americans.

MR. ZIEGLER: We have answered that question also.

Q: You are then leaving it open.

MR. ZIEGLER: We have answered the question regarding U.S. forces in Cambodia; that they will be completed by June 30 and there is no intention to reintroduce U.S. ground support into Cambodia.

Q: Ron, why are you fuzzing this up? Are you deliberately obfuscating this thing, or is it a matter of imprecise language? I must say in all candor that I am totally confused about what the policy is. Are you purposely fuzzing this up or not?

MR. ZIEGLER: Dan, I think I have answered these questions quite directly without fuzzing them up. I don't know how more precise we can be than to say that on June 30 U.S. forces will be out of Cambodia according to schedule. I don't know how more precise I can be than to refer you to a statement by the President of the United States in which he said that logistical and air support would be concluded on June 30. I don't know how more clear I can be and how more obvious I can be and how more obvious it should be to you and your colleagues that I am not going to discuss operations of ARVN forces beyond the completion of the sanctuary operation nor in precise terms at this time what action the United States may take in terms of air support beyond the June 30 deadline.

I think I have made that quite clear in Washington. I think this should be quite obvious to you why I am not being more precise in that area. However,

I have gone on to say that any U.S. air action which would be taken in the area, which I am not going to discuss one way or another, would be in relation to the security of U.S. forces in South Vietnam. That is, I think, quite precise.

Q: Ron, you are just insulting our intelligence. You are not being precise. It is obvious that you are deliberately obfuscating. If you would answer one simple question—

MR. ZIEGLER: Give it to me, and then we will conclude the Q&A.

Q: What we are trying to get at is are you reserving the right and the intention of the United States to give logistical and air support to the South Vietnamese after June 30? That is a fairly simple question.

MR. ZIEGLER: It is, and my response to you is exactly the way it has always been; that I am not going to discuss the operation of ARVN forces.

Q: We are not asking about ARVN forces.

MR. ZIEGLER: That is exactly right.

Q: We are asking about American forces.

MR. ZIEGLER: I have made the point clear on that.

Q: You have not, Ron. You have given both sides of the answer. You keep citing the President's saying we are not going to give that support and then you go on and imply that we are. All we are trying to do is get what you are trying to state straight.

MR. ZIEGLER: I shouldn't respond to you, but I will. U.S. air support following June 30 would relate to the security of U.S. forces in South Vietnam. Right? That is pretty clear.

That does not suggest the air support of ARVN forces in South Vietnam. It suggests U.S. air support in relation to U.S. forces in South Vietnam.

But the point we have made and will continue to make, no matter how belligerent the questions get in order to draw out an answer in relation to actions after June 30, I have made it clear that I have no intention at this time to discuss that. . . .

Whereupon the goats, frustrated, weary—and still hungry—called it a day. It's a tough business, being a goat at the White House. And it's none too easy on the rest of us.

The President's press secretary was more communicative—was almost gossipy, in fact—about the recent visit to the White House by a delegation of New York construction workers. He told how they pinned an American flag to Mr. Nixon's lapel, how they presented him with a white hard hat inscribed (in blue) with the title. "Commander-in-Chief." It was, Ziegler said, a "symbol of their support" for the President's action in Indochina.

The construction workers' massive Wall Street rally in support of the war was discussed, but their rampage against peace demonstrators somehow didn't come up, Ziegler reported.

How was it, a reporter inquired, that the construction workers had such ready access to the White House when others—including a member of the Cabinet and all the black members of the House of Representatives—had complained in recent weeks about Mr. Nixon's inaccessibility?

"I think that is kind of a loaded question," Ziegler replied, but he answered it: "They expressed an interest in seeing the President after the rally and they were invited down." The "hard hats" had a slightly different version; the invitation came first, they said, and was swiftly followed by the interest.

Law and Order:
Liberty, Law, and Violence

1968 was a vintage year for violence and social disruption. The assassinations of Martin Luther King and Robert F. Kennedy were followed by that infamous orgy of angry mobs and police brutality at the Democratic National Convention in Chicago. Coming on top of the earlier assassination of President John F. Kennedy, these and many other acts of violence set the tone for the 1968 campaign.

Law and order was its chief theme, and the public was treated to an excess of oratory which viewed with alarm and fixed blame. Solutions were offered, some of which were intelligent, many of which were naively simple, and some of which were dangerous violations of civil rights and liberties. When the voters went to the polls, however, it was difficult for many of them to escape the feeling that perhaps the system was coming apart and that all the men who made all the campaign promises could not put it back together again. Many people still wonder.

What has gone wrong? There is the argument that the courts are soft on "criminals, communists, and conspirators"; that society is too permissive; that there is a decline in religious belief; that there is too much pornography, profanity, and pot; that people are unpatriotic and desecrate national symbols, including the flag; that there is no respect for authority.

The list of symptoms is almost endless but the "deep disorder" causing the symptoms is much more serious. Military actions that are difficult to justify, such as Vietnam or the Bay of Pigs, racial injustices that must be righted, poverty of shameless dimensions, destruction and pollution of the environment, and estrangement between the young and their elders are but a few of the more obvious political problems that can and do lead to violence. In this section we look at the difficulties contingent upon enforcing

213

the law and maintaining order in the United States, where individual liberty is an essential part of the democratic form of government. This is particularly complicated when the society becomes so turbulent that violence flares up periodically. Indeed, violence as a political technique and its relationship to democratic politics is now a subject of serious inquiry, as some of the following articles will make clear.

There is always the possibility that the use of oppressive force to maintain order as a substitute for solving the causes of discontent can lead to the loss of liberty. Citizens in a democracy must remain constantly alert to this possibility, as some of the writers included in this section point out.

MARTIN LUTHER KING, JR.

Letter from Birmingham Jail [1]

April 16, 1963

MY DEAR FELLOW CLERGYMEN:

While confined here in the Birmingham city jail, I came across your recent statement calling my present activities "unwise and untimely." Seldom do I pause to answer criticism of my work and ideas. If I sought to answer all the criticisms that cross my desk, my secretaries would have little time for anything other than such correspondence in the course of the day, and I would have no time for constructive work. But since I feel that you are men of genuine good will and that your criticisms are sincerely set forth, I want to try to answer your statement in what I hope will be patient and reasonable terms.

I think I should indicate why I am here in Birmingham, since you have been influenced by the view which argues against "outsiders coming in." I have the honor of serving as president of the Southern Christian Leadership Conference, an organization operating in every southern state, with headquarters in Atlanta, Georgia. We have some eighty-five affiliated organizations across the South, and one of them is the Alabama Christian Movement for Human Rights. Frequently we share staff, educational and financial resources with our affiliates. Several months ago the affiliate here in Birmingham asked us to be on call to engage in a nonviolent direct-action program if such were

Source: The late Martin Luther King, Jr., was one of the great leaders in the Civil Rights Movement, President of the Southern Christian Leadership Conference, and winner of the Nobel Peace Prize in 1964. He was assassinated in 1968. This letter is reprinted from *Why We Can't Wait*, by Martin Luther King, Jr., Harper and Row, Publishers, pp. 77–100. Copyright © 1963, 1964 by Martin Luther King, Jr. Reprinted by permission of the publisher.

[1] *Author's Note:* This response to a published statement by eight fellow clergymen from Alabama (Bishop C. C. J. Carpenter, Bishop Joseph A. Durick, Rabbi Hilton L. Grafman, Bishop Paul Hardin, Bishop Holan B. Harmon, the Reverend George M. Murray, the Reverend Edward V. Ramage and the Reverend Earl Stallings) was composed under somewhat constricting circumstances. Begun on the margins of the newspaper in which the statement appeared while I was in jail, the letter was continued on scraps of writing paper supplied by a friendly Negro trusty, and concluded on a pad my attorneys were eventually permitted to leave me. Although the text remains in substance unaltered, I have indulged in the author's prerogative of polishing it for publication.

deemed necessary. We readily consented, and when the hour came we lived up to our promise. So I, along with several members of my staff, am here because I was invited here. I am here because I have organizational ties here.

But more basically, I am in Birmingham because injustice is here. Just as the prophets of the eighth century B.C. left their villages and carried their "thus saith the Lord" far beyond the boundaries of their home towns, and just as the Apostle Paul left his village of Tarsus and carried the gospel of Jesus Christ to the far corners of the Greco-Roman world, so am I compelled to carry the gospel of freedom beyond my own home town. Like Paul, I must constantly respond to the Macedonian call for aid.

Moreover, I am cognizant of the interrelatedness of all communities and states. I cannot sit idly by in Atlanta and not be concerned about what happens in Birmingham. Injustice anywhere is a threat to justice everywhere. We are caught in an inescapable network of mutuality, tied in a single garment of destiny. Whatever affects one directly, affects all indirectly. Never again can we afford to live with the narrow, provincial "outside agitator" idea. Anyone who lives inside the United States can never be considered an outsider anywhere within its bounds.

You deplore the demonstrations taking place in Birmingham. But your statement, I am sorry to say, fails to express a similar concern for the conditions that brought about the demonstrations. I am sure that none of you would want to rest content with the superficial kind of social analysis that deals merely with effects and does not grapple with underlying causes. It is unfortunate that demonstrations are taking place in Birmingham, but it is even more unfortunate that the city's white power structure left the Negro community with no alternative.

In any nonviolent campaign there are four basic steps: collection of the facts to determine whether injustices exist; negotiation; self-purification; and direct action. We have gone through all these steps in Birmingham. There can be no gainsaying the fact that racial injustice engulfs this community. Birmingham is probably the most thoroughly segregated city in the United States. Its ugly record of brutality is widely known. Negroes have experienced grossly unjust treatment in the courts. There have been more unsolved bombings of Negro homes and churches in Birmingham than in any other city in the nation. These are the hard, brutal facts of the case. On the basis of these conditions, Negro leaders sought to negotiate with the city fathers. But the latter consistently refused to engage in good-faith negotiation.

Then, last September, came the opportunity to talk with leaders of Birmingham's economic community. In the course of the negotiations, certain promises were made by the merchants—for example, to remove the stores' humiliating racial signs. On the basis of these promises, the Reverend Fred Shuttlesworth and the leaders of the Alabama Christian Movement for Human Rights agreed to a moratorium on all demonstrations. As the weeks and months went by, we realized that we were the victims of a broken promise. A few signs, briefly removed, returned; the others remained.

As in so many past experiences, our hopes had been blasted, and the shadow of deep disappointment settled upon us. We had no alternative except to prepare for direct action, whereby we would present our very bodies as a means of laying our case before the conscience of the local and the national community. Mindful of the difficulties involved, we decided to undertake a process of self-purification. We began a series of workshops on nonviolence, and we repeatedly asked ourselves: "Are you able to accept blows without retaliating?" "Are you able to endure the ordeal of jail?" We decided to schedule our direct-action program for the Easter season, realizing that except for Christmas, this is the main shopping period of the year. Knowing that a strong economic-withdrawal program would be the by-product of direct action, we felt that this would be the best time to bring pressure to bear on the merchants for the needed change.

Then it occurred to us that Birmingham's mayoral election was coming up in March, and we speedily decided to postpone action until after election day. When we discovered that the Commissioner of Public Safety, Eugene "Bull" Connor, had piled up enough votes to be in the run-off, we decided again to postpone action until the day after the run-off so that demonstrations could not be used to cloud the issues. Like many others, we waited to see Mr. Connor defeated, and to this end we endured postponement after postponement. Having aided in this community need, we felt that our direct-action program could be delayed no longer.

You may well ask: "Why direct action? Why sit-ins, marches and so forth? Isn't negotiations a better path?" You are quite right in calling for negotiation. Indeed, this is the very purpose of direct action. Nonviolent direct action seeks to create such a crisis and foster such a tension that a community which has constantly refused to negotiate is forced to confront the issue. It seeks so to dramatize the issue that it can no longer be ignored. My citing the creation of tension as part of the work of the nonviolent-resister may sound rather shocking. But I must confess that I am not afraid of the word "tension." I have earnestly opposed violent tension, but there is a type of constructive, nonviolent tension which is necessary for growth. Just as Socrates felt that it was necessary to create a tension in the mind so that individuals could rise from the bondage of myths and half-truths to the unfettered realm of creative analysis and objective appraisal, so must we see the need for nonviolent gadflies to create the kind of tension in society that will help men rise from the dark depths of prejudice and racism to the majestic heights of understanding and brotherhood.

The purpose of our direct-action program is to create a situation so crisis-packed that it will inevitably open the door to negotiation. I therefore concur with you in your call for negotiation. Too long has our beloved Southland been bogged down in a tragic effort to live in monologue rather than dialogue.

One of the basic points in your statement is that the action that I and my associates have taken in Birmingham is untimely. Some have asked: "Why didn't you give the new city administration time to act?" The only answer that I can give to this query is that the new Birmingham administration must be prodded about as much as the out-going one, before it will act. We are sadly mistaken if we feel that the election of Albert Boutwell as mayor will bring the millennium to Birmingham. While Mr. Boutwell is a much more gentle person than Mr. Connor, they are both segregationists, dedicated to maintenance of the status quo. I have hope that Mr. Boutwell will be reasonable enough to see the futility of massive resistance to desegregation. But he will not see this without pressure from devotees of civil rights. My friends, I must say to you that we have not made a single gain in civil rights without determined legal and nonviolent pressure. Lamentably, it is an historical fact that privileged groups seldom give up their privileges voluntarily. Individuals may see the moral light and voluntarily give up their unjust posture; but, as Reinhold Niebuhr has reminded us, groups tend to be more immoral than individuals.

We know through painful experience that freedom is never voluntarily given by the oppressors; it must be demanded by the oppressed. Frankly, I have yet to engage in a direct-action campaign that was "well timed" in the view of those who have not suffered unduly from the disease of segregation. For years now I have heard the word "Wait!" It rings in the ear of every Negro with piercing familiarity. This "Wait" has almost always meant "Never." We must come to see, with one of our distinguished jurists, that "justice too long delayed is justice denied."

We have waited for more than 340 years for our constitutional and God-given rights. The nations of Asia and Africa are moving with jetlike speed toward gaining political independence, but we still creep at horse-and-buggy pace toward gaining a cup of coffee at a lunch counter. Perhaps it is easy for those who have never felt the stinging darts of segregation to say, "Wait." But when you have seen vicious mobs lynch your mothers and fathers at will and drown your sisters and brothers at whim; when you have seen hate-filled policemen curse, kick and even kill your black brothers and sisters; when you see the vast majority of your twenty million Negro brothers smothering in an airtight cage of poverty in the midst of an affluent society; when you suddenly find your tongue twisted and your speech stammering as you seek to explain to your six-year-old daughter why she can't go to the public amusement park that has just been advertised on television, and see tears welling up in her eyes when she is told that Funtown is closed to colored children, and see ominous clouds of inferiority beginning to form in her little mental sky, and see her beginning to distort her personality by developing an unconscious bitterness toward white people; when you have to concoct an answer for a five-year-old son who is asking: "Daddy, why do white people treat colored people so mean?"; when you take a cross-country drive and find it necessary to sleep night after night in the uncomfortable corners of your automobile because no motel will accept you; when you are humiliated day in and day out by nagging signs reading "white" and "colored"; when your first name becomes "nigger," your middle name becomes "boy" (however old you are) and your last name becomes "John," and your wife and mother are never given the respected title "Mrs."; when you are harried by day and haunted by night by the fact that you are a Negro, living constantly at tiptoe stance, never quite knowing what to expect next, and are plagued with inner fears and outer resentments; when you are forever fighting a degenerating sense of "nobodiness"—then you will understand why we find it difficult to wait. There comes a time when the cup of endurance runs over, and men are no longer willing to be plunged into the abyss of despair. I hope, sirs, you can understand our legitimate and unavoidable impatience.

You express a great deal of anxiety over our willingness to break laws. This is certainly a legitimate concern. Since we so diligently urge people to obey the Supreme Court's decision of 1954 outlawing segregation in the public schools, at first glance it may seem rather paradoxical for us consciously to break laws. One may well ask: "How can you advocate breaking some laws and obeying others?" The answer lies in the fact that there are two types of laws: just and unjust. I would be the first to advocate obeying just laws. One has not only a legal but a moral responsibility to obey just laws. Conversely, one has a moral responsibility to disobey unjust laws. I would agree with St. Augustine that "an unjust law is no law at all."

Now, what is the difference between the two? How does one determine whether a law is just or unjust? A just law is a man-made code that squares with the moral law or the law of God. An unjust law is a code that is out of harmony with the moral law. To put it in the terms of St. Thomas Aquinas: An unjust law is a human law that is not rooted in eternal law and natural law. Any law that uplifts human personality is just. Any law that degrades human personality is unjust. All segregation statutes are unjust because segregation distorts the soul and damages the personality. It gives the segregator a false sense of superiority and the segregated a false sense of inferiority. Segregation, to use the terminology of the Jewish philosopher Martin Buber, substitutes an "I-it" relationship for an "I-thou" relationship and ends up relegating persons to the status of things. Hence segregation is not only politically, economically and sociologically unsound, it is morally wrong and sinful. Paul Tillich has said that sin is separation. Is not segregation an existential expression of man's tragic separation, his awful estrangement, his terrible sinfulness? Thus it is that I can urge men to obey the 1954 decision of the Supreme Court, for it is morally right; and I can urge them to disobey segregation ordinances, for they are morally wrong.

Let us consider a more concrete example of just and unjust laws. An unjust law is a code that a numerical or power majority group compels a minority group to obey but does not make binding on itself. This is *difference* made legal. By the same token, a just law is a code that a majority compels a minority to follow and that it is willing to follow itself. This is *sameness* made legal.

Let me give another explanation. A law is unjust if it is inflicted on a minority that, as a result of being denied the right to vote, had no part in enacting or devising the law. Who can say that the legislature of Alabama which set up that state's segregation laws was democratically elected? Throughout Alabama all sorts of devious methods are used to prevent Negroes from becoming registered voters, and there are some counties in which, even though Negroes constitute a majority of the population, not a single Negro is registered. Can any law enacted under such circumstances be considered democratically structured?

Sometimes a law is just on its face and unjust in its application. For instance, I have been arrested on a charge of parading without a permit. Now, there is nothing wrong in having an ordinance which requires a permit for a parade. But such an ordinance becomes unjust when it is used to maintain segregation and to deny citizens the First-Amendment privilege of peaceful assembly and protest.

I hope you are able to see the distinction I am trying to point out. In no sense do I advocate evading or defying the law, as would the rabid segregationist. That would lead to anarchy. One who breaks an unjust law must do so openly, lovingly, and with a willingness to accept the penalty. I submit that an individual who breaks a law that conscience tells him is unjust, and who willingly accepts the penalty of imprisonment in order to arouse the conscience of the community over its injustice, is in reality expressing the highest respect for law.

Of course, there is nothing new about this kind of civil disobedience. It was evidenced sublimely in the refusal of Shadrach, Meshach and Abednego to obey the laws of Nebuchadnezzar, on the ground that a higher moral law was at stake. It was practiced superbly by the early Christians, who were willing to face hungry lions and the excruciating pain of chopping blocks rather than submit to certain unjust laws of the Roman Empire. To a degree, academic freedom is a reality today because Socrates practiced civil disobedience. In our own nation, the Boston Tea Party represented a massive act of civil disobedience.

We should never forget that everything Adolf Hitler did in Germany was "legal" and everything the Hungarian freedom fighters did in Hungary was "illegal." It was "illegal" to aid and comfort a Jew in Hitler's Germany. Even so, I am sure that, had I lived in Germany at the time, I would have aided and comforted my Jewish brothers. If today I lived in a Communist country where certain principles dear to the Christian faith are suppressed, I would openly advocate disobeying that country's antireligious laws.

I must make two honest confessions to you, my Christian and Jewish brothers. First, I must confess that over the past few years I have been gravely disappointed with the white moderate. I have almost reached the regrettable conclusion that the Negro's great stumbling block in his stride toward freedom is not the White Citizen's Counciler or the Ku Klux Klanner, but the white moderate, who is more devoted to "order" than to justice; who prefers a negative peace which is the absence of tension to a positive peace which is the presence of justice; who constantly says: "I agree with you in the goal you seek, but I cannot agree with your methods of direct action"; who paternalistically believes he can set the timetable for another man's freedom; who lives by a mythical concept of time and who constantly advices the Negro to wait for a "more convenient season." Shallow understanding from people of good will is more frustrating than absolute misunderstanding from people of ill will. Lukewarm acceptance is much more bewildering than outright rejection.

I had hoped that the white moderate would understand that law and order exist for the purpose of establishing justice and that when they fail in this purpose they become the dangerously structured dams that block the flow of social progress. I had hoped that the white moderate would understand that the present tension in the South is a necessary phase of the transition from an obnoxious negative peace, in which the Negro passively accepted his unjust plight, to a substantive and positive peace, in which all men will respect the dignity and worth of human personality. Actually, we who engage in nonviolent direct action are not the creators of tension. We merely bring to the surface the hidden tension that is already alive. We bring it out in the open, where it can be seen and dealt with. Like a boil that can never be cured so long as it is covered up but must be opened with all its ugliness to the natural medicines of air and light, injustice must be exposed, with all the tension its exposure creates, to the light of human conscience and the air of national opinion before it can be cured.

In your statement you assert that our actions, even though peaceful, must be condemned because they precipitate violence. But is this a logical assertion? Isn't this like condemning a robbed man because his possession of money precipitated the evil act of robbery? Isn't this like condemning Socrates because his unswerving commitment to truth and his philosophical inquires precipitated the act by the misguided populace in which they made him drink hemlock? Isn't this like condemning Jesus because his unique God-consciousness and never-ceasing devotion to God's will precipitated the evil act of crucifixion? We must come to see that, as the federal courts have consistently affirmed, it is wrong to urge an individual to cease his efforts to gain his basic constitutional rights because the quest may precipitate violence. Society must protect the robbed and punish the robber.

I had also hoped that the white moderate would reject the myth concerning time in relation to the struggle for freedom. I have just received a letter from a white brother in Texas. He writes: "All Christians know that the colored people will receive equal rights eventually, but it is possible that you are in too great a religious hurry. It has taken Christianity almost two thousand years to accomplish what it has. The teachings of Christ take time to come to earth." Such an attitude stems from a tragic misconception of time, from the strangely irrational notion that there is something in the very flow of time that will inevitably cure all ills. Actually, time itself is neutral; it can be used either destructively or constructively. More and more I feel that the people of ill will have used time much more effectively than have the people of good will. We will have to repent in this generation not merely for the hateful words and actions of the bad people but for the appalling silence of the good people. Human progress never rolls in on wheels of inevitability; it comes through the tireless efforts of men willing to be co-workers with God, and without this hard work, time itself becomes an ally of the forces of social stagnation. We must use time creatively, in the knowledge that the time is always ripe to do right. Now is the time to make real the promise of democracy and transform our pending national elegy into a creative psalm of brotherhood. Now is the time to lift our national policy from the quicksand of racial injustice to the solid rock of human dignity.

You speak of our activity in Birmingham as extreme. At first I was rather disappointed that fellow clergymen would see my nonviolent efforts as those of an extremist. I began thinking about the fact that I stand in the middle of two opposing forces in the Negro community. One is a force of complacency, made up in part of Negroes who, as a result of long years of oppression, are so drained of self-respect and a sense of "somebodiness" that they have adjusted to segregation; and in part of a few middle-class Negroes who, because of a degree of academic and economic security and because in some ways they profit by segregation, have become insensitive to the problems of the masses. The other force is one of bitterness and hatred, and it comes perilously close to advocating violence. It is expressed in the various black nationalist groups that are springing up across the nation, the largest and best-known being Elijah Muhammad's Muslim movement. Nourished by the Negro's frustration over the continued existence of racial discrimination, this movement is made up of people who have lost faith in America, who have absolutely repudiated Christianity, and who have concluded that the white man is an incorrigible "devil."

I have tried to stand between these two forces, saying that we need emulate neither the "do-nothingism" of the complacent nor the hatred and despair of the black nationalist. For there is the more excellent way of love and nonviolent protest. I am grateful to God that, through the influence of the Negro church, the way of nonviolence became an integral part of our struggle.

If this philosophy had not emerged, by now many streets of the South would, I am convinced, be flowing with blood. And I am further convinced that if our white brothers dismiss as "rabble-rousers" and "outside agitators" those of us who employ nonviolent direct action, and if they refuse to support our nonviolent efforts, millions of Negroes will, out of frustration and despair, seek solace and security in black-nationalist ideologies—a development that would inevitably lead to a frightening racial nightmare.

Oppressed people cannot remain oppressed forever. The yearning for freedom eventually manifests itself, and that is what has happened to the American Negro. Something within has reminded him of his birthright of freedom, and something without has reminded him that it can be gained. Consciously or unconsciously, he has been caught up by the *Zeitgeist*, and with his black brothers of Africa and his brown and yellow brothers of Asia, South America and the Caribbean, the United States Negro is moving with a sense of great urgency toward the promised land of racial justice. If one recognizes this vital urge that has engulfed the Negro community, one should readily understand why public demonstrations are taking place. The Negro has many pent-up resentments and latent frustrations, and he must release them. So let him march; let him make prayer pilgrimages to the city hall; let him go on freedom rides—and try to understand why he must do so. If his repressed emotions are not released in nonviolent ways, they will seek expression through violence; this is not a threat but a fact of history. So I have not said to my people: "Get rid of your discontent." Rather, I have tried to say that this normal and healthy discontent can be channeled into the creative outlet of nonviolent direct action. And now this approach is being termed extremist.

But though I was initially disappointed at being categorized as an extremist, as I continued to think about the matter I gradually gained a measure of satisfaction from the label. Was not Jesus an extremist for love: "Love your enemies, bless them that curse you, do good to them that hate you, and pray for them which despitefully use you, and persecute you." Was not Amos an extremist for justice: "Let justice roll down like waters and righteousness like an ever-flowing stream." Was not Paul an extremist for the Christian gospel: "I bear in my body the marks of the Lord Jesus." Was not Martin Luther an extremist: "Here I stand; I cannot do otherwise, so help me God." And John Bunyan: "I will stay in jail to the end of my days before I make a butchery of my conscience." And Abraham Lincoln: "This nation cannot survive half slave and half free." And Thomas Jefferson: "We hold these truths to be self-evident, that all men are created equal . . ." So the question is not whether we will be extremists, but what kind of extremists we will be. Will we be extremists for hate or for love? Will we be extremists for the preservation of injustice or for the extension of justice? In that dramatic scene on Calvary's hill three men were crucified. We must never forget that all three were crucified for the same crime—the crime of extremism. Two were extremists for immorality, and thus fell below their environment. The other, Jesus Christ, was an extremist for love, truth and goodness, and thereby rose above his environment. Perhaps the South, the nation and the world are in dire need of creative extremists.

I had hoped that the white moderate would see this need. Perhaps I was too optimistic; perhaps I expected too much. I suppose I should have realized that few members of the oppressor race can understand the deep groans and passionate yearnings of the oppressed race, and still fewer have the vision to see that injustice must be rooted out by strong, persistent and determined action. I am thankful, however, that some of our white brothers in the South have grasped the meaning of this social revolution and committed themselves to it. They are still all too few in quantity, but they are big in quality. Some—such as Ralph McGill, Lillian Smith, Harry Golden, James McBride Dabbs, Ann Braden and Sarah Patton Boyle—have written about our struggle in eloquent and prophetic terms. Others have marched with us down nameless streets of the South. They have languished in filthy, roach-infested jails, suffering the abuse and brutality of policemen who view them as "dirty nigger-lovers." Unlike so many of their moderate brothers and sisters, they have recognized the urgency of the moment and sensed the need for powerful "action" antidotes to combat the disease of segregation.

Let me take note of my other major disappointment. I have been so greatly disappointed with the white church and its leadership. Of course, there are some notable exceptions. I am not unmindful of the fact that each of you has taken some significant stands on this issue. I commend you, Reverend Stallings, for your Christian stand on this past Sunday, in welcoming Negroes to your worship service on a nonsegregated basis. I commend the Catholic leaders of this state for integrating Spring Hill College several years ago.

But despite these notable exceptions, I must honestly reiterate that I have been disappointed with the church. I do not say this as one of those negative critics who can always find something wrong with the church. I say this as a minister of the gospel, who loves the church; who was nurtured in its bosom; who has been sustained by its spiritual blessings and who will remain true to it as long as the cord of life shall lengthen.

When I was suddenly catapulted into the leadership of the bus protest in Montgomery, Alabama, a few years ago, I felt we would be supported by the white church. I felt that the white ministers, priests and rabbis of the South would be among our strongest allies. Instead, some have been outright opponents, refusing to understand the freedom movement and misrepresenting its leaders; all too many others have been more cautious than courageous and have remained silent behind the anesthetizing security of stained-glass windows.

In spite of my shattered dreams, I came to Birmingham with the hope that the white religious leadership of this community would see the justice of our cause and, with deep moral concern, would serve as the channel through which our just grievances could reach the power structure. I had hoped that each of you would understand. But again I have been disappointed.

I have heard numerous southern religious leaders admonish their worshipers to comply with a desegregation decision because it is the law, but I have longed to hear white ministers declare: "Follow this decree because integration is morally right and because the Negro is your brother." In the midst of blatant injustices inflicted upon the Negro, I have watched white churchmen stand on the sideline and mouth pious irrelevancies and sanctimonious trivialities. In the midst of a mighty struggle to rid our nation of racial and economic injustice, I have heard many ministers say: "Those are social issues, with which the gospel has no real concern." And I have watched many churches commit themselves to a completely otherworldly religion which makes a strange, un-Biblical distincton between body and soul, and between the sacred and the secular.

I have traveled the length and breadth of Alabama, Mississippi, and all the other southern states. On sweltering summer days and crisp autumn mornings I have looked at the South's beautiful churches with their lofty spires pointing heavenward. I have beheld the impressive outlines of her massive religious-education buildings. Over and over I have found myself asking: "What kind of people worship here? Who is their God? Where were their voices when the lips of Governor Barnett dripped with words of interposition, and nullification? Where were they when Governor Wallace gave a clarion call for defiance and hatred? Where were their voices of support when bruised and weary Negro men and women decided to rise from the dark dungeons of complacency to the bright hills of creative protest?"

Yes, these questions are still in my mind. In deep disappointment I have wept over the laxity of the church. But be assured that my tears have been tears of love. There can be no deep disappointment where there is not deep love. Yes, I love the church. How could I do otherwise? I am in the rather unique position of being the son, the grandson and the great-grandson of preachers. Yes, I see the church as the body of Christ. But, oh! How we have blemished and scarred that body through social neglect and through fear of being nonconformists.

There was a time when the church was very powerful—in the time when the early Christians rejoiced at being deemed worthy to suffer for what they believed. In those days the church was not merely a thermometer that recorded the ideas and principles of popular opinion; it was a thermostat that transformed the mores of society. Whenever the early Christians entered a town, the people in power became disturbed and immediately sought to convict the Christians for being "disturbers of the peace" and "outside agitators." But the Christians pressed on, in the conviction that they were "a colony of heaven," called to obey God rather than man. Small in number, they were big in commitment. They were too God-intoxicated to be "astronomically intimidated." By their effort and example they brought an end to such ancient evils as infanticide and gladiatorial contests.

Things are different now. So often the contemporary church is a weak, ineffectual voice with an uncertain sound. So often it is an archdefender of the status quo. Far from being disturbed by the presence of the church, the power structure of the average community is consoled by the church's silent —and often even vocal—sanction of things as they are.

But the judgment of God is upon the church as never before. If today's church does not recapture the sacrificial spirit of the early church, it will lose its authenticity, forfeit the loyalty of millions, and be dismissed as an irrelevant social club with no meaning for the twentieth century. Every day I meet young people whose disappointment with the church has turned into outright disgust.

Perhaps I have once again been too optimistic. Is organized religion too inextricably bound to the status quo to save our nation and the world? Perhaps I must turn my faith to the inner spiritual church, the church within the church, as the true *ekklesia* and the hope of the world. But again I am thankful to God that some noble souls from the ranks of organized religion have broken loose from the paralyzing chains of conformity and joined us as active partners in the struggle for freedom. They have left their secure congregations and walked the streets of Albany, Georgia, with us. They have gone down the highways of the South on tortuous rides for freedom. Yes, they have gone to jail with us. Some have been dismissed from their churches, have lost the support of their bishops and fellow ministers. But they have acted in the faith that right defeated is stronger than evil triumphant. Their witness has been the spiritual salt that has preserved the true meaning of the gospel in these troubled times. They have carved a tunnel of hope through the dark mountain of disappointment.

I hope the church as a whole will meet the challenge of this decisive hour. But even if the church does not come to the aid of justice, I have no despair about the future. I have no fear about the outcome of our struggle in Birmingham, even if our motives are at present misunderstood. We will reach the goal of freedom in Birmingham and all over the nation, because the goal of America is freedom. Abused and scorned though we may be, our destiny is tied up with America's destiny. Before the pilgrims landed at Plymouth, we were here. Before the pen of Jefferson etched the majestic words of the Declaration of Independence across the pages of history, we were here. For more than two centuries our forebears labored in this country without wages; they made cotton king; they built the homes of their masters while suffering gross injustice and shameful humiliation—and yet out of a bottomless vitality they continued to thrive and develop. If the inexpressible cruelties of slavery could not stop us, the opposition we now face will surely fail. We will win our freedom because the sacred heritage of our nation and the eternal will of God are embodied in our echoing demands.

Before closing I feel impelled to mention one other point in your statement that has troubled me profoundly. You warmly commended the Birmingham police force for keeping "order" and "preventing violence." I doubt that you would have so warmly commended the police force if you had seen its dogs sinking their teeth into unarmed, nonviolent Negroes. I doubt that you would so quickly commend the policemen if you were to observe their ugly and inhumane treatment of Negroes here in the city jail; if you were to watch them push and curse old Negro women and young Negro girls; if you were to see them slap and kick old Negro men and young boys; if you were to observe them, as they did on two occasions, refuse to give us food because we wanted to sing our grace together. I cannot join you in your praise of the Birmingham police department.

It is true that the police have exercised a degree of discipline in handling the demonstrators. In this sense they have conducted themselves rather "non-violently" in public. But for what purpose? To preserve the evil system of segregation. Over the past few years I have consistently preached that non-violence demands that the means we use must be as pure as the ends we seek. I have tried to make clear that it is wrong to use immoral means to attain moral ends. But now I must affirm that it is just as wrong, or perhaps even more so, to use moral means to preserve immoral ends. Perhaps Mr. Connor and his policemen have been rather nonviolent in public, as was Chief Pritchett in Albany, Georgia, but they have used the moral means of nonviolence to maintain the immoral end of racial injustice. As T. S. Eliot has said: "The last temptation is the greatest treason: To do the right deed for the wrong reason."

I wish you had commended the Negro sit-inners and demonstrators of Birmingham for their sublime courage, their willingness to suffer and their amazing discipline in the midst of great provocation. One day the South will recognize its real heroes. They will be the James Merediths, with the noble sense of purpose that enables them to face jeering and hostile mobs, and with the agonizing loneliness that characterizes the life of the pioneer. They will be old, oppressed, battered Negro women, symbolized in a seventy-two-year-old woman in Montgomery, Alabama, who rose up with a sense of dignity and with her people decided not to ride segregated buses, and who responded with ungrammatical profundity to one who inquired about her weariness: "My feets is tired, but my soul is at rest." They will be the young high school and college students, the young ministers of the gospel and a host of their elders, courageously and nonviolently sitting in at lunch counters and willingly going to jail for conscience' sake. One day the South will know that when these disinherited children of God sat down at lunch counters, they were in reality standing up for what is best in the American dream and for the most sacred values in our Judaeo-Christian heritage, thereby bringing our nation back to those great wells of democracy which were dug deep by the founding fathers in their formulation of the Constitution and the Declaration of Independence.

Never before have I written so long a letter. I'm afraid it is much too long to take your precious time. I can assure you that it would have been much shorter if I had been writing from a comfortable desk, but what else can one do when he is alone in a narrow jail cell, other than write long letters, think long thoughts and pray long prayers?

If I have said anything in this letter that overstates the truth and indicates an unreasonable impatience, I beg you to forgive me. If I have said anything that understates the truth and indicates my having a patience that allows me to settle for anything less than brotherhood, I beg God to forgive me.

I hope this letter finds you strong in the faith. I also hope that circumstances will soon make it possible for me to meet each of you, not as an integrationist or a civil-rights leader but as a fellow clergyman and a Christian brother. Let us all hope that the dark clouds of racial prejudice will soon pass away and the deep fog of misunderstanding will be lifted from our fear-drenched communities, and in some not too distant tomorrow the radiant stars of love and brotherhood will shine over our great nation with all their scintillating beauty.

Yours for the cause of Peace and Brotherhood,
MARTIN LUTHER KING, JR.

RAMSEY CLARK

The Erosion of Civil Liberties

Q: In the light of recent events—the passage of certain anti-crime bills in Congress, for example—do you think this country is slipping back as far as civil rights are concerned?

CLARK: Natural pressures as well as human and social pressures bear on civil liberties. I think the greater risks to civil liberties are technology and the population increase. They put a heavy weight on the meaning and integrity of the individual, on his dignity, privacy, and the like. In the political context, it's clear today that the fight for individual freedom is not a popular cause. We have conditioned ourselves to be more concerned about other things—like profits, personal safety, quiet, order in the schools—than we are about

Source: Ramsey Clark served as Assistant Attorney General in the Kennedy administration and as Attorney General under Lyndon Johnson. Mr. Clark has long been committed to an interpretation of the meaning of justice which roots law and order in human rights and equal opportunity. This article is reprinted, with permission, from an interview published in the July 1970 issue pp. 51–58, of *The Center Magazine*, a publication of the Center for the Study of Democratic Institutions in Santa Barbara, California.

individual freedom and civil liberties. So you find an accumulation of specific encroachments on civil liberties and a high political popularity for those encroachments, a higher popularity than at any time, I would say, since the early nineteen-fifties. You also find a continuing erosion of civil liberties in the written law if not yet in the enforcement of the law.

This is particularly sad because there is no contest between liberty and security. You have both or neither. We can enlarge both.

Q: We are faced, it seems, with a circular situation here. Blacks, students, the poor, and the dispossessed, who feel helpless and repressed, strike out, sometimes violently, in their frustration. But when they do, all the strength and power of the majority gather and then even more repressive legislation and action are initiated. This, in turn, feeds the resentment of the blacks and the youth. How can we break out of that escalation of frustration and violence?

CLARK: There is polarization, but underneath the polarization and emotionalization we are seeing a new awareness that there is something profoundly wrong in our society causing people to act this way. Following the ghetto riots of 1967, for example, came the enactment, in April, 1968, of the federal open-housing statute. The Johnson Administration had submitted open-housing legislation to the Congress in 1966, the first time any Administration had favored enactment of a law prohibiting racial discrimination in the advertising, sale, and rental of housing. The Administration was unsuccessful in 1966. Then came the ghetto riots in 1967, followed by the backlash, high emotionalization, and polarization of black and white communities. Everybody thought it would be much more difficult to obtain civil-rights legislation after the 1967 riots. But in March 1968, the filibuster was broken and the Senate voted overwhelmingly for open housing. What happened was that, shocked and frightened and even outraged as white America thought it was about the 1967 riots, it found a new awareness of the problems that underlay those disturbances; and it came to believe that the problems were real and that something had to be done about them. So Congress passed the open-housing statute.

On the Vietnam issue, there has been a very significant change in national policy. It has come about because of the anti-Vietnam protest, which probably offended most people in this country. People saw unruly kids and were frightened. At the same time, other people were trying to frighten them by predicting holocaust and talking about communist conspiracies. But the long-range impact of that protest was a new awareness, a new concern about what we were doing in Vietnam and to ourselves—and it turned our policy around.

Q: That is one kind of response to protest and dissent we have seen. In recent months, we have seen other kinds of responses, from the Congress and from the Executive Branch of government. I am thinking now of legislation which the Senate has been passing with overwhelming votes, which clearly seems to reflect negative response to protest. The House recently voted to amend the Voting Rights Act of 1965, once again permitting local election

*boards in the South to change their voting laws so as virtually to exclude blacks
from the voting booth.*

CLARK: I didn't mean that all the responses to protest have been affirmative.
Perhaps Ronald Reagan is Governor of California in part because of the
Watts riots. Probably most responses to protest are negative. But protest does
create a new awareness of problems. In the area of civil rights we are now
undergoing a national reëxamination, one that is critically important. I think
that most of our people are now wondering whether racial integration as a
goal is right and, if it is right, whether it is possible. The reasons for this are
many, but the manifestations of it are efforts to amend the voting-rights law,
and half a dozen other significant administrative acts by the national Administration, as well as legislative acts in the Congress. This is no time for doubt;
we must integrate now.

*Q: Is Congress reflecting a regressive and negative national mood about
civil liberties, or is it helping to create such a mood by its actions?*

CLARK: It's a little of both, I believe. An anti-crime measure is very hard to
vote against when the country is seized by the fear of crime. The political situation is fairly equivocal anyway. Most politicians believe that getting reelected
is the first order of business. They just do not want to take on the burden of
fighting against, say, the no-knock law. The no-knock provision, to most
people, is not one of far-reaching impact. Congressmen do not figure that it
will be their door, or even the doors of most people who vote.

*Q: Senator Sam Ervin, of North Carolina, thought that that law was really
a sacrifice of something precious in the area of privacy and personal liberty.*

CLARK: Senator Ervin is a legal scholar with a very strong commitment to
some key protections in the Bill of Rights and the Constitution. He has provided important leadership in opposition to no-knock and preventive-detention
bills.

*Q: One of the criticisms of the no-knock law I have heard is that it could
be used to harass political activists. On the pretext of searching for marijuana,
so the criticism runs, law-enforcement people could break into meetings of
political activists without knocking at the door.*

CLARK: It certainly has that potential. In my judgment, the real harm in the
no-knock provision is that its passage indicates to the police that the public
wants this kind of law. It seeks to control conduct by police violence. Actually,
the no-knock provision by Congress would have concentrated application only
in the District of Columbia. But what it does is tell police, the legislatures,
and city councils in other parts of the country that this is something the
public condones. That sort of thing can get out of control. If you begin to
use such measures, you rarely limit them with any refinement. That has been
our experience. Once you encourage or cause law enforcement to use a technique that is essentially unfair and demeaning to human dignity, or a technique
that involves trickery, law-enforcement officers will use other techniques, and
non-professional police in the law-enforcement business do not tend to make

fine distinctions. Soon there is a general breakdown as far as respecting the personal and civil liberties of citizens is concerned.

Q: What is your guess as to the possibility of preventive-detention legislation being enacted?

CLARK: Preventive detention in the form now under consideration in Congress would permit federal judges to refuse bail for defendants in criminal cases if, in their judgment, the release of those defendants would be a threat to the community. The idea behind such a law is that there are habitual offenders who, while out on bail pending a court trial for one offense, commit a number of crimes. The problem with "preventive detention," of course, is that, at the discretion of the judge, it would begin punishing an accused even before his trial came up. With court calendars as crowded as they are, an accused person might spend months in jail waiting for his trial. The educated guess is that Congress will enact preventive-detention legislation this session. The federal government does not make criminal laws for the states, so this law would apply primarily to the District of Columbia. Actually, less than two per cent of pre-trial detention in the United States is within the federal system. The real action is at the state level. And, again, the impact of preventive-detention law would be in what it signals from Congress to the various law-enforcement and court jurisdictions.

Q: You have said that fear is at the bottom of many of the recent and current developments that are shrinking the area of personal and civil liberty. How can a nation begin to replace fear with confidence?

CLARK: The basic need is for education. And perhaps before education there must come research in many areas of crime, because education is impossible if the facts aren't known. Our ignorance of crime and criminal conduct is appalling. Our ignorance far exceeds our knowledge. We torture ourselves with assumptions, many of which are patently erroneous. Merely having an ideological debate about, for example, preventive detention has no real force. People can't relate such debates to anything that happens in their daily lives. But if the people are informed and educated about jails and conditions in jails, they will move for jail reform. If we do not have jail reform, preventive detention is simply going to cause crime, not reduce it. If we had preventive-detention laws, they would take the pressure off the courts to provide speedy trials—a man could be held in jail indefinitely until the law was good and ready to let him have his day in court. Provisions that trials must be held in thirty days or sixty days are not enforceable. And if we do not have speedy trials, then law is not a deterrent to crime. So some basic reforms that have to be made are inhibited by preventive detention. If people knew this, they would act on the basis of their knowledge.

Q: Why is it that the richest country in the world allows slums to fester, knowing slums breed crime, or why is it that the nation tolerates mental institutions that are disgraceful from almost every point of view? You suggest that if the American people were made more aware, in concrete detail, of such things as jail and slum conditions they would press for change and reform. More education and more research into the facts is part of the answer. And I suppose the mass communications media should be looked at critically, too. Perhaps the media should be rubbing our noses into these harsh realities, day after day.

CLARK: There is no doubt that lack of awareness is a major problem. We Americans are great problem-solvers when we really work at it and put our minds to it. But the average American has very little real knowledge of ghetto life. We structure our daily lives so that we do not have to see ghetto existence. Our freeways bypass it. The ghetto is another part of town, a strange culture. Mental illness and criminal behavior are also things that frighten people; they are the last to evoke compassion or sympathy. We are not willing to help them, even in self-interest. Most people who commit crimes and are in prison will be at large again someday, and the question is not how long did they spend in jail but what will they be like when they come out. We isolate them and then largely forget about them until they come out again, and if they come out with an increased capacity for crime, then watch out.

Q: In what sense, if any, is America a violent society?

CLARK: Violence may be a natural instinct for Americans. In our history, through a series of circumstances, violence has become a common method for solving problems. The frontier was an environment of violence. We had the brutalization of slavery for two and a half centuries. We have our heritage of guns, a heritage unlike practically any other nation in the world, and that increases the level of violence. We have had the merging of a great variety of cultures from different continents and races, and that creates and adds to the turbulence as we try to learn how to live together and to accommodate to each other. We have the vast urbanization and the technology and immense population growth, all of which contribute to the level of violence. If you look at our violence closely, it seems to be emotional and irrational and tends to be rather equivocal. In countries which we do not think of as being violent, you will find capacities for a deliberate and cruel type of violence that we Americans have not manifested. We know there are places where human hearts have been cut out and eaten, where heads are put on poles and carried around. We Americans are not that tough. We are not conditioned to that type of violence.

I think turbulence and instability and the anonymity of the individual in America all tend to cause us to seek violence as a problem-solver because we do not see any other way to solve our problems. In the American tradition, we have glorified the power of violence and ignored its pity. I think it is possible, within one generation, to condition the propensity for violence out of the American society. We have no greater challenge. Violence is no longer tolerable as an interpersonal or an international problem-solver.

Q: Is there such a thing as a moral equivalent for violence, a substitute for it that could engage, in acceptable ways, our energies and passions?

CLARK: Yes. But I think we have to approach it directly. We must condition violence from our character. It is most often an uncontrollable emotional reflex. People cannot see the relationship between the automobile and violence. But there is the closest relationship. Highway carnage cheapens life. Reverence for life will be essential to restrain life-injuring emotional impulses. Fifty thousand people are killed each year in this country in automobile accidents, with blood and broken bodies visible to millions. In half of those accidents the driver was under the influence of alcohol. This is controllable. Two-thirds of all murders are committed with firearms; eighty-five per cent of all murders are within families or among friends. They are crimes of sudden emotion. We know that if the gun had not been there many of these murders would not have been committed. It's a lot harder to kill somebody with a knife, and it takes a different kind of person to kill with a knife. If guns were not around, many murders just would not happen. To revere life, we will have to act to prevent its destruction.

Q: So this would be one way, a very specific and direct way, one could reduce crime?

CLARK: Yes. I think we have to try to create attitudes and traditions that make us incapable of resorting to violence. In an urban, technologically advanced, mass society, we have to recognize that, given our instincts for violence, we now have the technology to make that violence totally destructive. We have to come to grips with that fact and not let our instinct and our destructive technological capacity ever come together. I am talking in a much broader sense than the Bomb. It is forms of violence that threaten human dignity and the natural environment.

Q: You said earlier we must stop the encroachment on personal liberty and privacy, and the cheapening of the meaning of human life. I couldn't help but recall a newsphoto from Vietnam a few years ago which showed an American crane swinging a huge mesh bag filled with perhaps forty or fifty bodies of Vietnamese we had killed. The crane was simply slinging these bodies into a mass grave much as one would sling a load of cordwood into a pile. And it seemed to me that that one photo said a great deal about an "official" American attitude, as it were, toward human life. One wonders what value judgments the American young people are led to make by such practices. Does it tend to cheapen human life in their eyes? Does it encourage them to practice their kind of violence, which may degrade both them and those they attack?

CLARK: Human dignity is the central question of our times. We have not had a more tragic episode in our history than Vietnam. The dehumanization which the Vietnam experience has inflicted on the American people has been just devastating. We have to wonder what we have done to ourselves. The body-count by which the Vietnam war is officially and journalistically reported is as good an illustration as any of how we have depreciated the value of human life. We seem to want to derive some glory from the number of people we have killed, as if we were engaged in a baseball game: we killed ten of theirs for one of ours that they killed. Our lives won't be worth much until we value theirs equally.

Q: Is it that the pace of American life, at least in its frontier days when there was a lot of work to be done, precluded the possibility, or desirability, of analyzing and talking out our differences and problems rather than resorting to the violent solution?

CLARK: That's part of it. Another thing we have to understand is that we have been the first to experience high technological development, along with the population explosion. That will come to other countries. We must hope they cope with it as well as we have. By looking at crime statistics, you can see certain things: for instance, we know that crime varies between urban and rural areas, and between geographical parts of the country. The murder rate in the South is twice that of the rest of the nation. Rape is much more frequent in California than in the northeastern part of the country. Robbery tends to be a highly urban crime; robbery is thirty-five times more frequent per capita in cities of two hundred and fifty thousand or more than in rural areas. In frontier days you could avoid problems by walking away from them—finding your own place—today, you cannot escape. We are totally interdependent.

Q: Obviously, one can find slums in many countries. But it would be interesting to analyze crime incidence in countries where there is not great disparity of wealth on any significant scale (countries like Belgium and the Netherlands, for example) and compare that to crime figures in our own country.

CLARK: Some countries have been quite effective in ridding themselves of slums. Sweden, for instance. Its problems are relatively easy though. A simple culture or small population rich in resources, it can adapt easily to new welfare needs in an interdependent society. And there are some countries where the contrast between great wealth and great poverty is much sharper than our own. That would be true all through Latin America. A difference, however, is that in the United States our poor are a minority and that makes for difficulty; poverty is a stigma here. Poverty was never a stigma in those places where most of the people were poor; poverty was a common condition that was accepted. Also, our people are aware of the extent of their poverty and the relative general affluence of their fellow citizens. Lamennais, who was a youth at the time of the French Revolution and lived through the Napoleonic era and the Third Republic and the revolution of 1848, said that the stability of every society has depended upon the resignation of the poor to being poor. Our poor are not going to be resigned to their poverty. Infant mortality is four times greater among the poor; mental retardation is six to eight times greater because of malnutrition, lack of prenatal care, bad health generally, the use of stimulants during pregnancy. The poor know all this, not with the precision of statisticians or sociologists, but they know it because they are surrounded by it and feel it. When they look out there, through television, at the white suburb and at Marlboro country, they become enraged. They will not be resigned to their poverty and I would not want them to be.

Q: *Can the Justice Department, should it, interpret its responsibility as one that extends to the social conditions in which crime breeds? Does the Justice Department have a mandate that embraces the social as well as the strict law-enforcement concept of justice?*

CLARK: The Department of Justice, by law and by necessity, is far more than the flinty-eyed prosecutor. It needs to be and is becoming a ministry of justice in the broadest sense, and that includes social justice. Anatole France summed that up pretty well in *The Red Lily* when he said that the law in its majestic equality prohibits the rich as well as the poor from sleeping under bridges and begging in the streets and stealing bread. Where there is social and economic disparity there cannot be justice. There is no equality in law when people cannot fulfill their rights.

Q: *Specifically, what can the Department of Justice do in matters of social reform?*

CLARK: In the organization chart of the Department there is the Federal Bureau of Prisons. The mission of the Federal Bureau of Prisons is rehabilitation. I think that is the only mission that makes sense. We have a high obligation to use all the medical, physical, and social sciences at our command to provide the highest level of rehabilitation that can occur there. We also have such institutions as the Community Relations Service and the Civil Rights Division in the Department. Their roles in equal justice, understanding, and communication are critical to effective crime control as well as ends in themselves.

Q: *Are all these well budgeted, or are they institutions that exist mostly on paper?*

CLARK: The Federal Bureau of Prisons is the third largest within the Department of Justice. Its operating budget runs about sixty-five to seventy million dollars a year for programs, which is about half of what is needed to do the job.

Q: *I believe you once remarked that ninety-five per cent of prison budgets goes for custodial care, and five per cent for rehabilitation work with prisoners.*

CLARK: Ninety-five per cent is the national figure. The figure in the Department of Justice is much lower than that. But you can get the meaning of this when you realize that even in the federal prisons there aren't twenty psychiatrists for over twenty thousand prisoners; in some prisons virtually everyone needs some mental health care.

Q: *How might the federal government help with the problems of local communities?*

CLARK: As an illustration, we made a grant to the New York City Police Department and the sociology department of New York University for a program in a test precinct in New York through which police officers received formal training and education in such things as the handling of domestic and neighborhood disturbances, the range of referral agencies available to people who may need social or psychological or economic help, and the ways to prevent disturbances from becoming crimes. The Department has a large amount of such contract funds that should be used for social betterment. Law enforcement by itself cannot solve the crime problem. One-fourth to one-third of all arrests in the United States each year of the last decade were of people under the influence of alcohol. Alcoholism cannot be solved by getting more police. Alcoholics are a burden on the police; they impair effective police work in areas where police could be effective. Alcoholism is a medical and social problem, and just arresting the alcoholic over and over again until he has a lifetime of a hundred and fifty arrests and imprisonment for drunkenness is sheer insanity.

Q: *How much contact, systematic or casual, did you have when you were Attorney General with people in other departments such as Health, Education, and Welfare, or Labor, or Housing and Urban Development, or the Office of Economic Opportunity? Was there much close coördination and exchange of ideas and insights?*

CLARK: There was some interchange, but it is very difficult because people in those jobs are so busy attending to the myriad of little problems that they seldom have the opportunity to tackle the big ones. But we did have a variety of coördination and consultative efforts. We had an urban council at the Cabinet level that involved Justice, the Departments of Housing and Urban Development, O.E.O., the Department of Labor, and H.E.W. We tried to get together every two weeks just to see how we could be more effective. Through such interchange we developed, with H.E.W., the Juvenile Delinquency Prevention and Control Act. H.E.W., we felt, should have ninety per cent of the action in juvenile delinquency. The dominant role should belong to H.E.W., but we recognized there must also be a clear and direct relationship and coördination between H.E.W. and the Department of Justice. The Bureau of the Budget is also involved in the kind of inter-agency coördination you refer to. But bureaucratic management is not very effective science; it's just awfully hard to do.

Q: *Do you think that there is a calculated program on the part of the federal and/or local governments to break up the Black Panther organization?*

CLARK: I am a member of a commission which is sponsored by a number of agencies—the National Association for the Advancement of Colored People, the Urban League, the National Council of Churches, the American Civil Liberties Union, and six or eight other important agencies, plus twenty-some individuals. It has been set up to try to get at the truth of the relationship between the Black Panthers and the police. Those of us on the commission have thought it best not to comment on this question until we have had a chance to see what the commission comes up with.

Q: *You have said in a paper on "the death of privacy" that wiretapping and*

*bugging are the acts of an "incipient police state." It seems we are reading
of more and more incidents of such police surveillance in this country. Justice
William O. Douglas says in his most recent book that no phone in any federal
or state agency today is immune from the suspicion that it might be tapped;
it is also assumed that every conference room in government buildings is
bugged and that every embassy phone is an open transmitter. Under the circumstances, when does an "incipient" police state become an "actual" police
state?*

CLARK: This involves definitional problems. What is a police state? I think
perhaps it is better to speak generally. The acceptability of invasions of
privacy is probably as high in the United States today as it has ever been
in our history. The public seems to feel that it has got to sacrifice some
privacy for personal safety, so we condone such practices. There had been
legislation to authorize wiretapping before every session of Congress from
1961 to 1968, but nothing was done about it until 1968 and then Congress
authorized it. Public acceptance creates a major part of the threat to privacy.
Another part of that risk is technological development. We will soon have
the capacity to invade privacy totally and then there will be no sanctuary for
the individual person. Perhaps someday even the human skull will not be a
sanctuary. With the advent of the technological means to invade privacy, we
must establish now a clear and strong commitment to the value of privacy as
an end in itself or we will lose it. I don't think we have ever really examined
what privacy is. I think that privacy is the foundation of individual character.
I think it is the way you come to know who you are and what you are and how
you make value judgments as to what is right and what is wrong. If that kind
of personal, private judgment goes, then everything will become instinctive
or group reaction. I think one's character develops over a long period of time
through private reflection, by being by oneself and thinking about oneself, so
that when we tamper with privacy we tamper with the foundations of individual integrity.

*Q: This almost forces one to ask certain basic philosophical questions about
the nature of man, the nature of society, and the nature of the relationship
between man and society. If the view prevails that the importance of the
person is only to be found in his relationship to society or in what he can
contribute to society, then such things as individual privacy can be thought
of as quite expendable if they do not seem to contribute directly and obviously
to the good of society.*

CLARK: It may be that the meaning of mass population is that the individual loses his significance. I don't like that but I get glimpses of that
possibility. When you watch the Weatherman faction of Students for a
Democratic Society, you are seeing them reach the conscious conclusion that
the individual has no value, that all value is in the group. Perhaps this is
true of the Red Guard. That is so foreign to me. To me, everything that is
important must tend toward the fulfillment of the individual. In Jefferson's

time, he could correspond with leaders throughout the world, know them personally through correspondence and through meetings with them. He had some sense of who they were and what they were and what they thought. Today, that is almost impossible to do in one's own high school because of the mix, the movement, the anonymity, the size.

Q: *We have had young visitors to the Center describing their experiences in a commune. Typically, the size of such a community is about twelve to fifteen people ranging in age from nineteen to twenty-nine, and they tell us they want to achieve their "personhood," their fulfillment as persons, through living in such a community. In other words, they are totally committed to personalism and communitarianism.*

CLARK: We've had community experiments all through history. I wonder if many today don't reflect a vague desire for some transition from a society based on individualism, family, self-interest, acquisitiveness, and competition to a quieter, gentler environment of service to others equally with self, and non-materialism and non-involvement. This is a hard transition to make and these young people do not seem to be able to find it in their communities; they stumble around, and after a while come back out. With the mass numbers we have in our country, I doubt that you can structure the whole society by a proliferation of these small group activities. We have to question all of our institutions, even the family, but to me escapism is no longer possible. We are too interdependent.

Q: *But their argument is that even if their small community cannot be a model for mass society, at least they will find some meaning and dignity in life through these communal experiences in which there will be sharing, generosity, and a helping of one another.*

CLARK: I have my doubts about that. Even if true, it is basically selfish. We must be involved in the action.

Q: *What is your view of the anti-conspiracy and riot-control law under which the Chicago Seven were tried? How did that law get passed?*

CLARK: The law was designed to create a new federal crime, the crime of moving across a state line for the purpose of inciting a riot. The conspiracy provision was not embodied in that law. There is a general conspiracy statute that makes it a crime to conspire to commit a substantive crime. For example, it is a crime to rob a bank, and under the conspiracy statute it is also a crime to conspire to rob a bank. The first hearings on the substantive provision— moving across a state line to incite a riot—were, as I recall, in October of 1966. I had just become Acting Attorney General and we opposed the bill. The hearings were before a Housing judiciary subcommittee. We opposed it for several reasons. First, Americans are the most mobile people that ever lived; we are constantly on the move, crossing state and even national lines continually. We live in turbulent times. People come to university campuses, they speak, and sometimes there is violence in connection with a speech. To make it a crime to move across a state line to incite a riot has a terribly chilling effect on vitally important communications. We need to encourage the flow of communications, not make communication perilous. This law does make communication very perilous. So we raised strong constitutional questions about that bill. It inhibits free speech. There is some potential for violence when many important issues are discussed in mass assemblies. But mass assembly has had immense value for the whole country. It helped the awakening realization of the need to do something about civil rights.

Dr. King was not a universally popular man when he led the March on Washington in 1963. A lot of people wondered whether he was good or bad. A law that would say it is a crime, punishable by a long penitentiary sentence and a high fine, to move across a state line for the purpose of inciting a riot would place a heavy burden on a man who might organize something like that March on Washington. A person must be able to say what he believes to be true when he gets there. But what he believes may be provocative, and it may be said in an emotional setting. How can you tell what the speaker intends? The Vietnam protests are illustrations. Perhaps the First Amendment saved the nation from an even greater tragedy in Vietnam. Vietnam is an emotional issue, and yet there has been very little violence when you stop to think about the vast numbers of people and the episodes involved. The Poor People's Campaign might have been inhibited from assembling, because poverty and the problems of poverty are emotionally charged issues. Some people will tend to stay home for fear that they might be prosecuted. The poor are not very popular anyway; nobody wants poor people to come; and march in his city and say angry things.

Q: Who introduced the bill?

CLARK: I believe it was Representative William Cramer, of Florida. But it was favored by all those congressmen who think that all they have to do to make crime go away is to say: "You've got to respect the law," and then enforce it very vigorously. The Administration opposed that law successfully until Dr. King's assassination. In the very emotional climate that followed his death, with riots and all, and the later assassination of Robert Kennedy, it became law on June 19, 1968. In addition to the constitutional question, the law is defective on other grounds. The federal government doesn't have the capacity to enforce the anti-riot law. Our law enforcement is local. Crime control is generally a local responsibility and police manpower is overwhelmingly local. There are laws in every state against rioting, and police in every state with the presence and capacity to enforce them. Why would the prosecution want to take on the immensely difficult burden of trying to prove that someone started in one state and crossed a state line intending to start a riot? It's really a cruel joke for Congress to tell the American people that they can decrease riots by passing a federal statute like that. Such a statute will have no inhibitory effect; in fact, it might have an inflammatory effect.

But, above all, it does not have enforcement power behind it. The first need is to prevent riots. The second, to control them. Federal enforcement does not have the police manpower for either.

Q: But does not such federal action as the Chicago trial have an inhibiting effect on the exercise of free speech and assembly?

CLARK: It may inhibit free speech, but not riots. We saw what happened after the verdict and the sentencing in the Chicago trial. The statute did not inhibit disturbances around the country. In fact, there was a general outbreak of disturbances in widely scattered sections of the country in direct response to the results of the trial. During the trial, the biggest mass-protest meeting in the history of the United States took place on November 15th with the New Mobilization rally in Washington. The law did not inhibit some from trying to create disturbances. No, I think the motivation of this law was demogogic. It gave congressmen a chance to go back home and say, "Look, folks, we hate riots just as much as you do, and see what we have done about them!" In fact, the congressmen did not do anything but escalate emotions.

Q: Do you think liberalism still has an important role to play in American politics? Can such socially explosive problems as racism, the youth rebellion, the Vietnam war, be dealt with by peaceful reforms within the existing system? There is one view, as you know, which holds that the McCarthy-Kennedy movement represented what may prove to be the last chance to maintain the American system, to keep the society governable by peaceful means, and that liberalism, if it is to survive, will have to make an alliance with radicalism. Failing such an alliance, so this view holds, the right-wing forces will take over with a vengeance and stop at nothing in the restoration of law and order.

CLARK: By instinct, I am a maverick. I rather like the outside way. It's just more fun. But I have come to the conclusion that most change must be achieved from within institutions. Those who think in revolutionary terms are living in the past and do not see the present. They do not see that it is much too inhumane, too dangerous, to think of violent transformation of the system in a mass, urban, technologized society. Even when everything is peaceful in New York City it is very difficult just to keep the electricity coming, to keep the subways running, to get the garbage collected, to assure water and food and police and fire protection. To believe that man has the intelligence suddenly to do everything in a different way is to see something that I have never seen manifested within human capability.

So I think we have got to take the hard way. I think we have to find ways within the system for humanity's sake, because the cost in human suffering would be just too great to contemplate. Violence as a potential problem-solver in the nineteenth century in the United States was not so dangerous. But can you really think of violence as an acceptable tool today? The only thing violence could do today is restrict rather than open. That is true in the international order as well. When people say that the Russians have more nuclear missles than we do, we can say, "Too bad for them. Let's hope they don't hurt themselves or anybody else with them." Surely our response can't be that we will make even more weapons, when obviously both of us have too many already. Violence no longer works as a problem-solver.

Q: Do you tend, in the long run, to be optimistic or pessimistic about the future of personal and civil liberties in America, and the future of the human condition in general in this country?

CLARK: I am an optimist by nature. But I also think the notion that human nature is irrespressible and indomitable is not true today. Given the pressures of population and the impact of technology on the individual, and knowing that the individual can be conditioned to almost anything, this notion of the indomitability of the human spirit seems to me to be something romantic, something out of Rousseau. It is not realistic today. It will require all of our vision and courage and compassion to preserve human dignity.

Q: Do you tend to have ambiguous feelings about dissent: in favor of it, but also in favor of respect for the law?

CLARK: A society that wants to fulfill itself will not only tolerate dissent, it will provide means for the communication of dissent. I think government has an affirmative duty to find ways for the communication of dissent. Let dissent be tested in the marketplace. If we do that, we will reduce the potential for violence, but that is really a fringe benefit. The dissenting scientist, after all, has been the man who made the next discovery. And then, as Max Planck said, it takes another generation of scientists to accept and build on that discovery.

Q: What the young people are saying, I think, is that the freedom to dissent is fine, but if dissent never leads to any social changes or reforms, if legitimate grievances are never redressed, if the President, for example, simply tunes in on the Purdue-Ohio State football game when three hundred thousand people are standing on the streets outside the White House to protest the Vietnam war, then what is the practical value of dissent? Don't they have, then, some ethical justification for going beyond verbal petition and expression?

CLARK: Dissent will be the tool through which we develop sciences of institutional change and innovation, as well as attitudinal change. If it leads to violence, the system, too, must have integrity. If the system does not act in accordance with its rules, there cannot be a government of laws and there cannot be effective techniques for change, because there is no hard place to push against, and everything just washes away. Dissent is, of course, the view of the powerless. What we are really talking about is power. If people had power they would not dissent, they would do something. Confrontation is dissent in action, dissent seeking change. And if the confrontation violates the law, the man of the law has an obligation to enforce the law.

Q: In a rather neat sort of way, Governor Lester Maddox, of Georgia, is in the same box as Abbie Hoffman or Jerry Rubin, to the extent that all of them advocate deliberate breaking of the law. Governor Maddox has told the people of Georgia to disobey federal law with regard to desegregating the schools.

CLARK: Yes.

Q: But now we get down to the question of individual conscience, down to the dilemma of the Thoreaus and the Gandhis and others.

CLARK: That's not a dilemma for me. I think an individual must do what he thinks is right. He has to weigh his decision carefully. He has to judge the possible and probable consequences. And he must know that if he believes something is right and it is in violation of the law, he should pay the price of the law. For the system to work, the individual must not only expect to pay that price, he must consider it proper to do so. The thing that disappointed me about Thoreau is that he let Emerson, or his sister, or somebody, pay the tax for him and he got out of prison. In a sense, he did not have the strength of his convictions. It is hard to have that strength. It is traumatic for people, very strong and good people, to accept imprisonment for their beliefs. Gandhi spent years in prison when he could have got out.

Q: That raises another question: If a law is unjust and tyrannical and if the society itself is tyrannical, what is a man's obligation? Is it to obey the law, or is it to attempt to overthrow the law and perhaps the tyrannical society?

CLARK: I think history has just passed that kind of question by. The power, the firepower and the capacity for destruction are too great today. It isn't as though we were a lot of farmers in an agrarian age firing the shot heard around the world. Fire a shot today and you will get your head blown off. That is too bad—too dangerous—but I am afraid that is the way it is. This is why we must condition violence out of human character and also why it is now possible.

ARTHUR R. MILLER

The National Data Center and Personal Privacy

The modern computer is more than a sophisticated indexing or adding machine, or a miniaturized library; it is the keystone for a new communications medium whose capacities and implications we are only beginning to realize. In the foreseeable future, computer systems will be tied together by television, satellites, and lasers, and we will move large quantities of information over vast distances in imperceptible units of time.

The benefits to be derived from the new technology are many. In one medical center, doctors are already using computers to monitor heart patients in an attempt to isolate the changes in body chemistry that precede a heart attack. The search is for an "early warning system" so that treatment is not delayed until after the heart attack has struck. Elsewhere, plans are being made to establish a data bank in which vast amounts of medical information will be accessible through remote terminals to doctors thousands of miles away. A doctor will then be able to determine the antidote for various poisons or get the latest literature on a disease by dialing a telephone or typing an inquiry on a computer console.

A committee of the Bureau of the Budget has proposed that the federal government set up a National Data Center to compile statistical information on various facets of our society. Certainly the computer can help us simplify record-keeping by assigning everyone a "birth" number that will identify him for tax returns, banking, education, social security, the draft, and other purposes. This number could also serve as a telephone number, which, when used on modern communication mechanisms, would make it possible to reach its holder directly no matter where he might be.

But such a Data Center poses a grave threat to individual freedom and privacy. With its insatiable appetite for information, its inability to forget anything that has been put into it, a central computer might become the heart of a government surveillance system that would lay bare our finances, our associations, or our mental and physical health to government inquisitors or even to casual observers. Computer technology is moving so rapidly that a

Source: Mr. Miller is a professor of law at the University of Michigan and staunch defender of civil liberties. Reprinted from *The Atlantic Monthly*, November 1967, pp. 53–57. Copyright © 1967 by Arthur R. Miller. Reprinted by permission of the author.

sharp line between statistical and intelligence systems is bound to be obliterated. Even the most innocuous of centers could provide the "foot in the door" for the development of an individualized computer-based federal snooping system.

Since a National Data Center would be augmented by numerous subsystems or satellites operated by state and local governments or by private organizations, comprehensive national regulation of computer communications, whether of federal or nonfederal origin, ultimately will become imperative.

Moreover, deliberations should not be conducted in terms of computer capability as it exists today. New computer hardware is constantly being spawned, machine storage capacity and speed are increasing geometrically, and costs are declining. Thus at present we cannot imagine what the dimensions, the sophistication, or the snooping ability of the National Data Center will turn out to be ten or twenty years from now. Nor can we predict what new techniques will be developed to pierce any safeguards that Congress may set up in order to protect people against those who manipulate or falsify information they extract from or put into the center.

Of course, it would be foolish to prohibit the use of data-processing technology to carry out important governmental operations simply because it might be abused. However, it is necessary to fashion an adequate legal structure to protect the public against misuse of information handling.

In the past, privacy has been relatively easy to protect for a number of reasons. Large quantities of information about individuals have not been available. Generally decentralized, uncollected, and uncollated, the available information has been relatively superficial, access to it has been difficult to secure, and most people are unable to interpret it. During the hearings held recently by two of the congressional subcommittees investigating invasions of privacy, however, revelations concerning the widespread use of modern electronic and optical snooping devices shocked us.

In testimony before the House Subcommittee on Invasion of Privacy, Edgar S. Dunn, Jr., a research analyst for Resources for the Future, Incorporated, pointed out that information in the center would not be intelligible to the snooper as are the contents of a manila folder. Computerized data require a machine, a code book, a set of instructions, and a technician in order to be comprehended. Presumably Mr. Dunn's thesis is that if it is difficult or expensive to gain access to and interpret the data in the center, there is little likelihood of anyone's trying to pry; if the snooper's cost for unearthing a unit of dirt increases sufficiently, it will become too expensive for him to try to violate the center's integrity.

Mr. Dunn's logic fails to take into account other factors. First, if all the information gathered about an individual is in one place, the payoff for snooping is sharply enhanced. Thus, although the cost or difficulty of gaining access may be great, the amount of dirt available once access is gained is also great. Second, there is every reason to believe that the art of electronic surveillance will continue to become more efficient and economical. Third, governmental snooping is rarely deterred by cost.

Mr. Dunn also ignores a number of special dangers posed by a computerized National Data Center. Ever since the federal government's entry into the taxation and social welfare spheres, increasing quantities of information have been recorded. Moreover, as recording processes have become mechanized and less cumbersome, there also has been centralization and collation of information. In something akin to Parkinson's Law, the increase in information-handling capacity has created a tendency toward more extensive manipulation and analysis of recorded data, which, in turn, has required the collection of more and more data. The creation of the Data Center with electronic storage and retrieval capacity will accelerate this pattern.

Any increase in the amount of recorded information is certain to increase the risk of errors in reporting and recording and indexing. Information distortion also will be caused by machine malfunctioning. Moreover, people working with the data in Washington or at a distance through remote terminals can misuse the information. As information accumulates, the contents of an individual's computerized dossier will appear more and more impressive and will impart a heightened sense of reliability to the user, which, coupled with the myth of computer infallibility, will make it less likely that the user will try to verify the recorded data. This will be true despite the "softness" or "imprecision" of much of the data. Our success or failure in life ultimately may turn on what other people decide to put into our files and on the programmer's ability, or inability, to evaluate, process, and interrelate information. The great bulk of the information likely to find its way into the center will be gathered and processed by relatively unskilled and unimaginative people who lack discrimination and sensitivity. Furthermore, a computerized file has a certain indelible quality—adversities cannot be overcome simply by the passage of time.

There are further dangers. The very existence of a National Data Center may encourage certain federal officials to engage in questionable surveillance tactics. For example, optical scanners—devices with the capacity to read a variety of type fonts or handwriting at fantastic rates of speed—could be used to monitor our mail. By linking scanners with a computer system, the information drawn in by the scanner would be converted into machine-readable form and transferred into the subject's file in the National Data Center.

Then, with sophisticated programming, the dossiers of all of the surveillance subject's correspondents could be produced at the touch of a button, and an appropriate entry—perhaps "associates with known criminals"—could be added to all of them. As a result, someone who simply exchanges Christmas cards with a person whose mail is being monitored might find himself under surveillance or might be turned down when he applies for a job with the government or requests a government grant or applies for some other governmental benefit. An untested, impersonal, and erroneous computer entry such as "associates with known criminals" has marked him, and he is helpless to rectify the situation. Indeed, it is likely that he would not even be aware that the entry existed.

These tactics, as well as the possibility of coupling wiretapping and computer processing, undoubtedly will be extremely attractive to overzealous law-enforcement officers. Similarly, the ability to transfer into National Data Center quantities of information maintained in nonfederal files—credit ratings, educational information from schools and universities, local and state tax information, and medical records—will enable governmental snoopers to obtain data that they have no authority to secure on their own.

The compilation of information by unskilled personnel also creates serious problems of accuracy. It is not simply a matter of truth or falsity of what is recorded. Information can be entirely accurate and sufficient in one context and wholly incomplete and misleading in another. For example, the bare statement of an individual's marital status has entirely different connotations to the selective service, a credit bureau, the Internal Revenue Service, and the social security administration. Consider a computer entry of "divorced" and the different embellishment that would be necessary in each of those contexts to portray an accurate picture of an individual's situation.

The question of context is most graphically illustrated by the unexplained and incomplete arrest record. It is unlikely that a citizen whose file contains an entry "arrested, 6/1/42; convicted felony, 1/6/43; three years, federal penitentiary" would be given federal employment or be accorded the governmental courtesies accorded other citizens. Yet the subject may simply have been a conscientious objector. And what about the entry "arrested, disorderly conduct; sentenced six months Gotham City jail." Without further explanation, who would know that the person involved was a civil rights demonstrator whose conviction was reversed on appeal?

Finally, the risks to privacy created by a National Data Center lie not only in the misuse of the system by those who desire to injure others or who can obtain some personal advantage by doing so. There also is a legitimate concern that government employees in routine clerical positions will have the capacity to inflict damage through negligence, sloppiness, thoughtlessness, or sheer stupidity, by unintentionally rendering a record inaccurate, or losing it, or disseminating its contents to people not authorized to see it.

To ensure freedom from governmental intrusion, Congress must legislate reasonably precise standards regarding the information that can be recorded in the National Data Center. Certain types of information should not be recorded even if it is technically feasible to do so and a legitimate administrative objective exists. For example, it has long been "feasible," and from some vantage points "desirable," to require citizens to carry and display passports when traveling in this country, or to require universal fingerprinting. But we have not done so because these encroachments on our liberties are deemed inconsistent with the philosophical fiber of our society. Likewise, highly personal information, especially medical and psychiatric information, should not be permitted in the center unless human life depends upon recording it.

Legislation sharply limiting the information which federal agencies and officials can extract from private citizens is absolutely essential. To reinforce these limitations, the statute creating the Data Center should prohibit recording any information collected without specific congressional authorization. Until the quality of the center's operations and the nature of its impact on individual privacy can be better perceived, the center's activities should be restricted to the preservation of factual data.

The necessary procedural and technical safeguards seem to fall into two categories: those needed to guarantee the accuracy and integrity of the stored information, and those needed to control its dissemination.

To ensure the accuracy of the center's files, an individual should have an opportunity to correct errors in information concerning him. Perhaps a printout of his computer file should be sent to him once a year. Admittedly, this process would be expensive; some agencies will argue that the value of certain information will be lost if it is known that the government has it; and there might be squabbles between citizens and the Data Center concerning the accuracy of the file that would entail costly administrative proceedings. Nonetheless, the right of a citizen to be protected against governmental dissemination of misinformation is so important that we must be willing to pay some price to preserve it. Instead of an annual mailing, citizens could be given access to their files on request, perhaps through a network of remote computer terminals situated in government buildings throughout the country. What is necessary is a procedure for periodically determining when data are outmoded or should be removed from the file.

Turning to the question of access, the center's computer hardware and software must be designed to limit access to the information. A medical history given to a government doctor in connection with an application for veteran's benefits should not be available to federal employees not legitimately involved in processing the application. One solution may be to store information according to its sensitivity or its accessibility, or both. Then, governmental officials can be assigned access keys that will let them reach only those portions of the center's files that are relevant to their particular governmental function.

Everyone directing an inquiry to the center or seeking to deposit information in it should be required to identify himself. Finger- or voice-prints ultimately may be the best form of identification. As snooping techniques become more sophisticated, systems may even be needed to counter the possibility of forgery or duplication; perhaps an answerback system or a combination of finger- and voice-prints will be necessary. In addition, the center should be equipped with protector files to record the identity of inquirers, and these files should be audited to unearth misuse of the system. It probably will also be necessary to audit the programs controlling the manipulation of the files and access to the system to make sure that no one has inserted a secret "door" or a password permitting entry to the data by unauthorized personnel. It is frightening to realize that at present there apparently is no foolproof way to prevent occasional "monitor intrusion" in large data-processing systems. Additional protection against these risks can be achieved by exercising great care in selecting programming personnel.

In the future, sophisticated connections between the center and federal offices throughout the country and between the federal center and numerous state, local, and private centers probably will exist. As a result, information will move into and out of the center over substantial distances by telephone lines or microwave relays. The center's "network" character will require information to be protected against wiretapping and other forms of electronic eavesdropping. Transmission in the clear undoubtedly will have to be proscribed, and data in machine-readable form will have to be scrambled or further encoded so that they can be rendered intelligible only by a decoding process built into the system's authorized terminals. Although it may not be worth the effort or expense to develop completely breakproof codes, sufficient scrambling or coding to make it expensive for an eavesdropper to intercept the center's transmission will be necessary. If information in the center is arranged according to sensitivity or accessibility, the most efficient procedure may be to use codes of different degrees of complexity.

At a minimum, congressional action is necessary to establish the appropriate balance between the needs of the national government in accumulating, processing, and disseminating information and the right of individual privacy. This legislation must be reinforced by statutory civil remedies and penal sanctions.

Testimony before Congress concerning the intrusive activities of the Post Office, the Internal Revenue Service, and the Immigration and Naturalization Service gives us cause to balk at delegating authority over the Data Center to any of the agencies that have a stake in the content of data collected by the government. Some federal personnel are already involved in mail-cover operations, electronic bugging, wiretapping, and other invasions of privacy, and undoubtedly they would try to crack the security of any Data Center that maintains information on an individual basis. Thus it would be folly to leave the center in the hands of any agency whose employees are known to engage in antiprivacy activities. Similarly, the center must be kept away from government officials who are likely to become so entranced with operating sophisticated machinery and manipulating large masses of data that they will not respect an individual's right to privacy.

The conclusion seems inescapable: control over the center must be lodged outside existing channels. A new, completely independent agency, bureau, or office should be established—perhaps as an adjunct to the Census Bureau

ARTHUR R. MILLER *The National Data Center* 249

or the National Archives—to formulate policy under whatever legislative guidelines are enacted to ensure the privacy of all citizens. The organization would operate the center, regulate the nature of the information that can be recorded and stored, ensure its accuracy, and protect the center against breaches of security.

The new agency's ability to avoid becoming a captive of the governmental units using the center would be crucial. Perhaps with proper staffing and well-delineated lines of authority to Congress or the President, the center could achieve the degree of independence needed to protect individuals against governmental or private misuse of information in the center. At the other end of the spectrum, the center cannot become an island unto itself, populated by technocrats whose conduct is shielded by the alleged omniscience of the machines they manage and who are neither responsive nor responsible to anyone.

The proposed agency should be established *before* the center is planned. To date, there has been virtually no meaningful exchange among scientists, technicians, legal experts, and government people on the implications of the center. The center also might consider supporting some of the planned non-federal computer networks, such as the Interuniversity Communications Council's (EDUCOM) plan to link the major universities together, using them as models or operating laboratories to test procedures and hardware for the federal center.

To satisfy those who argue for the early establishment of a purely statistical Data Center, it might be possible for the proposed agency to set up a modest center in which information which does not invade privacy could be made available to government officials, educators, and private researchers. Other federal agencies might establish satellite centers that would contain information too sensitive to be recorded in the statistical center during that institution's formative period, although the data in satellites ultimately might be transferred to the national center.

The threat to individual privacy posed by the computer comes from the private sector as well as the proposed federal Data Center. Each year state and local governments, educational institutions, trade associations, and industrial firms establish data centers that collect and store quantities of information about individuals. Because the high cost of computer installation forces many organizations to operate on a time-share basis, the nonfederal centers pose a special danger to privacy. Without effective screening and built-in security devices, one participant, accidentally or deliberately, may invade and extract or alter the computer files of another participant. Moreover, because many time-share systems operate over large geographic areas, their transmissions will be vulnerable to tapping or malicious destruction unless they are scrambled or encoded. Right now, a mailing list containing 150 to 170 million names, accompanied by addresses and financial data, is being compiled. The list is so structured that it yields sublists of people in various vocational and avocational categories. Where the necessary information to produce this monster came from and how one gets *off* the list are mysteries.

Currently there are more than two thousand independent credit bureaus in the United States, many of whose files are being computerized. Eventually, these bureaus will make a network of their computers, creating a ready source of detailed information about an individual's finances. The accuracy of these records will become increasingly crucial; an honest dispute between a consumer and a retailer over a bill may produce an unexplained and unexpungeable "no pay" evaluation in the computer and result in considerable damage to the buyer's credit rating.

In testimony before the House subcommittee, the director of the New York State Identification and Intelligence System described a data bank containing files on "known" criminals that ultimately will contain millions of entries. He expressed a willingness to exchange information with police officials in other states as soon as the state systems could be meshed. If this system is tied into the National Data Center or New York's Bureau of Motor Vehicles or welfare agencies, it would permit someone to direct an inquiry to the computer file of "known" criminals, find an entry under the name of his subject, and rely on that entry to the subject's detriment without attempting to verify its accuracy.

Congress should consider the need for legislation setting standards to be met by nonfederal computer organizations in providing information about private persons and restraining federal officers from access to certain types of information from nonfederal data centers. Nonfederal systems should be required to install some protective devices and procedures. This is not to suggest that Congress should necessarily impose the same controls on nonfederal systems that it may choose to impose on the federal center. But a protector file to record the source of inquiries and modest encoding would probably prevent wide-scale abuse, although security needs vary from system to system. Since security may be facilitated by installing protective devices in the computer hardware itself, the possible need for regulation of certain aspects of computer manufacturing also should be taken into account.

The possibility of regulating transmission between federal and nonfederal centers and the interaction among nonfederal centers also should be considered. The specter of a federal agency, such as the Veterans' Administration, reaching into a citizen's medical file in a data center operated by a network of hospitals to augment the federal center's file is a disturbing one. Regulating the security of the transmissions and imposing sanctions for noncompliance and eavesdropping would preserve individual privacy against governmental snooping and bureaucratic spinelessness or perfidy.

J. EDGAR HOOVER

Message from the Director

To All Law Enforcement Officials

Atheistic Communism and the lawless underworld are not the only threats to the safety and welfare of our great Nation. Enemies of freedom come under many guises.

Our society today is in a great state of unrest. Many citizens are confused and troubled. For the first time, some are confronted with issues and decisions relating to the rights and dignity of their fellow countrymen, problems which heretofore they had skirted or ignored.

We have in our midst hatemongers, bigots, and riotous agitators, many of whom are at opposite poles philosophically but who spew similar doctrines of prejudice and intolerance. They exploit hate and fear for personal gain and self-aggrandizement. They distort facts, spread rumors, and pit one element of our people against another. Theirs is a dogma of intimidation and terror.

Almost every community of our land is infested with these opportunists, either organized or "freelance." They wage a continuing war of slander and vilification, undermining the orderly pursuit of decency and morality. Surrounded with dupes and miscreants, these merchants of hate and malice promote grief and strife. There is no limit to their outrageous deeds short of death. In the wake of their defiance of law and order lie the trampled rights of their fellow men.

Law enforcement, as a profession dedicated to preserving America's God-given heritage, is often caught in the crossfire of criticism and distrust coming from the opposing forces which clash on the issues involved. In each instance, our actions must be exemplary. We must not deviate from the solid principles and high traditions of our profession. We must not be compromised nor intimidated. We must demonstrate that the freedoms Americans cherish so highly are strengthened whenever law enforcement asserts itself not only against crime and subversion but also against any invasion upon the rights and dignity of all the people.

Source: Mr. Hoover is Director of the Federal Bureau of Investigation, United States Department of Justice. Reprinted from *FBI Law Enforcement Bulletin,* Vol. 33, No. 12, December 1, 1964, pp. 1–2.

Fortunately, the overwhelming majority of our citizens deplore rabble-rousing and mob action. They look to and abide by our laws and constitutional processes for guidance and redress of grievances. They know that our Nation's hopes rest on truth, justice, and individual dignity, not on discrimination, persecution, and mob rule.

As Americans, we have within our grasp the ideals which were but visions to our Founding Fathers—freedom under God with liberty and justice for all. We must not be satisfied merely to have these ideals exist. We must assure that they flourish—generation after generation—so all the world will know that America stands for brotherhood among all men.

John Edgar Hoover, *Director.*

December 1, 1964

JAMES VORENBERG AND JAMES Q. WILSON

Is the Court Handcuffing the Cops?

An Exchange of Views

James Vorenberg

In my view, the contest between the police and the United States Supreme Court is grossly exaggerated. In any event, that contest, to the extent that it exists at all, has very little to do with crime. What the Supreme Court does has practically no effect on the amount of crime in this country, and what the police do has far less effect than is generally believed. The nation seems

Source: James Vorenberg is a professor of law and director of the Center for the Advancement of Criminal Justice at the Harvard Law School. James Q. Wilson is a professor of government at Harvard and author of *Varieties of Police Behavior.* The article is adapted from a tape recording of a forum sponsored by the Harvard Club of New York City and the Associated Harvard Alumni at Town Hall, New York. Reprinted from *The New York Times Magazine,* May 11, 1969, pp. 32–33, 134–136, 139–140. © 1969 by The New York Times Company. Reprinted by permission.

to have its attention riveted on a largely irrelevant, overdramatized confrontation between the police and the Court, and thus is impeded in doing anything constructive about crime—or even understanding it.

The controversy over confessions is probably the best example of how the effect of Supreme Court decisions on the volume of crime has been exaggerated. The principal target of those who attack the Court is the *Miranda* decision of 1966. *Miranda* held that once a suspect was in police custody he had to be given a warning of his rights, including an offer of counsel if he was too poor to provide his own counsel.

What is suggested is that this decision is in some way accountable for a very large rise in crime that has occurred since 1966. But what are the facts? In the first place, the President's Commission on Law Enforcement and Administration of Justice, which is generally known as the Crime Commission, found that only something between one-tenth and one-third of the crimes committed are even reported to the police.

It's not very likely that a decision that deals only with people in custody is going to have much effect on crimes that are not even reported to the police.

We also found in one study that, of those crimes that are reported to the police, only one-quarter lead to arrest. And of those that do lead to arrest, only a small proportion are cases where a confession is crucial to solution. The others are cases where there is a witness or some piece of tangible evidence.

Already we are probably down to a maximum of 1 per cent or 2 per cent for cases in which *Miranda* could have a direct impact. Then we have to take account of the fact that, in many cases since *Miranda*, the suspect still confesses, and that, in many cases before *Miranda*, the suspect did not confess. The result is that the maximum direct statistical impact of this much-reviled decision is of the order of a fraction of 1 per cent.

But, it is said, there is more to it than that: *Miranda* in some way provides general encouragement to potential criminals. What that means is that, to get the encouragement *Miranda* is said to provide, before I set out to commit a crime I have to go through the following reasoning process: "If I commit this crime, and if I'm caught, and if I confess, that confession can be excluded if the police don't offer me counsel." I suggest that, in view of what little we do know about the people who are committing crimes, and the conditions under which those crimes take place, it is unlikely that that rather elaborate hypothetical reasoning process is going on.

Then it is said by the critics of *Miranda*: "It's not what *Miranda* actually says that has such a demoralizing effect on the police and encourages crime. It's what it is thought to mean, what the exaggerated view of it is." An obvious first step to remedying this effect of *Miranda* is for these very people to stop overstating the effect.

I am not a great champion of the *Miranda* decision. It is an unnecessarily confusing opinion for law-enforcement officers. It does not really make it clear whether confessions are or are not to be sought. I suspect it has had some demoralizing effect on law enforcement. But I strongly urge that it is not the culprit in any sense for the increase in crime, and I think the same is generally true of other Supreme Court decisions.

In one sense, it is true that Supreme Court decisions are responsible for some of the "crime problem." They are responsible for much of the improvement in police reporting of crime. For many years, it was the custom in our big cities for the police not to report all crimes because the figures were embarrassing. They might suggest the police were doing a poor job. Then, especially since *Miranda*, it became acceptable to report large crime increases in our cities because there was now an attractive scapegoat. So, in that sense, the Court probably is responsible for part of the reported increase.

But it is not just a reporting increase that we are facing. I am satisfied on all the evidence that enough of our cities are now reporting crimes sufficiently well so that what we see is not simply a paper increase. There is a significant increase in serious street crimes.

What is the explanation? The only honest answer is that we do not know, and as a nation we are doing very little to find out.

For example, in New York City between last year and this year, the number of reported robberies—which I think is in some ways the most important class of crime—increased from 36,000 to 54,000. That is a 50 per cent increase in one year, really an astonishing increase—particularly when you look at the gross numbers.

During that same period the number of robberies in Chicago as reported to the police stayed just about the same. That at least entitles one to ask the question: Why?

There are a number of possible theories. One is that the police in Chicago are better, that they're doing a better job in holding down crime. Those of us who watched the Democratic convention would be rather discouraged if that turned out to be the answer.

Another theory is that the Chicago police are much worse, that people don't report crimes to them because they don't have confidence in them. Take your pick.

Chicago and New York are not the only examples. Cleveland had no increase in robberies; Pittsburgh had a 70 per cent increase.

What I find striking is that virtually nothing significant is being spent in this country today to try to find out what is happening and why. Think what would happen in the medical field if there were an astronomical increase in cancer or polio cases in some cities, with no increase in other cities. Congress would be pouring money on medical researchers to try to find an answer.

If "curbing the Court" is not a constructive way of dealing with the nation's crime problem, what can be done? I would suggest three possible promising lines for change in dealing with the problems of crime.

First, we need to recognize that most defendants plead guilty, and thus, in the great majority of criminal cases, the crucial question is not whether the defendant committed a crime, but what should happen to him as a result of his conviction.

In spite of the fact that less than 1 per cent of the cases are tried by a jury, the general view of the criminal process is influenced by what might be called the Perry Mason syndrome. Too little attention and too few resources are devoted to the administrative process involved in accepting pleas of guilty and deciding on a sentence—as compared to the adjudicating process of the full criminal trial. The sentence often does not reflect a thoughtful and informed judgment as to what should be done with the defendant. It simply is a part of the process of keeping cases moving through the system in order to keep the traffic of criminal cases from grinding to a halt. Often there has been no real investigation as to what kind of treatment the defendant really needs.

We are thus losing our best opportunity to use the criminal system to reduce crime. We have identified somebody who is a potential future criminal (most crimes are committed by persons who have committed prior crimes), and in many cases we have identified him early in what may turn out to be a long and destructive criminal career. We have an opportunity to try to deal with him intelligently at that point, to devote some major resources to deciding what he needs. Does he really need to go to prison? Does he need some sort of medical or psychiatric treatment? Can he be released into some sort of job-training program?

There are some programs trying to deal with this problem. The Crime Commission proposed the establishment of Youth Service Bureaus which would take many nonserious juvenile cases out of the criminal system and offer the juvenile and his family helping services on a voluntary basis. In New York, the Manhattan Court Employment Project, run by the Vera Institute in cooperation with the court and the prosecutor's office, provides for the dismissal of a case after 90 days if the defendant is accepted in the program and is successfully placed in a job. This, I think, exemplifies the possibilities of private agencies taking over some of these nonadjudicatory cases.

The second major change we might consider is the way we deal with those who are convicted. Here we are presented with two polar theories. One is to be as tough as possible. The other extreme is the view of the therapist—lots of treatment in prison will lead to personal reformation.

On the hard-nosed view: We know very little about the deterrent effect of the possibility of a serious penalty. And since we are not really prepared to take every defendant out of circulation for the rest of his life, they are going to be released at some point. If we release them more dangerous than when they went into prison, we have not done much with the problem of public safety.

The therapist's view has not turned out to be much more promising. A recent California experiment took four groups of prisoners, 600 each. It offered three of these groups different kinds of intensive group counseling; the fourth group got the same prison treatment as the other three, except no group counseling. When they were all through, and had been followed up for five years, it turned out that there were no significant differences in the recidivism rates of the four groups.

Perhaps this suggests that maybe we should experiment with doing as little as possible in as many cases as possible. To the extent that any form of treatment takes away responsibility for handling one's life, it makes it harder to get back into society. Thus the use of half-way houses, probation, work release —anything that, in effect, permits the convicted person to begin living as soon as possible in the kind of world he's going to have to live in—may, in the end, turn out to be the most promising.

Finally, we have to recognize frankly the limits on what the criminal justice system can do for us in dealing with crime.

The first part of that is to recognize how overburdened the system is already, and to remove from it as many forms of conduct as possible that are not, and should not be, central areas of concern. The Crime Commission's proposal in 1967 that drunkenness should not be a crime has won increasing support. There are a variety of sex offenses, most of those between consenting adults, that should also be candidates for decriminalization, and a very hard look should be given to at least some of the drug crimes that are occupying more and more enforcement time.

More important than trying to take out of the system those cases that should not be there is to recognize how little the system itself can do in dealing with the problem of crime and to focus more on what broadly has been called prevention.

It is increasingly clear that the police, the courts, the prisons and the correctional services generally are engaged in what, at best, is a holding action. The most important finding of the Crime Commission is that any major reduction of the kind of predatory crime that is producing frustration and despair in the nation depends on ending the frustration and despair of the millions of Americans we have neglected for generations.

Simply put, this means that until we are willing to give poor people a stake in law and in order and in justice, we can expect crime to increase. The best hope of crime control lies not in better police, more convictions, longer sentences, better prisons. It lies in job training, jobs and the assurance of adequate income; schools that respond to the needs of their students; the resources and help to plan a family and hold it together; a decent place to live, and an opportunity to guide one's own life and to participate in guiding the life of the community.

Of course, these are things that a fair society does, not only in the name of crime control but in the name of social justice. Perhaps fear of crime will provide the added impetus that so far has been lacking in the nation's commitment to these programs. If not, and if there are new attempts to curb crime by new repressive measures, including possible constitutional changes, I think we can confidently predict that, 5, 10 or 25 years from now, crime will be an even more menacing part of the life of the nation than it is today.

James Q. Wilson

I would like to speak specifically about two possible roles that the police can play in dealing with crime: first of all, the police as an agency of crime prevention and, second, the police role in the detection and apprehension of criminals who are believed already to have committed a crime.

I am confining my remarks to street crime because I regard robberies, muggings, holdups and the like as the most serious kind of crime. I want to distinguish street crimes from consensual crimes—gambling, the narcotics trade, sexual crimes of various sorts—and from crimes of stealth—burglaries and larcenies that are committed when no victim is physically endangered—and even from private crime. Most assaults, most murders—perhaps most rapes—involve persons known or related to each other. They are crimes among friends, so to speak.

I think street crime is the most important crime. What is striking to me is that there have been so few serious, carefully evaluated experiments as to how the police can best be deployed to reduce street crimes in high-crime-rate areas. One important experiment did take place in 1954 in New York. In the 25th Precinct of Manhattan, an area about equally divided among whites, blacks and Puerto Ricans and with a high crime rate, the entire graduating class of the Police Academy was assigned as supplementary patrolmen with the result that the patrol force, largely on foot in that precinct, was doubled or tripled for a four-month period. In addition, detectives, juvenile, narcotics and other specialized officers were assigned to the area.

The results were striking. The murder rate did not go down. Those private crimes continued unabated behind drawn shades of apartments and hotel rooms. But street robberies in this four-month experimental period compared with the four similar months in the preceding year, fell from 69 to 7; auto thefts from 78 to 24; disorderly-conduct arrests from 177 to 77; other robberies, not street robberies but store-front, liquor-store, gas-station robberies and the like, declined from 97 to 43. And of those crimes that were committed, a substantially higher percentage were solved by the arrest of the person involved, usually by a foot patrolman who was near the scene of the crime.

Yet this experiment, dramatic as it was, did not answer all the questions one might ask of how the police might prevent crime. We do not know, for example, how many of the criminals in Precinct 25 went next door to the adjacent precinct to practice their enterprises there, or perhaps even to an adjoining borough. We do not know what would have happened if the experiment had been carried on for a year or two. Some people can get used to anything, even the presence of a police officer on every street corner, and it might have occurred to somebody to enter those buildings from the rear rather than the front. We do not know how the citizens felt about it—whether they felt they were being subjected to unnecessary police surveillance or whether they felt relieved that the streets were safer.

What disturbs me is that no one has tried to duplicate this experiment to see if similar results can be produced elsewhere under other circumstances. All that energy that was devoted to this project, which on the surface had promising results, has been dissipated elsewhere, perhaps in attacks on the Supreme Court.

The role of court restrictions on the use of the police as a device for deterring, though surely not eliminating, street crime has to do with the point at which the police officer ceases to deter crime simply by his presence or discourage criminals by his questioning but instead begins to set in motion the train of events that will lead to a person's being arrested and charged.

The *Miranda* decision holds that once a person is in custody, he must be warned of his rights, and I believe, for one, that it is entirely proper that he be warned of his rights. But at what point does custody begin? At what point does a casual questioning on the street of a suspicious person, asking him to identify himself and to give an account of his intentions and his activities— when does that end and when does an arrest begin?

I think it is extremely important for the police to have, under a carefully drawn statute, the right to stop and question citizens about their activities and their place of residence. I believe this is one way the police, without seriously infringing on our right of free movement, can help make the streets safer for all of us.

What concerns me is that the tendency of some lower courts may be to discourage the exercise of this police right, leading not to the ending of street stops by police officers, but leading to their becoming covert activities. Most police officers, if they take their responsibilities seriously, will stop and question persons they regard, on the basis of their experience, rightly or wrongly, as suspicious. But in many states it is not clearly legal for a police officer to do this. Consequently, a local police administrator, wishing not to court the disfavor of higher opinion, will ignore the problem, not lay down any policies for his officers, not train them on how to carry out this function responsibly, and allow his officers to carry it out, so to speak, covertly.

The question of frisks is a more complicated one. Under what circumstances should an officer be allowed to pat down a suspect, a person he meets on the street? Generally the courts are of the view that if it is necessary for the protection of the officer—that is, if he believes a person is likely to be carrying a concealed weapon—they will be tolerant of it. But, again, it is a controversial area of the law, and as long as it is controversial, police administrators will be derelict in their duty to define policies and to train officers in the proper exercise of these policies.

One study done for the Crime Commission indicated that one out of every

10 street frisks produced a concealed weapon. I believe this is enough of a gain to society to warrant giving police the right to stop and frisk persons on the street. What is needed is a very carefully drawn statute defining the right.

Let me turn now to the problem of the detection and apprehension of persons alleged already to have committed a crime. There have been a number of studies to see if the police were being inhibited by the rules of evidence that were being laid down by the Supreme Court. These studies are not clear-cut in their findings, but I think it is fair to say that on the whole they do not show any substantial loss in convictions as the result of the police being instructed to warn the suspect of his rights—the right to an attorney, the right to a court-appointed attorney if he cannot afford one, the right to remain silent, and the like.

One reason for this is that in many cases the warning is made in a perfunctory way, or perhaps not made at all, and the person is not adequately appraised of his rights. But there is also a large number of cases in which the warning is made in a serious way and the suspect chooses knowingly to waive his rights.

A study published in The Yale Law Journal suggests that in the case of the New Haven Police Department neither the investigating detectives nor the law-school observers were of the opinion, after examining a large number of cases, that the warnings had inhibited the giving of confessions, or that the confessions had been necessary for conviction.

It is important when talking about the role of confessions in convictions to distinguish among kinds of crimes. I think that the role of confessions may be extremely important in solving burglaries and other crimes of stealth where there is no witness to the crime. Confessions may be especially important in implicating accomplices. Confessions may be important in crimes of a consensual nature, where, of course, there is no complaining witness. But in street crimes there usually is a witness, a victim who was confronted face-to-face—or sometimes back-to-front.

Here the problem is usually first getting the witness or victim to report the crime to the police. Even with robberies, half are not reported to the police at all. The second problem, after the person reports the crime, is getting his cooperation in making an identification of such suspects as the police may turn up. This again is not an easy task.

I think the chief difficulty in making good cases against persons committing street crimes lies with us, the citizens, in not reporting crimes, or, when the crime is reported and a suspect is identified, in telling the police that we don't want to get involved and that we hope they'll understand if we don't come down there. That kind of citizen noncooperation with the police seems to me a far more serious impediment to law enforcement than most appellate court decisions in this area.

Beyond the question of getting a confession in a particular case is the question of the task the police are being asked to perform in the first place.

The police, in effect, are being asked to add their energies to spinning a revolving door through which pass the people they have arrested before. Eighty-five per cent of persons arrested, according to a Crime Commission estimate, for something more serious than a traffic offense have been arrested before. The average man who is arrested once will be arrested seven times. In California, which keeps especially careful records on these matters, 38 per cent of those persons imprisoned for armed robbery are reimprisoned for the same crime within two years.

Recidivism is the real crime—about which we are doing so little. If arrest has no deterrent value, then pouring additional resources into the detective function of the police—finding persons and getting statements and witnesses and trying to lock the person up—will have far less value than we would like, and perhaps far less value than equivalent resources put into trying to devise sentencing procedures and correctional programs that could make some difference in this revolving door.

There is evidence that if we attempt to classify first offenders carefully; if we try to assign them to community treatment centers where they will be employed or in school during the day and reporting to the centers in the evening and on weekends for close supervision; if we take people who are nominally on probation off the street, where they are unsupervised, and place them in institutions where they are both supervised and near their own communities—there is evidence that we can make real gains in recidivism. California, by dealing with youthful offenders through community treatment centers, has found it possible, at least in some circumstances, to cut the recidivism rate nearly in half—and at a lower cost per offender than for locking up the same persons in conventional prisons and reformatories.

The gains we would make might do no more than slow down the present increase in crime. But I for one think any gain is worth it. And yet we do not try these experiments. Correction is an uninteresting subject for most people when they deal with law enforcement. They think it is wholly a police problem.

I know that a lot of crime will occur no matter what we do. But I also know we cannot hold the police—or the courts—responsible for the fact that the crime that does occur is committed by people who have committed similar crimes in the past. I hold us responsible for that. I hold us responsible for not asking our state legislators to take their correctional programs more seriously. I hold us responsible for backing law and order with bumper stickers but not money. I hold us responsible for insisting that the only way to deal with offenders is to lock them up in some bucolic retreat behind high walls in the countryside, not recognizing that if we isolate them from the community their attitude toward the community will wreak a terrible price on us when, as they will be eventually, they are released.

In the question period that followed, one member of the audience raised the issue of President Nixon's tentative proposal for "preventive detention" of presumably dangerous persons. The scheme is a response to complaints arising from efforts to reform the generally existing bail system—which admittedly discriminates against the poor—by substituting a system of releasing an accused person in his own recognizance—possibly to commit more crimes while awaiting trial.

Professor Vorenberg answered: I think the starting point ought to be a recognition of the total corruptness and irrelevance of the money bail system in this country. It makes absolutely no sense to hinge release upon how much money an individual has. Unfortunately, that is the system that has built up. It is embodied in the Bill of Rights, where there is a reference to bail.

The question is: Are we prepared to abolish it altogether and have everybody be released? The answer is probably: "No." So, do we try to identify those people who are so dangerous, so likely to commit additional crimes, so likely not to show up for trial, that we hold them regardless of how much money they have?

If I thought a very limited form of preventive detention would be benignly administered by the courts, and if, in return for such a statute, we were able to get rid of money bail, and if I thought we really could identify those people who are dangerous—that third "if" is a very large one—I would be prepared to propose it.

I don't think it would be benignly administered. I think there are many judges today who are abusing the present bail system, and I think that this would simply be an added basis for detention. And I think we have really very little ability to predict who is and who is not dangerous.

For that reason, I would be very strongly opposed to a preventive-detention statute. I would continue to try to work within the present bail system.

Professor Wilson added: I would much prefer first to exhaust the possible remedies in increasing the speed with which hearings and trials are held. In the two or three years preceding 1966, when the President's Crime Commission reported, the average felony in the District of Columbia courts took in excess of five months to be adjudicated. That time length has since grown larger. At the same time, even though the rate of felonies was increasing dramatically in the District of Columbia and even though the police were arresting more and more people on felony charges, the number of persons being tried on felony charges was actually declining because prosecuting attorneys, in order to manage their growing work load, lacking judges—lacking also, sufficient counsel, both prosecuting and defense—were marking felonies down to misdemeanors in order to get the calendar cleared.

I think we need a major assault on restaffing and remanaging the lower criminal courts—not only with respect to judges, but with respect to prosecuting and defense attorneys as well—to have speedy dispositions. After that strategy is exhausted, then I might consider allowing judges substantial freedom in deciding who is a dangerous person even though he has not been convicted of anything.

The final question concerned the impact of greater community control upon crime prevention. Professor Vorenberg replied:

I think there are some very promising lines: correctional and delinquency-prevention projects—perhaps staffed and run by people in the community—to deal with those who are released on probation or parole, or young people who are arrested and turned over to such an agency rather than the courts. I think that is promising. On the other hand, I have very serious doubts at the moment that proposals for total community control of the police are promising.

Much more broadly, the real case for community control as a line of crime prevention lies in giving poor people their fair share of political control so they can express themselves, and demand the kinds of resources that are needed for effective social programs. These are, in the long run, the only effective forms of crime prevention.

J. ANTHONY LUKAS

On the Lam in America

As he hunched forward, rolling across the warped slats of the park bench his face passed into a patch of sunlight and I saw for the first time the depth of his prison pallor: slack skin the color of half-cooked porridge.

Then, with a sigh mixed of weariness and contentment, he sank back and stretched his legs across the grass. "I still can't quite believe I'm here in a real park on a Saturday morning just like anybody else," he said.

Source: Mr. Lukas is a staff writer for *The Times Magazine* and the author of the recently published book, *The Barnyard Epithet and Other Obscenities* about the Chicago Seven trial. Reprinted from *The New York Times Magazine*, Dec. 13, 1970, pp. 31, 54–77 passim. © 1970 by The New York Times Company. Reprinted by permission.

My companion that October morning in Washington Square was Bob—not his real name—who a month before had escaped from a Midwestern prison after serving four and a half years for armed robbery.

Around us the square shimmered in autumn glory. Nannies wheeled their strollers through the leaves; two N.Y.U. students spiraled a football under the elms, and up by the fountain three girls with a guitar were singing folk songs.

And there, on our bench, Bob told me what it was like to be on the lam in America in 1970.

"It's not like most people imagine from movies and True Detective and all that—you know, always on the run, looking over your shoulder. I mean, it used to be like that for most people, and it was once for me. But not any more."

On the lam! The term, we are told, comes from Africa, but it reverberates somewhere deep in the American soul. We have been a nation of fugitives from the start. Some colonists literally fled England's religious persecution or poor laws, but even the most law-abiding were fugitives in a larger sense. "No features of English society in the 18th century were more valued than security and dependence," writes Daniel Boorstin. "For men who had been caught in this ancient web, much of the appeal of America was escape."

But America's greatest fascination is reserved for another kind of fugitive: the outlaw, the man on the run from the law. Jesse James, Cole Younger, Bonnie and Clyde, "Baby Face" Nelson and John Dillinger are among America's folk heroes. One need only listen to this generation's songs to sense how alive that fascination still is: the Jefferson Airplane ("We are all outlaws in the eyes of America"), Bob Dylan ("I may look like Robert Ford but I feel like Jesse James") or Merle Haggard—who spent three years in San Quentin—singing, "I'm a Lonesome Fugitive":

> Down every road there's always one more city,
> I'm on the run, the highway is my home.
> I raised a lot of Cain back in my younger days
> While mama used to pray my crops would fail.
> Now I'm a hunted fugitive with just two ways—
> Outrun the law or spend my life in jail.[1]

And today, many of America's political dissenters—people as different as Angela Davis, Father Daniel Berrigan, Timothy Leary and Mark Rudd—have themselves become outlaws and have recognized their affinity with the criminal fugitive. So who could better describe today's life on the lam than one of those fugitives?

And Bob knows what he's talking about. He estimates he's been arrested 50 or 60 times, the first time when he was 11. Now 30, he's spent seven and a

[1] © Copyright 1966, 1967 by the 4-Star Music Co., Inc., Los Angeles, California. Reprinted by permission.

half years in Federal and state prisons. His first stretch began at 17 when he was arrested after a cross-country chase—his first experience as a traditional fugitive.

"We were like hunted animals. It was a four-month hassle for existence. Me and this other guy stole this car and we knew the police were after us. If we'd stayed in the state we might have got probation for a first conviction, but running like that make it a Federal charge and we kept making it worse. We have had to steal just to get something to eat, but every time we took something we increased the chance of getting caught. The pressure kept building up. We were so scared we never felt we could stay any place for more than a few days and, of course, we couldn't trust anybody. You know how we finally got caught? For speeding. Then they checked us out and found we were wanted in the other state. Speeding! Isn't that something."

Bob served three years on that charge, was out for a while, then got up to 20 years for armed robbery. In the Midwest prison where he served his time, he met a political prisoner—an antiwar activist. "We had some long talks and he told me that if I ever got out I should get in touch with Movement people who would help me."

Last September, Bob was among 25 model prisoners chosen to attend a religious retreat at a lake near the prison. The first night he waited until the others were asleep, then crept out of the unguarded cabin and into the woods.

At first, he followed the classic scenario of the criminal fugitive: seeking refuge in a nearby city with an ex-con, who gave him civilian clothes to replace his prison grays; hiding out there several days until "the heat was off"; finally making contact with another ex-con who gave him some money and arranged to get him a Social Security card and other "fake I.D."

"Now I could travel, but I was still acting on my old instincts, playing it cute. I had my friend make a reservation for me on a train to St. Louis, then I took a bus to New York. I was dressed up—new bellbottoms, a nice sweater and my hair tinted white. Why white? Well, people expect if you're on the lam you won't want to stand out. So I wanted people to notice me a little; not too much, but a little."

As his bus churned down the freeway, Bob had plenty of time to think. "Suddenly it hit me hard: I'm free now. I can be anything, anybody I want to be. So when I got to New York I contacted the political guy I'd met in prison and since then things have really been different.

"The Movement people are fabulous. They have a real underground that takes care of you. No matter where I went they made sure I had something to eat, they introduced me to others, they made me feel safe. The first night I slept on somebody's roof, but since then they've found me a place to stay regular, they found me a job with somebody they trusted.

"I've only been here three weeks now, but I feel completely different from all the other times I've been on the run. It's not a hassle like it was alone. I'm part of a real community. The underground is much bigger than you'd think.

It's all around. I could go from place to place for weeks and there'd always be a place I could stay and people to take care of me."

"I think more so-called criminals are going to find their way into the Movement because it's the best place of all to hide. Most people, they think there's this big criminal underworld out there. But that's only for the big Mafia types. The average guy who sticks up something has no place to turn when he's on the run. He's on his own and, believe me, it's the loneliest life in the world. But the Movement people, they really have something going here. And, you know, they're really a lot like us. They've made me see that. Whether you call us criminals or radicals, we've all been—by this society, we're all on the lam together."

"Donald Rogers Smelley, a holdup man who had reputedly vowed not to be captured alive, grunted a note of resignation on Nov. 7, 1966, when he was seized by F.B.I. agents in Hollywood, Calif. Smelley conceded, en route to a jail cell, 'I'm glad it's over. You guys are too hot for me.'"—From an F.B.I. press release.

Whatever its record with ordinary criminals, the F.B.I. isn't too hot at catching the new breed of fugitive.

Just the week before I spoke with Bob, three ex-convicts, former inmates at Walpole State prison in Massachusetts, allegedly joined with two radical women from Brandeis University in a daylight holdup of a Brighton, Mass., bank, during which a policeman was shot and killed.

The three experienced criminals were caught within a week, one as he stepped from a cab in front of his Somerville home; another as he boarded a plane in Grand Junction, Colo.; and the third, William "Lefty" Gilday, a paroled armed robber, after what Boston newspapers called "the largest and wildest manhunt in New England history."

After eluding 800 policemen in a twisting chase along the Massachusetts-New Hampshire border, Gilday hid out for a while in an apple tree and a cellar; then he seized two hostages for a last desperate dash for freedom down the Massachusetts Turnpike, only to be seized by State policemen at a Worcester traffic circle. "He was beat and he was tired," said State Police Staff Sergeant Thomas H. Peterson, one of the men who captured him. "And he was afraid. Anybody would be afraid when you have 500 officers looking for you and every one of them has a rifle or a shotgun."

But while the ex-cons were rounded up, the two Brandeis women—Kathy Power, a 20-year-old senior, and Susan Saxe, a 21-year-old June graduate—made their getaway. A purple dress supposedly belonging to Miss Power was found in a locker at Boston's Logan Airport and Miss Saxe wrote her mother a letter, enclosing a ring handed down from her grandmother. But there the trail ended. As of this writing, the ladies are still at large.

One reason the new fugitives are so hard to find is that there are so many of them. Nobody knows just how many—but there are now 75,000 fugitives listed in the F.B.I.'s central computer. (The F.B.I. has 7,000 agents, only a fraction of whom are assigned to fugitive squads.)

The best-known group of political renegades, of course, is the Weathermen, the violence-prone faction which split off from S.D.S. in mid-1969 and then went underground last winter. The attention they have drawn is out of all proportion to their numbers; most Weather-watchers believe they now number only 50 to 200. In addition, there are probably several hundred more underground radicals who like to think of themselves as Weathermen or who carry out "Weather" types of actions—e.g., the University of Wisconsin bombing.

Then there is a small but politically important Catholic underground, engaged in actions against draft boards. Politically less important but numerically far greater are the young people fleeing arrests for drug offenses or campus riot charges—not to mention the thousands of teen-age runaways who often commit minor offenses on the way.

Finally, there are the draft resisters and deserters. The Selective Service has no accurate figures for resisters, but their ranks are clearly growing every month. Desertions are increasing at an even faster rate. According to a Pentagon spokesman, there were 73,121 deserters from the armed forces in fiscal 1969, and 89,088 in fiscal 1970. Many deserters turn themselves in, others are caught, still others reach safety abroad. But exile groups in Canada estimate there are between 35,000 and 50,000 deserters underground in the United States today.

On the evening of April 21, 1968—17 days after he shot Martin Luther King—James Earl Ray walked into a Toronto tavern just in time to catch his favorite TV program: "The F.B.I." Ray liked the show particularly because of its regular feature showing one of the F.B.I.'s "10 most wanted fugitives." According to his biographer, William Bradford Huie, Ray had always yearned to be a member of the "Top Ten," a group he regarded as equivalent to Academy Award winners. Sitting there that night, drinking vodka and orange juice, he saw his own face flash onto the screen not only on the "Top Ten" but in a "special international category." According to Huie, Ray was elated.

"Jake!" a deserter shouted across the office of an American exile group in Canada the other day. "My folks say there's a wanted poster of me up in the post office."

"Hey! Wow!" cried Jake. "Congratulations."

In the new fugitive subculture, a wanted poster in your local post office is a status symbol. But the ultimate accolade, of course, is a place on the "10 most wanted" list. Since the list was inaugurated in 1950, it has been made up chiefly of bank robbers, rapists, kidnappers and the like. But in recent months they have been largely replaced by the new breed of fugitive until, at this writing, 9 of the 16 names on the expanded list are young radicals.

Alongside Benjamin Hoskins Paddock (alias "Big Daddy" and "Old Baldy"), a bank robber who escaped from a Texas prison, and Taylor Morris

Teaford, who is wanted for murdering his 74-year-old grandmother, and shooting his sister, a passing motorist and a deputy sheriff, one finds Miss Powers and Miss Saxe, the Brandeis ladies at large; Bernardine Dohrn, the leading Weatherwoman, who is under indictment for her role in the Weathermen's "Days of Rage" demonstrations in October, 1969, as well as for conspiracy to transport explosives in interstate commerce; Hubert Geroid (H. Rap) Brown, National Chairman of the Student Non-Violent Coordinating Committee, who is charged with inciting riot and arson in Cambridge, Md.; Cameron David Bishop, a Colorado State University student charged with sabotage in the dynamiting of Colorado power transmission towers; and Karleton Lewis Armstrong, Dwight Alan Armstrong, Leo Frederick Burt and David Sylvan Fine, all charged with last August's bombing of the Mathematics Research Center at the University of Wisconsin, in which a graduate student was killed.

The F.B.I.'s critics contend the "most wanted" list is largely a public relations gimmick designed to glorify the bureau by showing how quickly it catches fugitives. They suggest the F.B.I. often puts a fugitive on the list only after it has picked up his trail so he can then be caught quickly (the average fugitive spends 132 days on the list). The F.B.I. denies this.

Some critics see an even subtler purpose in the list. "It tells us whom we should see as our enemies," says one. "If the list is full of holdup men, the public is more likely to believe its problem is street crime. If it were full of Mafia types, we might see our problem is organized crime. Now, with it full of young revolutionaries, the F.B.I. is telling us *they're* the real threat."

The F.B.I. denies this, too. Harold Leinbaugh, a bureau spokesman, says: "We don't make that much distinction between the radicals and other criminals. Most of these young people are wanted for conspiracy, sabotage or unlawful flight. We regard them as ordinary criminals."

In many obvious respects—age, education, family background—the new breed of fugitive is very different from the old. Perhaps most important, the F.B.I. has accumulated a detailed "track record" on the traditional fugitives, while it seems to know very little at all about the political ones.

Most of the traditional fugitives have been in and out of prisons all their lives, while few of the political ones have ever been arrested; in two cases the bureau doesn't have their fingerprints or signatures on file. The bureau knows that one of the most wanted criminals, John William Clouser, likes to play poker, watches football, drinks bourbon, likes big cars and Western music, and that another, James Byron Rice, wears expensive clothing, enjoys bowling, likes steaks, eggs and veal, and reads religious literature; but of Karleton Armstrong it reports only that he speaks Spanish and is a strict vegetarian. Police say fugitives without a track record are very hard to track.

I was once on the lam myself. It was early in 1957 and I'd just completed my Army basic training and reported to Fort Bragg, N.C. But my thoughts were on a lovely Barnard girl, seemingly out of reach in New York.

I was lying dejectedly on my cot when a corporal asked me what the trouble was. I told him. "Oh, don't be a silly idiot," he said. "They'll never miss you around here the first few days. Come on, I'll drive you to the airport."

So I went AWOL for the weekend. The Barnard girl was as lovely as ever, but somehow I didn't enjoy it as much as I'd expected. One afternoon we went for a walk in Central Park and every time we passed a policeman I cringed behind a tree. I knew it was silly, but I was convinced they were looking for me.

When I told this story to a fugitive the other day, he smiled in recognition. "That's one of the hardest things to overcome," he said. "At first, you're sure everybody's looking for you. Every guy in a snap-brim hat is an F.B.I. man on your tail. But then you come to realize that the F.B.I. has a million other things to worry about before you. You find out nobody's after you, or at least not very hard. You see that there's a lot more space for a fugitive in this country than you'd ever dreamed. Only then, when you're relaxed like that, can you take the judicious risks you have to take."

According to reliable information, several leaders of the Weathermen who are among the most eagerly sought political fugitives spent part of last winter at a fashionable Puerto Rico hotel.

Not all fugitives are as radical as the Weathermen; but the very act of going on the lam can be a radicalizing experience. When Ralph, a soldier, walked off a Southern Army base in 1968, he was just trying to avoid Vietnam, where he knew his infantry unit was about to be sent. He took a bus to New York, got a room at the Y.M.C.A., and walked the streets, never daring to contact anyone. "I was scared and lonely and after a couple of weeks I just gave myself up. But I couldn't bear to turn myself in. So I just went home, knowing they'd come and get me. Within a week, they did."

Returned to his unit, Ralph waited until he was eligible for a weekend pass, then took off again. "But this time I got in touch with Peace Movement people in New York. I realized I'd failed the first time because I hadn't made contacts like that. The Movement people asked me what I wanted to do. I said I wanted to go to Canada. It was easy. I just took a train to Montreal."

Ralph stayed in Canada for two months. Through conversations with other deserters there, he began for the first time to think in political terms. "I was around Movement people all the time, taking part in demonstrations and meetings. I began to see that the Vietnam war was part of a whole militaristic foreign policy which I had to fight, and to do that effectively I had to come back to America. To stay in Canada, the safe sanctuary, would have been a copout."

Six months ago, Ralph returned to this country. Since then he has been traveling along the East Coast, "just feeling out the underground situation, looking for a group with which I can identify myself." He travels under several different names, but has not bothered to change his appearance. "Realistically, I know the F.B.I. can't be looking for me very hard. How can they? There are just too many deserters for them to handle."

In August, 1970, the New York Yearly Meeting of the Society of Friends passed a minute on "loving support to deserters." It said: "Friends approve helping deserters, despite possible conflict with the law, whenever such aid seems required by compelling human considerations."

John and Susan—not their real names—are two New York Quakers who were following this policy even before the meeting approved it. In the past year, they have harbored half a dozen deserters for periods of a day to a week. "I feel if a man's only crime is not wanting to kill, then, the laws of the country notwithstanding, he hasn't committed a crime," says John.

They have harbored all sorts of other people, too—draft resisters, alcoholics, teen-age runaways, even a waitress who didn't have a place to say. "We'll take in almost anybody who needs help," Susan says. "The two exceptions are people who commit acts of violence and people who insist on using drugs in our home."

John and Susan are part of a loose network of such families throughout the country. This network has been called the new "underground railway," after the group which harbored runaway slaves. But Susan says it's not really that organized. "Somebody just calls up and says, 'Can we bring some company over tonight?' and we say, 'Sure.' "

In the years before the Civil War, many runaway slaves, instead of heading north through the underground railway, sought refuge with Indian tribes. The slaves, writes Peter Farb, found in Indian society not only a safe haven but "hospitality and sharing, adoption and complete social integration."

Perhaps the most important asset to the new breed of fugitive is the presence in America today of self-contained subcultures almost as impervious to official penetration as the Indian tribes of the 19th century.

For the black fugitive, the ghetto has long provided succor, support and protection from the white (or black) pursuer.

But now the white fugitive can find much the same sanctuary in the "youth culture" which flourishes in most major cities and university towns like Berkeley, Cambridge, Ann Arbor or Boulder, Colo.

Many of today's new fugitives seek refuge with clans of "street people" in such areas, where few questions are asked of the newcomer and where long hair, a beard and granny glasses provide a simple but effective disguise.

CHICAGO, Nov. 12 (UPI)—A west side Selective Service office was firebombed early today. The police said they were searching for a long-haired, bearded suspect.

After they went underground, the Weathermen recognized that the "youth culture" would be their safest refuge. But this posed a problem. For, while overground, the Weathermen had been known as dogmatic, even grim radicals with little sympathy for the drugs and rock music celebrated in the youth culture.

Seeking to change this image overnight, they pulled what must rank as the most audacious caper in recent underground history: the freeing of Timothy Leary from a minimum-security prison at San Luis Obispo, Calif., last September.

The details of the escape are still not known, although one man who saw the high priest of hallucinogens recently at his hideout in Algiers says Leary related that he had been driven straight to San Francisco where he was given a fake passport in the name of "William John McNellis," then flew to Chicago, Paris, and on to Algiers.

But certainly the caper has paid off richly for the Weathermen. Leary now says he is a member of the Weathermen, whom he calls "acid revolutionaries, holy liberation saints." He advises his followers to "arm yourselves and shoot to live." And he even reports that while on the lam in this country, "I went to see 'Woodstock' with Bernardine Dohrn and Jeff Jones [another Weatherman leader]. We were stoned out of our minds."

"Where fish travel in schools, it is useless to work with even the most sophisticated reels. The only solution: metamorphose into a fish."—Father Daniel Berrigan, S.J.

Some observers familiar with the inner workings of the F.B.I. says its capacity for metamorphosis is limited.

One of these is Ramsey Clark, the former Attorney General.

"In the fifties, the F.B.I. was about as professionally excellent an investigatory body as could be developed," Mr. Clark said in a recent interview. "It's still very good at certain things, and finding certain types of criminal fugitives is one of them. But it's simply no longer the leader and innovator it once was."

Clark sees two reasons for the bureau's stagnation:

"It got saturated with hangups about Communism, and if there's anything a seeker of facts can't afford it's ideological convictions.

"It drained off diversity. All the pressures internally were toward likeness of viewpoint, attitude, even physical appearance."

And that, he says, is why the F.B.I. seems to be doing so poorly with the political fugitives. "How are all those straight, short-haired C.P.A.'s and L.L.B.'s going to infiltrate the youth culture? They don't even know how to talk to the sort of informant who can operate in there. If you want to know the truth about all segments of a diverse society, you have to have people from all areas of that society."

One of the few political fugitives the F.B.I. has captured recently is Angela Davis, the black Communist captured in a midtown Manhattan motel on Oct. 13. The next day, a New York Times editorial praised the F.B.I. for a "brilliant investigative effort."

But those who know how the F.B.I. operates are skeptical. They note that the one radical group the bureau is known to have heavily infiltrated is the

Communist party. And it appears that Miss Davis went underground through party channels rather than through the more flexible, imaginative New Left.

Moreover, the bureau apparently picked up her trail in Southern Florida, which Ramsey Clark says is probably the section of the United States heavily infiltrated by the bureau. "With all the Cuban activity down there," Mr. Clark says, "half the motel owners and gas station attendants are probably F.B.I. informants."

"Gosh, I don't know, dad," said Karleton Armstrong, one of the suspects in the University of Wisconsin bombing, when his father suggested he turn himself in to the F.B.I.

The current rash of political fugitives reflects a major shift in the American radical movement. There have been radical fugitives before—"Wild Bill" Haywood, for one, skipped bail and fled to Russia in 1921. But the model for recent Movement actions has been the civil rights struggle, in which people didn't flee jail, they positively courted it. Voluntary surrender to the law in Birmingham or Selma partook both of Christian witness for a holy cause and the hardheaded recognition that arrest and trial were the most effective means of drawing attention to injustice.

When the Movement's focus shifted to the Vietnam war, it retained this characteristic legalism. Even the Chicago Seven, who in the fall of 1969 became symbols of resistance to the judicial system, showed up in court every day of their four-and-a-half month trial and marched off to jail to begin serving their terms (they have since been released on bail pending appeal).

Yet only one year later, the situation has drastically altered. Virtually the only important Movement figures standing trial today are Black Panthers, who have always believed in legal confrontation. Convinced that black men have never enjoyed their basic legal rights under the Constitution, they are determined to make white Americans face up to that reality in the courtroom.

But nearly everywhere else, Movement people facing trial, indictment or merely police surveillance have gone on the lam.

Sometimes this shift has caught even their closest allies by surprise. William Kunstler, chief defense attorney in the Chicago trial, was retained as attorney for Rap Brown, who faced trial last spring in Cambridge, Md. He recalls his shock when Brown failed to appear in court.

"I didn't have the slightest inkling he wouldn't show," Kunstler says. "Rap had been in to see a colleague of mine once during February and I talked with him myself on the phone late that month. He said he'd be there. When he didn't show, I confess my first reaction was disappointment: that I'd been denied an opportunity to show what a good lawyer I was, and that the Movement had been denied an opportunity to win a winnable case.

"But then I came to see that the decision was really a very personal one involving a person's own fate and future. It's not something a lawyer has the right to intervene in."

Others have stood trial first and then, after being convicted, have become fugitives; notably Daniel Berrigan, the Jesuit priest convicted for destroying draft records at Catonsville, Md., who carried his mission underground for four and a half months before the F.B.I. caught up with him.

Dan Berrigan was influenced by Howard Zinn, the Boston University professor, who has written: "If the protest is morally justified . . . it is morally justified to the very end, even past the point where a court has imposed a penalty. If it stops at that point, with everyone saying cheerfully, as at a football match, 'Well we played a good game, we lost and we will accept the verdict like sports'—then we are treating social protest as a game."

He was also influenced by the example of the French worker-priests during the Resistance and by the revolutionary priests working underground in Brazil today. He determined to use his life underground creatively, regarding it primarily as "an experience in and of the spirit . . . otherwise, one is playing cat and mouse with the hunters and the chase becomes frivolous, thoughtless or pathetic, played out according to their feints and starts, exercised in their fears."

For four and a half months, Berrigan was a divinely inspired mouse, staying two or three jumps ahead of the cat while still managing to profoundly influence the lives of hundreds with whom he came in contact. He did that largely by confronting men and women not yet committed to the Movement with the fact of his own need. "I say to these people, 'Here I am and what are you going to do about it?'"

This mission gibed perfectly with his fugitive strategy. For the F.B.I. apparently assumed he would be harbored chiefly by the already committed Catholic Left. Radical nuns and priests known to be friendly with Berrigan were kept under close surveillance during the period. Meanwhile, Berrigan was harbored largely by Protestant or Jewish professional people—professors, lawyers, doctors, writers, who were usually no more than mildly "liberal."

Some other rudimentary precautions were taken. He stayed on the move, rarely spending more than a week in any one town. Only a tiny inner circle knew his itinerary. He was introduced only to people known intimately by his contacts in each town. All phone calls about his movements were made from pay phones and he was never referred to by name ("Dan McCarthy" or "Mr. Johnson" were among his pseudonyms).

But those who helped organize this loose network are still astonished that Berrigan wasn't caught earlier. "Dan just wasn't that far underground," says one of the key organizers. "He insisted on communicating regularly with people overground: sending articles to publications, giving a stream of interviews to the press, talking with some quite well-known Movement personalities, even giving a sermon in a Philadelphia church. Each one of those contacts increased his risk, but he couldn't be dissuaded. He said the whole purpose of becoming a fugitive was so he could keep communicating."

One of the men who harbored Berrigan in his home says:

Dan isn't a recluse and he didn't behave like one when he was with us. He's an open, giving man, who loves people and the things of this world. So he would take what often seemed like astonishing risks. He went to the movies, he'd take walks out along the open road, and once even went to the beach. Another time I took him for a drive and we passed this police car; he looked, I looked, but nothing was said. With us, he had no real disguise. He would have been instantly recognizable.

Dan Berrigan was one of five defendants from the original "Catonsville Nine" who did not surrender last April to begin serving their Federal prison sentences. Berrigan and three others—his brother, Phil, David Eberhardt and George Mische—have all been caught. That leaves only one of the Catonsville defendants still at large—Mary Moylan, a 34-year-old registered nurse from Baltimore.

I interviewed Mary one day in November on the terrace of the Central Park Zoo cafeteria. Since she is dedicated to Women's Liberation, a condition of our interview was that I should be accompanied by a female reporter who would ask many of the questions. Judy Klemesrud, a talented writer for The Times, agreed to perform that role.

The meeting was arranged by Mary's friends with great concern for her security. Judy and I met our contact in front of the Huntington Hartford Museum without knowing where the interview was to take place. Our contact then hailed a taxi and took us to the zoo cafeteria, where we found Mary Moylan bundled up in a coat over a steaming cup of coffee.

We moved to the terrace and took a table surrounded by a herd of small children and their harassed parents. I was nervous about being overheard, but Mary confidently began her story.

"I hadn't really intended to go underground. But we had a meeting about a week before we were supposed to turn ourselves in. When I found out that four of the men were going to become fugitives, I felt I had to try it, too, if only to show a woman could do it. And I wanted to rely exclusively on my sisters in the women's movement. I spoke with some of them and they said they'd help.

"The F.B.I. really thought I was with Dan, because when they caught Phil and George they asked them whether I'd been with them or with Dan. I resented this automatic assumption that it was impossible for me to do it without a man. But now I think I've showed them."

At first, Mary says, she found underground life difficult and oppressive. She lived for a while in a small, one-bedroom apartment, reading, drinking, smoking and sleeping, not daring to go outside, shunning most people, avoiding all forms of Movement activity.

"It really was depressing. I felt I was endangering sisters I really loved, afraid at any moment that the blankety-blank Feds would come knocking through the door. I thought about going to some town and becoming the town librarian or a waitress, just going completely straight and waiting until the whole thing blew over. I even considered turning myself in, just going up to some F.B.I. man and saying, 'Here I am, sweetie.' "

Her friends persuaded Mary to go to Canada instead and think things over awhile. "I stayed up there for two months and pondered my whole situation. I asked myself, 'If you really believe in a human revolution, how do you remain human hiding from the Feds?' Finally I decided that of course I'd have to take sensible precautions but I just couldn't spend all my time worrying about who was coming through the door."

At that point in Mary's story, a trench-coated figure appeared at the head of our table. Mary stopped and I looked up as the figure said:

"Excuse me, may I borrow the salt?"

We all laughed and Mary talked on. But just a minute later, the figure was back looming over us again. Somehow I was sure the F.B.I. had arrived. Prepared for anything, I looked up as he said:

"Sorry, but may I have the pepper, too?"

Since her return from Canada last June 29, Mary has lived a much more relaxed life. "I've kept on the move a lot but at a pretty easy pace. I travel pretty much by myself, but I know at least one sister in each city I go to, and if I can't stay with her she arranges for me to stay with some other sister. The people I stay with usually provide me with food and a little money and they look out for me. They are pretty careful about whom they invite when I'm with them."

Mary remembers only one frightening moment. "I was having dinner at the home of this couple (I stay with married people too, but it's always arranged through the woman). This guy dropped by and as soon as he saw me he said, 'I think we know each other. Where are you from?' Just like that I said, 'Ames, Iowa,' picking it because it was so insane; I don't even know where Iowa is. But he was sure he knew me and I guess he did because he said, 'Have you ever been through Baltimore?' I said I'd passed through, and then he dropped it. Even if he'd guessed who I was, I don't think he would have done anything, but that was scary."

Mary hasn't bothered to disguise herself very much, although she has changed her hair color. "I don't worry much about getting recognized on the street. I don't imagine the great majority of people have even heard of Mary Moylan, and I don't think there are too many photographs of me floating around." But she has prepared herself for the possibility of capture. "Time is certainly on their side. Eventually they may catch up with me."

"So I say, 'O.K., in the meantime how can I work with others to make things better than they are?' " She has begun speaking to small, carefully selected groups, and she is thinking about forming some kind of underground "collective."

When asked to sum up what it's like living underground, Mary pauses and then compares it to her two years as a missionary in Uganda. "When I got back from Africa people asked, 'What was it like over there?' And I'd always say, 'It's really not all that much different, it was a life like any other life.' Well, that's what I'd say about this. It's a life like any other life. In any life you have to work out a routine for yourself. I get up, have breakfast, read books, drink Scotch, turn on occasionally with pot or hash, see people, eat dinner, go to sleep. A human being can adapt to anything, and I've adapted myself to this."

Not everyone has adapted so well. Here is part of a letter from one fugitive to a friend:

"Images of myself: eyes bugged out, arms extended before me, running as fast as I can to escape the steam-roller which is almost on top of me, and casting an occasional glance from side to side to see if I can help someone who's out of breath or who's stumbled and about to succumb to destruction, all the while screaming in a hoarse, inaudible voice for help.

"Waiting for that unseen hand which will snatch me away to safety before I heave head first into the pit the Grand Inquisitor's steaming hot moving walls are pushing toward me.

"These are desperate images. That's not altogether true. Sometimes the steam-roller breaks down or gets gummed up with the bones of more intentional victims. Or I begin to think I'm imagining the whole thing and it's surrealist fantasy. . . .

"People keep asking what people *do* in the underground. Mostly grasp for another day of life in an ephemeral freedom. Soon as enough housing, food, clothing, transportation, I.D. and love is available to allow me to *think*, maybe I can come up with some ideas about what I can *do*, but right now I'll just settle for this race with oppression.

"Is this why they call it the human *race*? Because we have to move so fast to preserve ourselves from the phantoms that pursue us? Much better to be involved in a mass charge under a hail of bombs and artillery and small weapons fire! Then, at least, you can see what your death looks like. Here you don't dare peek over your shoulder for fear the lack of attention to the path ahead will cause you to trip on the unseen rock and be crushed. . . .

"Pa said over the phone yesterday—'If I knew where you were I'd turn you in!' "

Separation from family and friends is one of the cruelest prices of being on the lam. One fugitive told me: "There's this woman in Chicago I hoped to marry. But of course I can't contact her at all, or, naturally, my family either, because that's the first place the cops would look. That's really hard for me because I'm an extremely sensitive person. So I'm looking for a female companion now, but whenever I find one I tend to freeze up because I wonder whether I could promise her anything beyond the minute we have together. If I ever had a meaningful relationship, I couldn't tell her who I was; for her protection and for mine, the less she knows the better. And that makes me very lonely."

Once upon a time in 1969, a soldier deserted from the Army and went home to see his wife. She turned him in. Brooding in the stockade, he decided it had all been some horrible misunderstanding. So he deserted again and went back to straighten things out with his wife. She turned him in again.

On July 23, 1970, Pun Plamondon, Defense Minister of the radical White Panther Party, was rolling through Michigan's Upper Peninsula in the back of a Volkswagen bus.

Pun, wanted for bombing the C.I.A. office in Ann Arbor, was the first radical placed on the "most wanted" list this year. But he had successfully eluded the F.B.I. for eight months and that morning in northern Michigan he had every reason to be pleased with himself.

So he and his two companions—both officials of the party—picked up a six-pack of beer and guzzled it as they sped along, tossing the empties out the widow (in gross violation of the party's 10-point program pledging an end to "pollution of the land").

It was also a violation of Michigan's antilittering law, duly noted by a state trooper who stopped the van. After checking their identification (Pun's was false), the trooper let them go with a lecture. But when police ran a quick check and found out Pun's two companions were White Panthers, they realized who the third man might be and arrested the three again a few miles up the road.

"The whole incident caused a lot self-criticism in the party," a White Panther concedes. "It was not regarded as highly disciplined revolutionary action."

Life on the lam demands a degree of self-discipline. The fugitives I talked with agreed on certain basic rules that should be followed:

Avoid automobiles wherever possible. Even if you're the best driver in the world a careless one coming the other way, or sheer happenstance, may involve you in an accident and cause your identification to be checked. Moreover, cars can easily be traced through registration.

Avoid use of alcohol and drugs unless you are in extremely secure surroundings. Both slow your reactions and impair your judgment. Moreover, use of both can lead to arrest and further investigation of your background.

Don't say anything over the telephone you don't want the authorities to know. Assume any phone in the home of a known radical may be tapped. If you must pass messages by phone, use a pay phone.

If you change your name, do it carefully. Avoid such obvious mistakes as using your wife's maiden name, your uncle's middle name or an Anglicization of a foreign name. A private detective I talked with recalls a fugitive named Goldberg, who changed his name to Ormont. ("You don't have to be a linguist to know they both mean gold mountain.")

These are the most obvious cautions. Recently, a fugitive who has been on the lam for some time wrote an article for the Liberated Guardian in which he offered some other advice:

Cities are generally safer than rural areas or small towns. Avoid communes. Don't wear clothes that are likely to draw suspicion (i.e. military boots or jackets if you were in the Army). Don't turn up at well-known pads . . . your involvement in movement activities is up to you. But be aware that your jeopardy increases directly with the amount of involvement . . . once you have a name stick to it, unless you blow it and have to start again . . . use only a few trustworthy contacts in different locations to channel your mail. Place your letter in an envelope, omit the return address, send it in another envelope (with a covering sheet over the inner envelope) to your contact . . . avoid leaving fingerprints anywhere, wear gloves in handling letters. . . . Libraries are cool [but] don't check out books with suspicious titles [and] stay away from the out-of-town newspaper rack.

I finished my interview with Bob, the armed robber, in a hamburger joint at Eighth Street and Sixth Avenue. Later, in the street outside, we searched for a cab. Suddenly I became aware of noise and, looking up, I noticed that the prisoners in the Women's House of Detention were shouting from behind their bars. "This is a pigpen!," "Free us!" and, "Get me out of here!"

Glancing toward Bob, I asked, "How does that make you feel?"

"Damn glad to be on the lam," he said.

ABE FORTAS

The Limits of Civil Disobedience

The revolt of the young people, on and off the campus, is a fairly new phenomenon for this country. Hitherto, our young people have been submissive, hedonistic and practical-minded. Their idealism has been largely confined to dreams, poetry and abstractions. Even in the depths of the Depression, relatively few of them were activists. Generally, they have accepted

Source: Abe Fortas is a former Associate Justice of the Supreme Court of the United States. This article is adapted from his book *Concerning Dissent and Civil Disobedience.* It appeared in *The New York Times Magazine,* May 12, 1968, pp. 29, 90–98. Reprinted by permission of The World Publishing Company from *Concerning Dissent and Civil Disobedience* by Abe Fortas. An NAL book. Copyright 1968 by Abe Fortas.

the leadership of their elders, not uncritically, but passively. Their revolt has usually taken the form of social misbehavior, not of political activism.

Until the generation of John F. Kennedy, their participation in practical politics was marked by acceptance of "Junior" status: the Junior Chamber of Commerce, the Young Democrats, etc. Only a few years ago, during President Eisenhower's Administration, many of us despaired because the college generation was so passive, so docile and so uninvolved. It was apparently uninterested in anything that was not safe, conventional and serviceable in practical terms.

Now this has drastically changed. Young people have suddenly taken on distinctive character and quality. They are not merely junior-size editions of their elders. They have become a positive, differentiated factor in American life. They are no longer predictably proceeding in a straight line behind their parents and grandparents, preparing to receive the torch from their elders to run the next lap in the old relay race.

This refusal to accept the existing pattern of life and thought merely because it exists is, I think, the common element in the revolt of the youth generation. I do not suggest that most of this age group are active, conscious participants in the revolt. A sharp change in the philosophy of life of a generation is always the work of a few, although it may influence the destiny of all. Probably a majority of today's young people are going about their lives with little discernible difference in their basic actions and those of their parents' generation. But the existence of a special, independent outlook and orientation of the youth generation is an article of faith to which most of them subscribe. Even though it is ill-defined, hazy in outline and uncertain in context, the revolt profoundly affects the lives of all of them, even of those who do not participate in the new activities.

This refusal to accept the domination of the past—the insistence upon this generation's right and duty to make its own life decisions—has produced both count-me-outs and count-me-ins. It has produced the hippies, the psychedelic addicts and the flower-children. It has also produced other young people, not so picturesque in their appearance or habits, who have quietly divorced themselves from the main stream of life. These are the count-me-outs who decline to join in the agony and activity of their time, or in its customary preoccupations. They are immersed in the warm fluid of me-ness. They reject a world which they regard as crass or callous.

On the other hand, there are the activists, the militants, who are passionately devoted to the cause of the Negroes and the poor, and to promoting student domination of university management, and to such causes as opposition to the war in Vietnam and to the draft. They participate vigorously in the life around them to advance those causes. These are the count-me-ins. They have ideas, programs, convictions, energy and initiative. Some of them were significant participants in the Freedom Rides and marches and the early struggle to end discrimination against Negroes. They organize and participate in mass activities to achieve their objectives and to defeat governmental and university actions which they oppose.

Their actions raise basic questions which challenge all of us. I, for example, am a man of the law. I have dedicated myself to uphold the law and to enforce its commands. I fully accept the principle that each of us is subject to law; that each of us is bound to obey the law enacted by his Government.

But if I had lived in Germany in Hitler's days, I hope I would have refused to wear an armband, to *Heil Hitler*, to submit to genocide. This I hope, although Hitler's edicts were law until Allied weapons buried the Third Reich.

If I had been a Negro living in Birmingham or Little Rock or Plaquemines Parish, La., I hope I would have disobeyed the state laws that said I might not enter the public waiting room reserved for "whites." I hope I would have had the courage to disobey, although the segregation ordinances were presumably law until they were declared unconstitutional.

How, then, can I reconcile my profound belief in obedience to law and my equally basic need to disobey these particular laws? Is there a principle, a code, a theory to which a man, with honor and integrity, may subscribe? Or is it all a matter of individual judgment? Above all, it is critically important for us to know whether violence is essential, lawlessness necessary—or whether there are effective alternatives.

Many factors have contributed to the youth revolt: the affluence of our society and the resulting removal of the pressure to prepare oneself for economic survival; the deterioration of the family unit; the increasing involvement of universities and their faculties with non-teaching interests; the disruptive shock of the atom bomb, which gave a new uncertainty and instability to life; the prospect that one's life will be interrupted by compulsory military service; the opposition to the war in Vietnam; the shock of discovering that our national pride and progress concealed the misery and degradation in which Negroes and the poor were living; disillusionment with the standards of the older generation; the new awareness of the wretched state of most of the world's people which came with the end of colonialism, and the example of Negroes in this country and of the people of Africa and Asia who, by individual and group effort, courage and organization have fought and sometimes won heroic battles.

Most of all, the revolt has found impetus, reason and outlet in the opposition to the war in Vietnam and to the draft. Many of the younger generation, as well as some of their elders, have come (justifiably or not), to regard this as a war of a small people against oppression by a vast power, as a struggle for national unity, or as a purely civil war in which our country is "brutally" participating. This has reinforced the natural and familiar opposition of many young men to military service, and especially to compulsory military service. In the minds of these young people, the draft is bad enough; to be drafted to fight a war which they are led to believe is disreputable is intolerable.

The disaffection of youth is expressed by a great variety of activities, ranging from the amusingly juvenile to formidable, threatening assaults upon the institutions of our society. It is difficult for the young people who are moved to passionate action by these factors to resign themselves to the idea that they may be punished if their actions violate the law. They *know* they are right. They are certain that their motives are pure. And they do not accept the proposition that there is any virtue in obedience to authority. They are not broken to society's bridle.

Negroes and poor people are more likely than the young in general to have experienced conflict with the law and police. They are more likely to accept the fact that transgression of the rules carries with it the penalty of punishment. They may not like the consequences, but they do not react with the sense of injustice that the campus "radical" feels. He knows that he is both righteous and right. Generally, his background is middle-class and "respectable." It is impossible for him really to visualize a confrontation between himself and the power of the law. He cannot really see himself as a "criminal," even if he starts a scuffle with the police, destroys property or assaults persons engaged in recruiting for the armed forces or war industries.

But the rules apply to him as well as to the Negro and the indigent. The college youth who is protesting against the college administration or the war in Vietnam or the draft has, of course, the full scope of First Amendment rights. He is entitled to the full protection of the state and the courts in the exercise of speech and symbolic speech, however hostile. But he is not entitled to immunity if he directly and willfully incites violence or insists upon deliberately disrupting the work or movement of others.

A university may choose to refrain from complaining to the police if students disrupt classes by physical violence, or destroy university property, or manhandle recruiters for the armed services or for industries making war materials. If it does not take action itself or summon police assistance, the police are not likely to take the initiative on the campus. But if it lodges a complaint, the governing legal principles in this country are not essentially different from those applicable off campus.

Campus and university facilities are public facilities, but public use does not authorize either the general public or the university faculty and students to use them in a way which subverts their purpose and prevents their intended use by others. I know of no legal principle which protects students on campus from the consequences of activities which would be violations of law if undertaken elsewhere. This is the law, but we are now confronted with a problem which is not solved by mechanical application of the criminal law: the problem of readjusting campus life to the new attitudes and demands, and of coping with the disaffections which afflict so many students.

Here again, perhaps it is a beginning to separate student activities which are nonviolent from those which involve assault on persons or damage to property. Where the law violation is nonviolent or technical (such as blocking entrance to a campus building, or even orderly occupancy of a university facility), there may be sense in patient forbearance despite the wrong that the action involves. But violent activities, in my judgment, should be regarded and treated as intolerable. Punishment of on-campus violence involves risks. Particularly in respect to the youth generation, it should be undertaken only after all efforts to persuade, patiently applied, have been exhausted. But the toleration of violence involves, I think, even greater risks, not only of present damage and injury but of erosion of the base of an ordered society. The point, I think, is not whether the aggressor should be halted and punished, but how —and it is here that moderation, consideration and sympathetic understanding should play their part.

I do not know how profound in intensity or how lasting the current youth revolt may be. It may presage a new and welcome era of idealism in the nation. It may forecast the development of greater maturity and independence of outlook among our young people, and this may be productive of much good. It may even bring about the development of increased maturity in the educational and living rules of our colleges. In any event, it presents a challenge to the older generations as well as to youth to reconsider the goals of our society and its values, and urgently to reappraise the distribution of function and responsibility among the generations.

Conflict between the demands of ordered society and the desires and aspirations of the individual is the common theme of life's development. We find it in the family, where, first, the child is disciplined to accommodate himself to the needs of living with others, and then, as the years go by, he begins the painful process of achieving for himself relative freedom of action and a separate identity. The same is true in any organized society. The achievement of liberty is man's indispensable condition of living; yet liberty cannot exist unless it is restrained and restricted. The instrument of balancing these two conflicting factors is the law.

The term "civil disobedience" has been used to describe a person's refusal to obey a law which he believes to be immoral or unconstitutional. John Milton's famous defiance of England's law requiring licensing of books by official censors is in this category. He openly announced that he would not comply with it. He assailed the censorship law as an intolerable restriction of freedom, contrary to the basic rights of Englishmen.

But the phrase "civil disobedience" has been grossly misapplied in recent years. Civil disobedience, even in its broadest sense, does not apply to efforts to overthrow the government or to seize control of areas or parts of it by force, or by the use of violence to compel the government to grant a measure of autonomy to part of its population. These are programs of revolution. Revolutionists are entitled, of course, to the full benefit of constitutional protections for the advocacy of their programs. They are even protected in the many types of *action* to bring about a fundamental change, such as the organization of associations and the solicitation of members and support at the polls. But they are not protected in the use of violence. Programs of this sort, if they are pursued, call for law enforcement by police action.

But there is a form of civil disobedience other than the refusal to obey a law because of disapproval of that particular law. This is the violation of laws in order to publicize a protest and to bring pressure on the public or the government to accomplish purposes which have nothing to do with the law that is breached. The great exponent of this type of civil disobedience was Gandhi.

The first type, as in Milton's case—the direct refusal to obey the specific law that is the subject of protest—may sometimes be a means, even an essential means, of testing the constitutionality of the law. For example, a young man may be advised by counsel that he must refuse to report for induction in order to challenge the constitutionality of the Selective Service Act. This is very different from the kind of civil disobedience which is *not* engaged in for the purpose of testing the legality of an order within our system of government and laws, but which is practiced as a technique of warfare in a social and political conflict over other issues. Frequently, of course, civil disobedience is prompted by both motives—by both a desire to make propaganda and to challenge the law. This is true, for example, in many instances of refusal to submit to induction.

Here let me be clear about a fundamental proposition. The motive of civil disobedience, whatever its type, does not confer immunity for law violation. Especially if the civil disobedience involves violence or a breach of public order prohibited by statute or ordinance, it is the state's duty to arrest the dissident. If he is properly arrested, charged and convicted, he should be punished in accordance with the provisions of law, unless the law is invalid in general or as applied.

He may be motivated by the highest moral principles. He may be passionately inspired. He may, indeed, be right in the eyes of history or morality or philosophy. These are not controlling. It is the state's duty to arrest and punish those who violate the laws designed to protect private safety and public order.

So we must end by acknowledging that the rule of law is the essential condition of individual liberty as it is of the existence of the state.

We are now in the throes of a vast revolution. Considering its scope and depth, I think it has been relatively peaceful; I think that, even as of today, it is the most profound and pervasive revolution ever achieved by substantially peaceful means.

We have confessed that about 20 million people—Negroes—have been denied the rights and opportunities to which they are entitled. This national acknowledgment—typically American—is in itself a revolutionary achievement. We have proclaimed our national obligation to repair the damage that this denial has inflicted. We have made a beginning—an important, substantial beginning—in the long, difficult and enormously costly and disrupting task of reparation and reform.

At the same time, we have faced the revolt of the youth generation. Our young people have dramatically challenged the authority of their elders. They have asserted their right to frame their own standards and to hold a share of power in society. For the United States, this assertion is, in a sense, more disturbing than the Negro revolution to which it is dynamically related. We have precedents for the trials and disorders that attend the economic and political breakthrough of a segment of the population. But the breakup of patterns of authority—of the straight line of march—is new. Our prior experience of youth's rebellion has been limited to explosions within the pattern. Now, the design itself is challenged.

In both the Negro and the youth rebellions, the critical question is one of method, of procedure. The definition of objectives and the selection of those which will triumph are of fundamental importance to the quality of our society, of our own lives and those of our descendants. But the survival of our society as a free, open, democratic community will be determined not so much by the specific points achieved by the Negroes and the youth generation as by the procedures—the rules of conduct, the methods, the practices—which survive the confrontations. Procedure is the bone structure of a democratic society, and the quality of procedural standards which meet general acceptance —the quality of what is tolerable and permissible and acceptable conduct— determines the durability of the society and the survival possibilities of freedom within the society.

Our scheme of law affords great latitude for dissent and opposition. It compels wide tolerance not only for their expression but also for the organization of people and forces to bring about the acceptance of the dissenter's claim. Both our institutions and the characteristics of our national behavior make it possible for opposition to be translated into policy, for dissent to prevail. We have alternatives to violence.

Our present problems emerged as the result of militancy and aggressiveness by Negroes in pressing their dissent and demands. The forcefulness of their activity, in extent and depth, was new to our experience. The fundamental justice of their demands led to a national response, and produced substantial successes. These, in turn, fed the fires of dissent.

The disclosures of national discrimination against the Negroes and neglect of their demands, the example of their tactics, and the successes achieved, both stimulated and inspired the youth generation. Enough young people had participated in the Negro revolution to provide a nucleus of activists for the youth revolt.

The youth generation (except, of course, Negro youth) did not have specific grievances comparable to those of the Negroes, but they were stimulated to revolt by a breakup of established patterns in the arts and sciences; by the decline of the institution of the family, by the removal of most of the practical hazards of sex; and by the rude shattering of idealistic conceptions about their nation as a classless society in which all persons, regardless of race, were assured of basic rights and opportunity. The war in Vietnam and the draft focused their anxieties and fears and their desperate hunger.

It would be foolish to expect that these dissident groups—Negroes and youth—would confine themselves to the polite procedures that other segments of our society would wish. We can hardly claim that their deserving demands would be satisfied if they did not vigorously assert them. But we can, I think, insist that the methods which they adopt be within the limits which an organized, democratic society can endure.

An organized society cannot and will not endure personal and property damage, whatever the reason or occasion.

An organized society will not endure invasion of private premises or public offices, or interference with the work or activities of others if adequate facilities for protest and demonstration are otherwise available.

A democratic society must tolerate criticism, protest, demand for change, and organizations and demonstrations within the generally defined limits of the law to marshal support for dissent and change. It should and must make certain that facilities and protection where necessary are provided for these activities.

Protesters and change-seekers must adopt methods within the limits of the law. Despite the inability of anyone always to be certain of the line between the permissible and the forbidden, as a practical matter the lines are reasonably clear.

Any mass demonstration is dangerous, although it may be the most effective constitutional tool of dissent. But it must be kept within the limits of its permissible purpose. The functions of mass demonstrations, in the city or on the campus, are to communicate a point of view; to arouse enthusiasm and group cohesiveness among participants; to attract others to join; and to impress upon the public and the authorities the point advocated by the protesters, the urgency of their demand and the power behind it. These functions do not include terror, riot or pillage.

In my judgment, civil disobedience—the deliberate violation of law—is never justified in our nation when the law being violated is not itself the target of the protest. So long as our Governments obey the mandate of the Constitution and assure facilities and protection for the powerful expression of individual and mass dissent, the violation of law merely as a technique of demonstration constitutes an act of rebellion, not merely of dissent.

Civil disobedience is violation of law. Any violation of law must be punished, whatever its purpose, as the theory of civil disobedience recognizes. But violations directed not against laws or practices that are the subject of dissent, but to unrelated laws which are disobeyed merely to dramatize dissent, may be morally as well as politically unacceptable.

Earlier in this discussion, I presented the dilemma of obedience to law and the need that sometimes may arise to disobey profoundly immoral or unconstitutional laws. This is another kind of civil disobedience, and the only kind that, in my view, is ever truly defensible as a matter of social morality.

It is only in respect to such laws—laws that are basically offensive to fundamental values of life or the Constitution—that a moral (although not a legal) defense of law violation can possibly be urged. Anyone assuming to make the judgment that a law is in this category assumes a terrible burden. He has undertaken a fearful moral as well as legal responsibility. He should be prepared to submit to prosecution by the state for the violation of law and the imposition of punishment if he is wrong or unsuccessful. He should even admit the correctness of the state's action in seeking to enforce its laws, and he should acquiesce in the ultimate judgment of the courts.

After all, each of us is a member of an organized society. Each of us benefits from its existence and its order. And each of us must be ready, like Socrates, to accept the verdict of its institutions if we violate their mandate and our challenge does not succeed.

Animating all of this in our society is the principle of tolerance. The state must tolerate the individual's dissent, appropriately expressed. The individual must tolerate the majority's verdict when and as it is settled in accordance with the laws and the procedures that have been established. Dissent and dissenters have no monopoly on freedom. They must tolerate opposition. They must accept dissent from their dissent. And they must give it the respect and the latitude which they claim for themselves. Neither youth nor virtue can justify the disregard of this principle, in the classroom, in the public hall or on the streets. Protest does not justify hooliganism.

These are workable, viable principles in our nation, for we have alternatives to violence and alternatives to suppression. For the state, our constitutional principles, although they provide wide latitude for demonstration and dissent, permit strong and effective state response to violence. For the citizen, the guarantees of freedom of speech, of the press, of peaceable assembly, of protest, of organization and dissent provide powerful instruments for effecting change. Ultimately, the all-important power of the vote—access to the ballot box—furnishes the most effective weapon in the citizen's arsenal.

The experience of these past few years shows, more vividly than any other episode in our history, how effective these alternatives are. It is through their use—and not through the sporadic incidents of violence—that we have effected the current social revolution, and it is through their use that we have begun to create a new—and, we can hope, richer and better—set of institutions and attitudes.

In short, we have shown that our democratic processes do indeed function, and that they can bring about fundamental response to fundamental demands, and can do this without revolution, and despite the occasional violence of those who either reject or have not attained maturity and restraint to use, and not to abuse, their freedom. This is an extraordinary tribute to our institutions.

ROBERT TAYLOR

Decade of Violence

assassin: 1. One who kills for fanatical or monetary reasons: often restricted in usage to the murderer of a prominent person.

From Random House Dictionary

The United States of America last year had one of the highest homicide rates in the world—5.6 homicides for every 100,000 members of the population, as contrasted with 0.4 for Ireland, 0.7 for England, 1.4 for Canada and 1.5 for France and Japan.

Not until recent years, however, has political assassination become a prominent feature of our culture.

Three American Presidents prior to John F. Kennedy were the victims of assassins. (All three were murdered in a 50-year span, a sorry record that contrasts, say, with the tenures of English Prime Ministers.) But we tended to soft-pedal U.S. political violence—the product of what criminologists call "the subculture of violence."

The shooting of Sen. Robert F. Kennedy in Los Angeles, at least superficially, falls outside the normal range of American statistical murder. Most murderers kill someone they know (83 percent last year did) and indeed, 29 percent of homicides occur within the family itself.

Yet the alleged assassin of Sen. Kennedy is young, belonging to the age category susceptible to violence (the increase in the homicide rate coincides with the increase in the numbers of youth) and most prone to identifying public figures with paternalistic authority or familial roles.

If one accepts the dictionary definition of an assassin as "the murderer of a prominent person," many of the ghastly crimes of this decade do not precisely qualify.

Charles Joseph Whitman, climbing to the top of The University of Texas Tower at noon, Aug. 1, 1966, and with two rifles, a carbine and a shotgun, spraying the neighborhood with bullets, killing 15 and wounding 31, is no dictionary assassin. Valerie Percy, murdered in her bed in September, 1966, was not of sufficient prominence in herself to be called the victim of an

Source: Reprinted from *Boston Sunday Globe*, June 9, 1968, A–3, by permission of the publisher.

assassination—not in the sense of Sen. Kennedy. Although the distinction seems mere semantic quibbling, death by assassination, dealt by persons who kill for abstract aims rather than by compulsion, is spreading.

Compared to the lawless '20s, for example, a decade of simple gangster greed, the '60s are the decade of cold blood.

Consider the last five years, covering a critical phase of the civil rights struggle in America, years in which violent attempts were made on such disparate figures as Maj. Gen. Edwin Walker and James Meredith. A representative list of assassinations and near-misses would include:

MEDGAR EVERS—The field secretary of the N.A.A.C.P. was shot and killed from ambush on the night of June 12, 1963, outside his home in Jackson, Miss. Later one Byron de la Beckwith was tried for the crime; his trial ended in a hung jury. Beckwith later ran for lieutenant governor of Mississippi. He lost.

JOHN F. KENNEDY—The 35th President of the United States was assassinated Nov. 22, 1963, as he rode in a motorcade through downtown Dallas, with his wife and Texas Gov. and Mrs. John B. Connally.

LEE HARVEY OSWALD—The assassin of President Kennedy was fatally wounded by Jack Ruby, nightclub owner, in the basement of the Dallas Municipal Building, as Oswald was being transferred to jail, Nov. 24, 1963. Earlier, Oswald had slain patrolman J. D. Tippitt in Oak Cliff, a section of Dallas.

ANDREW GOODMAN, JAMES CHANEY, MICHAEL SCHWERNER—Shot to death June 21, 1964, in Philadelphia, Miss., purportedly by 19 Klansmen, when the trio went into Neshoba County on a civil rights mission. The victims' bodies were found 44 days later, buried in a freshly-built earthen dam.

JIMMIE LEE JACKSON—A 26-year-old Negro was clubbed and shot to death early in 1965 in Marion, Ala. The alleged killers were state policemen; but no charge was pressed.

REV. JAMES REEB—Beaten to death on a Selma, Ala., street, in early March, 1965. The white Unitarian minister from Boston was in Alabama on a civil rights demonstration.

MRS. VIOLA GREGG LIUZZO—A Detroit woman who had come to Selma on a protest march following the murder of James Reeb, she was killed by pistol shots while she drove a fellow protestor, Leroy Moten, from Selma to Montgomery.

JONATHAN M. DANIELS—An Episcopal Seminarian from New Hampshire, killed by a blast from a 12-gauge shotgun carried by a part-time deputy sheriff, Tom Coleman. A companion, Rev. Richard F. Morrisroe, a Catholic priest from Chicago, was critically wounded at the same time, when the two approached a grocery store to buy food.

MALCOLM X.—In February, 1965, the fiery black nationalist leader was murdered by shotgun blasts fired by three assassins in front of an audience of some 400 persons.

JAMES MEREDITH—In June, 1966, James Meredith, first Negro student to enroll at the University of Mississippi, was felled by two of three shots fired from ambush by Mississippi hardware dealer, Aubrey James Norvell. Meredith, on a solo march of protest through Mississippi, recovered from his wounds.

GEORGE LINCOLN ROCKWELL—The 49-year-old self-styled Fuehrer of the American Nazi Party, was shot to death last Aug. 25 as he sat in his car outside a laundromat in Arlington, Va. The slayer was John C. Patler, a disaffected Rockwell aide.

DR. MARTIN LUTHER KING—The advocate of non-violence was shot and slain from ambush as he stood on the porch of a Memphis motel, preparing to go to dinner last Apr. 4. The FBI is seeking an escaped Missouri convict, James Earle Ray.

Such a catalogue is not comprehensive, only an approximation of the '60s anguished toll.

Four years after a President of the United States was killed by shots fired from a mail-order rifle, a bill of Sen. Thomas J. Dodd to ban the mail-order sale of firearms, passed in highly adulterated form.

Opposition to gun control legislation comes mainly from western and rural states and from the National Rifle Assn. The gun lobby, however, is recognized as extremely powerful and well-organized. Congress, by amending various gun control bills, has not come up with effective controls. It is still possible to obtain mail-order weapons from free-wheeling firms—death on the installment plan.

Legislation, furthermore, does not define times that are out of joint, the climate and quality of a civilization.

The last year has seen the success of the film "Bonnie and Clyde," the Norman Mailer novel "Why Are We in Vietnam," the stage travesty called "Macbird," which rests on the the thesis that President Johnson engineered John F. Kennedy's assassination.

These works do not necessarily glorify violence; they may well be symptoms of an already existing disease, and the name of the disease may be called the 20th Century.

John F. Kennedy's assassination was on television; Lee Harvey Oswald's was on television; and now, Robert F. Kennedy's assassination has been on television. The medium is not responsible, TV is an electronic reporter—but also an emblem, a most visible emblem, of technology's impact on modern man.

"Precisely how certain television programs may affect young viewers is a matter of dispute about which we have relatively little evidence," Robert W. Sarnoff, board chairman of NBC, has declared.

Yet psychiatrists such as the late Frederick Wertham assert that TV does, in fact, influence behavior. The assassination of Sen. Kennedy occurred under conditions of nightmare; it is almost impossible to disentangle electronic fact and fantasy.

One of the characteristic images of the decade is the riot crowd in front of a smashed window, watching looters, the store being looted appearing on television screens.

Has the quality of our lives become unreal, abstract? "Americans are habituated to a high level of violence from childhood on," said Dr. John P. Spiegel, director of Brandeis University's Lemberg Center, after the Kennedy slaying.

In the fantasies of an age of technology, the simple gangster outlaw has vanished. Darkness stains the air shrouding a modern figure of violence, "one who kills for fanatical reasons," an idealist: the gangster has been succeeded by the dedicated assassin.

PAUL JACOBS

The Varieties of Violence

In April, 1937, seven prominent Bostonians, including the President Emeritus of Harvard University, sent a telegram to the United States Senate, stating, among other things, that "armed insurrection—defiance of law and order and duly elected authority—is spreading like wildfire. . . . It is the obligation of Congress and the state legislatures, of the President and the governors, in their Constitutional fields, to enact and enforce legislation that will put an end to this type of defiant insurrection."

The "armed insurrection" to which the Bostonians were referring was the sit-down strike in which thousands of General Motors employees took over the G.M. plants in Michigan. In fact, of course, these strikes were never "armed insurrections" and within a few years the strike leaders had become respectable defenders of the status quo.

Today, as in 1937, it is difficult to find phrases more commonly used than

Source: Reprinted with permission, from the January 1969 issue, pp. 17–19, of *The Center Magazine,* a publication of The Center for the Study of Democratic Institutions in Santa Barbara, California.

"law and order," "armed insurrection," or "violence." Even the distinguished head of the American Bar Association discusses "law and order" in the most general and meaningless way. Politicians vie for public favor by escalating their promises to restore or maintain "law and order," and police departments move immediately and in massive numbers with para-military "tactical forces" whenever a breakdown of "law and order" appears imminent.

The amount of public attention given to law and order, violence, and mobbism is a direct result of the racial crisis in America, which has disrupted our "domestic tranquility." Racial disorders always carry the potential of violence, affecting the sprawling city area, and bringing both property destruction and widespread theft. So public discussion of "law and order" and "violence," associated as they are with racial tensions, reflects feelings of fear or guilt or both on the part of the white population, while fear and hate underlie the minority's reaction. The general public, in such an atmosphere of terrible tension, embraces unspecific generalizations—"Law and Order!"—and remains unaware of the varying attitudes toward the use of violence and the varieties of violence that have been tolerated in our society.

Almost all the discussions about law and order in America begin as if there were certain commonly accepted propositions about law and order and violence. One of these propositions is that all violence is illegal. Another is that there is a common view about the destructiveness of violence against persons or property, and that all Americans know the fixed rules that exist for the preservation of law and order and accept those rules as being valid. The "lawbreaker," then, is seen as a deviant; his illegal behavior stems from some personality defect or a fault in his environment. But these propositions do not take into account that within American society there exist sharply differentiated views concerning violence and the meaning of law and order and that certain forms of collective violence are tolerated as the political power of the protesting groups increases.

In the case of the sit-down strikes of 1937, no one doubted that the strikers were violating the law. It was clear that they were occupying property that did not belong to them and were, in addition, prepared to defend their "right" to carry on this illegal activity. Yet, the state made no attempt to remove them forcibly from the G.M. property nor was there any prosecution of them after the strike ended. Political power and economic pressure outweighed the purely legal considerations. Even when economic pressure or political power is not enough to protect strikers from prosecution for acts of violence, the courts tend to be lenient because of the feeling that the workers are defending their job interests. One criterion arbitrators use in determining the penalty against a worker who violates either company procedures or the law itself by engaging in violence is length of employment: the longer an employee has served the company, the less severe the penalty is likely to be. Similarly, trade union political power has successfully worked to exempt union representatives from prosecution or punishment for carrying out acts that would be labeled crimes if participated in by others: trespassing upon or loitering near posted industrial property is a misdemeanor prohibited by the law in California unless the trespass or loitering is committed by a member of a union, an agent of a union, or a group of union members engaged in attempts to organize, or to investigate safety conditions, or to engage in picketing in order to inform the public of the existence of an alleged labor dispute.

In Europe there has been, until recently, another form of tolerated collective violence, and that is the riot. In the past, European riots were different, in very important ways, from the riots that have taken place in America. There they have tended to be limited, short-termed, directed at bringing about a specific end or specific reforms within the context of the system as it is, not for the purpose of transforming or overthrowing the system. The rioters may tear up the streets to build barricades, may overturn cars and even burn them. But generally shots are not exchanged, the police do not kill anybody, and there is little or no looting. In contrast to the European riots, as well as to American labor strikes, the racial disturbances in America today result from generalized, non-specific demands upon the society, demands that cannot or will not be met. After Watts, after Hough, after Detroit, the question that was always put by the whites to the people who participated in the riots was: "What do you want? What do you want?" And the answer: "I want what you want." This generalized demand is not understood because those who ask the question have a different perception about the nature of American society than those who answer.

Most whites believe our political and legal system embodies a shared system of values, a consensus about how changes take place. We also assume that no fundamental differences exist in the society in its view of property rights and violence. I suggest that these assumptions are incorrect and that no such consensus exists, especially among the non-white population. The American Indian perception of land and its use was—and in some cases still is—totally different from that of the white man's. The initial conflict that took place in this country between Indians and Europeans was over the concept of land as private property. In the Indian perception land was endowed with a magical quality, involving a relationship to the sun and the water and the earth all put together, and for the collective use of all. The notion of a fence to separate portions of the land was unknown to Indians, who believed that a fence defaced the land. They could not understand the concept of making land into private property and giving its "owners" the right to bar everyone else; land was for the communal use of all men—and all animals, too. "We suffer the little mouse to play," said the Indian, meaning that mouse as well as man had a right to use the land. And so the bloody conflict developed because the white European "bought" what the Indians did not understand they were selling.

Even today there are tribes who do not accept the white majority's view of private land. The Hopi Indans will not permit oil leases or the building of factories on their land. The belief that the land is the mother of all men is still so strong among some Indians that in the spring they will not walk over the land in hard-soled shoes or permit their horses out of the corral lest shoes harm the earth's pregnant body. In recent months, some tribes have started to resist, with force and violence, any attempt to arrest Indians accused of shooting deer out of season. To them, killing a deer for food cannot be considered a crime; killing for sport is far more criminal.

Another view of land as property is causing conflict between the state of New Mexico and the Alianza led by Reies Tijerina. A group of New Mexicans, Mexican-Americans, are challenging the government on a basic question of land ownership. Should the Alianza win, the entire state of New Mexico would belong to its members. Tijerina acts on his different vision, his different understanding, of land ownership; in the name of the Alianza he arrests police officers! Last year, he and his group marched into the county courthouse armed with rifles and arrested law enforcement officials whom he accused of violating the Alianza's rights to the land.

In the case of looting, there is again a different perception of property held by the looters and the property owners. Looting in the racial disturbances has had a number of special characteristics. Those involved seem to conceive of it as a kind of collective "taking," rather than stealing. The notion of taking is hoary with age in black-white relations in America; a slave "took" from the master with the approval of his fellow slaves; "stealing" was theft from fellow slaves and was disapproved in the slave community. To take from the master was one of the means the slaves resorted to in order to survive in both body and spirit. Looting, like "taking," assumes the quality of a political act, made more legitimate as it becomes a collective action.

A redistribution of goods—a forced redistribution of goods—is another justification, but it hardly matters what the goods are. The looters may be poor, but of greater significance is looting as a symbolic act, one marking identity and participation in a collective action. After the 1965 outbreak in Los Angeles some of the black hustlers bought all kinds of cheap merchandise to be resold throughout the ghetto, and people bought it because part of its sales appeal was its value for allegedly having been "taken" during the outbreak.

Eldridge Cleaver tells us, in *Soul on Ice*, that after the Watts rebellion took place jail prisoners who came from the area suddenly spoke up and said proudly, "I'm from Watts. I'm from Watts." In the months after Watts, sweatshirts with "I'm from Watts" printed on them were being worn, defiantly, by young men and women all over Los Angeles. To have participated even vicariously in that violence brought a collective identity they could be proud of, in contrast to how they had seen themselves before the event.

But how, most people ask, can a man be proud of an identity achieved through violence, looting, and burning? In the world of most non-whites there is no concept of a cause-and-effect relationship in politics, no belief that the political system is in any way responsive to their daily needs. In Washington, D.C., for example, there are black people living almost in the shadow of the Capitol who have no idea of what the white building on the hill is, or of what goes on there. And why should they? The fact is that there is no visible connection between what happens in that building and their lives. The daily little world of these people does not include what *we* think of as "normal" politics or the "normal" political system. Indeed, that micro-world has no conception of power-seeking or of finding relief and redress of grievances through our institutions. Instead, getting power or obtaining redress is seen as taking place through individuals, not through institutions. Implicit in this view of government is lack of knowledge about, or confidence in, the legal system as having any consequences—other than bad ones—affecting their lives. Demands for identity, for humanness, then, become expressed through outbreaks of violence.

It is clear that violent outbreaks have been frequently triggered by police action, and so the relationship of the police to the minority communities becomes very important. Here, again, a basic difference in viewpoint separates the majority from the minority. Most whites assume that the authorized representatives of society act with a minimum amount of bias in the over-all interests of society. We also believe that if they are not acting "properly," if they do display prejudice, we might still be able to develop better training techniques, better community and human relations programs, higher salaries, in order to reform them. There is no place in this view for the feeling of plain gut fear that a large number of black people and brown people have toward the police. When *we* walk down the street and see a police officer, it doesn't occur to us that he is going to shoot us or beat us. Instead, we expect that he will call us "Sir," that he will be polite even when he gives us a ticket, and that when we need him in an emergency he will help us.

A wide chasm separates these two views, and it is just as great at the institutional level of the police as it is at the level of what constitutes the total nature of American society. This means that our political structure is dysfunctional. When a political crisis occurs, no other mode of political expression is available to minorities except violence, because nonviolence as a technique for achieving political change can only function when there is a commonly shared view that change *within* a system is ultimately possible. We do not have that commonly shared view in America today. Our blindness in refusing to admit this has led us to such false ideas as that racial violence arises from the so-called "Lumpen-blacks." We ignore the fact that a great many middle-class, educated Negroes either participate in the disturbances or sympathize with those who do. This kind of superficial explanation for disorder and violence is extremely dangerous. To ignore the political injustices behind disorders and violence and to answer rebellion with repression is sheer blindness. Repression can only bring on the escalation of rebellion. If this happens, the country will become caught up in never-ceasing cycles of civil warfare.

RICHARD HOFSTADTER

The Future of American Violence

On the cover of the June 30, 1969, issue of *New Left Notes*, the organ of the Progressive Labor faction of Students for a Democratic Society, there is a large woodcut illustration which must surely be one of the minor signs of the times. Two young men, one white, one black, are seen crouching on a rooftop above a city in flames. Both are armed with automatic rifles, and both wear, Mexican-fashion, the crisscrossed bandoliers of the rural insurrectionary or *bandito*. They are revolutionaries, urban guerrillas. Alongside them is the legend: "We are advocates of the abolition of war, we do not want war; but war can only be abolished through war, and in order to get rid of the gun it is necessary to take up the gun." One must, I think, pass by the resemblance of this promise of a war-to-end-war to other such promises in the past; one must pass by also its hauntingly perverse echo of the words of the American officer in Vietnam that "In order to liberate the village we had to destroy it," to consider its larger meaning for American political culture.

There is in America today a rising mystique of violence on the left. Those who lived through the rise of European fascism, or who have watched the development of right-wing groups in this country over the last generation, or have fully recognized the amount of violence leveled at civil-rights workers in the South, are never surprised at violence cults on the Right. They still see them in action in such crank groups as the Minutemen, and hear their accents in some of the uninhibited passages in George Wallace's speeches. What has been more arresting is the decline of the commitment to nonviolence on the Left, and the growth of a disposition to indulge or to exalt acts of force or violence. What was once the Student Nonviolent Coordinating Committee has taken the "Nonviolent" out of its title. Frantz Fanon's full-throated defense of the therapeutic and liberating effects of violence has been one of the most widely read books of our time. During a summer of exacerbated rioting, *The New York Review of Books*, one of the most influential and

Source: Mr. Hofstadter is an eminent American historian, and his many books and essays are widely read and discussed. This article appeared in *Harper's Magazine*, April 1970, pp. 17, 48–53. Copyright © 1970 by Richard Hofstadter. Reprinted from *American Violence*, edited by Richard Hofstadter and Michael Wallace, by permission of Alfred A. Knopf, Inc.

294

fashionable periodicals on the American campus today, elected to feature on its cover a set of instructions, complete with diagram, for making a Molotov cocktail. In its columns, a widely read left-wing journalist, Andrew Kopkind, has told us that morality comes out of the muzzle of a gun. The Weatherman faction of SDS has made a primary tactic of violent encounters with the police. A young leader of the Black Panthers rises at the 1969 summer convention of the SDS to taunt the white delegates with the boast that the Panthers have "shed more blood than anyone" and that white Leftists have not even shot rubber bands. Dotson Rader, a young veteran of Columbia's wars, informs the readers of the *New York Times* in its correspondence columns that the justice the New Left seeks will be won by "fighting in the streets." Some, no doubt, are reminded of the Paris Commune. Others will be reminded of the promises of Mussolini.

Certain ironies in the new cult of violence are inescapable. The sidewalk Sorels who preach violence know very little about it, and sometimes prove pitifully ineffectual in trying to use it. Those who practice it with the greatest effect—the police and the military—find preaching superfluous. The new prophets of violence are almost certain to become its chief victims, if it becomes general and uncontrolled, especially when their own romanticism carries them from the word to the deed. Historically, violence has not been an effective weapon of the Left, except in that rarest of rare circumstances, the truly revolutionary situation. Under normal circumstances, violence has more characteristically served domineering capitalists or trigger-happy police, peremptory sergeants or fascist hoodlums. And even in our day, I think it should be emphasized, the growing acceptance of violence has been unwittingly fostered from the top of society. The model for violence, which has rapidly eroded the effectiveness of appeals to nonviolent procedures, has been the hideous and gratuitous official violence in Vietnam. And after having created and made heroes of such a special tactical force as the Green Berets, we should not be altogether surprised to find the Black Panthers wearing *their* berets and practicing close-order drill. It may be childishly irrelevant to cite the example of Vietnam as an answer to every reproach for domestic acts of force or violence, but there is in that answer a point of psychological importance that we should not overlook: now, as always, the primary precedent and the primary rationale for violence comes from the established order itself. Violence is, so to speak, an official reality. No society exists without using force or violence and without devising sanctions for violence which are used to uphold just wars and necessary police actions. But the frequency and the manner in which official violence is used is of signal importance to the legitimation of the civic order. Any liberal democratic state is in danger of wearing away its legitimacy if it repeatedly uses violence at home or abroad when a substantial number of its people are wholly unpersuaded that violence is necessary.

Neither establishments nor revolutionary movements can do without sanctions for violence. What any man sees as a just war or a necessary police action will, of course, depend upon his situation and his politics; but only a few pacifists quarrel with the idea that just wars are conceivable, and only a few utopian anarchists are likely to deny that under some circumstances authorities have to use force or violence to keep order. The right of revolution is itself an established and sanctified rationale for violence. It can hardly be banished from the established sanctions in a country like America that was born in a revolution. One of our most sacred texts lays down the circumstances under which revolutionary resistance becomes legitimate. "Prudence," it also remarks (there *were* revolutionaries for whom prudence was a consideration), "will dictate that governments long established should not be changed for light and transient causes. . . . But when a long train of abuses and usurpations, pursuing invariably the same object, evinces a design to reduce them under absolute despotism, it is their right, it is their duty, to throw off such a government, and to provide new guards for their future security."

In our own time we have no difficulty in thinking of some tyrants against whom the right of revolution was or could have been justifiably invoked, and responsibly so when the circumstances warranted hope of success. Unfortunately, in this age of verbal overkill, the epithet of tyranny can be hurled at any regime that is intensely disliked by a morally self-confident minority, and the prospects of revolutionary success may seem astonishingly good to those who gull themselves with their own miscalculations and fantasies. The classic rationale for revolution is now widely used to sanction piece-meal violence against democratic regimes in which no shadow of a revolutionary situation exists. The word "revolution" has been distended to apply to any situation in which there is rapid change or widespread discontent. Hence acts of forcible or violent adventurism can be given a superficial legitimacy by defining any situation one pleases as a "revolutionary situation." One radical thinker, Barrington Moore, Jr., who cannot be accused of lack of concern for the oppressed or of hostility to revolutions, has deplored the current disposition "to cast some vague universal cloak of legitimacy upon violence—even upon violent resistance to oppression," and has warned against occasions when "revolutionary rhetoric outruns the real possibilities inherent in a given historical situation." Today, in America, "talk about revolution is . . . pure talk with potentially dangerous and tragic consequences."

One of the essential difficulties in justifying violence is that its success is an ingredient in its justification, and such success is usually a matter of chance. There *are* some blunders that are worse than crimes, and among these are the blunders of those who, even in a good cause, precipitate violence without reasonable grounds for believing that violence will serve its purpose or that it can be contained within bounds that will be proportionate to the ends in view. No doubt it is tempting to think of putting a final end to some grave and massive social evil by a quick, surgical, limited act of violence. But the difficulty lies in being reasonably sure, before the event, that the evil will indeed be ended and not exacerbated or succeeded by some equal or greater evil; that the violence can really be limited both in time and in the casualties it inflicts, and that the reaction will not be more harmful than the surgery. For this reason all politicians, revolutionary no less than establishment politicians, must work with a terrible calculus in human misfortune.

In order to justify the use of violence as a means toward the accomplishment of some humane and "progressive" end, one must first believe that he knows, roughly at least, two things: first, that so-and-so much violence is in fact necessary to achieve the end; and second, what the countervailing human cost of the violence will be—that is, where its repercussions will stop. There are, of course, many people who imagine that they have this kind of command of the future; but some of us are not so sure, since we are not even sure that we can judge the necessity or usefulness of *past* violence in many cases where all the returns seem to be in hand.

But let us not deceive ourselves. Current credulity about the benefits of violence is rarely based upon a careful concern about when and how violence can be justified, or upon sober estimates of its past role or its prospects of future success. We are not living in a period of moral casuistry or measured calculation but in one of robust political romanticism. The protest politics of the 1960s threatened at times to break with the historic politics of liberal American reformers—who aimed to persuade a wide public, had scruples about methods, were willing to compromise, to move patiently from one limited end to another. For a decisive but now perhaps waning segment of the Far Left, politics has become all too much a matter of self-expression and of style, and such efforts as its more extreme exponents make at calculation and casuistry seem feeble as compared with the full-blown bravado of their actionist creed. There are moments when the aim of the political act seems to have become little more than the venting of a sense of outrage, and there have been activists more concerned with their freedom to carry the Vietcong flag in a peace parade or to use four-letter words than with their ability to persuade. There is less hope that any particular foray will yield visible results or affect public policy, more desire to get a sense of emotional satisfaction out of a mass happening. The demand for programmatic achievement has become less fixed, that of self-assertion central. The distinction between politics and theater has been systematically blurred by activists in politics and activists in the theater.

In the new politics, force or violence has a new place: for some it is satisfying merely to use it, but others have devised strategies to provoke counterviolence to show up the Establishment, as they put it, for what it is. In any case, violence has come to have the promise of redemption. "Violence alone," writes Franz Fanon in *The Wretched of the Earth*, one of the canonical works of the new politics, "violence committed by the people, violence organized and educated by its leaders, makes it possible for the masses to understand social truths and gives the key to them." Fanon, writes Sartre in presenting him, "shows clearly that this irrepressible violence is neither sound and fury, nor the resurrection of savage instincts, nor even the effect of resentment: it is man recreating himself. . . . No gentleness can efface the marks of violence, only violence itself can destroy them."

Violence, then, is not only useful but therapeutic, which is to say indispensable. It seems natural enough for those who have been victims of a great deal of violence, or simply of the constant threat of overwhelming force, to conclude that they can restore their dignity only when they use violence themselves. But the restorative power of violence, if indeed violence can have that power, must surely depend upon its being used successfully. The unsuccessful use of violence, ending in defeat and fresh humiliations, may in fact intensify the original malaise. It is hard, for example, to imagine that the survivors of the grim massacre of the Indonesian Communist party in 1965–66 would have the same enthusiasm for the restorative power of violence as the victorious Algerian rebels. And this is why the existential mystique of violence, which tries to circumvent the rational calculus of tactical probabilities, will not do: its claims for therapy or sanctification through violence rest upon an arbitrary assumption of success. There is no satisfactory refuge from political calculation in psychology or metaphysics.

But of course there *are* examples of success in our time—examples set by Mao, Castro, the Algerian rebels, Ho Chi Minh and the Vietcong. The circumstances in all these cases have a special quality: the successes have been among "backward" peoples with a firm territorial base and a history of colonial exploitation. It is now suggested that violence can be equally successful in modern industrial countries, that guerilla action suitable to the Sierra Maestre or the terror and sabotage that won in Algiers can be adapted to New York, Chicago, Oakland, or even, it appears, Scarsdale. A good deal of of tactical ingenuity has in fact been stimulated, but the chief intellectual consequences have been pathetic: many young blacks have begun to think of themselves as being a colonial people, and of their problems of liberation as having exactly the same characteristics.[1] The psychological similarities are, of course, there—and a book like Fanon's *The Wretched of the Earth*, the work of a psychiatrist, argues its case largely in psychological rather than in social structural terms. American blacks may have the psyches of other victims of colonialism but they lack all the essential features of the true colonial situation: a terrain suitable to guerrilla action, the prospect of becoming a majority, territoriality, and the promise of integral control of the economy

---

[1] Since so much has been accomplished by strategic minorities, it may not matter for the future of violence in America that the black militants have not yet converted a majority of Negroes. In *Newsweek*'s 1969 poll, 63 per cent (as against 21 per cent) thought that Negroes could win their rights without violence. Overwhelming majorities also repudiated separatism in response to questions about integrated schools and integrated neighborhoods. (*Newsweek*, June 30, 1969.) The appeal of militant ideas, however, is much higher among the young.

after the colonial power has been expelled. Except for these indispensable elements, the comparison is excellent, and therefore we may indulge ourselves in the fantasy that Watts is just like Algiers.

But in the end one must give the prophets of violence their due: violence *is* pervasive in human experience and has been pervasive in American history, and however it repels us, we must see it as an instrument of common use. The creed its proponents put before us is simple but forceful: Violence has been all but universal in the past. Violence changes things and nothing else does. Violence is therefore necessary. "Violence," said Rap Brown in what must surely remain one of the memorable utterances of our time, "is necessary and it's as American as cherry pie." Presumably he did not expect his listeners to be so uncritically patriotic as to think that violence must be good because Americans have so often used it. No doubt his hope was that if a decent respect for the normality and inevitability of violence could be instilled in the minds of his contemporaries, they would be less censorious about the violence supposedly necessary to black liberation. And one should grant all that is sound here: certainly violence that would in fact lead to a full realization of the rights of blacks would have a great deal to be said for it, and would stand in quite a different moral position from the violence, say, that many lynchers used for their own entertainment and for the edification of their children. Here, as always, however, one encounters the latent, the unexamined assumption: violence *will* deliver that which is expected of it. It is an assumption shared more and more among the very young, black or white: justice will be won by "fighting in the streets." Fighting in the streets as a revolutionary technique—it is one of the few old-fashioned ideas still alive.

Certainly world history yields plenty of cases in which some historical logjam seems to have been broken by an eruption of violence, which is then followed by a period of peaceful, gradualist improvement. It is always possible in such cases to argue (though difficult to prove) that the violence was a necessary precondition of the peaceful change that followed. The trouble is that there are so many other cases in which violence has decided issues in ways we are less likely to applaud. American experience with the large-scale violent resolution of fundamental crises is mixed. The Revolution and the Civil War pose an interesting antithesis. The question of American independence was settled by violence, and, as historical issues go, settled with considerable success. But one of the keys to that success may be found in the minimum of gratuitous violence with which the Revolution was carried out. There could be no regicide and there was no terror. There were frequent incidents, but there was no wholesale mobbing of dissidents. Few Loyalists outside the ranks of the British army were killed, though many were terrorized, many went into exile, and many lost large properties. Even the military action did not characteristically go beyond what we would call guerrilla warfare. Most important, the revolutionaries did not turn upon each other with violence or terror. The Thermidor, if the adoption of the Constitution can be correctly called that, was equally mild, and in part simply nationalized and embodied in institutional form some of the principles set forth in the Revolution itself. Not only was independence secured and the political life of the American states markedly democratized but some social reforms were given a strong impetus. In spite of the difficult questions of national organization that were not settled, and in spite of the tumultuous passions raised by the political issues of the Federal era, the episodes of domestic violence that followed the Revolution—and there were quite a number of them—were in a relatively low key and proved eminently controllable. The early rebellions mounted by Daniel Shays, the Whiskey rebels, and John Fries, though of much political consequence, were, as episodes of violence, kept at the level of skirmishes, and their leaders were afterwards treated with judicious consideration. The Revolution was followed by relative peace: on the whole, the era from 1790 to 1830, though far from violence-free, was one of the least violent periods in our domestic history.

The Civil War stands in marked contrast. Again, it did settle historical issues, the issues of union and of the legal status of slavery. But it was preceded by a decade of searing civic violence and climaxed by a war that cost 600,000 lives, and it left an extraordinary inheritance of bitterness and lethal passion that has not yet ended. The legal liberation of the slave was not followed by the actual liberation of the black man. The defeated states became less rather than more democratic. The violence of the war was followed by the resounding and horrifying episodic violence of Reconstruction, and the Thermidor in the South went on for a full generation after the guns were stilled. The war seems in retrospect to have been an intensely cruel and wasteful way of settling—if that is the right word—the issues that gave rise to it. I do not agree with the categorical form or exaggerated rhetoric of Barrington Moore's pessimistic world-historical estimates that "violence has settled all historical issues so far, and most of them in the wrong way," but in the considerable list of historical cases that could be drawn up to support his judgment, the Civil War would surely rank high.

If we look at the use of violence in social situations of less profound consequence than those which led to the Revolution and the Civil War, we can find instances when violence in the United States appears to have served its purpose. And it has been, on the whole, the violence of those who already had position and power. Many vigilante movements, for example, achieved their limited goal of suppressing outlaws. Lynching clearly added a note of terroristic enforcement to the South's caste system. For years employers used violence and the threat of violence against labor with success: in the main, the outstandingly violent episodes in industrial conflicts were tragic defeats for labor, although there were occasions when violence initiated on behalf of employers became too blatant for public acceptance and boomeranged. Labor has used violence less often than employers and with only rare success. There was, to be sure, one very effective series of extralegal actions by labor—the sit-downs of the 1930s. However, in these instances the workers though using illegal *force*, were using a tactical device that tended to avert rather than precipitate acts of outright violence. This may explain why they won considerable sympathy from the public, which was at the same time becoming acutely aware of the violence, intimidation, and espionage used by employers in many industries. In any case, the sit-downs were a transient tactic which labor leaders abandoned as soon as collective bargaining was achieved, and it is difficult to imagine the sit-downs repeatedly successful as a standard device.

In sum, violence can succeed in a political environment like that of the United States under certain conditions. Those who use it must be able to localize it and limit its duration. They must use it under circumstances in which the public is either indifferent or uninformed, or in which the accessible and relevant public opinion (as in the case of vigilantes and, usually, of employers in the nineteenth century) is heavily biased in their favor. If violence is accompanied by exceptional brutality (lynching, employer actions like that at Ludlow), it must be kept a local matter, and one must hope that it can somehow be screened from the attention of the larger polity. The conditions for its success, in this respect, seem to have become more problematical in the age of mass communications, where the most vital tactical problem is to set the stage so that the onus for violent action can be made to seem to rest entirely upon one's adversaries.

If violence sometimes works, it does not follow that nothing but violence works. Most of the social reforms in American history have been brought about without violence, or with only a marginal and inessential use of it, by reformers who were prepared to carry on a long-term campaign of education and propaganda. The entire apparatus of the welfare state, from child labor laws, wage-hour regulation, industrial safety laws, and workmen's compensation to legally regulated collective bargaining, social security, and medical care for the aged, is the achievement of active minorities which, while sometimes militant and always persistent, were also patient and nonviolent. Ours, however, is an age that cannot wait, and it is doubtful that young militants, black or white, are taking much comfort from the example of such predecessors in the tradition of American reform. The activists, according to their temperaments, will argue either that earlier reforms, being props to the Establishment, were of little or no value, or that they were all a generation overdue when they came. The first response is simply inhumane, but the second has much truth in it: such reforms were indeed long overdue. However, it does not follow that the use of violence would have hastened their coming. Under some conditions the fear or threat of violence may hasten social reforms, yet if actual outbreaks of violence were the primary force in bringing reform, one might have expected social-welfare laws to come in the United States before they came to such countries as Great Britain and Germany where there was less industrial violence. The important element seems to have been not the resort to violence but the presence of powerful labor movements with a socialist commitment and the threat of sustained action through normal political channels.

But the confrontationist politicians of our time seem to have hit upon an approach to violence that surmounts one of the signal disadvantages under which social dissidents have labored in the past: they have learned the value not of committing violence but of *provoking* it. It remains true today, as it has always been, that most political violence is committed by the agents of authority. In the past, for example, labor often got the blame for violent outbursts that were primarily the work of police or other agents of employers. Hence one speaks of "labor violence" but not of "capital violence." Today, however, a technique has been found to put official violence to work in the apparent interests of dissent. A small cadre of determined activists, enveloped in a large crowd of demonstrators, can radicalize a substantial segment of public opinion by provoking the police into violent excesses—if necessary by hurling objects, but better still by hurling nothing more than verbal abuse. The activists have correctly gauged the temper of the police, who are often quite ready to oblige by lashing out indiscriminately against both those who have offended them and those who have not—orderly demonstrators, innocent bystanders, reporters, cameramen. Young radicals have thus found a way to put the police and the mass media to work for them, as the public sees a hideous spectacle of beating, kicking, and clubbing by officers of the law against unarmed demonstrators and witnesses. Outrage becomes the more blatant to those who are aware of and attracted by the milky innocence of the majority of young demonstrators.

Whether the larger public effect of such confrontations will actually work to the ultimate advantage of the activists is problematical. What they can see with their own eyes at the moment of conflict is that many persons, hitherto vaguely sympathetic, become, at least for a time, energized and activated out of indignation. What they choose to ignore is the other, less visible but usually larger public, which puts the full blame on demonstrators and backs the police and the authorities. (The behavior of the Chicago police during the Democratic Convention of 1968, one of the most flagrant police actions of this era, was approved by a substantial majority of the public.) Still, activist leaders are aware of *their* converts, and converts there usually are. Why not rejoice in the converts and dismiss the backlash? Hence the ubiquitous New Left agitator, Tom Hayden, has called for "two, three, many Chicagos," and the young activists interviewed by Jerome Skolnick's researchers for the National Commission on the Causes and Prevention of Violence show a shrewd if limited understanding of the implications of such tactics. The purpose of confrontations, they argue with striking candor, is to educate the public by staging spectacles of repression. "Direct action is not intended to win particular reforms or to influence decision-makers, but rather to bring out a repressive response from authorities—a response rarely seen by most white Americans. When confrontation brings violent official response, uncommitted elements of the public can see for themselves the true nature of the 'system.' " The activists also believe that such experience lowers the "cultural fear of violence" natural among young middle-class radicals—a fear that is "psychologically damaging and may be politically inhibiting," and thus prepares them for a serious commitment to revolution. To some degree they have already been proved right: the "damaging" inhibitions against the use of guns, bombs, and arson have begun to break down.

Can this breakdown be extrapolated into an indefinite future? No doubt most Americans are more curious about where our penchant for violence is taking us than they are about a more precise explanation of its pattern in the past. But here prognosis is as hazardous as anywhere. In the past our violence has always been cyclical, and it is possible to believe that the 1960s will some day appear on the charts of the sociologists as another peak period, rather more pronounced than many, which is followed by relative calm. As the young never tire of reminding us, we live in a situation that is new and in some decisive respects unprecedented. (I sometimes think that *all* American experience is a series of disjunctive situations whose chief connecting link is that each generation repeats the belief of its predecessor that there is nothing to be learned from the past.) In any case, our social violence is not a self-contained universe that holds within itself all the conditions of its future development. In fact almost everything depends upon external forces which no ones dares to predict: the tempo at which we disengage from Vietnam, the national and international response to our undisguisable failure there, and our ability to avoid another such costly venture.

Who can really believe that he knows what to expect of the future of American violence? It is easy to draw up two plausible scenarios for the future, one apocalyptic, the other relatively benign though hardly exhilarating. Apocalyptic predictions are conventionally in order—indeed they have become so conventional that they constitute a kind of imperative intellectual fashion. But in them there is more of omniscience than of science, and their function seems more psychological than pragmatic. In a magical gesture one predicts evil in order to ward it off. Or worse, in moments of terrible frustration one threatens one's audience with some ultimate catastrophe by way of saying: This is what you will all get for not having followed the social policies I have prescribed for you. However, over the past generation the visions of the future that have prevailed among the most modishly apocalyptic intellectual circles in this country have been so largely wrong that they could almost be used like odd-lot buying in the stock market as a negative indicator of future realities. Perhaps the most cogent reason, aside from the perverse element of self-indulgence inherent in it, for not yielding too easily to the apocalyptic frame of mind is a pragmatic one: apocalyptic predictions, repeated too often and believed too automatically, could at best reduce men of good will to a useless passivity and at worst turn into self-fulfilling prophecies. Pragmatic wisdom argues for assuming that our difficulties are manageable, so that we may put our minds to thinking about how in fact they can be managed.

Still, it requires no remarkable ingenuity to see how some of the recent trends in American society, continued and magnified, could bring about the eclipse of liberal democratic politics. The danger is not that the alienated young and the militant blacks will wage a successful revolution. The United States is basically a conservative country, and its working class is one of the anchors of its conservativism. Its overwhelming majority is not poor, not black, and not in college. College activists, themselves only a fraction of the college population, command so much attention from the mass media that the actual state of mind of the American young has been obscured. Almost three-fourths of those in the 17–23 age bracket do not go to college, and their political direction is quite different from that of the college activists. Their responsiveness even to the cruder forms of backlash sentiment may be measured by their votes in the 1968 election; in which George Wallace had proportionately somewhat *more* support among white voters in the age groups 29 and under than in the age groups 30 and over.[2]

In a nation so constituted, the most serious danger comes not from the activities of young militants, black or white, but from the strength of the backlash that may arise out of an increasing polarization of the society. The apocalyptic scenario spells itself out rather easily: an indefinite prolongation of the war in Vietnam, or a re-escalation, or the launching of yet another such provocative and disastrous foreign undertaking; a continued unwillingness or inability to make adequate progress in accommodating the demand for racial justice; an intensification of confrontation politics in the colleges and on the streets; a heightened alienation of the intelligent young; violent scenes, vividly reported on TV, of provocative conduct by demonstrators and brutal responses by police; a continuing polarization of the political public into Right and Left which shuts off just such political and social efforts as might relieve the crisis; the formation of numerous armed groups of black and white citizens, highlighted perhaps by a few mass gunfights in the big cities; the breakdown of one or both of the major parties; the capture of the Presidency and Congress by a nationwide movement dedicated to political repression at home and a hard line in foreign policy.

Not altogether impossible, one must say, though to me it somehow fails to carry conviction. The particular forms of violence that flourished in the 1960s seem now to be on the decline: ghetto riots have been tapering off, and the crest of violence touched off by campus protest may have been reached in the years 1967 to 1969. Black militancy is certain to be with us for an indefinite future, and it is a sobering thought that the one major breakdown of the American political system came in association with an unresolved problem

[2] An American Institute for Public Opinion national sample showed that Wallace had the following support in four age brackets: 21–25, 13 per cent; 26–19, 18 per cent; 30–49, 13 per cent; 50 and over, 11 per cent.

of race; but black agitation tends to grow more selective about methods and goals, and it is by no means clear that it must involve large-scale violence or mass casualties. Student activism too seems likely to outlast the American withdrawal from Vietnam, since it rests on a profound cultural malaise that goes beyond any political issue, but it may work at a lower level of emotional intensity. An end to the war would bring about a political and economic climate in which the effort to relieve urban blight and poverty and to come to terms with the demand for racial justice can be resumed under far more favorable conditions than those of the past five or six years. It is a rare thing in our experience to be centrally preoccupied with the same problem for two successive decades, and it is quite conceivable that even a persisting and relatively high level of violence in the 1970s will come to be regarded as a marginal rather than a central problem. At some time in the near future the destruction of the environment, and the problems attendant upon pollution and over-population, are likely to take the center of the historical stage and to have such a commanding urgency that all other issues will be dwarfed. The styles of thought, the political mood that will be created by such problems, as well as the political alignments they will bring about, may be so startlingly different from those of the 1960s, that the mentality of the 1960s will seem even more strange by 1980 than the mentality of the 1950s has appeared during the past few years.

When one considers American history as a whole, it is hard to think of any very long period in which it could be said that the country has been consistently well governed. And yet its political system is, on the whole, a resilient and well seasoned one, and on the strength of its history one must assume that it can summon enough talent and good will to cope with its afflictions. To cope with them—but not, I think, to master them in any thoroughly decisive or admirable fashion. The nation seems to slouch onward into its uncertain future like some huge inarticulate beast, too much attainted by wounds and ailments to be robust, but too strong and resourceful to succumb.

section VI

The Agenda of American Politics: Race, the Military, the Economy, Poverty, and the Environment

Throughout the collection of articles in this book runs the theme that the United States is in a state of political crisis. Perhaps our country has simply grown out of its reckless youth and must face the fact that it can no longer waste its strength and resources with careless abandon. Nor can we any longer afford the luxury of ignoring problems with the hope they will solve themselves. "Benign neglect," as a deliberate approach to any of the major problems of the Seventies, is simply an invitation to disaster. At the same time, increasing numbers of citizens come to doubt whether, even with maximum effort, tolerable solutions can be worked out within the limits of pluralist politics.

The agenda of politics is long and we offer here only a few of the more obvious items. The crisis nature of politics extends all the way through our political structure, and such mundane problems as what to do with our garbage or how to keep automobiles moving become crises which confound our state and local governments. To those of a pessimistic nature the future looks grim indeed.

But despair is really the easy way out. The harder task is to confront the problems that demand attention and to make the institutional apparatus work toward their solution. The fact that we have recognized the serious nature of our predicament and are able freely to discuss ways of coping with it should give us some feeling of optimism.

This section takes up some of the issues high on the list of priorities. The problem of racial justice comes first—on grounds of both urgency and morality. It is followed by essays which deal with the political power of the military and the growth of militarism; the economic problems of inflation and recession; and the problem of poverty. But none of these things will matter much if we are unable to find ways to deal with our ecological problems and prevent the deterioration of our environment. Any other characteristics of the future are irrelevant if we all go gasping into oblivion with our last breath of carbon monoxide, strangle on our last bite of poisoned fish, or populate ourselves into extinction.

JAMES BALDWIN

A Letter to My Nephew

Dear James:

I have begun this letter five times and torn it up five times. I keep seeing your face, which is also the face of your father and my brother. I have known both of you all your lives and have carried your daddy in my arms and on my shoulders, kissed him and spanked him and watched him learn to walk. I don't know if you have known anybody from that far back, if you have loved anybody that long, first as an infant, then as a child, then as a man. You gain a strange perspective on time and human pain and effort.

Other people cannot see what I see whenever I look into your father's face, for behind your father's face as it is today are all those other faces which were his. Let him laugh and I see a cellar your father does not remember and a house he does not remember and I hear in his present laughter his laughter as a child. Let him curse and I remember his falling down the cellar steps and howling and I remember with pain his tears which my hand or your grandmother's hand so easily wiped away, but no one's hand can wipe away those tears he sheds invisibly today which one hears in his laughter and in his speech and in his songs.

I know what the world has done to my brother and how narrowly he has survived it and I know, which is much worse, and this is the crime of which I accuse my country and my countrymen and for which neither I nor time nor history will ever forgive them, that they have destroyed and are destroying hundreds of thousands of lives and do not know it and do not want to know it. One can be—indeed, one must strive to become—tough and philosophical concerning destruction and death, for this is what most of mankind has been best at since we have heard of war; remember, I said most of mankind, but it is not permissible that the authors of devastation should also be innocent. It is the innocence which constitutes the crime.

Now, my dear namesake, these innocent and well meaning people, your

Source: James Baldwin, novelist and essayist, is the author of *Notes of a Native Son* and *Nobody Knows My Name*, two books of essays, as well as three novels. "A Letter to My Nephew" appeared in *The Progressive*, December 1962, pp. 19–20. From *The Fire Next Time* by James Baldwin. Copyright © 1962, 1963 by James Baldwin. Reprinted by permission of the publisher, The Dial Press.

countrymen, have caused you to be born under conditions not far removed from those described for us by Charles Dickens in the London of more than a hundred years ago. I hear the chorus of the innocents screaming, "No, this is not true. How bitter you are," but I am writing this letter to you to try to tell you something about how to handle them, for most of them do not yet really know that you exist. I know the conditions under which you were born for I was there. Your countrymen were not there and haven't made it yet. Your grandmother was also there and no one has ever accused her of being bitter. I suggest that the innocent check with her. She isn't hard to find. Your countrymen don't know that she exists either, though she has been working for them all their lives.

Well, you were born; here you came, something like fifteen years ago, and though your father and mother and grandmother, looking about the streets through which they were carrying you, staring at the walls into which they brought you, had every reason to be heavy-hearted, yet they were not, for here you were, big James, named for me. You were a big baby. I was not. Here you were to be loved. To be loved, baby, hard at once, and forever to strengthen you against the loveless world. Remember that. I know how black it looks today for you. It looked black that day too. Yes, we were trembling. We have not stopped trembling yet, but if we had not loved each other, none of us would have survived, and now you must survive because we love you and for the sake of your children and your children's children.

This innocent country set you down in a ghetto in which, in fact, it intended that you should perish. Let me spell out precisely what I mean by that for the heart of the matter is here and the crux of my dispute with my country. You were born and faced the future that you faced because you were black and for no other reason. The limits to your ambition were thus expected to be settled. You were born into a society which spelled out with brutal clarity and in as many ways as possible that you were a worthless human being. You were not expected to aspire to excellence. You were expected to make peace with mediocrity. Wherever you have turned, James, in your short time on this earth, you have been told where you could go and what you could do and how you could do it, where you could live and whom you could marry.

I know your countrymen do not agree with me here and I hear them saying, "You exaggerate." They do not know Harlem and I do. So do you. Take no one's word for anything, including mine, but trust your experience. Know whence you came. If you know whence you came, there is really no limit to where you can go. The details and symbols of your life have been deliberately constructed to make you believe what white people say about you. Please try to remember that what they believe, as well as what they do and cause you to endure, does not testify to your inferiority, but to their inhumanity and fear.

Please try to be clear, dear James, through the storm which rages about your youthful head today, about the reality which lies behind the words "acceptance" and "integration." There is no reason for you to try to become like white men and there is no basis whatever for their impertinent assumption that they must accept you. The really terrible thing, old buddy, is that you must accept them, and I mean that very seriously. You must accept them and accept them with love, for these innocent people have no other hope. They are in effect still trapped in a history which they do not understand and until they understand it, they cannot be released from it. They have had to believe for many years, and for innumerable reasons, that black men are inferior to white men.

Many of them indeed know better, but as you will discover, people find it very difficult to act on what they know. To act is to be committed and to be committed is to be in danger. In this case the danger in the minds and hearts of most white Americans is the loss of their identity. Try to imagine how you would feel if you woke up one morning to find the sun shivering and all the stars aflame. You would be frightened because it is out of the order of nature. Any upheaval in the universe is terrifying because it so profoundly attacks one's sense of one's own reality. Well, the black man has functioned in the white man's world as a fixed star, as an immovable pillar, and as he moves out of his place, heaven and earth are shaken to their foundations.

You don't be afraid. I said it was intended that you should perish in the ghetto, perish by never being allowed to go beyond and behind the white man's definition, by never being allowed to spell your proper name. You have, and many of us have, defeated this intention and by a terrible law, a terrible paradox, those innocents who believed that your imprisonment made them safe are losing their grasp of reality. But these men are your brothers, your lost younger brothers, and if the word "integration" means anything, this is what it means, that we with love shall force our brothers to see themselves as they are, to cease fleeing from reality and begin to change it, for this is your home, my friend. Do not be driven from it. Great men have done great things here and will again and we can make America what America must become.

It will be hard, James, but you come from sturdy peasant stock, men who picked cotton, dammed rivers, built railroads, and in the teeth of the most terrifying odds, achieved an unassailable and monumental dignity. You come from a long line of great poets, some of the greatest poets since Homer. One of them said, "The very time I thought I was lost, my dungeon shook and my chains fell off."

You know and I know that the country is celebrating one hundred years of freedom one hundred years too early. We cannot be free until they are free. God bless you, James, and Godspeed.

Your uncle,
JAMES

CHARLAYNE HUNTER

A Homecoming for the First Black Girl at the University of Georgia

Athens, Ga.

Several days after Hamilton (Hamph) Holmes and I entered the University of Georgia in 1961 under court order as its first two black students, I sat in a world-history class, fighting desperately to stay awake and avoid confirming the stereotype that all blacks are lazy. The drowsiness was the result of my first few days on campus when white students, protesting our admission, rioted outside my dormitory.

Shortly after a brick and bottle had shattered the window in my room, sending chunks of broken glass within a foot of where I was standing, Hamilton, who lived off campus, and I were suspended for our "own safety." Our lawyers got the judge who had ordered us in to order us readmitted, but the girls who lived above me—I was the sole resident on the first floor—continued for a long time to pound the floor, night after night, late into the night, and I suffered the physical and mental exhaustion of those first few days throughout the winter quarter. Somehow, it was always in this mid-morning history class that I would find myself embarrassed as my head drooped and my eyes closed.

Almost nine years later, during my first visit to the campus since graduation, I entered that same classroom—this time wide awake, and found not a course in world history, but one in African history, part of a new black-studies program; and not one exhausted black girl, but five outspoken black men and women among the students and a young black man, with a heavy Afro haircut and wearing a turtleneck sweater, teaching the course. By the end of the hour, as the white students sat quietly taking notes, the black instructor was acting as referee for two of the black students who were engaged in a vehement clash of opinion on the subject of pan-Africanism.

"You won't believe your eyes when you see the changes," a Georgia English professor had told me when I called her from New York to say that I was

Source: Miss Hunter is a reporter for *The New York Times.* This article is from *The New York Times Magazine,* Jan. 25, 1970, pp. 24, 50–65 passim. © 1970 by The New York Times Company. Reprinted by permission.

coming to Athens. Then the professor, who, when I was a student, had lived in an apartment directly across the street, which she offered as a refuge whenever I needed it, went on to issue warning: "Come on down; just remember the stir you caused last time."

We both laughed. Nonetheless, as I stepped off the bus at the dingy little station a block from the campus, I felt a slight wave of anxiety sweep over me. But before I could dwell on that, I heard someone call my name. Looking around, I saw a familiar face, although I couldn't place it.

"I thought it was you," the man said, extending his hand. "I'm Pete Sasser from the journalism school." Pete had been a student there when I entered, and although I was a journalism major, I had little contact with the students when I was there, and have had almost none since I graduated. Pete said he was on the faculty now, and invited me over to see the new journalism school. I told him that I had heard that the dean had retired, but that I hadn't known that the old building had been retired, too. We settled on 3 o'clock, which would leave me time to have lunch with some professor friends and to get from them some suggestions about whom I should see this time around. I had my own ideas about whom I did *not* want to see.

Again, at lunch, I was told how impressed I would be with the changes. One of the group, my former classics professor, Ed Best, had just returned from the University of Alabama, where he had served as a judge in the Miss Homecoming contest. Among the contestants, he told me, were a Japanese girl and a black girl with an Afro, and they both finished in the top three, although Alabama was not ready for either one to reign as queen.

"You won't find anything like that here," Dr. Best said, "but I do think you'll find some things have changed."

After lunch, armed with a list of other names and places, I left the Holiday Inn and headed across the street to the first building I had ever set foot in at the university to have a talk with the new acting dean of student affairs, a young white Alabamian named O. Suthern Sims.

On my way over, I caught a glimpse of the Kappa Alpha house. It had been one of several trouble spots which I generally tried to avoid. The fraternity brothers of K.A. could always be counted on to yell at least one mouthful of obscenities if Hamp or I was passing by their house. Most of the time, we pretended to ignore them.

But every now and then, they would rile the normally calm, easy-going Hamp, and he would say, "Just look at the way they treat that flag they're supposed to love so much," referring to the Confederate flag. "They couldn't be serious the way they leave it out in all kinds of wind and rain." Even though it was a symbol of disgust to both of us, I think Hamp would have respected them a little more if they had shown some respect for what they were supposed to cherish. Now, there it was, tattered and rotting, but still flying.

Across the street and inside the academic building where Hamp and I had registered for our first classes, Dean Sims was a welcome change from the tight-jawed, closed-minded segregationists who proceeded him. Tall and slender and articulate, he greeted me warmly and said he hoped I had so far found the university to be a lot different from what it had been when I first came. I smiled noncommittally because I had not yet talked with any of the black students on campus, and urged him, instead, to tell me if he thought it had.

"We've now moved almost 180 degrees in regard to the psychology of *in loco parentis*," he said, and proceeded to outline the liberalization that had taken place in rules for students, particularly women, which had prohibited them from living off campus, staying out past 11 P.M. and wearing slacks. I found all this interesting, since along with the loosening up had come an end to the offices of dean of men and dean of women—in my years as a student there, the very personification of *in loco parentis*, particularly for Hamp and me, their unwanted children.

When, after two and a half years in one isolated room in a freshman dormitory, I had asked for a transfer to an upper-class dorm, it was the dean of women's office that said it couldn't be done—not because of segregation, but out of "consideration." Dean Edith Stallings told Calvin Trillin, a friend who helped me maintain my sanity while covering my entrance and who came back later to write a book about it: "We don't like to put any student in a position where she's not wanted. It's not race."

Her counterpart, Dean William E. Tate, took much of the credit for "protecting" Hamp and me during our stay here. I never had much to say to him, nor he to me, but he always seemed quite fond of Hamp. I was told that he often spoke of "Holmes," telling of Hamp's initiation into Phi Beta Kappa—an invitation which Tate himself extended by letter—as if he were his own.

By the end of this year, both will have been retired. "Tate has accepted this thing beautifully," Sims said. "He has a truly wonderful capacity to adapt."

And what about the capacity of the university to adapt to the presence of black students beyond the number of two, and without pressure from the courts?

Suthern Sims paused briefly, then said: "I think you can think of the integration of blacks into the university in two ways—legally and attitudinally. There is no question in terms of all the proper compliances. I do not believe you can find any forms of racial segregation that you can take any legal action against. I've looked for it, especially in student affairs. It's just not there."

He went on to outline the areas governed by Federal compliance regulations: "We will not list an apartment or job unless a compliance form is signed. We don't have any black rooms like they once had. To the best of my knowledge that stopped in '67." (My mind flashed back to my senior year when I had wanted Donald Hollowell, our lawyer, to go back to court for an order to desegregate the dorms. At that time, he had so many civil-rights cases pending, including some of Dr. Martin Luther King's, that he just didn't have the time and probably thought it wasn't worth it. I think the black students who eventually did have to push it five years later would have disagreed.)

In addition, Sims pointed out, of a total of 200 resident advisers—young women who live in the dorms, are paid $650 a year and offer nonprofessional guidance to their fellow students—five are black. "We hired every one that applied," Sims said, not altogeher unconscious of the two ways in which the remark could be taken.

"As to attitude," Sims said slowing down a little, "I can't measure it." Then he brought up the subject of the Black Student Union. In nine years, the university population has increased from about 7,200 students to about 18,000, with the number of blacks growing from two to "approximately 125" (no one admits to knowing for sure just how many black students there are). About 75 blacks are undergraduates, and of the total—including graduate students—about 30 belong to the B.S.U. For two consecutive years, the group has presented demands to the university administration.

"I think what they're really talking about is attitude, and this is a tough one," Sims said. "This might sound awfully inept, but I think it's improving. This current generation is the finest generation of college students that this country has ever seen. They've been more right about more issues than any before them. And here is where I think you'll find the meshing of legality and attitude."

He continued: "Our blacks come in and they're experiencing disgust and hostility, and it becomes really a paradox—'You do something about it now,' they say. But we can't just unilaterally rule against attitude. That's a fascist state." Back to 1961, in my memory: the white students who vowed not to accept desegregation, despite the fact that it was "being shoved down our throats." "You can't legislate morality," they were fond of saying.

Sims' personal assessment of the B.S.U. was, in general, favorable. He was but one of several administrators who conceded that without its pressure, some of the changes that were taking place within the university "probably wouldn't have happened so fast."

"I think I understand what they want," Sims said finally. "They want role models, not tokens." Then he pointed out what he considered gains in that area—blacks hold clerical positions throughout the university; there is even one in administration; there are black "public-safety officers." There are the five resident advisers.

But there were some ideas proposed by the B.S.U. that Dean Sims simply could not reconcile with his own personal code. He said they had asked for a separate dormitory and had refused to bring the organization officially on campus because they did not want to sign the compliance. "They told me frankly that, if they signed the compliance, they'd have to let whites in, and they don't want that.

"I make no bones about it. I'm an integrationist, not a separatist, because if you buy the separatist bag in the South, you positively re-enforce the white supremists. And to buy that would be to step back 75 years."

Next day, I stopped by the office of the dean of arts and sciences. He was not in, so I talked briefly with his assistant, Dr. Charles Wynes. Dr. Wynes had been in the history department when I was a student; since then, he has written a book, "The Negro in America Since 1865."

Dr. Wynes said that the university has really moved fast over the past few years. As evidence of the growth, he cited an appropriation by the State Legislature to increase the faculty by more than 500, citing it as "a breakthrough for educational excellence."

As I stood to leave, it occurred to me to ask Dr. Wymes how many of the 500 new faculty members were blacks. He said there was one, Dr. Richard Graham, a musical therapist.

My next stop was at the building where Dean Sims had told me I could find Ben Colebert, a young black who is also a kind of first. Although he is a graduate student in the art department, he is the first black admissions counselor, and it is his job to travel throughout the state to recruit black students.

A handsome medium brown, with a quiet Afro, Colebert, who is 27, moved with ease in what I was surprised to find was the office of M. O. Phelps. At the time Hamp and I were trying to get in, Phelps was freshman admissions counselor. I didn't have any problems with him in person, but he was one of a panel of three administrators who decided, on the basis of their interview with Hamp, that he was "not a suitable candidate" for admission.

In addition to the fact that he did not say "Sir," they said that he slumped in his chair, gave short answers to their questions, mumbled when he spoke and left them with "some doubt about his truthfulness." Hamp had a slight speech impediment, which often caused him to stutter or hesitate before he spoke.

Colebert said Phelps "admitted he had some prejudices," but that among the many dinner invitations he and his wife had received was one from Phelps.

"They really smoked me over," Ben said when I asked how he got the job. "I think they wanted to see how militant I was, but right away I knew I was the kind of nigger they wanted. In 1959, I did sit-ins, when I was an undergraduate at Savannah State. But that was a decade ago, and I don't have my master's yet, so I made myself very attractive to them."

Ben and I are the same age, and when he was sitting in at lunch counters in Savannah, I had just applied to the university. By the time I was admitted, it was 1961, and Ben, like me, would have been a sophomore. But he told me during my visit that he was encountering among black high-school students in the state the same problem he had had—as late as the year we graduated: "I simply didn't know the school existed, and neither do they."

Once they know, there is the problem of money. Even though the university is state-supported, expenses for an on-campus student can be $2,000 a year or more. "It *does* cost a lot of money," Ben said, "but there's a lot in this institution that needs to be channeled into the black community. The black community pays taxes, and supports this school." He added that 80 per cent of the black students at the university receive either work-study or graduate assistanceships or Federal aid. "If you have the guts to come here in the first place, then you got it made," he said.

(That wasn't necessarily so in my case, despite the rumor that the N.A.A.C.P. was paying me $50 a day. If I had been in it for the money that would hardly have been enough, but the rumor was totally groundless. The N.A.A.C.P. Legal Defense and Educational Fund donated its talents to fight our legal battles—but its support ended there, as it should have. Carl Holman, my closest friend, now a vice president of the National Urban Coalition, who was then a professor at Clark College and the editor of The Atlanta Inquirer, managed each quarter through friends to wangle some money from such groups as the Elks of Memphis, who paid the $83 a quarter or thereabouts for my room in the dormitory. And sometimes I made money speaking, although most of those engagements were for church groups that paid with "Praise the Lord" and "God bless you."

(It never occurred to me to apply for a job on campus, although I had worked at Wayne State University before I transferred. And I'm not sure that with all the other pressures at that time I would have been able to handle a job, too. Nor did I think of applying for any kind of loan or aid. Having had to force my way in, I guess I couldn't imagine their doing anything to help me stay.)

Admission requirements have stood in the way of black applicants, according to Ben Colebert. For starters, a combined score of 900 on the nationwide Scholastic Aptitude Test (S.A.T.) is required, in addition to a B-plus average. "The black school system just hasn't been geared toward passing these tests," he explained. "In a dual school system, black kids don't usually even come out with a foreign language. These tests are geared for kids who go to white, middle-class high schools. If a black kid does succeed in making 900 on the S.A.T., you know he could have made 1,500 with the proper background."

Most white students are, in addition, more test-conscious than blacks, having prepared for at least a couple of years for the S.A.T. by taking old tests and using books with prepared tests in them. My high school was one of the few black schools that did that when I was preparing for college. We had sessions for several weeks, on Saturday mornings, but my scores were still horrible. Fortunately, I never made below a B in any of my courses, and graduated third in my class. This, according to Colebert, would make a difference today, even with a low score.

At present, the mean score for the entire university for boys is 1,050, and for girls, about 1,060. "Less than half of 1 per cent" of the black students, according to Colebert, have even a 900 score. Their presence is the result of an admissions committee's recommendations. "The university does make some concessions," Colebert said.

I asked him about the football players—whites, many of whom could barely speak English. Surely they didn't have 900 S.A.T. scores. Colebert laughed. "We don't get into that," he said.

Because of inferior preparation, many black students have difficulties with their courses, particularly English—a bane to most Southern freshmen, regardless of color. Many of them flunked out. The B.S.U. demanded that they be readmitted, and that some special counseling program be set up. President Fred C. Davison responded in this way: "The admission and readmission policies of the university are conducted without regard to race. The proposal to readmit all black students who have flunked out of the university is not only educationally unsound but it, too, could be challenged on the grounds of racial discrimination. Moreover, such a policy would result in a serious impairment of academic standards of the university."

Ben does not think that the liberal grants to black students will continue for long—"particularly if they get a lot of black students." However, he plans to continue recruiting. "It *is* ironic," he said as I was leaving, "that now that the University of Georgia is concerned with admitting black students, comes the insurgence of pride in black institutions and black environments."

"How do you deal with that?" I asked.

"The only thing I tell them is that you get more awareness of being black here than in a black institution where it's taken for granted." It was a theme that I later heard expressed again and again by black students here.

Gradually, I made my way to the history department, which houses the black-studies program. I knew that there I would get not only some idea about the program, but also would probably run into some of the black students. Although 125 certainly increased the odds of coming across a black student, they still manage to get lost on the sprawling campus among 18,000 whites.

While waiting for Dr. David Foley, the young white professor in charge of the program, I looked at the paper. That morning, The Athens Daily News carried the headline: "Black Studies Panel Hears Local Professor," with a story out of Atlanta, which began: "While most speakers agreed Monday that more emphasis on black studies is needed in the state's public schools, a University of Georgia department head said this might result in building 'feelings of superiority among blacks.'" The man, who was quoted later in the story as saying that Negro history taught distinctly "could backfire badly," is chairman of the social studies department.

Dr. Foley, who taught for three years at the University of Sierra Leone, turned out to be pleasant, enthusiastic and intensely pleased with himself. "In most universities," he said, "whites ignore the existence of black culture. They're not anti—they just spend their time saying, 'What a wonderful fellow I am.' This is more degrading than anything. I don't know whether a black would like somebody to just come up and whack 'im one or ignore him."

Foley feels that students "cannot understand the demands or aspirations of Afro-Americans without an understanding of the black man as the inheritor of African culture." As for his own preparation, he said, "I'd like to think my two years in Africa helped me to rap here."

Downstairs, in an African history classroom, Anderson Williams, a young black graduate assistant who had just passed his Ph.D. orals, was lecturing on the "strong indigenous civilization in Africa that began a thousand years before the Europeans came to the continent."

After the class ended, I introduced myself to the black students sitting in front of me, and invited them to have lunch with me. Anderson Williams joined us, and we drove to a steak house in town—one of many that did not serve black people when I graduated.

On the way out, Benny Roberson, a junior from Athens, majoring in anthropology, started to chuckle. "Charlayne Hunter. You know how I remember you so well? The day you entered Georgia and all that stuff was going on with you, I started getting ready to go to town, and my mamma said, 'Boy, you are not going *nowhere* near that town *today*.' And I sat back down."

"When I first came here," said Joe Sales, a handsome senior from Columbus, Ga., who reminded me of Hamp, "I knew every black student on the yard, but not now."

Russell Williams, a graduate student who had been at the university off and on, having started his freshman year when I was a senior, concurred, and added, "There are even some black students nobody knows."

They explained that, although they and about 30 other black students belonged to the B.S.U., the majority did not. And while, they said, many of those who were not members sympathized, there were others who would not have anything to do with them.

Then Joe said: "You see, there's a basic division between those students who come from predominantly black schools and people who went to a white high school. The ones who went to a white high school are more willing to relate."

"Still," Russell interjected, "even those who participate are, at best, being tolerated. Those are the ones who catch it from both ends."

It was clear that my luncheon companions had no plans to get involved in university life or activities. I asked why. They all started to speak at once. Joe, who emerged strongest, said, "We tried it, but after all this time, we still feel like aliens in a strange land."

They explained that the B.S.U. was formed in 1967 because of that. "At first," Joe continued, "it just provided a social outlet—black-oriented functions. We would all meet at Bob Benham's house and party. It got to be known as 'The Black House.'"

Benham, now in his last year of law school, had been president of the

B.S.U. when it presented a list of 22 demands to the university—the first step the B.S.U. took after its members realized that 'partying all the time wasn't going to lead to any change in our lives within the university."

"The first year, we were concerned with getting a fair break," Joe explained. "We asked for things like an end to discrimination in housing—black people always ended up in the same rooms—and an end to discrimination in employment—as usual, they try to token you to death. We asked for a wider range of things because the whole idea was not just to represent the militants, but to represent a wide range of political opinion. Like, I'm not interested in fraternities, but the brother here is."

In that connection they asked for a ban on racist fraternities—specifically K.A. "There are still incidents in front of that house," they told me. "Black women are constantly subjected to all kinds of verbal abuse and getting things thrown at them."

During the next year, an expanded set of demands was presented to the university—some in the same vein as the previous year, but some more militant. Some of their optimism had waned. A young freshman from Atlanta, James Hurley, had gone out for football. He made the freshman team, the Bullpups, but as the year wore on and he began looking with anticipation toward playing with the Bulldogs, a sympathetic coach called him aside one day and told him that Georgia would probably dress him, but that if he was really serious about playing football, he'd better look elsewhere. (Subsequently Vanderbilt offered him a scholarship—and a chance to play—and he took it.)

Among the new demands that year was one for the establishment of a black dormitory. "If asking for an end to discrimination in housing one year, and a black dormitory the next sounds contradictory, it's not," Joe said. Then, talking all at once, they said that the demand was the logical next step to take with a university that says one thing, but does another.

Earlier, Ben Colebert had said it bothered him that some black students would want to request such a thing, but added, "The University should spend less of its energies condemning it, and more trying to find out why they want it." One indication of why might be revealed in the letter President Davison wrote to Benham in response to the demands. The letter, dated March 8, 1969, stated, in part:

"As for the recruitment of athletes, Athletic Director Evans has advised all coaches by memorandum that the university would recruit regardless of race, creed, or color. A Negro student has been designated to receive a tuition and books scholarship in the spring quarter if he is academically eligible to compete. To date, six Negro athletes have been offered full scholarships (three in football, two in track and one in basketball) or would have been had they been academically eligible. . . ." This sounded vaguely reminiscent of the series of technicalities on which Hamilton and I were denied admission to the university for a year and a half.

On K.A., President Davison wrote: "Kappa Alpha . . . is a duly constituted and recognized social fraternity and is in compliance with the provision of the department of student activities. The university cannot arbitrarily abolish such an organization."

It seemed almost as if the incidence of racism had risen in direction proportion to the number of blacks on campus. Joe put it this way: "To me racism is when you take English 101 and have to read 'Heart of Darkness,' and I point out that it's racist, just like 'Othello,' and the teacher takes points off my essay for it. In short, when you're looking at things from a black perspective, they can't understand it."

Several students at different times told me of a psychology professor who, upon seeing two black girls in his class, launched into a discussion of the high incidence of crime, illegitimacy, syphillis and gonorrhea among black people, and ended by saying that he knew of at least two people who were going to flunk the course. The girls withdrew from the class.

In some instances, escape was not so easy. One sociology major told me of a course required for a master's in his field. It was called "Community Reconnaissance." He was told that he could not take the course that time around because it involved a field trip to Oglethorpe County, where the class was to survey community leaders on what they felt was wrong with their communities.

The student, Leonard Lester, called Pie by the other blacks, said that he suspected there weren't any black leaders in the area, but he demanded that he be allowed to take the course. When an alternative—not involving the community reconnaissance—was offered, Pie said: "The professor told me, 'I understand your problem, but sometimes you have to go in the back door.'"

Pie went on: "I blew my stack. Then I went to the head of the department and they finally found some Negroes for me in the county. One was a black school principal, who wouldn't consent to the interview until I shaved my beard off." Pie subsequently dropped out of the university. He said he "just couldn't take it any more."

"The thing about segs," Bob Benham said to me later, "is that they're a lot more sophisticated than they used to be when you were a student. Last year, for instance, I belonged to the Demosthenian Society, and I was elected to the office of custodian. It was my duty to procure things for the organization, open up, and so on. One of the members was Albert Saye, a political-science professor and one of the most notorious segs around. He responded by proposing that the custodian be paid a salary of $20 a quarter."

Bob says he's given up "trying to get along with honkies." Last summer, he, along with several of his classmates, served as an intern in the office of Gov. Lester Maddox. He says he enjoyed it, but he doesn't think he could do it again.

"Time was, when a guy slipped and said 'colored' you'd consider it an accident and let him slide." Benham said. "You excused it even when you showed up for class in a shirt and tie and they responded by saying, 'Hi ya doin', preacher?' Or you'd try to study with them, and the first thing they're talking about was sex and how they'd like a black woman. Then you realize that their attitude toward blacks is still that the majority of them are low-life, slimy dogs, and I'm the exception. Their Booker T."

Although the black students say that what is called a black-studies program this year is what the school already had, plus two new courses, and that it doesn't tell blacks anything they don't already know, they are at least partially responsible for that much of a beginning.

Also, they are responsible for the removal of the segregated bathroom signs. Penny Mickelbury, a striking dark-skinned girl from Atlanta with a Kathleen Cleaver-style Afro, said that she and "a group of the brothers and sisters," went into a university cafeteria "determined that those signs were going to come down." They walked to the head of the food lines, she said, and simply refused to move.

I marveled at the story, even up to this point, since this was a cafeteria frequented by many of the Bulldogs. In my day, Bulldogs were known for their pugnacious character.

At any rate, a few of these types, according to Penny, took exception, and although there's some question as to who actually landed the first blow, it wasn't long before the cafeteria was in an uproar. Most of the whites and a few of the blacks left. Penny and a "few of the brothers," including Pie, remained to do battle.

"I climbed up on top of a table and started throwing forks and knives and trays," she recalled. "Anything I could get my hands on. That's one of the reasons they leave us alone. They think we're crazy. Imagine. Thirty black kids got 18,000 honkies scared to death."

Because at least a few of the black students make no secret of their readiness to retaliate, "much of the harassment" they say, "has all but disappeared." And despite the fact that the average black student does not participate in the B.S.U., many have benefitted from their protests. Bendelle Love, a young resident adviser in an all-white dorm, is there as a result of B.S.U. demands. She says she works nearly 40 hours a week advising others on their problems and that, because of the time consumed between that and her studies, she just doesn't have time for meetings. Of her own situation, she says: "There's no static."

Others, I think, feel there are some benefits. Pie and Floyd Williams, a graduate student in art, debated the point one evening. Pie said that all he wants to be is a soldier in the revolution. But Floyd argued that the revolution needs professionals—doctors, lawyers, technicians, even sociologists. The struggle, he said, benefits from those who know well their opposition.

But even the most militant of the black students say that things have improved "a little bit." Some say that the number of whites they can talk to is increasing.

I was, of course, particularly curious about how the white students felt about the blacks. In my own time, I had felt that most of them were too pre-occupied with fraternity and sorority parties really to concern themselves about us. And from what I was able to glean from various sources, this is still pretty much the case now.

Rebecca Leet, a junior from Atlanta and news editor of The Red and Black, said that she had talked to many white students who had come from integrated high schools, so that they did not consider Georgia's desegregation unusual. (High-school desegregation began the year after my entrance at the university.) "I just sort of don't feel anything toward them" one freshman from a small Georgia town told her adding: "But I don't feel anything against them." She said she saw "discrimination emanating, to some extent, from the way people talk about them and stuff."

A prelaw senior said that he had been disappointed last year when he tried to "get a human-relations seminar started." He said it was "a shock to him" that black students wouldn't accept him as being sincerely interested. "What do you do when you're sitting there and you are sincere and he doesn't believe you? Where do you go?" he asked.

(I recalled the all too numerous occasions when I was expected to provide easy answers to such questions as "What can we do?" so that they could go out and say, "Negroes say they want. . . .")

But charges made by the B.S.U. are confirmed unintentionally in other circumstances by white students who are neither pro nor con. "I wouldn't be comfortable if I were black on this campus," one white student said. "There's an awful lot of discrimination. It's just the way people have been raised to feel about blacks," he said.

At the end of my visit, of all the people I talked with, Joe Sales, the student who reminded me of Hamp, and Andy Williams, the graduate instructor in the African history class, are on my mind. Both bright and articulate, and by no means crazy—by my standards, at least—they came to the university under no other pressure than the knowledge of their communities that one of theirs had made it to a white school.

Now, with most of that behind them, they are disillusioned. "You'd have a lot more militant black people if they attended schools like this," Joe said. He also said: "A lot of things have happened that made me develop negative attitudes about whites that will be with me the rest of my life.

"Nothing here balances out the things I lost—like the inability to keep up with the tempo of the black community. Like I go home now, and I don't feel the same sense of belonging."

Andy feels that way, too, but desperately wants to "return to a black environment." If offered a job at the university, he says, he wouldn't take it. "I just couldn't function, because I think of the question Malcolm X raised and answered: 'You know what they call a black Ph.D.?'

" 'Nigger.' "

It has been more than six years since I left the University of Georgia and the South, and I am still weighing the things I lost against the things I gained. At one point, I even spent six months in graduate school because I felt I needed to fill in the gaps from the education I received from Georgia. Yet, before the six months were over, I realized that the education I received outside the classroom more than made up for what was lost inside. And, maybe, Joe and Andy will experience this, too.

They were not "firsts" in the sense that Hamp and I were firsts. So they are not getting the positive attention that we received from throughout the world. I would be less than honest if I did not admit that many ways were paved for me, at least, because I was a first. (Hamp now has his medical degree and is serving as an Army doctor in Germany.)

But they did come to the university out of the same backgrounds as Hamp and I, children of the black *bourgeoisie*, mentally, or in fact, protected by the same system that discriminated against us. Joe and Andy are appalled at the treatment they are receiving at the University of Georgia because for the first time in their lives, they are feeling it personally. Discrimination through separate and unequal schooling is not something you feel personally.

I remember resenting to the point of being rude that almost my only visitors in my dormitory were the girls whom no man would look at twice, the wallflowers who came because they had no Saturday dates, the overweight, the bookworms or the religious nuts. Not that there weren't exceptions—and some wonderful ones. But the former were the rule. And often, listening to records at night and dancing with the closet door, I would ignore their knocks because I found the whole charade disgusting.

And yet, I stayed, partly because I knew the world was watching. I think that, at that time, such a commitment was necessary. But the need is greater now, precisely because the world isn't watching. The move of black students to black colleges is fine for those who can afford it. But Benny Roberson lives here in Athens, where there is no black college, and he can't afford to go out of town. Things for blacks may improve now, not because the world is watching, but because there are more Benny Robersons.

The University of Georgia may not have prepared its black students for life in the orthodox way we have come to expect universities to do. But if they leave still unsatisfied with the treatment they received as blacks in a microcosmic white society, then I think the university will have succeeded far better than they may be able to realize now.

PETER SCHRAG

The Decline of the WASP

For most of us who were born before World War II, America was a place to be discovered; it was imperfect, perhaps—needed some reform, some shaping up—but it did not need to be reinvented. It was, all given, like a genetic code, waiting to unfold. We all wanted to learn the style, the proper accent, agreed on its validity, and while our interpretations and our heroes varied, they were all cut from the same stock. Cowboys, pioneers, athletes, entrepreneurs, men of letters: whatever we were offered we took pretty much as our own. Whether we were small-town boys or the children of urban immigrants, we shared an eagerness to become apprentices in the great open democracy, were ready to join up, wanting only to be accepted according to the terms that history and tradition had already established. It never occurred to us to think otherwise.

What held that world together was not just a belief in some standardized version of textbook Americanism, a catalogue of accepted values, but a particular class of people and institutions that we identified with our vision of the country. The people were white and Protestant; the institutions were English; American culture was WASP. We paid lip service to the melting pot, but if, for instance, one's grandmother asked, "Is it good for the Jews?" there wasn't any question in her mind about who was running the country. The critics, the novelists, the poets, the social theorists, the men who articulated and analyzed American ideas, who governed our institutions, who embodied what we were or hoped to be—nearly all of them were WASPs: Hemingway, Fitzgerald, Eliot, MacLeish, Sandburg, Lewis, Steinbeck, Dewey, Santayana, the Jameses, Beard, Parrington, Edmund Wilson, Van Wyck Brooks, Lester Frank Ward, Oliver Wendell Holmes; *The Saturday Evening Post* under George Horace Lorimer (with covers by Norman Rockwell); *The Atlantic* under Edward Weeks; *Harper's* in the days of Frederick Lewis Allen—to name only a few, and only from the twentieth century. Of all the major figures discussed by Henry Steele Commager in *The American Mind,* not one is a Jew, a Catholic, or a Negro. The American mind was the WASP mind.

We grew up with them; they surrounded us: they were the heroes of the

Source: Reprinted from *Harper's Magazine,* April 1970, pp. 85–91, by permission of Curtis Brown, Ltd. Copyright © 1970 by Peter Schrag.

history we studied and of the fantasy life we sought in those Monday-through-Friday radio serials. Even Hollywood, after all the creation of Jewish producers, never did much for pluralism. The stars were often ethnics—show business and sports constituting two major avenues for "outsiders" to make it into the mainstream—but their names and the roles they played rarely, if ever, acknowledged the existence of anything beyond that mainstream. The Hyman Kaplans were lovable jerks, immigrant Sambos; Rochester said, "Yassuh, Mr. Benny" (did we realize that Benny was a Jew?) and anything beginning with Mike, Pat, or Abie was set up for a laugh. Hollywood's Jews sold the American dream strictly in WASP terms.

They—the WASPs—never thought of themselves as anything but Americans, nor did it occur to others to label them as anything special until, about twenty-five years ago, their influence began to decline and they started to lose their cultural initiative and preeminence. There were, to be sure, regional distinctions, but whatever was "American" was WASP. Indeed, there was no "other"—was, that is, no domestic base of social commentary, no voice except their voice, for the discussion of "American" problems. The ethnics had their place and their strong loyalties, but insofar as that place was *American* it was defined by WASPs. We could distinguish Jews, Irishmen, Italians, Catholics, Poles, Negroes, Indians, Mexican-Americans, Japanese-Americans but not WASPs. When WASPs were alienated it was because, as in the case of Henry Adams, the country had moved away from them, not because, as with the others, they regarded themselves as alien in heritage or tradition. (Southerners who had lost their war and their innocence were—in that respect—alien, ethnically WASPs but also in some sense unwilling immigrants; they were among the first to be out of place in their own country.) For most WASPs, their complaints were proprietary. That is, the old place was going down because the tenants weren't keeping it up properly. They were the landlords of our culture, and their values, with rare exceptions, were those that defined it: hard work, perseverance, self-reliance, puritanism, the missionary spirit, and the abstract rule of law.

They are, of course, still with us—in corporations and clubs, in foundations and universities, in government and the military, maintaining the interlocking directorates that make sociologists salivate and that give the Establishment its ugly name: the Power Structure, the Military-Industrial Complex; the rulers of America. But while they still hold power, they hold it with less assurance and with less legitimacy than at any time in history. They are hanging on, men living off their cultural capital, but rarely able or willing to create more. One can almost define their domains by locating the people and institutions that are chronically on the defensive: university presidents and trustees; the large foundations; the corporations; government; the military. They grew great as initiators and entrepreneurs. They invented the country, its culture and its values; they shaped the institutions and organizations. Then they drew the institutions around themselves, moved to the suburbs, and became org-men.

Who and what has replaced them, then, in the invention and production of our culture? Jews and Negroes, Catholics and immigrants. "Of the Americans who have come into notice during the past fifty years as poets, as novelists, as critics, as painters, as sculptors, and in the minor arts," wrote Henry Mencken in 1924, "less than half bear Anglo-Saxon names. . . . So in the sciences, so in the higher reaches of engineering and technology. . . ." Mencken's declaration was premature then; it is an understatement now: Mailer and Roth; Malamud and Bellow; Ellison and Baldwin; Edward Teller and Robert Oppenheimer and Wernher von Braun; Ralph Nader and Cesar Chavez; Noam Chomsky and Allen Ginsberg; John Rock and Jonas Salk; Paul Goodman and Herbert Marcuse; Bruno Bettelheim and Erik Erikson; Eldridge Cleaver and Malcolm X and Martin Luther King. The 1969 Pulitzer Prize for nonfiction was divided between a Jew from Brooklyn (Mailer) and a French immigrant (René Dubos); the Pulitzer Prize for fiction was awarded to an American Indian (Scott Momaday). The spokesmen of American literature and culture tend increasingly to represent the pluralistic residues of a melting pot that—for better or worse—never worked as well as some Americans had hoped. It is not simply that many of the major postwar journals of criticism—*Commentary, The New York Review of Books, The New American Review*—are edited by Jews, or that *Time* is edited by a Jewish refugee from Hitler, or that *The Saturday Evening Post* is dead, or that the function of radical muckraking was revitalized by *Ramparts*, originally established as a Catholic magazine, or that William Buckley, a Catholic, is the most articulate conservative in America; we do, after all, still have WASP writers and journals —*Foreign Affairs*, for example, and *The Atlantic* (not to mention *Life* or *Reader's Digest*). It is, rather, that the style, ideas, traumas, perplexities, and passions tend to reflect other backgrounds and interests, and that the integrative capabilities of the WASP style have plunged into precipitous decline. The cultural issues of the 1960s enjoying the greatest cachet were not only ethnic and pluralistic, but also disintegrative—Alienation, the Identity Crisis, Black Power, Doing Your Own Thing, Dropping Out, the White Negro—and it seemed that any kind of material was acceptable as long as it was distinguishable from the old WASP mainstream: the life of the black ghetto, rock music and long hair and pot, Hindu gurus and Zen philosophers, Cuban guerrillas and Catholic radicals, black hustlers and Jewish anarchists. (The first thing I learned, coming from Brooklyn to Amherst in 1949 was that you didn't say "Bullshit" when you disagreed with someone, even your roommate. You said "Yes, but . . ." Now bullshit is back in style.) For the young, the chief villainy of the age is to be uptight, and who seems to them more uptight than WASPs, or the Jews and Irishmen trying to be like them? The 1960s was the decade of gaps—missile gaps, credibility gaps, generation gaps—when we became, in many respects, a nation of outsiders, a country in which the mainstream, however mythic, lost its compelling energy and its magnetic attraction. Now that the New Frontier and the Great Society have failed (not only as programs but as verbal rituals) so, at least for the moment, has the possibility of integration and, with it, traditional Americanism. The Average Man has become the Silent Majority. Both of these, of course, are merely convenient political fiction, but the change in labels points to a far deeper crisis of belief.

It is not that WASPs lack power and representation—or numbers—but that the once-unquestioned assumptions on which that power was based have begun to lose their hold. The foundation of WASP dominance in national politics and culture rested on the supposition that WASPdom was the true America, no subculture or special group. Now WASPs are beset by the need to enforce allegiance to something that their very place in power is supposed to take for granted. The problem is then compounded: government can become increasingly gray, trying to represent (or not to offend) "all the people," or it can begin to act as the voice of a distinctive group (the Forgotten Man, the Silent Majority)—in other words, to represent the majority as if it were a minority. (There is a third alternative, which I'll discuss later.) Nixon, characteristically, is trying to do both. When he was first elected in 1968 he brought to Washington a Cabinet of nonentities selected, it seemed, to illustrate the fix we were in: Winton Blount, Clifford Hardin, Maurice Stans, Walter Hickel, the old Agnew. (The exceptions—neither was then a regular Cabinet member—were Daniel Patrick Moynihan, an Irishman, and Henry Kissinger, a Central European immigrant.) They were men without visible personality, class, or place. Something of the same was true in Washington under Eisenhower, but then the Eisenhower atmosphere was tempered by an older lingering sense of independence, of region, a sense—finally—of principle. John Foster Dulles may have been a dangerous moralist, a stubborn Puritan, but he was not plastic. Nixon brought with him no John McCloy, no John Gardner, no Nelson Rockefeller (let alone a George C. Marshall or a Henry Stimson from an even earlier era of WASP assertion) nor does he carry Eisenhower's aura of small-town decency. (Eisenhower's men, like Nixon's, were or are institutional men, but many of them came from a tradition of "service" in which the social purposes of institutions tended to be more important than the problems of management.) We now have a government of "low profiles," gray men who represent no identifiable place, no region, no program. The security of the historic WASP position made regional roots and styles attractive; you weren't just an American but an American from a specific place, with a personality, with foibles and prejudices and attitudes. You didn't have to prove you were a WASP. But where is Nixon from? In what accent does he speak? What is his style, what are his convictions, even his hobbies? Nixon's campaign, his public conduct, and his tastes reflect not only the corporate-organization-man residue of WASPishness; they also symbolize the new insecurity of the mainstream culture.

There are advantages in all this: gray men are not crusaders; they don't speak about massive retaliation or final solutions (or, on the other hand, to be sure, the Great Society). But they are likely to regard any sort of noise as offensive and possibly dangerous. For a moment this afforded us some fun (Spiro Who?), but then Nixon, through the offices of Agnew and Mitchell, turned this quality of his Administration into a serious matter. The noise (of students, of Black Power, of protest) was, and is, scaring them. And for the first time in history—certainly for the first time since the 1920s—the majority has begun to act like a minority, like an ethnic group. The powerful are paranoid about the weak. (And needless to say, many ethnic groups are acting more like ethnic groups than they have at any time since the melting pot was pronounced a success.) This is what makes Agnew potentially more dangerous than Joe McCarthy. McCarthy's quarrels, finally, were those of an outsider attacking the Establishment, and the Establishment, which was still running the country, despite a bad case of nerves, ultimately put him down. But Agnew, Mitchell, and Nixon *are* the government, and among their most important targets are people who have no money, little organization, and access to nothing except the streets. The threat represented by Nixon's targets is not that of a foreign power, but that of a culture or cultures at odds with the mainstream. Inquisitions and witch-hunts generally mark the end, or the beginning of the end, of an age.

One of the major attributes of the WASP idiom was its self-confidence in its own Americanism. In following the ethic of the small town, in trying to make it, the WASP was operating in a system designed by his people, operated by his people, and responsive to his people. He wasn't trying to stand somebody else's ground or beat somebody else's game. But what is there for a nation that is urban (or suburban), in which the majority has (presumably) already made it, and where size and technology are rendering much of the system impersonal and unresponsive? It is no longer possible for anyone to control the country (or the world) as we once believed we could. With the exception of the balanced ticket (in politics or employment) we have no urban ethic. And so somewhere the self-confidence froze: what in the national spirit and imagery was expansive became conservative and restrictive, enterprise turned to management, ebullience to caution. Most of all, it tended to become dull. One of the most graphic illustrations of these differences in spirit is to be found in a book by John McPhee, *Levels of the Game*, an account of a tennis match between the Negro Arthur Ashe (then the highest-ranking American) and the WASP Clark Graebner (Shaker Heights suburban, churchy, the son of a dentist). Graebner speaks:

I've never been a flashy stylist, like Arthur. I'm a fundamentalist. Arthur is a bachelor. I am married and a conservative. I'm interested in business, in the market, in children's clothes. It affects the way you play the game. He's not a steady player. He's a wristy slapper. Sometimes he doesn't even know where the ball is going. . . . I've never seen Arthur really discipline himself. He plays the

game with the lackadaisical, haphazard mannerisms of a liberal. He's an underprivileged type who worked his way up. . . . There is something about him that
is swashbuckling, loose. He plays the way he thinks. My style is playmaking—
consistent, percentage tennis—and his style is shotmaking.

Ashe speaks:

There is not much variety in Clark's game. It is steady, accurate, and conservative.
He makes few errors. He plays stiff, compact Republican tennis.

Blacks, of course, can be disciplined grubbers as much as anyone else, and
WASPs certainly never used to lack for swashbuckling types—soldiers, tycoons,
ball players, frontiersmen, outlaws. Ashe, obviously, had to grub a lot harder
than any white man to break into the big time, or to become a player at all,
but he now manages his games with an aristocratic flair, not with what seems
to be bourgeois lack of grace. But Graebner's description is otherwise right: he
plays percentage tennis, Ashe takes chances. WASPs have learned to live by
percentages "steady" (as Ashe says), "accurate, stiff, compact." A little uptight. In taking risks there is more to lose than to gain.

A lot of people, needless to say, have only barely made it, or haven't made
it at all: prominent among them Negroes, Puerto Ricans, Poles, Irishmen,
Italians, and a good number of underclass WASPs.

For them the decline in confidence tends to be traumatic. At the very
moment that they are persuaded, or forced to believe, that the system will
work for them—that they can make it, that their children must go to college,
and all the rest—the signals from headquarters become confused and indistinct, and the rules seem to change. The children of the affluent march in
the streets; long hair and at least the outward signals of sexual freedom are
acceptable; hard work, stoicism, and perseverance aren't the ultimate values;
individual initiative is not sufficient; the schools are "in trouble." The cultural
colonies, forced by "modernization" (the supermarket, urban renewal, auto-
mated equipment, Vatican II) to abandon their own styles of life—the hierarchical family, ward politics, closed unions, old neighborhoods, religion,
language, food—become witnesses to behavior indicating that the (perhaps
mythic) mainstream has begun to stagnate, that a lot of people no longer
believe in it, or no longer believe in the old ways of getting there. Those on
the move upward and outward have, in other words, no attractive place to go.
Which is to say that the underclass tenants have discovered the neglect of
the landlord.

Blacks are alienated because they have been kept out of the running. The
white ethnics are frustrated because public attention, in defiance of the rhetoric
of individual initiative and equality, has gone to blacks. (And because affluent
WASPs, who had discriminated against all minorities, are trying to shift the
burden of blame on the white underclass.) All of them, sensing the decline
of WASP self-confidence and leadership, are left with choices among law and
order (meaning militant normalcy, the old ethic), a return to their own

cultural and political resources, or exotic combinations of the two. Following the lead, and to their eyes, success, of Black Power and Black Studies, a lot of minorities are trying to redevelop or to invent some exactly corresponding form of ethnic consciousness for themselves. Most of the whites, however, are or in the end will be content to cheer on the cops. For the first time we have Polish vigilantes and a Hebrew posse (the Jewish Defense League). Blacks and honkies, talking like frontiersmen, are buying guns. If the old WASP ethic was the ethic of making it, it isn't surprising that the most militant contemporary exponents of that ethic—those inclined to take its legends of force and action literally—should be among people outside the system trying to break in.

A measure of the decline of the WASP style—perhaps the best measure we have—is the conquest of space. From Lindbergh to NASA (or from Jack Armstrong to Neil Armstrong), from the man who was still a conqueror trusting his own bets and his own skills, and therefore an underdog (no dry runs, no simulators, no mission control) to the org-man, programmed and computerized to the last $24-billion step and the last televised statement, betting his life on the competence and devotion of anonymous technicians: courageous yes, underdog never. A symbol of modern man, to be sure (what if the trains stop or the electricity fails, what if the water becomes polluted and poisonous?), but also a sign of the decline of the great old WASP virtues of self-reliance, initiative, irreverence. Lindbergh was free enterprise; Apollo was the work of a crowd. No ape could have flown the *Spirit of St. Louis* from New York to Paris. But we could have sent an ape to the moon. Or a robot. With a fake flag artificially distended for a dead place where there is no wind.

It was a WASP enterprise all the way. Is it possible to conceive of NASA sending a Negro, a Jew—or a woman? Muhammad Ali perhaps? Joe Namath? Norman Mailer (who wanted to go)? Can one conceive of an astronaut who does not fit absolutely congruously into the background, like Muzak in a supermarket or Spiro Agnew at a picnic of Legionnaires? Can one conceive of an astronaut's wife living in a Jewish section of the Bronx, or expressing an opinion critical of the Vietnam war, or not taking the children to church on Sunday, or having a career of her own? Was it not inevitable that one of the wives would get down on her knees in front of the television set to pray for a safe reentry? (One can imagine, in that setting, that Walter Cronkite *is* God.) Can one expect Richard Nixon not to say that the mission was the greatest thing since the Creation—or Billy Graham not to suggest, in reply, that perhaps the Resurrection was more important?

What made the moonshot interesting was its unbelievably bad taste, the taste of a cultural style that has lost its juice: suburbs and corporation offices, network television and the electric toothbrush, airline pilots and airline hostesses, "the whole mechanical consolidation of force," as Henry Adams wrote in the *Education*, "which ruthlessly stamped out the life of the class into which Adams was born, but created monopolies capable of controlling the new energies that America adored." Clearly space travel is technologically impossible except as a collective enterprise. But that is precisely the point. There is no role for the American (i.e., WASP) hero. Heroes presumably defy great odds alone. Gary Cooper has been replaced by Dustin Hoffman.

You ask yourself: Does the Establishment live? And the answer, clearly, is Yes. And yet it does not live in the style to which it was accustomed. Ever since the development of large bureaucracies and tenure systems there has been a tendency among outside intellectuals to overestimate the influence of elites. Not that corporations and institutions are going out of style (and they may, in case of a recession, regain some of their allure to the ambitious because they offer security), but that they have become so large, so stiff, and so beset by critics and complexity as to have lost considerable influence and all the romance of their former connection to success. (In Nixon's Republican party there are disparaging references to "The Eastern Establishment" which suggest that there might now be more than one—meaning, of course, that there is none at all.) Here is Francis T. P. Plimpton, the former Deputy U.S. Ambassador to the U.N., and one of the finest representatives of the old style of WASP culture in America. A gentleman, a man of parts. From *Who's Who in America* (1964–1965):

PLIMPTON, Francis T. P., diplomat; b. N.Y.C., N.Y., Dec. 7, 1900; s. George Arthur and Frances Taylor (Pearsons) P.; grad. Phillips Exeter Acad., 1917; A.B., magna cum laude, Amherst Coll., 1922: LL.B., Harvard University, 1925; LL.D., Colby College, 1960; married Pauline Ames, June 4, 1926; children—George Ames, Francis T. P., Jr., Oakes Ames, Sarah Gay. Admitted to bar, 1926; assc. with Root, Clark, Buckner & Ballantine. N.Y. City, 1925–32, in charge of Paris office, 1930–31; gen. solicitor, Reconstruction Finance Corp., Washington, D.C., 1932–33; partner Debevoise, Plimpton & McLean, N.Y.C., and predecessor firms, 1933–61: dep. U.S. rep. to UN with rank ambassador E. and P., 1961—. Trustee U.S. Trust Co. of N.Y., Bowery Savs. Bank. Mem. U.S. delegation UN 15th–17th gen. assemblies. Trustee Tchrs. Ins. and Annuity Assn. (pres. trustees of stock), Coll. Retirement Equities Fund Corp., Amherst Coll., Barnard Coll. (vice chmn. bd.), Phillips Exeter Acad. (chmn. bd.), Union Theol. Sem., Athens Coll. (Greece), Lingnan U. (China), Dir. Philharmonic-Symphony Soc. N.Y., Roosevelt Hosp., Am.-Italy Soc. Fellow Am. Bar Found.; mem. Am., N.Y. State bar assns., Am. Law Inst., Bar Assn. City N.Y., Fgn. Policy Assn. . . .

The style is responsible, worldly involvement, directing institutions which nourished and arbitrated the culture; schools, universities, hospitals, the Council on Foreign Relations, the United Nations, the Church Peace Union, the missionary college in China, the Philharmonic. They were good institutions all, and many of them still do their good works, but with the possible exception of the federal courts, most of them are no longer sanctified as sources of social and cultural initiative, or even as mediators of conflict. There must have been a time when it was fun to be a university trustee.

The interest and action tend to come from others. George Plimpton, the son of Francis T. P. and probably the best-known WASP dealer in living culture, operates like a Paris salonist among Interesting People (Capote, Mailer, the Kennedys), writing brilliantly of his amateur involvement in The Real Stuff: fighting Archie Moore, playing quarterback for the Detroit Lions, pitching to the Yankees. (All sports are now saturated with ethnics.) It is a new role for the children of privilege. Is there a redeeming social utility in this work? Had Plimpton been Jewish he might have played *schlemiel* in a jockstrap, but as an upper-class WASP perhaps all he can do is represent the man whose dreams of command have turned to fantasy and whose greatest moments of glory come from watching other people do something well. A WASP playing honkie and nigger to find out how it feels to be upward bound. Does the aspiring WASP hero have a choice other than that between Apollo and *Paper Lion?*

The enervation of WASP culture may derive, more than anything, from a loss of place. The geographic and psychic worlds of the old mainstream become less distinct, but certain special neighborhoods, even if they are a generation away, survive as regions of the mind. The sense of place: Salem and Boston and Concord; Zenith and Winesburg; Yoknapatawpha County. It produced people with accents and fashions and biases—personalities—that they carried around as overtly as parasols and walking sticks. And because they knew who they were, they were quite willing to be eccentric and crazy. Now much of that material is gone. The black ghetto still remains as a real place, and so does the memory, if not the fact, of South Boston, of Brooklyn, of rural Mississippi and small-town Texas. But how much of a sense of place can grow in a bedroom suburb? What is the inner sense of Bronxville or Winnetka?

Because WASPs regarded themselves as the proprietors of history and the managers of destiny, there was a double displacement. While they were losing their regions they also began to lose their special role as the intrinsic Americans. When we discovered that the country and the world were no longer easily manageable—when we lost our innocence—it was the WASP role which was most affected. No matter how enthusiastically the ethnics waived the flag, they had always been partial outsiders. (Or perhaps better to say that they enjoyed dual citizenship.) In any case, their culture never depended on the assurance that they were running the show. They were tenants, had learned to survive as minorities. Obviously this produced problems, but it also created the tensions and identities of which modern literature (for example) is made. And these conditions of tenancy haven't yet been destroyed, may, indeed, have been strengthened through the mass media, which have nationalized isolated pockets of minority culture. Moreover, the media help create new minorities, new constituencies: students, for example, and women. What kids or blacks do in one town is now immediately communicated to others. Normalcy doesn't make good television, happenings do. The greatest effect of the melting pot, ironically, may not have been on immigrants and minorities, but on the mainstream.

The vacuum left by the old arbiters of the single standard—Establishment intellectuals, literary critics, English professors, museum directors, and all the rest—has produced a sort of cultural prison break. And not only by ethnics, by blacks and Indians, or by kids, but by a lot of others, including all sorts of WASPs themselves, who behave as if they have been waiting for this freedom all their lives. That a lot of what results from this new breakout is bad (and who, these days, can get away with saying that?), and that a lot will be transitory is hardly surprising. In a decade hundreds of thousands of "creative" people proclaimed themselves artists and poets, a million amateurs entered the culture biz, and God knows how many gurus, cultists, swamis, and T-group trainers hung out their shingles. No one could expect most of them to be good, or perhaps even to be serious. The wildcatters are working new territory and a lot are going to go bust. But for the moment they're thriving: the Stones and the Beatles, the groups and groupies, Polish Power and Black Studies, liberation schools and free universities, Norman Mailer's ego and Alexander Portnoy's mother. *The Graduate* and *Alice's Restaurant*, rebellious nuns and protesting priests, *Rat* and *Screw* and a hundred other underground papers, mixed-media shows and the Living Theater, bookstores of the occult, Tarot cards and freaks and hipsters, miniskirts and maxi coats, beads and joss sticks . . . all coexisting (barely, uneasily) with Lyndon Johnson's cornpone, Norman Vincent Peale's sermons, *I Love Lucy, Reader's Digest*, and Apollo 12. If the 1960s produced the beginning of any sort of renaissance, its characteristic instruments are the hand-held movie camera, the electric guitar, and the mimeograph machine, and if its efforts survive in nothing else, they will undoubtedly be remembered by the greatest outpouring of poster art in all history: peace doves and protest proclamations, the face of John Lennon, the pregnant Girl Scout over the motto "Be Prepared," and the pregnant black woman over the 1968 campaign slogan, "Nixon's The One." This is a counter culture—not high, not low or middle—but electric.

Until recently, when encounter groups, public therapy, and other psychic ceremonies became fashionable, reason had been more or less successfully keeping the dark night of the soul within the hidden closets of the mind. And WASPs were the most reasonable people of all. There were, obviously, advantages in that. Most people, I suspect, prefer dispassionate men for airplane pilots, surgeons, and commanders of nuclear-armed strategic bombers. Moreover, we may have survived the last twenty-five years precisely because we kept hot men from taking charge. But their style didn't do much for cultural enrichment. Now everything that a graying, nervous civilization kept jammed in those closets is coming out, whether it deserves to or not: sex in all forms, feelings, emotions, self-revelation, and forms of religion and ritual long condemned as superstition. "Honesty" replaces stoicism, and "love," however understood, overwhelms "work." It may well be that the kids are mining McLuhan's non-linear culture, that print and cool reason (and WASPs) will go under together. So far there is no way of knowing. What is certain is that the old media—books, newspapers, magazines—can no longer claim a monopoly on urgent cultural articulation, and that people who work the new territories have moved a long way from the old mainstream.

WASPs seem to have been crippled by their own sanity. They have become too levelheaded. Having confused their particular social order with the Immutability of Things (and with their own welfare), they have defaulted on their birthright of cussedness and irreverence. "This took courage, this took prudence, this took stoutheartedness," thinks Arthur Winner, Jr., James Gould Cozzens' hero, at the end of *By Love Possessed*. (He has just covered up—to his and Cozzens' satisfaction—some $200,000 worth of ledger-de-main perpetrated by one of his partners.) "In this life we cannot have everything for ourselves we might like to have. . . . Victory is not in reaching certainties or solving mysteries; victory is making do with uncertainties, in supporting mysteries." WASPs are willing to be "sick"—meaning that they can have their neuroses and their "reason" too—but never crazy. People who are willing to be crazy are almost invariably Something Else. We no longer have, or seem to have the possibility of having, a figure like Bertrand Russell; we no longer even have an Everett Dirksen or a John L. Lewis.

WASP crimes these days are invariably dull—price fixing, antitrust capers, tax fraud—which is why we are so fascinated by Jimmy Hoffa, Roy Cohn, and the Mafia, why we need the Mafia, would have to invent it were we ever to suspect (as has Daniel Bell) that it doesn't really exist.

Beyond the formal institutions of business and government—the banks, the corporations, the State Department, and Congress—the unique provinces of WASP domination tend to be conservative (in the pure sense) and mediating. WASPs, I think, still regard themselves as the principal heirs of an estate in which the streams flowed clear, the air was clean, and the language pure. In the growing number of conservation societies, and in their almost exclusive dominion over libraries, dictionary-making, and (surprising as it may seem to those familiar with only the current "celebrities" in the profession) the teaching of English, they are trying to preserve some of that estate. But as "the environment" becomes a national issue, they are going to lose ground (you should pardon the pun) even as conservationists. There are going to be new men—technicians, population planners, engineers—who will move in on the Audubon Society, the Sierra Club, and the Izaak Walton League. The urban environment (John Lindsay *vs.* the New York legislature and Nelson Rockefeller) will demand parity with the environment of Daniel Boone and the bald eagle. On some issues urban and rural conservationists can make common cause, but on others (mass transit, housing, street cleaning, and garbage collection) they cannot.

But it would be unfortunate, perhaps even fatal, if the WASP's mediating function (through courts and other institutions) were also to be seriously eroded. It is inconceivable that America could ever be integrated on ethnic terms. Can one imagine this country as essentially Negro or Italian or Polish;

or believe that the Republican party would nominate anyone named Spiro Agnopopoulos for Vice President; or visualize a trial in which the defendant is white and all the other participants—judge, jurors, lawyers, witnesses—are black? (It did, in fact, happen—in the preliminary proceedings against the Klansmen charged with plotting to murder Charles Evers, the black mayor of Fayette, Mississippi—but it may never happen again.) For if the minorities no longer accept the new style of the mainstream, they are even further from accepting each other. And somebody is going to have to help keep them from tearing each other apart: cops and kids, blacks and blue-collar whites, freaks and squares. Robert Kennedy, I think, recognized this need before he was killed (significantly by a crazy ethnic resenting Kennedy's sympathy with other ethnics). This is also what made the reelection of John Lindsay possible—and significant. The Jews and Negroes of New York may have distrusted him, but they trusted the Italians even less.

Even mediation, however, is no longer feasible on the old standard rigid WASP terms. For the first time, any sort of settlement among competing group interests is going to have to do more than pay lip service to minorities and to the pluralism of styles, beliefs, and cultures. The various commissions on violence and urban riots struggled with that problem but couldn't see beyond their assumptions to the logical conclusion. America is not on the verge of becoming two separate societies, one rich and white, the other poor and black. It is becoming, in all its dreams and anxieties, a nation of outsiders for whom no single style or ethic remains possible. The Constitutional prohibition against an established state religion was adopted because the Jeffersonians understood the destructive consequences of imposing a single set of cultural beliefs beyond the guarantees of freedom and due process.

The Establishment in America has, in part, lost its grip because it devoted itself too much to the management of its game, rather than to the necessary objective of making it possible for everyone to play his own. Minorities—cultural, ethnic, even minorities of one—are fighting over the wreckage of the WASP-abandoned cities and the WASP-forsaken culture. If the WASP Establishment is to act as umpire in this contest—and if we are not to become a police state—it will have to recognize the legitimacy of the contenders. One of the reasons that growing up in America is absurd and chaotic is that the current version of Americanization—what the school people call socializing children—has lost its appeal. We will now have to devise ways of recognizing and assessing the alternatives. The mainstream is running thin.

DAVID M. SHOUP

The New American Militarism

America has become a militaristic and aggressive nation. Our massive and swift invasion of the Dominican Republic in 1965, concurrent with the rapid buildup of U.S. military power in Vietnam, constituted an impressive demonstration of America's readiness to execute military contingency plans and to seek military solutions to problems of political disorder and potential Communist threats in the areas of our interest.

This "military task force" type of diplomacy is in the tradition of our more primitive, pre-World War II "gunboat diplomacy," in which we landed small forces of Marines to protect American lives and property from the perils of native bandits and revolutionaries. In those days the U.S. Navy and its Marine landing forces were our chief means, short of war, for showing the flag, exercising American power, and protecting U.S. interests abroad. The Navy, enjoying the freedom of the seas, was a visible and effective representative of the nation's sovereign power. The Marines could be employed ashore "on such other duties as the President might direct" without congressional approval or a declaration of war. The U.S. Army was not then used so freely because it was rarely ready for expeditionary service without some degree of mobilization, and its use overseas normally required a declaration of emergency or war. Now, however, we have numerous contingency plans involving large joint Air Force-Army-Navy-Marine task forces to defend U.S. interests and to safeguard our allies wherever and whenever we suspect Communist aggression. We maintain more than 1,517,000 Americans in uniform overseas in 119 countries. We have 8 treaties to help defend 48 nations if they ask us to—or if we choose to intervene in their affairs. We have an immense and expensive military establishment, fueled by a gigantic defense industry, and millions of proud, patriotic, and frequently bellicose and militaristic citizens. How did this militarist culture evolve? How did this militarism steer us into the tragic military and political morass of Vietnam?

Source: General Shoup, a hero of the Battle of Tarawa in 1943, rose to become Commandant of the United States Marine Corps for four years, until his retirement in December 1963. He wrote this essay in collaboration with another retired Marine officer, Colonel James A. Donovan. Reprinted from *The Atlantic Monthly*, April 1969, pp. 51–56, by permission of the publisher. Copyright © 1969, by The Atlantic Monthly Company, Boston, Mass.

Prior to World War II, American attitudes were typically isolationist, pacifist, and generally antimilitary. The regular peacetime military establishment enjoyed small prestige and limited influence upon national affairs. The public knew little about the armed forces, and only a few thousand men were attracted to military service and careers. In 1940 there were but 428,000 officers and enlisted men in the Army and Navy. The scale of the war, and the world's power relationships which resulted, created the American military giant. Today the active armed forces contain over 3.4 million men and women, with an additional 1.6 million ready reserves and National Guardsmen.

America's vastly expanded world role after World War II hinged upon military power. The voice and views of the professional military people became increasingly prominent. During the postwar period, distinguished military leaders from the war years filled many top positions in government. Generals Marshall, Eisenhower, MacArthur, Taylor, Ridgeway, LeMay, and others were not only popular heroes but respected opinion-makers. It was a time of international readjustment; military minds offered the benefits of firm views and problem-solving experience to the management of the nation's affairs. Military procedures—including the general staff system, briefings, estimates of the situation, and the organizational and operational techniques of the highly schooled, confident military professionals—spread throughout American culture.

World War II had been a long war. Millions of young American men had matured, been educated, and gained rank and stature during their years in uniform. In spite of themselves, many returned to civilian life as indoctrinated, combat-experienced military professionals. They were veterans, and for better or worse would never be the same again. America will never be the same either. We are now a nation of veterans. To the 14.9 million veterans of World War II, Korea added another 5.7 million five years later, and ever since, the large peacetime military establishment has been training and releasing draftees, enlistees, and short-term reservists by the hundreds of thousands each year. In 1968 the total living veterans of U.S. military service numbered over 23 million, or about 20 percent of the adult population.

Today most middle-aged men, most business, government, civic, and professional leaders, have served some time in uniform. Whether they liked it or not, their military training and experience have affected them, for the creeds and attitudes of the armed forces are powerful medicine, and can become habit-forming. The military codes include all the virtues and beliefs used to motivate men of high principle: patriotism, duty and service to country, honor among fellowmen, courage in the face of danger, loyalty to organization and leaders, self-sacrifice for comrades, leadership, discipline, and physical fitness. For many veterans the military's efforts to train and indoctrinate them may well be the most impressive and influential experience they have ever had— especially so for the young and less educated.

In addition, each of the armed forces has its own special doctrinal beliefs and well-catalogued customs, traditions, rituals, and folklore upon which it strives to build a fiercely loyal military character and esprit de corps. All ranks are taught that their unit and their branch of the military service are the most elite, important, efficient, or effective in the military establishment. By believing in the superiority and importance of their own service they also provide themselves a degree of personal status, pride, and self-confidence.

As they get older, many veterans seem to romanticize and exaggerate their own military experience and loyalties. The policies, attitudes, and positions of the powerful veterans' organizations such as the American Legion, Veterans of Foreign Wars, and AMVETS, totaling over 4 million men, frequently reflect this pugnacious and chauvinistic tendency. Their memberships generally favor military solutions to world problems in the pattern of their own earlier experience, and often assert that their military service and sacrifice should be repeated by the younger generations.

Closely related to the attitudes and influence of America's millions of veterans is the vast and powerful complex of the defense industries, which have been described in detail many times in the eight years since General Eisenhower first warned of the military-industrial power complex in his farewell address as President. The relationship between the defense industry and the military establishment is closer than many civilians realize. Together they form a powerful public opinion lobby. The several military service associations provide both a forum and a meeting ground for the military and its industries. The associations also provide each of the armed services with a means of fostering their respective roles, objectives, and propaganda.

Each of the four services has its own association, and there are also additional military function associations, for ordnance, management, defense industry, and defense transportation, to name some of the more prominent. The Air Force Association and the Association of the U.S. Army are the largest, best organized, and most effective of the service associations. The Navy League, typical of the "silent service" traditions, is not as well coordinated in its public relations efforts, and the small Marine Corps Association is not even in the same arena with the other contenders, the Marine Association's main activity being the publication of a semi-official monthly magazine. Actually, the service associations' respective magazines, with an estimated combined circulation of over 270,000, are the primary medium serving the several associations' purposes.

Air Force and Space Digest, to cite one example, is the magazine of the Air Force Association and the unofficial mouthpiece of the U.S. Air Force doctrine, "party line," and propaganda. It frequently promotes Air Force policy that has been officially frustrated or suppressed within the Department of Defense. It beats the tub for strength through aerospace power, interprets diplomatic, strategic, and tactical problems in terms of air power, stresses the requirements for quantities of every type of aircraft, and frequently perpetuates the extravagant fictions about the effectiveness of bombing. This, of course, is well coordinated with and supported by the multibillion-dollar aerospace industry, which thrives upon the boundless desires of the Air Force. They reciprocate with lavish and expensive ads in every issue of *Air Force*. Over 96,000 members of the Air Force Association receive the magazine. Members include active, reserve, retired personnel, and veterans of the U.S. Air Force. Additional thousands of copies go to people engaged in the defense industry. The thick mixture of advertising, propaganda, and Air Force doctrine continuously repeated in this publication provides its readers and writers with a form of intellectual hypnosis, and they are prone to believe their own propaganda because they read it in *Air Force*.

The American people have also become more and more accustomed to militarism, to uniforms, to the cult of the gun, and to the violence of combat. Whole generations have been brought up on war news and wartime propaganda; the few years of peace since 1939 have seen a steady stream of war novels, war movies, comic strips, and television programs with war or military settings. To many Americans, military training, expeditionary service, and warfare are merely extensions of the entertainment and games of childhood. Even the weaponry and hardware they use at war are similar to the highly realistic toys of their youth. Soldiering loses appeal for some of the relatively few who experience the blood, terror, and filth of battle; for many, however, including far too many senior professional officers, war and combat are an exciting adventure, a competitive game, and an escape from the dull routines of peacetime.

It is this influential nucleus of aggressive ambitious professional military leaders who are the root of America's evolving militarism. There are over 410,000 commissioned officers on active duty in the four armed services. Of these, well over half are junior ranking reserve officers on temporary active duty. Of the 150,000 or so regular career officers, only a portion are senior ranking colonels, generals, and admirals, but it is they who constitute the elite core of the military establishment. It is these few thousand top-ranking professionals who command and manage the armed forces and plan and formulate military policy and opinion. How is it, then, that in spite of civilian controls and the national desire for peace, this small group of men exert so much martial influence upon the government and life of the American people?

The military will disclaim any excess of power or influence on their part. They will point to their small numbers, low pay, and subordination to civilian masters as proof of their modest status and innocence. Nevertheless, the professional military, as a group, is probably one of the best organized and most influential of the various segments of the American scene. Three wars and six major contingencies since 1940 have forced the American people to become abnormally aware of the armed forces and their leaders. In turn the military services have produced an unending supply of distinguished, capable, articulate, and effective leaders. The sheer skill, energy, and dedication of America's military officers make them dominant in almost every government or civic organization they may inhabit, from the federal Cabinet to the local PTA.

The hard core of high-ranking professionals are, first of all, mostly service academy graduates: they had to be physically and intellectually above average among their peers just to gain entrance to an academy. Thereafter for the rest of their careers they are exposed to constant competition for selection and promotion. Attrition is high, and only the most capable survive to reach the elite senior ranks. Few other professions have such rigorous selection systems; as a result, the top military leaders are top-caliber men.

Not many industries, institutions, or civilian branches of government have the resources, techniques, or experience in training leaders such as are now employed by the armed forces in their excellent and elaborate school systems. Military leaders are taught to command large organizations and to plan big operations. They learn the techniques of influencing others. Their education is not, however, liberal or cultural. It stresses the tactics, doctrines, traditions, and codes of the military trade. It produces technicians and disciples, not philosophers.

The men who rise to the top of the military hierarchy have usually demonstrated their effectiveness as leaders, planners, and organization managers. They have perhaps performed heroically in combat, but most of all they have demonstrated their loyalty as proponents of their own service's doctrine and their dedication to the defense establishment. The paramount sense of duty to follow orders is at the root of the military professional's performance. As a result the military often operate more efficiently and effectively in the arena of defense policy planning than do their civilian counterparts in the State Department. The military planners have their doctrinal beliefs, their loyalties, their discipline—and their typical desire to compete and win. The civilians in government can scarcely play the same policy-planning game. In general the military are better organized, they work harder, they think straighter, and they keep their eyes on the objective, which is to be instantly ready to solve the problem through military action while ensuring that their respective service gets its proper mission, role, and recognition in the operation. In an emergency the military usually have a ready plan; if not, their numerous doctrinal manuals provide firm guidelines for action. Politicians, civilian appointees, and diplomats do not normally have the same confidence about how to react to threats and violence as do the military.

The motivations behind these endeavors are difficult for civilians to understand. For example, military professionals cannot measure the success of their individual efforts in terms of personal financial gain. The armed forces are not profit-making organizations, and the rewards for excellence in the military profession are acquired in less tangible forms. Thus it is that promotion and the responsibilities of higher command, with the related fringe benefits of quarters, servants, privileges, and prestige, motivate most career officers. Promotions and choice job opportunities are attained by constantly performing well, conforming to the exepected patterns, and pleasing the senior officers. Promotions and awards also frequently result from heroic and distinguished performance in combat, and it takes a war to become a military hero. Civilians can scarcely understand or even believe that many ambitious military professionals truly yearn for wars and the opportunities for glory and distinction afforded only in combat. A career of peacetime duty is a dull and frustrating prospect for the normal regular officer to contemplate.

The professional military leaders of the U.S. Armed Forces have some additional motivations which influence their readiness to involve their country in military ventures. Unlike some of the civilian policy-makers, the military has not been obsessed with the threat of Communism per se. Most military people know very little about Communism either as a doctrine or as a form of government. But they have been given reason enough to presume that it is bad and represents the force of evil. When they can identify "Communist aggression," however, the matter then becomes of direct concern to the armed forces. Aggressors are the enemy in the war games, the "bad guys," the "Reds." Defeating aggression is a gigantic combat area competition rather than a crusade to save the world from Communism. In the military view, all "Communist aggression" is certain to be interpreted as a threat to the United States.

The armed forces' role in performing its part of the national security policy —in addition to defense against actual direct attack on the United States and to maintaining the strategic atomic deterrent forces—is to be prepared to employ its *General Purpose Forces* in support of our collective security policy and the related treaties and alliances. To do this it deploys certain forces to forward zones in the Unified Commands, and maintains an up-to-date file of scores of detailed contingency plans which have been thrashed out and approved by the Joint Chiefs of Staff. Important features of these are the movement or deployment schedules of task forces assigned to each plan. The various details of these plans continue to create intense rivalries between the Navy-Marine sea-lift forces and the Army-Air Force team of air-mobility proponents. At the senior command levels parochial pride in service, personal ambitions, and old Army-Navy game rivalry stemming back to academy loyalties can influence strategic planning far more than most civilians would care to believe. The game is to be ready for deployment sooner than the other elements of the joint task force and to be so disposed as to be the "first to fight." The danger presented by this practice is that readiness and deployment speed become ends in themselves. This was clearly revealed in the massive and rapid intervention in the Dominican Republic in 1965 when the contingency plans and interservice rivalry appeared to supersede diplomacy. Before the world realized what was happening, the momentum and velocity of the military plans propelled almost 20,000 U.S. soldiers and Marines into the small turbulent republic in an impressive race to test the respective mobility of the Army and the Marines, and to attain overall command of "U.S. Forces Dom. Rep." Only a fraction of the force deployed was needed or justified. A small 1935-model Marine landing force could probably have handled the situation. But the Army airlifted much of the 82nd Airborne Division to the scene, including a lieutenant general, and took charge of the operation.

Simultaneously, in Vietnam during 1965 the four services were racing to build up combat strength in that hapless country. This effort was ostensibly to save South Vietnam from Viet Cong and North Vietnamese aggression. It should also be noted that it was motivated in part by the same old interservice rivalry to demonstrate respective importance and combat effectiveness.

The punitive air strikes immediately following the Tonkin Gulf incident in late 1964 revealed the readiness of naval air forces to bomb North Vietnam. (It now appears that the Navy actually had attack plans ready even before the alleged incident took place!) So by early 1965 the Navy carrier people and the Air Force initiated a contest of comparative strikes, sorties, tonnages dropped, "Killed by Air" claims, and target grabbing which continued up to the 1968 bombing pause. Much of the reporting on air action has consisted of misleading data or propaganda to serve Air Force and Navy purposes. In fact, it became increasingly apparent that the U.S. bombing effort in both North and South Vietnam has been one of the most wasteful and expensive hoaxes ever to be put over on the American people. Tactical and close air support of ground operations is essential, but air power use in general has to a large degree been a contest for the operations planners, "fine experience" for young pilots, and opportunity for career officers.

The highly trained professional and aggressive career officers of the Army and Marine Corps played a similar game. Prior to the decision to send combat units to South Vietnam in early 1965, both services were striving to increase their involvement. The Army already had over 16,000 military aid personnel serving in South Vietnam in the military adviser role, in training missions, logistic services, supporting helicopter companies, and in Special Forces teams. This investment of men and matériel justified a requirement for additional U.S. combat units to provide local security and to help protect our growing commitment of aid to the South Vietnam regime.

There were also top-ranking Army officers who wanted to project Army ground combat units into the Vietnam struggle for a variety of other reasons: to test plans and new equipment, to test the new air-mobile theories and tactics, to try the tactics and techniques of counterinsurgency, and to gain combat experience for young officers and noncommissioned officers. It also appeared to be a case of the military's duty to stop "Communist aggression" in Vietnam.

The Marines had somewhat similar motivations, the least of which was any real concern about the political or social problems of the Vietnamese people. In early 1965 there was a shooting war going on and the Marines were being left out of it, contrary to all their traditions. The Army's military advisory people were hogging American participation—except for a Marine Corps transport helicopter squadron at Danang which was helping the Army of the

Republic of Vietnam. For several years young Marine officers had been going to South Vietnam from the 3rd Marine Division on Okinawa for short tours of "on-the-job training" with the small South Vietnam Marine Corps. There was a growing concern, however, among some senior Marines that the Corps should get involved on a larger scale and be the "first to fight" in keeping with the Corps's traditions. This would help justify the Corps's continued existence, which many Marines seem to consider to be in constant jeopardy.

The Corps had also spent several years exploring the theories of counterinsurgency and as early as 1961 had developed an elaborate lecture-demonstration called OPERATION CORMORANT, for school and Marine Corps promotion purposes, which depicted the Marines conducting a large-scale amphibious operation on the coast of Vietnam and thereby helping resolve a hypothetical aggressor-insurgency problem. As always it was important to Marine planners and doctrinaires to apply an amphibious operation to the Vietnam situation and provide justification for this special Marine functional responsibility. So Marine planners were seeking an acceptable excuse to thrust a landing force over the beaches of Vietnam when the Viet Cong attacked the U.S. Army Special Forces camp at Pleiku in February, 1965. It was considered unacceptable aggression, and the President was thereby prompted to put U.S. ground combat units into the war. Elements of the 3rd Marine Division at Okinawa were already aboard ship and eager to go, for the Marines also intended to get to Vietnam before their neighbor on Okinawa, the Army's 173rd Airborne Brigade, arrived. (Actually the initial Marine unit to deploy was an airlifted antiaircraft missile battalion which arrived to protect the Danang air base.) With these initial deployments the Army-Marine race to build forces in Vietnam began in earnest and did not slow down until both became overextended, overcommitted, and depleted at home.

For years up to 1964 the chiefs of the armed services, of whom the author was then one, deemed it unnecessary and unwise for U.S. forces to become involved in any ground war in Southeast Asia. In 1964 there were changes in the composition of the Joint Chiefs of Staff, and in a matter of a few months the Johnson Administration, encouraged by the aggressive military, hastened into what has become the quagmire of Vietnam. The intention at the time was that the war effort be kept small and "limited." But as the momentum and involvement built up, the military leaders rationalized a case that this was not a limited-objective exercise, but was a proper war in defense of the United States against "Communist aggression" and in honor of our area commitments.

The battle successes and heroic exploits of America's fine young fighting men have added to the military's traditions which extol service, bravery, and sacrifice, and so it has somehow become unpatriotic to question our military strategy and tactics or the motives of military leaders. Actually, however, the military commanders have directed the war in Vietnam, they have managed the details of its conduct; and more than most civilian officials, the top military planners were initially ready to become involved in Vietnam combat and have the opportunity to practice their trade. It has been popular to blame the civilian administration for the conduct and failures of the war rather than to question the motives of the military. But some of the generals and admirals are by no means without responsibility for the Vietnam miscalculations.

Some of the credibility difficulties experienced by the Johnson Administration over its war situation reports and Vietnam policy can also be blamed in part upon the military advisers. By its very nature most military activity falls under various degrees of security classification. Much that the military plans or does must be kept from the enemy. Thus the military is indoctrinated to be secretive, devious, and misleading in its plans and operations. It does not, however, always confine its security restrictions to purely military operations. Each of the services and all of the major commands practice techniques of controlling the news and the release of self-servicing propaganda: in "the interests of national defense," to make the service look good, to cover up mistakes, to build up and publicize a distinguished military personality, or to win a round in the continuous gamesmanship of the interservice contest. If the Johnson Administration suffered from lack of credibility in its reporting of the war, the truth would reveal that much of the hocus-pocus stemmed from schemers in the military services, both at home and abroad.

Our militaristic culture was born of the necessities of World War II, nurtured by the Korean War, and became an accepted aspect of American life during the years of cold war emergencies and real or imagined threats from the Communist bloc. Both the philosophy and the institutions of militarism grew during these years because of the momentum of their own dynamism, the vigor of their ideas, their large size and scope, and because of the dedicated concentration of the emergent military leaders upon their doctrinal objectives. The dynamism of the defense establishment and its culture is also inspired and stimulated by vast amounts of money, by the new creations of military research and matériel development, and by the concepts of the Defense Department-supported "think factories." These latter are extravagantly funded civilian organizations of scientists, analysts, and retired military strategists who feed new militaristic philosophies into the Defense Department to help broaden the views of the single service doctrinaires, to create fresh policies and new requirements for ever larger, more expensive defense forces.

Somewhat like a religion, the basic appeals of anti-Communism, national defense, and patriotism provide the foundation for a powerful creed upon which the defense establishment can build, grow, and justify its cost. More so than many large bureaucratic organizations, the defense establishment now devotes a large share of its efforts to self-perpetuation, to justifying its organizations, to preaching its doctrines, and to self-maintenance and management. Warfare becomes an extension of war games and field tests. War justifies the existence of the establishment, provides experience for the military novice and challenges for the senior officer. Wars and emergencies put the military and their leaders on the front pages and give status and prestige to the professionals. Wars add to the military traditions, the self-nourishment of heroic deeds, and provide a new crop of military leaders who become the rededicated disciples of the code of service and military action. Being recognized public figures in a nation always seeking folk heroes, the military leaders have been largely exempt from the criticism experienced by the more plebeian politician. Flag officers are considered "experts," and their views are often accepted by press and Congress as the gospel. In turn, the distinguished military leader feels obliged not only to perpetuate loyally the doctrine of his service but to comply with the stereotyped military characteristics by being tough, aggressive, and firm in his resistance to Communist aggression and his belief in the military solutions to world problems. Standing closely behind these leaders, encouraging and prompting them, are the rich and powerful defense industries. Standing in front, adorned with service caps, ribbons, and lapel emblems, is a nation of veterans—patriotic, belligerent, romantic, and well intentioned, finding a certain sublimation and excitement in their country's latest military venture. Militarism in America is in full bloom and promises a future of vigorous self-pollination—unless the blight of Vietnam reveals that militarism is more a poisonous weed than a glorious blossom.

The opinions contained herein are the private ones of the author and are not to be construed as official or reflecting the views of the Navy Department or the naval service at large.

WARD S. JUST

Notes on Losing a War

The Pentagon is now the most melancholy building in Washington. Wracked with bitterness and dissension, near-paranoid since the enemy's successful assault at Tet, the Vietnamese New Year, and the assault on Saigon in May, the generals and their aides, in one of President Johnson's favorite phrases, are hunkered down like jackrabbits in a hailstorm.

The events at Tet are instructive, although the rot set in long before. The point is not whether the success was ours or theirs, for it can be argued either way depending on the definition of success, but the fact that Tet was done at all. No one, not the colonels, the diplomats, the intelligence agents, or the journalists, thought that the Viet Cong had the capacity to mount the offensive that they did; the enemy hit Saigon, every provincial capital in the country, more than thirty districts capitals, and held Hué for twenty-two days. The fact of it produced a crisis of confidence in the American ability to estimate the resources of the enemy, and confidence that when the enemy struck he could be quickly contained.

In America, the public perception of the war as something Out There in the rice paddies ended forever when the Viet Cong occupied the American Embassy—in living, vivid Cronkite color. Whatever the situation was (and who knew?), it was certainly different from what the public had been led to believe in November of 1967, when Ellsworth Bunker and William Westmoreland came marching home again to give positive accountings. The one reality did not square with the other, and it did not matter whether the spectator was thinking linearly or not; none of it jibed.

At any event, Tet was a sobering experience from which American officials in Washington still have not recovered. Could the estimates ever be trusted again? "It is very strange," said an embassy official in Saigon. "After Tet, Washington became very pessimistic, and we became very optimistic. Before, it was the other way around."

Why did Tet produce a surge of optimism in Saigon? It is quite simply

Source: Mr. Just is a correspondent for the Washington *Post* and author of *To What End: A Report from Vietnam* (Houghton Mifflin, 1968). This article is from *The Atlantic Monthly*, January 1969, pp. 39–44. Copyright © 1968 by Ward S. Just. Reprinted by permission of the author.

that officials there believed that for the first time the Vietnamese saw the seriousness of the struggle and therefore would take the steps required to deal with it. In Washington Tet was commonly analyzed as a military victory for the allies and a psychological victory for the Viet Cong. In Saigon, it was regarded as both a military and psychological triumph for the allies: the latter in the sense that everyone could plainly see that the situation was grim. The argument went that the Thieu government could no longer dither over reforms; the enemy was at the gates. It appeared to be true for a time that government efficiency increased. The prospect of imminent disaster concentrated the minds of Vietnamese officials wonderfully, the Americans said. For the first time, Saigon and Hué felt the effects of war; far from being demoralizing, the Americans said, the disaster would prove positively beneficial. The Vietnamese people would not now hesitate to place themselves in the center of the struggle against the Communists. It was for this reason that when the pessimism began to pour in from Washington, American diplomats fought against it. If only the Administration could hang on; victory was closer than ever. But Washington had concentrated its own mind and taken a reading. It had looked at the situation and decided to cut bait.

So there were no more optimistic readings from Washington. More important, the fact followed the logic: Westmoreland requested more men, and Lyndon Johnson refused to give them to him. The American command would have to make do with what it had, and the Vietnamese had to be made to understand that there was a bottom to the pit. As a practical matter, Tet seemed to confirm the belief here that the war would not end with a victory on the battlefield. However obvious that may seem, or have seemed, to the civilian strategists, it was never obvious to the American military, who customarily fought to win, nor to the principal civilians who dealt with the war, beginning with the President.

Wear him down. Wear the Cong down, and he'll quit. Put him through the meat grinder. Attrit him. He is hurting, said the American commander in mid-1967. *He can't take it much longer.* During the trip to Washington late that year, when he and the ambassador spoke so confidently of success, the general indicated that withdrawals of American troops could begin in 1969. They could begin because the war would be winding down, the beginning of the end begun. Of course there were other, more pessimistic estimates in Washington, most of them muted. "If we have not made marked progress in six months," said one of the ablest American experts in October, 1967, "then we ought to begin to disengage."

That is the meaning of Paris, and it also accounts for the odd silence in Washington, a silence that endured for most of the last half of 1968. The articles datelined Saigon, South Vietnam, appeared with merciless regularity on the front pages of the Washington *Post* and the New York *Times*, but they caused little comment. General Creighton Abrams, unlike his predecessor, made few pronouncements on the war's course: "No comment," he said time and time again. Any expression of optimism, either in Washington or in Saigon, was tolerantly smiled down.

Except that one day in October, Abrams slipped out of Saigon and flew to Washington to spend the early morning hours with the President. He told Lyndon Johnson that the allies could stand a bombing halt; so the bombing stopped. The action was in Paris, but no one could make sense of that pattern, if there was one. Less and less was heard from Robert Komer, the generalissimo in charge of the pacification program, and just days before the election the President nominated him to be American ambassador to Turkey. Komer left Saigon with relief.

Where have all the hawks gone? There are no new proposals for more and better bombing, no carefully leaked plans for 200,000 more troops. In Vietnam, save for the two northernmost provinces, the multidivision offensive operations have mostly ceased, to be replaced by sorties from B-52 bombers. In fact, the term "search and destroy" has been replaced by "reconnaissance in force," a phrase at once more and less descriptive. Search and destroy, as an offensive tactic born of an essentially defensive strategy, is dead. No one speaks now of a war of attrition. Even before the talks began, the war was existing largely as a holding action. To any American military man, to say this is to say that American forces have been held to a standoff. We have not won the war or even contained it. We have endured with it, and while that may be a triumph for American stamina, it is not as clear-cut as a colonel would like. The toughest colonels are calling it a defeat. And that is why the search for scapegoats has begun.

What this country does not need right now is a wave of recrimination over Vietnam, but that is what is likely to happen. If anything in the war was predictable, it was that at some point there would be a search for those responsible and a reckoning. *Who lost China?* The logic is inexorable: *Who lost Vietnam?* "We are in for a very bad period," said a senior official of the State Department early this summer. "They are getting ready for a stab-in-the-back thing." By "they," of course, the official meant the military in the Pentagon.

Since by everyone's agreement the situation in Vietnam is not satisfactory, someone, somewhere, must be held accountable for what went wrong. A nation of 200 million people with the most powerful army and air force in the world does not get stood off by a nation which collectively dresses out to 28 million, many of them half-naked natives, without there being something terribly wrong. Forget all the guerrilla books by Che Guevara or Vo Nguyen Giap; they say very little that Clausewitz does not, and in any case do not explain the disaster in terms that the ordinary citizen, or captain or colonel of infantry, can understand.

The most convenient scapegoat, now as in 1963, is the press; but it won't stick. Newspapermen were not doing the fighting, nor were they devising the strategy and the tactics or advising the Saigon government. There will be a postmortem on the war, and many will say that press accounts fortified morale in Hanoi. The officers, with Brigadier General (Ret.) S. L. A. Marshall in the vanguard, will say that an American victory was clear and present "if only the people were permitted to view it." There will be charges that the press lacked simple American patriotism, and charges that the war was covered from the bar of the Caravelle Hotel. Some of these charges will be accurate. Of course the press will counterattack. None of it will be very edifying. But the argument that the press lost the war will not stick for the elementary reason that it is demonstrably not true.

Similarly, civilians of one stripe or another will find generals in the wood-pile. If anything, the military is an even more convenient goat than the press: for every rum-soaked Hildy Johnson at the Caravelle, there is a Bat Guano at MACV (the acronym for the American military command). And from time to time, fascinating clues to the attitudes of the brass are uncovered. The most intriguing period is early 1965, when the President decided to send combat troops to South Vietnam. The initial domino was a bridge of the 173rd Airborne.

The late Robert F. Kennedy, in a conversation with this writer last fall, said it was his understanding that the Joint Chiefs of Staff sold the White House on the commitment by indicating that it was temporary. The Chiefs indicated that the single brigade would be enough to contain the insurgency, according to Kennedy, and would then be withdrawn before the end of 1965. If this is so, it was a miscalculation of staggering proportions; by the end of 1965, there were almost 200,000 troops in South Vietnam. Whether or not this account is correct, it is beyond dispute that from the beginning the military, led by their civilian Secretary of Defense, Robert S. McNamara, were relentlessly optimistic. Every day, in every way, the war was going better and better. The effect on the policy-makers in the White House and in the Cabinet was obvious.

Who then are the villains? First the press, from the point of view of the military. Second the generals in Washington, from the perspective of the demonologists. What of the generals in Saigon? An initial impression is that William C. Westmoreland is surely the least accountable commanding officer in American history, if not in the history of major conflicts since the beginning of warfare. The point is very tricky, since Westmoreland had the command and the authority, was the technically responsible official, and theoretically had full control over tactics in the South. But it is one thing to criticize his priorities: the emphasis on search and destroy; the failure prop-erly to retrain the Vietnamese Army (ARVN); the persistent misreading of enemy strength and intentions; and quite another to hold him responsible for the course of the war. Bombing was applied not massively and immedi-ately but piecemeal, by stages; Laos and Cambodia were off limits; as civilian casualties mounted, additional restrictions inhibited tactical bombing. In retrospect, many of MACV's decisions seem wrong; but in retrospect, almost everything about the war seems wrong, including the reasons for getting into it in the first place. If the Americans had cleared and held, rather than searched and destroyed, would the war have been won? If the ARVN had been equipped with M-16 rifles in 1965 rather than 1968, would Haunghia Province now be pacified? If the American command had known to a man how many Communists there were in South Vietnam, could it then have accomplished their extinction? If. If. If. If Nguyen Cao Ky had been Ho Chi Minh, the people would have rallied behind the government of South Vietnam.

In any case, Westmoreland was never permitted to run the war the way he wanted to run it—which is to say he wanted more aircraft, more men, and fewer limits on the targets permitted to be destroyed. Massive deployment of American troops, perhaps a million or more, was in fact the only way the Americans could make their startegy of attrition work. "Attrition," incidentally, was a word used by Westmoreland in Saigon, never by Lyndon Johnson in Washington. It is an ugly word, signifying a long-drawn-out struggle with many dead and one side or the other exhausted and beaten at the end.

So Westmoreland wanted to strike Laos and Cambodia, where the sanctuaries were, and he wanted to hit the port of Haiphong. He wanted more and heavier bombing of the North. Some members of his staff wanted to drop nuclear bombs in the South Vietnamese highlands ("nukes in the highlands," as one colonel put it), but the general stopped well short of that. He thought conventional power was sufficient, if applied in force.

None of this was done because the civilians in Washington controlled strategy.[1] Vietnam was a civilian-run war from the beginning, notwithstanding the paradox that in the war zone itself MACV entirely dominated the civilian establishment. But that was tactical; the rest was strategy. The principal philosophical difficulty was the absence of a clearly stated war aim; in an age of doubt and Tito, it is not enough to state that the enemy is Communist.

The closest that senior officials could come to defining what the United States wanted out of the war was the celebrated formulation of Dean Rusk: "We want them to stop doing what they are doing." The war would end, Rusk said, when the North decided to "leave its neighbors alone." While not subject to misinterpretation, Rusk's statement was not subject to much interpretation, either. It was to say everything and nothing, the use of simple arithmetic to solve a quadratic equation.

[1] It is a bit more complicated than that. Sometimes members of the JCS presented the service point of view only to get it on the record. The architects of the "civilian" decisions were often generals, and of course vice versa. It was often argued that the most important split was not civilian/military but Washington/Saigon, including elements of both on each side. Though some of the top military men who held office up to 1963 opposed a major land involvement in Vietnam, most generals after that time preferred a military solution applied massively. Most civilians were gradualists, uneasy to the end about the efficacy of arms to win a war whose roots lay in social revolution. Of course, Dean Rusk and his followers regarded the problem as one of external aggression.

So the object of the war became to kill the enemy. As the American techniques became more sophisticated, a pacification program was introduced. Its intent was to secure the countryside for the government, and induce the enemy to rally. The Americans prosecuted the war on the one hand and the pacification program on the other, never quite understanding where the one ended and the other began, if indeed there was a dividing line. The war part was run by the military, and the pacification part by the civilians.

The selection of bombing targets in North Vietnam was made by military officials but approved by the civilians, often by the President himself. The decision to introduce combat troops gradually was a civilian decision. The policy of restraint in the bombing of Laos and Cambodia was a political decision as, of course, were all the decisions relating to internal Vietnamese politics —to permit the fall of Ngo Dinh Diem, the establishment of Nguyen Cao Ky, the slow ascendancy of Nguyen Van Thieu.

It is impossible to say with certainty how important the internal situation was to the war effort, but my impression is that it was controlling. With the establishment of Ky, for example, the possibility of a neutralist government was foreclosed. But none of these decisions came flatly, by fiat. They are all characterized by gradualism, in Saigon as in Washington. They were hesitant policies, which flowed from the central presidential decision that America could have both guns and butter, could simultaneously win the war on poverty at home and the war against the Communists in Asia. That is, of course, if the war could be kept limited.

In his final eighteen months of the war, when visits to America became more frequent, Westmoreland began to learn something of the public dissatisfaction with the effort. He was honestly surprised, and appalled, when pickets appeared on his speaking tour. He shook his head, couldn't understand what was happening to the country. COMUSMACV picketed? Something had gone very wrong. Friends said that the general only began to understand the depth of disaffection when he returned to Washington in 1967 to speak at the Joint Session of Congress. He began then to comprehend what Lyndon Johnson was up against.

This is all by way of explanation why neither Westmoreland nor his command was finally accountable any more than anyone else. A brilliant tactician might have produced some startling temporary successes. A man with a more ironic turn of mind might have been able to convey the essential truth of the situation to the troops and the congressmen who invaded the war zone. But the war was more than public relations. There was no chance of structural change so long as the civilians were running it, and no chance for cosmetics so long as the soldiers were fighting it. Limited war, limited ends, as the President liked to say.

All of this, plus some other things as well, has produced in the military man something that can only be called rage, usually cold, sometimes hot.

And thus the search for some rational explanation of why it all went so wrong. To Lieutenant Colonel William R. Corson, the literate Marine whose superiors tried to suppress his book *The Betrayal* (Norton, 1968), the villains are the timid American official in Saigon who refuses to demand that the Vietnamese government rid itself of corruption, and the hidebound general at headquarters who refuses to permit deployment of American forces to protect the Vietnamese people in their hamlets. To Lieutenant Colonel David H. Hackworth, one of the most decorated officers in the American Army, it is the refusal of his superiors to cast aside World War II tactics and fight the Viet Cong and the North Vietnamese Army on their own terms, which is to say, a return to guerrilla warfare. To Lieutenant General Stanley R. ("Swede") Larsen it is the American press, which refused to support the success of the American pacification program. To a high-ranking Marine general, now retired, it is moral cowardice not to do what needs to be done. "We have told the Communists: 'Go ahead, take it over,'" he said last August; to the Marine general, American political leadership failed the men in the field.

The military establishment, of which the two generals can be said to be a part, tends to find its villains in high places. *They wouldn't let me do this . . . that . . . something else.* One man accuses the CIA, another the diplomats at State, a third the White House; a vacillating Congress, a self-indulgent public, left-wing journalists, men who were afraid, men who *wouldn't let us win it.* A single thread runs through these complaints: it is that if America had fought the war differently, it could have been won.

The American apparatus now sprawls over Vietnam like sleep. In the huge MACV headquarters at Tansonnhut—Pentagon East, it's called—colonels pad down well-lit noiseless corridors, the light a greenish hue from the special windows meant to withstand nearby explosions. There are heavy bunkers built of sandbags, with a concrete veneer all around the structure. A forest of antennas reaches over the buildings. Standing outside, looking up, you see aircraft of all kinds: Pan Am jets from Guam; an Army Caribou from Cantho; an Air Force C-130 from Pleiku; an RVNAF Skyraider returning from a sortie in Tayninh; a Navy Cod from an aircraft carrier on Dixie station in the South China Sea; a Phantom jet from an air strike in the Delta; and now the big four-engined 707 jets with unfamiliar names: Seaboard World Airlines, for example.

As if by rote, the old measurements are trotted out and dusted off for the visitor. At Camp Evans north of Hué, the intelligence officer of the 1st Cavalry Division (Air Mobile) talks of the body count for the past two months, avers that the commander of the 1st ARVN Division "is a real tiger" who, if unleashed, would willingly thrust north. Intelligence-gathering is now so improved that specialists can draw a circle around a house in a hamlet; beyond that, the enemy has moved away from Hué. He no longer commands the approaches into the city. "He knows he cannot win, and that is why he has pulled back," the intelligence officer says. "Every time we fight him, we win and he loses."

Chieu hoi (the program to induce enemy defections) figures are way up in Quangtri and Thuathien provinces, the two northernmost in the country. It is inexplicable, unless you assume that the enemy is losing badly, is coming apart at the seams, is prepared to give up the struggle. So that is what is believed. The best Viet Cong cadres are rallying to the government, supplying important data about enemy movements; some of the ralliers are of field-grade rank.

All this—the *chieu hoi*, the defectors, the KIA, and the rest—are now, as they have been since 1965 and before, quantified on charts and bar graphs. The colonels point to the bar graphs and say with pitiless simplicity: We are winning now . . . we are winning, yet the American people want to give up. They want to stop the bombing. The colonel shakes his head bitterly. If the bombing is stopped, it all might be lost. To the colonel, it is a question of the bombing; in Saigon, among the Vietnamese rulers, it is a question of the National Liberation Front. Simply a matter of proportion, or of perception of what the struggle means.

When the bombing was stopped, and the Saigon government was exercising its right not to participate in the talks at Paris, Nguyen Van Thieu talked of the NLF, and what recognition, at the talks or anywhere else, would mean: "They will become the winners," he said. "And the people will believe them. The regional force and popular force militia, quite a few of them I'm afraid, may be discouraged and lay down their weapons and go home, or worse join the Viet Cong. All the painfully built democratic institutions will collapse. Our existence is at stake." It was not precisely the remark of a man who saw victory around the corner; he was saying that the mere recognition of the existence of the Front would be sufficient to unravel the people of the South. The leaders of South Vietnam have never been as bullish on progress as the Americans; perhaps it is because the war has gone on so long.

Now that the end is in sight, it seems the cruelest irony that the Americans at last have an authentic hero (at least among themselves) in Saigon. He is General Creighton Abrams, who is admired and respected by literally all segments of opinion in Saigon; including, for what it is the worth, the most dovish and disbelieving of the American correspondents. They say he understands the political realities, is less impressed with his weight as a political figure. He understands the climate in the United States. He is offhand with journalists, does not cultivate them, apparently regards them as a necessary evil. He is a superb tactician. He listens to Mozart in his villa in the evening.

As Chief of Staff of the Army, Westmoreland himself spends as little time at the Pentagon as he can get away with. He has gathered much of his old staff around him: Lieutenant General Bruce Palmer, a corps commander in Vietnam, is vice chief of staff; and Major General Joseph McChristian, the controversial chief of intelligence for MACV, is now chief of intelligence for the entire Army. As in Vietnam, he tours Army bases giving pep talks and shoring up morale. He sees little of the press in Washington, but meets the locals occasionally when he turns up at Fort Benning or Fort Bragg. By at least one account, he is an unhappy man. "Why do they keep saying that Giap is such a great strategist?" he asked a recent visitor. The implication is obvious. "If Westy had had the good luck to leave Vietnam in late 1966, he would have looked pretty good. But the longer he stayed the worse it got," said an American official who has watched him here and there.

But Westmoreland is not much thought about in Saigon now, any more than is Henry Cabot Lodge or Ngo Dinh Diem. Memories are twelve or eighteen months long, no longer. The faces change, the war goes on. It has been for many of them a problem of bureaucracy. Officials working with the Hamlet Evaluation Survey (HES), the controversial method of computing which hamlets are friendly, which are unfriendly, and which are toss-ups in the race with the Communists, are in command of extraordinary facts which are said to ensure accuracy. Check and doublecheck; check and balance; check and recheck. Robert Komer until his ambassadorial nomination was in charge of it. Ask him or his extremely able aides about the HES, and they will display it and discuss it in the manner of a Swiss watchmaker discussing a Girard Perregaux. Wheels click and whir, mesh, and the machine runs. It does what its makers want it to do. It does not matter if the clock is five minutes fast or five hours slow. It is the mechanism that counts, and the mechanism is a marvel.

The Algerian analogy is now being used freely in Washington, and while very few men see a Secret Army Organization rising from the ashes of the Vietnam War, a number do see unprecedented bitterness and frustration among the officer corps at not being "permitted" to win the war. But this undercurrent is not evident in South Vietnam. For the first time, one hears majors and lieutenant colonels speaking of the war's absurdity. Creature comforts are at an unparalleled high (except for the wretch in the foxhole), and the sense of it is men watching the slow slide to the dark side of the moon. Marijuana is everywhere, casually available on street corners and in the bar of the Continental Palace Hotel. One finds bitterness, but the suspicion is that for the majority it is only skin-deep. The perversity of attitude allows a man to hate both the war and the press for "knocking" the effort, allows him to hate the Viet Cong and respect and admire him as a tough and tenacious fighter. It is a product of emotion. The war is not to soldiers an abstraction, but an existential event that must somehow be given meaning. To men accustomed to thinking in terms of honor and country, it is not enough to explain Vietnam away as a terrible mistake, an aberration in the American conscience, the result of nascent imperialism, a radical departure—as Eugene McCarthy says—from the traditional themes of American foreign policy.

Did all those men, the enlisted men for whom the officer corps is responsible, die in vain? If the war was worth fighting in 1966 and 1967, why is it not worth fighting in 1968 and 1969? It is one thing for a politician or a journalist to understand how it happened, how we got from here to there in Asia, denounce it as wrong, and say it will never happen again; quite another for a battalion commander who fought all three battles of Dakto. They have done the dirty work of the state, when all is said and done, and sooner or later if the enterprise fails they are entitled to explanations of why it failed. The rest of us are merely accomplices.

One returned finally to South Vietnam to talk to the inmates, to try to find out what lessons have been learned. We have been in it now for—what, three years? Five years? What do the people there think about it? How does it look inside the kaleidoscope?

"It really is a lot better now," a friend, an official, said, as if speaking of someone who was ill. "Really, it is. . . . The civil defense forces really are doing very well; the GVN has supplied the guns faster than we ever thought they could. The coordination has been fantastic. . . . You know about the new miracle rice. It's terrific. It is going to revolutionize farming in Southeast Asia. There is only one small trouble [smile]: the Vietnamese don't like the rice much [smile]; they don't like the taste of it. . . ."

He had been nodding, and speaking very slowly. Then his voice became an edge, and looking at me, he went on: "You know the GVN has beefed up the ARVN. They are past their 1968 quota and well into 1969. I *know* there are troubles with the officers and the rest; *none* of it is perfect. But the GVN has gotten off its ass better than we ever thought they could. It is a real government now; it's working."

Now he looked at me directly: "Look. We have proven one thing. We have proven that if something like this happens somewhere else in the world we have proven now that *we know how to do it*. We know how to contain an insurgency. We have made a hell of a lot of mistakes, but we've won this war, make no mistake about it. We have proven that we can win. We can do it. We have proven that now. . . ."

He went on for a little, but I did not pursue it. There was no point. I no longer lived in Vietnam; I lived in America. He had been in the country since the 1950s, had spent the better part of the last ten years dealing with the Vietnam problem. He knew more about it than I did. If he wanted to win the war, wanted to believe that it was won, it seemed to me that he had every right. There was nothing I could say that would help, because I saw it as an outsider. But as we left the restaurant I thought of the country, South Vietnam, as a corpse: molding, long dead, but with the hair and fingernails continuing to grow.

DAVID HALBERSTAM

The Vietnamization of America

I remember this incident. It was in 1962 and the Ngo Dinh Diem regime was at the height (if that word can be used) of its powers. The Viet Cong were stealing the country away at night out in the provinces; but in Saigon, which was all that mattered in that feudal society, Diem and his family controlled all. He won elections by a comforting 99 percent. His photo was everywhere; his name was in the national anthem. He controlled almost every seat in the assembly. He owned the Vietnamese press. The constitution was his. The American ambassador was his messenger boy; a four-star American general believed his every word. If Diem could not control the Viet Cong, he could control the Americans. All, unfortunately, but their press. That was the shame of it; if you accepted millions of their dollars, you had to let in their reporters. It rankled with Diem but even more with high-ranking members of the American mission. The press, not the Viet Cong, was the only problem in Vietnam, General Paul Harkins told Defense Secretary McNamara. If they could only control the American press, housebreak them. Censor them. Something like that.

It rankled in particular with the head of the Central Intelligence Agency there, a man we may call J. R. In those days, I did not think of J. R. as being a representative of a democracy. He was a private man, responsible to no constituency. Later, I was to think of him as being more representative of America than I wanted, in that he held power, manipulated it, had great money to spend—all virtually unchecked by the public eye. J. R., of course, bristled over the problems of working for a democracy. He disliked the press intensely. It was all too open. How could one counter communism, which was J. R.'s mission—little black tricks that never worked, lots of intelligence (mostly lies) coming in from his agents—with a free press that caused trouble and was read by suspicious Senators and Congressmen? How could one accomplish anything with them? He delivered these tirades from time to time and, one night, he made one to William Trueheart, then deputy chief of mission, one of the few high-ranking Americans to leave Vietnam with their

Source: Mr. Halberstam is a Pulitzer-prize-winning journalist. This article originally appeared in *Playboy Magazine*, December 1970, pp. 118, 166, 236, 237. Copyright © 1970 by Playboy. Reprinted by permission of the author and the publisher.

integrity intact. J. R. went to it—against a free press, free reporting, lack of controls—what could *serious* men do? We had to stop this. Look at the way Diem handled public information and the way the Communists handled theirs. Finally, Trueheart gently interrupted; yes, it was all true, but if we didn't watch out, if we did these things and controlled the press, we might very well end up just the same as the Communists.

We were all much younger then. Spiro Agnew was a better-than-average municipal official outside Baltimore; John Mitchell was selling municipal bonds; and SNCC was considered a radical and dangerous civil rights group. Who would have thought that the little war, this mockery of a war, would finally give the U. S. convulsions that would threaten its fiber, its confidence, its democratic traditions, so that what had seemed like the promise of a golden American era under Jack Kennedy would end under Lyndon Johnson and Richard Nixon with the darker shadows of another Weimar Republic hanging over us? Who would have thought that the tail would wag the dog; that as Saigon had seemed distant, arrogant and removed from its countryside —it was the duty of the peasant to honor the government, to get aboard, or the recourse would be force—Washington would seem ever more separated from the rest of its country, as though somehow there were a great moat around it? Each capital would come to be the mirror image of the other. Our country's nerves were jangled, its values were changing, it knew instinctively what did and did not work, and it regarded Washington as a manufacturer of most of what did not function. Washington was distant, removed and, yes, arrogant: there was a genuine swagger to Agnew. And there was an insensitivity to the real problems of the population and a belief that when those feelings were too openly and defiantly expressed, the only recourse was force.

We, who had been so sure, would export our values to Vietnam, where surely they would work. But our values would fail there, and, in failing, would so damage the major organism as to diminish belief in our democracy. The liberal democracy center, so damaged by the war, would begin to come apart. In its place would grow a new angry, alienated, militant and sometimes violent left (told not to be violent, its spokesmen would cite the national violence carried out in Vietnam); and then, in turn, on the right, a new menacing nationalism—angrier, anti-intellectual, bitter about the challenges to authority from the left, bitter about what *they* had done to the *flag*. Construction workers joyously beat up war protestors, encouraged, it occasionally seemed, by the White House.

The war had resurrected and given us Richard Nixon, who gave us Spiro Agnew, who would sound so much like J. R.; the problem was not the war and not the racial failure; it was those who wrote about them and those who protested them. Agnew spoke harshly and there was a touch of menace, an implicit threat in what he said when he talked about the press, particularly the TV networks. And Nixon gave us John Mitchell, who threatened, or promised—it was hard to tell the difference with him—that there was no such thing as the New Left, that the country was going so far right that we would not recognize it. One sensed with Mitchell, in those appearances on *Meet the Press,* a desperate attempt to control himself, not to say what he really thought; one could get a better glimpse of the real Mitchell through the words of his wife. A peace march reminded her of the Russian Revolution, with all those liberal-Communists in town. A shame they couldn't be deported. And, of course, her threatening late-hour phone calls to the Senators and newspapers that disagreed with her and her husband.

It wasn't surprising that Mitchell was an ominous figure in the country, for it was a sign of our times that we had politicized the police, that most dangerous of all acts in a democracy. The police had become a symbol, good or bad, depending upon which America you chose. They were a political force now and well aware of it. They had champions right through to the top; it was old-fashioned to be neutral about the cops, to think that their job was simply to enforce the laws. The laws themselves had become so controversial. So had the Presidency. The national anthem. The flag. The length of Marines hair. Bob Hope. Even football coaches. The outpouring of grief from the older and more authoritarian-minded America on the death of Vince Lombardi was extraordinary. He was the best of all possible symbols, a strict authoritarian and, better yet, a winner. When Lombardi died, the New York *Daily News,* perhaps the most patriotic if least informative of our major newspapers, gave him the space usually reserved for someone like Franklin Roosevelt or Dwight Eisenhower. And sportswriter Dick Young wrote: "Vince Lombardi has died and there is great sadness among the good people. He has left the world too soon, almost as though he couldn't stand to see what was happening to it. There is no longer a place for Vince Lombardi. He believed savagely in GOD, in COUNTRY and in FAMILY."

It was astonishing the way the war dominated the country and distorted the process of American life. There was an irony to this, because the men who had planned the war had realized that Asian jungles are tricky and had planned a technological and mechanistic war with low American casualties— a war that would infect American society as little as possible. In a limited sense, they were right; considering how much killing there was, American casualties remained low. But there was a special price, a price to the soul; what it did was change the values of a nation, turn it away from the technological thinking that had produced the war. We were at the height of our powers; we poured 80 billion dollars a year into the defense budget. (John McNaughton, a former Assistant Defense Secretary, once told a group of Senatorial aides: Well, yes, it would take about one billion dollars to defend the United States, so that anything more in the budget was simply a reflection of our view of ourselves as a world power.) Thus the New Romans, with 79 billion dollars' worth of empire. Technological Romans. Yet the iron of this power, a nation that sent men to the moon and brought them back, that has intercontinental missiles, nuclear submarines, all the hardware—seemed curiously threatened. When bombs went off in America, and they did despite the defense budget, they were bombs thrown from within, thrown by Americans, thrown in protest of the defense budget as much as anything else.

Vietnam had turned us upside down, challenged our fundamental assumptions. Indeed, as late as May 1970, Joseph Alsop, a hawk columnist who had helped invent the war and had written optimistically each year since 1962 about imminent victory, had noticed during one of his frequent trips to the U. S. that all was not well here. He had written an appeal to Senator Edward Kennedy, deploring "the political lunacy" of the young in "passionately demonstrating against your own country's successes on the battlefield." (Alsop's belief that Kennedy, by changing his stand on the war, could change the young showed that he knew almost as little about American politics as about Vietnamese politics.) To which Kennedy, youngest brother and political heir to two men who had helped initiate the war, wrote in one of the most eloquent dissections of what had happened here: "We are a nation constantly being reborn, and we can thank our God that those newly arrived in our society will not casually accept the views and presumptions of their fathers, much less their errors. They do not protest their 'country's successes on the battlefield,' doubtful as those successes may be; they protest the very existence of the battlefield, for it has no place in their vision of the country that is to be theirs. And I support them in that."

It was not just the war, of course, that was tearing the fabric of this society; there were many other factors that contributed to the division: the spiritual vacuum that seemed to accompany material affluence and technological success, the great racial sores in the country, the hypocrisy in much of American life. But finally, it was the war that magnified all faults, that eroded if not destroyed the faith of so many people in this country. We had set out to impose our values on a foreign land; we would help them, teach them good things. We found them a president, wrote them a constitution, bought them an army. What more could they want? But we learned that they did not want these things. Then, having seen our values fail there, we re-examined them here at home and found the definition of our society, and what constituted success, wanting. We had begun the Sixties sure of our values, willing to export them to all nations: advisors, Peace Corps people, Alliance for Progress workers. On reflection, there was a colossal arrogance to a nation that sought to aid the poor of the world but would not help its poor at home; to a Congress that would approve all kinds of programs to help the poor Vietnamese peasants fatten their pigs so they would have juicier pork than the Viet Cong but sat back and laughed and joked when a bill came up asking for Federal funds to be used against the rats in the nation's largest cities.

Mayor John Lindsay of New York, a city abounding in smog, racial failure and financial problems, would muse that perhaps he ought to discover a Communist guerrilla force in the city so he could get more Federal aid. We looked at Vietnam and found that what we claimed we were doing there was false; then we looked homeward and found that just as false. We were not the country we thought, not the country the history books taught us. And symbolically, if Vietnam was an example of technology used against human beings, then it was significant that the most important man of the past decade was not one of the great names of the era who had mastered that technology—McNamara, Bundy, Rusk, Kennedy—but a private citizen, Ralph Nader, who didn't work through any existing structure or political party. It was Nader who made the case against a kind of technology used only for bigness and profit, used *against* life rather than for it.

We were a democracy and were told often enough to be grateful for that privilege. We had choices, options, freedom. But they had snuck by us into the war, snuck by Congress, too. Then, as we went in deeper, as the reality of the failure out there came home to us, the Government seemed unable to do anything, only to get us in deeper, only to tell us that what we saw with our own eyes was not true. The feeling of frustration with the democratic process was enormous; we had elected Lyndon Johnson in 1964 because he wasn't Barry Goldwater and wouldn't get us into a war. We learned our lesson in 1968— and elected Richard Nixon because he wasn't Lyndon Johnson, for that reason and that reason alone. He would get us out of the war; he had a plan. So, having elected him, we found that all he had was the same old chauvinism of the past, the same rhetoric both harsh and foolish: peace with honor, we would not be humiliated, we would never lose a war. America somehow was different. We never lost wars. All our wars were just. Those of us who dreamed that it might be different, that a President could get up and speak humbly and tell the truth that the war was a great miscalculation, were struck once again by the arrogance of it all. We were told by Nixon that Vietnam was one of our finest hours (had it been one of our finest hours, he would have remained a New York City lawyer) and, to show it, he went into Cambodia. Vietnam begat Cambodia. Cambodia begat Kent State. Even his October 1970 peace proposals seemed to be aimed more at the American political scene than at the Vietnamese realities. Thus the widening of the gap between the two Americas.

I remember a dinner party for Nelson Rockefeller on the night of Kent State—not really a social occasion but a political one. Nelson and Happy wanted to meet some young people, writers and artists (it was lonely up there on Park Avenue; besides, it was an election year). A lovely evening, all black-tie, glittering women, great and famous men. Imported Cuban cigars. One's memories of Rockefeller were not necessarily bad; he had, after all, run against Nixon in 1960, been booed by the right wing in 1964 and had not been a particularly grievous governor, though being more fond of bomb shelters than most of us. That evening, however, he looked young but seemed old. It turned into an evening of unbelievable bitterness. Rockefeller had said no, he didn't plan to talk about the war or about the defense budget (he had cared about the war two years earlier, when it was an issue he could use against Nixon, but now he no longer cared, he had lost his passion on the war). He sensed our bitterness. He didn't share it, but he wanted to reassure us. It was great, fellas, just *great* that we could talk like this. Disagree. Express our feelings. It was the American way. What made us great as a country. I could not control myself that night, control my bitterness and anger and, in fact, hate, singling out this man, who (God save Standard Oil) was supposed to be one of our better politicians, this uniquely callous man. Didn't he know it had all gone beyond that, beyond his stupid Rotary Club speeches, that it was too late to congratulate us for having the opportunity to sit with him and smoke Cuban cigars and vent our impotence? Farewell to you, Nelson Rockefeller, you and all yours.

So in there somewhere was a loss of faith, a loss of confidence and belief. One sensed it in himself. I remember the first time I saw it, on opening day at Yankee Stadium in 1966 with a group of friends, mostly writers. One of them had a girlfriend along, and when they played the national anthem (a song that at its worst had been a bore), she refused to stand. She was already doing something called draft counseling. I thought her refusal to stand was a bit odd, but it was her business. Then later that year, watching the first major anti-war parade in the city, I remembered my own conflicting feelings, my anger when I saw the Viet Cong flag, a symbol of hostility toward our own country. I'm too numbed by it all now; I can't carry the Viet Cong flag *nor* my own. I find myself rebelling more and more against the symbols of my own country; the more patriotic the symbol, the more I withdraw. The more some speech invokes the greatness of the American past, the more dubious I am, not only of the present but of the past. I don't want any parades nor the national anthem nor the patriotic hanky-panky at half time (all, I suspect, that Nixon likes best; it is his America I withdraw from). The blind acceptance of it all: If it's American, it's good. Support it now and ask questions later. Trust in us, we know better.

All the old suspicions and doubts about the country are back, all the suspicions that must have been with my grandfather when he came to the country 80 years ago, which ebbed and disappeared through two generations of Americanization, better education, shorter hair, no beards—all to make it and then, having made it, to become alien again in one's own land. The police must have been very visible to him when he came to this country (just as he was visible to them, looking so different, so odd), and they must have disappeared from my father's view just as he disappeared from theirs. But now they are back in my view; for the first time, the sons of the upper class, disillusioned about the war, wearing their hair long, smoking pot, can see the police, and vice versa. Now I am alien again, my hair a bit longer; when I'm on an airplane, I look around and see all the nice young businessmen, out hustling, playing the game; I wonder what they think about the war and I look at their hair—after all, they look at mine. Our distaste is mutual. I judge them just as they must be judging me.

If this is happening with me (after all, I am a gentle 36—not too young, not too old—in the middle of the battlefield, and I can remember World War Two, and I'm grateful to this country for that, grateful for my education, largely liking my life), it is the same with others on both sides, driven from the center, driven from faith, reverting to what they had been, to older prejudices, be they right-wing prejudices against kids, against long-hairs, against Negroes and Jews or the other side's age-old prejudices against the military and the police. (Sometimes I wonder, when I see upper-class kids baiting the cops, if it isn't a new form of upper-class snobbism against the lower class.) There is a new arrogance to this country, a lack of willingness to compromise, to temper personal prejudice. Jerzy Kosinski, a writer who fled Poland for America and received a National Book Award in 1969, said that America has changed radically in the decade he has been here. It has become more European, less centrist; the people are more outspoken, more shrill. He is, I think, absolutely right: We have moved away from the rational concept of events (in part because the events themselves, engineered by men like Bundy, Kennedy and McNamara, who were supreme rationalists, turned out to be so irrational). We find reflections of our new doubts everywhere. It is not, I think, surprising that Richard Nixon liked the film *Patton* so much. It is an odd and brilliant film, a film for our time. The doves will see it and come out dovier; the hawks will emerge hawkier. Nixon surely found in it confirmation of the view he holds of himself, of the fact that authoritarian strength will triumph over soft dissent.

So we are all being Vietnamized, all a little differently, none of us the same. I grew up, like so many others, believing that this country worked, that it groped its way, sometimes slowly, sometimes awkwardly, toward a better life; and, essentially, that the future was going to be better. Now I'm not so sure. I see the tension and the hate and the bombings and the reaction to the bombings, and read *The New York Times Magazine* with its regular articles comparing us with the Weimar Republic, and I'm not sure that the future is so bright. Indeed, there are times when I am wide awake and rational and I get the cold chill of a bad dream, a sense that we may live through something very terrible in our lifetimes. To use the quotation from Emerson that George Ball, then Undersecretary of State, used when he made his valiant last desperate attempt to turn American policy around on Vietnam in 1965: "Events are in the saddle and tend to ride mankind."

ANSWER: It was a ditch. And so we started pushing them off and we started shooting them, so altogether we just pushed them all off, and just started using automatics on them. And then—

QUESTION: And babies?

ANSWER: And babies. And so we started shooting them, and somebody told us to switch off to single shot so that we could save ammo. So we switched off to single. . . .

—Excerpt from an interview with Paul Meadlo on the events at Song My.

The thing about us as a nation wasn't so much that we were different but that we *thought* we were different. In the early Sixties, we were a nation sure of our morality. We had our religion and, if it didn't really question the social and ethical problems of the day in most communities, it was booming ahead, nonetheless (in fact, it was a pretty good rule that the less the pastor questioned the local mores, the larger and more beautiful his church). We had our political system, which was free, and our capitalist enterprise, which worked miraculously. We were, it seemed, freer, richer and more pious than other nations. Our myths were our dogmas. When we went to war, we won those wars and found in the winning, in the prosperity that followed, proof that we were somehow different. Even in the brief flickering moment of doubt, the mid-Fifties, when Sputnik flashed (could the *Communist* system build a bigger rocket?), we doubted only our power, never our morality and decency.

Later in the decade, of course, we were secure again, even in our power. Our virility was restored, our space men flashed ahead of Soviet space men. We had harnessed our power to our morality, at least in space, where one could see it and boast of it, though perhaps not in our inner cities; we had resisted the temptation to be, most dangerous of all words, soft. Even our poets warned us against that. "Be more Irish than Harvard," Robert Frost had warned that Irish Harvard man John Kennedy at his Inauguration, not realizing that academe had produced a new brand of very tough bombardiers. We had always indulged ourselves in the belief in our nobility of intention, and the post-War years had confirmed our finest suspicions about ourselves. We became rich and the East was poor (that two oceans had separated us from the ravages of two great wars did not occur to us very often). More, it was not just financial superiority: The trail of refugees coming across Europe, east to west, confirmed our sense of values; capitalism was better than communism, more humane, its earlier abuses tempered by new liberal legislation that only a democracy could produce. President Kennedy could go to Berlin in 1963 and stand at the Wall, the symbol of our light and their darkness, and, carried away by the emotion of the moment, put aside his prepared statement and say that whether people felt that competition between East and West was judged on economics, politics or personal freedom—*let them come to Berlin.* Perhaps Europe, more cynical, torn by two terrible wars, more aware that no one ever wins a war, was tired of the old competitions; but here in America, we still believed that God was on the winning side. Ours.

While Europe had turned away from politics and war, tired and cynical after terrible bloodletting in this century, we still *believed.* (The French had failed in Indochina before us, but the men who planned our war were not deterred by that; they regarded the French as inferior people corrupted by too much defeat and too much good wine; they weren't a can-do society.) We were activists, believing that it could all change. This was the meaning of the Kennedy era—that we could elect a handsome young activist President who could diagnose the world's ills and then do something about them, that the establishment would, with a good deal of conniving and manipulation, respond. To be involved, that was it. Kennedy's favorite quotation was from Dante, that the hottest places in hell were reserved for those who sat neutral during a time of great crisis.

As Kennedy had challenged Americans to have higher hopes, to become involved, and as those years ended with the country mired in Vietnam, there would be an enormous disappointment and disillusion with the conventional processes. We were not different, we were the same as others. Just as powerless. But our sense of frustration was even greater because we had expected to share in the power and found that we could not and because we were living in a country that exercised such awesome power that when we failed to control it, the sense of disaster and horror was so much greater because we loosed so much more devastation on the world. Thus the withdrawal from conventional politics. Some would turn to more radical politics, seeing in Vietnam and the inability to reverse it a far deeper failure of the system, not just an aberration but a reflection. Some would become bombers, answering the violence around them with violence of their own. Some would become almost European in their attitudes toward politics, believing there are no answers, that politics is all, to use their word, shit; that the answer is in self, in humanism. The answer is to drop out, to turn to drugs, to become a mystic of sorts, away from the jarring crowded competitive race that is America. Drop out to communes, new villages, new, less competitive ways of life. Drop out of the existing political parties that seem so archaic and corroded into something newer, more personalized, narrower and angrier. If the party didn't include workers or farmers and was not a majority party, that was all right. The existing parties were throwing the vote away, in that they were a continuation of what existed, which was all false. Politics to them was something different than to their predecessors: It was a way of finding and expressing self; not, as it always had been before, the reverse, the individual going into politics to become part of something larger, greater, broader.

So the war in Vietnam began what will surely be an age of disillusion here at home, an age stunning in its speed, one more product of the incredible velocity of life that now marks the American culture. Ten years from grand illusion to loss of faith. Who would have thought of protesting Jack Kennedy's nomination at Los Angeles in 1960? Oh, perhaps there was a lingering hope of Stevenson, but Jack seemed to represent us at our best—handsome, stylish, intelligent, graceful, witty, tough. The fact that he was also very, very rich and thus able to use his money outrageously to bend the corrupt processes did not bother us then. He didn't represent the best of us, he represented the best of the rich. His concerns, therefore, were not necessarily our concerns, the pressures on him not necessarily the pressures on us. Thus, perhaps, Vietnam, and thus, perhaps, the Bay of Pigs. But the shadows had darkened by 1964. Kennedy was dead. Though the war in Vietnam was still a small one, it was growing and it seemed more in the tradition of the Bay of Pigs than of the

Peace Corps. The best of an entire generation had gone to Mississippi, a summer of deaths and cracked heads and tough sheriffs; and they had encountered local resistance and what appeared to be Washington's insensitivity.

In 1964, at Atlantic City, there was tension in the air, not within the processes; within what were deemed the processes, Lyndon Johnson had every vote. If he had signified Ho Chi Minh or Nasser as his running mate, he could have pulled it off. But for the first time, and this was significant, the people who were outside the processes, the disenfranchised, for whom the processes seemed distant and exclusive and arrogant, were demanding to get in. That was the significance of 1964; it was embryonic, but it was there. What would happen in the next four years would not end this sense of frustration, but, indeed, feed and fuel it.

By 1968, there was a full-scale war, a very big and dirty war, and those people who four years earlier had thought they were part of the processes, the very people who had helped keep the Mississippi Freedom Democratic Party out in 1964, now felt themselves excluded and powerless—the white liberal as nigger. So it was a great symbolic event, a bitter and violent confrontation, reflective of a country whose political system has not kept up with its needs, its politicians curiously insensitive to the demands of the occasion, the young people around them no longer interested in the old warnings: Be nice. Behave yourself. We may not be very good, but if you don't put on your good manners and swallow your disappointment, you may get something worse. The terrible thing about people who choose the lesser of two evils, Hannah Arendt once wrote, is that they soon forget they have chosen the lesser of two evils.

The young, who had said, in effect, it no longer works, you do not hear and you do not listen, your only answer to protest here and anywhere else is force, were, indeed, proved right in the streets of Chicago. This was not, after all, a challenge at some third-rate university where an insensitive university president had failed or a challenge at some bad local draft board or the protesting of a speech by the Secretary of State. Rather, this was a challenge to the heart of democratic society, in its (allegedly) most open function. The fact that, at this most democratic rite, the dominant role seemed to be played by the police was one more chilling lesson of what we had already lost and a warning of what might come next. We had gone through a jarring, tearing decade, torn apart by a stupid and senseless war, and we had lost much of our democratic balance.

Perhaps what we need now is for some great rich democratic nation to export its values to us, and its advisors, to teach us democracy, to help us with our values and institutions.

DWIGHT D. EISENHOWER

The Military-Industrial Complex

Until the latest of our world conflicts, the United States had no armaments industry. American makers of plowshares could, with time and as required, make swords as well.

But we can no longer risk emergency improvisation of national defense. We have been compelled to create a permanent armaments industry of vast proportions. Added to this, three and a half million men and women are directly engaged in the defense establishment. We annually spend on military security alone more than the net income of all United States corporations.

Now this conjunction of an immense military establishment and a large arms industry is new in the American experience. The total influence—economic, political, even spiritual—is felt in every city, every state house, every office of the Federal Government. We recognize the imperative need for this development. Yet we must not fail to comprehend its grave implications. Our toil, resources and livelihood are all involved; so is the very structure of our society.

In the councils of Government, we must guard against the acquisition of unwarranted influence, whether sought or unsought, by the military-industrial complex. The potential for the disastrous rise of misplaced power exists and will persist.

We must never let the weight of this combination endanger our liberties or democratic processes. We should take nothing for granted. Only an alert and knowledgeable citizenry can compel the proper meshing of the huge industrial and military machinery of defense with our peaceful methods and goals, so that security and liberty may prosper together.

Source: From Dwight D. Eisenhower's Farewell Address, January 1961.

G. WILLIAM DOMHOFF

The Power Elite

It is often said that the United States is a middle-class society. This may have been true generations ago when America was a land of small farmers and small businessmen, but it is hardly accurate today when farmers are a vanishing breed, twenty to twenty-five per cent of the population lives below the poverty line, sixty per cent of male heads of non-farm households are blue-collar and gray-collar workers, and a social upper class of .2 to .3 per cent of the population owns twenty-two per cent of all privately held wealth and sixty to seventy per cent of all privately held corporate wealth. In most of its aspects, then, the middle-class image of America is in need of considerable readjustment.

I would like to contribute to this readjustment by trying to show that major policy decisions in this country are made by members of a power elite which is the operating arm (or "executive committee" or "leadership group") of the enormously wealthy upperclass. Many members of this power elite are drawn from the upper class; others are high-level employees in institutions and associations controlled by members of the upper class. Whatever the social origins of any given member of the power elite, the important thing is that the power elite is rooted in and maintains the wealth and the privileges of a minuscule social group.

A distinction between upper class and power elite is important for two reasons. First, not all members of the upper class are involved in governing. Some may not even understand the policymaking process. Others may be personally opposed to some of the decisions made by their cousins and colleagues who have actively involved themselves in the upper-class organizations concerned with policy matters. Second, there are members of the power elite who are not members of the upper class. They are usually well-educated members of the middle class who have climbed the corporate ladder or have contributed ideas and leadership through the corporation law firm or the university. Many of these non-upper-class members of the power elite may become part of the upper class over a period of time. What is significant is

Source: Mr. Domhoff is a professor of psychology and author of *Who Rules America?* This is a brief version of a chapter from *The Higher Circles* by G. William Domhoff, which appeared in *The Center Magazine*, March 1970, pp. 87–90. Copyright © 1970 by G. William Domhoff. Reprinted by permission of Random House, Inc.

368

that these newcomers are advanced because of their ability to impress members of the upper class who—as directors, presidents, and advisers—control the organizations through which the non-upper-class employees must slowly advance.

In short, the distinction between upper class and power elite deals with two of the most typical objections to the idea that the upper class is a "governing" or "ruling" class, for there are upper-class playboys who are hardly "rulers," and there are leaders who are not members of the upper class.

Once the relationship between the upper class and the power elite is made clear, the next and most frequent objection to the thesis that a power elite dominates American society comes from those who are concerned with the actual policymaking process. Not content to infer "power" from such indicators as the distributions of wealth, income, tax benefits, and educational opportunities, these critics want to be shown in detail the means by which the rich and the well-born exercise their "power."

The challenge is a fair one to which there are several answers, including involvement in political campaigns and lobbying. Here I want to summarize what I think to be the major and least-known means by which the policy process is dominated. It is a fairly complex process and perhaps the best place to begin a discussion of it is with the interlocking group of organizations that I call the consensus-seeking and policy-planning institutions of the power elite. These groups—the Council on Foreign Relations, the Committee for Economic Development, the National Planning Association, and The Brookings Institution are among the most important and best known of them—are the means by which members of the power elite come together in groups of different sizes to discuss, to plan, to get to know each other better. It is primarily in these groups, I believe, and only secondarily in more social settings such as men's clubs, that attempts are made to iron out differences among themselves and to formulate reactions to events which are largely beyond their control.

Research, too extensive to recount here, shows that the members of these groups are for the most part corporate executives, bankers, financiers, and corporation lawyers, many of whom are, in turn, members of the upper class as indicated by criteria that have been carefully developed and substantiated as to their accuracy and utility (e.g. listings in certain blue books and social registers, attendance at certain private schools, membership in certain clubs). Further, research on these organizations indicates that they are financed in good measure by major corporations and foundations directed by the same men who participate in the work of the policy-planning and consensus-seeking organizations.

Ideas and policies generated by these groups reach the government in several ways. First, many members of these groups are appointed to positions in the Executive Branch of the federal government or to positions as advisers to legislative committees and subcommittees. Secondly, many members serve on the blue-ribbon commissions appointed by the President or departmental secretaries. Thirdly, some of these groups publish their policy suggestions, and thus, through books, pamphlets, the mass media, and discussion groups like the Foreign Policy Association and the World Affairs Council, reach people in government concerned with specific policies.

In general, then, these policy-planning groups serve as key links between the government and the social upper class of rich businessmen and their descendants. Financed by the major corporations and foundations controlled by members of the upper class, they are the training grounds for future governmental appointees and the generators of "idea-inputs" into the policy-formation process.

It is sometimes claimed that the social upper class is simply a collection of individuals who recognize no common interests and are therefore too unorganized to exercise power. It is true that some members of the upper class take no part in governing, but this does not deny the evidence that upper-class leaders from all over the country take part in interlocking consensus-seeking organizations of the power elite that are very much involved in the policy process. A. A. Berle, Jr., in his recent book on power and in his review of my book *Who Rules America?*, is wrong when he says that the upper class has no power because it does not get together and select leaders to represent it. I contend that the informal and peer-selected leadership provided by the Council on Foreign Relations, the Committee for Economic Development, the Twentieth Century Fund, and other such power-elite organizations is an adequate substitute for the overly formal criterion for cohesion set down by Berle.

It is often said, sometimes with heavy sarcasm, that the idea of a power elite is a conspiratorial fantasy of deluded, perhaps paranoid, individuals. It is, of course, almost axiomatic that those making this charge seldom have the humility to attempt to discover the psychiatric derivation of their own theories. Nor do they often note the existence of consensus-seeking and policy-planning organizations. When they do recognize their existence, as sociologist Arnold Rose did in the case of the Council on Foreign Relations in his book *The Power Structure*, they overlook the fact that the members of these organizations are members of the power elite. Instead, they characterize them as "experts."

When I use the term "power elite," I do not speak of a conspiracy of twelve or sixteen men who meet secretly in the bathroom of the University Club in New York, as George Kirstein caricatured my view in his *The Rich: Are They Different?* On the contrary, I speak of several thousand men from all over the country who meet quite openly in a variety of organizations that should be studied in detail by the academicians who so often serve as consultants to them.

One of the most prevalent beliefs I encounter is that it is really the "experts" who run America. This is true only in the limited sense that some middle-class experts housed in the M.I.T.-Harvard-Yale-Princeton-Columbia-University of

Chicago complex provide some of the information and ideas which members of the power elite use in making their decisions. Experts, especially economists, have been important for some time, but they hardly play the leading policy-forming role that social scientists and ultraconservatives have assigned to them.

I have not mentioned all the consensus-seeking and policy-planning organizations within the power elite. There are many. However, it would be misleading if I did not discuss two others: the National Association of Manufacturers and the U.S. Chamber of Commerce. They represent the die-hard conservatives within the power elite, just as such groups as the Council on Foreign Relations, the Committee for Economic Development, and the American Assembly represent what C. Wright Mills called the "sophisticated conservatives" or "business liberals," within the power elite.

Most American social scientists mistakenly think the N.A.M. and the U.S. Chamber of Commerce are key spokesmen of the entire power elite. These scholars note how often this extremely conservative clique is defeated by "liberals," and this is then used as evidence that the power elite doesn't have very much power.

This confusion concerning "liberal" victories over the power elite is so important that it deserves to be underlined by a consideration of two studies of the Social Security Act of 1935. That act is one of the favorite pieces of evidence against a power-elite theory. The implication of these two studies is that social security was a victory for "experts" or "liberals," thus apparently challenging my view that the power elite dominate the policy process. The first of these studies is by Roy Lubove, and it is entitled *The Struggle for Social Security, 1900–1935.* For my purposes here the key sentences are:

"The American Association for Labor Legislation (A.A.L.L.) created and sustained the organized social insurance movement in the United States. . . . The A.A.L.L. testified to the emergence of the social scientist as an influence in social legislation and reform."

Two points are noteworthy. First, nowhere in the book is the financing and leadership of the A.A.L.L. discussed. One learns from other sources that a few rich families and two or three power-elite foundations supported the work of this now-defunct organization. The A.A.L.L. had as its directors some of the important members of the power elite in the early years of this century. Second, the emphasis is put on the role of the social science expert, when in fact the handful of economists the author has in mind were merely the day-to-day spear-carriers.

The other study that overlooks the role of the sophisticated conservatives within the power elite in creating the social security system is by Arthur M. Schlesinger, Jr. It appears as a chapter in *The Coming of the New Deal.* The scene opens with a small but hardy band of liberals struggling to develop the social security program. Several names are mentioned, and it is noted that the A.A.L.L. and a few liberal businessmen played a role:

"From the outset of the Depression it [unemployment insurance] had been earnestly discussed among economists and social workers and within the American Association for Labor Legislation.

"In the fall of 1933 the Rauschenbusches met in Washington (the meeting was in the Brandeis apartment; the Justice was absent) with a group of liberal businessmen like Henry Dennison and Edward Filene, and young New Dealers, among them Charles E. Wyzanski, Jr., and Thomas H. Eliot of the Labor Department, and Thomas G. Corcoran."

There are several deficiencies in this account. First, nothing is told about the A.A.L.L. It could not be guessed that it is an organization of one element within the power elite. Second, the account does not connect the liberal businessmen Filene and Dennison to the A.A.L.L. Nor does it note that they are also important members or founders of other power-elite organizations, such as the Twentieth Century Fund and the Business Advisory Council. Third, it does not mention that the young New Dealers Wyzanski, Eliot, and Corcoran are corporation lawyers—Wyzanski in Boston's most eminent firm, Eliot from an "old" Boston family, and Corcoran with the Wall Street firm of Cotton & Franklin, which did considerable business for the investment house of Dillon Read & Co.

After painting an incomplete picture of the insurgent liberals, Schlesinger later warns that the enemies of social security were not asleep. Who were they? The forces of "organized business," Schlesinger writes. "While the friends of social security were arguing out the details of the program, other Americans were regarding the whole idea with consternation, if not with horror. Organized business had long warned against such pernicious notions."

What is the evidence for the notion that "organized business" viewed social security with consternation or horror? The answer is found in pronouncements from the National Industrial Conference Board, the National Association of Manufacturers, the Illinois Manufacturers Association, the Ohio Chamber of Commerce, and Alfred P. Sloan of General Motors. However, Schlesinger has committed a serious error in identifying organized business with these organizations and their views. In fact, they represent only one part of the power elite. The other, more sophisticated, sector manifested itself in at least three major ways on this issue:

1. Through the A.A.L.L., which Schlesinger does not connect to the business community.

2. Through the Business Advisory Council, whose social insurance committee consisted of Gerard Swope, president of General Electric; Walter Teagle, president of Standard Oil of New Jersey; Morris Leeds, president of Leeds & Northrup; and Colonel Robert G. Elbert, chairman of the board of the Aeolian Corporation and the International Holding Company. (Swope, who was very close to President Roosevelt, and Leeds were also leaders within the A.A.L.L.) This committee worked with the special government committee that formulated the social security legislation. The Business Advisory Council as a whole played its most important public role when twenty of its members

appeared at the White House to counter publicly the sharp criticism of the program by the U.S. Chamber of Commerce.

Among those present for this meeting were the retiring president of the U.S. Chamber of Commerce and representatives of Chase National Bank, Remington Rand, Kennecott Copper, U.S. Rubber, Cannon Mills, Procter & Gamble, Grace National Bank, Goldman Sachs, and Brown Brothers Harriman. None of this information on the Business Advisory Council (some of which figured prominently at that time in *The New York Times'* accounts of the Social Security Act) appears in Schlesinger's account.

3. The final example of a concerted effort for social security by a leading institution of the power elite concerns the Rockefeller Foundation. It brought two prominent British leaders to the United States in 1933 to tell American businessmen how pleased British businessmen were with the social security system already established in their country. According to Frances Perkins, then Secretary of Labor, writing about it years later in *The Roosevelt I Knew*, the visits to various parts of the country by these Rockefeller Foundation-sponsored Englishmen helped to allay the fears of many businessmen. Again, there is no mention of this in the Schlesinger account.

The net effect of Schlesinger's chapter, then, is to range "organized business" against the seemingly scattered forces of the A.A.L.L., a few liberal businessmen, and a handful of young New Dealers, when in fact big business was divided into "moderate" and conservative factions on the issue, with the moderate group well organized, quite articulate, and very much involved in the formulation and passage of the act. What we really have is a conflict between the two basic tendencies within the power elite, the sophisticated conservatives and the diehard conservatives (who, of course, are as one on a great many issues and on most general principles).

From a perusal of several other published case studies, and from the unpublished work on Congress by political scientist Edward Malecki of California State College at Los Angeles, I believe that the alignment of forces on the Social Security Act represents a fairly typical pattern. According to this view (and I realize I am being very cryptic in this brief account) the National Association of Manufactures-U.S. Chamber of Commerce clique gets its way with Congress unless the all-important sophisticated conservatives within the power elite side with labor and the liberals.

Against the united opposition of the power elite, labor and liberalism can get nowhere. Another way of putting this would be to say that the sophisticated conservatives within the power elite, founded upon larger and more internationally based wealth, and operating primarily through the Council on Foreign Relations, the Foreign Policy Association, the Committee for Economic Development, the Business Advisory Council, the National Planning Association, the Twentieth Century Fund, The Brookings Institution, the Urban Coalition, the National Municipal League, the Ford Foundation, the three Carnegie Foundations, the Rockefeller Foundation, and the moderate wings of both political parties, are the key determinant in the American policy-formation process. The coalition the sophisticated conservatives decide to form, whether it be with labor and liberals, or with fellow power elitists of the National Association of Manufacturers mentality, is going to be the winner in the long run in any American political struggle.

RALPH NADER

GM and the Auto Industry: The Threat of Corporate Collectivism

Getting around on the ground in private transport is America's biggest business. Whether in input-output analysis or simple aggregate data, the automobile industry stands as the private economic activity with the greatest multiplier effect for the rest of the economy. The industry consumed eleven per cent of the aluminum, twenty per cent of the steel, thirty-five per cent of the zinc, fifty per cent of the lead, and more than sixty per cent of the rubber used in the United States in 1967.

The automobile industry's capacity for insatiable depletion of public and private pocketbooks can be painful. One of every six retail dollars goes to buy or provide for motor vehicles. More than a hundred billion dollars a year are expended on new cars, used cars, gasoline, tires, auto repair and replacement parts, auto insurance and finance, the construction and upkeep of roads, and other supportive facilities. Numerous ancillary industries and public services rely on the continuous multi-million volume production of America's most visible industrial art form.

It is often said by auto industry boosters that one of every six business

Source: Ralph Nader, whose book *Unsafe at Any Speed* spurred the nation to long overdue reforms in automobile safety, has also pressed Congress and executive agencies on such diverse consumer causes as radiation hazards, pipeline safety, meat inspection, environmental pollution, and corporate concentration. Reprinted from *The Progressive*, September 1968, pp. 13–18, by permission of the publisher.

establishments is dependent on the purchase and use of motor vehicles. In terms of unused capacity, fuel consumption per passenger, injuries and pollution, and total time loss of passengers, automotive travel is probably the most wasteful and inefficient mode of travel by industrial man. This is not to mention the highway lobby's appropriation and gross misuse of urban land for highway belts and its stifling of investment in mass transit. Yet, automobiles will be here for some time to come, and the market structure, performance, and profits of an industry that so dominates the economy and is in turn so dominated by one corporation—General Motors—demand careful scrutiny to determine if it is functioning in the best interest of the public.

The domestic automobile industry is composed of four companies, three of which account for more than ninety-seven per cent of the domestic car market. General Motors delivered 54.7 per cent of the North American-type passenger cars sold in the United States last year. In most of the post-war period, GM's share of the market has consistently been between fifty and fifty-five per cent of the domestic market.

The dimensions of the world's largest industrial giant require some statistical etching. For 1967, the company's net sales reached $20,026,000,000, the third highest in its history. Net income was reported at $1,627,000,000, down from $1,793,000,000 for 1966, and still a distance from its profit record of $2,126,000,000 in 1965 (4.7 per cent of the total of U.S. corporate after-tax earnings).

First half reports for 1968 point to at least a near record year for GM sales and profits. Its profit rate is regularly far higher than that of other auto manufacturers. GM's shares of total domestic automobile manufacture sales and earnings for 1966 were fifty-two per cent and sixty-nine per cent respectively. For the period 1947–1966, GM's profits after taxes averaged 22.7 per cent return on net worth, almost twice the 12.2 per cent national average. This is the most conservative estimate, based on GM's accounting practices which understate its income.

The very size and diversity of GM provides an awesome leverage against any competitors. General Motors Acceptance Corporation, the company's wholesale and retail financing subsidiary, is the single largest seller of short-term commercial paper with such outstandings rivaling the U.S. Treasury itself. Motors Insurance Corporation, a wholly owned subsidiary of GMAC, is one of the nation's largest underwriters of physical damage insurance.

The nearly 13,000 substantial GM dealers, whom GM has made financially dependent upon it by its policy of dealer exclusivity, comprise a powerful force at the retail level to further GM's hegemony. Bending dealers to their will has resulted in a greater and greater captive or exclusive market for parts and accessories (trumpeted publicly by the saturation advertising campaign to "KEEP YOUR CAR ALL GM") and has put a merciless squeeze or squeezeout on independent manufacturers and wholesalers.

Power begets power. The former chief of the Justice Department's Anti-trust Division, Donald Turner, in June, 1966, spoke on the anti-competitive effects of advertising flowing from firms possessing inordinate market power in their industry. GM's annual advertising budget exceeds $200 million, touting, among other things, excellence and "genuineness" of their parts. With a liquidity position in excess of three billion dollars distributed in variable proportions among more than 100 of the country's largest banks, GM exerts a powerful influence in the world of finance. Considerations other than economics dictate such geographical placement.

Flexibility in the exercise of market power by GM is facilitated by keeping its financial reporting on the most general level. GM publishes only consolidated figures on its operations, refusing to break down its profits and financial data by divisions. Close observers of GM's operations indicate that one reason for such non-disclosure is that exceptionally high profits are made from its spare parts and accessories business—a particularly sensitive fact in view of the fancification, poor durability, and expensive replacement (owing to original design decisions) of various portions of its automobiles.

Another reason for no divisional reporting is to cover up which lines are subsidizing other company activities for the purpose of driving competitors out of business. Non-disclosure of divisional operations relates also to the spectacular profit rate, even for GM, of certain divisions. The Cadillac division, for example, before the construction of its new plant in the early 1960s, is reliably reported to have had a return on investment of more than 100 per cent *after* taxes. One can imagine the reaction of a Cadillac purchaser on learning that little more goes into a Cadillac than a top-line Buick or fully equipped Chevrolet, in terms of production cost.

Perhaps the most intriguing expression of inordinate market power is GM's long established practice of a target rate of profit. The method used is basically similar to that of a public utility, except that GM sets its own upper limit several orders of magnitude above the average utility and there is no public supervision of its cost formulations and pricing practices. To set its target rate of return, ranging from fifteen to twenty per cent on net worth but always managing to exceed it substantially, GM has to possess the market power requisite for fixing its prices in advance of the new model year without having to concern itself with the possible effects of competitive pricing on its planned percentage profits and on its share of the market.

Analysis of the yearly outcome of GM's pricing formula suggests that a sufficient margin is taken into account to cover estimated income taxes. Income tax rates have not affected GM's rate of return. Taxes for GM have been treated as another cost which it can pass on to its customers. After taxes, the 1929 rate of return was 36.2 per cent, while the 1950 rate of return was 37.5 per cent on average stockholders' investment; in 1950 GM made a pre-tax profit of 77.4 per cent to earn 37.5 per cent after taxes.

In an article that appeared in *The Corporate Director* (July, 1956), the American Institute of Management marveled at GM's phenomenal rate of return:

The astonishing fact emerges . . . that, from 1949 through 1955, the average rate of operating profit [net sales less cost of sales, selling and administrative expense and depreciation in proportion to total assets employed, including debt] has exceeded forty per cent per annum. The operating profit on net stock and surplus, defined to include minority interest and special reserves, has exceeded fifty-five per cent per annum in the average of these years. It has averaged 140 per cent of the average net plant account in these same years.

At the 1955 rate of profit, the AIM noted that GM's net earnings (after interest and income taxes) were sufficient to recoup the company's entire net plant investment in two years. AIM took note that this kind of return is "in fact, a continuing characteristic of the enterprise, being equaled or bettered in twelve of the preceding twenty years."

The price leadership of GM *vis-a-vis* Ford and Chrysler, for example, is indicative of its power. On occasion Ford and Chrysler have announced their annual model prices before GM, but they generally have to adapt closely to GM's prices if they guessed wrong. In 1957, Ford guessed wrong and *raised* its prices to meet GM's.

There is even less incentive to compete on price, under a target pricing policy by the dominant firm in the industry, when that firm has pursued a product policy that emphasizes non-price competition. With little price competition at the producer level and with the camouflaging complexities of financing, and trade-in gimmicks, the emphasis long ago shifted to the area of style, intimations of aggression, power, vacation-land image, and the "personality" of the particular make or model.

The bulk of the communication process between auto company and customer stresses these themes and garnishes them with animistic appellations taken from the mountains, jungles, and ocean depths. In the attenuated competition of a tight oligopoly, the range of competition is continually narrowed as each company competes more and more about less and less. In this game, GM has excelled. It has led the way with wrap-around windshields, hard-top models, protruding dash panels, low profile vehicles (partly through tire size reduction), dagger fins and ornaments, and other creative lethalities which the other domestic companies felt compelled to emulate.

As George Romney said ten years ago, when he was head of American Motors, GM's share of the market was so great that its styles determined the modernity of American cars. The stage was repeatedly set for what economists call "protective imitation." On the other side of vehicle design, although disc brakes and radial ply tires were available on some mass production cars in Europe as early as 1953 and 1949 respectively, only when GM, commencing in 1965, tiptoed into these radical offerings, as extra cost options, did the other companies follow suit.

Clearly, a competitive industry would have seen one or more companies forge ahead here with such tested innovations. But again and again, one hears and has heard the plaint of Ford and Chrysler personnel bemoaning the risks attendant upon not following the product leadership of GM. GM's planning in these price and product areas is made possible, of course, by the effective insulation from a critical consuming body having available real choices whose differences are revealed at the point of sale. Again, Romney stated it candidly:

When you get an adequate number of companies in an industry, the customer ceases to be king. He begins to be dictated to by the concepts that a few have as to what he ought to have. . . .

The domestic industry is no more competitive than it was a decade ago, although the operation of the auto safety law has the potential to provide a discernible point of sale differentiation in terms of safety performance, that may stimulate some safety competition. One worsening area is that the price of entry into automobile production with national distribution most certainly has gone up from the figure of one billion dollars estimated by Romney in 1958. Very high barriers to entry, including the exclusive dealer franchise, help preserve the status quo.

The history and attainments of GM's market power make it a classic candidate for anti-trust enforcement under the Sherman and Clayton Acts. In law and in economics there are solid grounds for proceeding toward dissolution or divestiture of General Motors under the two anti-trust laws. The only obstacle is political. How ironic indeed, for the political power of highly concentrated economic firms was a fundamental concern of the Republican Congress that passed the Sherman Anti-trust Act in 1890. History has come full circle, when General Motors can succeed in transforming a *fait accompli* into *de facto* immunity from this basic anti-trust action.

This is not the place for a detailed legal analysis of such an action. It is enough to say that General Motors passes the test of unreasonable market power in terms of its size and the source of that power growth through mergers and acquisitions of more than 100 companies, including the Olds Motors Works, Cadillac Motor Company, and Fisher Body. The Standard Oil, Alcoa, and Dupont cases, among others, are relevant authoritative interpretations of the anti-trust laws for application to the GM situation.

The Justice Department knows, more than anyone, the case against General Motors. Beginning near the end of the Eisenhower Administration and continuing into the Kennedy and Johnson Administrations, Anti-trust Division lawyers conducted a detailed examination into the company's anti-competitive and monopolistic behavior, both vertically and horizontally. A grand jury was convened in New York for eighteen months. In May, 1966, a 120-page memorandum, together with a 104-page draft complaint, was completed by the staff. Succeeding inquiries to the Department of Justice have received the same reply: "The matter is still under study." Anti-trust chiefs come and go, and the reply remains the same.

There are skeptics who say, "What difference does it make whether there are four or eight domestic automobile companies, or whether GM remains as is or is subjected to dissolution or divestiture proceedings?" I maintain that it makes a great deal of difference. Before giving my reasons, I should like to itemize a few of the many deficiencies associated with the auto industry's performance so there is a clearer idea of the gap between performance and promise:

One. The auto industry has been mired in a rut of technological stagnation unparalleled in a consumer goods industry. The record would have been worse were it not for innovations pressed on a reluctant industry by suppliers and European manufacturers. Henry Ford II and Donald Frey, Ford vice president, have recognized this lack of product innovation in public addresses. Professor Richard Morse of MIT recently sharply criticized the auto industry for neglecting research and development, particularly in engine innovation.

Auto thefts have been a serious problem for decades; yet only next year will the auto industry begin to adopt some long-standing engineering "fixes" that make cars difficult to steal. All the published research on crash safety by the industry since 1920 can be digested in a day's reading.

In the safety area generally, research and development facilities and manpower allocations have been almost insignificant. The most impressive evidence of this situation is available in the public docket of the National Highway Safety Bureau. This docket is full of statements about what automobile companies cannot do, what they do not know, and what they are unable even to measure. Under the pressures of modest, proposed safety standards, the companies owned up to their barren heritage, in marked contrast to their previous self-congratulatory catatonia. With the advent of the safety law, a capability for safety innovation is being built up slowly. Competition may be induced by legal compulsion in this area.

Two. An institutionalized, Byzantine-like secrecy has been nurtured by the leading auto companies. Several purposes are thereby served. One is the myth that secrecy is necessary to preserve the bitter competition between companies. This has to be a big joke in Detroit, where there are few auto secrets. Secrecy is really directed against the public pursuant to the tried precept that concealing the facts prevents the criticisms.

Just how phony is their continual plea of confidentiality for competitive reasons can be judged by an episode during the Kefauver hearings on administered prices. The big three auto companies turned down the Subcommittee request for a listing of materials costs on grounds that disclosure would place them at a serious competitive disadvantage. American Motors supplied the subcommittee with figures on their cost of materials and components. (The year was 1958 and AMC had its best years to come.) The companies know each others' costs, if not to the fourth decimal point. But if the public knew, for example, that the direct and indirect labor cost of a medium priced car does not exceed $300, the handy pretext of wage increase employed by management for raising car prices would tend to diminish to its real, not fancied, significance.

Three. Because it conflicted with GM's sales formula of visible obsolescence and invisible permanence, safety became encapsuled in a slogan that was merchandised: *"Safety doesn't sell."* Taking safety out of the competitive race occurred years ago and the consumer was never asked. His choice was made for him by corporate planning. To illustrate this, consider the argument that safety can be incorporated as part of competitive behavior. Safety is mostly engineered into the vehicle and is not visible to a consumer's supposed aesthetic rejection. Better brakes, tires, handling, safer instrument panels, steering columns, and door locks are all "passive" safety features hardly in the category of engaging a car buyer. Viewed as an innovative segment of product quality, it becomes part of vehicular progress, not a nasty nuisance.

A few safety features were add-on components and required passenger cooperation. The companies deliberately ignored these features (seat belts were prominent in aviation in the 1920s) and when they could no longer ignore them offered some as optional extra-cost equipment with very little communication of their protective qualities. Later they added seat belts as standard equipment, but their unnecessarily awkward design and installation (reflecting low seat and door pillar strength in part) impeded usage. Finally, by requirement of law for 1968 cars, shoulder harnesses of the most discommodious design were installed over the objections of General Motors.

In a classic episode of corporate deception, General Motors, in the summer of 1967, hastily forgot its own graphic displays of the shoulder harnesses' superior safety shown in the lobby of its Detroit headquarters (in May) and dispatched some misleading films to Washington in a last ditch attempt to get rid of the "spaghetti" (as harnesses are derisively called by auto stylists) for at least another year. The attempt failed, in no small part because one small auto manufacturer, Volvo, produced data on some 25,000 accidents involving Volvos equipped with harnesses that convincingly established the safety of their harnesses in even high speed collisions. This was a lesson in the benefits of competitive dissent because there was diversity. For decades, millions of unrestrained flying objects called Americans were flung inside their vehicles, crushing bones and ending life, because the industry's leaders focused competition toward variations of stylistic pornography instead of toward engineering integrity. (The policy of delivering style as standard equipment and safety as extra cost option is still hanging on wherever possible in the industry.)

Four. One of the neglected needs is that of breathing pure air. Roughly half of the nation's air pollution proceeds from the internal combustion engine and its emissions of hydrocarbon, carbon monoxide, nitrogen oxides, and lead. Here, once again, it was not the industry that defined the problem but a professor (Haagen-Smit) at Cal Tech, who observed the connection between photochemical smog and auto emissions in 1951.

The agonizing experience of Los Angeles County and the state of California in trying to move the auto industry toward less polluting engines has been told elsewhere. Here one may note that the Anti-trust Division of the Justice

Department thought there was enough serious evidence of concerted and collusive behavior by the domestic auto companies in restraining the development and marketing of auto exhaust control systems to keep a grand jury busy for eighteen months. But just as a ground-breaking suit for "product fixing" was about to be filed, the expected criminal action was dropped over the dissent of Government counsel who handled the proceedings before the grand jury. This was in January, 1968. A civil complaint ("go and sin no more" relief) was to be instituted instead. As of this day, there has been no action at all.

A particularly clear illustration of continuing industry intransigence on pollution-free engines was afforded last May during Senate hearings on steam cars. Testimony by GM and Ford was so patently misleading that independent authorities in the room blinked with incredulity. These company statements could be ascribed to ignorance, but it would be more accurate to describe them as exercises in corporate prevarication.

Five. Even in the area of supposed consumer acceptance, that of product differentiation over style, comforts, and gadgetry, the industry maintains an aversion to factual disclosure.

a. Would the consumer crave for styling changes if he knew that they are costing him at least $700 of the price of his new car? Especially if he had a choice of not having them and saving the difference?

b. Do consumers really want those chrome eyebrows, called bumpers, whose chief function appears to be self-protection or the fostering of a multi-million dollar industry selling bumper guards to make up for stylistic idiocy? Ask them after they see that $200 repair bill following a three mile-per-hour crash into another car while parking.

c. Was there a clamor by consumers to put eyelids on Cougars, particularly the kinds of eyelids that sometimes refuse to flutter open at night (such a defect led to the recall of 85,000 Cougars last spring)? These eyelids were standard equipment.

d. What popular demonstration demanded hidden windshield wipers and the consequent freezing problem in northern climates?

e. Do consumers know that, when asked to buy a fully-tinted windshield, they are paying more in order to see substantially less?

f. How about the discomfort in just getting in and out of cars and in having sufficient head room for many passengers while seated?

Six. What of the internal democracy of these corporations? Like any bureaucratic structure staffed by professionals with allegedly professional missions conflicting with prevailing corporate dictates, the climate can suppress or liberate, be fair or be unjust, be accountable, or be a buck-passer. The practices of exploiting the employed inventor or insuring the indemnification of directors have weakened incentive and responsibility:

Too often, those who wish to change an institution place an exclusive emphasis on external controls. Clearly, Ford's Donald Frey (himself an engineer and former professor) was thinking of problems internal to the industry's environment when he wrote:

It's a sad commentary, but some of the most reactionary people in industry are engineers. Fresh new departures that require creative thinking and innovation can wind up in the file marked NIH—NOT INVENTED HERE. It is up to management to prevent this waste by creative engineering organizations that are mentally attuned to trying the new.

Old line conservatives, believing in the open market and free enterprise, instead of the controlled market and closed enterprise characteristic of modern day oligopolies, might recommend some old-fashioned competition for meeting human needs of sober design, health and safety, economical operation and repair. Meaningful competition has a good deal of motivational force.

Looking over these less than optimum practices, it is apparent that anti-trust is relevant more in a structural rather than a strictly substantive sense. By fostering competition, it increases the probability of diversity, dissent, and risk-taking. It also attenuates the fear of the giant by the intermediates or the midgets. Anti-trust enforcement has other points to commend it. It is law; it has traditions deep in both conservative and liberal thinking; it has doctrines of great flexibility resembling the common law more than statutory law. Above all, anti-trust enforcement articulates the ideal of decentralized economic power and is a marvelous engine for disclosure of inaccessible facts having a spin-off into supplementary reforms which must be undertaken to do the tasks that anti-trust action is not equipped to perform.

It is instructive that while corporate planning seeks to obtain security at the expense of consumer or market sovereignty and at the expense of needed anti-trust enforcement, more and more managers are wondering how to generate innovation just to solve the problems that they define as important for commercial success. Studies of innovation find a strong and unyielding contribution by the individual inventor or small business unit. The cause of auto safety has suffered grievously because of the unjust and unsupportive environment for the lone inventor who is still the main source of creativity in the world of automobiles, although he rarely receives the recognition.

I have urged that anti-trust needed a constituency that supported its active enforcement. This is a constituency not just of professional manpower but of legal reforms and tools. Corporate accountability must necessarily be fostered with a variety of controls and incentives. These range from disclosure requirements, effective sanctions, determining the scope of corporate involvement in political campaigns, more independent roles by professional engineering, scientific and medical societies, a comprehensive rewriting of corporate charters for large corporations, and other reforms to take the myth out of people's capitalism and put the people in it.

In many ways these problems have deepened because of unchecked corporate concentrations. In 1965, the Assistant Attorney General for Anti-trust, William

Orrick, described the broader motivations behind the anti-trust laws in a manner often conveniently forgotten by those who give lip service to these laws:

The Sherman Act in 1890, the Clayton Act in 1914, the Celler-Kefauver Act in 1950 reflected Congressional fear of the political power that might be wielded by our largest corporations; fear of the inability of the small businessman to survive and prosper in an economy dominated by huge corporate structures; fear of the absence of shareholder democracy in the big corporations; fear of local concerns being acquired by national companies operated by absentee management unresponsive to local problems. . . . Finally, and perhaps most important of all, Congress' dedication to anti-trust goals as a means of preserving our way of life has always rested on its recognition that concentration of industrial power may lead to the police state.

The atrophy of anti-trust enforcement and the absence of sufficient appreciation for its doctrines can be appraised by the surprise with which the following selections will be met:

On March 8, 1956, President Eisenhower's Anti-trust chief, Stanley N. Barnes, urged General Motors voluntarily to give up one or more of its automobile divisions in order to lessen a dangerous concentration in the industry.

In the late 1940s, Henry C. Simons, one of the leading advocates of the "Chicago school of economics" and free-enterprise economics in the United States, wrote that reasonable monopoly is a contradiction in terms. There can be no such thing. Wide dispersion of political and economic power is the only foundation on which a democratic, free-enterprise system can long exist. The role of government, in Professor Simons' view, was to (1) maintain active competition within a general framework of free-enterprise rules of the game so as to stimulate efficiency and to disperse economic power; and to (2) own and operate directly those few industries where competition cannot be made to function effectively. He specifically urged these steps that are at least as urgent as they were two decades ago:

1. Federal incorporation of all private corporations.

2. Forbidding any manufacturing or merchandising corporation to own stock in any other such corporation.

3. An upper limit on the asset size of all corporations, far below the size of the present giants.

4. Provision that no firm may be big enough to dominate its industry, the Federal Trade Commission to determine this size limit in each industry.

5. Complete prohibition of interlocking directorates, except between unrelated industries.

6. Simplification of corporate securities to two simple types, to minimize the possibility of hidden or indirect control of corporations.

The distance of corporate behavior and influence from these norms declared by Orrick and Simons is the measure of the intensity of the radicalism of corporate collectivism. For if radicalism be defined as the operational aberration from the traditional and acknowledged norms of a society and if its intensity be gauged by the power of that aberration, then the issue is industrial autocracy and the corporate state. This is the real challenge to the consumer.

JOHN A. SCHNITTKER

The Farmer in the Till

John F. Kennedy is reported to have remarked that he didn't want to hear about agriculture from anyone except John Kenneth Galbraith, and didn't want to hear about it from him either. As President, Lyndon Johnson nursed an incurable longing for the rustic pleasures of the LBJ Ranch, but he avoided farm-policy questions when he could. Public officials are alternately wary and weary of agricultural policy. There is an ample reason for both attitudes. Farm voters are notoriously hard to please, and farm-policy debates are seldom stimulating. Yet the need for agricultural policy will not go away simply because frustrated politicians wish it. Advanced technology on the farm assures plenty of food for consumers. It also requires stable prices, and there are far too many farmers to arrange such a result without federal help.

Official lethargy on this score was shattered late in May this year when the House of Representatives, reacting against million-dollar payments to big farms, overwhelmingly approved a ceiling of $20,000 on direct subsidy payments to any farm. This revolt against the old order in farm policy was a replay of a surprising House action in 1968, an action later reversed by the Senate.

Congressional advocates of a farm-payment ceiling have some good things going for them. Farm-program costs, at $4 to $5 billion a year, are high and moving higher. In a careful survey made late in 1968, 85 percent of the farmers

Source: Mr. Schnittker speaks from his experience as Undersecretary of Agriculture, 1965–1969. He teaches now at Kansas State University. This article is from *The Atlantic Monthly*, August 1969, pp. 43–45. Copyright © 1969 by John A. Schnittker. Reprinted by permission of the author.

favored limiting farm benefits. City people are nearly unanimous in objecting to the big budget drain for farm programs when other priority needs beg for funds. Most important, advocates of farm-program reform in the House of Representatives and the Poor People's Lobby have skillfully contrasted giant federal payments to a few farms with the hand-to-mouth budget granted federal food programs by Southern-dominated Agriculture Committees in both houses of Congress, despite evidence of widespread malnutrition. Congressman Paul Findley (R., Ill.) has reported to the House that the cotton and wheat areas with the largest number of big farm payments were doing least about hunger and malnutrition. Finally, a study prepared last year at the request of President Johnson has destroyed the claim of the agricultural establishment in both political parties that surpluses and economic chaos would inevitably accompany a ceiling on farm benefits. Budget savings of $250 million per year are now anticipated by those who favor payment reform, and the savings could be doubled if the payment ceiling were set at $10,000 instead of the $20,000 that was proposed.

Those members of the Congress who opposed the ceiling on farm benefits claimed that such a plan could not be administered, that it was unworkable and unfair, and that it would not save money. Fortunately for the public, none of this is believed any more, at least not in the House of Representatives.

Parity Parity Parity

It helps to know some of the words and symbols, if one is to understand the need for change in farm programs. Parity, price supports, and direct payments are the key words.

Parity has been the battle cry of farmers since the 1920s. Public discussion of farm policy, however, has been clouded by three parity doctrines. Parity in the abstract is hard to argue with; it is essentially a fairness doctrine. The effort to find out what is fair for farmers, however, has spawned two competing statistical measures of farm parity.

Parity prices originated a generation ago out of what seemed to be a sensible notion: that farm-product prices should increase in step with the general price level; this would maintain the farmer's purchasing power. Conceived before the new technology revolutionized farming, the parity-price system has failed to account for recent rapid gains in productivity. If farmers were guaranteed 100 percent parity prices in 1969 (instead of the present 65 to 70 percent of parity), wheat, corn, and cotton prices would increase by about 50 percent. Crop surpluses would be inevitable, and the Agriculture Department budget would soon rival the Defense budget. Clearly, the parity-price doctrine is obsolete, although not quite dead.

Parity income is a more recent standard. Simply put, the parity-income doctrine says that a good farmer investing his capital in an operation large enough to employ him more or less fully should be able to earn as much farming as he would earn operating any other small business. A recent Department of Agriculture study showed that a half million of the biggest farmers producing two thirds of our farm products are meeting this standard, at least on the average if not on every farm every year. Net incomes on the largest farms, thanks partly to big payments, are generally far above parity; rapid land-price escalation as farms are enlarged is a clear sign of this. In contrast, the smallest and poorest two million farms could not earn parity incomes on the farm even if market prices were doubled or tripled.

Price Supports and Payments

Farm prices left to themselves are notoriously unstable. Price support programs, begun in 1933, grew out of that fact and out of the general economic depression. The new programs were supposed to raise prices by reducing crop production and by removing surpluses from the market. But neither the farm programs nor pump-priming expenditures in the rest of the economy brought real recovery in the 1930s. World War II did that, pushing farm prices so high that price ceilings and consumer food subsidies were applied. After the war, the farm bloc in Congress succeeded for a time in maintaining the high wartime prices under peacetime conditions, even though agricultural prices around the world were declining as Europe recovered and began producing again. The results were predictable. By the late 1950s high market-price guarantees and halfhearted production control were creating huge surpluses. More than that, farmers were gearing their expectations to high prices and buying their land at inflated values. Thus they were generating their own cost increases to justify future demands for even higher prices. By 1960, every grain- and butter-storage structure in the United States was filled. The annual cost of simply owning and storing the $9 billion farm surplus reached $1 billion in 1961. "How to let go of the bear's tail" became the principal preoccupation of the reform-minded farm officials and economists.

The answer was a system of direct payments to farmers in place of high price supports. In the early 1960s, payments became the key instrument of farm-policy reform, cushioning the impact of an abrupt shift from high to lower price guarantees for wheat and cotton, and providing farmers the cash incentives required to reduce acreages and limit farm output. Big farmers, who had profited handsomely from high market-price guarantees in the 1950s, became identified in the 1960s as the recipients of huge government checks. The stage was set for the present struggle to reduce the size of those checks.

Recent developments in farming have also helped to focus public attention on farm-program benefits. When farm programs were introduced in 1933, there were 7 million farms in the United States. A few were huge holdings, but most were small, one-family enterprises. Benefits were geared to production, and so farm aid was spread fairly evenly. By 1968, more than half of those farms had disappeared. Today there are 3 million farms, but 2 million of them are small, part-time, residential, or hobby farms. One million top farmers produce nearly all of the farm products marketed, and they get most of the money spent on farm programs. A new study just published by the Joint Economic Committee of Congress, for example, shows that the largest 5 percent of sugarcane and cotton growers get 63 and 41 percent respectively of all the direct benefits from those programs. The largest one percent of cotton growers in California and Mississippi get 25 percent of all the direct federal benefits in those states. Under such circumstances, public concern is certainly understandable.

Clearly, the large payments are not going to the traditional American farm, still typically a one-family enterprise. Instead, they help ensure financial security for such well-heeled enterprises as the J. G. Boswell Company of King's County, California, which collected direct farm payments of $3 million in 1968 and $4.1 million in 1967. The Boswell Company is a multimillion-dollar diversified cotton operation with good connections in Washington. Senators and congressmen are not excluded from farming, nor do they always disqualify themselves when the Congress votes on big farm payments. Family interests of Senator James Eastland of Mississippi (the Eastland Plantation, Inc., and H. C. Eastland) collected payments totaling $142,078 in 1968, down from $189,050 in 1967. In October, 1968, Senator Eastland voted against the payment ceiling which would have cut the Eastland farm payments to $60,000, or $20,000 on each of three farms. Campbell Farming of Big Horn County, Montana, often cited as the model of a modern wheat-farming operation, got $162,897 in 1968. Garst Farms, run by Roswell Garst, the international seed-corn figure and one-time host in Iowa to Premier Khrushchev, got $70,923 in 1966, but only $45,212 in 1968.

Nearly two and a half million farmers get federal payments, but only 10,000 farmers get over $20,000 per year. Most of the big payments go to cotton farmers in California, Texas, Mississippi, Arkansas, and Arizona. When Congressman Findley placed the names of all recipients of $25,000 or more in the *Congressional Record* this year, the list from the five biggest cotton states filled twenty-one pages. Five leading grain states required only four pages. Concentration of federal payments in a few cotton states makes them really ripe for reform, although sugar and wool, with powerful political support, are also involved.

Late this spring, when the House of Representatives voted a $20,000 ceiling on farm payments, the Majority and Minority Leaders were opposed, as were most committee chairmen. Understandably, the bulk of the opposing votes were from Texas, California, Mississippi, Arkansas, Kansas—the states with the biggest payments. The Senate could vote a ceiling this summer, if urban senators and the leadership take the initiative. If the Senate fails, final action may have to wait until the farm program is reviewed in 1970.

The White House does not seem to have learned anything from President Johnson's 1968 experience in this matter. When the House voted a payment ceiling last year despite intense Administration opposition, President Johnson began to have second thoughts about supporting his own farm bill, which continued the increasingly vulnerable big payments in a year when most budgets were being cut. Official embarrassment mounted after the Poor People's March when the Administration's expected assault on hunger fell before the tax surcharge, the $6 billion budget retrenchment, and higher Vietnam spending. When the Senate-House conferees on the farm bill dropped the payment-limiting amendments, last year's official White House strategy was designed to get the conference report stalled or rejected, so that the entire farm issue would have to be reviewed in 1969. That failed in a parliamentary maneuver designed without the President's knowledge by the Administration's own lobbyists. After that, President Johnson reluctantly signed the farm bill and directed "the Department of Agriculture to study the effect of a payment limitation on programs which require voluntary diversion of productive land."

That study was conducted in the Department of Agriculture and became public after President Johnson left office. Its findings flatly contradicted the principal argument the Administration and farm congressmen had made in recent years: that payment limits would destroy the production-control programs and would lead to new farm surpluses. The study also documented the potential budget savings associated with a payment ceiling. All this, even the potential budget savings, seems to have been lost on the new Administration.

The advocates of unlimited payments are now left without any sensible arguments for their position. Previous opposition to the ceiling rested on the argument that big payments are needed *to prevent too much corn and wheat production*. This spurious claim had a limited validity in the 1961–1964 period of heavy surplus removal, but it has none in 1969 when grain surpluses are down. The Department of Agriculture simply did not know the distribution of payments by size of farm until around 1965. Acting on faulty information, Department officials took an early stand against a payment ceiling, and never found a way to change their position. Now we know that only 2 percent of all feed grains and 4 percent of all wheat would be affected by a $20,000 limit. Even a $5000 ceiling would not materially affect the stability of the feed-grain economy.

Cotton is more concentrated; one third of the crop is grown on some 5000 big farms (out of more than half a million cotton farms) which would be affected by a $20,000 ceiling. Legislative leaders who had insisted that a payment ceiling would cause a grain *surplus*, now said it would cause a cotton *shortage*, an argument so symmetrical it seemed plausible. Senator Holland said last year that the prospect of lower payments made "it appear very unlikely that such producers could continue to supply the mills with low priced cotton. . . ." This is a proposition that ought to be tested: if American cotton growers cannot compete on even terms in world fiber markets without unconscionably high federal payments, it is not too early to discover it. Major changes in addition to a payment ceiling are required in the cotton program. The most important is to remove a provision of the 1965 act which ingeniously exempted cotton from any future payment ceiling. This must be repealed before the ceiling can be effective for the crop and the areas with most of the huge payments.

What to Do

No firm principles have emerged to direct the Congress toward a particular maximum level for farm payments. Budget savings are the best guide. By that test the $20,000 ceiling is too generous; the figure should be no higher than $5000 per crop or $10,000 per farm, in order to save more money. Reduced payments will not undermine farm-price stability as long as top payments are not forced below those levels. Inevitably, the maximum payment level will be set somewhat arbitrarily: a $20,000 limit will save $200 to $300 million a year; a maximum of $5000 per crop or $10,000 per farm would save $500 million or more. If farms are allowed to split up to circumvent the new policy, however, some of these savings will be lost. This will bear watching; Congress should give the Department of Agriculture firm directions against farm splitting.

These reforms will not silence the sharpest critics of farm programs, who have never accepted the policy of limiting farm production to stabilize prices while anyone anywhere is hungry. So long as the agricultural economy remains inherently unstable, with too many producers to combine effectively to set their own prices the way industrial combines do, the opponents of any farm stabilization effort will probably be disappointed. We need a farm policy as well as a responsive fiscal policy and a compassionate food policy. But a sensible farm policy does not require giant payments.

Farm payments and food programs will inevitably be paired off in the coming debate, although ending big payments will not automatically ensure more food for the poor. The public can't help seeing tragic irony in Congress' tight-fisted approach to hunger, in contrast to its open-handed financing of farm programs. Budget pressures alone ought to encourage the Administration to sense its interest in this matter, if principle does not, although White House help may never materialize, given Mr. Nixon's dependence on the South. Political advantage seems assured for those members who help drive farm-payment reform through the Congress. Big payments lack any legitimacy in real program objectives. It is right, therefore, to end them. Only the most twisted sense of priorities will let us continue to pay millions every year to a few big farms while we procrastinate about ghetto reconstruction, postpone remedial education, close Job Corps Camps, and let poor people starve.

MICHAEL HARRINGTON

The Betrayal of the Poor

In the seventies the poor may become invisible again. And even if that tragedy does not occur, there will still be tens of millions living in the other America when the country celebrates its two-hundredth anniversary in 1976.

This prediction should be improbable. Lyndon B. Johnson declared an "unconditional war" on poverty in 1964, Congress agreed, and for the next four years the White House recited awesome statistics on the billions which were being spent on social betterment. The sixties was a time of marches and militancy, of students and churches committing themselves to abolish want, and of documentary presentations of the nation's domestic shame by all the mass media. Indeed, the impression of frenetic government activity was so widespread that Richard Nixon campaigned in 1968 with a promise to slow down the pace of innovation. So how, then, argue that poverty will persist in the seventies and perhaps once again drop out of the society's conscience and consciousness?

The fact is that society has failed to redeem the pledges of the sixties and has taken to celebrating paper triumphs over poverty. Thus in August of 1969 the Department of Commerce announced that the number of the poverty-stricken had dropped from 39.5 million to 25.4 million in a matter of nine years (1959 to 1968). The only problem, as will be seen, is that the numbers prettied up the reality.

When Lyndon Johnson declared his social war in the State of the Union message of 1964, the Council of Economic Advisers defined poverty as a family income of less than $3000 a year. This was a rough measure, since it didn't take into account family size or geographic location, yet it was extremely useful in identifying the groups which were particularly afflicted.

In the next few years the criteria were made much more sophisticated. In a brilliant attempt to define poverty objectively, the Social Security Administration took the Department of Agriculture's Economy Food Plan as a

Source: Michael Harrington is chairman of the Socialist Party of the United States and author of *Toward a Democratic Left*. This essay is adapted from his introduction to a new Penguin edition of his *The Other America* as it appeared in *The Atlantic Monthly*, January 1970, pp. 71–74. Reprinted with permission of The Macmillan Company, from *The Other America*, by Michael Harrington. Copyright © by Michael Harrington, 1962.

base figure for the poverty level. This was about 80 percent of the Low Cost Plan which many welfare agencies had used to estimate budgets; it consisted in a temporary emergency diet. In 1964, the Economy Plan had provided $4.60 per person a week, or 22 cents a meal, and the poverty income "line" was $3100 a year. In 1969, it was $4.90 a week, and a four-member family was said to be poor if its income was below $3553 a year.

These definitions were drawn up by concerned public servants, some of them with a deep personal commitment to abolish the outrage they were defining. But note an extraordinary fact. Between 1964 and 1969, the poverty level was raised by only $453 a year, or about 14 percent for the five years. Yet during this same period, union workers, with an average increase in wage settlements in 1968 of 6.6 percent, were not making any substantial gains in purchasing power. In other words, the statistics enormously underestimate the disastrous impact of inflation upon the poor. And this problem was not simply a matter of personal income, for some of the most dramatic inflationary increases took place in the area of medical services and thereby canceled out all of the increases in Medicare benefits and forced some people out of Medicaid.

But there was another optimistic assumption in the official definition. When the Economy Food Plan was taken as the base figure, it was assumed that all other needs would cost twice the amount of the grocery bill. But, to keep up with changes in the economy and society since then, one should compute the other items at three times the price of food, not two. By using the erroneous assumptions of the Eisenhower fifties, the government abolished the poverty of 12 million Americans who were still poor.

If it seems extreme to suggest that honest, and even concerned, experts could thus overlook the anguish of 12 million of their fellow citizens, consider the famous Census undercount in 1960: almost 6 million Americans, mainly black adults living in Northern cities, were not enumerated. Their lives were so marginal—no permanent address, no mail, no phone number, no regular job—that they did not even achieve the dignity of being a statistic. Again the extent of misery was underestimated.

In 1967 there were roughly 12 million citizens whom the Council of Economic Advisers called the "near poor" (with incomes between $3335 and $4345 for families of four). If these numbers were underestimated in the same way as were the poor, there are 16 million Americans who are but one illness, one accident, one recession away from being poor again. If, as now seems so possible, America in the seventies should reduce its social efforts, this group will lose almost as much as the poor.

And there is another, and even larger, segment of the population whose destiny is related to that of the other Americans. In late 1966, the Bureau of Labor Statistics figured that it would take $9191 for a "moderate standard of living"—you could buy a two-year-old used car and a new suit every four years. It should be remembered that raising the minimum wage for the lowest paid workers tends to help raise the take of those who are organized and much better off, but turning our back on the poor creates a political and social atmosphere in which the needs of an increasing number of people can be overlooked.

Perhaps the simplest way to get a summary view of the dangerous trends is to examine one generation of broken promises in the area of housing.

The government promised every citizen a decent dwelling in 1949. Under the leadership of a conservative Republican, Senator Robert A. Taft, the Congress agreed that the private housing market was not serving the needs of the poor. They therefor pledged to build 810,000 units of low-cost housing by 1955. In 1970, one generation later, that target has not yet been achieved. But the problem is not what the government did not do, but what it did instead. For while Washington was providing cheap money and princely tax deductions for more than 10 million affluent home builders in suburbia, it was taking housing away from the poor. As the President's National Commission on Urban Problems, chaired by former Senator Paul Douglas, reported in January, 1969, "Government action through urban renewal, highway programs, demolition on public housing sites, code enforcement and other programs has destroyed more housing for the poor than government at all levels has built for them." In 1968 a law was passed pledging the United States to do in the seventies what it had pledged to do in the fifties. Within a year it became clear that it was unlikely that the nation would redeem this second promise. To build 26 million new housing units in ten years, 6 million of them low-cost, would require speeding up the production of dwellings for the poor to twenty times the present rate. And as George Romney, the Secretary of Housing and Urban Development, admitted in 1969, it is quite possible that we will fall 10 million units behind the goal.

What this means for the seventies is the further decay of the central cities of America, an increase in the already massive level of housing poverty which afflicts a third of the people—and the emergence of ghost towns in the middle of metropolis.

For the plight of the cities is becoming so grievous that even slums are not as profitable as they used to be. As a result, the Real Estate Research Corporation told the *Wall Street Journal* in 1969, between ten and fifteen thousand buildings are being abandoned in the course of the year.

When Richard Nixon was elected President he told the people that the federal government had tried to do too much and that he would therefore decentralize social programs and set more modest goals. There was a half-truth and a dangerous falsehood in his analysis, which bodes ill for the poor in the seventies.

Under Lyndon Johnson the Administration talked as if it were undertaking and accomplishing prodigies. One of the reasons why a disturbing number of white workers turned to George Wallace in 1968 was that they were under the impression that Washington had done so much for the poor, and particularly the Negroes. They confused the bold rhetoric with action and did not understand that life in the ghettos had changed very little. Insofar as Nixon takes Johnson for having talked too loudly, he is right. But the rest of his thesis—that the federal government was too activist, and that efforts must be cut back and turned over to the states—is wrong.

In order to destroy this myth of the favored, pampered poor, one need only consider official figures. In 1968 the National Advisory Commission on Civil Disorders—the "Riot" Commission—reported that in Detroit, New Haven, and Newark, the cities where the violence was the most destructive in 1967, the median percentage of those eligible who were actually covered by any one of the major social programs was 33 percent. In other words, in the United States, a majority of the poor are not on welfare at all. And, the Commission showed, the national average for welfare payments is "a little more than one half of need," and in some cases one fourth of need. In January, 1969, a special Cabinet committee reported to Lyndon Johnson that the existing domestic programs were already underfunded by $6 billion and that a moderate expansion of civilian efforts along lines already suggested by various commissions and study groups would cost another $40 billion by 1972. So the government by its own standards is falling billions of dollars behind what should be done.

To many citizens, people who receive welfare are regarded as a burden upon the hardworking common man. But what is really happening is that many of the poor are being undercompensated for humiliations which the government and the economy, or both, have visited upon them. The most dramatic case in point is the rural poor who were driven into the cities in recent years. Billions of dollars in federal subsidies were paid to rich individuals and corporate farmers—including hundreds of thousands to Senator James O. Eastland, the impartial plantation owner who sits on the Senate Agriculture Committee and helps determine his own rewards. These handsome welfare payments to the wealthy allowed them to make a profit by reducing the land under cultivation and also provided them with funds for mechanization. Productivity in the fields increased twice as fast as in the factories, but millions of the rural poor became economically superfluous.

Between 1950 and 1966 federal monies helped to force 5.5 million black farm workers into the cities. They came from areas where education for Negroes was substandard, and these black migrants were required to relate to a bewildering, complex urban environment and compete in a sophisticated labor market. They brought with them, as Harold Fleming has said, "the largest accumulation of social deficits ever visited upon an identifiable group."

In short, it is not that Washington has done too much but that it has so often done the wrong thing. And the central thesis of Mr. Nixon's 1969 welfare message—"a third of a century of centralizing power in Washington has produced a bureaucratic monstrosity, cumbersome, unresponsive, ineffective"—is not an accurate description of what happened. Moreover, Mr.

Nixon's major welfare proposal to establish a minimum income for families contradicts his own analysis, for it proposes to *federalize* welfare benefits at a certain level. Mr. Nixon was quite rightly disturbed that Mississippi pays an average of $39.35 a month to support an entire family while New York has much higher standards. He therefore wants to use the federal power to force Mississippi from abusing its states' rights in such an inhumane way, which is hardly decentralization.

One of the most disturbing facts about the poor is that roughly half of them are young. They will be flooding the labor market so fast in 1975 that the Department of Labor expects 25 percent more sixteen-to-nineteen-year-olds looking for jobs than in 1965—and 50 percent more black youths. This will happen at a time when blue-collar positions for which they will be competing will be opening up at a rate of about 15 percent a year. In other words, there is a very real possibility that many, even most, of the children of the poor will become the fathers and mothers of the poor.

These dangerous trends did not explode in the sixties, but two of the reasons were Vietnam and inflation. The nation's tragic commitment to the horror in Southeast Asia created 700,000 new "jobs" in the Armed Forces and a million new openings in defense industry. Since 80 percent of the draftees had high school diplomas, the Army did not actually take the poor in but removed some of their competition from the labor market. Then with inflation after 1965—which was triggered by a $10 billion "mistake" in federal spending based upon optimistic assumptions about a victory in the war in 1966—the labor market tightened up even more. But with peace in Vietnam, what are the acceptable substitutes for the employment generated by war and inflation?

In his message to Congress on population problems in the summer of 1969, President Nixon attacked a sweeping proposal made by the National Committee on Urban Growth Policy for not being sufficiently daring. The Committee, which included Democratic regulars like Hale Boggs and John Sparkman and even a Goldwater Republican, John Tower, had said that the nation must build ten new cities for one million citizens each and ten new towns for 100,000 inhabitants. After noting that there will be 100 million additional Americans by the year 2000, three quarters of them living in urbanized areas, the President said of the Committee's suggestion, "But the total number of people who would be accommodated if even those bold plans were implemented is *only* 20 million—a *mere* one fifth of the expected thirty-year increase." (Emphasis added.)

As the seventies open there is every indication that housing poverty will become even more acute, and that the children of the last decade's poor will, as parents in an economy without enough decent jobs, increase the size of the other America. To avoid such tragedies, certain things must be done.

First of all there must be planning. There should be an Office of the Future attached to the presidency and a Joint Congressional Committee on the

Future which would receive, debate, and adopt or modify annual reports from the White House.

Suburban home builders, automobile manufacturers, and trucking companies all pick up their huge federal subsidies without a thought of pollution. And now—not simply if poverty is to be abolished, but if the quality of life in America is to be kept from deteriorating—we must consider the "side effects" of new technologies even more scrupulously than we do those of new drugs. A year before his death, Dwight Eisenhower urged the building of new cities, racially and socially integrated and with new jobs. Mr. Nixon apparently agrees. But the enormously complex planning needed to accomplish such a task is not going to be done by the invisible hand of "Adam Smith."

Second, there must be billions of dollars in social investments. President Nixon, like President Johnson before him, hopes that private enterprise can do the job. His first version of this philosophy was called "black capitalism," and he ordered the concept extended to all the impoverished minorities when he took office. But the blunt economic facts of life are that costs in the slums are twice as high as in the suburbs, congestion much more serious, the labor market relatively untrained, and the neighborhoods unprofitable for big business. Minority enterprises can, of course, make a contribution to their areas and should be helped generously, but for the vast majority they offer no real hope.

As the sixties were ending, there did seem to be one area in which the cooperation of the public and private sector worked: employment. The National Association of Businessmen, with strong federal help, is trying to put poverty-stricken and minority workers into good jobs, and the measurable gains have been highly publicized. However, a 1969 analysis by the *Wall Street Journal* was not so sanguine. The main reason for the hirings, Alan Otten wrote, was the tight labor market, and any increase in unemployment—which is inevitable given the Nixon strategy against inflation—would turn these people back out on the streets. Yet when the Automobile Workers Union proposed to the Ford Corporation that its older members be permitted to take a voluntary layoff so that the new men could stay on, the company refused. The reason was simple: the supplementary unemployment compensation for a veteran is costlier than for a new worker. The profit motive was stronger than social conscience.

Early in the seventies the gross national product of the United States will pass the $1 trillion mark. As an article in *Fortune* calculated this trend, there would be a fiscal "dividend"—the automatic increase in government income without any rise in taxes which takes place when the GNP becomes larger— of $38 billion in 1974 and around $80 billion by 1980. The problem under these circumstances is not finding the resources but being intelligent enough to use them democratically and creatively.

In his 1969 welfare message, President Nixon made a sharp attack on the unevenness of the present states' rights welfare system. But in his proposals he urged Congress to delegate even more power to the very local administrations which had previously abused it, and he came out for a federal minimum which would leave people well below the poverty line. In the Nixon program, Washington would provide the funds to bring family payments up to $1600 a year, and the twenty states which now pay less than that would be required to contribute only half of their present welfare spending up to the total.

Instead of thus institutionalizing a federal minimum which is less than 50 percent of the way to the poverty line, the United States should adopt the principle that all of its citizens are legally entitled to a decent income. Lyndon Johnson's outgoing Cabinet computed that one version of such a social involvement, a negative income tax, would cost between $15 and $20 billion a year. Given the *Fortune* prediction of an $80 billion dividend by 1980, that amount is clearly within the country's means.

Such a program should have a work incentive. Instead of the typical American practice of taxing the earnings of the welfare recipient 100 percent (by reducing his benefits by the amount of his wages), the individual should be allowed to keep a decreasing proportion of his income supplement as his pay goes up. But this also means that there must be a vast increase in the number of decent jobs. In New York City, where Aid to Dependent Children payments approximate the level of menial jobs in the economy, there is no motive for the mothers to look for work, and they haven't. So a guaranteed income with a work incentive means a commitment to genuine full employment.

And that is where the notion of a guaranteed income ties in with the right to work. It was Franklin Roosevelt who first urged, in the campaign of 1944, that if the private economy does not provide jobs for the people, then the public economy must. If the promises of the Housing Acts of 1949 and 1968 were carried out, there would be a labor shortage and the country would discover that it really needs the unused work potential of the poor and the near poor. The effect of such a program would not be inflationary because workers would be producing valuable goods and services for their wages.

As the seventies begin, the nation needs planned long-range social investments to provide a decent home for every citizen and to guarantee either a living income or a good job for all. If the cities continue to sprawl and technology revolutionizes the land in a casual, thoughtless way, polluting our natural resources, it is the poor who will be the most cruelly used, but the entire nation will suffer as well.

ELIZABETH B. DREW

Going Hungry in America

From time to time during the past few years, there has come to public attention the jarring news that a great many Americans do not get enough to eat
because they are too poor. The words "starvation," "hunger," and "malnutrition" have all been used to describe the phenomenon. Each of these conditions is difficult to isolate, or even describe, or to separate from related
diseases, because there has been little scientific or official interest in the problem. Yet it is generally agreed, even among government circles, that, at a
minimum, ten million Americans are malnourished, and some of these are
chronically hungry, even starving, because they are poor.

In 1967, a group of doctors, including Robert Coles of Harvard University,
Joseph Brenner of MIT, Alan Mermann and Milton J. E. Senn of Yale, and
private practitioners from Yazoo City, Mississippi, and Charlotte, North
Carolina, took a foundation-sponsored trip to Mississippi to investigate the
problem and returned to tell the Senate Subcommittee on Poverty what they
had seen:

In Delta counties . . . we saw children whose nutritional and medical condition
we can only describe as shocking—even to a group of physicians whose work
involves daily confrontation with disease and suffering. In child after child we
saw: evidence of vitamin and mineral deficiencies; serious untreated skin infestation
and ulcerations; eye and ear diseases, also unattended bone diseases secondary to
poor food intake; the prevalence of bacterial and parasitic disease, as well as severe
anemia . . . in boys and girls in every county we visited, obvious evidence of
severe malnutrition, with injury to the body's tissues—its muscles, bones, and
skin as well as an associated psychological state of fatigue, listlessness, and exhaustion. . . . We saw children who don't get to drink milk, don't get to eat fruit,
green vegetables, or meat. They live on starches—grits, bread, Kool Aid. . . . In
sum, we saw children who are hungry and who are sick—children for whom
hunger is a daily fact of life and sickness, in many forms, an inevitability. We do
not want to quibble over words, but "malnutrition" is not quite what we found.
. . . They are suffering from hunger and disease and directly or indirectly they are
dying from them—which is exactly what "starvation" means.

Source: Elizabeth B. Drew is Washington editor for *The Atlantic Monthly*. This article
is from *Atlantic's* December 1968 issue, pp. 53–61. Copyright © 1968 by Elizabeth B.
Drew. Reprinted by permission of the author.

There is developing, moreover, a disturbing body of scientific information that indicates a connection between malnutrition in children, in particular insufficient protein, and brain damage. Seventy-five percent of the mental retardation in this country is estimated to occur in areas of urban and rural poverty.

The situation in the Mississippi Delta has been particularly acute because of unemployment as a result of mechanization, and among other things, other government programs: controlled planting, and a new one-dollar-an-hour minimum wage, which led many plantation owners to lay workers off rather than pay it. Mississippi's welfare program pays an average of $50 a month to a family with four children, but payments are made only if the wage earner is old or disabled or blind or has left his family. Thus there are thousands of families in the Delta with no jobs and no income.

There are two basic government programs which are intended to improve the diet of the poor—the sale of food stamps and the distribution of food. The local county chooses one or the other—or neither. Government officials point out that for some time every county in Mississippi has had one of the programs. In response to the reports that people still were not getting enough to eat, the Secretary of Agriculture said to the same Senate subcommittee: "They got some food because they were obviously walking around. I don't know where they got it."

For some time, in fact, it has been known within the government that the food programs had serious shortcomings, in the number of people being reached and in the form of the assistance. In addition, over the past year and a half or so, domestic hunger has been the subject of a great deal of publicity. A solution would not be all that expensive: government studies have indicated that adequate food distribution for everyone who needed it would cost between $1.5 billion and $2 billion more than the roughly half billion being spent on stamps and commodities now. (No one has calculated, in terms of illness and wasted and dependent lives, what it costs not to provide everyone with an adequate diet.) There were also short-range and less expensive actions that could have been taken to alleviate the most severe distress. While it would be inaccurate to say that nothing was done, the response was slow, piecemeal, and, it often seemed, reluctant. More thorough responses, including a national commitment to see that no one was denied an adequate diet because of low income, were considered, and at several points they were almost made. Because of the impact on the lives, every day, of several million people, the reasons why they were not are worth exploring.

The food programs are run by the Department of Agriculture because they were begun not so much to help the poor as to dispose of embarrassing agricultural surpluses. Food packages are distributed once a month to the poor who live in counties which happen to want the distribution and are willing to pay for it. (Only recently, the federal government began to pay for the packages in a few of the poorest counties.) "But," Orville Freeman, the

Secretary of Agriculture, has testified to Congress, "that doesn't mean that every person gets it, because a poor person who lives miles away from the distributing point where 100 pounds of food is made available for a month may very well (a) not even know about the distribution; (b) not be able to get there; and (c) not be able to carry it away." (One congressman replied: "I know dead soldiers who didn't miss out because they lived 10 miles from a recruiting office.")

The commodity packages have only recently approximated what even the Agriculture Department considers a "minimum adequate" diet, but the cheerful assumption is made that they are a "supplement" to a family's food supply. The commodity package has been periodically expanded, to the point where last summer, under public pressure, the Department announced that it would now contain some twenty-two items. The list is theoretical, however; whether the various items actually end up in the package depends on whether they are in sufficient supply and whether the local community elects to include them. It takes tolerance for tedium and some culinary ingenuity to make edible meals of the surplus packages, which until last summer consisted mainly of such things as flour, cornmeal, rice, dried peas, dried beans, bulgur. Formerly they contained thirty ounces of meat for each person for an entire month; now the packages are supposed to contain more meat, dried eggs, evaporated milk, canned chicken, canned vegetables, and some others. The wrapping is to be prettier, and recipes are to be supplied, although many of the recipients can't read.

The food stamp program, in which participants buy stamps which are worth more than the purchase price and use them to buy groceries, is preferred by just about everyone, including the local grocers. Long part of the Democrats' agenda, food stamps were started on a pilot basis in 1961, and were finally authorized by Congress three years later. The stamps are actually a form of income supplement, but that is not the sort of thing that is said out loud, and thus a great emphasis is always placed on how this, too, is to supplement a family's "normal" expenditure for food. It is difficult to divine just what was in the minds of the federal officials who worked out the details of how the food stamp program should work. Each month, a family may purchase a given amount's worth of stamps, depending on their income, in exchange for a given amount of bonus. Somehow, although people in general pay about 18 percent of their income for food, the poor, under the food stamp plan, are sometimes required to pay as much as 35 to 50 percent in order to obtain any stamps at all. If they cannot afford that because of the other demands on their income, or if they do not happen to have enough cash on hand on the day that the stamps are sold, they get no help at all. For example, after eight counties in Mississippi switched from commodity distribution to food stamps, some 32,000 fewer people were receiving food aid one year later. In Arkansas, of the 54,531 households on welfare in counties with the food stamp program, only 9700 buy the stamps. This is not peculiar to these states;

while some 6 million people are estimated to be receiving either commodities or food stamps now—roughly 3 million under each program—it is seldom mentioned that six years ago even more people were being helped, albeit the great part by the inferior commodities program.

Another quirk is that the bonuses go up as the income goes up, so that the higher-income poor end up with more food than those at the bottom of the scale. The Agriculture Department explains that this is because it would not be wise to give those who are accustomed to being worst off too much too soon. In order to be certified as eligible for the program, families must run the gauntlet of the welfare agencies, many of which are not known for their sympathies toward Negroes. The food programs are sometimes used as an instrument of control: people who participate in civil rights activities or who are needed when it is time for the crops to be picked find that the programs are suddenly unavailable. In many areas, food prices go up on the day the stamps are issued.

When the uproar over these failings developed in 1967, the Agriculture Department made a study of the situation in Washington County, Mississippi. It found, among other things, that more than half of those qualified to receive food stamps were not doing so. The investigators were not, however, greatly perturbed. "In general," they reported, "the study indicates that low-income households in this Mississippi Delta county accommodate themselves to a diet which low-income families elsewhere would reject. . . . It may be that low-income families place less value on food than we think."

The Department of Agriculture should not, in all fairness, be expected to demonstrate dazzling expertise in the needs and life-styles of the poor. Its essential mission is to nurture the agricultural economy; the poor are somebody else's department. The typical employee in Agriculture has been there a long, long time. He may have come in with Henry Wallace, or he may have been a dirt farmer who was down and out during the Depression, got a government job measuring acreage, moved up through the ranks, and was promoted to Washington when he was in his fifties.

Nobody envies Orville Freeman his job, frequently described as "the worst one in town." Freeman's own official biography says it all: "He has been shot at not only by Congressmen, rural and urban, but also by consumers protesting food prices, farmers protesting farm prices, and dissidents of all job descriptions and all colors protesting food programs and poverty." Freeman is a liberal out of the Democratic-Farmer-Labor movement, where he was a three-term boy-wonder governor. From the time that John F. Kennedy appointed him in 1961, Freeman has probably stirred up less than the traditional amount of controversy for Secretaries of Agriculture. "The Administration wanted him to cultivate the farmers, not the poor of the civil rights crowd," said one of his associates. "His tendency, in the earlier years, when the subject of hungry people came up, was to look embarrassed and change the subject." When it could no longer be ignored, Freeman behaved like a man in a trap. Moreover, he could, and frequently did, claim with justification that during his tenure, through initiating food stamps and expanding food packages, an unprecedented amount had been done toward feeding the poor. His injured pride and his combative nature served to deepen his troubles.

Jamie Whitten, a fifty-eight-year-old congressman from Charleston, Mississippi, chairman of the subcommittee which provides funds for the Agriculture Department's programs and one of the most powerful members of the House of Representatives, does not believe that anybody in this country is unavoidably hungry, "except," he says, "when there has been parental neglect through drunkenness or mental illness. You're dealing with people who for some reason or other are in a condition of poverty. If they had the training and foresight of other people, they wouldn't be in poverty."

Whitten has installed a number of employees at the Agriculture Department, and there is little that Orville Freeman does that Jamie Whitten doesn't know about. Whitten expects Freeman to consult him before he makes any policy move, and Freeman has decided it is the better part of wisdom to do just that. The congressman is a skilled legislator, however, and knows better than to stand intransigently against the majority opinion of the House. He hasn't often, in fact, made significant cuts in the food stamp program's funds once the House has approved the program. Neither, if he doesn't like what Freeman is doing, is he likely to cut into crop-support funds of such importance to the farm bloc. Whitten had denied money for work in the general area of rural poverty; Freeman is also anxious not to annoy Whitten to the point where he might cut funds which the Department lends to rural areas to build ski slides and golf courses that Freeman feels are important community programs. After a while, the relationship between a Cabinet officer and his House appropriations subcommittee chairman blurs beyond a rational if-I-do-this-he-will-do-that situation. "He simply becomes part of your thinking," says one former Cabinet officer. "He is an automatic part of all your decisions."

The House Agriculture Committee, which sets the policies for which Whitten's group then provides the money, is, to state it gently, disinterested in the poor. The committee's concerns are sheep scrapie and hog cholera and agriculture subsidies. The members of most committees see to it that the benefits of programs they preside over reach their constituents in full measure, but it is no accident that the home districts of a number of the Agriculture Committee members do not have food stamp programs. "These programs are not desired by the power structures back home," says one close observer, "and that's what elects them. The recipients of these programs don't vote."

The situation is similar in the Senate. In all cases, the Agriculture committees are almost entirely populated by representatives of Southern and Midwestern farm districts, with, in a Democratic Congress, the representatives of Southern landholders in charge. Senator James O. Eastland, for example, is the third-ranking member of the Senate Agriculture Committee and its most important determiner of cotton policy. Last year, the Eastland family planations in Sunflower County, Mississippi, received $211,364 in subsidies. Despite the slipping popularity of the farm programs, and the increasing urban and suburban orientation of Congress, these men have enough seniority, and serve on enough other important committees, to make their influence felt. To the extent that the Agriculture Department budget is under attack, they try to keep the budget down by curbing the Department's noncrop programs. "Freeman decided as a matter of policy," says one of his former colleagues, "that he was not going to antagonize these men. He checked out appointments with them and went to enormous lengths to cultivate them socially. When the food issue came up and he got caught in his conspiracy with the Southerners on the Hill, his instinctive reaction was to deny that anything was wrong. After all, he was relying on memos from his staff, and they were defending themselves, too."

In April, 1967, the Senate Labor and Public Welfare Committee's Subcommittee on Employment, Manpower, and Poverty went to Mississippi. The subcommittee, headed by Senator Joseph S. Clark of Pennsylvania, was making a nationwide study of the poverty program, and since Senator Robert Kennedy was a member of the group, wherever it went, the press went too. At a hearing in Jackson, Mississippi, Marian Wright, an attractive, soft-spoken attorney for the NAACP's Legal Defense Fund, Incorporated, who had been working in Mississippi, talked about welfare, poverty, and the situation in the Delta. "They are starving," she concluded. "They are starving, and those who can get the bus fare to go north are trying to go north. But there is absolutely nothing for them to do. There is nowhere to go, and somebody must begin to respond to them."

Kennedy and Clark said they would take it to the Department of Agriculture when they returned to Washington. Senator George Murphy went them one better and said that the group should "notify the President of the United States that there is an emergency situation, and send investigators and help in immediately." On the following day, Clark and Kennedy toured the Delta. The cameras were not there when Robert Kennedy sat on the floor in one particularly fetid shack watching a listless child toy with a plate of rice, feeling the child's body, trying to get the child to respond, and trying to comprehend. Until then, the senators really had not known how bad it was.

After they returned to Washington, all nine members of the subcommittee signed a letter to the President describing the situation as "shocking" and constituting an "emergency," and calling for specific Administration action. The White House, after trying not to receive it at all, bucked the letter to the Office of Economic Opportunity, which runs the poverty program, and OEO responded with a press release, its outlines dictated by the White House. The release said there was poverty in each of the senators' home states, too; that the crisis of poverty had been greater before Lyndon Johnson took office; that the Administration had started a lot of programs in Mississippi;

that the Congress had cut funds for the poverty program; that "every recommendation in the letter by the Senators has the hearty concurrence of the administration," but there were some legal problems; and "we already know what needs to be done."

The senators' concern and the attendant publicity might, of course, have been seen by the White House as an opportunity to make major moves to correct the problem, just as it had made it a point to get out in front on any number of issues, such as auto safety or home ownership for the poor, raised in Congress. But this time the President was in no mood to be pushed. Neither he nor Freeman believed that the problem was as serious as Clark and Kennedy said, and both saw "politics" in the whole affair. (Department officials say that Clark and Kennedy were taken on a "pre-arranged" tour by "professionals.") The President knew that neither senator had influence with, in fact they had highly angered, the Agriculture establishment on Capitol Hill, and to the White House these were important people not to anger. When he did move, and it was not doubted that he would, it would be at a time and in a manner of his choosing.

The problem of malnutrition had, like most conceivable domestic problems, been put before a secret interagency task force by the White House the year before, as part of the preparations for the Administration's 1967 legislative program. The appointment of the task force, the task force was told, reflected the White House's deep conviction that every American should have an adequate nutritional diet. The task force, headed by Agriculture Department representatives, did not, in the view of the White House, provide sufficient information on either the dimensions of the problem or possible new approaches. Neither presidential aide Joseph Califano, who had hoped to be able to propose a food program, nor his new assistant, James Gaither, was familiar enough with the complexities of the food programs to ask the right questions. Therefore nothing of any consequence was proposed. Following the senators' letter, renewed efforts within the Administration to work something out devolved into angry disputes between OEO, particularly Director Sargent Shriver, who accused Agriculture of incapacity to deal with the problem, and Agriculture, particularly Freeman, who accused OEO of trying to damage their Department and take away the programs. It was a classic bureaucratic fight over turf.

There were two basic issues between the subcommittee and the Administration: the price of the food stamps, and the Secretary's authority to declare an emergency in the Delta and send in extra food. After several months of subcommittee pressure and after prodding by the White House and harassment by Shriver, the Agriculture Department did lower the price of food stamps for those with an income of less than $20 a month to 50 cents per person a month, with a maximum of $3 per family. (This buys $72 worth of food for a family of six, about half what the Department estimates such a family needs.) It also decided to charge all families only half the price in the first month.

Prices could not be lowered generally until there was substantially more money for the program, a decision the President would have to make.

The Department resisted the argument that there were people with no income at all who should be charged nothing for their food stamps. For one thing, the Department thought that this was a problem in a small number of cases, and therefore not worthy of great concern. For another, the Secretary believed, as he told congressional committees on several occasions, that the poor could not be trusted with free stamps. "If you proceed, then, to have free stamps," he said, "and you give free stamps to everybody who wants them, what will happen to those stamps? Those stamps, I am afraid, in many cases will be bootlegged. That is what happened back in the 1940s and the 1930s, with the food stamp program. That destroyed the program. The food stamp program was discredited because those stamps became common currency for all kinds of things, from a wild party, to a beer party, to legitimate uses, to buy shoes." Another view of what ended the earlier program was the almost full employment during World War II.

The senators and others argued that the Secretary should have invoked his emergency power to send extra food to the Delta, using money from a special multipurpose fund (known as Section 32 for its place in an agriculture law), as he had used it to begin the food stamp program and expand the commodity packages. The Department argued that it didn't really have the power (despite the precedents), that the money really hadn't been budgeted, that it would be bad precedent and administratively inefficient to distribute free food where there were already food stamps; and there was also that danger that if there were two programs the people might start bootlegging. There was also the problem that the Agriculture committees frown on such use of the money.

As the argument tumbled forth at one private meeting, Kennedy looked at Freeman and shook his head. "I don't know, Orville," he said, "I'd just get the food down there. I can't believe that in this country we can't get some food down there."

Oddly, the one senator who took matters in his own hands and introduced a bill was John Stennis of Mississippi. The Stennis bill would have provided money for emergency food and medical programs, and required a government study of the true extent of malnutrition. (The government had made almost no studies of malnutrition in the United States; the Public Health Service had not seen that to be its concern. The Pentagon, wanting to know about the connection between malnutrition and defense preparedness of foreign countries, had sponsored several studies of nutrition overseas, and there were minor studies of the eating habits of Eskimos and Indian tribes in the United States.)

The Stennis bill went through the Senate quickly. But his shrewd move to cut off talk about his state was not appreciated by the House Agriculture Committee, which let the bill die. Through other congressional routes, OEO was given $10 million in emergency food money and the Department of

Health, Education, and Welfare was ordered to study the extent of malnutrition.

In September of 1967, in the only public statement on the issue he was to make for a long time, President Johnson said that "we want no American in this country to go hungry. We believe that we have the knowledge, the compassion, and the resources to banish hunger and to do away with malnutrition if we only apply those resources and those energies." He ordered the Department of Agriculture to see to it that, one way or the other, every one of the thousand poorest counties in the nation had a food program. The Department said that there were 331 of those counties that did not, and, to give it a little of the old pizzazz, it embarked on "Project 331." As it turned out, it was a full year before each of the 331 was said to have a program, for the Department remained highly reluctant to fly in the face of tradition by using federal money and federal personnel to establish a program if the counties resisted. It was also concerned about what it felt was a bad precedent of having the federal government pay the full costs. In May of the following year, with the Poor People's Campaign beating at his door, Freeman finally announced that this would be done.

Extending the programs to more counties had nothing to do with improving matters for recipients, as in Mississippi. Since greater amounts of money were not committed, it also meant that other less poor counties that were on the waiting list for the food stamp program would have to continue to wait. Finally, sometime after Project 331 was under way it was discovered that Agriculture defined a "poorest" county as one with the lowest average income, rather than one with the largest number of poor people. Therefore, poor people who had the misfortune of living near too many rich people were out of luck. This covered more counties at less expense, and fewer people were helped.

The President's encouraging statement may have been prompted by the fact that by the fall of 1967 the White House had set up another secret task force, which once more reflected their deep conviction, they said, that every American should have an adequate nutritional diet. The task force, now headed by representatives of the Budget Bureau, reported that for another $1.5 to $2 billion and in relatively short time the government could provide that adequate diet to every American. Now, however, and for months to come, the Administration was locked in its fight to secure a 10 percent income surtax from Congress, and Congress' demand that there be substantial cuts in government spending in return. "I don't think anyone realizes how paralyzed we became by that fight," says one Administration official. "I don't think even we realized it." With the White House feeling under particular pressure to do something about the cities (the Detroit riot had just taken place), and with their own expertise tending in that direction, Califano's staff that fall concerned itself with devising new programs for jobs and housing. Whatever the limitations of these programs in terms of delayed spending, they at least represented a commitment and an effort at new approaches, which were not made on giving the poor sufficient food. Through it all, Mr. Johnson remained unconvinced that the problem was as serious as the critics said, reluctant to take the fight to the Hill, where he had enough problems, and annoyed that no one could tell him exactly how many people were going hungry. (No one knows exactly how many unemployed or how much substandard housing there is either.)

Moreover, there was now no great public pressure on the White House to act on hunger, as there was on behalf of the cities. During all of 1967 and 1968, only a small coterie made the issue a continuing preoccupation: Miss Wright; Peter Edelman of Kennedy's staff; William Smith of Clark's staff; and Robert Choate, a young businessman of some means who took a sabbatical to become a free-lance, largely behind the scenes, and highly effective crusader on the issue. Of the enormous Washington press corps, only Nick Kotz of the Des Moines *Register* saw the hunger issue as worthy of continuing coverage, whether or not it was "in the news." Of all the lobby organizations, only a few of the more liberal labor groups found the issue to be of even intermittent concern.

The Citizens' Crusade Against Poverty, an organization with United Auto Workers backing, was the closest there was to a group with a full-time concern. Early in 1968, it had established a Citizens' Board of Inquiry, which published "Hunger, U.S.A.," a stinging indictment of the food programs. Around the same time, a coalition of women's organizations published a study of the federal school lunch program which could help children of the poor secure a better meal at least while they were in school. The women's groups found that of the 18 million children receiving free or reduced-price lunches under the program, only 2 million were poor; another 4 million poor children were not being helped. The Johnson Administration had tried to get Congress to restructure this so that less would go to the middle class and more to the poor, and Congress had adamantly refused. On May 21, CBS broadcast a powerful documentary called *Hunger in America.*

Several members of Congress reacted to all of this with outrage at the idea that anyone would charge that people in their areas were going hungry. Representative W. R. Poage of Texas, chairman of the House Agriculture Committee, wrote to county health officials, the very ones who would be most culpable, and asked if they personally knew of anyone in their county who was starving or seriously hungry. No, replied most of the health officers, and if the people were hungry it was mostly because they were lazy or ignorant. A few said the food programs were inadequate, but Poage did not emphasize that in his report to his colleagues.

The response of the politicians was understandable. More puzzling, in light of his professed zeal to get more done, were Freeman's own persistent attacks on the reports. Finding factual errors in the small (they didn't mention that grandma had a pension of $82-a-month), he condemned them in the large. The CBS telecast, he said, was "a biased, one-sided dishonest presentation of a serious national problem."

As the Poor People's Campaign, under the direction of the Southern Christian Leadership Conference, prepared for its March on Washington in the spring of 1968, strategists for both the SCLC and the federal government knew that, as always in these situations, there would have to be a governmental response which would enable the Campaign's leaders to make an honorable withdrawal from the city. First Attorney General Ramsey Clark, then the President himself asked the various government agencies to draw up a list of administrative actions—which would not cost money—which could alleviate some of the difficulties of the poor. A March on Washington by a grand coalition of white, black, brown, and red poor, who would encamp in the federal city, bringing their plight to the attention of the country, had been the idea of Martin Luther King. After Dr. King was assassinated, the leadership of the SCLC under Dr. Ralph Abernathy was in disarray. Goals and tactics became difficult to resolve. Miss Wright, who had moved to Washington, was placed in charge of the Campaign's dealings with the government agencies, and worked exhaustingly for weeks for a semblance of order and progress in the demands and responses. On the advice of Miss Wright and others, the Campaign leaders decided upon hunger as the central, most dramatic issue.

Now the issue was at its highest point of public attention. Most of the government agencies did what they could to respond to the marchers' demands. Agriculture, however, remained defensive. In the end, the Agriculture response consisted of promising to get a food program into each of the thousand counties—which the President had already done nine months earlier; making more commodities available for surplus distribution; regulations to improve the school lunch program; and improved food packages for infants and expectant mothers. Some Administration officials think the poor were not grateful enough.

As it happened, the major reason this response was so paltry was that the White House was preparing one on a grander scale for the President himself to present, probably in the form of a special message to Congress. It would have revised the entire food stamp schedule and perhaps lowered the cost to the very poorest to either nothing or a token amount; it would have expanded the size of the food programs so that many more areas could receive them; and it would have carried a commitment to build the programs over time, to the point where every American had an adequate diet. The Budget Bureau squirreled away some money to go with the message. The thought was that it would be delivered around the time of "Solidarity Day," on June 19, when thousands of others were to come to Washington to join the poor in a climatic march.

A number of reasons have been offered for why the President's Solidarity Day Message was never delivered: the mail in the White House was overwhelmingly against the Poor People's Campaign, and Resurrection City was out of control; Abernathy's final speech was likely to carry a stinging denunciation of the war in Vietnam; and the House of Representatives was going to vote at last on the tax bill the following day, and any move at that point by the President to increase government spending might jeopardize the long-negotiated compromise. The most important reason, however, was that the President simply did not want to be in the position of appearing to "respond to pressure." More startling to many was that after the poor had left town and the tax bill had passed, he still declined to move. He was focusing on the budget cuts that had to be made, annoyed at Freeman for getting out in front of him on the issue, still concerned at appearing to respond to pressure, and convinced that now that some legislation was moving on the Hill, it would be unseemingly for him, the President, to appear to be running to catch up.

By this time, things were most uncomfortable for Freeman, and he began to press hard at the White House for help—belatedly, in the opinion of many. His friend Vice President Humphrey tried to help. First Humphrey offered his services as a mediator with the Poor People's Campaign, but the offer was rejected by the White House. Then the Vice President of the United States tried indirect means of communicating with the President. Humphrey wrote to Mrs. Arthur Krim, wife of the President's chief money raiser: "It is just intolerable to me that there is such a problem of malnutrition and under-nourishment in the United States. . . . Through it all, there are ways the President could have helped—in approving some of Orville Freeman's budget requests, in supporting legislation on the Hill, and suggesting administrative change—but he has not. The thought came that you might be the person who could say a word or two to encourage him."

On Capitol Hill, a bill to expand the food stamp program was moving forward. Originally an Administration request to make a minimal expansion of $20 million (over the $225 million already authorized), under pressure from urban liberals, who threatened to retaliate against a farm bill that was also in the mill, the bill ultimately authorized the program to grow by $90 million in the first year and more after that. After endorsing a substantial increase in the program, Freeman was reprimanded by both Poage and the White House, but when an increase seemed probable, the White House joined in. More spending for the school lunch program was approved, and a special Senate committee was established to "study" the food problem, with a view to trying to maneuver the food programs away from Agriculture committees.

In the very last days of the congressional session, with the President about to make a routine request for additional funds for various agencies that had fallen short of funds, the machinery around the government—in the Agriculture Department, in the Budget Bureau, in his own staff—geared up once more for a presidential request for more funds for food stamps and a major statement on the issue. Instead, he simply requested the $90 million and in the closing rush Congress gave him $55 million. Wait, it was said, for his farewell messages in 1969.

The failure of the Johnson Administration to make substantial progress toward feeding the poor is viewed by many as its most serious domestic failure.

It is the cause of disappointment and even anguish on the part of many people within the government. Orville Freeman, for one, professes himself satisfied: "Everything I suggested from the beginning that should be in Lyndon Johnson's program, or damn near it, I have gotten. If he had gone up to Congress with a big feeding program like a bull in a china shop he'd have been under fire, and what would he have gotten? Some newspaper accolades and plaudits in some liberal magazines, and trouble with Congress."

The food issue is an unhappy example of a great deal that can go wrong in Washington. It is also an example, however, of the dangers of the latest fad of "local control." The food programs are examples of programs that *are* subject to local control—the local governments request, pay for, and run them —with the result that those areas which are least responsive to the needs of the poor can also deny them federally proffered food.

The problem is not nearly so insoluble as the events of the past two years would suggest. First of all, given enough money and flexibility, it is generally agreed the food stamp program is not at all a bad device. Choate, for one, suggests that in addition the program be federalized and computerized, to work as automatically and without continual harassment for the recipient as social security. He and a number of others believe that ultimately the food programs ought to be recognized as income supplements and become part of an income maintenance system. That, however, seems a long way off. When asked by the space agency, the food companies have found ingenious ways to pack meals for astronauts in Tootsie-Roll-sized bars or toothpaste-sized tubes. The Pentagon seems to have no trouble keeping the troops in the field well nourished. There are problems of tastes and habits to meet, but if the food industry were less apprehensive about change, or did less cohabiting with the farm bloc in that great combine they call "agribusiness," a lot more could be done to feed the poor efficiently and inexpensively. The food companies have lately shown more interest in exploring this field—with government subsidies, of course.

Yet so little was accomplished not because of mechanical or industrial failures, but because of what can happen to men in policy-making positions in Washington. When they stay in a difficult job too long, they can be overwhelmed by the complexity of it all, and they become overly defensive. Man's pride, particularly the pride of a man who can tell himself he has done some good, can overtake his intellectual honesty. Thus, not Southern politicians, not Orville Freeman, not Lyndon Johnson could face the fact when it was pointed out that many people were hungry, that they weren't wearing any clothes. In this way they reflected a national trait: it has been easier to stir sustained national concern over hunger in Bihar or Biafra than places at home for which we are more directly responsible. The problems are looked at in terms of the workings of Washington, not in terms of the problems. Decent men could sit and discuss statistical reliability and administrative neatness and the importance of good precedents while people went hungry.

The niceties of consensus politics were more important than the needs of some 10 million people. A new Congress and a new Administration ought to be able to improve on that kind of government.

PETER F. DRUCKER

A Warning to the Rich White World

The newest and greatest threat abroad in the world today may well be the threat of a war of the poor and largely colored peoples against the rich and largely white. There is greater disparity between the rich and the poor today than there has ever been before. It is increasingly a disparity within one community of information. And it is a disparity between races rather than a cleavage between classes.

This is new. China was much richer in the sixteenth century than England. But the Chinese gentleman of the times lived on a very similar standard to that of the Elizabethan gentleman. And so did the poor in the two countries. Today, however, the English workingman (not to mention the American) lives much better than any but the exceedingly rich in most countries of the world. The globe has become divided into nations that know how to manage technology to create wealth, and nations that do not. Within the rich nations technology has succeeded to an amazing extent in overcoming the cleavage between the rich and the poor, not by making the rich poorer—as the Marxists predicted—but by making the poor richer. Between the rich and the poor nations, however, technology has created a gap in income and opportunities which never existed before.

Even if such a gap had existed in earlier times, it would not have mattered much. If, 400 years ago, the poorest Chinese had lived as well as the English duke, no one in England would have known about it. It would have been a

Source: Mr. Drucker is an internationally known management consultant, teacher, and author. This article is from *Harper's Magazine*, December 1968, pp. 67–75. Copyright © 1968 by Minneapolis Star and Tribune Co., Inc. Reprinted from the December 1968 issue of *Harper's Magazine* by permission of the author.

traveler's tale on a par with stories about mermaids, unicorns, and other fables. Today, however, we see how other people live every day on the TV screen in our living room, as direct, personal, immediate experience. This is a gap, therefore, within one and the same community.

The gap is primarily a gap between races. It has lately become fashionable to talk about the "North-South gap," which implies that climate is responsible for the inability of two-thirds of mankind to break out of pre-industrial poverty. This is one of the theses of Gunnar Myrdal's recent book, *Asian Drama*. It is a dangerous, self-deluding euphemism. The Chinese, the largest single group among the pre-industrial peoples, are northerners to a man. All India lies north of the Equator; and the great bulk of the Indian population lives well north of the tropics. Every single population center of Latin America lies climatically in the temperate zone. The fact is that all the world's rich nations, excepting only the Japanese, are white and all the world's poor nations, excluding only part of Latin America, are colored. Within Latin America, too, the cleavages are largely racial, e.g., between the fast-developing and largely white industrial triangle of Brazil—Rio, São Paulo, Belo Horizonte—and the wretchedly poor and entirely black northeast; or between the growth of primarily Spanish Lima and the misery of the Andean Indians.

That the cleavage is above all racial shows clearly in the United States, where the poor are predominantly Negro. The American Negro is the representative of the poor races within the richest nation. The American Negro problem is, therefore, the most important, the most acute, and perhaps the most dangerous instance of the worldwide problem. If the United States, the world's richest, technologically most advanced, and managerially most accomplished country, cannot bring about economic and social development of a nonwhite minority in its midst, then it will be taken as proved, by white and colored alike, that there is an unbridgeable race conflict. By the same token, however, our ability in this country to resolve the problem of Negro destitution and to bring about rapid Negro development may also be the greatest possible contribution to the world race problem.

Yet race is not the explanation for "underdevelopment." Clearly nonwhite races are capable of development—as witness the Japanese. And the three non-Communist Chinese communities—Hong Kong, Formosa, and Singapore—have shown tremendous capacity for rapid economic and social growth in the last twenty years. At the same time, there are people of European stock, for instance the South Americans, who apparently do not have this capacity. And few areas in Latin America are as "underdeveloped" or as "colonial" as most of Spain or Sicily.

Whatever the reasons for the cleavage (and we know a good deal about them by now), it is clear that it will be overcome one way or another. Ideally, man will find ways to make the poor countries richer. Alternatively, the rich countries will not be allowed to remain rich.

That no country has developed to become a wealthy, advanced industrial nation since World War I, more than fifty years ago, is, therefore, a central social and political problem of the world economy. Between 1860 and 1910 a new major industrial nation emerged every twenty years or so. This created confidence throughout the world that economic development could be taken for granted. But for fifty years now it has not happened. We must make it happen—and in enough places to show that development is not a matter of race but of the right policies and efforts.

Almost twenty years ago President Truman proclaimed the goal of economic development for the poor nations in his Point Four program. Since then, statistically, economic growth has been a good deal greater than even the optimists of 1950 would have dared predict. Industrial production has been growing very fast indeed in a good many parts of the underdeveloped world. And agricultural production and productivity are suddenly jumping ahead, just when everyone had given up hope that world hunger could be averted. One could cite innumerable figures to prove that the last twenty years have validated our development policies. Yet the public would remain unconvinced. And the public would be right. Development, as President Truman conceived it and as we envisaged it these last twenty years, has been a failure. It has failed to produce the one essential result: the example of a new major growth economy. Development aid has resulted in the production of a lot of goods and a lot of jobs. But it has, so far, failed to generate the new vision.

The demands of economic development are more exacting than we believed when President Truman announced his Point Four program. We need intelligence much more than money—and intelligence is a great deal scarcer.

We must now understand that development can no longer be financed by agriculture, as it was in the nineteenth century. We must understand that it can, therefore, no longer be "automatic." We must understand that to provide investment capital from abroad on a planned and directed basis will not automatically produce development either, although it did in the nineteenth century. And we must understand the severe limitations on the effectiveness of foreign aid, and of government action altogether.

1. In the nineteenth century, agriculture in the settled countries was touched by the new industrial civilization only superficially. The countrysides I knew when I grew up—the English counties and the villages of Austria, Switzerland, and Northern Italy—still lived in their traditional culture and civilization as late as the 1920s. To be sure, they had a good many new tools, such as the railroads or electricity. But these had little impact on their way of life, on their view of themselves, on their social, political, or intellectual vision. They had had only limited impact on their economy. And this was even more true in France and Scandinavia.

At the same time, the population explosion of the nineteenth century was economic opportunity rather than threat. Population in the industrializing countries then—that is, in Europe, in North America, and finally in Japan—grew almost as rapidly as it is growing now in the developing countries. But instead of putting pressure on the food base of the economy, it created markets for the agriculture of the new "breadbaskets" in Eastern Germany, Hungary, Western Russia, the Ukraine, Romania, America, Argentina, Canada, and Australia. Thus, the new countries, whether in Central and Eastern Europe or overseas in the Americas and in the Pacific, could finance their development by farm exports from their new soils. Agriculture in these countries was not "advanced" technologically. Nor did it need to be. It took into cultivation new lands, where anything produced was so much increment, so much surplus. In this way developing nations not only obtained the manufactured goods for their own population, they also financed their capital imports.

The United States obtained more capital between 1870 and 1890 to build transcontinental railroads than all the money (adjusted for changes in purchasing power) the United States has spent in aid to developing countries in the last twenty years. Very little of it was ever paid back. The American railroads as a rule defaulted on the bonds and wrote off the shares. The money was, however, given against ample security: the new fertile soil the railroads were opening to settlement. Europe was repaid by cheap food to feed her urban masses.

It is no longer possible, however, to finance development out of agriculture. It is equally impossible nowadays to keep the village out of modern society and insulated from modern technology. The automobile and the truck, the transistor radio and the loudspeaker, as well as electric power, integrate rural society into city society. They abolish rural society as such, dissolve it into a poor and underprivileged component of an urban world. A hundred years ago the city was the exception and society was essentially the countryside. Today rural society rarely exists anymore and can only be defined by whatever city blessings it does not enjoy.

In the nineteenth century the then developed areas of the West could not have survived without steadily increasing food imports. Today most of the developed countries have become food-surplus producers. And most of the underdeveloped countries need all the food they can produce to feed their own people, in any event.

Moreover, agriculture in the developed countries (excepting only Russia) is now the most technologically advanced and the most industrialized of basic industries. Consequently, productivity differentials in agriculture between developed and underdeveloped economies far outrun the differentials in manufacturing. We expect a new steel mill in an underdeveloped country to be one-third to one-half as productive as a steel mill in the old industrial areas of Europe. But we are not surprised to see productivity differentials of ten to one or even twenty-five to one between the agricultures of the developed, highly industrial countries and the agricultures of the underdeveloped countries.

Fifty years or so ago, rice yields per acre in China, and even in India, were higher than those in the West. Today the yield per acre of irrigated rice in

California is ten times (or more) that of similar land in China. China, in turn, produces three times as much rice on the same irrigated acre as does Indonesia —and at least twice as much rice as even well-managed and well-watered farms in India.

Under these conditions, agriculture in the poor countries simply cannot compete, no matter how low the income of their farmers. Where agriculture provided the investment capital for industry in the nineteenth century—and still did in Stalin's Russia—today it requires very large capital investments of its own. "Forty acres and a mule" no longer make a productive farmer. They make a rural pauper. The fundamental agricultural equation on which nineteenth-century development was based no longer balances out.

2. Capital investment from abroad is no longer the answer to development. In fact, heavy capital investment from abroad may become a barrier to development rather than a spur. The nineteenth century, as the example of the American railroads illustrates, invested a great deal more capital abroad, especially in development areas, than we have invested in aid since World War II. Indeed, although international trade has been growing fast and is at a higher level than it was then—both absolutely and in relation to total production—capital investment lags far behind. The American investments in multinational corporations, large though they have been, represent a much smaller fraction of national income than did the European investments in American railroads a century ago.

But the nineteenth-century capital investment was investment "abroad" only in a geographic sense. Most of it, whether put into harbors or railroads or mines, served to produce food and raw materials for the lender's industrial centers. In financial terms this meant that the foreign investor was being repaid out of what his own countrymen paid for the grain, the cotton, or the copper whose supply his investment had made possible. There was no "transfer problem." The investment liquidated itself. To service it financially did not entail withdrawal of currency from the debtor country.

Such investment is by no means unknown today. Most of the billions invested in petroleum production around the world, for example, are being serviced out of the monies paid by the users—who, of course, are the developed industrial countries. But the bulk of development investment today is of a different kind. It aims at creating capacity to produce for the domestic markets of the country in which the investment is made. It does not, in other words, generate the exports with which to repay the investment.

Investment of capital in the developing countries, therefore, tends to create a foreign-exchange liability. This has been painfully demonstrated in Latin America. It explains in large measure why the last ten years have been years of trouble there. Latin America, through the mid-1950s, attracted almost as much capital as her development economists wanted. As a result, Latin America grew very fast during that period. But when the inflow diminished a little, crisis immediately set in. Payments on the loans and dividends remitted abroad began to use up whatever foreign exchange was available. If a country suspended payments abroad to counteract this, its credit promptly disappeared —and so did foreign capital. If, on the other hand, a country maintained its foreign payments to maintain its credit, its growth came to an end as its capital base shrank, thus creating a deflationary crisis. This too ended the influx of foreign capital.

We need all the trade we can get. We also need capital investment, and more than we have had in the last ten years. But we can no longer depend on either as the motive power of economic development.

3. But if "trade not aid," however beguiling, is an unrealistic slogan, "aid" alone will also not do the job of economic development.

Whenever we face the problem of poverty, whether domestic or international, our first impulse is to solve it through distributing wealth. Unfortunately, there is not enough wealth around to get us anything except disillusionment.

John Pincus of the RAND Corporation has recently computed how much it would take to tackle the world's poverty problems through distributing the wealth of the rich nations. To raise per capita income everywhere to $1,000 a year—still less than one-third the United States figure—would require $1.4 thousand billion a year, that is, more than the total annual income of all the developed countries and more than 200 times as much as we have ever spent on aid in any one year.

Aid, in other words, can only be a stimulant. The main growth has to come out of the resources of the poor countries themselves. Effective aid acts as a catalyst releasing local energies. But aid, unless carefully planned and ruthlessly administered, may also tend to inhibit the energies of the recipient. This has become apparent in our surplus food aid, which, so very well intentioned, is actually causing development failure. It has encouraged policies that cut back rather than improve food production at home. It has led to gross misallocation of resources, as recipient countries—and India is only one example—felt free to invest in politically palatable but economically dubious prestige projects—steel mills, typically, or jet planes—rather than in agriculture. Beyond relief for people actually threatened with starvation, food relief should be given only sparingly. It destroys the incentive of the local farmer to increase his output.

Aid, by its very nature, will flow toward problems rather than toward opportunities. It will go where the needs are greatest rather than were the results are. It will, therefore, tend to create—or, at least, to perpetuate—dependence.

This is true of aid at home fully as much as of aid abroad. It has dawned on us lately that the social worker in the big city often causes the very misery she works so hard to relieve. She causes dependence. Her clients are treated as "relief cases" and—unintentionally—prevented from even attempting to get back on their own feet, indeed often penalized if they try (by termination of relief payments, for instance).

In any aid program, the economist, especially the development economist employed by government, tends to impose his own values on the choice of priorities and projects. Understandably he likes things that look big, impressive, and "advanced": a petrochemical plant, for instance. He likes the things he knows the poor "ought" to have. He has nothing but contempt for the "frivolous," e.g., small luxuries.

The factory girl or the salesgirl in Lima or Bombay (or the Harlem ghetto) wants a lipstick. She lives in a horrible slum and knows perfectly well that she cannot, in her lifetime, afford the kind of house she would like to live in—the kind of house her counterpart in the rich countries (or the white suburbs) can afford. She knows perfectly well that neither she nor her brothers can get the kind of education they would like to have. She probably knows perfectly well that—if lucky—she will marry some boy as poor as herself and as little educated who, within a few years, will start beating her out of sheer despair. But at least she can, for a few short years, try to look like the kind of human being she wants to be, respects, and knows she ought to be. There is no purchase that gives her as much true value for a few cents as cheap cosmetics.

A cosmetic plant gives more employment per dollar of investment than a petrochemical plant. It trains more people capable of developing and running a modern economy. It generates managers, technicians, and salesmen. Yet the economist despises it. And the reliance on aid makes it possible for his moralism to prevail and for his desire for control to prevent development.

We did not, during the late nineteenth and early twentieth centuries overcome class war by philanthropy. What overcame class war was, first, new technology, particularly electric power. This new technology created new, more productive, and therefore better-paid jobs. Secondly, the class war was overcome by education, which gave an increasing number of the children of the poor the opportunity to break out of the "class" to which in Marxist ideology they were condemned. But above all, what overcame the class war was Frederick Taylor's *Scientific Management*, which first applied knowledge to work and thereby made the laborer productive for the first time.

We achieved whatever success we had through making the poor productive. The test for aid to poor nations is therefore whether it makes them capable of being productive. If it fails to do so, it is likely to make them even poorer in the—not so very—long run.

To be sure, development requires substantial amounts of money both in aid and in investment. But to succeed, these must come as support to effective and going efforts of the local community. Aid, for instance, might be in the form of matching grants conditional upon the organization of local efforts by the recipient. Investment might be geared to a country's development rate.

We must favor nations that have proved their ability to build if times are propitious. Examples are Brazil, Colombia, Iran, and Pakistan. At the same time, we need to be able to say to other areas, "Prove your willingness to develop and then we will help you. So far, you have wasted opportunity." An example is Argentina, which, during the last fifty years, has turned herself from a highly developed and rich country into an underdeveloped and poor one. Another example might be Indonesia. No matter how serious a "problem" such countries are, we cannot afford to waste exceedingly scarce resources on them. But we need to be able to go to work where the projections of the economists did not predict development, but where, nonetheless, it is happening. The non-Communist Chinese communities are examples.

This may sound very hard-boiled—and it is. But the choice before us is between wasting aid (and investment) and obtaining real development from it. All aid can do is encourage and stimulate. We, therefore, had better use it to give us what we need the most: highly visible examples of rapid, self-generated growth.

4. "Intergovernmental programs" do not produce development. An economy cannot be developed from the outside anyhow—but least of all by "government-to-government" efforts, be the foreigners "democratic" or "Communist."

Foreign governments cannot impose priorities on other countries. They cannot, therefore, resist local pressures to divert scarce development resources into unproductive projects. Consider the United States "military aid" to South America. It has served mainly to feed the ego of generals and colonels. Yet military aid not only uses up scarce funds—an airplane or a destroyer is not much use unless fuel for it, lubricants, and spare parts are supplied year-in and year-out. Thus, every dollar spent on military aid for Latin America has not only taken a dollar that should have gone into development, it has created a demand for an additional five or ten dollars to be diverted out of slender foreign exchange resources to maintain the general's toys.

Concentration on a few major priorities is fundamental to any successful effort at development; yet no principle has been so consistently violated in the last twenty years. We have spent a fair amount of money. We have invested very substantial human energies of good, able, dedicated people. But we have wasted resources by spreading them out so thin that they could not have substantial impact.

To concentrate development efforts is elementary; but the rule will be disregarded if intergovernmental efforts are central to development policies. Governments must be problem-oriented, for governments are, of necessity, protective institutions. But there is no development potential in problems; all one can do in taking care of a problem is to prevent collapse. One cannot build the new this way. Since governments have to act as governments, they cannot subordinate other goals to the priorities of economic development. They must put other considerations—military or political—first. They must, therefore, misallocate development resources. This is a fancy way of saying that there are always noneconomic strings to a relationship between governments.

Government is needed in a worldwide development policy. The governments of the developed countries must give direction to such a policy. The governments of poor countries must be effective and purposeful.

But there is one thing government can never provide: the individual's sense of achievement. Yet this is the essential element of development. What the world needs today is a vision. It is the individual's conviction that there is opportunity, energy, purpose to his society, rather than problems, inertia, and hopelessness.

If wealth were the one prerequisite for development, America's black ghettos would be no problem at all. Black Harlem is one of the world's wealthiest communities—fifth or so in per capita income of all communities outside of North America and Europe, and easily the richest of all Negro communities in the world. Altogether, three-fifths of all American Negro families are above the "poverty line." And what is considered "poverty" in the United States— i.e., a family income below $3,500 a year—is considered great wealth almost everywhere else. What makes Harlem, and our other black ghettos, a slough of despond and a cesspool of hatred is the feeling of hopeless stagnation and impotent despair that pervades it.

Development is thus largely a matter of the dynamics of individuals and of a local community. These can be supplied only by generating local, responsible initiative and multiplying human energies. Government can stimulate them —or stifle them. But it cannot provide them.

I said earlier that everyone in the nineteenth century took economic development for granted. An exception is Japan. In Japan there was a famous debate, lasting two decades, over the conditions of economic development and the forces making for it. But the debate was not between economists. It was between practical entrepreneurs who founded and built businesses.

The names Yataro Iwasaki (1834–1885) and Eiichi Shibusawa (1840–1931) are known outside of Japan only to a few specialists. Yet their achievements were a good deal more spectacular than those of Rothschild, Morgan, Krupp, or Rockefeller. Iwasaki founded and built the Mitsubishi group of industries— to this day the largest manufacturing complex in Japan and one of the world's largest and most successful business groups. Shibusawa founded and built more than 600 industrial companies during his ninety years of life. Between them, these two men founded something like two-thirds of Japan's enterprises in manufacturing and transportation. No other two men in any economy have had a similar impact.

And for twenty years, till Iwasaki's early death at fifty-one, these two men engaged in a public and often acrimonious debate. "Maximize profits," said Iwasaki. "Maximize talents," said Shibusawa. Today we know that both were right. Both Iwasaki and Shibusawa worked for a strong and achieving, rather than for a rich, Japan. Both men knew that the essence of development is not to make the poor wealthy; it is to make the poor productive. For this, one needs to make productive the fundamental resources. One needs to multiply both talent and capital.

Japan was exceptional in the nineteenth century. She was the one nonwhite, non-Western country to become a modern economy. She was poorer than any of the white countries—probably poorer than any of the developing countries of today (except perhaps Bolivia or Tibet). She was an old country and densely populated. She had silk to export and this paid for imports of manufactured goods and industrial raw materials. But she did not have new land to take under cultivation. She could not, therefore, as the new countries outside of Western Europe did, rely on imported capital. She could not have serviced such capital through exports of food or industrial raw materials.

What made Japan atypical for the nineteenth century makes her typical for today. Thus, the model of development today has to be Japan rather than the United States or Russia or, indeed, any of the white countries.

Japan accomplished development Iwasaki's way, that is, by attracting and moblizing every penny of capital within the country. As a result, shortage of capital never impeded Japan's development, though she did not borrow abroad or depend on foreign investors.

Japan also walked Shibusawa's way and attracted, trained, and mobilized every ounce of human energy. She put to work on growth opportunities all the talent a gifted people could muster.

Yet, the two men differed in their emphasis only. Iwasaki could not have succeeded had he not known how to find and develop large numbers of brilliant young men whom he formed into a worldwide management team of the highest *esprit de corps* and competence. And Shibusawa's command post was the Dai-Ichi Bank which he built into one of the major financial institutions of the country.

Today, we need to organize the "contract growing" of money and the "contract growing" of people. Of the two tasks, "contract growing" of money is actually old and familiar. To do the job the nineteenth century invented the venture banker. First conceived around 1820 by the French social philosopher Saint-Simon, the venture banker's task is to mobilize and multiply the financial resources of society and to switch them from less to more productive investments, that is, from yesterday to tomorrow.

It was the venture bank, as first embodied around 1850 in Paris, in the famous "Crédit Mobilier" of the Brothers Péreire, that industrialized Continental Europe. And in far-off Japan, without benefit of European theory, Iwasaki built his Mitsubishi empire around a major venture bank.

The one difference between those days and today is that we know much better how to organize development banks. In fact, the World Bank and its affiliate, the International Finance Corporation, started to encourage such banks all over the world in the 1950s and they have produced more development than all the aid programs together, even though the amount of money invested in them from foreign sources is negligible.

These banks multiply the capital resources of the community. For every dollar of capital imported from abroad, they attract five additional dollars of domestic capital. Their own capital thus represents a multiplication by six of the imported dollars from abroad. Then, for every dollar they themselves invest in a venture out of their own capital, they raise another five dollars of investment capital from other sources in the community. By the time they have finished financing a venture, every dollar of imported capital should have triggered the investment of another thirty dollars of local capital. And then each of these thirty dollars should trigger an additional very large amount of indirect investment from local sources—the way every dollar invested in automobile manufacturing leads to the investment of many more dollars in tire plants, roads, motels, service stations, and so on.

Perhaps the best example of development banking is a totally private "contract grower," ADELA, an international investment company started in 1964 by some 150 leading banks and manufacturing companies of the developed countries as their vehicle for venture banking in, and the development of, Latin America. By investing less than $30 million of its own money, it had mobilized almost half a billion of investment, most of it local. It had created at least 25,000 jobs. And it had mobilized for growth opportunities a large number of entrepreneurs, managers, and technical people.

To speak of "lack" of capital is a euphemism for mismanagement of capital. The capital is there. But it is kept where it should not be—often locked up in economically marginal land ownership as it was in eighteenth-century France and on today's West Coast of Latin America. Or it is not invested at all—the treasure of the Indians, from peasant to Maharaja, is an example. Or it is employed productively but without any "multiplier" impact. One dollar does the work of one where it should do the work of one hundred.

Capital without people is sterile, but people can move mountains without capital. Development, therefore, requires rapid growth of human talents and opportunities to employ them. It requires leadership of a high order and also followers who can convert the leader's vision into reality.

In the 'fifties the American aid program invested a small sum, barely one million dollars, to form management associations and institutes throughout Latin America. This program was at first not very popular with the American government. It seemed so insignificant and needed so little money. And the Latin-American governments pointed out, with good reason, that associations were one of the few things in abundant supply throughout the continent.

Admittedly, management associations are unromantic. Nor did these do anything unusual. They held meetings, gave speeches and listened to them, ran courses, distributed literature, and so on. Yet the impact can hardly be exaggerated.

That Latin America has managed to move forward during the last ten years, despite almost crushing deflationary pressures, is due largely to these programs for the development of human energies and vision.

Out of them came, for instance, the upsurge of development in the Cauca

Valley of Colombia, in and around the city of Cali. The young men who met in the courses of the new Colombian management association rapidly organized themselves to take responsibility for the local university, the Universidad del Valle. There they pushed a public health program which, for the first time in the whole region, is systematically training and organizing villagers for public health. They started a series of management courses—especially courses for the top management people in which the most successful citizens of the area went to school (something almost unimaginable to an older generation of Latin Americans), and in which each of their businesses was examined, diagnosed, and prescribed for by the whole group. Then they began to supply young and well-trained people to local governments, both in state and city.

Cali is still poor, and unemployment is still too high. But out of the work at the Universidad del Valle have come at least 30,000 jobs in the last ten years. More important, out of it has come an entirely different leadership—for the entire community and all major community activities.

Quite different is the approach taken by a small semiprivate group called the Development Advisory Service. Located at Harvard University and staffed mainly with Harvard economists, this small group—no more than seventy-five —works in small teams as senior advisers and civil servants to developing nations from Pakistan to Indonesia, and from Liberia to Jamaica. It decides itself what countries and projects it will work on so that it will get the most results from its small staff. It insists that the host country put its own best people on these projects. And it aims in all its projects at creating human competence and vision throughout a whole area. There were never more than two dozen men from the Development Advisory Service in Pakistan, for instance. But largely through them, Pakistan's industrial output during the last fifteen years has grown at the rate of 15 per cent a year or more, and farm output at better than 5 per cent a year.

The most effective agent of rapid human development in the economy has been the multinational corporation. In the developing countries, the multinational business should be less concerned with capital investment and ownership control than with developing management skills. The multinational company should get paid—and paid exceedingly well—for developing both local business and local people. And where the multinational corporation has been primarily in manufacturing, we need to focus its skills on agriculture.

Farmers everywhere are highly receptive to monetary incentives. No one is more willing to do something new than the farmer, provided he sees a clear gain. But the farmer in the poor countries cannot take much risk. He knows that one crop failure or price drop for his harvest may mean total destruction for himself and his family: famine, forced selling of his daughters into prostitution, loss of what little land he has. And he knows also that he has little skill.

What farmers have needed therefore—and what has proven successful wherever tried—is the contract growing of the new crops, the improved seeds, the better breeds. This, however, requires the skills and resources of a major corporation.

A food processor or food marketer works out the best way to grow the new crop or the new animal, provides the farmer with the necessary supplies— seeds, day-old chicks, feed, implements, fertilizer, and so on—and with the instructions on how to use them. He then guarantees the farmer a definite income at the end of the growing season, regardless of drought, of animal diseases, of market price. For these are the risks the farmer in the poor countries cannot himself take. Most of the crops for canning in the United States— most of the tomatoes, for instance, or the cherries—are now contract grown.

In the developing countries where farmers lack the necessary skills, the risks of "agribusiness" have to be reinsured, obviously by government, at least for a few early years. But the risks are capable of being identified and defined. And except for weather in a few places, the risks are not particularly great (though greater than a private business or a farm cooperative could take by itself at the start).

Such contract growing, in which the cultivation of crops is being used to change the capacities, aspirations, competence, self-confidence, and performance of the farmer—that is, of the majority in the poor nations—is perhaps the only way in which real progress can be made in the most dangerous areas of human erosion.

The idea underlying contract growing needs to be extended from growing crops to growing skills, self-confidence, and the capacity to achieve. It needs to be extended to contract-grow people.

One promising approach is being worked out in one of our worst black ghettos, in Oakland, California. There a small local group first obtains definite jobs. It gets a contract to service the electric typewriters at the university or the cars of the telephone company. Then it goes out and trains unemployable and unemployed young Negroes for those already existing jobs. This way it can both guarantee a job and demand high performance standards.

There is much more to development than economics. There are cultural and social institutions, for instance. It is still fashionable, especially among academicians, to believe that development requires the destruction of traditional society. To be sure, development will change a society and its traditions. But it must at the same time be based on existing social and cultural institutions and on existing values.

Again Japan offers an instructive example. Japan's Westernization, a hundred years ago, overturned within a few short years the rigid class structure under which for almost three hundred years no commoner could become a soldier (a *sumurai*), and no *sumurai* (with rare exceptions) a noble. Japan became a country of great upward mobility. Shibusawa, for instance, came from the peasantry. Yet he, while still quite young, was given one of the top positions in the new ruling group, the Ministry of Finance.

At the same time, however, Japan built her new institutions on the basis of the old tribal concepts of mutual loyalty and of "belonging." All modern institutions of Japan—the government agency, the university, the business enterprise—no matter how modern and "Western" their methods and how efficient their output, were *hans*—extended tribal families based on lifelong, indissoluble mutual loyalty. And the Confucian ethic, with its demand for service, governed both Iwasaki and Shibusawa.

The problem of the traditional culture and values is much subtler than most of us still think. Gunnar Myrdal, the Swedish economist and sociologist, asserts that development cannot occur unless there are first massive social and cultural reforms. But in the ten years during which Myrdal worked on his Survey, major development did occur in Pakistan without prior social change. Rather, development initiated social changes while at the same time reaffirming traditional social values and using them as an engine of development. Unfortunately, there seems to be no way to decide in advance which cultural traditions are "remnants of feudalism" and must go and which are "cultural values" and must be used.

Similarly, the most fundamental disagreement about development, that between the Marxists and the capitalists, is fraught with subtleties. Our experience indicates that government control may be a transitory phase in development rather than either its essence or its denial. In the early stages of development, government ownership may be essential. Only government may command the high-grade human resources needed. The army, in particular, is often the only educational institution in the nation. As development proceeds, however, government becomes less and less necessary and effective. Other institutions—businesses, hospitals, universities, and so on—become more highly developed and more complex, and increasingly require managerial autonomy as well as control by nongovernmental forces such as the market. (This is what underlies the much-publicized "new new economics" of the Communist countries of Europe.)

Whatever the political, social, and cultural problems and uncertainties, development still remains primarily an economic process. Economic success does not by itself solve all problems. It creates many new ones. But it makes it much easier to live with problems, to assuage them, and perhaps ultimately even to solve them.

Development is no panacea. Indeed it is very dangerous. It is growth; and growth is never orderly. It is also change. And change in society and culture is dislocation. The period during which a society takes off in sustained development is a most dangerous time. Economically speaking, development has become a success and an accomplished fact. But the leaders still act in terms of the traditional society instead of responding to the new reality. At present there is a grave danger of social and political catastrophe.

No country that has gone through the development process has been able so far to avoid this transition period and its dangers. We can see the makings of such crises today wherever there has been development. In Brazil, for instance, the tremendous growth of the central region has made the non-development of the northeast region increasingly unbearable and increasingly a threat to the country's social fabric. In India it is clear that economic development, limited though it has been, has made language into a problem that threatens cohesion of the whole subcontinent. Even in France, as the events of the spring of 1968 showed, development into an economy of mass affluence created a severe crisis of the still largely Napoleonic institutional structure.

Development, in other words, is risky. But the alternative is infinitely riskier. At least we can direct, lead, control, and inspire development. The alternative we can barely hope to survive.

ALDOUS HUXLEY

The Politics of Ecology

In politics, the central and fundamental problem is the problem of power. Who is to exercise power? And by what means, by what authority, with what purpose in view, and under what controls? Yes, under what controls? For, as history has made it abundantly clear, to possess power is *ipso facto* to be tempted to abuse it. In mere self-preservation we must create and maintain institutions that make it difficult for the powerful to be led into those temptations which, succumbed to, transform them into tyrants at home and imperialists abroad.

For this purpose what kind of institutions are effective? And, having created them, how can we guarantee them against obsolescence? Circumstances change, and, as they change, the old, the once so admirably effective

Source: Mr. Huxley authored many notable works and was a member of a distinguished English family of scientists and scholars. Of his many works, Mr. Huxley is probably best known for his *Brave New World*, written in 1932. Reprinted, by permission, from *The Center Magazine*, March 1969, a publication of the Center for the Study of Democratic Institutions in Santa Barbara, California.

devices for controlling power cease to be adequate. What then? Specifically, when advancing science and acceleratingly progressive technology alter man's long-established relationship with the planet on which he lives, revolutionize his societies, and at the same time equip his rulers with new and immensely more powerful instruments of domination, what ought we to do? What *can* we do?

Very briefly let us review the situation in which we now find ourselves and, in the light of present facts, hazard a few guesses about the future.

On the biological level, advancing science and technology have set going a revolutional process that seems to be destined for the next century at least, perhaps for much longer, to exercise a decisive influence upon the destinies of all human societies and their individual members. In the course of the last fifty years extremely effective methods for lowering the prevailing rates of infant and adult mortality were developed by Western scientists. These methods were very simple and could be applied with the expenditure of very little money by very small numbers of not very highly trained technicians. For these reasons, and because everyone regards life as intrinsically good and death as intrinsically bad, they were in fact applied on a world-wide scale. The results were spectacular. In the past, high birth rates were balanced by high death rates. Thanks to science, death rates have been halved but, except in the most highly industrialized, contraceptive-using countries, birth rates remain as high as ever. An enormous and accelerating increase in human numbers has been the inevitable consequence.

At the beginning of the Christian era, so demographers assure us, our planet supported a human population of about two hundred and fifty millions. When the Pilgrim Fathers stepped ashore, the figure had risen to about five hundred millions. We see, then, that in the relatively recent past it took sixteen hundred years for the human species to double its numbers. Today world population stands at three thousand millions. By the year 2000, unless something appallingly bad or miraculously good should happen in the interval, six thousand millions of us will be sitting down to breakfast every morning. In a word, twelve times as many people are destined to double their numbers in one-fortieth of the time.

This is not the whole story. In many areas of the world human numbers are increasing at a rate much higher than the average for the whole species. In India, for example, the rate of increase is now 2.3 per cent per annum. By 1990 its four hundred and fifty million inhabitants will have become nine hundred million inhabitants. A comparable rate of increase will raise the population of China to the billion mark by 1980. In Ceylon, in Egypt, in many of the countries of South and Central America, human numbers are increasing at an annual rate of 3 per cent. The result will be a doubling of their present populations in approximately twenty-three years.

On the social, political, and economic levels, what is likely to happen in an underdeveloped country whose people double themselves in a single generation, or even less? An underdeveloped society is a society without adequate capital resources (for capital is what is left over after primary needs have been satisfied, and in underdeveloped countries most people never satisfy their primary needs); a society without a sufficient force of trained teachers, administrators, and technicians; a society with few or no industries and few or no developed sources of industrial power; a society, finally, with enormous arrears to be made good in food production, education, road building, housing, and sanitation. A quarter of a century from now, when there will be twice as many of them as there are today, what is the likelihood that the members of such a society will be better fed, housed, clothed, and schooled than at present? And what are the chances in such a society for the maintenance, if they already exist, or the creation, if they do not exist, of democratic institutions?

Not long ago Mr. Eugene Black, the former president of the World Bank, expressed the opinion that it would be extremely difficult, perhaps even impossible, for an underdeveloped country with a very rapid rate of population increase to achieve full industrialization. All its resources, he pointed out, would be absorbed year by year in the task of supplying, or not quite supplying, the primary needs of its new members. Merely to stand still, to maintain its current subhumanly inadequate standard of living, will require hard work and the expenditure of all the nation's available capital. Available capital may be increased by loans and gifts from abroad; but in a world where the industrialized nations are involved in power politics and an increasingly expensive armament race, there will never be enough foreign aid to make much difference. And even if the loans and gifts to underdeveloped countries were to be substantially increased, any resulting gains would be largely nullified by the uncontrolled population explosion.

The situation of these nations with such rapidly increasing populations reminds one of Lewis Carroll's parable in *Through the Looking Glass*, where Alice and the Red Queen start running at full speed and run for a long time until Alice is completely out of breath. When they stop, Alice is amazed to see that they are still at their starting point. In the looking glass world, if you wish to retain your present position, you must run as fast as you can. If you wish to get ahead, you must run at least twice as fast as you can.

If Mr. Black is correct (and there are plenty of economists and demographers who share his opinion), the outlook for most of the world's newly independent and economically non-viable nations is gloomy indeed. To those that have shall be given. Within the next ten or twenty years, if war can be avoided, poverty will almost have disappeared from the highly industrialized and contraceptive-using societies of the West. Meanwhile, in the underdeveloped and uncontrolledly breeding societies of Asia, Africa, and Latin America the condition of the masses (twice as numerous, a generation from now, as they are today) will have become no better and may even be decidedly worse than it is at present. Such a decline is foreshadowed by current statistics of the Food and Agriculture Organization of the United Nations. In some underdeveloped regions of the world, we are told, people are somewhat less adequately fed, clothed, and housed than were their parents and grandparents thirty and forty years ago. And what of elementary education? UNESCO recently provided an answer. Since the end of World War II heroic efforts have been made to teach the whole world how to read. The population explosion has largely stultified these efforts. The absolute number of illiterates is greater now than at any time.

The contraceptive revolution which, thanks to advancing science and technology, has made it possible for the highly developed societies of the West to offset the consequences of death control by a planned control of births, has had as yet no effect upon the family life of people in underdeveloped countries. This is not surprising. Death control, as I have already remarked, is easy, cheap, and can be carried out by a small force of technicians. Birth control, on the other hand, is rather expensive, involves the whole adult population, and demands of those who practice it a good deal of forethought and directed willpower. To persuade hundreds of millions of men and women to abandon their tradition-hallowed views of sexual morality, then to distribute and teach them to make use of contraceptive devices or fertility-controlling drugs—this is a huge and difficult task, so huge and so difficult that it seems very unlikely that it can be successfully carried out, within a sufficiently short space of time, in any of the countries where control of the birth rate is most urgently needed.

Extreme poverty, when combined with ignorance, breeds that lack of desire for better things which has been called "wantlessness"—the resigned acceptance of a subhuman lot. But extreme poverty, where it is combined with the knowledge that some societies are affluent, breeds envious desires and the expectation that these desires must of necessity, and very soon, be satisfied. By means of the mass media (those easily exportable products of advancing science and technology) some knowledge of what life is like in affluent societies has been widely disseminated throughout the world's underdeveloped regions. But, alas, the science and technology which have given the industrial West its cars, refrigerators, and contraceptives have given the people of Asia, Africa, and Latin America only movies and radio broadcasts, which they are too simple-minded to be able to criticize, together with a population explosion, which they are still too poor and too tradition-bound to be able to control by deliberate family planning.

In the context of a 3, or even of a mere 2 per cent annual increase in numbers, high expectations are foredoomed to disappointment. From disappointment, through resentful frustration, to widespread social unrest the road is short. Shorter still is the road from social unrest, through chaos, to dictatorship, possibly of the Communist party, more probably of generals and colonels. It would seem, then, that for two-thirds of the human race now suffering from the consequences of uncontrolled breeding in a context of industrial backwardness, poverty, and illiteracy, the prospects for democracy, during the next ten or twenty years, are very poor.

From underdeveloped societies and the probable political consequences of their explosive increase in numbers we now pass to the prospect for democracy in the fully industrialized, contraceptive-using societies of Europe and North America.

It used to be assumed that political freedom was a necessary pre-condition of scientific research. Ideological dogmatism and dictatorial institutions were supposed to be incompatible with the open-mindedness and the freedom of experimental action, in the absence of which discovery and invention are impossible. Recent history has proved these comforting assumptions to be completely unfounded. It was under Stalin that Russian scientists developed the A-bomb and, a few years later, the H-bomb. And it is under a more-than-Stalinist dictatorship that Chinese scientists are now in process of performing the same feat.

Another disquieting lesson of recent history is that, in a developing society, science and technology can be used exclusively for the enhancement of military power, not at all for the benefit of the masses. Russia has demonstrated, and China is now doing its best to demonstrate, that poverty and primitive conditions of life for the overwhelming majority of the population are perfectly compatible with the wholesale production of the most advanced and sophisticated military hardware. Indeed, it is by deliberately imposing poverty on the masses that the rulers of developing industrial nations are able to create the capital necessary for building an armament industry and maintaining a well equipped army, with which to play their parts in the suicidal game of international power politics.

We see, then, that democratic institutions and libertarian traditions are not at all necessary to the progress of science and technology, and that such progress does not of itself make for human betterment at home and peace abroad. Only where democratic institutions already exist, only where the masses can vote their rulers out of office and so compel them to pay attention to the popular will, are science and technology used for the benefit of the majority as well as for increasing the power of the State. Most human beings prefer peace to war, and practically all of them would rather be alive than dead. But in every part of the world men and women have been brought up to regard nationalism as axiomatic and war between nations as something cosmically ordained by the Nature of Things. Prisoners of their culture, the masses, even when they are free to vote, are inhibited by the fundamental postulates of the frame of reference within which they do their thinking and their feeling from decreeing an end to the collective paranoia that governs international relations. As for the world's ruling minorities, by the very fact of their power they are chained even more closely to the current system of ideas and the prevailing political customs; for this reason they are even less capable than their subjects of expressing the simple human preference for life and peace.

Some day, let us hope, rulers and ruled will break out of the cultural prison in which they are now confined. Some day . . . And may that day come soon! For, thanks to our rapidly advancing science and technology, we have very little time at our disposal. The river of change flows ever faster, and somewhere downstream, perhaps only a few years ahead, we shall come to the rapids, shall hear, louder and ever louder, the roaring of a cataract.

Modern war is a product of advancing science and technology. Conversely, advancing science and technology are products of modern war. It was in order to wage war more effectively that first the United States, then Britain and the USSR, financed the crash programs that resulted so quickly in the harnessing of atomic forces. Again, it was primarily for military purposes that the techniques of automation, which are now in process of revolutionizing industrial production and the whole system of administrative and bureaucratic control, were first developed. "During World War II," writes Mr. John Diebold, "the theory and use of feedback was studied in great detail by a number of scientists both in this country and in Britain. The introduction of rapidly moving aircraft very quickly made traditional gun-laying techniques of anti-aircraft warfare obsolete. As a result, a large part of scientific manpower in this country was directed towards the development of self-regulating devices and systems to control our military equipment. It is out of this work that the technology of automation as we understand it today has developed."

The headlong rapidity with which scientific and technological changes, with all their disturbing consequences in the fields of politics and social relations, are taking place is due in large measure to the fact that, both in the USA and the USSR, research in pure and applied science is lavishly financed by military planners whose first concern is in the development of bigger and better weapons in the shortest possible time. In the frantic effort, on one side of the Iron Curtain, to keep up with the Joneses—on the other, to keep up with the Ivanovs—these military planners spend gigantic sums on research and development. The military revolution advances under forced draft, and as it goes forward it initiates an uninterrupted succession of industrial, social, and political revolutions. It is against this background of chronic upheaval that the members of a species, biologically and historically adapted to a slowly changing environment, must now live out their bewildered lives.

Old-fashioned war was incompatible, while it was being waged, with democracy. Nuclear war, if it is ever waged, will prove in all likelihood to be incompatible with civilization, perhaps with human survival. Meanwhile, what of the preparations for nuclear war? If certain physicists and military planners had their way, democracy, where it exists, would be replaced by a system of regimentation centered upon the bomb shelter. The entire population would have to be systematically drilled in the ticklish operation of going underground at a moment's notice, systematically exercised in the art of living troglodytically under conditions resembling those in the hold of an eighteenth-century slave ship. The notion fills most of us with horror. But if we fail to break out of the ideological prison of our nationalistic and militaristic culture, we may find ourselves compelled by the military consequences of our science and technology to descend into the steel and concrete dungeons of total and totalitarian civil defense.

In the past, one of the most effective guarantees of liberty was governmental inefficiency: The spirit of tyranny was always willing; but its technical and organizational flesh was weak. Today the flesh is as strong as the spirit. Governmental organization is a fine art, based upon scientific principles and disposing of marvelously efficient equipment. Fifty years ago an armed revolution still had some chance of success. In the context of modern weaponry a popular uprising is foredoomed. Crowds armed with rifles and home-made grenades are no match for tanks. And it is not only to its armament that a modern government owes its overwhelming power. It also possesses the strength of superior knowledge derived from its communication systems, its stores of accumulated data, its batteries of computers, its network of inspection and administration.

Where democratic institutions exist and the masses can vote their rulers out of office, the enormous powers with which science, technology, and the arts of organization have endowed the ruling minority are used with discretion and a decent regard for civil and political liberty. Where the masses can exercise no control over their rulers, these powers are used without compunction to enforce ideological orthodoxy and to strengthen the dictatorial state. The nature of science and technology is such that it is peculiarly easy for a dictatorial government to use them for its own anti-democratic purposes. Well financed, equipped and organized, an astonishingly small number of scientists and technologists can achieve prodigious results. The crash program that produced the A-bomb and ushered in a new historical era was planned and directed by some four thousand theoreticians, experimenters, and engineers. To parody the words of Winston Churchill, never have so many been so completely at the mercy of so few.

Throughout the nineteenth century the State was relatively feeble, and its interest in, and influence upon, scientific research were negligible. In our day the State is everywhere exceedingly powerful and a lavish patron of basic and *ad hoc* research. In Western Europe and North America the relations between the State and its scientists on the one hand and individual citizens, professional organizations, and industrial, commercial, and educational institutions on the other are fairly satisfactory. Advancing science, the population explosion, the armament race, and the steady increase and centralization of political and economic power are still compatible, in countries that have a libertarian tradition, with democratic forms of government. To maintain this compatibility in a rapidly changing world, bearing less and less resemblance to the world in which these democratic institutions were developed—this, quite obviously, is going to be increasingly difficult.

A rapid and accelerating population increase that will nullify the best efforts of underdeveloped societies to better their lot and will keep two-thirds of the human race in a condition of misery in anarchy or of misery under dictatorship, and the intensive preparations for a new kind of war that, if it breaks out, may bring irretrievable ruin to the one-third of the human race now living prosperously in highly industrialized societies—these are the two main threats to democracy now confronting us. Can these threats be eliminated? Or, if not eliminated, at least reduced?

My own view is that only by shifting our collective attention from the merely political to the basic biological aspects of the human situation can we hope to mitigate and shorten the time of troubles into which, it would seem, we are now moving. We cannot do without politics; but we can no longer afford to indulge in bad, unrealistic politics. To work for the survival of the species as a whole and for the actualization in the greatest possible number of individual men and women of their potentialities for good will, intelligence, and creativity—this, in the world of today, is good, realistic politics. To cultivate the religion of idolatrous nationalism, to subordinate the interests of the species and its individual members to the interests of a single national state and its ruling minority—in the context of the population explosion, missiles, and atomic warheads, this is bad and thoroughly unrealistic politics. Unfortunately, it is to bad and unrealistic politics that our rulers are now committed.

Ecology is the science of the mutual relations of organisms with their environment and with one another. Only when we get it into our collective head that the basic problem confronting twentieth-century man is an ecological problem will our politics improve and become realistic. How does the human race propose to survive and, if possible, improve the lot and the intrinsic quality of its individual members? Do we propose to live on this planet in symbiotic harmony with our environment? Or, preferring to be wantonly stupid, shall we choose to live like murderous and suicidal parasites that kill their host and so destroy themselves?

Committing that sin of overweening bumptiousness, which the Greeks called *hubris*, we behave as though we were not members of earth's ecological community, as though we were privileged and, in some sort, supernatural beings and could throw our weight around like gods. But in fact we are, among other things, animals—emergent parts of the natural order. If our politicians were realists, they would think rather less about missiles and the problem of landing a couple of astronauts on the moon, rather more about hunger and moral squalor and the problem of enabling three billion men, women, and children, who will soon be six billions, to lead a tolerably human existence without, in the process, ruining and befouling their planetary environment.

Animals have no souls; therefore, according to the most authoritative Christian theologians, they may be treated as though they were things. The truth, as we are now beginning to realize, is that even things ought not to be treated as *mere* things. They should be treated as though they were parts of a vast living organism. "Do as you would be done by." The Golden Rule applies to our dealings with nature no less than to our dealings with our fellow-men. If we hope to be well treated by nature, we must stop talking about "mere things" and start treating our planet with intelligence and consideration.

Power politics in the context of nationalism raises problems that, except by war, are practically insoluble. The problems of ecology, on the other hand, admit of a rational solution and can be tackled without the arousal of those violent passions always associated with dogmatic ideology and nationalistic idolatry. There may be arguments about the best way of raising wheat in a cold climate or of re-afforesting a denuded mountain. But such arguments never lead to organized slaughter. Organized slaughter is the result of arguments about such questions as the following: Which is the best nation? The best religion? The best political theory? The best form of government? Why are other people so stupid and wicked? Why can't they see how good and intelligent *we* are? Why do they resist our beneficent efforts to bring them under our control and make them like ourselves?

To questions of this kind the final answer has always been war. "War," said Clausewitz, "is not merely a political act, but also a political instrument, a continuation of political relationships, a carrying out of the same by other means." This was true enough in the eighteen thirties, when Clausewitz published his famous treatise; and it continued to be true until 1945. Now, pretty obviously, nuclear weapons, long-range rockets, nerve gases, bacterial aerosols, and the "Laser" (that highly promising, latest addition to the world's military arensals) have given the lie to Clausewitz. All-out war with modern weapons is no longer a continuation of previous policy; it is a complete and irreversible break with previous policy.

Power politics, nationalism, and dogmatic ideology are luxuries that the human race can no longer afford. Nor, as a species, can we afford the luxury of ignoring man's ecological situation. By shifting our attention from the now completely irrelevant and anachronistic politics of nationalism and military power to the problems of the human species and the still inchoate politics of human ecology we shall be killing two birds with one stone— reducing the threat of sudden destruction by scientific war and at the same time reducing the threat of more gradual biological disaster.

The beginnings of ecological politics are to be found in the special services of the United Nations Organization. UNESCO, the Food and Agriculture Organization, the World Health Organization, the various Technical Aid Services—all these are, partially or completely, concerned with the ecological problems of the human species. In a world where political problems are thought of and worked upon within a frame of reference whose coordinates are nationalism and military power, these ecology-oriented organizations are regarded as peripheral. If the problems of humanity could be thought about and acted upon within a frame of reference that has survival for species, the well-being of individuals, and the actualization of man's desirable potentialities as its coordinates, these peripheral organizations would become central. The subordinate politics of survival, happiness, and personal fulfillment would take the place now occupied by the politics of power, ideology, nationalistic idolatry, and unrelieved misery.

In the process of reaching this kind of politics we shall find, no doubt, that we have done something, in President Wilson's prematurely optimistic words, "to make the world safe for democracy."

FRANK M. POTTER, JR.

Everyone Wants to Save the Environment But No One Knows What to Do

It is difficult to find a newspaper today that doesn't have at least one story on environmental problems. People who read these stories react to them and, with increasing frequency, their reaction is sympathetic. Environmental concerns are no longer the private preserve of the birdwatchers: the same bell tolls for us all.

In 1969, the National Wildlife Federation commissioned two polling organizations to investigate American attitudes on environment. The polls reached the conclusion that most people are actively concerned about environmental problems and would prefer that a greater proportion of their taxes be devoted to the costs of solving them. The level of concern here rose with income and varied inversely with age. Over fifty per cent of those interviewed felt that the government was devoting insufficient attention to environmental problems

Source: Mr. Potter is executive director of Environmental Clearinghouse, Inc. Reprinted with permission from the March 1970 issue, pp. 35–40, of *The Center Magazine*, a publication of the Center for the Study of Democratic Institutions in Santa Barbara, California.

and was providing insufficient funds to resolve them. Over eighty per cent felt a personal concern, and most of these registered "deep concern." What, then, keeps them from the barricades?

Apathy, one might think, but the surveys rule that out. The most significant inhibitor of action may be that we are too easily convinced of our own political impotence. The larger the grouping, the more difficult it is for any person to make a significant impact upon social decisions.

On the other hand, when they are really aroused, people can take and have taken effective action. For example, a coalition of citizens joined forces in 1969 to require a reluctant U.S. government to quadruple the amount of funds to be used for waste-water facilities. They did so by informing their elected representatives that this was a matter of specific, personal, and urgent priority; their representatives listened and responded. Again, a few years ago, a small group of citizens banded together against the largest utility in the United States, opposing plans to construct a major hydroelectric plant within fifty miles of New York City. They stopped the utility company in its tracks. That company was Consolidated Edison, the plant was the Storm King project. The Federal Power Commission, which must decide whether or not the plant should be built, has still not made its decision. The strong case made by the citizens depended in large measure on the fact that they were able to propose alternatives to the project and to support their case by a wealth of technical and engineering detail that showed New York's serious power problems could be met by less damaging methods. Although Con Edison has not yet given up the project, it has adopted the alternatives, and many sophisticated agency-watchers now consider it unlikely that the Storm King plant will ever be built.

Collective action, then, can make a difference. Individually or collectively, we are confronted with a clear option: Are we to live well only for a short period, or must we cut back economic growth in favor of long-term survival for the species? For the most part we appear to have adopted the former course of action, and it is by no means clear that we would act much differently if the choice were clearer. "*Après moi, le déluge*" is an attitude confined neither to France nor to the eighteenth century. As individuals, we tend to be somewhat ambivalent about the importance of what might be called an environmental conscience.

With very little effort, we could educate our children about the importance of environmental responsibility; yet it is the children who seem to be taking the lead in educating us. A national Environmental Teach-In is scheduled for April, 1970, in schools and colleges across the country, and there are signs that problems of pollution are occupying a rapidly increasing portion of the attention of young people.

It is important to distinguish between the actions and attitudes of individuals and those of the citizen groups organized to consider environmental problems. The biggest problem faced by such groups is seldom a lack of motivation; it is financial. It is still rare for anyone whose economic interests are involved to oppose a polluter; this means that concerned citizens must themselves assume these costs, although the financial burdens of speaking out and working against a powerful and well-financed industry or government agency may be great. The costs of carrying on a major controversy may exceed five hundred thousand dollars. We cannot reasonably expect any private group to bear such a burden, nor should we as long as the group is acting to protect assets that are common and valuable to all of us.

It is important to note, though, that even concerned citizens do not always organize themselves to protect the environmental system as a whole—one group may be interested only in visual pollution while another is interested in noise. It is an unfortunate fact of life that a normal resolution of a pollution problem often means pushing it into another area which may not be so vigorously defended. For example, the public concerned with power-generation facilities producing air pollution in the form of coal dust, oil droplets, and increased sulphur dioxide emissions encouraged the building of nuclear plants, which involve none of these pollutants but may well present other problems in terms of radioactive and thermal pollution of cooling water.

To look to private business for solutions to pollution may be futile. Its horizons are deliberately limited to those factors which are considered to be of immediate importance, principally economic, and the hidden costs to the society at large tend to be ignored. These costs still exist, however, and they must be borne by everyone if not by the industry which creates them. A classic example would be a pulp processing plant which emits fumes of hydrogen sulphide, causing foul air and peeling paint for miles downwind. The resulting inconvenience, possible health hazards, and certain increases in maintenance costs have not traditionally been imposed upon the agency which created them. Instead, they have been borne by our whole society, regardless of the capability or willingness of individual members to bear them.

To be sure, some private companies have taken steps to limit the anti-social consequences of their operations and have done so at considerable cost, quite beyond what they have been required to assume by law. But a voluntary approach to reducing environmental problems, it is clear, is just not good enough. For one thing, the forces of competition tend to minimize such voluntary efforts. Few men or companies, however public-spirited they may be, are prepared to expend large sums on the internalization of indirect costs. Nor can they do so without incurring the wrath of profit-seeking stockholders, who are even further removed from the environmental mischief they have indirectly created.

Polluting industries have most often resisted pressure to clean up their operations by claiming that the measures proposed are unduly prohibitive or confiscatory. Their chief means of resistance has usually involved threats to pull up stakes and move elsewhere. This last resort has been adopted infrequently, if at all, and is only likely to occur where a producer has found himself impossibly squeezed between falling profits and rising costs. It has also been alleged that these are the marginal producers whom the next strong wind will blow away in any case, so that little lasting economic damage to the area ever occurs.

The mechanics for balancing social costs against economic values, then, must be found outside the private institutions themselves, and they are—this is a major function of government. The laissez-faire philosophy which at one time characterized the attitude of American government toward American industry won't work today. It is also apparent that the government is likely to expand its program in this area. Public attention has already been focused on air and water pollution. But there are other areas in which governmental action must be anticipated—among them, noise, solid-waste disposal, and the by-products of energy transfer are mentioned with increasing frequency.

Governmental over-view, if impartially and reasonably imposed, need not be hostile to the private sector; it may even be in its interest, both short-termed and long-termed. The National Association of Manufacturers has never been known as a hotbed of social activists, yet members of N.A.M. operating committees have endorsed proposals for a strong federal body to oversee environmental issues. Businessmen have to breathe, too, and most of them are prepared to accommodate themselves to the ecological imperative—as long as their competitors are subject to the same rules. We cannot assume, however, that increased governmental concern will take place without some economic disruption. Marginal producers will feel the pinch most strongly, and some may not survive. Nevertheless, the important consideration is that the rules must be enforced fairly and impartially upon all parties.

It is important to bear in mind that the mass of government workers—the *Lumpenbürokratie*—marches to a drumbeat that only it can hear. Higher levels of government, presumably more responsive to broad social needs, generally find their choices so circumscribed by business-as-usual decisions farther down the line that their options are dissipated by the inertia of the machinery. This is by no means peculiar to the solution of environmental problems, though these tend to be somewhat more acute because of the high stakes involved and because the new issues do not fit easily into the existing bureaucratic patterns.

In practically every agency of government, at almost every level, strong pressures to maintain the status quo are built up. As one progresses from local to national bureaucracy the inertia increases. A random example: early in the nineteen-fifties the Eisenhower Administration stated a strong preference for private power development as against public power, but it was not until the Kennedy Administration took office eight years later that the direction of bureaucratic thinking had changed enough to give effective support to the idea of private power. Nor could the Democrats reverse the trend.

There are also powerful personal influences that, in current bureaucratese, are "counter-productive." As one observer put it, "the paramount objective of the permanent bureaucracy is permanence." This contributes directly to the institutional resistance to change. Agency employees tend to react self-protectively. This was probably the principal roadblock encountered by Ralph Nader's "Raiders" in their government agency investigations during the past two summers. They often ran up against a bureaucratic wall which blocked the publication of several unfavorable agency reports on the controversial supersonic transport until the reports were wrenched from unwilling bureaucratic hands by actively concerned congressmen. To combat this reaction Congress passed the Freedom of Information Act, requiring disclosure of all but certain specified documents—a public law which has been honored far more in the breach than in the observance.

This problem is compounded by a frequent lack of clear policy guidance from the upper levels of government to the lower. New policies may be found in new regulations and pronunciamentos which either go unheeded or trickle down by word of mouth. This communications system serves as an efficient filter for any content that may fortuitously have crept into the public statements of the man or men at the top.

Such difficulties should not be ascribed solely to bureaucracy. The problem for bureaucrats is essentially the same as that of the private citizen: they are unable to relate everyday decisions to any specific action of the government machinery. Moreover, the results of yesterday's decisions are rarely communicated to the decision-makers as a corrective for tomorrow's programs. To be sure, there is enough feedback for everyone to know when a dam doesn't hold water (which happens), but when a dam destroys a delicate ecological balance and wreaks havoc in the local community, the mischief is rarely perceived as a genuine problem.

Still another troublesome aspect is that government agencies compete with one another. For decades, to cite an example, the Departments of the Interior and Agriculture have carried on a polite war; its prime casualties have frequently turned out to be considerations of the environment. Countless examples of this competition have been observed: timber-cutting practices on public lands and in national forests, pesticide regulation (if that is the correct term for it), dam building, and soil conservation are just a few. The same kind of competition may occasionally be found between the public and private sectors of the economy; once again, concern for the environment usually loses out.

In some respects, such competition is healthy. Occasionally, the public may even benefit from it. Several years ago, for instance, the Army Corps of Engineers conceived a plan to build a high dam on Alaska's Yukon River which would flood hundreds of thousands of acres of land in the process. The dam was successfully opposed by the Fish and Wildlife Service of the Interior Department on the ground that it would do untold damage to the wildlife in the region. The operative word here is "untold"; no one knew just how much damage would have been done and the Corps was not really interested in finding out.

There are other consequences of governmental competition. Although they operate with public funds, governmental agencies are under pressure to make the most of the funds they expend. The budgetary restrictions placed upon the head of a large operating government agency are no less severe than those upon the directors of a large corporation, and the body to which they report is no more aware of the importance of environmental factors than the average stockholder of American Telephone & Telegraph. This comparison ought not to be pressed, however, since while it will be difficult to improve the ecological understanding of the average citizen, it is not beyond our grasp to educate Congress.

The essential function of the Legislative Branch of government is to formulate and to review policy. In so doing, it operates under constitutional or other social restraints, and it must of necessity paint with a broad brush. Translating basic policy decisions into specific go and no-go decisions, never an easy task, is often complicated by pressures within the Executive Branch to change the policy decisions themselves. More important, policy is only as good as the information upon which it is based, and this information tends to be biased, conflicting, fragmentary, and/or out-of-date.

Consider the effect of the following factors upon the theoretical non-bias with which a congressional policy decision is supposed to be approached:

1. *The Nature of the Proposal.* Most legislation enacted by the Congress is originally proposed by agencies in the Executive Branch. (This, incidentally, may not be quite so common today; the legislative proposals of the present Administration have been criticized as somewhat sporadic. Many of the bills now before the Congress, however, are holdovers from earlier years, and the basic pattern seems to have changed very little.) Support for these measures tends to be channeled well in advance of their consideration—facts are marshaled, charts are drawn up, witnesses are prepared. A frequent result of this process is that the Congress may focus on the wrong issues.

2. *The Congressional Committee Structure.* Committees of the Congress, and especially their ranking members, are among the principal focal points of power in Washington. This apparatus determines which bills are considered, whether testimony in opposition will be considered, and if so, how it will be rebutted. Unless the issue is getting the attention of the press and the public, or unless a maverick congressman digs in his heels, those controlling the committee have a relatively free hand in developing the arguments for and against the bill; hence they control its future.

3. *The Bias of Congressional Leaders.* The environmental crisis is a relatively new phenomenon, and the young are more concerned with the problems than their elders. This is as true in the Congress as elsewhere. The result is that

many of the older members, who exercise greater control over legislative action than their younger colleagues, are less inclined to meet the new challenge. Exceptions can easily be found, but the general truth of this observation is not seriously questioned. There is, then, a bias favoring inaction. It ought not to be discounted.

4. *The Adequacy of the Testimony Itself.* Assuming that the measure is reasonable and that the controlling committee is interested in developing the real issues, the witnesses called to testify may nonetheless not be the best available. Witnesses on environmental issues have tended to be the elder statesmen—established scientists and professionals whose views on new problems and on the need for new approaches have been colored by their own studies and viewpoints, which are frequently considerably out-of-date. A review of non-governmental scientific testimony over the past few years shows that several names pop up again and again; these individuals (who may be spectacularly well qualified in their own areas of competence) occasionally edge into areas in which they are not well qualified to speak, and they often seem to be responding to the unspoken needs of some committee members to be reassured that things are not all that bad, and somehow technology will find a way. Although not every expert witness falls into this category, it happens often enough to constitute a real problem. There is, consequently, a need to develop a base of scientific testimony available to the Congress on environmental issues and to see that younger scientists, whose factual knowledge is more current, are heard.

5. *The Context of the Legislative Decision.* Another conflict, not at all restricted to environmental issues, faces the legislator who must decide whether to favor the good of his own constituency over national interests. Thus congressmen and senators from the West are generally inclined to favor legislative proposals to open public lands for development (mining, grazing, lumbering, oil exploration, etc.), whereas the interests of the entire country might seem to favor retaining these lands in a less exploited condition. How to measure the interests of local areas against those of society is a serious question. Resolving the conflict may be one of the most significant functions of government.

The broad nature of the authority and responsibility of the legislature may prevent it from exercising effective control over the actions of the organizations theoretically under its direction. The policies the legislators are called upon to define are so broad they cannot possibly be spelled out in detail, and yet it is in such details that the actions of government become manifest.

The legislative mechanism may also be criticized for its slow reaction time. The Congress is a highly conservative body—deliberate in adopting new courses of action, and slower to change them once they are adopted. This is, of course, a source of strength, preventing today's fad from becoming tomorrow's straitjacket. But it is also a real source of danger to the system. Science and technology have transformed the world of the mid-twentieth century into something that was quite unimaginable fifty years ago. The rate of change is accelerating, and it is a brave man who will claim that he can predict the state of the world in the year 2000. Shrill voices may decry technology and demand that there be a halt to new technological development; they are no more likely to be heeded than were the machinery-wrecking Luddites of nineteenth-century England. Whether they are right or wrong is quite beside the point; barring massive catastrophe, technology will not be significantly curbed and the rate of technological change will almost certainly continue to speed up.

New technology creates new social conventions, which in turn affect legislative policy. Yet the mechanisms for determining that policy are keyed to technological considerations that may have already been out-of-date in 1800, and to decision-making processes that have remained essentially unchanged since the days of Roger Bacon.

Consider massive changes in climate. Scientists tell us that urban development and energy transfer now have a significant effect upon global weather patterns. We hear on the one hand of the "greenhouse effect," which tends to raise atmospheric temperature as a function of increased carbon dioxide production, and on the other of increased amounts of pollution in the air, which tend to raise atmospheric temperature by decreasing the amount of solar radiation reaching the earth's surface. Some scientists, extrapolating present activities, speculate that it would take ten years to decide which is the more powerful effect, and that by then large-scale climatic changes may be irreversible. This view is by no means commonly held, but it is under serious consideration by men whose voices ought to be heard. They are not given a hearing before Congress; if they were, they might well be outnumbered ten to one by men saying, "We are not certain, we do not know, and we should take no action until we do."

Our ecological problems, then, are not the exclusive province of the Congress; they are those of the scientific community and of all of us who have an interest in human survival. There seems as yet no way to force these problems to the forefront, conjoined as they are with an historically validated precedent for doing nothing—at least not yet.

Legislators tend to focus upon institutions rather than individuals—to see the needs of the larger groups whose existence depends upon traditional thought patterns and legal fictions. A water pollution problem is perceived as that of a municipality or an oil company, an air pollution problem as that of a manufacturer. Yet it is individual citizens whose favor the legislator must seek if he is to survive. This suggests in turn that if individuals can organize themselves to be heard as an institution concerned with environmental survival the legislators will respond. This has not yet happened generally. No significant environmental lobby has yet made its voice heard on the national level.

The courts exist to see that the written and unwritten rules of society are followed; that the policies formed by the people and their elected representatives are observed. Within narrow limits, the courts have been successful in this function. As a means of achieving rational decisions on environmental issues, however, the courts are usually ineffective. Their influence could increase, but this would require a significant departure from the usual legalistic approach. It would involve the recognition of a basic and inalienable human right to a livable environment. Such a decision appears to be a remote possibility. Without this new constitutional approach, the courts will almost certainly be hamstrung by inadequate policies adopted by the legislature and by common-law rights which were defined centuries before the current environmental problems appeared.

Only in rare instances can the courts make decisions with more than local force and effect. The U.S. Court in southern New York may properly hold that the federal Department of Transportation must observe certain procedures specified by statute that may have escaped the Department's notice, and for this reason a highway shall not be built over the Hudson River. At the same time, the same Department favors the construction of longer runways into the Columbia River. Technically, the decision of the New York court is not binding in Oregon; the Oregon courts are free to disagree with their East Coast brethren and such disagreements are in no way uncommon. A means does exist for resolving interjudicial disputes—the Supreme Court of the United States. The Court, however, is already operating under a fearful load and can devote only a limited amount of its energies to environmental questions, however important they may appear to be.

The courts also lack the information upon which to base their decisions. The common-law system is grounded upon the adversary system, the theory being that each side will present the most favorable case it can and that the court will then resolve the dispute on the basis of the evidence before it. The environmental problems arising today are very complex—very different from the land disputes and tort actions of centuries ago. In theory, expert testimony ought to be available to both sides to support their cases; in practice, this simply does not work. Even if environmentalists can afford to hire experts (and often they cannot), experts cannot always be found. It is a rare electrical engineer who will agree to take the witness stand on behalf of opponents to a power plant or transmission line; he knows that other utilities may thereafter hesitate to contract with him for services even in circumstances that may be wholly unrelated to the present controversy. Conscientious men do exist and some may be found to testify, but it is not easy to find them. Cases have been lost and will continue to be lost for this reason alone. Without that interplay of expert testimony, the court is at a major disadvantage.

Even if experts can be found by all parties, the court's information problems are not thereby solved. Technical questions are already difficult, and they are growing more complex every day. Judges spring from different backgrounds, but the law operates according to the theory that their experience is essentially irrelevant to the issues that they must decide. Historically, ignorance has been a prime virtue, the court acting as the *tabula rasa* upon which the cases of the opposing parties may be written. This is a manifest absurdity, but it is the way the law grew, and it is a fact that lawyers with weak technical cases prefer judges with little technical competence.

Another weakness built into the judicial system is its tendency to delay decision. Combined judicial and administrative delays have postponed the Storm King decision by five years already. If the parties fight down to the wire, a longer delay is likely. In many respects this delay has worked in favor of the conservation group, but this happy state of affairs is not the rule. Citizens opposed to a particular proposal or project are usually forced to seek injunctive relief from the courts; they may and often do find that this relief cannot be obtained without their posting a substantial bond which is quite beyond their means. The result is that while they work their way through the courts, the opposition is busily building or digging or chopping down. By the time that the court is ready to decide, the essential question has become moot. Injunctive relief is typically the only possible hope for environmentalists, since the alternative is a damage suit, and it is a basic tenet of such organizations that money cannot replace what is threatened.

Constitutional revision has been proposed as a means of providing a clearer and more enforceable definition of our rights to a satisfactory environment. New York State has adopted such a program, and similar efforts have been mounted on a national level. An Environmental Bill of Rights would indeed be a valuable tool, but no such proposal has a chance of even being seriously considered without vastly increased pressure upon the Congress and upon the legislatures of the several states.

Pollution will be inevitable until we can develop adequate tools for dealing with it. The government will never do the job by itself. The solution seems to lie, rather, in putting stronger weapons into the hands of the public—helping it to bring about the necessary reforms through legislative and judicial channels.

RALPH NADER

Corporations and Pollution

The modern corporation's structure, impact, and public accountability are the central issues in any program designed to curb or forestall the contamination of air, water, and soil by industrial activity. While there are other sources of pollution, such as municipalities dumping untreated or inadequately treated sewage, industrial processes and products are the chief contributors to the long-term destruction of natural resources that each year increases the risks to human health and safety.

Moreover, through active corporate citizenship, industry could soon overcome many of the obstacles in the way of curbing non-corporate pollution. The mighty automobile industry, centered around and in Detroit, never thought it part of its role to press the city of Detroit to construct a modern sewage treatment plant. The automobile moguls, whose products, according to Department of Health, Education and Welfare data, account for fifty-five to sixty per cent of the nation's air pollution, remained silent as the city's obsolete and inadequate sewage facilities dumped the wastes of millions into the Detroit River. Obviously, local boosterism does not include such elementary acts of corporate citizenship.

The toilet training of industry to keep it from further rupturing the eco-system requires an overhaul of the internal and external levers which control corporations. There are eight areas in which policies must be changed to create the pressures needed to make corporate entities and the people who run them cease their destruction of the environmnt:

One. The conventional way of giving the public a share in private decisions that involve health and safety hazards is to establish mandatory standards through a public agency. But pollution control standards set by governmental agencies can fall far short of their purported objectives unless they are adequately drafted, kept up to date, vigorously enforced, and supported by sanctions when violated. Behind the adoption of such standards, there is a long administrative process, tied to a political infrastructure. The scientific-engineering-legal community has a key independent role to play in this vital and complex administrative-political process. Almost invariably, however, its

Source: From *The Progressive,* where it appeared under the title "The Profits in Pollution," April 1970, pp. 19–22. Reprinted by permission of the author.

talents have been retained on behalf of those to be regulated. Whether in Washington or in state capitals around the country, the experts demonstrate greater loyalty to their employers than to their professional commitments in the public interest.

This has been the regular practice of specialists testifying in behalf of coal and uranium mining companies on the latters' environmental contamination in Appalachia and the Rocky Mountain regions. Perhaps the most egregious example of willing corporate servility was a paper entitled "We've Done the Job—What's Next?" delivered by Charles M. Heinen, Chrysler's vehicle emissions specialist, at a meeting of the Society of Automotive Engineers last spring.

Heinen, whose paper bordered on technical pornography, said the auto industry had solved the vehicle pollution problem with an eighty per cent reduction of hydrocarbons and a seventy per cent reduction of carbon monoxide between the 1960 and 1970 model years. He avoided mentioning at least four other vehicle pollutants—nitrogen oxides, lead, asbestos, and rubber tire pollutants. He also failed to point out that the emissions control performance of new cars degrades after a few thousand miles, and that even when new they do not perform under traffic conditions as they do when finely tuned at a company test facility. The overall aggregate pollution from ever greater numbers of vehicles in more congested traffic patterns also escaped Heinen's company-indentured perceptions.

Two. Sanctions against polluters are feeble and out of date, and, in any case, are rarely invoked. For example, the Federal air quality act has no criminal penalties no matter how willful and enduring the violations. In New Jersey, New York, and Illinois, a seventy-one year old Federal anti-water pollution law was violated with total impunity by industry until the Justice Department moved against a few of the violators in recent months. Other violators in other states are yet to be subjected to the law's enforcement. To be effective, sanctions should come in various forms, such as non-reimbursable fines, suspensions, dechartering of corporations, required disclosure of violations in company promotional materials, and more severe criminal penalties. Sanctions, consequently, should be tailored to the seriousness and duration of the violation.

It is expressive of the anemic and nondeterrent quality of existing sanctions that offshore oil leaks contaminating beaches for months, as in Santa Barbara, brought no penalty to any official of any offending company. The major controversy in Santa Barbara was whether the company—Union Oil—or the Government or the residents would bear the costs of cleaning up the mess. And even if the company bore the costs initially, the tax laws would permit a considerable shifting of this cost onto the general taxpayer.

Three. The existing requirements for disclosure of the extent of corporate pollution are weak and flagrantly flouted. The Federal Water Pollution Control Administration (FWPCA) has been blocked since 1963 by industrial polluters (working with the Federal Bureau of the Budget) from obtaining information from these companies concerning the extent and location of discharges of pollutants into the nation's waterways. For three years, the National Industrial Waste Inventory has been held up by the Budget Bureau and its industry "advisers," who have a decisive policy role. Led by the steel, paper, and petroleum industries, corporate polluters have prevented the FWPCA from collecting specific information on what each company is putting into the water. Such information is of crucial importance to the effective administration of the water pollution law and the allocation of legal responsibility for violations.

Counties in California have been concealing from their citizens the identity of polluters and the amounts of pollution, using such weak, incredible arguments to support their cover-up as the companies' fear of revealing "trade secrets." California state agencies have refused to disclose pesticide application data to representatives of orchard workers being gradually poisoned by the chemicals. Once again the trade secret rationale was employed.

The real reason for secrecy is that disclosure of such information would raise public questions about why government agencies have not been doing their jobs—and would facilitate legal action by injured persons against the polluters. What must be made clear to both corporate and public officials is that no one has the right to a trade secret in lethality.

Massive and meticulous "fish bowl" disclosure requirements are imperative if citizens are to be alerted, at the earliest possible moment, to the flow of silent violence assaulting their health and safety, and that of unborn generations as well. This disclosure pattern, once established, must not lapse into a conspiracy between private and public officials, a conspiracy of silence against citizens and the public interest. A good place to start with such company-by-company disclosure is in the corporation's annual report, which now reveals only financial profits or losses; it should also reveal the social costs of pollution by composition and tonnage.

Four. Corporate investment in research and development of pollution controls is no longer a luxury to be left to the decision or initiative of a few company officers. Rather, such research and development must be required by law to include reinvestment of profits, the amount depending on the volume of pollution inflicted on the public. For example, in 1969 General Motors grossed $24 billion, yet last year spent less than $15 million on vehicle and plant pollution research and development, although its products and plants contribute some thirty-five per cent of the nation's air pollution by tonnage. A formula proportional to the size of a company and its pollution could be devised as law, with required periodic reporting of the progress of the company's research and its uses. A parallel governmental research and development program aimed at developing pollution-free product prototypes suitable for mass production, and a Federal procurement policy favoring the purchase of less-polluting products, are essential external impacts.

Five. Attention must be paid to the internal climate for free expression and due process within the corporate structure. Again and again, the internal discipline of the corporate autocracy represses the civic and professional spirit of employes who have every right to speak out or blow the whistle on their company after they have tried in vain, working from the inside, to bring about changes that will end pollution practices. Professional employes—scientists, engineers, physicians—have fewer due process safeguards than the blue collar workers in the same company protected by their union contract.

When Edward Gregory, a Fisher Body plant inspector for General Motors in St. Louis, publicly spoke out in 1966 on inadequate welding that exposed Chevrolet passengers to exhaust leakage, the company ignored him for a few years, but eventually recalled more than two million cars for correction. GM knew better than to fire Gregory, a member of the United Auto Workers.

In contrast, scientists and engineers employed by corporations privately tell me of their reluctance to speak out—within their companies or outside them—about hazardous products. This explains why the technical elites are rarely in the vanguard of public concern over corporate contamination. Demotion, ostracism, dismissal are some of the corporate sanctions against which there is little or no recourse by the professional employe. A new corporate constitutionalism is needed, guaranteeing employes' due process rights against arbitrary reprisals, but its precise forms require the collection of data and extensive study. Here is a major challenge to which college faculty and students can respond on the campus and in field work.

Six. The corporate shareholder can act, as he rarely does, as a prod and lever for jolting corporate leaders out of their lethargy. The law and the lawyers have rigged the legal system to muffle the voice of shareholders, particularly those concerned with the broader social costs of corporate enterprise. However, for socially conscious and determined stockholders there are many functions that can be performed to help protect the public (including themselves) from industrial pollution.

Shareholders must learn to take full advantage of such corporate practices as cumulative voting, which permits the "single-shot" casting of all of a shareholder's ballots for one member of the board of directors. Delegations of stockholders can give visibility to the issues by lobbying against their company's ill-advised policies in many forums apart from the annual meeting—legislative hearings, agency proceedings, town meetings, and the news media, for example. These delegations will be in a position to expose company officers to public judgment, something from which executives now seem so insulated in their daily corporate activities.

Seven. Natural, though perhaps unexercised, countervailing forces in the private sector can be highly influential incentives for change. For example, the United Auto Workers have announced that pollution will be an issue in the collective bargaining process with automobile company management this year; the union hopes to secure for workers the right not to work in polluting activities, or in a polluted environment. Insurance companies could become advocates for loss prevention in the environmental field when confronted with policyholder, shareholder, and citizen demonstrative action. Through their political influence, their rating function in evaluating risks and setting premium charges, and their research and development capability, insurance companies could exert a key countervailing stress on polluters. Whether they do or not will first depend on citizen groups to whip them into action.

Eight. Environmental lawsuits, long blocked by a conservative judiciary and an inflexible judicial system, now seem to be coming into their own—a classic example of how heightened public expectations, demands, and the availability of facts shape broader applications of ancient legal principles. Environmental pollution is environmental violence—to human beings and to property. The common law has long recognized such violence against the person as actionable or enjoinable. What has been lacking is sufficient evidence of harm and avoidability to persuade judges that such hitherto invisible long-range harm outweighed the economic benefits of the particular plant activity in the community.

It now appears that such lawsuits will gain greater acceptance, especially as more evidence and more willing lawyers combine to breathe contemporary reality into long-standing legal principles. An amendment to the U.S. Constitution providing citizens with basic rights to a clean environment has been proposed; similar amendments to state constitutions are being offered. Such generic provisions can only further the judicial acceptance of environmental lawsuits. Imaginative and bold legal advocacy is needed here. The *forced consumption* of industrial pollutants by 200 million Americans must lead to a recognition of legal rights in environmental control such as that which developed with civil rights for racial minorities over the last two decades.

Three additional points deserve the attention of concerned citizens:

First, a major corporate strategy in combating anti-pollution measures is to engage workers on the company side by leading them to believe that such measures would threaten their livelihood. This kind of industrial extortion in a community—especially a company town—has worked before and will again unless citizens anticipate and confront it squarely.

Second, both industry spokesmen and their governmental allies (such as the President's Science Adviser, Lee DuBridge) insist that consumers will have to pay the price of pollution control. While this point of view may be an unintended manifestation of the economy's administered price structure, it cannot go unchallenged. Pollution control must not become another lever to lift up excess profits and fuel the fires of inflation. The costs of pollution control technology should come from corporate profits which have been enhanced by the use of the public's environment as industry's private sewer. The sooner industry realizes that it must bear the costs of cleanups, the more likely it will be to employ the quickest and most efficient techniques.

Finally, those who believe deeply in a humane ecology must act in accordance with their beliefs. They must so order their consumption and disposal habits that they can, in good conscience, preach what they actually practice. In brief, they must exercise a personal discipline as they advocate the discipline of governments and corporations.

The battle of the environmentalists is to preserve the physiological integrity of people by preserving the natural integrity of land, air, and water. The planet earth is a seamless structure with a thin slice of sustaining air, water, and soil that supports almost four billion people. This thin slice belongs to all of us, and we use it and hold it in trust for future earthlings. Here we must take our stand.

HAL BORLAND

Spring, and a Time to Listen

There's something about the vernal equinox that takes me right back to fundamentals. It reminds me, for one thing, that the year began with March, not January, before the Roman emperors began tinkering with the calendar. It makes me thankful that winter doesn't last six months instead of three. It reminds me that April is at hand—April, a teen-age girl with a bunch of daffodils in her hand, stars in her eyes, a taunt in her laughter, and an inclination to play practical jokes. And the equinox makes me glad I live where I do. Doubly glad this year.

Up here in the hills we know that we always have to earn spring by enduring January and February and sometimes March. This year, by the middle of February we began to think the price had been inflated a good deal more than the six per cent they concede for everything else. We had the snowiest December and the coldest January on record. Groundhog Day was dour and lowery, as usual, and spring didn't come early, also as usual. However, here

Source: Hal Borland, conservationist, essayist, and novelist, is probably best known for his distinguished nature writing. Reprinted from *The Progressive,* April 1970, pp. 44–46, by permission of Collins-Knowlton-Wing, Inc. Copyright © 1970 by Hal Borland.

is April, bought and paid for. April, with blue sky, an early thunderstorm, a late snowstorm, cursed with March's leftovers, blessed with a foretaste of May. April, yellow rocket and shadblow and dandelions, pink buds on the apple trees, purple leaves on the lilacs, peepers in the twilight, robins in the dawn.

And high time. It's much easier to listen to and believe the facts of conservation in April than in January, and the tide of environmental concern has been rising all winter. For years a handful of us have been warning that things were getting out of hand, but we were largely talking to a vacuum. The technologists, the industrial chemists, the public officials, and most of the general public, when they heard us at all, said, "Nonsense! Who cares about a little smog and smoke? They are signs of full employment. What does a little sewage and industrial waste matter in the rivers and lakes? Water is water, isn't it? And what if the miracle pesticides do kill a few songbirds? We are prosperous, the most prosperous nation in the world, with the highest standard of living in history. That's what really matters."

But finally even they began to choke on their own fumes and gag on their own water. And conservation became a popular cause.

A few weeks ago my friend John and I went to Hartford to attend a meeting of the Governor's committee to develop an environmental policy for Connecticut. John taught English in an Ivy League college for some years, then quit and came up here and became a dairy farmer to get back to reality. "Isn't it ironic," John said as we were driving to Hartford that day, "that we destroy so many comfortable, satisfying things in our environment before we decide it's time to develop a policy to save that environment?" And from that question we went on to discuss the comfortable, satisfying things in life the way we try to live it, the things any sensible policy would try to preserve.

There are the three fundamentals, of course—the land, the air, the water. Curb their pollution and we will all live much healthier lives. Our committee, we knew was going to try to work out a program to do just that, clean up the land, the air, the water, improve the environment. But there were factors beyond those obvious ones which were almost impossible to codify and, as we said after discussing the matter for ten minutes, those were the factors that make the life we live, as countrymen, worth while.

We didn't even try to discuss those factors. We named a few of them, but that was all. The sense of belonging to the land. The look of a pasture after a snowfall. Birch trees in first leaf. The cool air that flows down from a mountainside at dusk on a summer evening. Autumn in New England. The taste of spring water. A deer in the home pasture at dawn. A catbird singing in a lilac bush. The smell of fresh-cut hay in June. The smell of a newly plowed field in April. A whippoorwill calling from 3 a.m. till 3:45, without one real pause for breath. The taste of wild grape jelly.

It sounds ridiculous, in a way, I suppose, unless you have experienced all those things and know what they mean. Of what possible importance can things like that be in a conservation program or an environmental policy?

Well, the best answer I can come up with offhand is that without such things life as we know it would be not merely stagnant but sterile. An environment is more than the air you breathe, the water you drink, and the people around you. It is the land around you, and the wind and rain and trees and grass, the sun, moon, and stars. It is all those things and the subtleties inherent which go into your thinking and your dreams, or lack of them.

As I say, John and I didn't discuss such matters. We merely named a few of them that seemed important in a very personal way. But I intend to discuss and try to explain those matters here, or at least a few of them, so that when we are tempted to immerse ourselves in air and water and soil we can perhaps be aware, at least, of some of these intangibles.

I am sure there are plenty of other writers and talkers to expatiate on the need for open space, breathing room, grass, trees, potable water, breathable air, and the lethal nature of biocides. Others undoubtedly will discuss our incredible mountains of trash and garbage, our billion of tons and gallons of industrial waste, our mad population growth.

But beyond the scientific fact that a tree is the best source of oxygen on earth is the fact that a tree is a tree. Not board feet of lumber, or gallons of turpentine, or rolls of newsprint. But a tree, a growing plant, a marvel of fiber and sap and bud and leaf and blossom. Shade in summer, and shelter for nesting birds. Nuts in autumn for hungry squirrels. And a beauty forever, with its haze of new leaves in the spring; its mass of green, fluttering in the breeze, pattering in the rain, casting shade, making life more pleasant in the summer; its color in the autumn, sheer beauty that not even the most enterprising chemist has yet been able to sell as a pigment or a flavor or a food. A tree, one of the most beautiful things on earth.

The land, of course, is a commodity. It is a building site, a field for corn or hay, a sand and gravel pit, a place to put a superhighway, or an airport, or a parking field. It is open space between houses, between towns. It is room for cities and suburbs to expand. But the land is also the only place where the fundamental green of the leaf grows. And that green is the fundamental sustenance of life. It manufactures the oxygen and it is the ultimate food of all of us, ant to elephant, horse to human being. That is the land. And when we want to have a piece of that land to stand on, to walk upon, to know intimately, it is more than mere acquisitiveness. It is fundamental with us, for we need to know and be in daily contact with the earth of our own origins. It's as simple as that. And we want some of the wild places preserved wild because that is where we can come close to the truth of life and the earth itself. We smell it when we plow a field in spring. We see it when we cut and cure hay in June. We taste it when we take in the garden crop in September. But we feel it, we are a part of it, when we go to a wilderness area at any time of the year.

Be practical and point out that every one of our songbirds and even our game birds is a partner of the farmer who is producing food for the millions.

Nobody has yet invented a better insecticide than the birds in our dooryard. That is a basic reason the outcry was first made against DDT and its chemical kindred—it killed birds as well as insects. Later we found that it was far more harmful than that, but when we first pointed to the bird kill the chemical people scoffed at "the loss of a few songbirds." And they missed the whole point—missed it twice, in fact. First, a bird killed by DDT was only a symptom of far greater damage being done. Second, a songbird is more than a few ounces of flesh and feathers. It is song, for one thing. The birds were the first songsters on earth, and quite probably they taught man to sing. And it is beauty, of form and color and motion. It is that superb chorus which makes a summer dawn so memorable. It is the hummer at the petunias and the indigo bunting in the apple tree full of blossom, it is the scarlet tanager and the goldfinch and the cockaded cardinal. It is the catbird making sweet music and then making a travesty of his own song. It is, yes, the whippoorwill yelping interminably in the small hours of the night and you lying awake, counting. It is the eagle and the falcon and the soaring hawk.

Water is the most abundant element on earth, but clean water is becoming rare. Even clean ocean water has become scarce along the continental margins, thanks to the filthiest animal alive and his cities. Without water we all perish, of course. And it is fouled by every element of society and industry. What is a river? A place to dump something you don't want or can't use. Just recently New York's Consolidated Edison atomic plant up the Hudson from New York City sucked fish into its cooling system through a defective screen. Conservationists complained of the fish kill, so Con Ed plugged the leaky screen and dumped 150,000 dead fish back into the river! Where else? The river was handy, and it would carry the dead fish away, to someone else's waterfront.

Water, to be used and abused. But also a majestic river, a beautiful, remote brook, a sweet mountainside spring. Give the countryman a good supply of sweet water and he can make a home anywhere. Give him a clean brook and he will fish for trout, a clean lake and he will catch bass for his supper. Water, the wet sweetness of this earth, the mountaintop cloud made tangible, the morning dew gathered into a stream. Water to refresh the air and the earth and all its creatures. Man is of that long line of red-blooded life which first appeared in the water. We are no longer aquatic, but from the time we stand in youthful wonder beside a spring brook till we sit in old age and watch the endless roll of the sea we feel a strong kinship with the waters of this earth. We marvel at the magnificence of a snowflake, a water crystal. We sleep content with the drone of rain on the roof. We slake our thirst, we cool our faces, we bathe our bodies with water. The blood that courses our veins is largely water. Small wonder the countryman cherishes his brooks and ponds and will fight to keep them and keep them clean.

Perhaps you begin to understand. More than air and water and soil are at stake. Conservation and environment are not so simple. There are ways of life, and there are fundamentals of living, that also need conserving, if only as reminders of what is possible for man if he ever again is master of his own life. Not as an example of the antique or the historical, not Grandfather's way, but a simpler way of life possible even today without privation or hardship or flight from reality.

What I am talking about is receptivity. Perhaps that sounds pretentious, but it really isn't. It is understanding and a willingness to participate. I have heard someone speak of "appreciation," but that is too precious a term; it smacks of the esthetic, and this a thoroughly practical matter. Perhaps that is why I said at the start that April is a better time to discuss such matters than January. In April the world around you, particularly here in the country, cannot be ignored. You are receptive, or you are deaf, dumb, and blind, and an utter clod to boot. And I am not talking about the traveler out to see how many miles he can cover in a weekend, or about the bird watcher out to accumulate a longer list than her neighbor down the street. I am talking about understanding what is all around you, not merely counting or identifying.

We keep hearing that population is the ultimate cause of all these environmental problems, and in many areas that is true. Certainly some way should be found to make 1980, or 2000, less of a terminal deadline for human survival. Maybe disease will take care of that, or famine, or a cataclysmic war. But I have less fear of the standing-room-only prophecies than I have of the tendency to emulate the ants. And of the sophisticated disdain for all things rural, coupled with blind legislative insistence, largely of urban origin, that all farmland be vacated and all country folk be taken to the cities. You don't conserve anything that way, and you certainly don't improve environments. It often seems that the urban majority of our population, now up around eighty per cent I believe, is afraid of the open country except when passed through safely inside a speeding automobile or high above it in a supersonic transport. Afraid of open spaces and distrustful of their relatively few inhabitants.

Why? Not simple agoraphobia, I am sure. And not wholly a matter of thinking everyone living five miles from a metropolitan center is an oaf or a dolt. I think we all know now that a city lunkhead is just as witless as a rural simpleton, and the averages don't vary much per thousand. Can it be because they have forgotten so many things that should be remembered?

Actually, we all once lived close to the soil, even here in America. Well over half of us were still there within the memory of men barely old enough for Social Security. The ways of the country are in our blood, if not in our hearts, as a nation. We turn our back on them at our peril, and we embrace the technologies that have done so much to destroy our environment. We listened too long to the factory whistles, thinking that more was better, and bigger was best of all. Bigger cities, bigger industry, bigger armament, bigger wars.

And that is what this is all about, this sudden surge of concern over the environment. That's what some of us have been saying for twenty years or more. And now it's another April, another spring, and maybe it will be easier to listen to what was said all this time. As I said just a few paragraphs back, in April you are receptive, you listen and try to understand, or you are deaf, dumb, and blind, and an utter clod to boot. Let's stand on that for now. Let this be the time to separate the men from the clods.